Karl Baedeker

Central Italy and Rome

Karl Baedeker

Central Italy and Rome

ISBN/EAN: 9783337386672

Printed in Europe, USA, Canada, Australia, Japan

Cover: Foto ©Andreas Hilbeck / pixelio.de

More available books at **www.hansebooks.com**

HANDBOOK FOR TRAVELLERS

BY

K. BÆDEKER.

SECOND PART:

CENTRAL ITALY AND ROME.

With 3 Maps and 8 Plans.

Second Edition, Revised and Augmented.

COBLENZ:
KARL BÆDEKER.
1869.

LONDON:
WILLIAMS & NORGATE.
14 Henrietta Street, Covent Garden.

PARIS:
HAAR & STEINERT.
9 rue Jacob.

Right of translation reserved.

"Go, little book, God send thee good passage,
And specially let this be thy prayere
Unto them all that thee will read or hear,
Where thou art wrong, after their help to call,
Thee to correct in any part or all."

CHAUCER, 1380.

PREFACE.

The object of the present Handbook, like that of the Editor's other works of the same description, is to render the traveller as independent as possible of the services of guides, valets-de-place, and others of the same class, to supply him with a few remarks on the progress of civilisation and art among the people with whom he is about to become acquainted, and to enable him to realise to the fullest extent the enjoyment and instruction of which Italy is the fruitful source.

The Handbook is, moreover, intended to place the traveller in a position to visit the places and objects most deserving of notice with the greatest possible economy of time, money, and, it may be added, temper; for in no country is the traveller's patience more severely put to the test than in some parts of Italy. The Editor will endeavour to accompany the enlightened traveller through the streets of the Italian towns, to all the principal edifices and works of art; and to guide his steps amidst the exquisite scenery in which Italy so richly abounds.

With a few very trifling exceptions, the entire book is framed from the Editor's *personal experience*, acquired at the places described. As, however, infallibility cannot be attained, the Editor will highly appreciate any *bonâ fide* information with which travellers may favour him. That already received, which in many instances has been most serviceable, he gratefully acknowledges.

The Maps and Plans, the result of great care and research, will abundantly suffice for the use of the ordinary traveller. The inexperienced are strongly recommended, when steering their course with the aid of a plan, before starting, to mark with a coloured pencil the point for which they are bound. This will enable them to avoid many a circuitous route. For the benefit of those who desire to become more intimately acquainted with the country than the limits of the present work admit of, the admirable *Supplementary Sheets of G. Mayr's Atlas of the Alps* (for Central and Southern Italy) may be mentioned. They are most easily procured in Germany (price, mounted, 2 dollars each). For Naples the map of the *Real Officio Topografico* (Naples, 1835) will be found useful.

Altitudes are given in Parisian feet (1 Par. ft. = $1^{1}/_{15}$ Engl. ft.).

Distances are generally given in English miles. The Italian "miglia" varies in different districts. Approximately it may be stated that 1 Engl. M. = $6/_{7}$ Ital. migl. = $11'/_{14}$ Roman migl.

Railway, Diligence and Steamboat Timetables. The most trustworthy are contained in the *"Guida-Orario ufficiale di tutte le strade ferrate d'Italia contenente anche le indicazioni dei Piroscafi* (steamboats), *Corrieri, Diligenze"* etc., with map, published at Milan (price 40 c.).

Hotels. In no country does the treatment which the traveller experiences at hotels vary so much as in Italy, and attempts at extortion are probably nowhere so outrageous. The asterisks are therefore to be received as indicating those hotels which the Editor believes to be *comparatively* respectable, clean and reasonable. The average charges stated in the Handbook will at least enable the traveller to form a fair estimate of the demands which can be justly made.

CONTENTS.

	Page
I. Travelling Expenses. Monetary System	XIII
II. Period and Plan of Tour	XV
III. Language	XVI
IV. Passports and Custom-houses	XVII
V. Public Safety. Mendicity	XVIII
VI. Traffic	XIX
VII. Locomotion	XXII
VIII. Hotels	XXVI
IX. Restaurants, Cafés etc.	XXVIII
X. Churches, Theatres, Shops etc.	XXX
XI. Postal Arrangements	XXXI
XII. Calculation of Time	XXXI
XIII. Climate. Mode of Life	XXXI
XIV. Historical Sketch of Italian Art	XXXIII

Route.
1. From Marseilles (Genoa) to Leghorn (Civita Vecchia and Naples) ... 1
2. From Florence to Rome (by sea) viâ Leghorn and Civita Vecchia ... 8
   1. From Civita Vecchia to La Tolfa ... 12
3. From Florence to Rome by the Maremme ... 13
   1. Piombino and Populonia ... 14
   2. From Grosseto to Rusellæ ... 16
   3. Orbetello. Monte Argentario ... 16
   4. From Montalto to Vulci ... 17
   5. Corneto ... 17
4. From Leghorn to Volterra ... 19
   1. Monte Catini. La Cava. Lagoni di Monte Cerboli ... 22
5. Elba and the Tuscan Islands ... 22
6. From Florence to Rome by Siena, Orvieto and Viterbo ... 24
   1. From Poggibonsi to San Gimignano ... 24
   2. From Asciano to Torrenieri. Monte Oliveto Maggiore ... 31
   3. Monte Pulciano. Pienza ... 32
   4. Excursions from Viterbo. Castel d'Asso. Norchia. Toscanella. Bomarzo ... 39
   5. Caprarola ... 41
   6. From Ronciglione to Monterosi by Sutri ... 41
7. From Siena to Perugia (and Rome) by Chiusi ... 43
8. From Florence to Rome by Arezzo, Perugia and Foligno ... 44
   From Florence to Arezzo and Cortona ... 44
   From Cortona to Perugia ... 50
   1. From Perugia to Narni by Todi ... 56
   2. From Perugia to the Upper Valley of the Tiber ... 57

CONTENTS.

Route	Page
From Perugia to Foligno by Assisi	57
3. Bevagna. Montefalco	61
From Foligno to Rome	61
4. From Narni to Otricoli	66
From Borghetto to Rome by Città Castellana and Rignano	68
5. Falerii	69
6. From Città Castellana to Rome by Nepi	71
9. From Bologna to Rome by Ancona (Falconara) and Foligno	71
1. From Rimini to San Marino	74
2. From Pesaro to Urbino	75
From Fano to Foligno and Rome viâ Gubbio	77
10. From Trieste to Ancona	80
11. From Ancona to Rome	82
1. From Fabriano to Sassoferrato	83
2. From Ancona to Foligno by Civitanuova, Macerata, Tolentino, San Severino and Camerino	84
12. Rome	86
Arrival. Consulates. Money. Bankers. Hotels. Private Apartments	86
Restaurants. Cafés	87
Gratuities. Baths. Physicians. Chemists. Booksellers. Teachers. Studios	88
Permessi. Export of works of art	89
Shops. Theatres. Church Festivals	90
Popular Festivals. Carnival	92
Street-scenes. Promenades. Fiacres and Omnibuses	93
English Church Service. Post and Telegraph Office. Cigars. Vetturini. Railways. Steamboats	94
Collections, Villas etc.	95
Diary	96
History of the City of Rome	97
Topography	105
I. Strangers' Quarter and Corso	109
*Piazza del Popolo. English Church	109
*S. Maria del Popolo	110
*The Pincio	110
Villa Medici. SS. Trinità de' Monti	112
Casa Zuccari. Piazza di Spagna. Propaganda	113
S. Andrea delle Fratte. *Fontana di Trevi	114
The Corso. Pal. Rondinini. S. Giacomo in Augusta. Gesù e Maria	115
S. Carlo al Corso. S. Lorenzo in Lucina	116
Palazzo Fiano. Palazzo Chigi	116
*Piazza Colonna. Piazza di Monte Citorio	117
*Dogana (Temple of Neptune). Palazzo Sciarra-Colonna	117
S. Ignazio. Collegio Romano. *Museo Kircheriano	118

CONTENTS. IX

	Page
S. Marcello. S. Maria in Via Lata	119
*Palazzo Doria	119
*SS. Apostoli	121
*Palazzo Colonna	121
Piazza di Venezia. Palazzo di Venezia. Palazzo Torlonia	122
S. Marco. Monument of Bibulus	123
*Gesù	124
*Villa Borghese	124

II. The Hills of Rome. Quirinal, Viminal, Esquiline . 126

*Fontana del Tritone. S. Maria della Concezione	127
**Villa Ludovisi	127
Gardens of Sallust	128
*Villa Albani	129
*Palazzo Barberini	131
Piazza di Monte Cavallo. Palazzo della Consulta	132
*Palazzo Apostolico al Quirinale	133
*Palazzo Rospigliosi. S. Silvestro a Monte Cavallo	134
S. Bernardo. Piazza di Termini	135
S. Maria della Vittoria	136
Porta Pia. Villa Torlonia. *S. Agnese fuori.	136
S. Costanza. Railway Station. Thermae of Diocletian.	
*S. Maria degli Angeli	137
Campo Militare	138
S. Pudenziana	139
S. Lorenzo in Paneperna	140
**S. Maria Maggiore	140
S. Antonio Abbate. *S. Prassede	141
Porta S. Lorenzo. *S. Lorenzo fuori le Mura	142
Arch of Gallienus. S. Eusebio	143
S. Bibiana. Temple of Minerva Medica. Porta Maggiore.	
*S. Croce in Gerusalemme	144
Amphitheatrum Castrense. S. Martino ai Monti	145
*S. Pietro in Vincoli	146

III. Rome on the Tiber 147

Mausoleum of Augustus	147
*Palazzo Borghese	148
*S. Agostino	151
S. Luigi de' Francesi	152
Università della Sapienza	153
Piazza della Rotonda. **Pantheon	153
S. Maria sopra Minerva	155
Palazzo Madama. *Piazza Navona	156
S. Agnese. *S. Maria dell' Anima	157
*S. Maria della Pace. Palazzo Vidoni	158
S. Andrea della Valle. Palazzo Massimi alle Colonne	159
Palazzo Braschi. Piazza di Pasquino. Chiesa Nuova	160
*Palazzo della Cancelleria. S. Lorenzo in Damaso	161
*Palazzo Farnese	162

CONTENTS.

Route	Page
°Palazzo Spada alla Regola	163
S. Giovanni de' Fiorentini	164
S. Carlo a' Catinari	164
Palazzo Costaguti. Palazzo Mattei	165
S. Maria in Campitelli	166
Ghetto	166
Colonnade of Octavia. Theatre of Marcellus	167

IV. Ancient Rome 167

°S. Maria in Araceli	168
°°Piazza del Campidoglio. Palazzo del Senatore	169
Tarpeian Rock. °Tabularium	170
°°Forum Romanum. °Temple of Saturn	171
Colonnade of the Twelve Gods. °Temple of Vespasian. Temple of Concordia	172
Triumphal Arch of Septimius Severus	172
Rostra. °Column of Phocas. Basilica Julia	173
°Temple of Castor and Pollux. °Carcer Mamertinus	173
°Temple of Faustina. °SS. Cosma e Damiano	175
Basilica of Constantine. S. Francesca Romana	175
Triumphal Arch of Titus. Temple of Venus and Roma	176
°°Colosseum	177
Triumphal Arch of Constantine	179
°Thermæ of Titus	180
Forum of Nerva. Accademia di S. Luca	181
Forum of Augustus. °Forum of Trajan	182
The Palatine	183
Janus Quadrifrons. S. Giorgio in Velabro. °Arcus Argentarius	186
°Cloaca Maxima. S. Maria in Cosmedin	186
°Temple of Vesta. °S. Maria Egiziaca	187
Circus Maximus	188
The Aventine	189
Protestant Cemetery. °Pyramid of Cestius. Monte Testaccio	190
S. Sabina	191
S. Alessio. S. Maria Aventina	192
Porta S. Paolo. °°S. Paolo fuori le Mura	193
Via Appia. °Thermæ of Caracalla. SS. Nereo ed Achilleo	195
S. Cesareo. S. Giovanni a Porta Latina	196
°Tomb of the Scipios. Arch of Drusus	197
The Cælius. S. Gregorio. SS. Giovanni e Paolo. S. Maria in Domnica. S. Stefano Rotondo	198
S. Clemente. SS. Quattro Coronati	200
S. Giovanni in Laterano	204
Gregorian Museum	204
Villa Massimo. Villa Wolkonsky	207
Collections of the Capitol	208

V. Quarters of the City on the Right Bank 213

Castello S. Angelo	214
Palazzo Giraud. Ospedale S. Spirito	215

CONTENTS. XI

oute	Page
Piazza di S. Pietro	216
S. Pietro in Vaticano	217
Cimiterio dei Tedeschi	223
Longara. S. Onofrio	223
Villa Farnesina	224
Palazzo Corsini	226
Trastevere. S. Pietro in Montorio	227
Villa Doria Pamfili	229
Isola di S. Bartolommeo. Ponte Rotto	231
S. Crisogono. S. Maria in Trastevere	232
S. Cecilia in Trastevere. Ospizio S. Michele	233
The Vatican	234
Sala Ducale. Sala Regia. Sixtine Chapel. Pauline Chapel	235
Raphael's Loggie	237
Raphael's Stanze	238
Cappella Niccolina	242
Museum of Statues. Galleria Lapidaria	242
Braccio Nuovo	243
Museo Chiaramonti	244
Museo Pio-Clementino	245
Raphael's Tapestry	249
Museo Gregoriano of Etruscan Antiquities	250
Egyptian Museum	252
Picture Gallery	252
Library of the Vatican	254
The Catacombs	256
3. Environs of Rome	261
A. Short Excursions in the Campagna	262
Beyond Porta S. Paolo. Tre Fontane	262
Beyond Porta S. Sebastiano. Via Appia. Domine Quo Vadis. S. Sebastiano	263
Circus of Maxentius. Tomb of Cæcilia Metella	265
Temple of the Deus Rediculus. Grotto of Egeria. S. Urbano	267
Beyond Porta S. Giovanni. Via Latina. Porta Furba	268
Beyond Porta Maggiore. Torre Pignattara. Tor de' Schiavi	269
Beyond Porta S. Lorenzo	270
Beyond Porta Pia	270
Beyond Porta Salara. Fidenæ	271
Beyond Porta del Popolo. Acqua Acetosa	271
Beyond Porta Angelica. Monte Mario. Villa Mellini. Villa Madama	272
B. Longer Excursions from Rome to the Mountains and the Sea	273
The Alban Mountains	273
Frascati	274
Grotta Ferrata	276

CONTENTS.

Route	Page
Marino	277
Rocca di Papa	277
Monte Cavo	277
Palazzuola. Lago di Albano. Alba Longa	278
Albano	279
Castel Gandolfo. The Emissarius	280
Ariccia. Genzano	281
Città Lavinia. Velletri	282
Nemi and its lake	282
The Sabine Mountains	**283**
Tivoli	283
Subiaco	287
Palestrina	290
Olevano	292
Genazzano	292
Monte Gennaro	293
Valley of Licenza	294
The Volscian Mountains	**294**
Cori	295
Norma	296
Segni	296
Etruscan Towns	**297**
Veii	297
Galera	299
Bracciano	299
Cære	301
The Sea-coast of Latium	**302**
Ostia. Castel Fusano. Tor Paterno. Pratica. Ardea	302
Porto. Fiumicino. Isola Sacra	304
Porto d'Anzio	305
Nettuno. Astura	306
Index	307
List of streets in the plan of Rome	315

List of Maps and Plans.

1. Map of Italy, facing title-page.
2. Plan of Marseilles, between pp. 2 and 3.
3. Plan of Siena, between pp. 24 and 25.
4. Plan of Perugia, between pp. 50 and 51.
5. Plan of Ancona, between pp. 80 and 81.
6. Large Plan and
7. Key-Plan of Rome, at the end of the volume.
8. Plan of Ancient Rome, between pp. 166 and 167.
9. Plan of the Forum Romanum, between pp. 170 and 171.
10. Map of the Environs of Rome, between pp. 260 and 261.
11. Map of the Roman Campagna, between pp. 272 and 273.

INTRODUCTION.

> "Thou art the garden of the world, the home
> Of all Art yields, and Nature can decree;
> Even in thy desert, what is like to thee?
> Thy very weeds are beautiful, thy waste
> More rich than other climes' fertility,
> Thy wreck a glory, and thy ruin graced
> With an immaculate charm which cannot be defaced."
> Byron.

From the earliest ages down to the present time Italy has ever exercised a powerful influence on the denizens of more northern lands, and a journey thither has often been the fondly cherished wish of many an aspiring traveller. At the present day this wish may be gratified with comparative facility. Northern Italy is now connected by a direct "iron route" with the southern portion of the peninsula, as far as Naples and Brindisi, and the approaching completion of the great network of railways will soon enable the traveller to penetrate into the interior of provinces hitherto untrodden by the ordinary tourist. Prior to 1860 the peninsula possessed but few railways, and these of insignificant extent, and exclusively of local importance. Rapidity of locomotion is not, however, the sole advantage which has been attained since that period. A single monetary system has superseded the numerous and perplexing varieties of coinage formerly in use; the annoyances inseparable from passports and custom-houses, with which the traveller was assailed at every frontier, and even in many an insignificant town, have been greatly mitigated; and energetic measures have been adopted in order to put an end to the extortions of vetturini, facchini, and other members of this irritating class. Whilst those in search of adventure and excitement will miss many of the characteristic elements of former Italian travel, those who desire the more rational enjoyments derived from scenery, art or science will not fail to rejoice in the altered state of the country.

I. Travelling Expenses. Monetary System.

The cost of a tour in Italy depends of course on the traveller's resources and habits. Generally it may be stated that the expenses need not exceed those incurred in the more frequented parts of the continent. The average expenditure of a single traveller may be estimated at 25 l. per diem, or about half that sum when a prolonged stay is made at one place. Travellers acquainted with the language and habits of the country may succeed in reducing their expenses to still narrower limits. Persons travelling as members of a party may effect a considerable saving, and will find their respective shares of the cost of carriages, guides, hotels and fees reduced to two-thirds, or one-half of what they would have to pay when alone. Where ladies are of the party the expenses are always unavoidably greater; not merely because the better hotels, and the more comfortable modes of locomotion are selected, but because the Italians regard the traveller in this case as wealthier, and therefore a more fitting object for extortion.

In the *Kingdom of Italy* the French monetary system is now universal. The franc (lira or franco) contains 100 centesimi. 1 l. 25 c. = 1 s. = 10 silbergroschen = 35 German kreuzer = 50 Austrian kreuzer. The silver coins in common circu'ation are Italian pieces of 1 and 2 l., and Italian or French 5 l. pieces; gold coins of the Italian or French currency of 10 and 20 l. are the commonest (those of 5 and 40 l. rare). Since the war of 1866 a paper-currency, at a compulsory rate of exchange, has been introduced, in consequence of which the valuable metals have entirely disappeared from ordinary circulation. Copper and banknotes down to 2 l. are almost exclusively employed. The change for gold or silver should always be given in silver; and paper should be declined, unless 6—7 per cent in excess of its nominal value be proffered, a premium which the money-changers generally give. In the same way paper may be exchanged for gold or silver, at a loss of 8—10 per cent. Two points, however, should in the latter case be observed: (1) the notes of small amount (2 and 5 l.) should be preferred, owing to the difficulty of changing those of greater value in ordinary traffic: (2) public and railway offices refuse to give change when payment is made in paper. In the latter case the precise sum should be tendered, as any amount in excess, or short of the fare is alike declined. In case of emergencies, the traveller should of course be provided with a reserve of silver. French banknotes are on a par with gold. — In the *States of the Church*, scudi, paoli and bajocchi are still in use besides the recently introduced lire. 1 scudo = 10 paoli = 100 baj. 1 scudo = 5 l. 37$^{1}/_{2}$ c. = 4 *s.* 4$^{1}/_{4}$ *d.*; 1 paolo = 55 c. = 5$^{1}/_{4}$ *d.*; 1 baj. = 5 c. (1 soldo) = $^{1}/_{2}$ *d.* Banknotes of 5, 10, 20 and 50 scudi are also in common use; silver pieces of 1 scudo, and 5, 2 and 1 paolo; copper pieces of 2, 1 and $^{1}/_{2}$ bajocco. Since the introduction of the new system, coins of 2$^{1}/_{2}$, 2, 1, $^{1}/_{4}$ lire in silver, and of 4, 2, 1, $^{1}/_{2}$ soldo in copper have been issued. The papal paper and silver currency is always considerably depreciated when exchanged for French or Italian gold. The nominal value of a napoleon at Rome is 3 scudi 72 baj., whereas the real equivalent is 3 sc. 90, to 4 sc. 10 baj. French and Italian silver also is generally taken at a higher rate than papal.

In some parts of Italy the former currency is still employed in keeping accounts, and the coins themselves are occasionally seen. Thus the francesconi and crazie of Tuscany, the Roman scudi and bajocchi still used in Umbria, the piastri and grani of Naples, and the uncie and tari of Sicily. An acquaintance with these now nearly obsolete currencies is, however, not essential unless the traveller diverges from the beaten track, in which case the necessary information will be afforded by the Handbook.

The traveller should, before entering Italy, provide himself with *French Gold*, which he may procure in England, France or Germany on more advantageous terms than in Italy. *Sovereigns* are received at the full value by most of the principal hotel keepers, but this is not the case in the less frequented districts.

II. Period and Plan of Tour.

The *season* selected, and the *duration* of the tour determined on must of course depend on the traveller himself. Suffice it to remark that the colder months are those usually preferred. The majority of travellers bound for the South proceed to cross the Alps in September and October, and arrive in Rome about the beginning of November. Rome is the favourite winter-residence of strangers until the Carnival, but at the commencement of Lent the city is deserted by many for the gayer scenes of Naples. At Easter it is again inundated by a vast concourse of visitors, who flock thither in order to witness the sumptuous ecclesiastical pageantry of the "Holy Week", and depart as soon as their curiosity has been gratified. Some then proceed to Naples, Florence or other parts of Italy; the majority, however, prepare to quit the country before the commencement of summer. In this vast and ever-varying influx of travellers the English element is always greatly predominant.

No month in the year can be pronounced absolutely unfavourable for travelling in Italy, but the seasons recommended are the late autumn months (Sept. 15th to Nov. 15th), and the months of April and May. The rainy winter months should, if possible, be avoided for the commencement of a tour, and may be most profitably spent by those who winter in Italy in one of the larger cities, of which Rome offers by far the most numerous and varied attractions. The months of June, July and August are hardly less unfavourable for a tour. The scenery indeed is then in perfection, and the long days are hailed with satisfaction by the active traveller; but the fierce rays of an Italian sun seldom fail to exercise a prejudicial influence upon the physical and mental energies. This result is not occasioned so much by the intensity, as by the protracted duration of the heat, the sky being frequently cloudless, and not a drop of rain falling for several months in succession. The first showers of autumn, which fall about the end of August, again commence to refresh the parched atmosphere.

The *Plan* of a tour in Italy must be framed in accordance with the object which the traveller has in view. Florence, Rome and Naples are the principal centres of attraction; the less frequented districts of the interior, however, are also replete with inexhaustible sources of interest. In order to obtain a more than superficial acquaintance with Italy, the traveller must not devote his attention to the larger towns exclusively. The farther he diverges from the beaten track, the better opportunities he will have of gaining an insight into the characteristics of this fascinating country.

III. Language.

The time and labour which the traveller has bestowed on the study of the Italian language at home will be amply repaid as he proceeds on his journey. It is by no means impossible to travel through Italy without an acquaintance with Italian or French, but in this case the traveller cannot conveniently deviate from the ordinary track, and is moreover invariably made to pay *(alla Inglese)*, by hotel-keepers and others, considerably more than the ordinary charges. A knowledge of French is of very great advantage, for the Italians are extremely partial to that language, and avail themselves of every opportunity of employing it. For those, however, who desire to confine their expenditure within the average limits, a slight acquaintance with the language † of the country is indispensable.

† "*Baedeker's Manual of Conversation in four Languages (English, French, German and Italian) with Vocabulary etc.*" (18th Edit.) will be found serviceable for this purpose. With the addition of a pocket-dictionary, the traveller may safely encounter the difficulties of the situation. A few brief remarks on the pronunciation may here be made for the benefit of those unacquainted with the language. *C* before *e* and *i* is pronounced like the English ch, *g* before *e* and *i* like j. Before other vowels *c* and *g* are hard. *Ch* and *gh*, which generally precede *e* or *i*, are hard; *sc* before *e* or *i* is pronounced like sh, *gn* and *gl* between vowels like ny and ly. In other respects the pronunciation of Italian more nearly resembles that of German than French or English. The prosody occasionally presents difficulties, being different from what one would naturally expect: e. g. Brindȳsi, Gaëta, Nisȳta. — In addressing persons of the educated classes "lei", with the 3rd pers. sing., should always be employed (addressing several at once,

Nowhere more than in Italy is the traveller who is ignorant of the language so much debarred from the thorough enjoyment of travelling, and from the opportunity of forming an independent opinion of the country, its customs, history, literature and art.

IV. Passports and Custom-houses.

On entering the kingdom of Italy, the traveller's passport is rarely demanded; but it is unwise not to be provided with one of these documents, as it may occasionally prove useful. Registered letters, for example, will not be handed over to strangers, unless they exhibit a passport as a guarantee of their identity.

For Rome the visa (gratis) of a papal nuncio is necessary (obtainable in Paris, Vienna, Munich, Lucerne etc.). Those who have omitted this formality before entering Italy may procure the visa (5 l.) on application to the Spanish consul at Genoa, Leghorn or Naples, these officials being at the same time the representatives of the pope in these places (it is, however, probable that this will be altered in consequence of the events of Sept., 1868). The same thing may be accomplished at Marseilles through the medium of the steamboat offices. On quitting Rome, the visa of the ambassador of the traveller's nationality, and that of the Papal police (1 sc.) are necessary. The traveller who returns from Naples to Rome is required to be furnished with another Spanish visa, which must be preceded by that of the consul of the traveller's nation. Those who return to Rome by other lines are not required to be provided with this second visa.

In the larger towns, and on the ordinary routes, the traveller is never exposed to annoyance from the police. In the remote districts, however, where the public safety demands a more rigorous supervision, the traveller who cannot exhibit his credentials is liable to detention. As a rule the passport is an essential companion during excursions in the country, especially in the vicinity of Naples and the southern provinces. It must, however, be admitted that the Italian and Papal police are uniformly polite and obliging.

The examination of luggage at the Italian Custom-houses is usually extremely lenient. Tobacco and cigars are the articles especially sought for. Books and photographs are the principal objects of suspicion in the States of the Church, on the frontier of which the scrutiny is occasionally rigorous. The questions of

---

"loro" with the 3rd pers. pl.). "Voi" is used in addressing waiters, drivers etc., "tu" by those only who are proficient in the language. "Voi" is the commonest mode of address employed by the Neapolitans, but is generally regarded as inelegant or uncourteous.

the officials are best answered by "*sono libri di professione*". Books in the Italian language are often inspected one by one.

Those who travel to Rome by the high road may escape these annoyances by giving a gratuity to the official at the frontier (1—2 l.), and another on passing the gate of the city. These individuals are said to depend on such fees for their livelihood, according to the system formerly prevalent throughout Italy. On arriving by railway, however, and in the kingdom of Italy generally, the traveller is not recommended to resort to such expedients.

V. Public Safety. Mendicity.

Italy is still frequently regarded as the land of Fra Diavolo's and Rinaldo Rinaldini's — an impression fostered by tales of travellers, sensational letters to newspapers etc. The fact, however, is, that travelling in Northern and Central Italy is hardly attended with greater hazard than in any of the more northern European countries. At the same time the traveller may be reminded of the danger of seeking quarters for the night in inferior or remote inns in large towns. Rome and Naples are deservedly notorious in this respect. Even in the most secure districts temporary associations of freebooters are occasionally formed with a view to some predatory enterprise, but the attacks of such bands are directed against wealthy inhabitants of the country, who are known to be travelling with large sums of money, and seldom if ever against strangers, with whose resources and plans such marauders cannot easily be acquainted. Strangers, however, especially when accompanied by ladies, should not neglect the ordinary precaution of requesting information respecting the safety of the roads from the authorities, gensdarmes (carabinieri, generally respectable and trustworthy) etc.

The *Brigantaggio*, properly so called, is a local evil, which the traveller may always without difficulty avoid. Owing to the revolution of 1860 it had increased in the Neapolitan provinces to an alarming extent. The Italian Government has done its utmost to suppress this national scourge, and its efforts have in a great measure been crowned with success; but the evil still resembles a conflagration which has been imperfectly extinguished, and from time to time bursts forth anew. The demoralisation of the inhabitants of the southern provinces is still deplorably great, and the brigandage there is not only fostered by popular discontent and a professed sympathy for the Bourbons, but is actually carried on as a speculation by landed proprietors. These "gentry" frequently equip and harbour gangs of banditti, with whom they share the spoil; or they at least aid and abet them, on condition that their own property is respected. The evil is moreover favoured by the mountainous character of the country, into the remote recesses of which troops cannot easily penetrate. The most notorious districts are the frontier range of mountains between the Neapolitan provinces and the present States of the Church, the mountains of Campania and the whole of Calabria. Sicily has also of late years been much infested by brigands, especially the provinces of Palermo and Girgenti; but even in the most dangerous localities those who adopt the ordinary precautions may travel with tolerable safety. Under such circumstances some acquaintance with the language and the country is indispensable.

Weapons cannot legally be carried without a licence. For the ordinary traveller they are a mere burden, and in case of a rencontre with brigands only serve greatly to increase the danger.

Mendicity, countenanced and encouraged according to the former system of Italian politics, still continues to be one of those national nuisances to which the traveller must habituate himself. The system is energetically opposed in Naples by the new regime, but in Rome and many of the smaller towns it prevails to the same extent as formerly. Begging in Italy, in a still greater degree than in other places, is rather a trade than a genuine demand for sympathy. The best mode of liberation is to bestow a small donation, a supply of the smallest coin of the realm being provided for the purpose. A beggar, who in return for a donation of 2 c. thanked the donor with the usual benedictions, was on another occasion presented with 50 c., an act of liberality, which, instead of being gratefully accepted, only called forth the remark in a half-offended tone: "ma signore è molto poco!"

VI. Traffic.

Travelling in Italy differs essentially in many respects from that in France, Germany, Switzerland etc., and the experience there acquired here avails comparatively little. An acquaintance with the language will prove the best aid in supplying the deficiency.

The traveller is regarded by landlords, waiters, drivers, porters, and others of the same class, as their natural and legitimate prey. Deception and imposition are regarded as very venial offences by Italians of the lower class, who view a successful attempt as a proof of superior sagacity. The traveller, therefore, who submits complacently to extortion is regarded with less respect than he who stoutly resists the barefaced attempt upon his credulity. Among the Swiss Mountains the judicious traveller knows well when to make the tender of his cigar-case or spirit-flask; in this country such amiable manifestations are only calculated to awaken a further spirit of cupidity and discontent.

On the principal routes, and especially in Naples, the insolence of the mercenary classes has attained to such an unexampled pitch, that the doubt not unfrequently presents itself to the traveller's mind whether such a thing as honesty is known in Italy. It is to be hoped that a more intimate acquaintance with the people and their habits will satisfy him that his unpleasant misgivings apply to the above classes only, and not to the community generally.

In Italy the highly pernicious custom of demanding considerably more than will ultimately be accepted is universal; but a knowledge of the custom, as it is based entirely upon the presumed ignorance of one of the contracting parties, tends greatly to mitigate the evil.

Where tariffs and fixed charges exist, they should be carefully consulted. In other cases a certain average price is generally established by custom, under which circumstances the traveller should make a precise bargain with respect to the service to be rendered, and never rely on the equity of the other party.

Those individuals who appeal to the generosity of the stranger, or to their own honesty, or who, as rarely happens, are offended by the traveller's manifestation of distrust, may well be answered in the words of the proverb: *"patti chiari, amicizia lunga"*. In the following pages the prices, even of insignificant objects, are stated with all possible accuracy; and although they are liable to constant fluctuations, they will at least serve as a guide to the stranger, and prove a safeguard against many gross extortions. The Editor ventures to offer the homely hint, that the equanimity of the traveller's own temper will greatly assist him if involved in a dispute or bargain, and no attention whatever should be paid to vehement gesticulations or an offensive demeanour. The more imperfect the traveller's knowledge of the Italian language is, the more careful should he be not to involve himself in a war of words, in which he must necessarily be at great disadvantage.

It need hardly be observed that the representations of drivers, guides etc., with whom even the inhabitants of the place often appear to act in concert, are unworthy of the slightest reliance. Thus in Naples the charge for a single drive is $1/2$ l. and yet the driver would find no difficulty in summoning 20 individuals ready to corroborate his assertion that the proper fare is 5 l. *"Ebben mostrami la tariffa!"* "Ma signore siamo galantuomini." *"Voglio vedere la tariffa!"* "Non l'abbiamo." *"Va bene allora ti do mezza lira!"* The driver, thus discomfited, is compelled to accept the precise fare, and a boisterous laugh at his expense is raised by the bystanders. In all such cases the traveller may generally implicitly rely on the data given in the handbook. Where farther information is required, it should be sought from fellow-travellers, gensdarmes, respectably dressed persons present, occasionally from landlords, but seldom or never from waiters.

Caution is everywhere desirable in Italy; but if exaggerated, it may be construed as the result of fear or weakness on the part of the traveller, whose best safeguard is often his own self-confidence; and it must be admitted, that, the preliminaries once adjusted, the trustworthiness exhibited by members of the fraternity in question is often greater than at first anticipated.

An abundant supply of copper coins should always be at the traveller's command in a country where donations, as frequent as trifling, are in constant demand. Drivers, guides, porters, donkey-attendants etc. invariably expect, and often demand as their right, a gratuity *(buona mano, mancia, da bere, bottiglia, caffè, fumata)* in addition to the hire agreed on, and varying according to circumstances from 2—3 sous to a franc or more. The traveller need feel no embarrassment in limiting his donations to the smallest possible sums. Liberality is often a fruitful source of future annoyance and embarrassment. Half-a-franc bestowed where two sous would have sufficed may be fraught with disagreeable results to the injudicious traveller; the fact speedily becomes known, and other applicants make their appearance, whose demands it becomes utterly impossible to satisfy. It may be laid down as a rule, that parsimony, however much at variance with the generous feelings of the traveller, is so essential to his enjoyment, that he must endeavour to practise it on every possible occasion.

The demeanour of the stranger towards the natives must be somewhat modified in accordance with the various parts of the country through which he travels. The Italians of the north resemble the inhabitants of the south of France, and those of Italian Switzerland. The character of the Tuscans is more effeminate, their language and manners more refined. The bearing of the Roman is grave and proud. With all of these, however, the stranger will find no difficulty in associating; and acts of civility or kindness will not be misplaced, even when conferred on persons of the lower ranks. With the class of Neapolitans with whom the traveller generally comes in contact the case is entirely different. Dishonest and perfidious to an almost incredible extent, cringing and obsequious, they seem to conspire to embitter the traveller's enjoyment of their delightful country. It is to be hoped a better era is dawning under the new regime, and the "policy" of honesty will at length begin to penetrate the Italian mind.

The traveller who possesses more than a mere superficial acquaintance with the language will probably derive far greater instruction and gratification from a tour in Italy if he travels alone, than if accompanied by others; whilst, on the other hand, those who have attained little proficiency in the language will find it more enjoyable, as well as economical, to be members of a party.

VII. Locomotion.

Railways. With regard to the rapid advance of this modern essential of civilization the remarks already made (p. XIII) may suffice. — It may be added that the greatest speed attained by the trains is extremely moderate.

Porters who convey luggage to and from the carriages are sufficiently rewarded with a few sous. where there is no fixed tariff. It is a wise, and often necessary precaution (see p. XIV) to be provided with the exact fare before taking tickets.

The most trustworthy information respecting hours of starting. fares etc. is afforded by the "*Guida-orario ufficiale di tutte le strade ferrate d'Italia*" (see p. VI), containing a map, published at Milan by Edoardo Sonzogno (price 40 c.), with which the traveller should not fail to provide himself. The local time-tables of the Tuscan. Roman. and Neapolitan lines will also be found useful. and may be procured at the railway-stations for a few sous.

Steamboats. A voyage on the Mediterranean or Adriatic is almost inseparably connected with a tour in Italy and Sicily, irrespective of the fact that the latter can be reached by water only. If the vessel plies near the coast, the voyage is often extremely entertaining: and if the open sea is traversed, the magnificent Italian sunsets, which light up the deep blue water with their crimson rays, present a scene not easily forgotten.

Tickets should be purchased by the traveller in person at the office of the company, and no attention paid to the proffered services of loiterers in the vicinity. The ticket is furnished with the purchaser's name and destination, the name of the vessel, and the hour of departure. Fares, duration of voyage etc. are stated in each instance in the following pages (pp. 1, 9, 80). Family-tickets for the first or second class, for not fewer than three persons, are issued by all the companies at a reduction of 20 per cent on the fare, but not on the cost of food. A child of 2—10 years pays half-fare, but in this case must share the berth of its attendant. Two children are entitled to a berth for themselves. The tickets of the Messageries Impériales are available for four months, and the voyage may be broken at the passenger's discretion. It may here again, be remarked that the rival French companies Fraissinet and Valéry (p. 1, 9) reduce their fares from 20 to 30 per cent according to circumstances. At the same time it should be borne in mind that these vessels usually stop to discharge their cargoes during the day, and proceed on their voyage at night.

The saloons and berths of the first class are comfortably and elegantly fitted up, those of the second tolerably. Passengers of the second class have free access. like those of the first, to every part of the deck. Officers of the Italian and French armies, up to the rank of captain inclusive, are entitled to berths of the second class only, when travelling at the expense of government.

Luggage. First-class passengers are allowed 100 kilogr. (= 2 cwt.), second class 60 kilogr. (= 135 lbs.), but articles not intended for the passenger's private use are prohibited.

Food of good quality and ample quantity is included in the first and second-class fares. The difference between that provided for first and for second-class passengers is inconsiderable. A déjeûner à la fourchette is served at 10, consisting of 3—4 courses, tolerable table wine ad libitum, and a cup of coffee. Dinner is a similar repast between 5 and 6 o'clock. At 7 tea is served in the first, but not in the second class. Passengers who are too ill to partake of these repasts are furnished with lemonade etc. gratuitously. Refreshments may of course be procured at other hours on payment.

Fees. The steward expects 1 l. for a voyage of 12—24 hrs., more if the passenger has made unusual demands upon his time or patience.

Embarcation. Passengers should be on board an hour before the advertised time of starting. The charges for conveyance to the steamboat (usually 1 l. for each pers. with luggage) are fixed by tariff at all the sea-ports, and will be found in the Handbook. Passengers should therefore avoid all discussions on the subject with the boatmen, and simply direct them to row "al Vaticano", "alla Bella Venetia", or whatever the name of the vessel may be. En route, the boatman generally makes a demand extravagantly in excess of the tariff: "Signore, sono cinque lire!" to which the passenger may simply reply: "avanti!"

On arriving at the vessel, payment should not be given to the boatman until the traveller with all his luggage is safely on deck. The wild gesticulations of the boatman, who has perhaps calculated upon the credulity of his passenger, but receives no more than his due (ample remuneration), may be enjoyed with malignant serenity from the deck, as on that "terra sacra" disputes are strictly prohibited.

On board the passenger gives up his ticket, receives the number of his berth, superintends the stowing away of his luggage, and finally repairs to the deck to observe the progress of the vessel as it quits the harbour, of which it generally commands a fine view.

On board the vessels of the Messageries everything is conducted with military precision. Complaints should be addressed to the captain. Questions addressed to the subalterns or crew are generally responded to somewhat laconically.

Diligences. *Corrieri* are the swifter conveyances which carry the mails, and accommodate two or three passengers only at high fares. *Diligenze*, the ordinary stage-coaches, convey travellers with tolerable rapidity, and generally for the same fares as similar vehicles in other parts of the continent. They are in the hands of private companies, and where several run in competition the more expensive are to be preferred. The company is usually far from select, the carriages uncomfortable. When ladies are of the party the coupé ($^1/_3$rd dearer) should if possible be secured. Regular communication cannot be depended on except on the principal routes. The importunities of the coachmen at the end of each stage should be disregarded.

The communication between many towns is maintained by **Vetturini**, who convey travellers neither very comfortably nor rapidly, but at moderate cost. Inside places cost somewhat more than those in the cabriolet. The driver receives a trifling fee, the ostler 1 soldo; for the removal or replacement of luggage 2 soldi. These conveyances afford the best opportunity of obtaining an insight into the customs of the country. The institution has, however, received a death-blow from the more modern diligences and railways. The ordinary tourist will probably rarely have occasion to submit to a style of conveyance rapidly becoming obsolete, except on the route between Florence and Rome. The vetturini are generally respectable and trustworthy, and show no less zeal for the comfort and safety of their employers than in the care of their cattle. With three horses and a vehicle to accommodate six passengers 35—40 M. are daily accomplished. At midday a halt of several hours is made. The vetturini also engage to provide the traveller with hotel accommodation, which, when thus contracted for, is considerably less costly than when the traveller caters for himself. In this case it is advisable to draw up a carefully worded contract, to which the vetturino affixes his signature or mark. This should also be made to include the gratuity (tutto compreso); and, if satisfaction is given, an additional fee may be bestowed at the termination of the journey. The entire vehicle, or the interior only, may be engaged. It should be distinctly arranged before starting, where the night is to be passed, where breakfast and dinner taken. The aid of some one acquainted with the customs of the country is desirable in a transaction of this description. The agreement having been concluded, the vetturino gives the traveller a small sum as earnest-money (caparra), by which both parties are bound. The following formula will serve as a basis for a contract of this nature.

Contratto tra il Sgr. N. N. e il Vetturino N. N.

Io sottoscritto Vetturino m'obbligo, di condurre il Sgre. N. N. e sua famiglia etc. in una buona carrozza con tre etc. buoni ca-

valli, *ed incaricare la loro roba di viaggio cosi ben servata*, *che non prenda nessun danno*, *e non si perda niente*, *da* . . . . *per* . . . . *a* . . . . *in* . . . . *giorni*, *cioè a dire il primo giorno a* . . . . *il secondo a* . . . . *etc. ed arrivare sempre a buon ora*, *sotto le seguenti condizioni:*

La vettura tutta intiera (non eccettuato il gabrioletto, or if the traveller engages the interior only, *eccettuato il g.)*, *appartiene per questo viaggio ai detti Sgri. Passeggieri. Al vetturino non è permesso*, *di prendere un altro viaggiatore*, *sotto qualunque nome sia.*

Gli passeggieri ricevono ogni giorni di viaggio salvo quello dell' arrivo al conto del vetturino in un albergo di prima qualità la cena di (sei) *piatti e* . . . *stanze separate ben ammobigliate e pulite con* . . . . *letti netti e buoni.*

Il sopradetto Signore spende al sopradetto vetturino la somma di . . . . *senza altera obbligazione di pagare mancia*, *pedaggio*, *barriera*, *cavalli*, *bovi*, *poste o altra cosa sia. Il pagamento detto sara pagato nelle proprie mani del medesimo vetturino* . . . . *dopo l'arrivo a* . . . .

La partenza da . . . . *è fissata per il* . . . . *del mese* . . . .

In caso che il vetturino non tenga un punto del contratto, *il viaggiatore non è tenuto di pagare un quattrino.*

Date . . . . Signature of the vetturino, or . . . . *per non sapere scrivere fece la croce.*

A single traveller may also bargain with a vetturino for one seat, the charge for which varies. The back-seats are "i primi posti", which are generally secured by the first comers, who are first consulted with regard to the arrangement of the journey. For a single traveller a written contract is hardly necessary. A previous understanding should, however, be made with regard to the gratuity; and a separate room (stanza separata) at the inns should be stipulated for, otherwise the traveller will run the risk of being compelled to share the apartment of his travelling companions.

The stranger who travels with little luggage, and desires to become acquainted with the customs of the country, need not bind himself to the regular stages on the high roads, but may arrange his journey so as to stop at the less frequented towns and villages. Besides the above-mentioned conveyances, carriages may be hired everywhere (with one horse about 65 c. per Engl. M.).

Pedestrianism. An Italian never walks if he can possibly drive; to him it is an inexplicable mystery how walking can afford pleasure. The remark has been frequently made to the Editor: "*lei è signore e va a piedi?!*" In the more frequented districts, such as the vicinity of Rome, the inhabitants are accustomed to this mania of strangers, who may wander in the Campagna, and among the Sabine and Alban Mts. without exciting much surprise. Excursions on foot in other parts of Italy also possess their peculiar attractions, and among other advantages that of procuring for the pedestrian the enviable reputation of being a *pittore*, or needy individual from whom little is to be extorted.

Prolonged walking-tours, such as are undertaken in more northern climates, and fatiguing excursions will be found wholly unsuitable to the Italian climate. Cool and clear weather should if possible be selected, and the sirocco carefully avoided. The height of summer is totally adverse to tours of this kind.

A *horse* (cavallo) or *donkey* (sommaro, Neapol. ciucio), between which the difference of expense is inconsiderable, often affords a pleasant and inexpensive mode of locomotion, especially in mountainous districts, where the attendant (pedone) acts at once as a servant for the time being, and as a guide. This mode of travelling is especially in vogue on the Alban and Sabine Mountains, and may without hesitation be adopted by ladies. A previous bargain should here be made, tutto compreso, a gratuity being added if the traveller is satisfied. It should also be observed that the attendants often avoid the most picturesque points on account of the ruggedness of the paths. Moreover they frequently indulge in a habit of urging on the animals to an alarmingly rapid pace at first starting, or when passing through a town or village. The éclat attending such a proceeding, though a source of gratification to them, tends neither to the safety nor the dignity of the rider! At the beginning of the excursion, therefore, a check should be imposed upon these impulsive gentry by a threat of withholding the buona mano.

VIII. Hotels.

The idea of cleanliness in Italy is in arrear of the age; the brilliancy of the southern climate perhaps in the opinion of the natives neutralizes dirt. The traveller will not, however, suffer much annoyance in this respect in hotels and lodgings of the best class. Those who quit the beaten track, on the other hand, must be prepared for privations. In the villages the pig (animale nero) appears as a domestic animal, and a privileged inmate of the houses, to which the poultry also have free access. Iron bedsteads should if possible be selected, as affording less accommodation to the active class so hostile to repose. Insect-powder *(polvere di Persia*, or Keating's) or camphor is some antidote to their advances. The *zanzare*, or gnats, are a source of great annoyance, and often suffering, during the autumn months. Windows should always be carefully closed before a light is introduced into the room. Light muslin curtains (zanzieri) round the beds.

masks for the face, and gloves are employed to ward off the attacks of these pertinacious intruders.

In all the more frequented places good hotels of the first class are always to be found, the landlords of which are frequently German. Rooms $2^1/_2$—5 l., bougie 75 c.—1 l., attendance 1 l.. table d'hôte 4 l., and so on. Families, for whose reception the hotels are often specially fitted up, should make an agreement with the landlord with regard to pension (8—10 l. each). Strangers are expected to dine at the table d'hôte, otherwise the price of the room is raised. or the inmate is given to understand that it is "wanted". French spoken everywhere. Cuisine a mixture of French and Italian.

The second-class inns are thoroughly Italian. rarely very clean or comfortable; charges about one-half the above: no table d'hôte. but a trattoria will generally be found connected with the house. where refreshments à la carte may be procured at any hour. These establishments will often be found convenient and economical by the voyageur en garçon, but are of course rarely visited by ladies.

In hotels in the Italian style, especially in the smaller towns, it is advisable to institute enquiries as to charges beforehand. If exorbitant demands be made, they may be generally reduced without difficulty to reasonable limits. An extortionate bill may even be reduced although no previous agreement has been made, but this is never effected without long and vehement discussions.

The best hotels have fixed charges. Attendance, exclusive of boots and commissionaire. is charged in the bill. This is not the case in the smaller inns, where 1 [l. per diem is usually divided between the waiter and the facchino, or less for a prolonged stay. Copper coins are never despised by such recipients.

Hôtels Garnis are much frequented by those whose stay extends to 10—14 days and upwards, and the inmates enjoy greater quiet and independence than at a hotel. The charges are moreover considerably more moderate. Attendance about $1/_2$ l. per diem.

Lodgings of various degrees of comfort and accommodation may also be procured for a prolonged residence. Here, likewise. a distinct agreement respecting the rent should be made beforehand. Where a whole suite of apartments is hired . a written contract should be drawn up with the aid of some one acquainted with the language and customs of the place (e. g. a banker). For single travellers a verbal agreement with regard to attendance, linen, stoves and carpets in winter, a receptacle for coal etc., will generally suffice.

A few hints may be here added for the benefit of the less experienced:

If a prolonged stay is made at a hotel, the bill should be demanded every three or four days, by which means errors, whether accidental or designed, are more easily detected. When the traveller contemplates departing at an early hour in the morning, the bill should be obtained on the previous evening, but not paid until the moment for starting has arrived. It is a favourite practice to withhold the bill till the last moment, when the hurry and confusion render overcharges less liable to discovery.

The mental arithmetic of waiters is apt to be exceedingly faulty, though rarely in favour of the traveller. A written enumeration of the items charged for should therefore invariably be required, and accounts rejected in which, as not unfrequently happens, *"colazione, pranzo, vino, caffè* etc." figure in the aggregate.

Information obtained from waiters, and others of a similar class, can never be implicitly relied upon. Enquiries should be addressed to the landlords or head-waiters alone, and even their statements received with considerable caution.

IX. Restaurants and Cafés.

Restaurants *(trattorie)* are chiefly frequented by Italians, and travellers unaccompanied by ladies. Dinner may be obtained à la carte at any hour between 12 and 7 or 8 p. m., for $1^{1}/_{2}$ —3 l. The waiters expect a gratuity of 2—4 soldi. The diner who desires to confine his expenses within reasonable limits should refrain from ordering dishes not comprised in the bill of fare. A late hour for the principal repast of the day should be selected in winter, in order that the daylight may be profitably employed.

The following list comprises most of the commoner Italian dishes:

Zuppa, soup.
Consumè, broth or bouillon.
Santè, or *minestra*, soup with green vegetables and bread.
Gnocchi, small puddings.
Riso con piselli, rice-soup with peas.
Risotto, a species of rice pudding (rich).
Maccaroni al burro, with butter; *al pomidoro*, with paradise-apples.
Manzo, boiled beef.
Fritti, fried meat.

Arrosti, roasted meat.
Bistecca, beefsteak.
Coscietto, loin.
Arrosto di vitello, roast-veal.
Testa di vitello, calf's head.
Fegato di vitello, calf's liver.
Braccioletta di vitello, veal-cutlet.
Costoletta alla minuta, veal-cutlet with calf's ears and truffles.
Patate, potatoes.
Quaglia, quail.
Tordo, field-fare.
Lodola, lark.
Sfoglia, a species of sole.

CAFÉS.

Principi alla tavola, hot relishes.
Funghi, mushrooms (often too rich).
Prezciutto, ham.
Salami, sausage.
Pollo, fowl.
Pollastro, turkey.
Umidi, meat with sauce.
Stufatino. ragout.
Erbe, vegetables.
Carciofi, artichokes.
Piselli, peas.
Lenticchie, lentils.
Cavoli fiori. cauliflower.
Fave. beans.
Fagiuolini, French beans.
Mostarda, simple mustard.
Senape, hot mustard.
Ostriche. oysters (good in winter only).
Giardinetto, fruit-desert.
Crostata di frutti, fruit-tart.
Crostata di pasta sfoglia, a species of pastry.
Fragole, strawberries.
Pera, pear.
Persiche, peaches.
Uva, bunch of grapes.
Limone, lemon.
Portogallo. orange.
Finocchio, root of fennel.
Pane francese, bread made with yeast (the Italian is made without).
Formaggio, cheese.
Vino nero. red wine; *bianco*, white: *asciutto*, dry: *dolce*. sweet; *nostrale*, table-wine.

Cafés are frequented for breakfast and lunch, and in the evening by numerous consumers of ices. Café noir *(caffè nero)* is usually drunk (10—20 c. per cup). *Caffè latte* is coffee mixed with milk before served (20 c.); or *caffè e latte*, i. e. with the milk served separately, may be preferred (30—40 c.). *Mischio* is a mixture of coffee and chocolate (15—20 c.), considered wholesome and nutritious. The usual viands for lunch are ham, sausages. cutlets and eggs *(uova da bere*, soft; *toste*, hard; *uova al piatto*, fried). .

Ices *(gelato)* of every possible variety are supplied at the cafés (30—90 c. per portion); a half portion *(mezza)* may always be ordered. *Granita*, or half-frozen ice *(limonata*, of lemons; *aranciata* of oranges), is especially in vogue in the forenoon. The waiter *(bottega)* expects a sou or more, according to the amount of the payment; he occasionally makes mistakes in changing money if not narrowly watched.

The principal Parisian newspapers are to be found at all the larger cafés, English rarely.

Wine-shops *(osterie)* are much frequented, especially in Rome, by the lower classes, and are generally primitive and dirty. Habitués of these localities resort thither in the evening to sup, having previously provided themselves with comestibles procured at the sausage-monger's *(pizzicarola)*.

Valets de Place *(servitori di piazza)* may be hired at 5 l. per diem, the employer previously distinctly specifying the services to be rendered. They are generally trustworthy and respectable.

but implicit reliance should not be placed on their statements respecting the places most worthy of a visit, which the traveller should ascertain from the guide-book or other source. Their services may always be dispensed with, unless time is very limited. Travellers are cautioned against employing the *sensali*, or commissionaires of an inferior class, who pester the stranger with offers of every description. Contracts with vetturini, and similar negociations should never be concluded through such a medium, or indeed any other. Interventions of this description invariably tend considerably to increase prices, and are often productive of still more serious contretemps. This remark applies especially to villages and small towns, whether on or out of the regular track.

X. Churches, Theatres, Shops etc.

Churches are open till noon, and usually again from 4 to 7 p. m.; St. Peter's the whole day. Visitors may inspect the works of art even during the hours of divine service, provided they move about noiselessly, and keep aloof from the altar where the clergy are officiating. The verger (*sagrestano*, or *nonzolo*) receives a fee of $1/2$ l. or upwards, if his services are required.

Theatres. The representations in the large theatres begin at 8, and terminate at midnight or later. Here operas and ballets are exclusively performed; the first act of an opera is usually succeeded by a ballet of 3 or more acts. Verdi is the most popular composer. The pit (*platea*) is the usual resort of the men. A box (*palco*) must always be secured in advance. — A visit to the smaller theatres, where dramas and comedies are acted, is especially recommended for the sake of habituating the ear to the language. Representations in summer take place in the open air, in which case smoking is allowed. The charming comedies of Goldoni are still among the greatest favourites. — The theatre is the usual evening-resort of the Italians, by whom during the performance of the music profound silence is never observed.

Shops, with the exception of those of German and English booksellers, rarely have fixed prices. As a rule two-thirds or three-quarters of the price demanded should be offered. The same rule applies to artizans, drivers and others. "*Non volete?*" (then you will not?) is a remark which generally has the effect of bringing the matter to a speedy adjustment. Purchases should never be made by the traveller when accompanied by a valet-de-place. These individuals, by tacit agreement, receive at least 10 per cent of the purchase-money, which naturally comes out of the pocket of the purchaser. This system of extortion is carried so far that, when a member of the above class observes a stranger enter a shop, he presents himself at the door, and afterwards claims his percentage under the pretext that by *his* recommendation the purchase has been made. In such cases it is by no means superfluous to call the attention of the shopkeeper to the imposition (*"non conosco quest' uomo"*).

Cigars in Italy and the States of the Church are a monopoly of Government, and bad; those under 3—4 sol. scarcely smokable. Passers-by freely avail themselves of the light which burns in every cigar-shop, without making any purchase.

XI. Postal Arrangements.

The address of letters (whether *poste restante* or to the traveller's hotel) should, as a rule, be in the Italian or French language. Postage-stamps are sold at all the tobacco-shops. Letters to England cost 60 c., France 40 c., Germany 60 c., Switzerland 30 c., Belgium 40 c., Holland (via France) 70 c., Denmark 85 c., Norway and Sweden 1 l., Russia 1 l.

Letters by town-post 5 c.; throughout the kingdom of Italy 20 c. prepaid, 30 c. unpaid. Letters to Rome must be prepaid as far as the frontier (20 c.), also vice versà.

In the larger towns the post-office is open daily from 9 a. m. to 10 p. m. (also on Sundays and holidays).

XII. Calculation of Time.

The old Italian reckoning from 1 to 24 o'clock is now disused, except by the people. Ave Maria = 24. The hours are altered every fortnight, being regulated by the sunset. The ordinary reckoning of other nations is termed *ora francese*. The traveller will find little difficulty in employing the Italian reckoning when he has occasion to do so.

XIII. Climate. Mode of Life.

Travellers from the north must in some degree alter their mode of living whilst in Italy, without however implicitly adopting the Italian style. Strangers generally become unusually susceptible to cold in Italy, and therefore should not omit to be well supplied with warm clothing for the winter. Carpets and stoves, to the comforts of which the Italians generally appear indifferent, are indispensable in winter. A southern aspect is an absolute essential for the delicate, and highly desirable for the robust. Colds are most easily caught after sunset and in rainy weather. — Even in summer it is a wise precaution not to wear too light clothing. Flannel is strongly recommended.

Exposure to the summer-sun should as much as possible be avoided. According to a Roman proverb, dogs and foreigners (Inglesi) alone walk in the sun, Christians in the shade. Umbrellas, and spectacles of coloured glass (grey, concave glasses to protect the whole eye are best) may be used with advantage when a walk in the sun is unavoidable. Repose during the hottest hours is advisable, a siesta of moderate length refreshing. Windows should be closed at night.

English and German medical men are to be met with in the larger cities. The Italian therapeutic art does not enjoy a very high reputation in the rest of Europe. German and English chemists, where available, are recommended in preference to the Italian. It may, however, be a wise discretion, in the case of maladies arising from local causes, to employ native skill.

Italian Art.
An Historical Sketch by Professor Springer of Bonn.

One of the primary objects of the enlightened traveller in Italy is usually to form some acquaintance with its treasures of art. Even those whose ordinary vocations are of the most prosaic nature unconsciously become admirers of poetry and art in Italy. The traveller here finds them so interwoven with scenes of everyday life, that he involuntarily encounters their impress at every step, and becomes susceptible to their influence. A single visit can hardly suffice to enable any one to form a just appreciation of the numerous works of art he meets with in an extended tour, nor a guide-book to initiate him into the mysterious depths of Italian creative genius, the past history of which is especially attractive; nevertheless a few remarks on this subject will be found materially to enhance the pleasure, and assist the penetration of even the most unpretending lover of art. Works of the highest class, the most perfect creations of genius, lose nothing of their charm by being pointed out as specimens of the culminating point of art; whilst, on the other hand, those of inferior merit are invested with far higher interest when regarded as necessary links in the chain of development, and when, on comparison with subsequent or preceding works, their relative defects or superiority are recognised. The following observations, therefore, will hardly be deemed a superfluous adjunct to a work designed to aid the traveller in deriving the greatest possible amount of enjoyment and instruction from his sojourn in Italy.

The two great epochs in the history of art which principally arrest the attention are those of classic antiquity, and of the 16th century, the culminating period of the so-called Renaissance. The intervening space of more than a thousand years is usually, with much unfairness, almost entirely ignored. But this interval not only continues to exhibit vestiges of the first epoch, but gradually paves the way for the second. The erroneousness of the view, that in Italy alone the character of ancient art can be thoroughly appreciated, may here be demonstrated. This opinion dates from the period when no precise distinction was made between Greek and Roman art, when the connection of the former with a particular land and nation, and the tendency of the latter to pursue an independent course were alike overlooked. Now, however, that we are acquainted with more numerous Greek originals, and have acquired a deeper insight into the development of Hellenic art, an indiscriminate confusion of the Greek and Roman styles is no longer to be apprehended. We are now well aware that the highest perfection of ancient architecture is visible in the Hellenic temple alone. The Doric order, in which majestic gravity is expressed by massive proportions and symmetrical decoration, and the Ionic structure, with its lighter and more graceful character, exhibit a creative spirit entirely different from that manifested in the sumptuous Roman edifices. Again, the most valuable collection of ancient sculptures in Italy is incapable of affording so admirable an insight into the development of Greek art as the sculptures of the Parthenon, and other fragments of Greek temple-architecture preserved in the British Museum. But, although instruction is afforded more abundantly by other than Italian sources, ancient art is perhaps thoroughly admired in Italy alone, where works of art encounter the eye with more appropriate adjuncts, and where climate, scenery and people materially contribute to intensify their impressiveness. As long as a visit to Greece and Asia Minor is within the reach of comparatively so few travellers, a sojourn in Italy will be best calculated to furnish information respecting the growth of ancient art. An additional facility, moreover, is afforded by the circumstance, that in accordance with an admirable custom of classic antiquity the once perfected type of a plastic figure was not again arbitrarily abandoned, but rigidly adhered to, and continually reproduced. Thus in numerous cases, where the more ancient Greek original had been lost, it was preserved in subsequent copies, and even in the works of the Roman imperial age Hellenic creative talent is still reflected.

The non-professional traveller will hardly be disposed to devote much of his attention to the works of the earliest dawn of art, to the so-called Cyclopean walls, constructed of polygonal blocks of stone (as those of Pyrgi, Cosa, Saturnia, but more commonly met with in Lower Italy), or to the artistic progress of the mysterious Etruscan nation (man'fested in their tombs, cinerary urns, implements of metal and mural paintings). But the eye will not fail to rest with interest upon their magnificent golden ornaments, their beautiful designs engraved on metal (bronze-mirrors: the finest engraved design handed down by antiquity is on the Ficoronian cista in the Museo Kircheriano at Rome), and their numerous painted vases. The latter not only disclose to the observer a wide sphere of ancient artistic ideas, and prove how intimately a love of the beautiful and graceful was associated with the pursuit of a mere trade, but at the same time present one of the earliest instances of artistic industry. Although most of these vases were discovered in Etruscan tombs, they are not all to be regarded as specimens of Italian workmanship, for many of them were imported from Greece, where they were systematically manufactured, originally perhaps at Corinth, subsequently at Athens (vases with red figures).

The artistic dependence of ancient Italy on Greece was not confined to this single, and comparatively subordinate branch of art, but gradually extended to every other department, including those of architecture and sculpture. This supremacy of Greek intellect in Italy was established in a twofold manner. In the first place Greek colonists introduced their ancient native style into their new homes. This is proved by the existence of several Doric temples in Sicily, such as those of Selinunto (but not all dating from the same period), and the ruined temples at Syracuse, Girgenti and Segesta. On the mainland the so-called Temple of Neptune at Pæstum, as well as the ruins at Metapontum, are striking examples of the fully developed elegance and grandeur of the Doric order. But, in the second place, the art of the Greeks did not attain its universal supremacy in Italy till a later period, when Hellas, politically ruined, had learned to obey the dictates of her mighty conqueror, and the Romans began to combine the refinements of more advanced culture with their political superiority. The ancient scenes of artistic activity in Greece (Athens for example) became re-animated at the cost of Rome; Greek works of art, and Greek artists were introduced; ostentatious pride in the magnificence of the booty acquired by victory, merged, by an easy transition, into a taste for such objects; to surround themselves with artistic decoration became the universal custom, and the foundation of public monuments an indispensable duty of government.

Although the Roman works of art of the imperial epoch are deficient in originality compared with the Greek, yet their authors never degenerate into mere copyists, or entirely renounce independent effort. This remark applies especially to their Architecture. Independently of the Greeks, the ancient Italian nations, and with them the Romans, had acquired a knowledge of stone-cutting, and discovered the method of constructing arches and vaulting. With this technically and scientifically important art they aimed at combining Greek forms, the column supporting the entablature. Moreover the sphere of architecture became extended. One of the chief requirements was now to construct edifices with spacious interiors, and several stories in height. No precise model was afforded by Greek architecture, and yet the current Greek forms appeared too beautiful to be voluntarily abandoned. The Romans therefore preferred to combine them with the arch-principle, and apply this combination to their new architectural designs. The individuality of the Greek orders, and their originally so unalterable coherence were thereby sacrificed, and divested of much of their importance; that which once possessed a definite organic significance frequently assumed a superficial and decorative character; but the aggregate effect is always imposing, the skill in blending contrasts, and the refinement of the directing taste admirable. The lofty gravity of the Doric † style must not be sought for at Rome. The Doric column in the hands of Roman architects lost the finest features of its original character, and was at length entirely disused. The Ionic column also, and corresponding entablature were regarded with less partiality than those of the Corinthian order, the decorative sumptuousness of which was more in unison with the artistic taste of the Romans. As the column in Roman architecture was no longer destined exclusively to support a superstructure, but formed a projecting portion of the wall, or was merely of an ornamental character, a form in which the enrichments were most conspicuous was the most appropriate. It is, moreover, intelligible that the graceful Corinthian capital, formed by slightly drooping acanthus-leaves, was at length regarded as insufficiently

---

† Those unacquainted with architecture may without difficulty learn to distinguish the different Greek styles. In the Doric the shafts of the columns (without bases) rest immediately on the common pavement, in the Ionic they are separated from it by bases. The flutings of the Doric column are immediately contiguous, separated by a sharp ridge, whilst those of the Ionic are disposed in pairs, separated by broad unfluted intervening spaces. The Doric capital, expanding towards the summit, somewhat resembles a crown of leaves, and was in fact originally adorned with painted representations of wreaths; the Ionic capital is distinguished by the volutes (or scrolls) projecting on either side, which may be regarded rather as an appropriate covering of the capital than as the capital itself. The entablature over the columns begins in the Doric style with the simple, in the Ionic with the threefold architrave; above which in the Doric order are the metopes (originally openings, subsequently receding panels) and triglyphs (tablets with two angular channels in front, and a half channel at each end, extremities of beams, as it were), in the Ionic the frieze with its sculptured enrichments. In the temples of both orders the front culminates in a pediment. The so-called Tuscan, or early Italian column, approaching most nearly to the Doric, exhibits no decided distinctive marks; the Corinthian, with the rich capital formed of acanthus-leaves, is essentially of a decorative character only. The following technical terms should also be observed. Temples in which the columns are on both sides enclosed by the projecting walls are termed "in antis" (antæ = end-pilasters); those which have one extremity only adorned by columns, prostyle; those with an additional pediment in the rear, supported by columns, amphiprostyle; those entirely surrounded by columns, peripteral. In some temples it was imperative that the image of the god erected in the cella should be exposed to the rays of the sun. In this case an aperture was left in the ceiling and roof, and such temples were termed hypaethral. Temples are also named tetrastyle, hexastyle, octastyle etc. according to the number of columns at each end. — A most attractive study is that of architectural mouldings and enrichments, and of those constituent members, which indicate superincumbent weight, or a free and independent existence. Research in these matters will enable the traveller more fully to appreciate the strict harmony of ancient architecture.

enriched, and was superseded by the so-called Roman capital (first applied in the arch of Titus), a union of the Corinthian and Ionic. As an impartial judgment respecting Roman architecture cannot be formed from a minute inspection of the individual columns, so the highest rank in importance is not to be assigned to the Roman temples. The sole circumstance of the different (projecting) construction of their roofs excludes them from comparison with the Greek. Attention must be directed to the several-storied structures, in which the tasteful ascending gradation of the component parts, from the more massive (Doric) to the lighter (Corinthian), especially attracts the eye; and the vast and artistically vaulted interiors, as well as the structures of a merely decorative description, must be examined, in order that the chief merits of Roman art may be recognised. In the employment of columns in front of closed walls (e. g. as members of a façade), in the disposition of domes above circular interiors, and of cylindrical and groined vaulting over oblong spaces, the Roman structures served as models to posterity, whose workmanship has often fallen short of the originals. No dome-building has yet been erected which will bear comparison with the simple and strikingly effective Pantheon, originally a pertinent of the Thermæ of Agrippa; nor does there exist any edifice so sumptuous, combining so varied an aggregate of structures, and yet bearing so harmonious and monumental a character, as from their ruins we presume the Thermæ of Caracalla and Diocletian to have been. Boldness of design, skill in execution, accurate estimation of resources, consistent prosecution of the object in view, and practical utility combined with imposing splendour characterise most of the Roman fabrics, whether destined for public traffic like the basilicas of the fora, to gratify the popular love of pageantry like the amphitheatres, theatres and circuses, to commemorate the achievements of the living by means of triumphal arches, or those of the dead by monumental tombs. Finally it is worthy of note that architecture resisted degradation longer than any other art, and does not betray palpable signs of declension until the commencement of the 4th century, after having considerably earlier attained its culminating point under the Flavii.

The history of the Art of Sculpture among the Romans, which moreover never evidenced their national greatness in the same degree as architecture, is of briefer duration. Two different methods of investigation may here be pursued. Those who possess sufficient preliminary information, and do not shrink from an arduous although interesting task, should examine the numerous statues representing gods and heroes in accordance with the Greek models, of which we possess written records, and compare them with the descriptions. In the statue of Zeus from the house of the Verospi, and in the bust of Otricoli (Vatican), the lineaments of the Olympic Zeus created by Phidias will be sought for, in the statues of Hercules their derivation from the ideal of Lysippus, in the Juno Ludovisi, and the other head of Hera in the Museum at Naples, their descent from the Juno of Polycletes: whilst the discus-throwers of Myron, the Amazons of Phidias, Ctesilaus etc., the Ares and Apollo of Scopas, the statues of Venus by Praxiteles and others will be recognised in their imitations and slight variations. By these means a correct judgment will be formed with regard to the position of the individual work in the development of ancient art, and the relation of the later sculpture of the Romans to that of the earlier Greeks will be clearly understood. By this systematic criticism the science of archæology has of late years arrived at brilliant results; it has proved that a series of Greek works, once regarded as irrecoverably lost, still survive in their copies, and it has correctly explained other misinterpreted sculptures (e. g. the Apollo Belvedere). The amateur, however, will probably prefer to adhere to the course which was formerly enthusiastically pursued by the scientific, and be satisfied with contemplating the mere artistic beauty of the sculptures, irrespective of their historical significance. This æsthetic mode of investigation is justified by the fact that the sculpture of antiquity presents to our eye a harmonious whole, in which the same principles and the same bias of imagination almost invariably prevail. Be the distinction between Greek and Roman views of art, and between the earlier and later development of the plastic art ever so strongly emphasized, yet the existence of numerous common elements, and the voluntary subordination of the later artists to the once established type cannot be disputed. This will be rendered clearer by an example. A universally predominant ideal of the Madonna, on which the images of mediæval and modern art are based, cannot possibly be discovered. Between the Madonnas of Raphael, and Our Lady of the old German and Dutch schools, not the faintest resemblance can be traced; were the former lost, their character could never be divined from the latter. In ancient art, on the contrary, the image of a god, even of the later Roman period, continues to exhibit the distinctive character of the original ideal, and often serves admirably to throw light upon defects in the earlier images; moreover every plastic work of antiquity, whether remote or more recent, faithfully embodies for us the precepts of sculpture, and enables us to recognise the treatment of the nude, the disposition of the drapery, and the just standard of expression and movement. Whether the archæological or æsthetical interest be placed in the foreground, opportunities will always present themselves for an examination of the characteristic features of Roman sculpture. This art developed itself most freely between the reigns of Augustus and Hadrian, flourishing contemporaneously with the most brilliant period of the Empire, and constituting its artistic adornment. Aptitude in imparting a living and attractive character to allegorical representations, as is well exemplified by the charming group of the Nile (Vatican), is not to be regarded as a peculiar feature of Roman art so much as the strikingly individualizing stamp expressed in portrait-busts and statues, and the realistic element from which the creation of historical reliefs has emanated. Specimens of this faithful and detailed historical representation, which however occasionally violates the plastic standard, are afforded by the triumphal arches of Titus and Constantine (reliefs partly transferred from the arch of Trajan), the columns of Trajan and Marcus Aurelius. As late as the time of Hadrian a new ideal was sought in Antinous, but after that period the art rapidly declined, although even down to the latest era of the Empire great technical skill was still frequently exhibited. The most interesting of these later works are sarcophagus-sculptures, owing to their almost encyclopædic richness in representations, and the extensive sphere of ideas which they embrace. They constituted the most important school of art for subsequent generations, whence their historical significance; but the same cannot be said of monumental architecture. although the latter now exhibits the most diversified and attractive picture of the artistic life of antiquity. The ruins of Herculaneum and Pompeii prove more forcibly than any record, how universally art was applied in the ancient world, and how even the humblest implements were ennobled by artistic forms; they form an inexhaustible mine of decorative enrichment, and refute the prevailing idea that an entirely subordinate rank is to be assigned to ancient painting. As they were not rescued from oblivion till the 18th century, they exercised no influence on the art of the middle ages or the Renaissance, whilst on the other hand we no longer possess the decorative paintings of the Roman Thermæ, which wrought so powerfully on the artistic imagination as late as the 16th century.

In the 4th century the heathen world, which had long been in a tottering condition, at length became Christianised, and a new period of art commenced. This is sometimes erroneously regarded as the result of a forcible rupture from the ancient Roman art, and à sudden and spontaneous invention of a new style. But the eye and the hand adhere to custom more tenaciously than the mind. Whilst new ideas, altered views of the character of the Deity and the destination of man were entertained, the wonted forms were still necessarily employed in the expression of these thoughts. Moreover the heathen sovereigns had by no means been unremittingly hostile to Christianity (the most bitter persecutions did not take place till the 3rd century). and the new doctrines were permitted to expand, take deeper root, and organize themselves in the midst of heathen society. The consequence was, that the transition from heathen to Christian ideas of art was a gradual one, and that in a formal respect early Christian art prosecuted the tasks of the ancient. The best proof of this is afforded by the paintings of the Roman Catacombs. These, forming as it were a subterranean belt around the city, were by no means originally the secret and anxiously concealed places of refuge of the primitive Christians, but constituted their legally recognised, publicly accessible burial-places (e. g. the catacombs of Nicomedes and of Fl. Domitilla), and were not enveloped in intentional obscurity until the periodically recurring. persecutions of the 3rd century. Reared in the midst of the customs of heathen Rome, the Christian community perceived no necessity to deviate from the artistic principles of antiquity. In the embellishment of the catacombs they adhered to the decorative forms handed down by their ancestors; and in design, choice of colour, grouping of figures, and treatment of subject, they were entirely guided by the customary rules. The earlier the date of the paintings in the catacombs, the more nearly they approach the ancient forms. Even the sarcophagus-sculptures of the 4th and 5th centuries differ in purport only, and not in technical treatment, from the type exhibited in the tomb-reliefs of heathen Rome. Five centuries elapsed before a new artistic style was awakened in the pictorial, and the greatly neglected plastic arts. Meanwhile architecture had developed itself commensurately with the requirements of Christian worship, and, in connection with the new modes of building, painting acquired a different character.

The term Basilica-Style is often employed to designate early Christian architecture down to the 10th century. The name is of great antiquity, but it is erroneous to suppose that the early Christian basilicas possessed anything beyond the mere appellation in common with those of the Roman fora. The latter structures, which are proved to have existed in most of the towns of the Roman empire, and served as courts of judicature and public assembly-halls, differ essentially in their origin and form from those of the Christian church. The forensic basilicas were neither fitted up for the purposes of Christian worship, nor did they serve as models for the construction of Christian churches. The latter are rather to be regarded as extensions of the private dwelling-houses of the Romans, where the first assemblies of the community were held, and the component parts of which were reproduced in ecclesiastical edifices. The most faithful representative now extant of the architectural character and internal arrangements of an early Christian basilica is the church of S. Clemente at Rome. A small portico borne by columns leads to the anterior court (atrium), surrounded by colonnades and provided with a fountain (cantharus) in the centre; the eastern colonnade is the approach to the interior of the church, which usually consisted of a nave and two aisles, the latter lower than the former, and separated from it by two rows of columns, the whole terminating in a semicircle (apsis). In front of the apse a transverse space (transept) sometimes extended; the altar, surmounted by a columnar structure, occupied a detached position in the apse; the space in front of it, bounded by cancelli or railings, was occupied by the choir of officiating priests; and the two pulpits (ambones) where the gospel and epistles were read. Unlike the ancient temples, the early Christian basilicas exhibit a neglect of external architecture, the chief importance being attached to the interior, the decorations of which, however, especially in early mediæval times, were often procured by plundering the ancient Roman edifices, and transferring them to the churches with little regard to harmony of style and material. Thus the churches of S. Maria in Trastevere and S. Lorenzo fuori le Mura each possess columns of entirely different workmanship and materials. Other instances of a similar transference of columns are afforded by the churches of S. Sabina, S. Maria Maggiore etc. The most appropriate ornaments of the churches were the metallic objects, such as crosses and lustres, and the tapestry with which papal piety presented them: whilst the chief decoration consisted of mosaics, especially those covering the background of the apse and the (triumphal) arch which separates the apse from the nave. The mosaics, as far at least as the material was concerned, were of a sterling monumental character, and contributed to give rise to a new style of pictorial art: in them ancient tradition was for the first time abandoned, and the harsh and austere style erroneously termed Byzantine gradually introduced. Some of the earliest mosaics (composed of fragments of glass) are in the church of S. Pudenziana, dating like those of S. Costanza and the Baptistery of Naples from the 4th century, whilst those of S. Maria Maggiore and S. Sabina belong to the 5th. The mosaics in the church of SS. Cosma e Damiano in the Forum (date 526—530) are regarded as the finest compositions of the description.

Christian art originated at Rome, but its development was greatly promoted in other Italian districts, especially at Ravenna, where during the Ostrogothic supremacy (493—552), as well as under the succeeding Byzantine empire, architecture was zealously practised. The basilica-type was there more highly matured, the external architecture enlivened by low arches and projecting buttresses, and the capitals of the columns in the interior appropriately moulded with reference to the superincumbent arches. At Ravenna the occidental style also appears in combination with the oriental, and the church of S. Vitale (dating from 547) may be regarded as a fine example of a Byzantine structure. The term "Byzantine" is often totally misapplied. All the works of the so-called dark centuries of the middle ages, everything in architecture that intervenes between the ancient and the Gothic, everything in painting which repels by its uncouth, ill-proportioned forms, are designated as Byzantine: and it is commonly supposed that the practice of art in Italy was entrusted exclusively to Byzantine hands from the fall of the Western Empire to an advanced period of the 13th century. A belief in the universal and unqualified prevalence of the Byzantine style is entirely unfounded, as well as the idea that it exhibits no other characteristics than unsightliness and a clumsy, lifeless character. The forms of Byzantine architecture are at least strongly and clearly defined. Whilst the basilica appears as a long-extended hall, over which the eye is compelled to range until it finds a natural resting-place in the recess of the apse, every Byzantine structure may be circumscribed with a curved line. The aisles, which in the basilica run parallel with the nave, degenerate in the Byzantine style to narrow and insignificant passages; the apse loses its intimate connection with the nave, and is separated from it; the most conspicuous feature in the architecture consists of the central square space, bounded by four massive pillars which support the dome. These are the essential characteristics of the Byzantine style, which culminates in the magnificent church of S. Sophia, prevails throughout oriental Christendom, but in the West, including Italy, only occurs sporadically. With the exception of the churches of S. Vitale at Ravenna, and St. Mark at Venice, the edifices of Lower Italy alone exhibit a frequent application of this style. When baptisteries and mortuary chapels are styled Byzantine on account of their circular form, this is not more justifiable than the popular classification of the whale among fishes. External points of resemblance must not be confounded with essential relationship.

The influence of the Byzantine imagination on the growth of other branches of Italian art appears to have been no greater. A brisk traffic in works of art was carried on by Venice, Amalfi etc. between the Levant and Italy; the position of Constantinople resembled that of the modern Lyons; silk-wares, tapestry, jewellery were most highly valued when imported from the Eastern metropolis. Byzantine artists were always welcome visitors to Italy, Italian lovers of art ordered works to be executed at Constantinople, especially those in metal, and the superiority of Byzantine workmanship was universally acknowledged. All this, however, does not justify the opinion that Italian art was entirely subordinate to Byzantine. In the main, notwithstanding various external influences, it experienced an independent and unbiassed development, and never entirely abandoned its ancient principles. A considerable interval indeed elapsed before the fusion of the original inhabitants with the early mediæval immigrants was complete, before the aggregate of different tribes, languages, customs and ideas became blended into a single nationality, and before the people attained sufficient concentration and independence of spirit to devote themselves successfully to the cultivation of art. Unproductive in the province of art as this period is, yet an entire departure from native tradition, or a serious conflict of the latter with extraneous innovation never took place. It may be admitted, that in the massive columns and cumbrous capitals of the churches of Upper Italy, and in the art of vaulting which was here developed at an early period, symptoms of the Germanic character of the inhabitants are manifested, and that in the Lower Italian and especially Sicilian structures, traces of Arabian and Norman influence are unmistakable. The pointed arches of the cathedral of Amalfi, and those in the cloisters of the monastery-church of Ravello, the interior of the Cappella Palatina at Palermo etc. point to Arabian models; whereas the façades of the churches at Cefalu and Monreale, and the enrichments of their portals recal Norman types. In the essentials, however, the foreigners continue to be the recipients; the might of ancient tradition, and the national idea of form could not be repressed or superseded. About the middle of the 11th century a zealous and promising artistic movement took place in Italy, and the seeds were sown which three or four centuries later yielded so luxuriant a growth. As yet nothing was matured, nothing completed, the aim was obscure, the resources insufficient: meanwhile architecture alone satisfied artistic requirements, whilst attempts at painting and sculpture were barbarous in the extreme; these, however, were the germs of the subsequent development observable as early as the 11th and 12th centuries. This has been aptly designated as the Romanesque period, and the then prevalent forms of art as the Romanesque Style. As the Romance languages, notwithstanding alterations, additions and corruptions, maintain their relation of daughtership to the language of the Romans, so Romanesque art, in spite of its rude and barbarous aspect, reveals its immediate descent from the art of that people. The Tuscan towns were the principal scene of the prosecution of mediæval art. There an industrial population gradually arose, treasures of commerce were collected, independent views of life were acquired in active party-conflicts, loftier common interests became interwoven with those of private life, and education entered a broader and more enlightened track. — whence a taste for art also was awakened, and æsthetic perception developed itself. When Italian architecture of the Romanesque period is examined, the difference between its character and that of contemporaneous northern works is at once apparent. In the latter the principal aim is perfection in the construction of vaulting. French, English and German churches are unquestionably the more organically conceived, the individual parts are more inseparable and more appropriately arranged. But the subordination of all other aims to that of the secure and accurate formation of the vaulting does not admit of an unrestrained manifestation of the sense of form. The columns are apt to be heavy, symmetry and harmony in the constituent members to be disregarded. On Italian soil new architectural ideas are rarely found, constructive boldness is not here the chief object; on the other hand, the decorative arrangements are richer and more grateful, the sense of rythm and symmetry more active. The cathedral of Pisa, founded as early as the 11th century, or the church of S. Miniato near Florence, dating from the 12th, may be taken as an example. The interior with its rows of columns, the mouldings throughout, and the flat ceiling recal the basilica-type; whilst the exterior, especially the façade destitute of tower, with the small arcades one above the other, and the variegated colours of the layers of stone, present an aspect of decorative pomp. But the construction and decoration of the walls already evince a taste for the elegant proportions which we admire in subsequent Italian structures; the formation of the capitals, and the design of the outlines prove that the precepts of antiquity were not entirely forgotten. In the Baptistery of Florence (S. Giovanni) a definite Roman structure (the Pantheon) has even been imitated. A peculiar conservative spirit breathes throughout the mediæval architecture of Italy; artists do not aim at an unknown and remote object; the ideal which they have in view, although perhaps instinctively only, lies in the past; to conjure up this and bring about a Renaissance of the antique appears to be the goal of their aspirations. They apply themselves to their task with calmness and concentration, they indulge in no bold or novel schemes, but are content to display their love of form in the execution of detail. What architecture as a whole loses in historical attraction is compensated for by the beauty of the individual edifices. Whilst the north possesses structures of greater importance in the history of the development of art, Italy boasts of a far greater number of pleasing works.

The position occupied by Italy with regard to Gothic architecture is thus rendered obvious. She could not totally ignore its influence, although incapable of according an unconditional reception to this, the highest development of vault-architecture. Gothic was introduced into Italy in a mature and perfected condition. It did not of necessity, as in France, develop itself from the earlier (Romanesque) style, its progress cannot be traced step by step; it was imported by foreign architects (practised at Assisi by the German master Jacob), and adopted because in consonance with the tendency of the age; it found numerous admirers among the mendicant orders of monks and the humbler classes of citizens, but could never entirely disengage itself from Italianising influences. It was so far transformed that the constructive constituents of Gothic are degraded to a decorative office, and the national taste thus became reconciled to it. The cathedral of Milan cannot be regarded as a fair specimen of Italian Gothic, but attention should be directed to the mediæval cathedrals of Florence, Siena, Orvieto, as well as numerous secular edifices, such as the loggia of the Lanzi at Florence, and the communal palaces of mediæval Italian towns. An acquaintance with true Gothic construction, so contracted notwithstanding all its apparent richness, so exclusively adapted to practical requirements, can assuredly not be acquired from these cathedrals. The spacious interior inviting, as it were, to calm enjoyment, whilst the cathedrals of the north appear to call forth a sentiment of longing, the predominance of horizontal lines, the playful application of pointed arches and gables, of finials, canopies etc. prove that an organic coherence of the different architectural distinguishing members was here but little regarded. The characteristics of Gothic architecture, the towers immediately connected with the façade, and the prominent flying buttresses are frequently wanting in Italian Gothic edifices — whether to their disadvantage, it may be doubted. It is not the sumptuousness of the materials which disposes the spectator to pronounce a lenient judgment, but a feeling that Italian architects pursued the only course by which the Gothic style could be reconciled with the atmosphere and light, the climate and natural features of Italy. Gothic lost much of its peculiar character in Italy, but by these deviations from the customary type it there became capable of being nationalised. This was the more infallibly the case as at the same period the other branches of art also aimed at a greater degree of universality, and entered into a new combination with the fundamental trait of the Italian character, that of retrospective adherence to the antique. The apparently sudden and unprepared-for revival of ancient ideals in the 13th cent. is one of the most interesting phenomena in the history af art. The Italians themselves could only account for this by attributing it to chance. The popular story was that the sculptor Nicola Pisano was induced by an inspection of ancient sarcophagi to exchange the prevailing style for the ancient. We are, however, in a position to trace the course pursued by Italian sculpture more precisely: we conjecture that Nicholas of Pisa was stimulated by the example of Lower Italy, where during the Hohenstaufen sway a golden era of civilisation was developed: we moreover know that this inclination towards antiquity was by no means confined to Italy, but was equally active at an even earlier period in the north (e. g. in the ancient district of Saxony); nevertheless Nicola Pisano's influence was instrumental in inaugurating a new epoch in the development of Italian imagination. His sculptures on the pulpits in the Baptistery of Pisa and the Cathedral of Siena introduce us immediately into a new world. Their obvious resemblance to the works of antiquity does not alone arrest the eye; a still higher interest is awakened by their peculiarly fresh and lifelike tone, betokening the enthusiastic concentration with which the master devoted himself to his task. During the succeeding period (Pisan School) ancient characteristics were placed in the background, and importance was attached solely to life and expression (e. g. reliefs on the façade of the Cathedral at Orvieto). Artists now began to impart to their compositions the impress of their own peculiar views. Art, moreover, became more interwoven with the public taste, which had already fully manifested itself in poetry also. From this period (14th century) therefore the Italians date the origin of their modern art. Contemporaneous writers who observed the change of views, the revolution in sense of form, and the superiority of the more recent works in life and expression, warmly extolled their authors, and proclaimed how greatly they surpassed their ancestors. But succeeding generations began to lose sight of this connection between ancient and modern art. A mere anecdote was deemed sufficient to connect Giotto di Bondone (1276—1336), the father of modern Italian art. with Giovanni Cimabue, the most celebrated representative of the earlier style (Cimabue is said to have watched Giotto, when as a shepherd-boy he relieved the monotony of his office by tracing the outlines of his sheep in the sand, and to have received him as a pupil in consequence). But it was forgotten that a revolution in artistic ideas and forms manifested itself at Rome and Siena still earlier than at Florence, that both Cimabue and his pupil Giotto possessed numerous professional brethren, and that the composition of mosaics was still successfully practised, as well as mural and panel-painting. Subsequent investigation has rectified these errors, pointed out the Roman and Tuscan mosaics as works of the transition-period, and restored the Sienese master Duccio, who was remarkable for his sense of the beautiful and the expressiveness of his figures, to his merited rank. At the same time, however, Giotto is fully entitled to rank in the highest class. The amateur, who before entering Italy has become acquainted with Giotto from insignificant panel-pictures only, often arbitrarily attributed to this master, and even in Italy itself encounters little else than obliquely drawn eyes, clumsy features, and cumbrous masses of drapery as characteristics of his style, will regard Giotto's reputation as unfounded. He will be at a loss to comprehend why Giotto is regarded as the inaugurator of a new era of art, and why the name of the old Florentine master is only second in popularity to that of Raphael himself. The fact is, Giotto's celebrity is not due to any single perfect work of art. His indefatigable energy in different spheres of art, the enthusiasm which he aroused in all directions, and the development for which he paved the way, must be taken into consideration, in order that his place in history may be understood. Even when, in consonance with the poetical sentiments of his age, he embodies allegorical conceptions, as poverty, chastity, obedience, or displays to us a ship as an emblem of the Church of Christ, he shows a masterly acquaintance with the art of converting what is perhaps in itself an ungrateful idea into a speaking, life-like scene. Giotto is an adept in narration, in imparting a faithful reality to his compositions. The individual figures in his pictures may fail to satisfy the expectations, and even earlier masters, such as Duccio, may have surpassed him in execution, but intelligibility of movement and dramatic effect were first naturalized in art by Giotto. This is partly attributable to the luminous colouring employed by Giotto in place of the dark and heavy tones of preceding masters, enabling him to impart the proper expression to his artistic and novel conceptions. On these grounds therefore Giotto, so versatile and so active in the most extended spheres, was accounted the purest type of his century, and succeeding generations constituted a regular school of art in his name. As in the case of all the earlier Italian painters, so in that of Giotto and his successors, an opinion of their true merits can be formed from their mural paintings alone. The intimate connection of the picture with the architecture, of which it constituted the living ornament, compelled artists to study the rules of symmetry and harmonious composition, developed their sense of style, and, as extensive spaces were placed at their disposal, admitted of broad and unshackled delineation. Almost every church in Florence boasted of specimens of art in the style of Giotto, almost every town in Central Italy during the 14th century practised some branch of art akin to Giotto's. The most valuable works, however, are preserved in the Churches of S. Croce and S. Maria Novella at Florence (in the latter the Cappella degli Spagnuoli is especially important). Beyond the precincts of the Tuscan capital the finest work of Giotto is to be found in the Cappella dell' Arena at Padua, where in 1303 he executed a representation of scenes from the life of the Virgin. The Campo Santo of Pisa affords specimens of the handiwork of his pupils. In the works on the walls of this unique national museum the spectator cannot fail to be struck by their finely-conceived, poetical character (e. g. the Triumph of Death), their sublimity (Last Judgment, Trials of Job), or their richness in dramatic effect (History of St. Rainerus, and of the Martyrs Ephesus and Potitus).

In the 15th century, as well as in the 14th, Florence continued to take the lead amongst the capitals of Italy in matters of art. Vasari attributes this merit to its pure and delicious atmosphere, which he regards as highly conducive to intelligence and refinement. We are, however, now in a position to offer a sounder explanation. The fact is, that Florence did not itself produce a greater number of eminent artists than other districts. During a long period Siena successfully vied with her in artistic fertility, and Upper Italy in the 14th cent. gave birth to the two painters d'Avanzo and Aldighieri (paintings in the Chapel of S. Giorgio in Padua), who far surpass Giotto's ordinary style. On the other hand, no Italian city afforded in its political institutions and public life so many favourable stimulants to activity in so marked a degree, or combined a love of enjoyment with dignified principles so harmoniously as Florence. What therefore was but obscurely experienced in the rest of Italy, and manifested at irregular intervals only, was usually here first embodied with tangible distinctness. Florence became the birthplace of the revolution in art effected by Giotto, and Florence was the home of the art of the Renaissance, which began to prevail soon after the commencement of the 15th cent., and superseded the style of Giotto. The word R e n a i s s a n c e is commonly understood to designate a revival of the antique. It must be admitted that ancient art now began more strongly to influence artistic taste, and that its study was more zealously prosecuted. But the essential character of the Renaissance by now means consists exclusively, or even principally, in the imitation of the antique; nor must the term be confined merely to art, as it may be said to embrace the entire progress of civilisation in Italy during the 15th and 16th centuries. How the Renaissance manifested itself in political life, and the different phases it assumes in the scientific and the social world, cannot here be discussed. It may, however, be observed that the Renaissance in social life was chiefly promoted by the "humanists", who preferred general culture to great professional attainments, who enthusiastically regarded classical antiquity as the golden age of great men, and who exercised the most extensive influence on the bias of artistic views. In the period of the Renaissance the position of the artist with regard to his work, and the nature and aspect of the latter are changed. Personal education, individual taste leave a more marked impress on the work of the author than was ever before the case; his creations are pre-eminently the reflection of his intellect; his alone is the responsibility, his the reward of success or the mortification of failure. Artists now seek to attain celebrity, they desire their works to be examined and judged as testimonials of their personal endowments. Skilful workmanship by no means satisfies them, although they are far from despising the drudgery of a handicraft (many of the most eminent quattrocentists received the rudiments of their education in the workshop of a goldsmith), the exclusive pursuit of a single sphere of art is regarded by them as an indication of intellectual poverty, and they aim at mastering the technicalities of each different branch. They work simultaneously as painters and sculptors, and if they apply their abilities to architecture, it is deemed nothing unwonted or anomalous. A comprehensive and versatile education, united with refined personal sentiments, forms their loftiest aim. This they attain in but few instances, but that they eagerly aspired to it is proved by the biography of the illustrious Leo Battista Alberti, who is entitled to the same rank in the 15th century, as Leonardo da Vinci in the 16th. Rationally educated, physically and morally healthy, keenly alive to the calm enjoyments of life, and possessing clearly defined ideas and decided tastes, the artists of the Renaissance necessarily regarded nature and her artistic embodiment with different views from their predecessors. A fresh and joyous love of nature seems to pervade the entire epoch. In accordance with the diversified tendencies of investigation, artistic imagination also strives to approach her, at first by a careful study of her various phenomena. Anatomy, geometry, perspective, and the study of drapery and colour are zealously pursued and practically applied. External truth, fidelity to nature, and a correct rendering of real life in its minutest details are among the necessary qualities in a perfect work. The realism of the representation is, however, only the basis for the expression of life-like character and enjoyment of the present. The earlier artists of the Renaissance exhibit no partiality for pathetic scenes, or events which awaken painful emotions and turbulent passions; their preference obviously inclines to cheerful and joyous subjects. In the works of the 15th century strict faithfulness, in an objective sense, must not be looked for. Whether the topic be derived from the Old or the New Testament, from history or fable, it is always transferred to the immediate present, and adorned with the colours of actual life. Thus Florentines of the genuine national type are represented as surrounding the patriarchs, visiting Elisabeth after the birth of her son, or witnessing the miracles of Christ. This transference of remote events to the present bears a striking resemblance to the naïve and not unpleasing tone of the chronicler. The development of Italian art, however, by no means terminates with mere fidelity to nature, a quality moreover displayed by the contemporaneous art of the north. A superficial glance at the works of the Italian Renaissance enables one to recognise the higher goal of imagination. The carefully selected groups of dignified men, beautiful women and pleasing children, occasionally without internal necessity placed in the foreground, prove that attractiveness was pre-eminently desired. This is also evidenced by the early-awakened enthusiasm for the nude. by the skill in disposition of drapery, and the care devoted to boldness of outline and accuracy of form. This aim is still more obvious from the keen sense of symmetry observable in all the better artists. The individual figures are not coldly and accurately drawn in conformity with systematic rules. They are executed with refined taste and feeling; harshness of expression and unpleasing characteristics are sedulously avoided, whilst in the art of the North physiognomic fidelity is usually accompanied by extreme rigidity. A taste for symmetry does not prevail in the formation of the individual figure only; obedience to rythmical precepts is perceptible in the disposition of the groups also, and in the composition of the entire work. The intimate connection between Italian painting (fresco) and architecture naturally leads to the transference of architectural rules to the province of pictorial art, whereby not only the invasion of a mere luxuriant naturalism was obviated, but the fullest scope was afforded to the artist for the execution of his task. For to discover the most effective proportions, to inspire life into the representation by the very rythm of the lineaments, are not accomplishments to be acquired by extraneous aid; precise measurement and calculation are here of no avail; a happily organised eye, refined taste, and a creative imagination, which instinctively divines the appropriate forms for its design, can alone excel in this sphere of art. This enthusiasm for external beauty and just and harmonious proportions is the essential characteristic of the art of the Renaissance. A veneration for the antique is thus also accounted for. At first an ambitious longing for fame caused the Italians of the 15th and 16th centuries to look back to classical antiquity as the era of illustrious men, and ardently to desire its return. Subsequently, however, they regarded it simply as an excellent and appropriate resource, when the study of actual life did not suffice, and an admirable assistance in perfecting their sense of form and symmetry. They by no means viewed the art of the ancients as a perfect whole, or as the product of a definite historical epoch, which developed itself under peculiar conditions; but their attention was arrested by the individual works of antiquity and their special beauties. Thus ancient ideas were re-admitted into the sphere of Renaissance art. A return to the religious spirit of the Romans and Greeks must of course not be inferred from the veneration for the ancient gods during the humanistic period; belief in the Olympian gods was extinct; but precisely because no devotional feeling was intermingled, because these forms could only receive life from creative imagination, did they exercise so powerful an influence on the Italian artist. The significance of mythological characters being entirely due to the perfect beauty of their forms, they could not fail on this account pre-eminently to recommend themselves to artists of the Renaissance.

These remarks will, it is hoped, convey to the reader a general idea of the significance of the Renaissance. Those who examine the architectural works of the 15th or 16th century should refrain from marring their enjoyment by the not altogether justifiable reflection, that in the Renaissance style no new system was invented, as the architects merely employed the ancient elements, and adhered principally to tradition in their constructive principles and selection of component parts. Notwithstanding the apparent want of organization, however, great beauty of form, emanating from the most exuberant imagination, will be observed in all these structures, from the works of Brunelleschi (1377—1446) to those of Andrea Palladio of Vicenza (1518—1580), the last great architect of the Renaissance. The style of the 15th century may without difficulty be distinguished from that of the 16th. The Florentine palaces (Pitti, Riccardi, Strozzi) are still based on the type of the mediæval castle. A taste for beauty of detail, coeval with the realistic tendency of painting, produces in the architecture of the 15th century an extensive application of graceful and attractive ornaments, which entirely cover the surfaces, and throw the true organisation of the edifice into the background. For a time the true aim of Renaissance art appears to have been departed from, anxious care is devoted to detail instead of to general effect; the re-application of columns did not at first admit of spacious structures, the dome rose but timidly above the level of the roof. But this attention to minutiæ, this disregard of effect on the part of these architects, was only, at is were, a restraining of their power, in order the more completely to master, the more grandly to develop the art. The early Renaissance is succeeded by Bramante's epoch (1444—1514), with which the golden age of symmetrical construction commenced. With a wise economy the mere decorative portions were circumscribed, whilst greater significance and more marked expression were imparted to the true constituents of the structure, the real exponents of the architectural design. The works of the Bramantine era (High Renaissance) are less graceful and attractive than those of their predecessors, but superior in their well defined, ,lofty simplicity and finished character. Had the Church of St. Peter been completed in the form originally designed by Bramante, we should be in a position to pronounce a more decided opinion respecting the ideal of the church-architecture of the Renaissance. The circumstance that precisely the mightiest work of this style has been subjected to the most varied alterations (for vastness of dimensions was the principal aim of the bold plans of the architects) teaches us to refrain from the indiscriminate blame which so commonly falls to the lot of Renaissance churches. It must at least be admitted that the favourite form, that of a Greek cross (with equal arms) with rounded extremities, crowned by a dome, possesses concentrated unity, and that the pillar-construction relieved by niches presents an aspect of imposing grandeur; nor can it be disputed that in the churches of the Renaissance the same artistic principles are applied as in the universally admired palaces and secular edifices. If the former therefore excite less interest, this is not due to the inferiority of the architects, but to causes altogether beyond their control. The succeeding generation of the 16th century did not adhere to the style established by Bramante, but never reduced it to a finished system. They aim more sedulously at general effect, so that harmony among the individual members begins to be neglected: they endeavour to arrest the eye by boldness of construction and striking contrasts; or they import new modes of expression from antiquity, the precepts of which had hitherto been applied in an unsystematic manner only. Throughout the diversified stages of development of the succeeding styles of Renaissance architecture, felicity of proportions is invariably the aim of all the great masters. To appreciate their success in this aim should also be regarded as the principal task of the spectator, who with this object in view will do well to compare a Gothic with a Renaissance structure. This comparison will prove to him that other elements than harmony of proportion are effective ingredients in architecture; for, especially in the cathedrals of Germany, the exclusively vertical tendency, the attention to form without regard to measure, the violation of the precepts of rythm. and a disregard of proportion and the proper ratio of the open to the closed cannot fail to strike the eye. Even the unskilled amateur will thus be convinced of the abrupt contrast between the mediæval and the Renaissance styles. Thus prepared, he may. for example, proceed to inspect the Palace of the Pitti at Florence, which, undecorated and unorganised as it is, would scarcely be distinguishable from a rude pile of stones, if a judgment were formed from the mere description. The artistic charm consists in the simplicity of the mass, the justness of proportion in the elevation of the stories, and the tasteful adjustment of the windows in the vast surface of the façade. That the architects thoroughly understood the æsthetical effect of symmetrical proportions is proved by the mode of construction adopted in the somewhat more recent Florentine palaces, in which the roughly hewn blocks (rustica) in the successive stories recede in gradations, and by the careful experiments as to whether the cornice surmounting the structure should bear reference to the highest story, or to the entire façade. The same bias manifests itself in Bramante's imagination. The Cancelleria may justly be designated as a beautifully organized structure; and when, after the example of Palladio in church-façades, a single series of columns superseded those resting above one another. symmetry of proportion was also the object in view.

Every guide-book and every cicerone points out to the traveller in Italy the master-pieces of Renaissance architecture which he should inspect. Of that of the 15th century the Tuscan towns afford the finest selection, but at the same time the brick structures of the cities of Lombardy, which display a taste for copious and florid decoration, should not be overlooked. An acquaintance with the style of Bramante and his contemporaries (Peruzzi, San Gallo the younger) may best be formed at Rome, although the architecture of the 17th century is most characteristic of the Eternal City. The most important works of the middle and latter half of the 16th century are also to be sought for in the towns of Upper Italy (Genoa, Vicenza, Venice). In Venice especially, within a very limited space, the development of the Renaissance architecture may conveniently be surveyed. The fundamental type of the domestic architecture here continues with little variation. The nature of the ground afforded little scope for the caprice of the architect, whilst the conservative spirit of the inhabitants gave rise to a definite consuetude in style. The nicer distinctions of style are therefore the more observable, and that which emanated from a pure sense of form the more appreciable. Those who by careful comparison have discovered the great superiority of the Biblioteca (in the Piazzetta) of Sansovino over the new Procurazie of Scamozzi, although the two edifices exactly correspond in many respects, have made great progress towards an accurate insight into the architecture of the Renaissance. Much, moreover, would be lost by the traveller who exclusively devoted his attention to the master-works which have been extolled from time immemorial, or solely to the great monumental structures. As even the insignificant vases (majolicas, manufactured at Pesaro, Urbino, Gubbio and Castel-Duvante) bear testimony to the taste of the Italians, their pleasure in classical models, and their enthusiasm for purity of form, so also in inferior works, some of which fall within the province of a mere handicraft, the peculiar beauties of the Renaissance style are detected, and in remote corners of the towns charming specimens of a prolific architectural imagination are discovered. Nor must the vast domain of decorative sculpture be disregarded, as such works, whether in metal, stone or stucco, in inlaid or carved wood, often verge on the sphere of architecture.

On the whole it may be asserted that the architecture of the Renaissance, which in consonance with the requirements of modern life manifests its greatest excellence in sumptuous secular structures, cannot fail to gratify the taste of the most superficial observer. With the sculpture of the same epoch the case is different. Italian architecture of the 15th and 16th centuries possesses a practical value for us, and is frequently imitated at the present day; the painting of the same period we believe to have attained its highest consummation; the sculpture of the Renaissance, on the other hand, does not appear to us worthy of revival, and cannot in this respect compete with that of antiquity; and we are wont to regard its position as subordinate in the sphere of art of that age. The latter opinion, however. is erroneous. Sculpture, far from enjoying a lower degree of favour, was viewed by artists as the true centre of their sphere of activity. Sculpture was the first art in Italy which was launched into the stream of the Renaissance, in its development it was ever a step in advance of the other arts. and in the popular opinion possessed the advantage of most clearly embodying the current ideas of the age, and of affording the most brilliant evidence of the re-awakened love of art. It is probably to be ascribed to the intimate connection between Italian Renaissance sculpture and the peculiar national culture, that the former lost much of its value after the decline of the latter, and was less appreciated than pictorial and architectural works. in which adventitious historical origin is obviously of less importance than general effect. In investigating the rise of the plastic art of the Renaissance, the enquirer at once encounters serious deviations from its strict precepts. and numerous infringements of æsthetical rules. The execution of reliefs constitutes by far the widest sphere of action of the Italian sculpture of the 15th century. These, however, contrary to the precepts of immemorial usage, are executed in a pictorial style. Ghiberti, for example, in his celebrated (eastern) door of the Baptistery of Florence. is not satisfied with grouping the figures as in a painting, and placing them in a rich landscape copied from nature. He treats the background in accordance with the rules of perspective; the figures at a distance are smaller and less raised than those in the foreground. He oversteps the limits of the plastic art, and above all violates the laws of the relief-style, according to which the figures are always represented in an ideal space, and the usual system of a mere design in profile is seldom departed from. So also the painted reliefs in terracotta by Luca della Robbia do not quite coincide with the current views of purity of plastic form. But if it be borne in mind that the sculptors of the Renaissance did not derive their ideas from a previously defined system, or adhere to abstract rules, the fresh and life-like vigour of their works (especially those of the 15th century) will not be disputed, and prejudice will be dispelled by the great attractions of the reliefs themselves. The sculpture of the Renaissance adheres as strictly as the other arts to the fundamental principle of representation; scrupulous care is employed in the faithful and attractive rendering of the individual objects; the taste is gratified by expressive heads, graceful female figures, and joyous children; the sculptors have a keen appreciation of the beauty of the nude, and the importance of a calm and dignified flow of drapery. Fidelity of representation, however, becomes for them a source of poetry in a higher degree than for their contemporaries in art. Actuated by a sense of the value of personality, true disciples of the humanistic precepts, they do not shrink from harshness of expression or rigidity of form; and by imparting the impress of their individual genius to the intractable exterior, they approach to the verge of the sublime. A predilection for bronze-casting accords with this inclination for the characteristic. In this material, decision and pregnancy of form are expressed without restraint, and almost, as it were, spontaneously. Works in marble also occur, but these generally trench on the province of decoration, and seldom display the bold and unfettered aspirations which are apparent in the works in bronze. It is remarkable that the reformatory character of the earlier sculpture of the Renaissance is confined to form alone, whilst in the selection of subjects tradition is invariably followed. The majority of these works bear the impress of ecclesiastical destination. The best museum of Italian sculpture of the 15th century is constituted by the external niches of Or San Michele in Florence, where, besides Donatello the principal master, Ghiberti. Verocchio and others have immortalised their names. These with other statues on church-façades (the best specimens of the second generation of sculptors of this period are perhaps the works of Rustici and Sansovino in the Baptistery of Florence), reliefs of pulpits, organ-parapets, altar-enrichments, church-doors etc. form the principal sphere of plastic activity. The most admirable specimens of the earlier Renaissance sculpture are to be found in Central Italy. Besides Florence, the towns of Lucca (where Civitali wrought), Pistoja, Siena and Prato should be explored. At Rome (S. Maria del Popolo) and Venice (school of the Lombardi, Bregni and of Leopardo) the monumental tombs especially merit careful examination. We may perhaps frequently take exception to their inflated and somewhat monotonous style, which during an entire century remained almost unaltered, but we cannot fail to derive sincere pleasure from the inexhaustible freshness of imagination so richly manifested within these narrow limits.

As a museum cannot convey an adequate idea of the 15th century, so a visit to a picture gallery will not afford an accurate insight into the painting of that period. Sculptures are frequently removed from their original position, as has been the case with the Florentine churches, which within the last few years have been deprived of many of their treasures, whilst mural paintings are of course generally inseparable from the architecture. Of the frescoes of the 15th century of which a record is preserved, perhaps one-half are destroyed or obliterated, but those still extant are the most instructive and attractive examples of the art of this period. The mural paintings in the Church del Carmine (Cappella Brancacci) at Florence, executed by Masaccio and others, are usually mentioned as the earliest specimens of the painting of the Renaissance. This is a chronological mistake, as some of these frescoes were not completed before the second half of the

15th century; but in the main the classification is justifiable, as this cycle of pictures may be regarded as a programme of the earlier art of the Renaissance, and served to maintain the significance of the latter even during the age of Raphael. Here the beauty of the nude was first revealed, here a calm dignity in the single figures, as well as in the general arrangement, was for the first time faithfully embodied; and the transformation of a group of indifferent spectators in the composition into a sympathizing choir, which as it were forms a frame to the principal actors in the scene, was first successfully effected. It is, therefore, intelligible that these frescoes should be still regarded as models by the succeeding generation, and that, when in the preceding century the attention of connoisseurs was again directed to the beauties of the pre-Raphaelite period, the works of Masaccio and Filippino Lippi should have been eagerly rescued from oblivion.

A visit to the churches of Florence is well calculated to convey an idea of the subsequent rapid development of the art of painting. The most important and extensive works are those of Domenico Ghirlandajo: the frescoes in S. Trinità (a comparison with the mural paintings of Giotto in S. Croce, which also represent the legend of St. Francis, is extremely instructive; so also a parallel between Ghirlandajo's Last Supper in the monasteries of S. Marco and Ognissanti, and the work of Leonardo), and those in the choir of S. Maria Novella, which in sprightliness of conception are hardly surpassed by any other work of the same period. Beyond the precincts of Florence, Benozzo Gozzoli's charmingly expressive scenes from the Old Testament on the northern wall of the Campo Santo of Pisa, forming genuine biblical genre-pictures, then Filippo Lippi's frescoes at Prato, Piero della Francesca's Finding of the Cross in S. Francesco at Arezzo, and finally Luca Signorelli's representation of the end of the world in the Cathedral at Orvieto, present the most brilliant survey of the character and development of Renaissance painting in Central Italy. Arezzo and Orvieto should by no means be passed over, not only because the already-mentioned works of Piero della Francesca and Luca Signorelli show how nearly the art even of the 15th century approaches perfection, but because both of these towns afford an immediate and most attractive insight into the artistic taste of the mediæval towns of Italy. Those who cannot accomplish a visit to the provincial towns will find several at least of the principal masters of the 15th cent. united in the mural paintings of the Sixtine Chapel at Rome, and by studying the pictures in the gallery of the Florentine Academy will obtain a general idea of the development of Renaissance-painting. At the same time an acquaintance with the Tuscan schools alone can never suffice to enable one to form a judgment respecting the general progress of art in Italy. Chords which are here but slightly touched vibrate powerfully in Upper Italy. Mantegna's works (Padua and Mantua) derive their chief interest from having exercised a marked influence on the German masters Holbein and Dürer. The Umbrian school, which originates with Gubbio, and is admirably represented early in the 15th century by Ottaviano Nelli, blending with the Tuscan school in Gentile da Fabriano and Giovanni da Fiesole, and culminating in its last and greatest masters Perugino and Pinturicchio, also merits attention, not only because Raphael was one of its adherents during his first period, but because it in fact supplements the broadly delineating Florentine style, and notwithstanding its peculiar and limited bias is impressive in its character of lyric sentiment and religious devotion (e. g. Madonnas). The fact that the various points of excellence were distributed among different local schools pointed to the necessity of a loftier union. Transcendant talent was requisite, harmoniously to combine what could hitherto be viewed separately only. The 15th century, notwithstanding all its attractiveness, shows that the climax of art was not yet attained. The forms employed, graceful and pleasing though they be, are not yet lofty and pure enough to be regarded as embodying the purest and loftiest conceptions. The figures still present a local colouring, having been selected by the artists rather because sensually attractive, than because characteristic and expressive of their ideas. A portrait style still predominates, the actual representation does not appear always wisely balanced with the internal significance of the event, and the dramatic element is insufficiently emphasised. The most abundant scope was therefore now afforded for the labours of the great triumvirate, Leonardo da Vinci, Michael Angelo Buonarotti and Raphael Santi, by whom an entirely new era was inaugurated.

Leonardo's (1452—1519) remarkable character can only be thoroughly understood by means of prolonged study. His comprehensive genius was only partially devoted to art; he also directed his attention to scientific and practical pursuits of an entirely different nature. Refinement and versatility may be described as the goal of his aspirations; a division of human power, a partition of individual tasks were principles unknown to him. He laid, as it were, his entire personality into the scale in all that he undertook. He regarded a careful physical training as scarcely less important than a comprehensive culture of the mind; the vigour of his imagination aroused the application of his intellect also, his minute observation of nature developed his artistic taste and organ of form. One is frequently tempted to regard Leonardo's works as mere studies, in which he tested his powers, and which occupied his attention so far only as they gratified his love of investigation and experiment. At all events his personal importance has exercised a greater influence than his productions as an artist, especially as his prejudiced age strenuously sought to obliterate all trace of the latter. But few of Leonardo's works have been preserved in Italy, and these sadly marred by neglect. A reminiscence of his earlier period, when he wrought under Verocchio at Florence, and was a fellow-pupil of Lorenzo di Credi, is the fresco (Madonna and donor) in S. Onofrio at Rome. Several oil-paintings, portraits, Madonnas etc. (in the Galleria Sciarra at Rome) are attributed to his Milan period, although careful research inclines us to attribute them to his pupils. The best insight into Leonardo's style, his reforms in the art of colouring etc., is obtained by an attentive examination of the works of the Milan school (Luini, Salaino), as these are far better preserved than the original works of the master, of which (his battle-cartoon having been unfortunately lost with the exception of a single equestrian group) the Last Supper in S. Maria delle Grazie at Milan is now the only worthy representative. Although this in its damaged condition may be termed the shadow of a shadow, it is still well calculated to convey to the spectator, who has been prepared by the engravings, an idea of the new epoch of Leonardo. He should first examine the delicate equilibrium of the composition, how the individual groups are complete in themselves, and yet simultaneously point to a common centre, and impart a monumental character to the work; then the remarkable physiognomical fidelity which pervades every detail, the psychological distinctness of character, the dramatic life, together with the calmness of the entire bearing of the picture; he will then comprehend that with Leonardo a new era in Italian painting was inaugurated, that the development of art had attained its perfection.

The accuracy of this assertion will perhaps be regarded by the amateur as dubious when he turns from Leonardo to Michael Angelo (1474—1563). On the one hand he hears Michael Angelo extolled as the most celebrated artist of the Renaissance, whilst on the other it is said that he exercised a prejudicial influence on Italian art, and was the precursor of the decline of sculpture and painting. Nor is an inspection of this illustrious master's works calculated to dispel the doubt. Unnatural and arbitrary features often appear in juxtaposition with the perfect, the profoundly significative, and faithfully conceived. As in the case of Leonardo, biographical studies alone afford an explanation of these anomalies, and lead to a just appreciat'on of Michael Angelo's artistic greatness. His principles do not differ from those of his contemporaries. Educated as a sculptor, he exhibits partiality to the nude, and treats the drapery in many respects differently from his professional brethren. But, like them, his aim is to inspire his figures with life-like expression, which he endeavours to attain by imparting to them an imposing and impressive character. At the same time he occupies an isolated position, at variance with many of the tendencies of his age. Naturally predisposed to melancholy, concealing a gentle and almost effeminate temperament beneath a mask of austerity, Michael Angelo was confirmed in his peculiarities by adverse political and ecclesiastical circumstances, and wrapped himself up within the depths of his own absorbing thoughts. His sculpture especially bears testimony to the profound sentiment of the artist, to which however he sacrifices symmetry and precision of form. His figures are thus converted into anomalous types, in which a grand conception, but no distinct or tangible thoughts, and least of all the traditional ideas are apparent. It is difficult now to comprehend what hidden sentiments the master embodied in his statues and pictures, which often present nothing but a massive and clumsy form, and appear to lose themselves in meaningless mannerism. The deceptive effect produced by Michael Angelo's style is best exemplified by some of his later works. His Moses in S. Pietro in Vincoli is of impossible proportions; such a man can never have existed: the huge arms and the gigantic torso are utterly disproportionate; the robe which falls over the celebrated knee could not be folded as it is represented. Nevertheless the work is grandly impressive: so also are the monuments of the Medicis in S. Lorenzo at Florence, in spite of the forced attitude and arbitrary moulding of some of the figures. Michael Angelo only sacrifices the accuracy of constituents in order to enhance the aggregate effect, in the inspection of which we forget to examine the details. Had so great and talented a master not presided over the whole, the danger of an inflated style would have been incurred, the forms selected would have been exaggerated, and a professional coldness apparent. Michael Angelo's numerous pupils, desirous of faithfully following the example of the master's Last Judgment in the Sixtine, succeeded only in representing complicated groups of unnaturally foreshortened nude figures, whilst Baccio Bandinelli. thinking even to surpass Michael Angelo, produced in his group of Hercules and Cacus (in the Piazza della Signoria at Florence) a mere caricature of his model.

Amateurs will best be enabled to render justice to Michael Angelo by first devoting their attention to his earlier works, among which in the province of sculpture the group of Pietà (in St. Peter's) occupies the highest rank. The statues of Bacchus and David (at Florence) likewise do not transgress the customary precepts of the art of the Renaissance. Paintings of Michael Angelo's earlier period are rare; the finest, whether conceived during his youthful development, or his maturer years, is unquestionably the ceiling-painting in the Sixtine. The architectural arrangement of the ceiling, and the composition of the several pictures are equally masterly; the taste and discrimination of the painter and sculptor are admirably combined. In God the Father.

Michael Angelo produced a perfect type of its kind; he understood how to inspire with dramatic life the abstract idea of the act of creation, which he conceived as motion in the prophets and sibyls. Notwithstanding the apparent monotony of the fundamental intention (foreshadowing of the Redemption), a great variety of psychological incidents are displayed and embodied in distinct characters. Finally, in the so-called ancestors of Christ, the forms represented are the genuine emanations of Michael Angelo's genius, pervaded by his profound and mystically obscure sentiments, and yet by no means destitute of gracefulness and beauty.

Whether the palm be due to Michael Angelo or to Raphael (1483—1520) among the artists of Italy is a question which formerly gave rise to vehement discussion among artists and amateurs. The admirer of Michael Angelo need, however, by no means be excluded from enjoying the works of Raphael. We now know that it is far more advantageous to form an acquaintance with each master in his peculiar province, than anxiously to weigh their respective merits; and the more minutely we examine their works, the more firmly we are persuaded that neither in any way impeded the progress of the other, and that a so-called higher combination of the two styles was impossible. Michael Angelo's unique position among his contemporaries was such, that no one, Raphael not excepted, was entirely exempt from his influence; but the true result of preceding development was turned to account, not by him, but by Raphael, whose susceptible and discriminating character enabled him at once to combine different tendencies within himself, and to avoid the faults of his predecessors. Raphael's pictures are replete with indications of profound personal sentiment, but his imagination was so constituted that he did not distort the ideas which he had to embody, in order to accommodate them to his own views, but rather strove to identify himself with them, and to render them with the utmost possible fidelity. In the case of Raphael, therefore, a knowledge of his works and the enjoyment of them are almost inseparable, and it is difficult to point out any single sphere with which he was especially familiar. He presents to us with equal enthusiasm pictures of the Madonna, and the myth of Cupid and Psyche; in great cyclic compositions he is as brilliant as in the limited sphere of portrait-painting; at one time he appears to attach paramount importance to strictness of style, architectural arrangement, symmetry of groups etc., at another one is induced to believe that he regarded colour as his most effective auxiliary. His excellence consists in his rendering equal justice to the most varied subjects, and in each case as unhesitatingly pursuing the right course, both in his apprehension of the idea and selection of form, as if he had never followed any other. In each period of his development worthy rivals trench closely on his reputation. As long as he adhered to the Umbrian School, Pinturicchio, and to some extent the Bolognese goldsmith Francia, contested the palm with him, and when he went over to the Florentine School (1504) numerous competitors maintained their reputation by his side. Leonardo's example had here given a great impetus to art, and his works had yielded an insight into a new world of ideas and forms. Without entirely quitting local ground, the artists of Florence became familiar with the loftier spheres of imagination, and proceeded far beyond the original goal of life-like fidelity of representation. It is hardly necessary to direct the attention to Fra Bartolommeo (1467—1517) and Andrea del Sarto (1488—1536): those who visit the Pitti Gallery only may form an adequate idea of the styles of these masters (the altar-piece in the cathedral of Lucca by Fra Bartolommeo, however, should not be overlooked): but other Florentine painters of the 16th century deserve more notice than usually falls to their share. It is commonly believed that all the gems of the Galleria degli Uffizi are collected in the Tribuna, and the other pictures are therefore passed over with a hasty glance; yet on entering the second Tuscan room the visitor encounters several highly finished works, such as the Miracles of St. Zenobius by the younger Ghirlandajo; nor is the enjoyment and instruction afforded by the portraits of artists, most of them by their own hands, to be despised. There is nothing unintelligible in the fact that Raphael did not at once rise above all his contemporaries in art during the first period of his development. The enthusiastic admirer of Raphael will be still more unwilling to admit that even in his Roman period (1508—1520) his then matured qualities, especially his charming gracefulness of representation, were most successfully cultivated by another artist. This was Razzi or Sodoma, who has been most unfairly treated by the biographers of Italian artists. His frescoes in the Farnesina and his numerous mural paintings at Siena, where he spent the greater part of his life, are worthy rivals of Raphael's works of the same description, and even surpass them in the colouring. But, whilst Sodoma, like all other rivals of the master of Urbino, vie with him in a single branch of art only, the latter excels equally in all. Raphael's versatility, therefore, constitutes his principal merit.

Several of Raphael's most celebrated easel-pictures are distributed throughout different parts of the world, but Italy still possesses a valuable collection, together with the three works which correspond to the terminations of the three distinct periods of the master's development (Nuptials of Mary, at Milan, at the close of the Umbrian period; Entombment of Christ, in the Galleria Borghese, at the close of the Florentine period; Transfiguration, in the Vatican, left uncompleted by Raphael), as well as a great number of portraits, among which the so-called Fornarina in the Barberini Gallery derives a still higher interest from its subject. The amateur, moreover, should on no account omit to see the St. Cecilia in Bologna, and the Madonna della Seggiola in the Pitti Gallery. The latter is a characteristic specimen of Raphael's Madonnas, which are by no means calculated to awaken feelings of devotion. The fundamental ecclesiastical idea generally yields to feelings of a less elevated character; and maternal happiness, the bless of unsullied family-life, or the perfection of female beauty are the predominating features. In Italy only, or rather in Rome (the mural painting in S. Severo at Perugia is a solitary specimen of his earlier period), Raphael's merits as a fresco-painter can be appreciated. Like all the great Italian painters, his finest productions have been in the province of art. The highest rank must be assigned to his works in the papal chambers of state in the Vatican. In order to understand them, the spectator should on the one hand bear in mind that fresco-painting is never entirely divested of a decorative character, and on the other keep in view the peculiar position of papacy at the commencement of the 16th century. In the Palace of the Vatican the same courtly tone, the same taste for pleasure and enjoyment as in the residences of other Italian princes are exhibited; secular views here met with a willing reception, and humanistic tendencies especially appear not to have been repugnant to the dignity of the Roman court. All these qualities are more or less apparent in Raphael's frescoes; the courtly tone is repeatedly assumed, even the refined compliment paid to the patron of the artist is not disdained, the ceremonial representation not excluded, and personal allusions are not less frequent than political. We must finally remember that Raphael was always compelled to employ with discrimination the space at his command, and to distribute his decorative paintings appropriately on walls and ceilings, and that the limits imposed on him could not fail frequently to hamper his movements, and oblige him to alter his plans. His theological and philosophical erudition, exhibited in the Disputa and the School of Athens, his address in combining the most disconnected subjects, such as the expulsion of Heliodorus from the Temple, and the retreat of the French from Italy, and his unvarying success in the treatment of all the complicated series of subjects in the Stanze are sources of just astonishment. Raphael is, moreover, worthy of the highest admiration on account of his discrimination in selecting what was capable of artistic embodiment from a heterogeneous mass of ideas, and on account of the energy with which he asserts the privileges of imagination and his sense of the beautiful, thus rendering the most intractable materials obedient to his designs. This is most strikingly exemplified in the picture which represents the conflagration of the Leonine city, the so-called Borgo, or rather, in accordance at least with the design of the donor, the extinction of the fire by means of the papal benediction. No spectator can here detect the unreasonableness of the demand that a miracle should be materially represented. Raphael transfers the scene to the heroic age, paints a picture replete with magnificent figures and lifelike groups, which have stimulated every subsequent artist to imitation, and depicts the confusion, and preparations for flight and rescue, accompanied by the corresponding emotions. The painting does not perhaps contain what the donor desired, but on the other hand is transmuted into a creation inspired by imagination, and suggested by the most versatile sense of form. Raphael executed his task in a similar manner in the case of the celebrated frescoes in the first Stanza, viz. the Disputa and the School of Athens. Although he was not precisely desired to illustrate a chapter in the history of ecclesiastical dogmas (development of the doctrine of transubstantiation), or to produce a sketch in colours of the history of ancient philosophy, yet the task of representing a mere series of celebrated philosophers and propounders of church doctrine could possess but little attraction. By interspersing ideal types amid historical characters, by representing the assembled congregation of believers in the Disputa as having beheld a vision, which necessarily called forth in each individual evidence of profound emotion, and by emphasising in the School of Athens the happiness of knowledge and the pleasure of being initiated in the higher spheres of science, Raphael has brilliantly upheld the rights of creative imagination.

After these observations the amateur scarcely requires another hint respecting an impartial examination of Raphael's works. If he directs his attention solely to the subjects of the representation, and inquires after the name and import of each figure, if he feels bound to admire the versatility of the artist, who derives the different forms from remote provinces of learning and abounds in erudite rallusions, he loses the capability of appreciating the special artistic value of Raphael's works. He will then perceive no material distinction between them and the great symbolical pictures of the middle ages; nay, he will even be tempted to give the latter (e. g. the mural paintings in the Cap. degli Spagnuoli, in S. Maria Novella) the preference. These unquestionably comprise a wider range of ideas, aim with greater boldness at the embodiment of the supersensual, and may boast of having cultivated the didactic element in the most comprehensive manner. It is a matter of doubt to what extent Raphael's scientific knowledge was based on the communications of contemporaneous scholars (as such, Castiglione, Bembo, Ariosto etc. have been mentioned), or whether he was entirely independent of these. In the former case the merit of versatility would be due to these savants; but in the latter, had Raphael independently collected all the recondite allusions which the paintings in the Stanze are said to exhibit, his artistic character would not thereby be more clearly revealed to us; his intellect, not his imagination, would have been exercised. Raphael's pictures will not only be enjoyed in a higher degree, but a better insight into his character and greatness acquired, if the attention be principally directed to the manner in which the artist, by the power of his imagination, imparted a living form to ideas in themselves devoid of life, in which he distinguished the various figures by a marked psychological impress, so that the bearers of historical appellatives at the same time appear to the spectator as actual human characters, and in which he skilfully produced an equilibrium of movement and repose in his groups, and not only devoted attention to beauty of outline, but effected a happy reconciliation of profound intellectual contrasts. It must not, however, be imagined by those who undertake such an investigation, that their task and its interest will speedily be exhausted. Numerous questions still present themselves to the enquirer: by what motives Raphael was actuated in the entirely different colouring of the Disputa and the School of Athens; how far the architectural background of the latter contributes to the general effect; why the predominance of portrait-representation is in one part limited, at another (Jurisprudence) extended; what considerations gave rise to the various alterations in the compositions which we discover by comparison with the numerous sketches etc. Unfortunately the condition of the paintings in the Stanze is little calculated to produce pleasure in their examination; and we cannot now without difficulty appreciate in the Loggie the ancient magnificence of this unique decorative painting, or in the sadly disfigured tapestry recognise the culminating point of Raphael's art. A clue to the details of the composition of the latter is indeed afforded solely by the cartoons, now preserved in the Kensington Museum; but the designs at the base, and the marginal arabesques, partially preserved in the original tapestry, contribute materially to convey an idea of the festive impression which these representations, originally destined for the Sixtine Chapel, were intended to produce.

Raphael's frescoes in the cheerful Farnesina present an apparently irreconcilable contrast to his works in the Vatican. The latter bear the impress of religious fervour, aspiration to the sublime, a tendency to serious reflection, whilst in the former the art of the master is dedicated to joyous scenes, and every figure beams with pleasure and innocent happiness. But even the frescoes of the Farnesina are a characteristic manifestation of Raphael's genius. He derived his knowledge of the myth of Cupid and Psyche from the well-known work of Apuleius, which was as eagerly perused in the 16th century as during Roman antiquity.

No author of ancient or modern times can boast of a more charming illustration than that of Apuleius by Raphael, although the subject is somewhat freely treated. In Raphael's hands the myth acquires a new form. Well aware that his task was the decoration of a festive hall, Raphael has carefully avoided everything of a sombre character. Psyche's sufferings are placed in the background; her triumph alone occupies the artist's attention. The confined limits of the hall appear transformed into stimulants of the artist's sense of form. He embodies the myth in an abridged form, suggests many scenes in a superficial manner, yet without omitting any essential point, and thus without constraint contrives to render the historical compatible with the decorative. Harmony in conception and design, symmetrical precision, and capacity of concentration in adhering strictly to the subject, without admixture of personal caprice, — all genuine attributes of Raphael, — are as distinctly manifested by the frescoes of the Farnesina as by those of the Vatican. The ceiling-paintings in the principal hall are far inferior in execution to the so-called Galatea in the adjoining apartment; but the contemplation of both works affords the highest enjoyment, a repetition of which is longed for by every spectator.

The traveller cannot duly prepare himself north of the Alps for a just appreciation of the works of Leonardo, Michael Angelo and Raphael; however familiar he may imagine himself to be with them, he will be forcibly struck by the new light in which they appear on their native soil. The case is different with Coreggio and Titian, who are frequently extolled in the same breath as heroes of art, and elevated to equal rank with these three great masters. An approximate idea of Coreggio's merits may easily be formed in the galleries of the north, but some peculiarities will be detected for the first time in Italy. He will be discovered to tend to a naturalistic bias; it will be observed that not only his treatment of space (perspective cupola-painting) is devoid of delicacy, but that the individual characters possess nothing beyond their natural charm. Coreggio cannot be regarded as a perfect and comprehensive character, embracing as it were an entire world, but merely as an attractive colourist, who highly matured one branch of his artistic education, but totally neglected the other. Giorgione and Titian, the great masters of the Venetian school, cannot, on the other hand, be duly appreciated as artists of the Renaissance except in Italy. These are not mere colourists, they are not indebted exclusively to local impulses for their peculiar art; the joyous and festive scenes which they are unwearied in depicting are a true emanation of the culture of the Renaissance (Titian's connection with the "divine" Aretino is in this respect very suggestive); the happy individuals, rejoicing in the soft delights of love, whom they so often represent, remind one of the ancient gods, and afford a clue to the manner in which the revival of the antique is associated with the Renaissance-period.

Coreggio, as well as subsequent Venetian masters, were frequently regarded as models by the Italian painters of the 17th century, and the influence they exercised could not fail to be detected even by the amateur, were not the entire post-Raphaelite period usually overlooked. Those who make the study of the great cinquecentists their principal object will doubtless be loth to examine the works of their successors. Magnificent decorative works are occasionally encountered (those of Giulio Romano at Mantua, and Perino del Vaga at Genoa), but the taste cannot but be offended by the undisguised love of pomp and superficial professionalism which they generally display. Artists no longer earnestly identify themselves with the ideas which they embody; they mechanically reproduce the customary themes, they lose the desire, and finally the ability to compose independently. They are, moreover, deficient in taste for beauty of form, which, as is well known, is most attractive when most simple and natural. Their technical skill is not the result of mature experience, slowly acquired and justly valued; they came into easy possession of great resources of art which they frivolously and unworthily squander. The quaint, the extravagant, the piquant alone stimulates their taste; rapidity, not excellence of workmanship, is their aim. Abundant specimens of this mannerism are encountered at Rome and Naples (cupola of the cathedral at Florence by Zuccaro, frescoes in the Roman churches of S. Maria Maggiore and S. Prassede by d'Arpino, in S. Stefano by Tempesta etc.). The fact that several works of this class produce a less unfavourable impression does not alter the general judgment, as it is not want of talent so much as of conscientiousness which is attributed to these artists. The condition of Italian art, that of painting at least, improved to some extent towards the close of the 16th century; a species of second efflorescence, known in the schools as the "revival of good taste", took place, and is said to have manifested itself in two main directions, the eclectic and the naturalistic. But these are terms of little or no advantage in the study of art, and the amateur is recommended entirely to disregard them. The difficulties, however, of forming a fair judgment are not thereby terminated. Down to the close of the preceding century the works of Bernini, Guido Reni, Domenichino, and even of Carlo Dolce and Maratta were in high repute. Scaffoldings were erected in the Tiber in order to afford an opportunity of inspecting Bernini's statues on the Ponte S. Angelo more closely, and travellers indulged in unbounded admiration of the paintings of the 17th century. At a later period a reaction took place; under the influence of the modern "romantic" period the public became averse to fluent beauty and easy gracefulness of form. Censure of the 17th century and the barock style was hailed as a sign of the revival of better artistic taste. At the present day the bias of the preceding period has again become a subject of investigation, and Bernini's architecture is now less frequently stigmatized as "barock". The Italian art of the 17th century has already become a constituent of modern art, and the estimation in which it is held is therefore often dependent on the fashion of the day. The safest course to be pursued here also is that of historical investigation. The principal monuments of the architecture of the 17th century are the churches of the Jesuits, which unquestionably produce a most imposing effect; but the historical enquirer will not easily be dazzled by their meretricious magnificence. He will perceive the absence of organic forms, and the impropriety of combining totally different styles, and he will steel himself against the gorgeous, but monotonous attractions of the paintings and other works of the same period. The bright Renaissance is extinct, simple pleasure in the natural and human obliterated. A gradual change in the views of the Italian public, and the altered position of the church did not fail to influence the tendencies of art, which in the 17th century again devoted itself more immediately to the service of the church. Devotional pictures now became more frequent, but at the same time a sensual, naturalistic element gained ground. At one time it veils itself in beauty of form, at another it is manifested in the representation of voluptuous and passionate emotions; classic dignity and noble symmetry are never attained. Allori's Judith should be compared with the beauties of Titian, and the frescoes of Caracci in the Palazzo Farnese with Raphael's ceiling-paintings in the Farnesina, in order that the difference between the 16th and 17th centuries may be distinctly comprehended; and the enquirer will be still farther aided by consulting coeval Italian poetry, and observing the development of the lyric drama or opera. The latter especially furnishes a suitable key to the mythological representations of the School of the Caracci. Gems of art, however, were not unfrequently produced during the 17th century, and many of the frescoes of this period are admirable (the Aurora of Guido Reni in the Pal. Rospigliosi, Life of St. Cecilia in S. Luigi, Life of St. Nilus in Grottaferrata, paintings on the cupola and vaulting of S. Andrea by Domenichino etc.). Beautiful oil-paintings by various masters are also preserved in the Italian galleries. Besides the public collections of Bologna (St. Jerome by Ag. Caracci, Slaughter of the Innocents and Il Pallione by Guido Reni), Naples, and the Vatican and Capitol (Guercino's Petronilla), the private galleries of Rome are of essential importance. The so-called gallery-pieces, figures and scenes designated by imposing titles, and painted in accordance with the prevailing taste of the 17th century, were readily admitted to, and indeed most appropriately placed in the palaces of the Roman nobles, most of which owe their origin and decoration to that age. This retreat of art to the privacy of the apartments of the great may be regarded as a symbol of the universal withdrawal of the Italians from public life. Artists, too, henceforth occupy an isolated position, unsustained by reliance on a healthy national culture, exposed to the caprices of amateurs, and themselves inclined to an arbitrary deportment. Several qualities, however, still exist of which Italian artists are never entirely divested; they retain a certain address in the arrangement of figures, they uphold their reputation as ingenious decorators, and understand the art of occasionally imparting an ideal impress to their pictures; even down to a late period in the 18th century they excel in effects of colour, and by devoting attention to the province of genre and landscape-painting they may boast of having extended the sphere of their native art. At the same time they cannot conceal the fact that they have lost all faith in the ancient ideals, that they are incapable of new and earnest tasks. They breathe a close, academic atmosphere, they no longer labour like their predecessors in an independent and healthy sphere, and their productions are therefore devoid of absorbing and permanent interest.

This slight outline of the decline of Italian art brings us to the close of our brief and imperfect historical sketch, which, be it again observed, is designed merely to guide the eye of the enlightened traveller, and to aid the uninitiated in independent investigation and discernment.

1. From Marseilles *(Genoa)* to Leghorn *(Civita Vecchia and Naples)*.

Steamboats. Those who travel for pleasure, especially when accompanied by ladies, should invariably select the vessels of the **Messageries Impériales** on account of their superior organization, punctuality and comfort (comp. Introd.). The subjoined data are only designed to convey an idea of the usual routine, as alterations usually take place every spring and autumn. On these occasions the Company issues a new edition of their "*Livret des lignes de la Méditerranée et de la mer Noire*", which may be procured at the offices gratis, or may be written for by prepaid letter addressed "*A l'Administration des Services Maritimes des Messageries Impériales.*"

Messageries Impériales (Office at Marseilles, 16 Rue Cannebière; at Paris, 28 Rue Notre-Dame des Victoires): every Thursday by Leghorn and Civita Vecchia to Naples. Departure from Marseilles at 10 a. m.; arrival at Leghorn on Friday about 11 a. m.; departure thence at 7 p. m., arrival at Civita Vecchia about 8 a. m.; departure at 3 p. m.; arrival at Naples on Sunday about 2 p. m. — Return-voyage: Tuesday at 11 a. m. from Naples; Wednesday at 9 a. m. from Civita-Vecchia; Thursday at 7 a. m. from Leghorn; Friday at 5 p. m. arrival at Marseilles.

By the vessel bound for the Piræus and Constantinople, direct to Messina every Saturday in 64 hrs.

By the vessel for Alexandria, to Messina direct on the 9th, 19th and 29th of every month at 2 p. m., returning on the 3rd, 13th and 23rd of every month at 4 p. m.

By the vessel for Syra, Smyrna and Alexandria, to Palermo and Messina direct on the 8th, 18th and 28th of every month.

Last summer the company's vessels ceased to run between Marseilles, Genoa and Malta.

Besides the Messageries Impériales the following companies despatch vessels to the Italian ports (Genoa, Leghorn, Civita Vecchia and Naples):

Marc Fraissinet père et fils (Office at Marseilles, 6 Place Royale): steamers every Sunday and Wednesday at 8 a. m. to Naples viâ Genoa, Leghorn and Civita Vecchia; every Thursday 8 p. m. to Genoa and Leghorn; every Monday 8 p. m. to Nice, Savona and Genoa.

Valery frères et Comp. (Office at Marseilles, 3 Quai Napoléon): every Wednesday, Friday and Sunday at 9 a. m. to Naples viâ Genoa, Leghorn and Civita Vecchia.

Peirano Danovaro et Comp. (Office at Marseilles, 7 Rue Beauveau): every Wednesday at 10 a. m. to Genoa; departure thence for Leghorn and Naples on Monday, Wednesday, Friday and Saturday at 9 p. m.

Average voyage from Marseilles to Genoa 18—20 hrs., from Genoa to Leghorn 9 hrs., from Leghorn to Civita Vecchia 12 hrs., from Civita Vecchia to Naples 12—14 hrs., from Naples to Messina direct in 20 hrs., from Messina to Palermo in 9—10 hrs. — From Marseilles direct to Leghorn in 24 hrs., to Civita Vecchia in 30 hrs., to Messina in 64 hrs., to

Palermo in 53 hrs. — From Leghorn to Naples direct in 28 hrs., to Palermo in 38 hrs. — From Naples to Palermo direct in 20 hrs.

Fares (comp. Introd.): from Marseilles to Genoa, 1st class 76 fr., 2nd class 58 fr.; to Leghorn 1st 98 fr., 2nd 71 fr.; to Civita Vecchia 1st 133 fr., 2nd 95 fr.; to Naples 1st 181 fr., 2nd 128 fr.; to Messina direct 1st 220 fr., 2nd 154 fr., viâ Palermo 1st 235 fr., 2nd 164 fr., viâ Leghorn, Civita Vecchia and Naples (i. e. the entire circuit, comp. Introd.) 1st 250 fr., 2nd 174 fr.; to Palermo direct 1st 220 fr., 2nd 154 fr.; viâ Leghorn etc. and Messina 1st 260 fr., 2nd 184 fr.; to Malta direct viâ Messina 1st 253 fr., 2nd 183 fr., viâ Leghorn etc. and Messina 1st 274 fr., 2nd 199 fr.

All the above vessels start from the *Bassin de la Joliette* at Marseilles; embarcation and landing are therefore unattended with expense. An omnibus conveys passengers gratis from the office (p. 1) of the Messageries Impériales to the vessel, where the "facteurs" are forbidden to accept gratuities.

The **Visa of Passports** for Rome (3 fr. 75 c.) is procured without additional charge by the officials of the steamboat company.

Marseilles, the principal sea-port of France, termed *Massalia* by the Greeks, *Massilia* by the Romans, an important place even at an early period of antiquity, now a city with 260,000 inhab., is the capital of the Department of the embouchures of the Rhone and the depôt of a brisk and flourishing trade with the East, Italy and Africa (Algiers).

Hôtels. °Grand Hôtel du Louvre et de la Paix, °Grand Hôtel de Marseille, Hôtel de Noailles, Rue de Noailles. all in the Cannebière-Prolongée and fitted up in the style of the great Parisian hotels, containing 250 rooms from 2 fr. upwards, table d'hôte at 6 p. m. 5, B. 1½, A. and L. 3 fr.; °Hôtel du Petit Louvre, R. 2 fr., Rue Cannebière; °Hôtel de l'Orient, Rue Grignan 11, R. on 1st floor 5, on 2nd 4, on 3rd 3 fr., D. at 6 p. m. 4½, B. 1½, A. 1 fr.; Hôtel du Luxembourg, Rue St. Ferréol 25. R. 3, L. and A. 1½, D. 4 fr.; °Hôtel des Colonies, Rue Vacon; Hôtel des Ambassadeurs, Rue Beauveau, R. 1½ fr.; Hôtel du Parc, Rue Vacon, "journée" 6½ fr.; Hôtel du Var, Rue des Récollettes, "journée" 6 fr. — The atmosphere of the town in summer is hot and oppressive. Those therefore who contemplate a sojourn of several days during the warm season are recommended to select the °Hôtel des Catalans, in the immediate vicinity of the sea-baths (Pl. E, 6) and near the so-called *Résidence Impériale* (p. 6); the situation is delightful, and the house spacious and comfortable; omnibus to and from the station. A small establishment, somewhat more distant, is the °Hôtel Victoria, situated at the extremity of the Cours du Prado, at the point where it approaches the sea; there is a good bathing-place near, and the house is recommended for a prolonged stay.

Restaurants. De la Cannebière; Hôtel d'Orient; Roubion, beautifully situated on the new road La Corniche; Hôtel du Luxembourg (Parrocel); *Bouillabaisse*, good fish. *Chablis, Graves* and *Sauterne* are the white wines usually drunk.

Cafés. De France et de l'Univers, on the E. side of the Cannebière. Bodoul, Rue St. Ferréol; Café Turc in the Parisian style, but quieter.

Post-office, Rue de Grignan.

Bookseller. Veuve Camoin, in the Cannebière, with reading-rooms (25 c. per day). French newspapers, Galignani etc.

Carriages are of two descriptions. First, the *voitures du service de la gare*, destined for the conveyance of travellers to and from the railway-station, and posted there only. The passenger on entering receives a detailed tariff, in which even the driver's name is stated: one-horse carr. 1 fr.

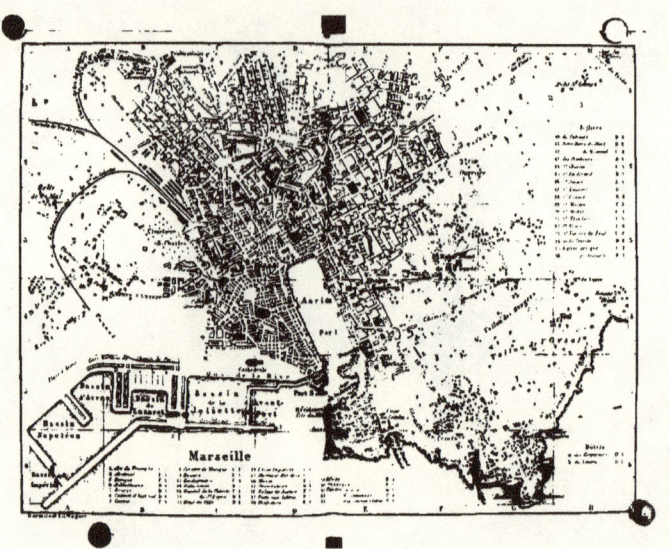

25 for 1 pers., for each additional pers. 25 c.: two-horse carr. 1 fr. 75 c. for 1 pers., for each additional pers. 25 c., for a drive at night 25 c. more; each article of luggage 25 c.; if the traveller fail in obtaining accommodation at the hotel, 25 c. more for driving to another. Secondly, the *voitures de place (fiacres)*: one-horse 1 fr. 50 c. per drive, 2 fr. 25 c. for the first, and 2 fr. for each succeeding hour; two-horse 2 fr. per drive, 2 fr. 50 c. for the first and 2 fr. for each succeeding hour. From 6 p. m. to 6 a. m. one-horse 1 fr. 75 c., two-horse 2 fr. 50 c. per drive. — *Omnibus* 30 c., each article of luggage 25 c.

Boats in the Ancien Port at the extremity of the Rue Cannebière: 1½ fr. for the first, 1 fr. for each succeeding hour. In fine weather a delightful excursion may be made to the islands of Ratonneau, Pomègues, and the Château d'If (p. 6).

Sea-Baths, handsomely fitted up, in the *Anse des Catalans*, on the E. side of the town, below the conspicuous *Résidence Impériale*; also warm sea-water baths, douche, vapour etc. for gentlemen and ladies. Adjacent is the large *Hôtel des Catalans* (see p. 2), with restaurant. Omnibus to or from the baths 30 c.

English Church Service performed by a resident chaplain.

Theatres. Grand Opéra (Pl. 41), W. of the Place Royale, and Théâtre du Gymnase (Pl. 42), in the Allée de Meilhan, both good. There are also two smaller theatres frequented by the humbler classes.

Massilia was a colony founded about B. C. 600 by Greeks from Phocæa in Asia Minor, who soon became masters of the sea, conquered the Carthaginians in a naval battle near Corsica, and established new colonies in their neighbourhood, such as *Tauroeis* (near Ciotat), *Olbia* (near Hyères), *Antipolis* (Antibes) and *Nicaea* (Nice), all of which, like their founders, rigidly adhered to the Greek language, customs and culture. Massilia maintained this reputation until the imperial period of Rome, and was therefore treated with leniency and respect by Julius Cæsar when conquered by him B. C. 49. Tacitus informs us that his illustrious father-in-law Agricola, a native of the neighbouring Roman colony Forum Julii (Fréjus), even under Claudius found ample opportunities for completing his education at Massilia in the Greek manner, for which purpose Athens was usually frequented. The town possessed temples of Diana (on the site of the present cathedral), of Neptune (on the coast), of Apollo and other gods. Its government was aristocratic. After the fall of the W. Empire Marseilles fell successively into the hands of the Visigoths, the Franks and the Saracens, by whom it was destroyed; in the 10th cent. it was restored and became subject to the *Vicomtes de Marseille*; in 1218 it became independent, but shortly afterwards succumbed to Charles of Anjou. In 1481 it was united to France, but still adhered to its ancient privileges, as was especially evident in the wars of the Ligue, against Henri IV. In 1660 Louis XIV. divested the town of its privileges, so that it retained its importance as a sea-port only. In 1720 and 1721 it was devastated by a fearful pestilence. During the revolution it remained unshaken in its allegiance to royalty and was therefore severely punished. In 1792 hordes of galley-slaves were sent hence to Paris, where they committed frightful excesses. It was for them that *Rouget de l'Isle*, an officer of engineers, composed the celebrated *Marseillaise:* "Allons, enfants de la patrie", which subsequently became the battle-hymn of the republican armies.

The town contains few objects worthy of special mention. The harbour whence it derives its commercial importance, is one of the most interesting points. Since 1850 it has been extended to four times its former size, notwithstanding which there is still a demand for increased accommodation. In 1853 the *Bassin de la Joliette* was added to the *Ancien Port* and is now the starting-point of most of the steamboats. The *Bassin du Lazaret*, *d'Arène*

1*

and *Napoléon* were next constructed. It is now proposed to form two new docks and an entrance-harbour *(avant-port)*, which will render Marseilles one of the greatest sea-ports in the world. Nearly 10,000 vessels on an average, of an aggregate burden of 1,800,000 tons, enter and quit Marseilles annually. The annual amount of customs-dues exceeds 60 million francs (i. e. 2,400,000 *l.*). The old harbour is long and narrow. Its entrance is defended by the forts of *St. Jean* and *St. Nicolas*. La *Cannebière*, a broad street, intersects the town from W. to E., from the extremity of the Ancien Port to the centre of the town where the ground rises. In this street, a few paces from the harbour, stands the *Bourse*, with a portal of Corinthian columns, and adorned with the statues of (r.) Euthymenes and (l.) Pytheas, two natives of Massilia who distinguished themselves as navigators in the 4th (?) cent. B. C. To the latter we are indebted for the earliest data with respect to the length of the days in the different northern latitudes and the ebb and flow of the tide. The opposite *Place Royale* is used as a fish-market.

A short distance further, on the l., the *Cours de Belsunce* is reached, a shady promenade generally thronged with foot-passengers, at the S. extremity of which stands the statue of Bishop Belsunce, "*pour perpétuer le souvenir de sa charité et de son dévouement durant la peste qui désola Marseille en 1720*". This intrepid prelate, during the appalling plague which carried off 40,000 persons, alone maintained his post and faithfully performed the solemn duties of his calling. From this point the Rue d'Aix ascends to the *Arc de Triomphe*, erected originally to commemorate the Spanish campaign of the Duke of Angoulême (1823), now decorated with sculptures by *Ramey* and *David d'Angers* of the battles of Marengo, Austerlitz, Fleurus and Heliopolis, and bearing the inscription: "*A Louis Napoléon Marseille reconnaissante*". The railway-station is situated to the N. of this point; the cemetery adjoins it.

We now return to the Cannebière. Opposite to the Place Belsunce opens the *Cours St. Louis*, continued by the *Rue de Rome* and the *Cours du Prado*, which is $2^1/_2$ M. in length. At the S. extremity of the latter is the *Château des Fleurs*, a small park with fish-ponds, affording various kinds of entertainments, a poor description of "Tivoli". The following pleasant drive of several hours is recommended, especially for the afternoon and evening: From the Porte de Rome or the Place Castelane (both Pl. E, 2) up the Cours du Prado, passing the Château des Fleurs; then down to to the coast, where some charming views are obtained, and by the Chemin de Ceinture to the village of *Endoume*; hence, skirting the Anse des Catalans (baths and hotel p. 3), to the Promenade Bonaparte. The stranger may now either return to the town, or ascend on foot to the r. to the church of Notre Dame de la Garde (see below).

To the l. in the Cours St. Louis, at the entrance to the narrow Rue de la Palud, is a fountain, adorned with an insignificant bust of *Pierre Puget*, the celebrated sculptor, who was a native of Marseilles.

The W. prolongation of the Cannebière is formed by the animated *Allée de Meilhan*, with fountains, and the new *Boulevard de la Madeleine*, which leads to the *Zoological Garden*, 1 M. distant. The latter (admission 1 fr.) contains a valuable collection of animals. All these streets are traversed by omnibuses, of which the stranger may avail himself.

A short distance S. of the Zoological Garden, at the extremity of the Boulevard de Longchamp, is the new *Museum*, a handsome edifice, opened Aug. 15th, 1868 (admission gratis on Sundays and holidays from 10 to 4, at other times by payment of a fee). It contains relics of statues, Greek and other inscriptions, sarcophagi etc.; also a collection of pictures, of which the following merit inspection: *198. *Philippoteaux*, Parting repast of the Girondists on the eve of their execution; 231. *Curzon*, Female weavers of Naples; 123. Portrait of the Flemish school; 170. St. John writing the Apocalypse, a copy from Raphael; 169. *Perugino*, Madonna with saints.

The ancient cathedral of *St. Lazare* on the harbour, recently condemned to demolition, is still suffered to stand. Opposite to it, on the E. side of the Ancien Port, rises the church of *St. Victor*, with crypt of the 11th cent., superstructure of 1200, towers added in 1350 by Pope Urban V. who was once abbot here.

The stranger whose time permits is recommended to visit the harbour and docks, which afford the most interesting walks at Marseilles, especially the new basins on the N. side. The Bassin de la Joliette contains the large passenger-steamers. At the commencement of the pier there is an omnibus-station. The principal hall of the *Consigne* (sanitary department of police) contains several good pictures: *Horace Vernet*, The cholera on board the frigate Melpomene; *Guérin*, The Chevalier Rose directing the sepulture of those who have died of the plague; *Gérard*, Bishop Belsunce during the plague of 1720 (see above); *Puget*, The plague at Milan, a relief in marble; *David*, St. Rochus praying to the Virgin, painted at Rome in 1780.

The finest point in the environs of Marseilles is to the E. of the Ancien Port, near the fort of **Notre Dame de la Garde*, with the church of that name, which contains an image of the Virgin and innumerable votive tablets of those who have been rescued from the dangers of shipwreck or disease. It has recently been restored and decorated with frescoes by a Dusseldorf artist. The eminence to the r. above the chapel affords an admirable survey of the extensive city, occupying the entire width of the valley, the innumerable white villas *(bastides)* on the surrounding hills, the harbour and the group of barren islands at its entrance, with the Château d'If, where Mirabeau was once confined (also mentioned in Dumas' "Monte Christo"), and a portion of the Mediterranean. That part of the sea which is concealed by the projecting angle of the fort may be surveyed from the rear of the chapel: grey mountains, light-brown houses with red roofs, scanty vegetation, numerous barren rocks and a beautiful view of the sea. This point is reached in $1/_2$ hr. from the old harbour, by the Promenade Bonaparte, adorned with beautiful southern vegetation and affording charming views of the town, harbour and mountains (the unfinished *Résidence Impériale* is situated here), and finally by steps, a somewhat fatiguing ascent. Here the full force is often felt of the prevailing *Mistral*, or piercing N.W. wind, the scourge of Provence.

Departure. The vessel slowly extricates itself from the Bassin de la Joliette and emerges into the Avant-Port. To the l. above the lighthouse rises the imperial château, surrounded by pleasure-grounds; beyond it Fort Nicolas. Notre Dame de la Garde on the more distant height long remains a conspicuous object. The view of the town of Marseilles itself is by no means imposing. The vessel steers towards the S.; to the l. the *Batterie du Phare*, adjoining the Anse des Catalans and the baths (p. 3). To the r. the islands of *Ratonneau* and *Pomègues;* then the *Château d'If*, described in Dumas' novel Monte Christo; to the l. the rugged coast, presenting a picturesque appearance.

At 10. 45 a. m. (Marseilles having been quitted at 10. 30) the *Cap de la Croisette* is passed, Marseilles gradually disappears and the steamer directs its course towards the E. At 11. 20 a rocky basin is traversed, 1 hr. later the vessel passes between the *Iles de Calseraigne* and shortly afterwards affords a view of the town and bay of *Cassis*. 12. 20, to the l. in the sea the *Rochers de Cassidaine* with a lighthouse, beyond which the bay of *Lecques* and the small town of *La Ciotat*. After passing the *Cap Notre Dame* the steamboat nears

(2 p. m.) **Toulon,** the principal naval depôt of France, surrounded by barren mountains and commanded by forts, the strongest of which are *La Malgue*, *Aiguillette* and *Balaguier* and the *Fort Napoléon*, surnamed "le petit Gibraltar". The latter was defended by English troops in 1793, but was compelled to surrender to the French under the command of Buonaparte, lieutenant of artillery, then 23 years of age.

(3. 30 p. m.) The steamboat steers between the *Iles d'Hyères* and the mainland. *Porquerolles*, the first of these islands, is defended by the *Fort du Grand Langoustier*. To the l. in the bay rise the *Salines d'Hyères* in terrace-like gradations; in the background the wooded heights of the *Montagnes des Maures*. The rocky character of the landscape has disappeared. To the r. the island of *Porteros* is next passed; then the long *Ile du Titan*, or *du Levant*, with two forts, the last of which rises from a rocky prominence. To the l. *Cap Benat*, in the distance *Cap Camaret*. The vessel now proceeds in the direction of Leghorn and gradually leaves the coast behind, which however still continues visible.

The following morning at 6 o'clock the steamer nears *Genoa*, the forest of masts in the harbour of which may be distinguished with the aid of a telescope. Then to the r. the island of *Corsica*, afterwards that of *Capraja* (p. 22); 8. 45 a. m., the islet of *Gorgona* (p. 22) rises abruptly from the sea; to the N. the coast of Spezia with its lofty mountains. After Gorgona is passed, *Elba* (p. 23) becomes visible in the distance to the S. — 10. 15, *Leghorn* is sighted, the Apennines become more conspicuous (to the r.), and (11 o'clock) the harbour is entered (debarcation p. 10). A visit to Pisa (comp. Part I. of this Handbook) is strongly recommended to the traveller and may easily be accomplished by railway if the train departs in time (by carriage not to be recommended). About 6, sometimes 7 p. m., the steamer again weighs anchor and proceeds on its course to Civita Vecchia (see p. 11).

From Genoa to Leghorn (Civita Vecchia and Naples).

The Ital. Mail Steamers (comp. p. 1 and Introd.; fares and duration of voyage see p. 2) of the *Società Rubattino* start on Mondays, Wednesdays, Thursdays and Saturdays at 11 p. m. for Leghorn, those of the *Società Peirano* on Mondays, Wednesdays, Fridays and Saturdays at 9 p. m. for Leghorn and Naples. The vessels of the French *Compagnie Fraissinet* leave on Mondays and Thursdays at 8 p. m. Those of the *Compagnie Valery* on Thursdays and Saturdays at 7 a. m. for Leghorn and on Monday at 7 p. m. (comp. p. 1 and Introd.) for Naples viâ Leghorn and Civita Vecchia. The Messageries Impériales have discontinued touching at Genoa. — Boat to or from steamer 1 l. for each pers. incl. luggage. — Travellers arriving at Genoa by sea and intending to proceed thence by railway avoid trouble and annoyance by at once booking their luggage for their destination at the harbour, immediately after the custom house examination. For this purpose a facchino of the douane (20 c.), distinguished by a badge, should be employed and not one of the unauthorized and importunate bystanders.

Hotels at Genoa, all externally unprepossessing. °Hôtel Feder, now Trombetta, formerly palace of the admiralty, R. 3 l. and upwards, B. 1½, D. inc. W. at 5 o'clock 4, L. 1, A. 1 l.; Hôtel d'Italie, with view of the harbour, R. from 2½, D. inc. W. 3½, L. 1, A. 1 l.; Quattro Nazioni; °Hôtel de la Ville, R. from 2½, D. inc. W. 4½. L. 1, A. ¾ l., omnibus 1¼ l. — Hôtel Royal; Croce di Malta; Grande

Bretagne: *Hôtel de France; Pension Suisse, R. 2, D. 3, A. 1½; all good hotels of moderate pretensions. All these houses are situated on the harbour in the Via Carlo Alberto, behind the harbour-terrace, and command seaward views.

Cafés-Restaurants. *Concordia, Via Nuova, opp. the Palazzo Rosso, handsome rooms, not expensive; *di Genova, formerly Lega Italiana (near the Teatro Carlo Felice).

Boats for 2—4 pers. with 1 boatman 2 l. per hour.

Carriages, two-horse 15, one-horse 10 l. per day of 6 hrs.; one-horse 1½ l. for the first hour, 75 c. for every additional half-hour, per drive 80 c.

Money. The Genoese *Soldo* = 4 centesimi only (1 l. = 25 Gen. soldi; 1 Gen. lira = 80 c., used principally by the poorer classes). The ordinary soldo of 5 c. is termed in Genoa, as in Tuscany, *palanca*.

Passports (comp. Introd.). Travellers en route for Rome, who are as yet unprovided with the visa, should here repair the omission by applying to the Spanish consul (Via al Ponte di Carignano, close to the church of S. Maria di Carignano, open from 10—4). No visa required for Florence, Naples etc.

English Church Service performed by a resident chaplain.

For a description of the town and its sights see Part I. of this Handbook.

As the vessels for Leghorn and Civita Vecchia generally start at night, the charming retrospect of Genoa "la superba" is lost, unless indeed the beautiful picture is illumined by moonlight. The steamer pursues its course within sight of the coast, which from Genoa southwards to Spezia is termed *Riviera di Levante*, passes the towns of *Nervi*, *Recco*, *Rapallo* (sea-port with shrine of the Madonna di Montallegro), *Chiavari* and *Sestri a Levante*, and after a run of about 6 hrs. nears *Porto Venere* and the island of *Palmaria*, at the entrance to the bay of Spezia. In the background rise the Apennines. As Leghorn is approached the island of Gorgona (p. 22) appears to the S.; arrival at Leghorn see pp. 9, 10; excursion to Pisa see p. 7. Passage to Civita Vecchia and Naples see pp. 11, 14.

2. From Florence to Rome *(by sea)* viâ Leghorn and Civita Vecchia.

From Florence to Rome the traveller has a choice of different routes. The shortest is by railway viâ Foligno, the longest viâ Orvieto. Two other routes are viâ Leghorn and Civita Vecchia, one by sea, the other by railway, traversing the Tuscan and Roman "Maremme". The cost of each is about the same; the land-route the shorter by a few hours, but far more fatiguing. A selection between the two must depend on the season, the weather, the traveller's inclination etc. The sea-voyage is very pleasant in favourable weather. The vessels steam in the vicinity of the coast; they generally weigh anchor in the afternoon, pass between the island of Elba and the Punta di Piombino in the evening, and arrive at Civita Vecchia on the following morning. Average passage about 12 hrs.

PISA. *2. Route.* 9

Passports (see Introd.), which must be furnished with the visa of a papal nuncio (Paris, Vienna etc.) or that of the Spanish consul at Leghorn, are surrendered at the booking-office and restored at Civita Vecchia.

Offices of the different steamboat-companies (comp. Introd. and p. 1) at Florence: *Comp. Fraissinet, Comp. Valery, Società Rubatino, Messageries Impériales* (corner of the Via della Farina), all in the Piazza della Signoria; that of the *Società Peirano* in the Piazza S. Margherita, adjoining the Badia.

Fares from Florence to Leghorn: 1st class 9 l. 35, 2nd 7 l. 70, 3rd 6 l. 5 c.; from Leghorn to Civita Vecchia: 1st cl. 45, 2nd 34 l. (comp. p. 2 and Introd.). Railway-fares from Civita Vecchia to Rome: 1st cl. 10 l. 95 c., 2nd 7 l.; 1st class alone tolerable, 2nd bad and not recommended to ladies.

The line skirts the N. bank of the Arno, passing the Cascine and numerous villas. Beyond stat. *S. Donnino* the valley of the Arno expands. Stat. *Signa* with its grey pinnacles and towers is celebrated for its straw-plaiting establishments. The line intersects undulating vineyards, crosses the *Ombrone*, which falls into the Arno, and enters the defile of the *Gonfolina* which separates the middle from the lower valley of the Arno. Stat. *Montelupo* is approached by an iron bridge across the Arno. Beyond it the *Villa Ambrogiana* is visible on the r., founded by Ferdinand I. on the site of an old castle of the Ardinghelli. Then crossing the small river *Pesa* the train reaches

Stat. *Empoli* (described in Part I. of this handbook), a small town (6000 inhab.) with antiquated buildings and narrow streets, situated in a fertile district. Here the line to Siena (R. 6) diverges to the S. The following stations are *S. Pierino, S. Romano* and *La Rotta*. To the r. rise the *Apennines;* to the l. on the height *San Miniato dei Tedeschi*, a small town which the Emp. Frederick II. in 1226 elevated to the rank of the seat of the Vicar of the empire. Stat. *Pontedera* at the influx of the *Era* into the Arno, where the road to Volterra (p. 19) diverges. Stat. *Cascina* on the Arno, where on the day of S. Vittorio, July 28th, 1364, the Pisans were defeated by the Florentines. Stat. *Navacchio;* to the r. the *Monti Pisani* with the ruins of a castle on the summit of Verruca.

Pisa, a quiet town with 25,000 inhab., is considered a favourable winter-residence for invalids on account of the mildness and moisture of its atmosphere. The heat in summer is oppressive. The *Pisae* of the ancients was one of the oldest cities of Etruria. It lay at the confluence of the *Arnus* and *Auser* (Serchio), which latter now empties itself into the sea. The present town, through which the *Arno* flows, lies about $2^1/_2$ M. from the coast.

The railway from Pisa to Leghorn traverses flat meadow-land intersected by cuttings, and near Leghorn crosses the Arno-Canal.

Leghorn, Ital. *Livorno,* French *Livourne.*

The vessels generally anchor in the inner harbour *(porto vecchio* or *Mediceo)*, sometimes also in the outer harbour *(porto nuovo)*. The different charges for landing are: from the Porto Nuovo 1 l. for each pers., 1½ for 1 pers. with ordinary luggage (trunk, carpet-bag, hat-box), 30 c. for each additional article; from the Porto Vecchio 50 c. for each pers., 1 l. for 1 pers. with luggage; children under 8 years free, others half-fare. Payment is made to the superintending official and not to the boatmen. — Facchino with ordinary luggage between the railway-station and the wharf, or to any other part of the town, 1 l.; for a box alone 80 c., hat-box 20 c. (according to tariff).

Hotels. *Hôtel Victoire et Washington, on the harbour and canal; adjacent to it, on the canal, *Hôtel de l'Aigle Noire; in both R. from 3—4 l. upwards, D. at 5 o'clock 3½ l.; *Gran Bretagna with Pension Suisse on the harbour, Via Vittorio Emanuele 17, R. from 2 l., good table d'hôte at 5 o'cl. 3½ l.; Hôtel du Nord on the harbour; Hôtel d'Angleterre, Via Vitt. Eman. 24; Iles Britanniques, No. 33 in the street.

Cafés. *Vittoria, Piazza d'Armi; *Posta, Via Vittorio Emanuele, opp. the post-office; in the same street Borsa, Americano, Minerva. — *Beer:* Mayer, Via Ricasoli.

Restaurants. Fenice; Giardinetto; Pergola, all in the Via Vittorio Emanuele; Ghiaccaio, Piazza d'Armi.

Carriages. Per drive in the town 85 c., without the town 1 l. 70 c.; per hour 1 l. 70 c., each additional ½ hr. 60 c.; to or from the station 1 l. Portmanteau 10 c., trunk etc. 40 c. The services of the facchini of the railway in the transference of luggage to or from the train are gratuitous; trifling fee for additional trouble.

As Leghorn is a free harbour, passengers' luggage is superficially examined when leaving the town. A second examination may be avoided by the purchase (20 c.) of a ticket which exempts the bearer from the formality.

Consulates. Great Britain: *Alex. Macbean Esq.*, Via Borra 17; American: *John Hutchinson Esq.*; Spain: Via Maremmana 34, where a visa for Rome is procured for 5 l.; fee to commissionaire of hotel for procuring visa 1 l.

As late as the 16th cent. Leghorn was a mere village (in 1551 the population amounted to 749). For its present importance it is indebted to the Medicis, who attracted hither the oppressed and disaffected from every country, Roman Catholics from England, Jews and Moors from Spain and Portugal, and merchants from Marseilles who sought to escape from the civil war. Montesquieu therefore termed Leghorn the "master-piece of the Medicis dynasty". Population 84,000, among whom are 29,000 Jews. It is a free harbour and defended by fortifications.

Leghorn is a well-built, entirely modern town, containing few objects to arrest the traveller's attention, and may be sufficiently explored in a few hours. The *Harbour*, where extensive improvements are now in progress, presents a busy scene. The inner harbour *(porto vecchio* or *Mediceo)* cannot accommodate vessels of great draught of water; a second *(porto nuovo)* was therefore constructed during the present cent. to the S. of the former, and protected by a semi-circular molo. On the harbour stands the **Statue of the Grand-duke Ferdinand I.* by *Giovanni dell' Opera*, with four Turkish slaves in bronze by *Pietro Tacca*.

The *Via Grande* or *Vittorio Emanuele* (formerly Via Ferdinanda) is the principal street. Proceeding from the harbour, it leads to the extensive *Piazza d'Armi* with the cathedral, the Palazzo Comunale (or town-hall) and a small royal palace. From this point it then leads to *Piazza Carlo Alberto*, formerly *Piazza dei due Principi*, with the colossal *Statues of the Grand-dukes Ferdinand III. and Leopold II.*, which bear reliefs and inscriptions recording their beneficence to the town.

Departure. On quitting the harbour, the steamboat commands a beautiful retrospect of the town. To the W. the island of *Gorgona* rises abruptly from the sea. The vessel now proceeds in a S. direction, and the island of *Capraja* soon appears; in the distance the dark outlines of *Corsica*. To the E. the coast continues visible, to the N.E. the Apennines. The steamer then threads its way between the island of *Elba* (p. 23), with the *Porto Longone* and the islands of *Palmajola* and *Cerboli*, and the *Punta di Piombino* (p. 14), a beautiful passage. The retrospect of the small rocky islands, furnished like the numerous promontories of the coast with lighthouses, is particularly picturesque. Somewhat later the island of *Pianosa* is passed; farther S. *Giglio* and *Argentaro* with the beautifully-formed *Monte Argentario* (p. 16), rising immediately from the sea; farther off is the small island of *Giannutri*.

The coast becomes flat. *Civita Vecchia*, situated picturesquely on an eminence, soon becomes visible in the distance.

Arrival at Civita Vecchia. After arriving in the harbour the traveller is often detained one or two hours on board until the passport formalities are settled, for without that document no one is permitted to land. During this annoying delay the train for Rome occasionally starts, a trial of the temper to the traveller eager to behold the glories of the eternal city. At length the harbour-commissary appears and proceeds to distribute the passports to their respective owners. Once in possession of |the precious document, the traveller orders his luggage to be placed in one of the boats in attendance, bestows (unless dissatisfied) 1 l. on the steward, and is speedily conveyed on shore. On landing, a wooden gate is passed through, where to the r. the passport is again exhibited (occasionally the passport is here returned to the traveller who gives up a *rincontro di passaporto*, which he has received on board), and on the l. by the outlet the fare for conveyance on shore is paid. The tariff is 1|2 l. (9¹|2 baj.) for each pers.: for a box from the steamboat to the station 1 l. (18¹|2 baj.); travelling bag or hat-box ¹|2 l. The strict custom-house examination, directed chiefly against books, newspapers, manuscripts and photographs, takes place at the railway-station, situated in the vicinity without the town. One-horse carr. for this short distance ¹|2 l., two-horse 1 l. All the above charges are the same for embarcation. Travellers from Rome who spend the night at Civita Vecchia pay for a box from the stat. to the town 40 c., thence to the harbour 25 c., from the harbour to the vessel ¹|2 l., travelling-bag half these charges. Omnibus from the station to the town 25 c.

If time permit, the traveller may obtain a glimpse of the town before the departure of the train. It is not necessary that he should accompany his luggage to the station; it will be kept at the dogana until his arrival. Its transport having been paid for in advance at the harbour, no farther payment need be made at the station.

Civita Vecchia (** Orlandi* at the entrance to the town, expensive, dinner may be ordered at a fixed sum; *Europa*, more moderate; *Railway-restaurant*), the fortified sea-port of the States of the Church with about 8000 inhab., the ancient *Centum Cellae* founded by Trajan, and sometimes termed *Portus Trajani*. The town was destroyed by the Saracens in 828, but in 854 the inhabitants returned into the "*ancient city*". The entrance to the harbour, in front of which a small fortified island with a lighthouse is situated, is defended by two strong towers, which have lately been restored by the French. Visitors are permitted to inspect the Bagno, where the galley-convicts are at work.

The town contains little that is interesting. The traveller may spend a leisure hour in walking on the quay, the archæologist in inspecting the inscriptions and antiquities in the ante-room of the *Delegazione della Polizia*, or in visiting the shop of Bucci, a dealer in old-books, in the Piazza.

A good road leads from Civita Vecchia to the volcanic mountains of *La Tolfa* and the loftily situated village of that name, in the vicinity of which are extensive mines of alum. The scenery is picturesque, and the locality interesting to geologists. Some mineral springs, with the ruins of ancient baths (*Aquae Tauri*) are situated about 3 M. from Civita Vecchia.

A diligence runs 3 times weekly in 7 hrs. to *Viterbo* (p. 38) alternately by *Corneto* and *Toscanella* (p. 40) and by *Monte Romano* and *Vetralla* (p. 40).

The Railway from Civita Vecchia to Rome (express in 2, ordinary train in 3—4 hrs.; fares see p. 9.; views to the r. till Rome is approached, when a seat on the l. should if possible be secured) traverses a dreary tract, running parallel with the ancient *Via Aurelia* near the sea-coast as far as Palo. On clear days the Alban and Volscian mountains are visible in the distance, and still farther off the promontory of Circeii. The first stat. *Santa Marinella* possesses a mediæval castle rising above a small bay, in the garden of which a date-palm flourishes. Stat. *Rio Fiume*; then the picturesque baronial castle of *Santa Severa* (stat.), formerly the property of the Galera, afterwards of the Orsini family, now of the Hospital Santo Spirito at Rome. Here in ancient times was situated *Pyrgos* or *Pyrgi*, harbour of the once powerful Etruscan city *Caere*, formerly termed *Agylla* or the "circular city" by the Phœnicians, with whom the town carried on a flourishing trade. It is now *Cervetri* (p. 301), situated on the height 6 M. farther to the l. Next stat. *Furbara*. The solitary towers on the shore were erected during the middle ages for protection against the dreaded Turkish Corsairs.

Stat. **Palo** (poor railway-restaurant), with a château and villa of the Odescalchi, occupies the site of the ancient *Alsium*, where Pompey and Antoninus Pius possessed country-residences. Relics of antiquity now scanty. Stat. *Palidoro*, on the river of that name, which rises on the heights by the Lago di Bracciano. The line now approaches the plantations of *Maccarese* (stat.) to the r.. believed to be the ancient *Freyenae*, situated near the mouth of the *Arrone*, a river which descends from the Lago di Bracciano. The *Lago di Ponente* or *Stagno di Maccarese* is now skirted. Stat. *Ponte Galera*, beyond which the line runs in the vicinity of the Tiber.

Beyond stat. *Magliana* a more unbroken view is obtained of the extensive *Campagna di Roma* and the Alban Mts., at the base of which glitter the white houses of Frascati (p. 274), and of the Sabine Mts. in the background; in the foreground the handsome Benedictine monastery of *S. Paolo fuori le mura* with its sumptuous new basilica. To the l. is disclosed a view of Rome, the *Aventine* (p. 189), the *Capitol* (p. 170) and *Trastevere* (p. 227). The train crosses the Tiber by a new iron bridge and slowly approaches the walls of Rome, of which the S.E. side is skirted. Above the wall rises *Monte Testaccio* (p. 190); adjacent is the *Pyramid of Cestius* (p. 190) with the cypresses of the Protestant cemetery; in the vicinity, the *Porta S. Paolo*, farther distant the *Aventine* with S. Sabina (p. 191). The line then traverses gardens and unites with the railway from Naples. The *Porta S. Sebastiano*, approached by the *Via Appia* (p. 264), is visible. The latter having been crossed, the *Lateran* (p. 202) appears with the numerous statues of its façade; then the monastery of *S. Croce in Gerusalemme* (p. 144), with lofty Romanesque tower. The train now enters a tunnel beneath the aqueduct of the *Acqua Felice* and passes the *Porta Maggiore* (p. 144), which is crossed by two ancient water-conduits. The line then intersects the city-wall; to the l. a decagonal ruin, usually termed a *Temple of Minerva Medica* (p. 144), two stories in height. A view is next obtained of *S. Maria Maggiore* (p. 140), a handsome edifice with two domes and Romanesque tower. To the r. insignificant remnants of the ancient *Wall of Servius*, discovered and destroyed by the construction of the railway. The train now enters the station at the N.W. extremity of the town, opposite the *Thermae of Diocletian*, and the traveller is in the Imperial City (p. 86).

3. From Florence to Rome by the Maremme.

One of the most direct routes between *Florence* and *Rome*. Departure from Florence at 6. 35 a. m., arrival at *Leghorn* 9. 50 a. m., departure thence at 10. 5 a. m., arrival at Civita Vecchia 6. 30 p. m., departure 6. 40 p. m., arrival at Rome 8. 47 p. m. Fares from Leghorn to Rome 36 l. 45 c., 27 l. 40 c., 22 l. 30 c.; from Florence to Rome 46 l. 5 c., 35 l. 30 c., 28 l. 45 c.

The direct route from Florence to Naples is viâ Foligno and Rome (R. 8).

This route is coincident with the ancient *Via Aurelia*, constructed by Æmilius Scaurus, B. C. 109. During the present century the Tuscan government caused a road to be constructed here, in order to benefit the coast-district. Although the most direct route, it is of greatly inferior importance to the others. This tract of country is by no means destitute of picturesque scenery, and the traveller who desires to explore it may devote a few days to the journey. Owing to the malaria, however, this is not practicable between June and the end of October (comp. p. 15). During that period the majority of the inhabitants remove to the mountainous district of Siena. Even in October entire villages are still deserted. — Views always on the right.

From Florence to Leghorn see p. 9; Leghorn p. 10.

The Maremme-railway is for a short distance coincident with the Pisan (p. 9), and then diverges to the S. It runs inland as far as Cecina, where it approaches the coast, commanding fine views of the sea with its promontories and islands. Soon after Leghorn is quitted, a view is obtained of *La Madonna di Monte Nero*, situated on one of the hills which intervene between the railway and the coast. This celebrated place of pious resort, especially revered by seafaring men, possesses an ancient picture of the Virgin brought from the East in the middle ages, with which a variety of legends are connected.

Stations *Colle Salvetti, Acciajolo, Orciano, Acquabuona*. The adjacent villages are all of recent origin and contain nothing of interest; they testify, however, to the rapid improvement which has taken place during the present century in this formerly so dreary district. The line crosses the *Cecina*, the ancient *Caecina;* the family of that name was settled in this district, as is proved by numerous inscriptions at Volterra.

Stat. *Cecina*, halt of 8 min. (indifferent café), where a branch line to Volterra (see p. 19) diverges. The village of Cecina, situated in the vicinity, is of modern origin.

The line now approaches the coast. The loftily-situated, ancient Etruscan *Populonia* becomes visible on a chain of hills projecting into the sea; beyond it the island of *Elba* (p. 22).

Stat. *Bambolo;* then stat. *S. Vincenzo*, with a small fort and harbour. Stat. *La Cornia*, on the small river of the same name; to the l. on the height the small town of *Campiglia*, with a ruined castle and Etruscan tombs of no great interest.

Piombino and Populonia. On the arrival of the last train from Leghorn a diligence runs in about 2 hrs. from *La Cornia* to *Piombino*, returning thence at noon. A forenoon suffices for a visit to Populonia.

Piombino, situated at the S. extremity of a wooded promontory, which towards the land is bounded by a flat district, is a small town (poor inn). A weather-beaten tower on the harbour commands a magnificent prospect of the sea and the neighbouring island of *Elba* (in front of which rise the cliffs of *Cervoli* and *Palmarola*), of *S. Giglio* and the coast and *Corsica* in the distance.

Piombino originally belonged to Pisa, in 1399 became a principality of the *Appiani*, in 1603 was acquired by Spain and finally by the family of *Buoncampagni-Ludorisi*, from whom it was wrested by Napoleon in 1805 in favour of his brother-in-law the Corsican *Felix Bacciocchi*. In 1816 it was restored, and till 1859 remained under the Tuscan supremacy.

The mail ferry-boats maintain the communication between this point and Porto Ferrajo, starting from Piombino at noon daily, from Porto Ferrajo in the morning. The duration of the passage depends on the state of the weather and other circumstances (comp. p. 22).

About 6 M. from Piombino, at the N. extremity of the peninsula, is situated the ancient Populonia, the Etruscan *Pupluna*. A shorter route through the woods should not be attempted without a guide. The town with its mediæval castle, 'situated on a lofty and precipitous eminence, is a conspicuous object from all sides. Once a prosperous seaport. it suffered greatly from a siege by Sulla; in the time of Strabo it had fallen to decay, and is now a poor village. In ancient times the iron of Elba was here smelted. The old town-walls may still be distinctly traced, and are especially well preserved on the side towards the sea; they consist of huge blocks, approaching the polygonal style. The views towards the land and the sea are striking and extensive. Several vaults, erroneously said to belong to an amphitheatre, and a reservoir may also be mentioned as relics of the Roman period. The Etruscan tombs in the vicinity are objects of no great interest.

The district now begins to exhibit the distinguishing characteristics of the Maremme: a world of its own, consisting of forest and swamp, uncultivated, and in summer poisoned by malaria. During the Etruscan period the Maremme were richly cultivated and possessed several considerable towns: *Populonia*, *Vetulonia*, *Rusellae*, *Cosa*. On the decline of agriculture in Italy and the conversion of the farms into pasture-land, the desolation of the Etruscan coast-district made rapid progress; for in this flat district, where the water easily becomes stagnant, high cultivation is alone capable of keeping the poisonous exhalations in check. Even Pliny describes this district as unhealthy. In the middle ages the desolation was still more complete; during the present century, however, under the wise administration of the grand-dukes of Tuscany, much was done to counteract the evil by the drainage and filling up of swamps and the establishment of new farms: but the evil is still very great. Charcoal-burning and in winter cattle-grazing are the chief resources of the inhabitants, who in May, when the malaria begins, all withdraw to the Tuscan hill-country. A few only of the densely populated localities enjoy a tolerably healthy atmosphere. Those of the natives who are compelled to remain suffer severely from fever, and their gaunt and emaciated countenances distinctly betoken the curse of the district.

Stat. **Follonica** near the sea, a small but industrial place which is deserted in summer, possesses considerable smelting-foundries for the iron from Elba. Beautiful view towards the sea; to the r. the promontory of Piombino and Elba, to the l. the promontory of Castiglione with a lighthouse, and the small, grotesquely shaped island of *Formica*. On an eminence inland rises *Massa*, one of the largest villages of the Maremma, with 3—4000 inhabitants. The line again quits the coast in order to avoid the *Promontory of Castiglione*.

Stat. *Potassa*. Farther to the l. an ancient château is visible. to the r. at the mouth of the small river *Bruna*, is situated the small fortified harbour of *Castiglione della Pescaia*. Here, as in the other seaports of the Maremma, wood and charcoal form the principal exports.

Stat. *Monte Pescali*.

On the hills to the l. (not easily distinguished from the railway) are situated the ruins of *Rusellae*, one of the 12 capitals of the Etruscan confederation. The place has been deserted since the middle of the 12th cent. and is thickly overgrown with underwood. The walls, in most places accessible, consist partly of horizontal layers, partly of polygonal blocks (6—8 ft. high, 7—12 ft. long). They are usually visited from Grosseto. The route is by the sulphureous *Bagni di Roselle*, 5 M. distant, whence the ruins are reached in 1½ hr.

To the l. stat. **Grosseto** (*Aquila*), the fortified capital of the Maremme, a cheerful little town with 3000 inhab. The curé *Chelli* possesses a collection of Etruscan antiquities.

Around Grosseto and in the direction of Castiglione extends a plain of considerable magnitude, in ancient times a lake (the *Lacus Prelius* of Cicero), which gradually became shallower (*Palude di Castiglione* and *di Grosseto*), and by its exhalations formed one of the chief sources of the malaria. By means of skilful drainage, and by conducting hither the deposits of the neighbouring rivers, the government has succeeded in almost entirely filling up the morass and converting it into a valuable pasture, 15 M. in length.

A short distance beyond Grosseto the *Ombrone* is crossed. The line skirts the wooded *Promontory of Talamone*; towards the S. the imposing *Monte Argentario* (see below) becomes visible.

Stat. *Talamone*, where a beautiful view of the sea is disclosed. The village lies at the extremity of the promontory and possesses an anchorage sheltered by the island of Giglio and the M. Argentario. The creek has been greatly encroached on by alluvial deposits. Here, B. C. 224, the Roman legions landed and signally defeated the Gauls who were marching against Rome.

The line crosses the small river *Osa*, then the more important *Albegna* (ancient *Albinia*), at the mouth of which salt-works are situated. Stations *Albegna*, *Orbetello* (halt of 20 M.). Here passports are given up, on receipt of a counter-mark, and are returned again at Montalto. The horizon is bounded by *M. Argentario* (1662 ft.), on the N. side of which lies the harbour *Porto S. Stefano*.

On the arrival of the train an omnibus (1 l.) starts for **Orbetello** (poor inns, the best is the *Trattoria del buon gusto*, or "*Saccoccione*"), 1½ M. distant, a visit to which will amply repay the lover of the picturesque and the archæologist. *M. Argentario*, an isolated promontory, is connected with the mainland by two narrow tongues of land, thus forming a large salt-water lagoon. Into the latter a third promontory projects, at the extremity of which the small fortified town, with 3000 inhab., is situated. Beyond its remarkable situation the place contains nothing of interest except the polygonal walls on the side towards the sea, which testify to the great antiquity of the town, although its ancient name is unknown. An embankment has been constructed from the town across the shallow lake, which however abounds in fish, to M. Argentario. A carriage-road leads to the N. harbour *Porto S. Stefano* and to *Port' Ercole* on the S. side. The mountain culminates in two peaks, on one of which a monastery of the Passionists is situated. The ascent is extremely interesting and is accomplished from Orbetello in 2—3 hrs. (with guide). The "view embraces the coast of Tuscany and the States of the Church as far as M. Amiata, and the sea with its numerous rocky islands as far as Sardinia. If time is limited, the first and lower eminence, 3/4 hr. from Orbetello, commanding a picturesque view of the coast, should be visited. — Orbetello is also the most convenient point from which an excursion to the interesting ruins of the ancient *Cosa*, the present *Ansedonia*, 4½ M. distant, may be undertaken. — It is likewise a suitable starting-point for a visit to the ancient towns of *Saturnia* and *Sovana*, about 30 M. inland.

On an eminence to the r. beyond Orbetello lie the ruins of *Cosa*, an ancient Etruscan town, deserted as early as the 5th cent. of our era (see above). The polygonal walls with their towers are admirably preserved. Beautiful prospect of the sea and coast.

The Italian frontier is soon crossed. The line traverses the Roman Maremma, the district is unattractive. The *Fiora* is crossed and stat. *Montalto* reached (halt of 25 min.), a poor village, where the passports are returned and luggage examined.

From Montalto the traveller may ascend by the bank of the Fiora to the ancient *Ponte della Badia* and the site of *Vulci*, where since 1820 most successful excavations have been made, and thousands of Etruscan vases etc. discovered.

Beyond Montalto the country becomes more undulating. The road crosses the small rivers *Arrone* and *Marta*, the outlet of the Lake of Bolsena. Stat. *Corneto*. The town with its numerous towers is loftily situated, and conspicuous from several points of the line which passes at its base. A visit to this interesting place, unfortunately inconvenient to the passenger who travels direct from Florence to Rome, requires 4—5 hrs. The excursion is generally made from Rome.

Corneto (*Palazzacio*, in a palace of the Vitelleschi dating from 1437, bargaining necessary. *Agapito Aldanesi*, a well-informed old man, is the custodian of the tombs; fee for 1 pers. 1½ l., for 2 pers. 2 l., for a party more in proportion), a small town of antiquated appearance and loftily situated, commands fine views of the sea with M. Argentario and the neighbouring islands. The interiors of the Romanesque churches have been sadly modernized. The town arose at the commencement of the middle ages after the decline of Tarquinii. A genealogical tree al fresco in the Palazzo Comunale professes to trace the origin of the place to a remote mythical era — a striking instance of the disregard for history often manifested by similar small towns. At the extremity of the principal street (*Il Corso*), near a spot on the town-wall termed *Il Belvedere*, an interesting survey is obtained of the bleak environs. On the stony hill opposite (*Turchina*), separated from *Montarozzi*, the hill of the tombs, by a ravine, lay *Tarquinii*, anciently one of the 12 Etruscan capitals, and remarkable for the influence which it exercised on the development of the national religion of Etruria. It participated in the war of the Etruscan confederation against Rome, but was compelled to surrender after the Samnite war and to receive a Roman colony. The town continued to flourish during the empire, but subsequently declined and was devastated by the Saracens; it was, however, inhabited till 1307, when its last remnants were totally destroyed by the inhabitants of Corneto. No ruins are now visible save the scanty vestiges of walls and foundations. Of its seaport *Graviseae* a few fragments on the r. bank of the *Marta*, 1½ M. from its mouth, still remain.

The principal interest attaching to Corneto is derived from its tombs, which are scattered in great numbers over the hill where the town itself stands. This Necropolis of the ancient Tarquinii was accidentally discovered in 1823 by Carlo Avvolta, a native of Corneto, who whilst digging penetrated into a tomb, and through an aperture beheld a warrior extended, accoutred in full armour. The influence of the air caused the body to collapse after a few minutes' exposure. The unsophisticated discoverer subsequently described the spectacle as the happiest moment of his life. Even in ancient times the tombs were frequently plundered for the sake of the precious trinkets they contained, and modern excavations have despoiled them of every moveable object which remained, so that the empty vaults alone are now left. A visit to them is nevertheless extremely interesting to those who desire to form an idea of the civilisation, art and religion of the Etruscans; and for this purpose the tombs of Corneto, the paintings in which are in the best state of preservation, are well adapted. The painting of the chambers is peculiar to the towns of southern Etruria, and indicates a particularly close relationship to Hellenic art. The *Tumuli* which externally distinguished the tombs have in the lapse of ages been entirely destroyed; the subterranean chambers now alone remain, of which the following are the most interesting:

1. *Grotta della caccia del cignale* (boar-hunt), or *Grotta Querciola*. The paintings, copied in the Museo Gregoriano, are much faded; they represent a banquet with music and dancing, and a boar-hunt. — Opp. to the latter: *2. *Grotta del Convito funebre*, or *del Triclinio*, also containing the representation of a banquet. The men are here, as in all the others, sketched in outline on the walls in dark red, the women in whitish colours. — 3. *Grotta del Morto*, small; scene of mourning for the deceased and of dancing. — *4. *Grotta del Tifone*, more extensive, supported in the centre by a pillar, on which are Typhons, winged genii of death terminating in serpents. The sarcophagi bear Latin as well as Etruscan inscriptions, a proof that they belong to a comparatively recent epoch. To the r. on the wall souls escorted by genii; beneath Charon, with the hammer. — 5. *Grotta del Cardinale*, the most spacious tomb of Tarquinii, supported by 4 pillars, opened in the last century; colours almost entirely faded. — 1½ M. from Corneto is: 6.' *Grotta delle Bighe;* a copy of the paintings is preserved in the Vatican. — In the vicinity: 7. *Grotta del Mare*, small, with sea-horses. — *8. *Grotta del Barone*, so called from the Hanoverian ambassador by whom it was opened, contains warlike games, riders etc., partly in the archaic style; colours well preserved. — 9. *Grotta Francesca* or *Giustiniani*, with dancers and races, much faded; copies in the Museo Gregoriano. — 10. *Grotta delle Iscrizioni*, so called from the numerous Etruscan inscriptions, with warlike trials of skill.

Toscanella is now best visited from Corneto, see p. 40.

The railway skirts the foot of the hill of Corneto. Farther to the r. the traveller perceives the insignificant *Porto Clementino*, entirely abandoned in summer on account of the malaria. The horizon is bounded inland by the mountains of *Tolfa*, which yield an abundant supply of alum and sulphur. The line then crosses the small river *Mignone*, at the mouth of which is situated the *Torre Bertaldo* (where according to a legend an angel refuted the doubts which St. Augustin entertained respecting the Trinity), and soon reaches Stat. C i v i t a V e c c h i a (halt of 10 M.).

From Civita Vecchia to Rome see p. 12.

4. From Leghorn to Volterra.

Railway from Leghorn to Cecina in 1¹/₂ hr., fares 5 l. 20, 4 l. 20 or 3 l. 15 c.; from Cecina to Saline in 1¹/₄ hr., fares 3 l., 2 l. 40 or 1 l. 80 c. From Saline to Volterra diligence in 2 hrs., fare 1 l.

A visit to Volterra, interesting on account of its antiquities, may be most conveniently and inexpensively accomplished from Leghorn and combined with the prosecution of the traveller's journey to Rome, if luggage be left at Cecina. — From *Pontedera* (p. 9), a stat. on the line from Florence to Pisa, Volterra is reached by carriage through the valley of the *Era* in 5—6 hrs.; from *Poggibonsi* (p. 24), stat. on the line from Empoli to Siena, by a hilly road in 3—4 hrs.

From Leghorn to *Cecina (Maremme Railway)* see p. 14. Our line here diverges and ascends on the r. bank of the *Cecina*, traversing a district remarkable for its mineral wealth. Stations *San Martino, Casino di Terra, Ponte Ginori* and *Saline*, the terminus, in a bleak situation where the malaria prevails in summer. The extensive salt-works in the vicinity supply the whole of Tuscany with salt and yield a considerable revenue.

The road from Saline to Volterra ascends. The country presents a peculiarly bleak aspect.

Volterra *(Unione; Nazione)*, the ancient *Volaterrae*, Etruscan *Velathri*, one of the most ancient Etruscan cities, now containing 5000 inhab., an episcopal residence, loftily situated (1602 ft.), commands in clear weather charming prospects, extending to the heights of Pisa, the Apennines, and the sea with the islands of Gorgona, Elba, Capraja and Corsica. The environs are dreary and desolate; the effect of the rain on the soft and spongey soil is most prejudicial to agriculture.

Volterra was one of the 12 ancient confederate cities of Etruria and was so strongly fortified that during the civil wars it withstood a siege by Sulla's troops for two years. It subsequently became a Roman muncipium, but gradually fell to decay and was totally destroyed in the 10th cent. It was re-erected under the Othos but does not now extend to one-third of its ancient magnitude. In the middle ages it was a free town, until it became subject to Florence.

Among the *Antiquities* the ancient *Town Walls, once 6 M. in circumference, of double the extent of those of Fiesole and Cortona, are especially worthy of notice. Their dimensions (40 ft. in height, 14 ft. in thickness) and construction of horizontal layers of sandstone blocks (panchina) are best inspected outside the Porta S. Francesco and in the garden of the monastery of Santa Chiara. One of the ancient gateways is also still in existence, the *Porta all' Arco, 21 ft. in height. The corbels are adorned with almost obliterated heads of lions or guardian deities of the city, imitated on an urn in the museum which represents the

2*

battle of Thebes. Another gateway, outside the Porta Fiorentina, termed *Porta di Diana*, has been much altered. Without the same gate, below the burying-ground, is situated the ancient *Necropolis*, about midway on the slope of the hill, at the place which is now termed *S. Marmi*. A number of the curiosities in the museum were found here, but the tombs have all been reclosed.

The *Piscina*, without the fortifications, a reservoir resting on 6 columns, is only accessible by permission from the bishop and is entered by a long ladder.

The *Thermae*, near the fountain of S. Felice, are of Roman origin. Traces of an *Amphitheatre* near the Porta Fiorentina.

The *Museum* in the *Palazzo Pubblico* in the piazza is the most interesting object which the town possesses. The handsome edifice, begun in 1208, completed in 1257, is unfortunately somewhat modernized; the exterior adorned with mediæval coats of arms.

The museum, established in 1731, greatly enriched by the collections of the erudite *Mario Guarnacci* in 1761, contains in 10 rooms a valuable collection of inscriptions, coins, bronzes, statues, vases etc. and upwards of 4000 *cinerary urns*. A few of the latter, 2—3 ft. in length are constructed of terracotta and sandstone, most of them of the alabaster of the environs. On the lid the greatly reduced recumbent effigy of the deceased, the sides adorned with reliefs; traces of painting and gilding distinguishable on some. The collection is admirably calculated to afford an insight into the customs, faith and art of this remarkable people. The representations on the urns are partly derived from the peculiar sphere of Etruscan life, partly from Greek mythology. From the former, parting scenes are the most frequent; the deceased, equipped as a rider, is escorted by a messenger who bears a long sack containing his good and evil deeds, or is accompanied by Charon with the hammer. The flowers which are often observed, when half in bloom, denote the youth, when completely opened the riper age of the departed. Sacrifices and funeral-processions occur frequently, as well as banquets, races, contests of skill etc. Greek mythology has supplied an abundant selection of subjects, e. g. Ulysses with the Sirens and with Circe, the abduction of Helen, death of Clytemnestra, Orestes and the Furies, the Seven before Thebes, Polynices and Eteocles, Œdipus with the Sphynx, Œdipus slaying his father, Rape of Proserpine. An austere bias is exhibited in the choice of subjects and in their treatment. A certain degree of technical perfection has been attained, but the realism of art has been carried so far that ease and harmony are almost entirely wanting.

The *Sala della Magistratura* contains a *Library* of 13,000 vols., ivory carving, diptychs etc. On the wall the Annunciation, a large fresco by *Orcagna*, greatly damaged.

The * *Cathedral*, consecrated in 1120 by Pope Calixtus II., enlarged in 1254 by Nicola Pisano, restored in the 16th cent., the façade dating from the 13th cent., is remarkable for the rich marble decorations and sculptures of the interior. The * *Oratorio di S. Carlo* in the S. transept resembles a complete picture-gallery, containing works of *Luca Signorelli*, *Leonardo da Pistoja*, *Benvenuto da Siena*, *Filippo Lippi* and *Daniele da Volterra*.

The chapel of the Virgin is adorned with a fresco by *Benozzo Gozzoli*.

S. Giovanni, in the vicinity, of octagonal form, supposed to date from the 7th cent., occupies the site of an ancient temple of the sun. The entrance-archway and the capitals of the columns, decorated with animals and birds, as well as the fine arch of the high-altar, are by *Balsimelli da Settignano* (16th cent.), the octagonal font by *Andrea di Sansovino* (1502), and the ciborium by *Mino da Fiesole* (1471).

S. Lino, a church and monastery, founded in 1480 by *Raffaele Maffei*, contains the tomb of that scholar with a recumbent statue by *Silvio da Fiesole*.

The churches of *S. Francesco*, with the Gothic chapel of the *Confraternità della Croce di Giorno* of 1315, *S. Agostino* and *S. Michele* (of 1285) also contain frescoes and pictures worthy of inspection.

The *Citadel* consists of two portions, the *Cassero* or *Rocca Vecchia*, erected on the ancient town-walls in 1343 by Walther de Brienne, Duke of Athens, and the *Rocca Nuova* by the Florentines after the capture of the town. At the same time they constructed the prison *Il Mastio* for the incarceration of political offenders, into which the mathematician *Lorenzo Lorenzini* was thrown as a suspected individual in 1682 by the Grand-duke Cosimo III. and where he was confined for 11 years. The citadel has been converted into a house of correction and may be visited with permission of the Sotto Prefetto.

The *Casa Guarnacci*, opposite the church of S. Michele, with its three towers, the oldest dating from the 13th cent., is an interesting edifice.

The *Casa Ducci* bears the Roman epitaph of a boy of 5 years, probably a member of the family of the poet *Persius*, who was born A.D. 34 at Volaterræ.

In the *Casa Ricciarelli*, *Daniele da Volterra*, the celebrated pupil of Michael Angelo, was born in 1509; he died at Paris in 1567. The house still belongs to the family of *Ricciarelli*, who possess the artist's *Elias.

The *alabaster-works* of Volterra are celebrated, and afford occupation to nearly two-thirds of the population. The ordinary descriptions are found in the vicinity, the more valuable in the mines of La Castellina, S. of Leghorn. A visit to the work-shops is interesting, where suitable objects for presents or reminiscences of Italy may be purchased far more advantageously than at Florence or Leghorn.

In the neighbourhood of Volterra, in the valley towards the E., is situated the *Villa Inghirami*, with the rocky labyrinth termed *Le Buche de' Saracini*. About $3/4$ M. to the N.W. of the town, between the churches of S. Giusta and La Badia, lies a deep ravine which has been comparatively recently formed by the action of water and continues to increase in extent, termed *Le Balze*. Several buildings have already been undermined and destroyed, and the celebrated abbey of *San Salvatore* of the order of Camaldoli is now threatened with the same fate. It was founded in the 11th cent, and possesses Doric cloisters and several treasures of art: *St. Romuald by *Domenico Ghirlandajo*, frescoes by *Volaterrano* etc.

A pleasant excursion may be made to the copper-mines of *La Cava*, near *Monte Catini*, 11½ M. from Volterra. The road leads by the eminence of *La Bachetona* to *Monte Catini* on the summit of the *Selagite*, a mountain of volcanic origin; the square tower of the old castle commands an extensive prospect. The mines have been worked since the 15th cent., and have since 1837 been successfully conducted by an English firm (Sloane and Hall). M. *Schneider*, the director (a German) readily affords information respecting the extremely interesting geological peculiarities of the locality, and admits visitors to the mines. A red species of rock, resembling porphyry, here known as *gabbro rosso*, of which a number of peaks, such as *Monte dell' Abete*, *Poggio alla Croce* and *Monte Massi*, consist, has been upheaved at a comparatively recent period through the surrounding sand and limestone.

The view from *Monte Massi* (1910 ft.) or from *Poggio alla Croce* (½ hr. from Monte Catini) extends from the heights near Massa and Carrara towards the N. to Monte Amiata on the S., and embraces the sea with the islands of Elba, Capraja and Corsica.

From *Le Saline* a walk of 3 hrs., by the village of *Pomarance*, may be undertaken to the borax-works of Count Lardarello, the *Lagoni di Monte Cerboli*, where 300 persons are employed, an establishment of great interest to experts. In 1856, 4½ million lbs. were prepared and exported to England for the use of potteries and glass-manufactories. Count Lardarello possesses 8 other similar establishments, all situated between the sources of the Cornia and Cecina, a fact which appears to indicate one vast common receptacle of these gaseous emissions.

5. Elba and the Tuscan Islands.

A visit to Elba, strongly recommended to the scientific and admirers of the picturesque, is most conveniently accomplished from Leghorn. A small steamboat (Società *Rubattino & Comp.*) runs thence in 7 hrs. to *Piombino* and *Portoferrajo*, starting every Sunday at 10 a. m. (fares 13½, 9½ or 6 fr.) and returning to Leghorn at 8 a. m. on Mondays. Every Wednesday at 8 a. m. to *Gorgona*, *Capraja*, *Portoferrajo*, *Pianosa*, *Giglio* and *S. Stefano* (the N. harbour of M. Argentario). From Porto S. Stefano Thursdays 3. 30 p. m., and from Portoferrajo Fridays 8 a. m. to Leghorn by Capraja and Gorgona. Another mode of conveyance is afforded by the mail-boats which run every morning from Portoferrajo to Piombino and correspond with a diligence to the Maremme-line, thus abridging the sea-passage.

Half-an-hour after the harbour of Leghorn has been quitted, the cliff *Meloria* comes in sight, near which the Pisans were defeated in a naval battle by the Genoese in 1283 and thus deprived of their supremacy. Farther W. *Gorgona*, inhabited by fishermen, sterile and affording pasture to wild goats only. Between the latter and Elba lies *Capraja* ("island of goats", so called by the ancients also), with 2000 inhabitants, and producing wine.

Elba, Lat. *Ilva*, Greek *Æthalia*, consisting of an imposing mountain-group, is reached from Piombino in 1½ hr. The *Torre di Giove*, situated on the highest point, serves as a landmark to sailors. The vessel rounds the *Capo della Vita* and enters the beautiful bay of *Porto Ferrajo*, enclosed amphitheatrically by mountains. The island was celebrated in ancient times for its iron ore; in the middle ages it appertained to the Pisans, then to Genoa, to Lucca and to the Appiani of Piombino, and was finally presented by the Emp. Charles V. to the Grand-duke Cosimo I. of Florence, who in 1548 fortified the harbour of *Porto Ferrajo*. As the name of the town indicates, the export of iron and its manufacture constitute the principal occupation of the inhabitants (22,000), others of whom are supported by the tunny and sardine fisheries. Elba has acquired a modern celebrity as the retreat of Napoleon, after his abdication, from May 5th, 1814, to Feb. 26th, 1815, after which he again embarked on his last and desperate venture. A few days later (March 1st) he landed at S. Raphael near Fréjus. The small palace occupied by the emperor is still shown at *Porto Ferrajo*, on the height above the harbour, between the forts *Stella* and *Falcone* erected by Cosimo I., and commanding a view of the bay in front and of the sea in the direction of Piombino in the rear. It is now the residence of the governatore, and contains reminiscences of its former imperial occupant. The cathedral, theatre, arsenal etc. of which the island boasts contain nothing which requires comment. After the fall of Napoleon in 1815 Elba was restored to Tuscany, in the fortunes of which it has since then participated. Length of the island about 18 M., breadth 6½ M., area 152 sq. M.; it contains two fertile valleys, but lofty and precipitous mountains predominate. *Monte Capanne*, the highest point, near the village of *Marciana*, is upwards of 3000 ft. in height. The coast towards the mainland of Italy is less abrupt and produces wine and fruit of remarkably fine quality, especially in the environs of *Capoliveri*, where an excellent quality of Aleatico is grown. Most of the villages, e. g. the picturesque stronghold of *Porto Longone*, founded by the Spaniards, are situated on the coast. *Rio*, where the iron-mines are worked, lies more inland. The yield of ore is still abundant, and in ancient times formed a source of wealth to the Etruscans. The strata containing the ore lie on the surface, and are recognised at a distance by the reddish-black appearance of the hills.

Between Elba and the mainland are the two small islands of *Palmaiola* and *Cerboli*.

To the S. lies *Pianosa*, the ancient *Planasia*, which, as its name indicates, is perfectly flat, the place of banishment of Agrippa

Posthumus, grandson of Augustus. To him are referred the considerable Roman remains still existing in the island. Farther S. rises *Monte Cristo*, consisting of granite-rock, 6 M. in circumference. It contains numerous springs and the ruins of a monastery destroyed by pirates in the 16th cent. Nearer the coast is *Giglio*, Lat. *Igilium*, containing a village and the vestiges of Roman palaces.

6. From Florence to Rome by Siena, Orvieto and Viterbo.

Railway from *Florence* to *Orvieto* in 7½ hrs., fares 24 l. 25, 17 l. 25, 12 l. 50 c. From *Florence* to *Siena* in 3½ hrs., fares 9 l. 40, 7 l. 30, 5 l. 40 c.; from *Siena* to *Orvieto* in 4 hrs., fares 14 l. 30, 10 l. 5, 7 l. 15 c. From Orvieto the line is in course of construction to Orte (p. 67) on the Tiber, a station on the line between Rome and Ancona (R. 11). Since the opening of the railway line Florence-Foligno-Rome, the former diligence-communication between *Rome* and *Orvieto* has been suspended, thus rendering this route more difficult, although opportunities often offer for going to Viterbo and thence to Rome. Carriage from Orvieto to Rome 40 l., to Orte viâ Viterbo 20—25 l. Unless the traveller has a particular desire to see Viterbo, it is better to return from Orvieto, either to Florence or Chiusi and thence to go to Perugia (R. 7); or he can drive to Poggibonsi and thus reach the Maremme Railway to Rome viâ Volterra and Saline (p. 19).

From Florence to Empoli see p. 9. Passengers to Siena change carriages here; halt of 23 min.

The line to Siena traverses the fertile valley of the *Elsa*, on the r. bank of the stream. To the r. on the height *S. Miniato dei Tedeschi*, picturesquely situated, and possessing a lofty mediæval tower. Stat. *Osteria Bianca*, beyond which a fruitful valley is traversed. Stat. *Castel Fiorentino;* the town, on the height to the l., is the principal place in the *Val d'Elsa*.

Stat. *Certaldo;* the town, on the hill to the l., was the native place of the poet *Giovanni Boccaccio*, who died here, Dec. 21st, 1375, at the age of 62. Until 1783 his tomb was in the church of *S. Michele e Giacomo (La Canonica);* it was erected in 1503 and adorned with a statue of the poet, who held the "Decamerone" in his hand. The monument was subsequently removed and the bones scattered. The house of Boccaccio was restored in 1823 by the Countess *Carlotta Lenzoni-Medici* and fitted up in the antique style. The remains of his monument were also brought hither.

Stat. *Poggibonsi;* the town (3500 inhab.) lies to the r. From this point to Volterra in 3—4 hrs. (comp. p. 19). Carriage 10 l.

S. Gimignano, which may be reached in 2 hrs. from Poggibonsi, is an ancient, loftily-situated town, possessing a number of lofty square towers and presenting a thoroughly mediæval aspect, whence its appellation "*S. Gi-*

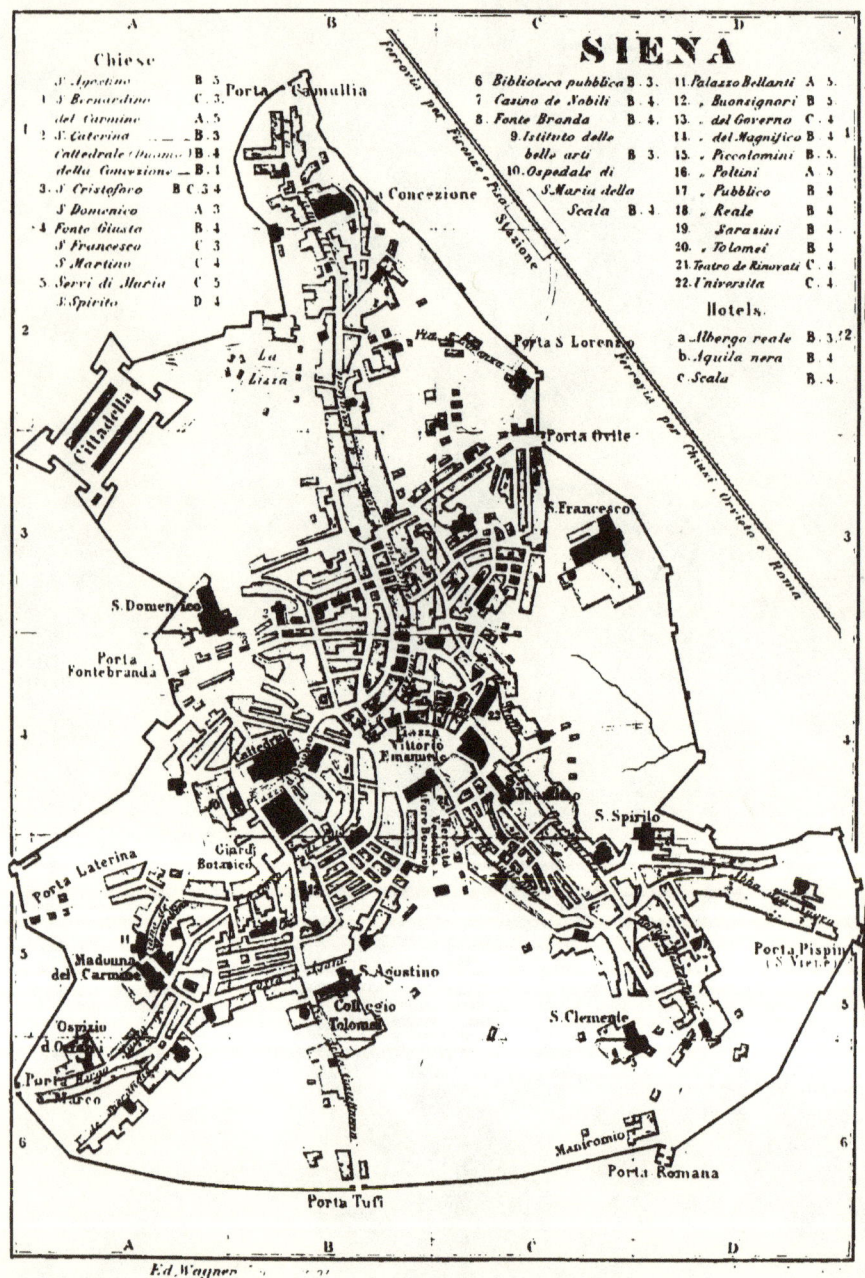

mignano delle belle torri". The *Palazzo Pubblico* of the 14th cent. contains a large fresco by *Lippo Memmi* of 1317, restored by *Benozzo Gozzoli* in 1467; also several ancient pictures by *Taddeo Bartoli*, *Filippino Lippi* etc. Adjacent to the latter: *Torre del Comune*, the loftiest of the 13 towers (175 ft.), erected 1298. The largest of the three bells dates from 1328. The double towers of *Ardinghelli* are of the 13th cent.

Of the 36 churches which formerly existed here, the following should be noticed:

*La Collegiata of the 11th cent., altered in the 15th by *Giuliano da Majano*, contains frescoes (badly preserved) by *Bartolo di Fredi* of Siena (1356), *Barna di Siena* and *Giovanni da Ascanio* (1380). *Martyrdom of St. Sebastian by *Benozzo Gozzoli* (1465). *Chapel of S. Fina with altar by *Benedetto da Majano*, frescoes by *Dom. Ghirlandajo*, pictures by *Benozzo Gozzoli*, *Piero di Pollajuolo* and *S. Mainardi*. Chapels of S. Gimignano, della Purificazione, della Concezione, all adorned with frescoes; likewise the sacristy and oratorium of S. Giovanni.

S. Agostino, erected 1280, contains frescoes by *Benozzo Gozzoli*, *S. Mainardi* and *Bartolo Fredi*.

S. Girolamo, *S. Giacopo* (of the 11th cent., church of the Knights Templar), *S. Lorenzo in Ponte* and the church of the monastery of *Monte Oliveto*, 3 M. distant, also contain good pictures.

Beyond Poggibonsi the line begins to ascend considerably. To the r. *Staggia* with a mediæval château; farther to the r. the ancient and picturesque château of *Monte Riggioni*; then through a long tunnel (3 min.).

Siena [*A l b e r g o R e a l e (Pl. a), formerly *Arme d'Inghilterra*; *A q u i l a N e r a (Pl. b), more unpretending, near the cathedral, R. 2 l.; S c a l a (Pl. c); C a f f è G r e c o, by the Casino de' Nobili. — Carriage from the stat. to the town, one-horse 1½, two-horse 2 l., after sunset 2 and 2½ l.; smaller articles of luggage free]. — When time is limited the traveller may engage one of the ciceroni who offer their services, and some of whom are well-informed; fee 2—3 l. according to circumstances.

Siena, the ancient *Sena Julia* or *Colonia Julia Senensis*, is said to have been founded by the Senonian Gauls and converted into a Roman colony by Augustus, whence it derives its arms, the female-wolf and the twins. Of Etruscan antiquities there is no trace. The town attained the culminating point of its prosperity in the middle ages, after at the commencement of the 12th cent. it had become a free state, and having banished the nobility had united with the party of the Ghibellini. Farinata degli Uberti and the Ghibellini from Florence were welcomed in Siena, and on Sept. 4th, 1260, a great victory over the Guelfs was gained near *Monte Aperto* (6 M. distant). The nobility now returned to Siena, but the city kept a jealous watch over its privileges and increased to such an extent that it numbered 200,000 inhab., and vied with Florence in wealth and love of art. At length the supremacy was usurped by tyrants, such as (about 1500) Pandolfo Petrucci (whom Macchiavelli represents as a model of a tyrant), by whose aid the Medicis of Florence gradually exercised an influence and finally obtained the sovereignty over the city. During this period, under the Grandduke Cosimo I., the savage Count of Marignano devastated Siena with fire and sword, and cruelly massacred the population of the Maremme, in consequence of which the malaria obtained so fatal an ascendancy in that district.

The *School of Painting* of Siena is remarkable for its delicacy and pathos, pervaded with a deep sentiment of devotion, and is no mean rival of that of Florence. The most illustrious names of the 13th cent. are *Diottisalvi*, *Guido* and *Ugolina da Siena* and *Duccio di Buoninsegna*. The most celebrated master was *Simone di Martino*, the friend of Petrarch, who died in 1344. Among his pupils were his brother-in-law *Lippo Memmi*, *Pietro* and *Ambrogio*

Lorenzetti and *Barna di Siena*. Somewhat later (15th cent.) *Andrea di Vanni*, *Taddeo Bartolo* and *Jacopo Pacchiarotto*. After a short period of decline in the 15th cent., *Gianantonio Razzi*, a contemporary of Raphael, surnamed *Il Sodoma* (1480—1549), distinguished himself above his predecessors. He was born at Vercelli, was a pupil of Leonardo da Vinci and subsequently settled in Siena. His works are remarkable for their earnestness and tenderness of expression. His contemporaries were *Domenico Beccafumi* of Siena, surnamed *Meccherino*, and *Baldassare Peruzzi* (1481—1536), especially distinguished as an architect.

Siena possesses a population of 23,000 souls, a university founded in 1203, an archbishop, several libraries and scientific societies, a thriving trade and manufactories, and is one of the busiest and most agreeable towns in Tuscany. The climate is healthy, the atmosphere in summer being tempered by the lofty situation; the language and manners of the inhabitants pleasing and prepossessing. The pronunciation of Italian is here purer and less guttural than in Florence. The town is situated on undulating ground; the streets are for the most part narrow and crooked, but contain a considerable number of palaces and handsome churches, in the architecture of which (as is rarely the case in Italy) the Gothic style predominates.

The handsome *Piazza Vittorio Emanuele*, formerly named *del Campo* from some verses of Dante (Purgat. 11, 134), forms the central point of the town. Its form is that of an elongated semicircle, in some degree resembling an ancient theatre. Here the popular assemblies and festivals of the ancient republic took place. Horse-races are still annually held here *(Il Palio)* on Aug. 15th.

On the diameter of the semicircle of the piazza stands the *Palazzo Pubblico* (Pl. 17), or Town-Hall, erected in 1293—1309 from designs by the Sienese architects *Agostino* and *Agnolo*. In front of it is a small chapel of the Virgin *(Cap. di Piazza)* with damaged frescoes by *Sodoma*, built after the cessation of the great plague of 1348 which is said to have carried off 80,000 persons. The frescoes in the interior of the palace merit inspection (custodian $1/2$—1 l.). The beautiful chapel is adorned with frescoes from the life of the Virgin by *Taddeo di Bartolo;* the *altar-piece a Holy Family by *Sodoma*. The beautifully carved choir-stalls are by *Domenico di Niccolò* (1429). The contiguous vestibule contains a fresco by *Taddeo di Bartolo*, in which are represented in quaint juxtaposition St. Christophorus, Judas Maccabæus and six statesmen of the Roman republic. Here is the entrance to the *Sala del gran consiglio* or *delle Balestre* which contains large frescoes: *Madonna and Child under a canopy borne by saints, by *Simone di Martino* (1315); opposite *S. Ansano, *S. Victor and B. Bernardo by *Sodoma*. The *Sala dei Priori* with *Events in the life of the Emp. Frederick I. and of Pope Alexander III. by *Spinello Aretino*, and a Madonna by *Matteo da Siena* (1484). The *Sala del Concistoro* is adorned with ceiling-paintings by *Beccafumi* from

Roman history, and with portraits of 8 popes and 39 cardinals who were natives of Siena. The *Sala dei Nove* or *della Pace* is decorated with frescoes by *Ambrogio Lorenzetti* (1337), representing "good and bad government". In the *Sala del Sindaco* is a *fresco by *Sodoma*, the Resurrection. Above the palace rises the tower, *della Mangia*, begun in 1325, finished after 1345, which commands an extensive panorama (fee $1/2$ l.).

The *Fonte Gaja, a fountain adorned with bas-reliefs in marble (damaged) of subjects from the Scriptures, executed by *Jacopo della Quercia*, who is therefore surnamed *della Fonte*, has been conveyed to a place of safety, and a copy by *Sarrochi* erected on the same spot. A subterranean conduit conveys hither the most excellent water, the merits of which were extolled by Charles V., from a distance of 18 M.

From the Piazza the visitor ascends to the cathedral, passing the *Loggia di S. Paolo*, the hall for the sessions of the commercial tribunal, erected in 1417, now *Casino de' Nobili*. To the r. in the cathedral-square is a royal palace, to the l. the archiepiscopal palace; opposite to the cathedral a hospital, the *Spedale di S. Maria della Scala*, founded in 832.

The ** Cathedral, occupying the most elevated position in the town, commenced in the 11th cent., stands on the site of the older church of S. Maria Assunta, which is said to have superseded an ancient temple of Minerva. In 1339 it was intended to erect a much larger edifice; as, however, only a part of the principal aisle was completed, now fallen to decay, after the plague of 1348 the design was abandoned, and (1356) the present cathedral (which formed the transept in the original plan) built. The *Façade, constructed in 1270—1380, a combination of the pointed and round-arch styles, is adorned with red, white and black marble, and numerous sculptures representing prophets and angels by *Jacopo della Quercia* of Siena (1368—1442). The campanile was erected by *Bisdomini*.

The interior contains clustered columns with beautiful capitals; at the extremities °circular windows. Above the arches of the nave are placed the busts of the popes down to Alexander III. in terracotta. Two large columns at the door (of 1483) support a graceful tribune, with 4 bas-reliefs: Annunciation, Nuptials, Exaltation and Assumption of the Virgin. One of the basins for the consecrated water was executed by *Jacopo della Quercia*. The dome is an irregular hexagon, with small columns. The °*pavement* is unique: dark grey marble inlaid on white, shaded with lines, with representations from the Old Testament: Moses, Samson, Judas Maccabæus, Solomon, Joshua by *Duccio;* the sacrifice of Isaac, Adam and Eve, Moses on Mt. Sinai etc. by *Beccafumi;* the emblems of Siena and the towns allied with it, Hermes Trismegistus, Socrates and Crates, the Sibyls etc. by less celebrated masters. (Some of these are covered by boards which the visitor may cause to be removed.) The choir contains beautiful °carving from designs by *Bartolo Negroni*, named *Riccio*, completed in 1569, and inlaid work (tarsia) by *Fra Giovanni da Verona*. A °tabernacle in bronze by *Lorenzo da Pietro* (1472), octagonal °pulpit, reading-desk of white marble by

Nicola Pisano, his son *Giovanni* and his pupils *Arnolfo* and *Lapo* (1266). By the columns of the dome are two poles of the flag-waggon *(carroccio)* of the Florentines, captured at Montaperto in 1260, and on an altar near them the crucifix which the Sienese carried with them on that occasion. The two chapels in front of the entrance to the choir contain the two halves of a *picture by *Duccio di Buoninsegna:* in the chapel of the Eucharist the life of the Saviour in 27 compartments, and (in the chapel of S. Ansano) the Madonna and Child with saints, of the year 1311. For this work the artist received the sum of 3000 ducats. In the chapel of St. John a *statue of the saint by *Donatello* and font by *Jacopo della Quercia*. The 5 small frescoes are by *Pinturicchio*.

In the l. aisle is the entrance to the **Library (libreria)*, formerly *Sala Piccolominea*, built (1495) by order of Cardinal Francesco Piccolomini, afterwards Pope Pius III., and (1502—1506) adorned with ten *frescoes by *Bernardino di Betto* of Perugia, surnamed *Pinturicchio*, a fellow-pupil of Raphael under Pietro Perugino, representing scenes from the life of the celebrated *Æneas Sylvius Piccolomini* of Siena (or Pienza), born 1405, subsequently pope Pius II. (1458—1464). On the exterior another fresco of the coronation of his nephew Pius III. (1503), who reigned 27 days only. Raphael is said to have assisted in the execution of these frescoes, but apparently only in the drawings and cartoons; the colouring is admirably preserved, especially in that to the r. by the window, representing the journey of Æneas Sylvius to the Council of Bâle with Cardinal Capranica. On the ceiling mythological representations.

The 29 choir-books contain beautiful *miniatures by *Ansano di Pietro, Liberale di Verona, Girolamo di Cremona* etc. A few modern monuments, as that of Giulio Bianchi by *Tenerani* and the anatomist Mascagni (b. 1752 near Siena, d. 1815 at Florence), by *Ricci*.

To the l. of the door the monument of Bandino Bandini, with Christ and angels after the resurrection, an early work of *Michael Angelo*. Farther l. the *Altar dedicated to the Piccolomini family with statues of SS. Peter, Pius, Gregory and James (?) by *Michael Angelo*. St. Franciscus, begun by *Torrigiani*, completed by *Michael Angelo*.

In the r. transept the *Chapel of the Chigi*, erected by Alexander VII. (Fabio Chigi of Siena, in 1648 papal nuncio at the conclusion of the Peace of Münster, Pope 1655—67), sumptuously decorated with lapis lazuli, marble and gold, and statues of S. Jerome and Mary Magdalene (said originally to have represented Andromeda) by *Gior. Bernini* of Naples (1598—1680).

In the rear of the cathedral and beneath the choir is the ancient *Baptistery*, now the church of St. John the Baptist, with Gothic *façade and beautiful brazen *font, with sculptures by *Lorenzo Ghiberti*, *Donatello* and *Jacopo della Quercia*, and frescoes of the 15th cent.

Opposited the façade of the cathedral is the * *Pellegrinajo*, a hospital with the church of *S. Maria della Scala*. On the l. of the beautiful entrance hall is a *room with frescoes by *Dom. Bartoli* (1440—1443) and other masters (fee $^{1}/_{2}$ l.).

S. Agostino was completed by *Vanvitelli* in 1755. 2nd altar r., *Crucifixion, by *Pietro Perugino;* chap. r., *Slaughter of the Innocents, by *Matteo da Siena*, and a statue of Pius II. by *Dupré;* altar-piece, *Adoration of the Magi, by *Sodoma*.

S. Domenico (1220—1465), in the nave r. *chapel of S. Catherine of Siena with frescoes by *Sodoma*. Altar-piece, l. Legend of the Stigmata r. Vision of the Saints; l. wall, execution of an infidel. Last altar r., *Adoration of the shepherds by *L. Signorelli*. 2nd chap. l. of the high-altar, Madonna by *Guido da Siena* (1221?). 2nd chap. r. Madonna by *Matteo da Siena* (1478).

Il Carmine (S. Niccolò), a beautiful brick-structure, with tower and cloisters by *Baldassare Peruzzi*, now a barrack.

SS. Concezione (dei Servi): 4th altar r., Slaughter of the Innocents, by *Matteo da Siena*. Behind the high-altar: Madonna by *Giov. di Pietro* (1436).

S. Francesco, completed in 1236, now dilapidated and robbed of most of the pictures. 2nd chap. l. of the high-altar two frescoes by *Lorenzetti*, formerly in the refectory. Adjoining, the

* *Confraternità di S. Bernardino*. (Keys to be had of the bastiere Giuseppe Fineschi, saddler, in the Piaggio di Provenzano, fee 1 l.). On the 1st floor, oratorium with frescoes: *Mary visiting the temple; *Annunciation of the Nativity of Christ, Visitation, *Assumption and Coronation of the Virgin by *Sodoma*; the others by *Pacchiarotto* and *Beccafumi*.

Confraternità di Fontegiusta (1482) with a fresco by *B. Peruzzi*: Sibyl announcing to Augustus the Nativity of Christ.

S. Spirito, façade by *Bald. Peruzzi* (1519). 1. chap. r., altar-wall with frescoes by *Sodoma;* in the cloisters the Crucifixion, a fresco by *Fra Bartolommeo* (1/2 l.).

Two Oratories in the *House of St. Catherine of Siena*, daughter of a dyer and fuller (in fullonica) deserve special mention. Born in 1347, a nun at the age of 8, and celebrated for the visions and inspiration alleged to have been vouchsafed to her, she prevailed on Pope Gregory XI. to re-transfer the papal throne from Avignon (1377) to Rome. She died in 1380 and was canonized in 1461. The lower oratory contains pictures from the life of the saint, by *Sodoma*, *Pacchiarotto* and *Salimbeni*. The upper one the miraculous crucifix, a work of *Giunta da Pisa*, from which Catherine, according to the legend, received her wounds. The floor here is beautifully inlaid (1/2 l.).

The *Istituto delle Belle Arti* (Pl. 9, in the Via della Misericordia near S. Domenico) contains a valuable collection of pictures, principally of the older Sienese school, formed at the commencement of the present century from the works of art procured from suppressed monasteries and from the Palazzo pubblico, and subsequently enlarged. Admission gratis 9—3 o'clock daily, except on holidays, when access may be obtained for a gratuity. The interest attaching to this collection is especially of a historical nature.

At the entrance reliefs of little value. The first section contains pictures of the old school of Siena. 1—5. in the Byzantine style; 6. Madonna, by *Guido da Siena*. The following unknown. 18. S. Francis, by *Margaritone d'Arezzo;* 20 and 21. Chamberlains of Siena, *Diotisalvi Petroni* (1264);

27. Madonna with 4 saints, *Duccio di Buoninsegna;* 43. Madonna with 4 saints, *Simone di Martino* (?); 48—52. by *Ambrogio Lorenzetti* (49. Annunciation, 1344); 54, 56—63. by *Pietro Lorenzetti* (about 1330); 70. Crucifix, *Nicolò di Segna* (1345); *94. Madonna, *Lippo Memmi.* — 113. Madonna, *Mino del Pelliciaio* (1362); 130—136. by *Taddeo di Bartolo* (1409); 139—144. by *Giovanni di Paolo* (1445); 145. S. Bernardino, *Pietro di Giovanni;* 146—153. by *Sano di Pietro* (1479); 160. Madonna and Saints, *Neroccio di Bart. Landi* (1476); 175—179. by *Matteo da Siena* (1470); 209. Madonna appearing to Calixtus III., *Sano di Pietro;* *211. Christ about to be scourged, al fresco, from the cloisters of S. Francesco, by *Sodoma;* 224 and 225. two frescoes with beautiful frames (Æneas departing from Troy, Liberation of captives), *Luca Signorelli;* 245 and 246. Death and Coronation of the Virgin, *Spinello Aretino* (1384); 302. Nativity, *Francesco di Giorgio.* — In the centre of the following large saloon the celebrated marble-group of the *Three Graces, of Greek workmanship, found in the 13th cent. at the foundation of the cathedral. *336. Descent from the Cross, *Sodoma;* *333, 334. Christ on the Mt. of Olives and in Paradise, frescoes by *Sodoma;* 347. Madonna, *Beccafumi;* 346. Judith, *Sodoma;* 358. Fall of the angels, *Beccafumi.* — The following apartment contains upwards of 100 pictures of different schools, among which: 26. Copy of Raphael's Madonna della Perla (at Madrid); 36. Five morra-players, *Caravaggio;* 39. Portrait, *Morone;* 45. Holy Family, *Pinturicchio;* *53. Portrait, *Schongauer* (?); *54. Portrait of Charles V., *German School;* 63. St. Catherine of Siena with the wounds, *Beccafumi;* 71. Same, by *Sodoma;* 73. Portrait, *German School;* 85—87. Nativity, *Sodoma;* 91. St. Catharina, *Fra Bartolommeo;* 99. Mary Magdalene, same artist; 103. Brazen Serpent, *Palma Giovine;* 105, 106. Pietas and Madonna, *Sodoma.* — The large saloon of the casts of ancient statues contains the seven original cartoons of *Beccafumi* from the history of Moses, executed in mosaic on the pavement of the cathedral. Here, too, are specimens of wood-carving, an art in which Siena surpassed all the towns of Italy. In the 15th and 16th centuries the family of *Barili* excelled in the art; at the present day the workshop of *Giusti*, near the monastery of S. Domenico, merits a visit.

The *Palaces* of Siena are more interesting on account of their architecture than their collections of objects of art. Most of them were designed by the architects *Agostino* and *Agnolo* (about 1300).

The *Palazzo del Magnifico* (Pl. 14), near the cathedral, was erected in 1504 for the tyrant Pandolfo Petrucci, surnamed il Magnifico; decorations in bronze on the exterior by *Cozzarelli* and *Mazzini*. *Palazzo Saracini* (Pl. 19). *Palazzo Buonsignori* (Pl. 12), in the Gothic style, with façade of brick. *Palazzo Piccolomini* (Pl. 15), with two halls painted by *Bernard van Orley*, who abandoned the school of Van Eyck for that of Raphael. *Palazzo Piccolomini*, now *del Governo*, with handsome loggia, begun in 1469, with the inscription: "Gentilibus suis", i. e. for his relations. In 1859 the great *Archives* (Director *Cav. Bianchi)* were placed here. They form one of the largest collections in Italy and consist of 30,000 parchment documents dating from 814. Interesting specimens of records, the hand-writings of celebrated men, miniatures etc. are arranged in glass-cases. *Palazzo Pollini*, ascribed to Peruzzi, with frescoes by *Sodoma;* Susanna, Scipio, Burning of Troy, Judgment of Paris. *Palazzo Tolomei*, erected by *Tozzo* in 1205.

The *Fonte Fullonica*, near the Palazzo Piccolomini, was erected in 1249.

The early-Gothic *Fonte Branda* (Pl. 8), at the S.W. base of the hill of S. Domenico, dating from 1198, was praised by Dante (Inferno 30, 78), and after it the nearest gate is named.

The *University* (Pl. 22) is in the Via Ricasoli, not far from the Piazza; in the vestibule the monument of the celebrated jurist *Nicolò Aringhieri* (1374), with a bas-relief representing the professor in the midst of his audience.

The *Library* (Pl. 6), in the spacious hall of the *Accademia degli Intronati*, is reputed the most ancient in Europe (in the 17th cent. Siena possessed 16, and in 1654 even one for women), and contains 40,000 vols. and 5000 MSS.; among the latter the *Greek Gospels, formerly in the chapel of the imperial palace at Constantinople, of the 9th cent., magnificently bound with workmanship in silver; *Treatise on architecture by *Francesco di Giorgio*, with sketches and drawings by the author; Sketch-books of *Baldassare Peruzzi* and *Giuliano da Sangallo*.

The *Citadel*, constructed by the Grand-duke Cosimo I., rises at the N. extremity of the town, contiguous to *La Lizza*, the favourite promenade of the inhabitants, occupying the site of a fortress founded by Charles V. in 1551.

Near Siena is the Franciscan Monastery *L'Osservanza*, erected in 1423, where Pandolfo Petrucci, who died in 1512, is interred.

From Siena a pleasant excursion may be made to the neighbouring castle B e l C a r o (carr. 1 h.), whence there is a splendid view of Siena and the surrounding country. On the ground-floor a frescoed ceiling, Judgment of Paris, by *B. Peruzzi*, who also painted the chapel, now undergoing restoration.

The train backs out of the station and is transferred to another line of rails, on which it passes Siena on the N. side. It now traverses the hills which form the watershed between the *Ombrone* and the valley of the *Chiana*, and passes through 6 tunnels. This district is one of the bleakest in Italy; grotesquely shaped hills of sand, barren and rugged mountains, interesting to the palæontologist alone.

Stat. *Asciano* is reached; village to the r., $1/2$ hr. from the railway, with several beautiful churches.

A railway is in course of construction from this point to *Grosseto* (p. 16), the capital of the Maremma, and is now open as far as the second stat. *Torrenieri* (18$1/2$ M., one-third of the entire distance). This line is of little importance to the ordinary traveller except from the fact, that the first station (two trains daily, I. cl. 1 l. 35 c., II. cl. 1 l., III. cl. 75 c.) *S. Giovanni d'Asso* (Locanda della Stella d'Oriente, tolerable) is only half an hour's walk (to save time a guide had better be taken; one-horse carr. also procurable) from the Benedictine monastery, now dissolved, of **Monte Oliveto Maggiore** near *Chiusure* with celebrated °frescoes by *Luca Signorelli* and *Sodoma*. Entrance to the monastery-yard to the r. of the church. The r. wall, except the first (by *Sodoma*) and the last picture (by *Riccio*), is painted by

L. Signorelli, the other three by *Sodoma*, whose earliest-known and perhaps most important work this is. The scenes commence. on the wall opposite that painted by *Signorelli*, with the departure of S. Benedict from his father's house. — This line, when completed, will enable the traveller conveniently to combine a visit to Siena with the direct route to Rome through the Maremme.

Stat. *Rapolano*, reached in 10 min.; the village (on the r.) possesses baths which are frequently visited in July and August.

The country becomes more attractive: several villages on the hills to the l. Then stat. *Lucignano:* the mediæval village lies on the hill to the l. The higher cultivation of the soil indicates the proximity of the charming valley of the *Chiana*. To the l. in the distance the chain of the Apennines is visible above Cortona.

Stat. *Sinalunga* or *Asinalunga*. village on the r. where Garibaldi was taken prisoner on his march to Rome. Sept. 24th 1867.

From this point the traveller may proceed in 3 hrs. through the luxuriant *Valley of the Chiana* to *Cortona*, and thence by the *Trasimene Lake* to *Perugia* (see p. 50). This route is far more attractive than that by Chiusi; a visit to Cortona is also extremely interesting. One day more, however, is necessary [quarters for the night at *Camuscia* (p. 48) or *Cortona*] to visit the extensive and well-conducted farms *(fattorie)* of *Bettole*, *Foiano*, *Crete* etc., which are situated on this route.

Stat. *Torrita*, beyond which the lofty *Monte Pulciano* is visible to the r. Stat. *Salarco*.

From Salarco the picturesque town (XXX) inhab.) of **Monte Pulciano**, with mediæval walls, may be reached in 1½ hr. The principal church, *S. Biagio*, was erected by *Sangallo*; the *Palazzo Buccelli* contains Etruscan and Roman antiquities. The full-bodied wine produced here enjoys a high reputation. Here in 1454 the erudite *Angelus Politianus* was born, the confidant of Lorenzo the Magnificent and preceptor of his children (d. at Florence 1494). — About 10½ M. from M. Pulciano is situated *Pienza*, birthplace of Pope Pius II. (Æneas Sylvius Piccolomini) and his nephew Pius III., who embellished the town with sumptuous edifices, e. g. the extensive *Palazzo Piccolomini*.

To the r. the *Monti di Cetona* become visible, with which *M. Amiata* (5000 ft.), the highest point of the Tuscan Apennines is connected. To the l. extends the long *Lake of Monte Pulciano;* beyond and connected with it by a canal, the similar *Lake of Chiusi*. The exhalations from these lakes render the neighbourhood unhealthy in summer.

Stat. *Chiusi*, town on the height to the r. Carriage (¼ hr.) 1 l. for 1 pers.; to the r. of the road are the small catacombs of *S. Caterina*, to the l. a Roman tomb.

Chiusi *(Leon d' Oro*, no fixed charges. The landlord offers Etruscan relics for sale at exorbitant prices. Travellers are cautioned against making purchases of this description at Chiusi, where the manufacture of spurious "antiquities" is greatly in vogue), the ancient *Clusium*, one of the 12 Etruscan capitals, frequently mentioned in the wars against Rome and as the headquarters of Porsenna. The town was fearfully devastated by the malaria in the middle ages and now scarcely numbers 3000 inhab. The walls are mediæval; a few relics of those of the Etruscan period may be distinguished near the cathedral, outside the *Porta delle Torri*. A walk thence round the town to the *Porta Romana* affords pleasing views of the S. portion of the Chiana Valley, Città della Pieve, the mountains of Cetona, to the N. the lakes of Chiusi and Montepulciano and the latter town itself.

Beneath the town is a labyrinth of subterranean passages, the object of which has not yet been precisely ascertained. The Etruscan tombs in the vicinity have yielded a rich spoil, consisting of vases, bronzes, mirrors. sarcophagi, and especially of cinerary urns, most of them of terracotta, a few of alabaster and travertine. The Bishop Msgr. Ciofi and Sgr. Mazetti possess valuable collections of these objects.

The *Cathedral (S. Mustiola)* consists almost entirely of fragments of ancient structures; the 18 columns of unequal thickness in the interior, and the tomb of S. Mustiola are derived from a similar source. The walls of the arcades in the cathedral-square bear numerous Etruscan and Roman inscriptions.

The *Etruscan Tombs* are numerous; four of the largest compete for the honour (probably without reason) of being the *Mausoleum of Porsena* mentioned by Pliny and Varro. The tombs, situated in isolated mounds, are generally closed. As they are scattered and at some distance from the town, the visitor may consult the guide (Zeppotoni can be recommended, 3—4 l. per diem) respecting the time to be devoted to each. The most interesting are: the *Deposito del poggio Gajelli*, 3 M. to the N.E. of the town, very distant and much damaged; *Deposito del Granduca*, $2^1/_4$ M., and *Deposito della Scimia*, $^3/_4$ M. to the N.E.; *Deposito de' Dei*, $2^1/_4$ M. (now filled up), and *Deposito dei Monachi*, $1^1/_2$ M. to the N.W.; **Deposito del Colle*, with mural paintings. The *Tombs of the early Christians* (near S. Caterina and S. Mustiola) may be glanced at in passing (the custodian must be ordered beforehand).

From Chiusi to Perugia, see R. 7.

The Railway proceeds through the Chiana Valley to stat. *Carnaiola* or *Ficulle;* village 3 M. distant, on the hill to the l. Thence the line follows the valley of the *Paglia*, an impetuous tributary of the Tiber, which in rainy seasons frequently occasions great damage. The formation here consists of tertiary sandstone, whilst at Orvieto the volcanic district begins, of which the central point is the lake of Bolsena (p. 36).

The station lies at the base of the hill occupied by Orvieto. The corriere starts hence after the arrival of the 3 p. m. train. A long and winding road (omnibus 1 l.) ascends to

Orvieto (the principal hotel and post-office, *delle Belle Arti*, was formerly much complained of, but is now improved; *Aquila Bianca*, unpretending; the *Caffetiere Agostino* also lets comfortable apartments; bargaining as usual), situated on an isolated tuffstone rock, 720 ft. above the *Paglia*, 1250 ft. above the sea-level, the *Urbibentum* of Procopius, termed *Urbs Vetus* in the 8th cent., whence its name. In the middle ages it was a stronghold of the Guelphs which often afforded an asylum to the popes, and is now a small town and episcopal residence.

The ** *Cathedral*, one of the most magnificent specimens of Italian Gothic, consists, like those of Florence and Siena, of alternate blocks of black and white marble; the façade richly decorated with mosaic and sculptures, the interior with frescoes and statuary of the 16th cent. Founded in consequence of the "miracle of Bolsena" (comp. p. 36) the edifice was begun in 1290 by *Lorenzo Maitani*, and continued till the end of the 16th cent. Pope Nicholas IV. laid the first stone. The *Façade is said to be the largest and most gorgeous "polychromatic" structure in existence. The lower portions of the pillars are adorned with *bas-reliefs by *Giovanni Pisano*, *Arnolfo* and other pupils of Nicola Pisano, representing Scripture scenes: 1st pillar l., from the creation down to Tubalcain; 2nd, Abraham, genealogy of the Virgin; 3rd, history of Christ and Mary; 4th, Last Judgment with Paradise and Hell; above are the bronze emblems of the 4 Evangelists. Above the principal portal a Madonna under a canopy, in bronze. Above the doors and in the three pointed pediments are modern *mosaics on a golden ground: Annunciation, Nuptials of the Virgin, Baptism of Christ, Coronation of the Virgin.

The interior, of black basalt and greyish-yellow limestone (from quarries in the vicinity), is in the form of a Latin cross, 278 ft. long, 108 ft. broad and 115 ft. high. The windows pointed, upper parts filled with stained glass. The nave is separated from the aisles by 6 arches supported by columns 62 ft. in height, above which is a gallery adorned with rich carving. The framework of the roof is visible, and was formerly richly ornamented. At the sides of the principal entrance, r. St. Sebastian by *Scalza*, l. St. Pellegrino. Immediately to the l. a fresco of the *Madonna and St. Catherine, by *Gentile da Fabriano*. Before this stands a marble *font, the lower part by *Luca di Giovanni* (1390), the upper by *Sano di Matteo* (1407). In front of the columns the statues of the 12 Apostles, by *Mosca*, *Scalza*, *Toti*, *Giovanni da Bologna* and other masters. On the high altar the *Annunziata and Archangel, by *Mocchi*. In the choir frescoes from the life of the Virgin by *Ugolino d'Ilario* and *Pietro di Puccio;* the tarsia (inlaid wood-work) in the choir by artists of Siena of the 14th cent.; altars on either side with *reliefs in marble: l. Visitation of Mary, executed by *Moschino* when 15 years of age, from designs by *Sammicheli* of Verona; r. Adoration of the Magi, by *Mosca*.

In the r. aisle the *Chapel of the Madonna di S. Brizio*, with a miraculous image of the Virgin and a Pietà by *Ippolito Scalza*. The *Frescoes here, by *Luca Signorelli* and *Fra Angelico da Fiesole*, are celebrated. On the ceiling: Christ as Judge, and prophets, by *Fra Angelico*; apostles, signa judicii, patriarchs and doctors, virgins and martyrs, by *Luca Signorelli*, partly from the drawings of Fiesole. The pictures on the walls are entirely by *Signorelli*. On the wall of the entrance: Announcement of the end of the world by Sibyls and prophets, rain of fire; on the window-wall: Summons to Judgment, archangels beneath. On the l.: Arrival of Antichrist (in the corner portraits of Luca Signorelli and Fra Angelico) and Paradise; r. Last Judgment and Hell. (These admirable frescoes of Signorelli bear no mean comparison with those of Michael Angelo in the Sixtine chapel at Rome.) *Beneath these pictures are, r. the portraits of Cicero, Ovid and Horace, l. Seneca, Dante and Virgil, surrounded by medallions representing scenes from their works. On the r. wall, in a niche behind the Pietà of Scalza: *Entombment of Christ by *Signorelli*. Opposite, in the N. aisle, is the *Cappella del Corporale*, containing the large silver shrine (400 lbs. in weight) by *Ugolino Vieri* of Siena, with brilliant enamel representing the Passion and miracles, covered and visible only on the festivals of Corpus Christi and Easter Sunday. Modernized frescoes representing the "Miracle of Bolsena" (p. 36), by *Ugolino*. Altar l., Madonna by *Filippo Memmi*.

Opposite the cathedral, Nr. 39, the *Opera del Duomo (if closed apply to the sacristan of the cathedral). In a room on the first story are preserved: *Designs for the façade of the cathedral and a pulpit (which was never completed) on parchment; a beautifully carved reading-desk; a precious *Reliquary by *Ugolino da Siena*; a *Magdalene by *L. Signorelli* (1504); two specimen-frescoes by *Signorelli*, portraits, one of himself.

S. Giovenale (if closed, visitors knock at the door r. of the façade, whence access can be obtained to the older church at the back), a basilica .with nave and two aisles, open roof and remains of old paintings (1312 and 1399).

S. Domenico contains (in the r. transept) the monument of Cardinal di Brago, by *Arnolfo* (1282).

Near the dilapidated *Fortress* a celebrated fountain, *Il Pozzo di S. Patrizio*, begun in 1527 by *Sangallo*, completed in 1540 by *Mosca*, partly hewn in the tuffstone, partly consisting of masonry. Visitors descend by a flight of 250 steps and quit it by another of the same height (fee 1/2—1 l.). Near the fountain a fine view is obtained of the valley of the Tiber and the Umbrian Mts. The *Palazzo Comunale* and several towers have a mediæval aspect.

A short distance beyond Orvieto the present dominions of the papal see are entered. Passports scrutinized. The main-road from Orvieto to Montefiascone (18 1/2 M.) traverses a somewhat dreary district on the E. side of the *Lake of Bolsena*, which is partly concealed from view by the surrounding crater-wall.

About 14 M. from Orvieto a road to the l. leads to (4 3/4 M.) *Bagnorea*, situated on a hill surrounded by ravines, the ancient *Balneum Regis*. The modern village is connected by a narrow strip of land with the older *Civitá*, which, owing to the gradual erosion of the earth, is threatened with slow but certain destruction. The situation of the village is strikingly peculiar and picturesque, and especially interesting to geologists.

A far more interesting route than the above-mentioned is that by Bolsena, about 2 1/2 M. longer. From the mainroad the traveller diverges to the r. and descends to the lake, the vast crater of an extinct volcano which formed the central point of a wide sphere of volcanic agency extending as far as Orvieto.

The *Lake of Bolsena*, the ancient *Lacus Vulsiniensis*, 910 ft. above the sea-level, is 28 M. in circumference, and abounds in fish (its eels are mentioned by Dante, Purg. 24, 24). Its form is circular, the banks, especially towards the W., bleak and deserted, owing to the malaria, which, confined in the basin of the lake, is not easily dispelled by the wind. The monotony of the surface is relieved by the two picturesque islands, *Bisentina* and the rocky *Martana*. On the latter Amalasuntha, Queen of the Goths, only daughter of Theodoric the Great, was imprisoned in 534, and afterwards strangled whilst bathing, by order of her cousin Theodatus, whom she had elevated to the rank of co-regent. The church in the island of Bisentina (formerly a monastery, now private property) was erected by the Farnese family and embellished by the Caracci. It contains the relics of St. Christina, a native of Bolsena.

Bolsena (*Hotel* in the Piazza) is a small town situated below the Roman *Volsinii* (birthplace of Sejanus, the favourite of Tiberius), of which fragments of walls, columns etc. are still seen. It was one of the 12 capitals of the Etruscan League, and after various vicissitudes was at length conquered and destroyed by the Romans. The spoil is said to have comprised 2000 statues. Its wealth is proved by the discovery, in the vicinity, of numerous vases, trinkets, statues etc., among the latter the statue of an orator, termed "l'Arringatore", now in the museum at Florence. The present town contains inscriptions, columns and sculptures of the Roman municipium which superseded the Etruscan city. The ancient site is reached in a few minutes by an antique causeway of basalt. Among the ruins is an amphitheatre, worthy of special attention, now converted into a vegetable-garden. Beautiful views of the lake.

The triple church of *S. Cristina* possesses a façade embellished with bas-reliefs from an ancient temple, and a sarcophagus with the triumph of Bacchus.

<small>The "*Miracle of Bolsena*", the subject of a celebrated picture by Raphael in the Vatican, occurred in 1263. A Bohemian priest, who entertained doubts respecting transubstantiation, was convinced of the truth of that doctrine by the miraculous appearance of drops of blood on the host which he had just consecrated. In commemoration of this, Pope Urban IV., then present in Orvieto, instituted the festival of Corpus Christi.</small>

From Bolsena the road ascends on the bank of the lake through woods to (6 M.) Montefiascone, where luggage is examined by the papal officials, a formality from which a donation of 1—2 l. (for a party) will liberate the traveller. With regard to this the vetturino should previously be consulted.

Montefiascone (*Aquila Nera*, outside the gate), a town with 2600 inhab., is situated 1700 ft. above the sea-level. The uncompleted cathedral of *S. Margareta*, with octagonal dome, was one of the earliest works of *Sammicheli*. Near the gate, on the road to Viterbo, is *S. Flaviano*, a structure of 1030, restored by Urban IV. in 1262, in the Gothic combined with the round-arch style. In the subterranean chapel the *tomb of the Canon *Johannes De Foucris* of Augsburg, with the inscription:

*Est, Est, Est. Propter nimium est,
Johannes de Fuc., D. meus, mortuus est.*

It is recorded of this ecclesiastic that, when on a journey, he made his valet precede him with orders to inscribe the words "Est, Est" on the doors of the taverns where the wine was of a superior quality. The good canon relished the produce of Montefiascone so highly that he never got any farther. The best muscatel of the district is still known as Est Est, and may be procured for 1 l. per flask.

The traveller should not omit to ascend into the town for the sake of the magnificent view: N. the lake of Bolsena as far as the chain of M. Amiata, E. the Umbrian Apennines, S. as far as the Ciminian forest, W. as far as the sea. The extensive plain of ancient Etruria with its numerous villages may be surveyed from this point: the conjecture that the celebrated *Fanum Voltumnae*, the most sacred shrine of the Etrurians, stood here, has much in its favour.

The old high-road from Siena to Rome, little used since the construction of the railway to Orvieto, leads by *Torrenieri*, *Radicofani*, *Acquapendente*, *S. Lorenzo*, *Bolsena* and *Montefiascone*, where it unites with that above described. From Siena to Montefiascone is a distance of 84 M. *Monte Amiata* is sometimes ascended from Radicofani. *Acquapendente* is the frontier-town where luggage and passports are inspected. The route is picturesque, but in other respects uninteresting.

From Montefiascone to (14 M.) Viterbo the road traverses the somewhat bleak and unattractive plain between the *Ciminian Forest* and the *Lake of Bolsena*. Midway, near the *Osteria della Fontanella*, a portion of the ancient *Via Cassia* lies to the r. About 2½ M. farther, ¾ M. to the l. of the road, are situated the ruins of *Ferento*, the Etruscan *Ferentinum*, birthplace of the Emperor Otho. In the 11th cent. it was destroyed by the inhabitants of Viterbo on account of its heretical tendencies, for the Ferentines represented the Saviour on the cross with open eyes, instead of closed, as was thought more orthodox. Such is the account of the chroniclers. Among the extensive mediæval, Roman, and Etruscan remains, a *Theatre* of a peculiar and primitive construction, with subsequent additions, deserves special attention.

About 2 M. farther is situated *Bulicame*, a warm sulphureous spring, mentioned by Dante (Inferno, 14, 79), still used for baths.

Viterbo *(Aquila Nera*, a spacious hotel, no fixed charges; *Tre Re*, less pretending, and *Angelo*, new, both in the *Piazza)*, situated in the plain on the N. side of the Ciminian Forest, 1700 ft. above the sea-level, was the central point of the extensive cession made by the Countess Matilda of Tuscia to the papal see, the so-called patrimony of St. Peter, frequently mentioned as a residence of the popes and as the scene of the papal elections which took place here in the 13th cent. The town, surrounded by ancient Lombard walls and towers, an episcopal residence with 14,000 inhab., is termed by old Italian authors the "city of handsome fountains and beautiful women". The objects of interest may, however, be inspected in the course of a brief visit.

The *Cathedral of S. Lorenzo*, occupying the site of a temple of Hercules, contains the tombs of the Popes John XXI., Alexander IV. and Clement IV., a few pictures of little value etc. At the high-altar of this church, in 1279, Count Guido de Montfort, the partizan of Charles of Anjou, assassinated Henry, son of Count Richard of Cornwall, King of the Germans and brother of Henry III., in order thereby to avenge the death of his father who had fallen at the battle of Evesham in 1265 when fighting against the latter. Dante mentions this deed and places the assassin in the seventh region of hell (Inferno 12, 120). In front of the church is the spot where in July, 1155, Pope Hadrian IV. (Nicholas Breakspeare, an Englishman) compelled the Emperor Frederick I., as his vassal, to hold his stirrup. Adjacent is the dilapidated *Episcopal Palace* of the 13th cent. The hall is shown in which, by order of Charles of Anjou, the Conclave assembled in 1271 and elected Tebaldo Visconti of Piacenza Pope as Gregory X., and in 1281 De Brion, a Frenchman, as Martin IV. On the latter occasion Charles excited a tumult and caused the roof to be removed in order to compel the cardinals to proceed with the election. Here, too, is the apartment in which, on May 16th, 1277, John XXI., a Portuguese (elected here in 1276), was killed by the falling in of the ceiling.

The church and monastery of *S. Rosa* contain the remains (a blackened mummy) of that saint, who was born here in the 13th cent. She urged the people to rise against the Emp. Frederick II., was expelled by the Ghibellini and after the death of the emperor returned in triumph to Viterbo.

S. Francesco (in the rear of the Aquila Nera), a Gothic structure, contains (in the l. transept) a *Descent from the Cross by *Sebastiano del Piombo* (design by Michael Angelo) and (r.) the *Tomb of Adrian V. (de' Fieschi of Genoa, elected July 11th, died Aug. 16th, 1276, at Viterbo), with recumbent effigy. The church of the *Osservanti del Paradiso* also possesses a picture by *Seb. del Piombo*, the Scourging, and on the exterior a fresco (Madonna and saints) ascribed to *Leonardo da Vinci*.

S. Maria della Verità contains a *fresco by *Lorenzo di Giacomo* of Viterbo (1469), representing the Espousals of the Virgin, with numerous portraits introduced as characters.

In front of *S. Angelo in Spata*, a Roman *sarcophagus bears an inscription to the memory of the beautiful *Galiana* (1138), in behalf of whom, like Helen of old, a war was once kindled between Rome and Viterbo, in which the latter was victorious.

In the court of the *Palazzo Pubblico* are five large Etruscan sarcophagi with figures and inscriptions. The hall of the *Accademia degli Ardenti* possesses frescoes by *Baldassare Croce*, pupil of Annibale Caracci. In the *Museum* Etruscan and Roman antiquities and paintings; also the "decree of Desiderius, king of the Lombards" and the Tabula Cibellaria, forgeries of the infamous *Annius* of Viterbo, a Dominican of the monastery in front of the Porta Romana, who died at Rome in 1502.

The most remarkable fountains are: *Fontana Grande*, begun in 1206; that in the market-place; that in the Piazza della Rocca, of 1566. ascribed to *Vignola;* and one in the court of the Palazzo Pubblico.

The *Palazzo S. Martino*, property of the Doria Pamfili, contains a magnificent staircase "a cordoni", by which a carriage may ascend, and a portrait of the well-known Olympia Maldachini Pamfili, sister-in-law of Innocent X. who reigned 1644—55.

From Viterbo a number of remarkably attractive excursions, especially interesting to the antiquarian, may be made to the ruins of the surrounding Etruscan towns.

The farther the traveller deviates from the main route, the more miserable do the inns become. The principal places can be attained by carriage only, but some of the excursions must be performed on horseback or on foot.

The volcanic nature of the district, betokened by the profound ravines and fissures of the rock, and the dreary desolation which prevails, combined with the proximity of the graves of 2000 years' antiquity, tend to awaken a sentiment of awe.

Castel d'Asso, popularly known as *Castellaccio*, 4³|₄ M. to the W. of Viterbo, may be visited on horseback or on foot (guide necessary; lights should not be forgotten by those who purpose exploring the interior of the tombs). Passing the Bulicame, the road traverses a moor and leads to the valley, which contains a succession of *Etruscan Tombs*, hewn in the rock. The fronts of these are architecturally designed, and bear some resemblance to the rock-tombs of Egypt. The numerous inscriptions in an enigmatical language have bidden defiance to all the efforts of modern research. On the opposite hill the picturesque ruins of a mediæval castle; scanty remains of an ancient village, probably the *Castellum Azia* of Cicero.

The traveller may from this point proceed to *Vetralla*, 9¹|₂ M. from Viterbo and connected with it by diligence, in the vicinity of the Roman *Forum Cassii*. A carriage-road gradually ascends thence to (14 M.) *Sutri* (p. 41) and leads to Rome. On certain days the diligence runs from Viterbo to Corneto and Civitavecchia by Vetralla and M. Romano (comp. p. 12).

From Vetralla a bridle-path, traversing a bleak moor, leads in 1½ hr. to the necropolis of **Norchia** (with guide), similar to Castel d'Asso, but more imposing. Two of the tombs manifest a bias to the Hellenic style. Adjacent are picturesque ruins of a Lombard church; in the 9th cent. the village was named *Orcle*, ancient name unknown.

A similar locality is at *Bieda*, the ancient *Blera*, a miserable village, 4½ M. from Vetralla, with rock-tombs and two ancient bridges. Scenery strikingly grand.

Toscanella (*Inn* at the gate), the ancient *Tuscania*, a small town 14 M. from Viterbo, reached by the diligence to Corneto 3 times weekly (since the completion of the railway it is better to make this excursion from Rome viâ Corneto, see p. 18). The walls and towers impart a mediæval aspect to the place, which contains two noble Romanesque structures of that epoch: *S. Pietro*, on the height, with crypt and antique columns, and on the exterior fine sculptures. Smaller but even more interesting: *S. Maria*. Both churches now disused. On the hill of S. Pietro stood the ancient citadel. Etruscan tombs in the vicinity.

Campanari's small garden, situated in the lower part of the town, embellished with sarcophagi and other relics and containing an imitation of an Etruscan tomb, is an extremely interesting spot. The sarcophagi, with the life-size portraits of the deceased framed in the living green, produce a profound impression, and the traveller will nowhere acquire a more accurate idea with respect to the contents of an Etruscan tomb than here. Sign. *Carlo Campanari*, as obliging as well-informed, has with his father conducted many of those extensive excavations which have filled the museums of Europe with Etruscan vases, goblets, mirrors etc. — From Toscanella to Corneto 16½ M.

Interesting excursions may also be made to the E. into the *Valley of the Tiber*. The road to (11½ M.) *Bomarzo* leads by the Dominican monastery of the *Madonna della Quercia*, designed by Bramante, and *Bagnaia* with the now deserted *Villa Lante*, erected by Vignola. The route by *Ferento* (p. 37) and *Le Grotte* is more interesting and not much longer; from the latter a guide necessary; both routes inaccessible to carriages.

Bomarzo, a village in a remarkably picturesque situation on a precipitous rock near the *Tiber;* opposite to it lay the ancient *Polimartinm*, where considerable excavations have been made. From Bomarzo to Orte a beautiful route of 9½ M., on which, near *Bassano*, is situated the small *Laghetto di Bassano*, the *Lacus Vadimonis*, celebrated in ancient history for the signal victories of the Romans over the Etruscans, B. C. 309 and 283, and described by the younger Pliny (Epist. 8, 20) with its floating islands; at the present day, however, it is greatly reduced in extent.

From Viterbo the ancient *Mons Ciminius*, now usually termed *Monte di Viterbo*, is slowly ascended. The culminating point (2673 ft.) of the road is attained in 1½ — 2 hrs. at the post-station *l'Imposta;* the summit of the mountain is 3000 ft. above the sea-level. These wooded heights, now clothed with heath and brushwood, intermingled occasionally with oaks and chestnuts, were regarded as an insuperable barrier for the protection of central Etruria, until the Consul Q. Fabius, B. C. 308, successfully traversed it and signally vanquished the Etruscans. The road is lonely; piquets of papal gensdarmes, who effectually watch over the public safety, are encountered at intervals. The culminating point commands an admirable *survey of the plain towards the N., as far as the chain of Cetona and M. Amiata, and W. as far as the sea. A more imposing view is soon disclosed, towards the S., of the vast Campagna di Roma; E. the long chain of the Umbrian and Sabine Apennines as far as Palestrina and the Alban Mts.; then the sinuous course of the Tiber and the isolated Soracte, and, in clear weather, the dome of St. Peter's and the distant Volscian Mts. Beneath lies the small *Lago di Vico*, the *Lacus Ciminius* (1400 ft.), the E. bank of which the road skirts, of circular form, surrounded by wood, and doubtless an extinct crater (similar to the Laacher See in the Rhenish Province of Prussia). This entire range is of volcanic origin. In the centre of the ancient crater rises the beautifully wooded *Monte Venere*. According to a tradition of antiquity a town, overwhelmed by the lake, may be distinguished beneath the surface.

Midway between l'Imposta and Ronciglione a path to the l. leads through a beautiful wood to (1½ M.) the château of *Caprarola, of pentagonal form, surrounded by a rampart and fosse, erected by *Vignola* for Cardinal Alexander Farnese, nephew of Paul III. (1534–49). The saloons and other apartments are adorned with frescoes, representations from the history of the Farnese family, allegories etc., by *Federigo*, *Ottaviano* and *Taddeo Zucchero*, *Tempesta* and *Vignola*. A magnificent prospect is enjoyed from the upper terrace of the *Palazzuolo*, a pretty structure (by *Vignola*) situated in the grounds.

Beyond the Lago di Vico, with its miserable village, the traveller soon reaches *Ronciglione* (Posta, Aquila Nera, both good), a beautifully situated little town, with ruined castle on the height (1300 ft.), on the verge of the extensive *Campagna di Roma*, a plain which stretches hence S. to the promontory of Circeii near Terracina, E. to the Sabine Apennines, and W. as far as the sea.

From Ronciglione to *Monterosi* by the main road is a distance of 8 M., by *Sutri* 1¼ M. farther.

Sutri, the ancient Etruscan *Sutrium*, frequently mentioned in the pages of history as the ally of Rome in the wars against the Etruscans, from whom it was wrested by Camillus, B. C. 365 *(Claustra Etruriae)*, converted into a Roman colony in 383, is most picturesquely situated on an isolated volcanic ridge. The deep ravine contains numerous Etruscan tombs, and, on the S. side, fragments of the ancient walls. Of the 5 gates 3 are ancient, two towards the S., and the Porta Furia on the N. side (said to be so named because once entered by M. Furius Camillus), now closed by masonry. Outside the Porta Romana at the foot of an eminence, near the Villa Savonelli and shaded by dense forest, is situated an admirably preserved *Amphitheatre, hewn in the rock, dating from Augustus, erroneously regarded by some as Etruscan. The rocks above contain numerous tomb-chambers, one of which has been converted into a *church, where, according to the various local traditions, the early Christians celebrated divine service. A legend attaching to the *Grotta d'Orlando*, near the town, describes it as the birthplace of the celebrated paladin of Charlemagne.

A bridle-path leads in 2 hrs. from Sutri to the *Lake of Bracciano* and *Trevignano* (p. 300).

The road from Monterosi to Rome (23 M.) is almost entirely coincident with the ancient *Via Cassia*, which led by Sutri, Bolsena and Chiusi to Florence. *Sette Vene*, an *inn 3 M. beyond Monterosi, is recommended in preference to the latter as a halting-place. About 3 M. farther the verge of the crater is attained in which the somewhat unhealthy village of *Baccano* (*Posta) lies; in the vicinity a mephitic pond, to the W. the two small lakes of *Martignano (Lacus Alsietinus)* and *Stracciacappa*. Traces of ancient drains (emissarii) are distinguished on the l. side of the road. Immediately beyond Baccano the road rises and surmounts the S. extremity of the crater, whence (better from one of the hills to the l.) in favourable weather a beautiful panorama of Rome and its environs is enjoyed. E. the chain of the Umbrian and Sabine Apennines, snow-clad in winter and spring, the Tiber winding through the plain; from a lower point of the road appears the summit of Monte Gennaro, the ancient Lucretilis (comp., however, p. 294), at its base the eminences of Monticelli and Sant' Angelo; more towards the S., the opening whence the Anio issues, with Tivoli, and still more distant the precipitous rocks on which Palestrina, the ancient Praeneste, stands. The broad plain of the valley of the Liris extends between the Apennines and the Volscian range. Nearer the spectator are the Alban Mts., now Monte Cavo, and the towns of Frascati, Marino and Castel Gandolfo. The dome of St. Peter's appearing above the low ridge of Monte Mario, is now all that is visible of Rome.

The road descends gradually to the *Osteria del Fosso*, on the verge of a ravine through which a branch of the *Cremera* (now *Valchetta*) flows, a river celebrated as the scene of the defeat of the three hundred Fabians by the Veientines, July 16th, B. C. 477. The mountain-slope, which is skirted on the l., was the site of *Veii*, once the rival of Rome, conquered at length by Camillus in 396. The precise position which it occupied is not visible from this side (see p. 297).

La Storta, last post-station before Rome is reached. The Campagna retains its bleak aspect, relieved only by an occasional dilapidated tower of the middle ages, the remains of a Roman tomb or a miserable farm-house, and betrays no symptom of the proximity of the ancient capital of the world, until after an angle at the 7th milestone the dome of St. Peter's and the castle of S. Angelo become distinctly visible. To the r. Monte Mario, clothed with cypresses; opposite the traveller the heights of Frascati and Albano, to the l. the plain of the Tiber, beyond it the Sabine Mts. Between the 4th and 5th milestones, to the r. of the road, on a dilapidated basement, stands a sarcophagus with a long inscription, commonly termed, although without the slightest foundation, the *Tomb of Nero*; for the inscription (at the back, facing the line of the ancient road) expressly records that it was erected by *Vibia Maria Maxima* (probably about the close of the 2nd cent. after Christ) to the memory of her father P. Vibius Marianus and her mother Regina Maxima.

The pleasant valley of the *Acqua Traversa* (ancient *Tutia*), in which Hannibal encamped when retreating from Rome, is now entered, a height with villas and farm-houses traversed, and the traveller descends to the tawny *Tiber*. The river is crossed by the *Ponte Molle*, which occupies the site of the ancient *Pons Milvius* or *Mulvius*, constructed B. C. 109 by the Censor M. Æmilius Scaurus. Here, in the night of Dec. 3rd, B. C. 63, Cicero caused the emissaries of the Allobrogi, who were in league with Catiline, to be captured. Here, too, Oct. 27th, A. D. 312, Maxentius, who had been defeated at Saxa Rubra by Constantine under the auspices of the labarum or sign of the cross, was precipitated into the river and drowned. The present bridge was almost entirely rebuilt in 1815 under Pius VII., and embellished with statues of Christ and John the Baptist by *Mocchi*, and a species of triumphal arch. In May, 1849, one of the arches was blown up, but shortly afterwards restored. Beyond the bridge, on the l., stands a chapel erected by Pius II. on the spot where he met the procession with the head of St. Andrew, which was brought from the Peloponnesus in 1462. The road, now straight and tedious, and enclosed by garden-walls, leads to the *Porta del Popolo*. Arrival in Rome see p. 86.

7. From Siena to Perugia *(and Rome)* by Chiusi.

This is a favourite land-route between Florence and Rome, as it combines Siena (and Orvieto, compare p. 32, R. 6) with Perugia and a tour through Umbria (R. 8). It is necessary to perform part of this route by diligence, but the traveller has the advantage of visiting the most interesting towns of Central Italy. The country is admirably cultivated and produces a very different impression from the bleak and melancholy route from Orvieto to Rome. Inns generally good.

On the arrival of the train from Siena and Florence at Chiusi a diligence starts from the stat. at 1. 25. p. m. for Perugia, arriving there in 7 hrs. and departing again on the following morning. When necessary two diligences run daily (enquiry should be made at the railway-station at Siena). Fares: interior 8, coupé 9 l.; 35 lbs. of luggage free; for overweight 15 c. per lb.

Ascending from the valley of the *Chiana*, the traveller reaches (1 hr.) **Città della Pieve,** where horses are changed, a loftily (1700 ft.) situated town, birthplace of *Pietro Vannucci* in 1446, surnamed *Perugino* because he afterwards became the founder of a new school of painting at Perugia. He was the master of Raphael, and died at Perugia in 1524. His native place possesses some of his finest works. Thus in the oratory *de' Disciplinati*, or *S. Maria dei Bianchi*, the *Adoration of the Magi. Two letters from the artist at Perugia are shown relative to the price of this fresco, reducing it from 200 to 75 ducats. The remains of the Crucifixion, another fresco by Perugino, are still seen in the church of the *Servites* (outside the gate, towards Orvieto); in the cathedral (interior modernized) the Baptism (1st chap. l.) and *Madonna with saints (Peter, Paul, Gervasius and Protasius) in the choir, date 1513. In the church of *S. Antonio* a picture of St. Antony with S. Paulus Eremita and S. Marcellus, all by *Pietro Perugino*.

The road intersects the chain of hills which separate the Chiana Valley from the Tiber, passes through extensive woods and commands fine views of the Chiana Valley, and in some places of the Trasimene Lake towards the N. At the small village of *Tavernelle* (midway) horses are again changed. To the l. on the height the much-frequented shrine of the *Madonna di Mongiovino*. With the aid of auxiliary oxen the diligence slowly ascends to Perugia.

A far more picturesque route from *Sinalunga* by *Cortona* and the Trasimene Lake to Perugia requires an additional half-day, see p. 50.

Perugia, and thence by Spoleto to Rome see pp. 57 and follg.

8. From Florence to Rome by Arezzo, Perugia and Foligno.

This is the most interesting, and since the completion of the railway, the shortest and cheapest route from Florence to Rome. If the traveller desire to visit the principal points, 4—5 days are required: 1st, *Arezzo* and *Cortona*; 2nd, *Perugia*; 3rd, *Assisi* and *Spoleto*; 4th, *Terni* and the waterfalls, in the evening to *Rome*; but this is reckoning very closely, and Spello and Foligno are passed by. — From Florence to Rome two trains daily (express leaves in the night) in 12—16 hours; fares 39 l. 90 c., 31 l., 22 l. 70 c.

From Florence to Arezzo and Cortona.

Railway to Arezzo in 3½ (express 2½) hrs.; fares 8 l. 70, 7 l. 15, and 5 l. 55 c.; to Cortona (from Florence) in 4½ hrs.; fares 11 l. 50, 9 l. 40 and 7 l. 35 c. Those who wish to see Arezzo and Cortona and arrive at Perugia all on one day, had better leave in the afternoon or evening for Arezzo and there pass the night.

From the central station near S. Maria Novella the train describes a circuit round the town to the *Porta S. Croce*, where travellers who reside in that neighbourhood may join it. The line intersects the valley of Florence on the N. bank of the Arno; the valley contracts; *Fiesole* to the l. on the height long remains visible. Stat. *Compiobbi*. The surrounding heights are barren, the slopes and valley well-cultivated; to the l. the mountain-chain of the Pratomagno, on which the monastery of Vallombrosa lies, and which bounds the upper valley of the Arno, is visible. To the l. stat. *Pontassieve*, at the influx of the *Sieve* into the Arno. From the valley of the Sieve mountain-passes cross the Apennines to Forli and Faenza. From this point Vallombrosa and the Casentino, or upper valley of the Arno, are usually visited. In crossing the Sieve the train commands a beautiful glimpse of the valley to the l.; farther on a small tunnel is passed through. The line crosses to the l. bank of the Arno; beautiful view to the r. and l. as the bridge is crossed. The valley contracts. To the r. stat. *Rignano*. The fortress of *Incisa* is a conspicuous object from a distance. The train passes through another tunnel and reaches (r.) stat. *Incisa*. Here the river forces its way through the limestone rock, whence the name of the village. R. stat. *Figline*. In the environs, and also near Montevarchi and in the plain of Arezzo, bones of the elephant, rhinoceros, mastodon, hippopotamus, hyæna, tiger, bear etc. have frequently been discovered, often erroneously believed to be the remains of Carthaginian elephants of the train of Hannibal. Collections at Florence and Arezzo.

Stat. *S. Giovanni*, small town to the l., where in 1402 the celebrated painter *Masaccio* was born (d. at Florence, 1443); also *Giovanni da S. Giovanni*, one of the best fresco-painters of the 17th cent. Pictures by the latter in the *Cathedral:* Beheading of John the Baptist, Annunciation etc. The chapel to the r. of the high-altar in the church of *S. Lorenzo* contains a Madonna by *Masaccio* (?).

To the l. stat. *Montevarchi* (Locanda d'Italia, in the main street, Per gli Ortaggi: names of streets here always introduced by "per"), a small town with 9500 inhab. The loggia of the principal church in the piazza is embellished with a richly sculptured terracotta-relief by *della Robbia*. Opposite is the house of *Benedetto Varchi*, the Florentine historian and independent favourite of Cosimo.

Views as far as Arezzo on the left. The train ascends, passing through four tunnels, to stat. *Bucine;* the village close to the line on the r. Four more tunnels in rapid succession; r. and l. large embankments, often supported by walls. Stations *Laterina* and *Ponticino*, beyond which the train gradually ascends to the level of Arezzo, visible to the l. from a distance.

Arezzo *(Victoria;* * *Chiari d'Oro*, in the Via Cavour opposite, R. 2—2½ l.; *Café Italia*, Corso; *dei Constanti*, Via Cavour), the ancient *Arretium*, seat of a bishop and prefect, a clean and pleasant town with 10,000 inhab., in a beautiful and fertile district, abounding in historical reminiscences.

Arretium was one of the most powerful of the 12 confederate cities of Etruria, and (like Cortona and Perusia) concluded peace with the Romans in the great war of B. C. 310, after which it continued to be an ally of Rome. In 187 the Consul C. Flaminius constructed the *Via Flaminia* from Arretium to Bononia (Bologna), of which traces are still distinguishable. In the civil war Arretium was destroyed by Sulla, but was subsequently colonized *(Colonia Fidens Julia Arretium)* and again prospered. Its manufactures were red earthenware vases of superior quality, and weapons. The town suffered greatly from the Goths and the Lombards, and at a later date rom the party-struggles of the Guelphs and Ghibellini. In the 14th cent. it was for a time subjected to the dominion of the Tarlati, in 1337 temporarily, and in the 16th cent. under Cosimo I. finally to that of Florence. In 1799 an insurrection against the French broke out here, which was sanguinarily avenged.

Here *C. Cilnius Macenas*, the friend of Augustus and patron of Virgil and Horace, scion of the ancient and originally royal family of the Cilnii, was born; also *Petrarch*, *Vasari*, *Cesalpini* the botanist, *Spinello Aretino* the painter, *Pietro Aretino* the satirist, *Guido Aretino* founder of the modern school of music, *Leonardo Aretino* historian of Florence, *Margaritone* painter and sculptor of the 13th cent., Count *Vittorio Fossombrone* the statesman, and *Pietro Benvenuti*, painter of the chapel of the Medicis at Florence.

The *Via Cavour* forms a right angle with the *Corso Vittorio Emmanuele*, the principal street, which ascends from the gate to the cathedral-square. Ascending this street, the visitor perceives to the r. the interesting church of

S. Maria della Pieve, said to have been erected in the commencement of the 9th cent. on the site of a temple of Bacchus; tower and façade of 1216. The latter is very peculiar, consisting of 4 series of columns, distributed with extraordinary incongruity. Ancient sculptures over the door. The interior, now undergoing restoration, consists of a nave and two aisles and a dome. Above the high-altar *St. George by *Vasari*; r. an altar-piece by *Pietro Laurati* in sections, Madonna surrounded by saints: both of these are temporarily placed in the Badia.

Higher in the street, l. is the *Palazzo Pubblico* of 1332, sadly modernized; in front numerous armorial bearings of the ancient Podestà. It now serves as a prison.

Somewhat farther the Via dell' Orto diverges to the l., near the entrance to which a long inscription indicates the house in which *Francesco Petrarca* was born, July 20th, 1304. His parents, like Dante, the victims of a faction, were expelled from Florence. The visitor now proceeds to the not far distant

* *Cathedral*, a fine specimen of Italian Gothic, begun in 1177, with additions of 1290; façade unfinished. The interior contains painted glass *windows, dating from the beginning of the 16th cent., by *Guillaume de Marseille*; the middle window in the choir is modern. In the r. aisle is the *Tomb of Gregory X., of 1276, by *Margaritone*. This indefatigable prelate expired at Arezzo, Jan. 10th, 1276, whilst returning from France to Rome, after having proclaimed a new crusade. On the high-altar marble sculptures by Giovanni da Pisa of 1286: Madonna with St. Donatus and Gregory and bas-reliefs from their lives. In the l. aisle is the tomb of the poet and physician *Redi* (d. 1698). Near it is the chapel of the *Madonna del Soccorso* with two altars of the

Robbia school. Farther on the *Tomb of Guido Tarlati di Pietramala, the warlike bishop of Arezzo, the work of *Agostino* and *Agnolo da Siena* about 1330, from the design of *Giotto*, as Vasari conjectures, in 16 compartments, representing the life of this ambitious and energetic prelate, who, elected governor of the town in 1321, soon distinguished himself as a conqueror, and afterwards in S. Ambrogio at Milan crowned the Emperor Louis the Bavarian. These events, as well as his death in 1327, are all represented here.

In front of the cathedral, the marble statue of Ferdinand de Medicis, by *Giovanni da Bologna*, erected in 1595. In the cathedral-square (No. 1) is the *Pal. Comunale*, ornamented with numerous armorial bearings.

Opposite the Palazzo Pubblico a street, containing the *Loggie* erected by *Vasari*, soon leads to the Piazza. In the centre a monument to Ferdinand III., erected in 1832. Contiguous to the tribune of S. Maria della Pieve is the *Museum, in the cloister of the *Fraternità della Misericordia*, with handsome façade in the Gothic style, of the 14th cent. On the first floor the museum and library. If closed, visitors ring for the custodian at the door opposite the entrance.

1st and 2nd Rooms. Minerals and fossils; among them a stag's-head found in the Chiana Valley not far from Arezzo. 3rd Room. At the wall of entrance antique and modern bronzes. R. wall: Roman inscriptions and reliefs. On the wall of egress: antique utensils in bronze. In the centre: °mediæval and antique seals. 4th Room: majolicas, in the centre an °antique vase, Combat of Hercules and the Amazons. In the cupboards, cinerary urns and other vessels of red clay (vasa Arretina). 5th Room: Etruscan cinerary urns. In the centre an °antique vase, the abduction of Hippodamia by Pelops.

At the extremity of the Corso, near the gate, the Via dell' Anfiteatro leads to the church of *S. Bernardo;* in the sacristy a fresco by *Spinello*. From the corridor to the l. are seen in the garden the insignificant remnants of a Roman amphitheatre.

In the Via Cavour is the church of *S. Francesco* with frescoes: History of the Cross by *Pietro della Francesca* (behind the high-altar); others in the body of the church, of the school of *Spinello*, have been white-washed. In front of the church the monument of the praiseworthy *Fossombrone* (p. 48). In the same street *Badia di S. Fiora;* in the refectory the Banquet of Ahasuerus by *Vasari*.

Other churches also possess objects of interest, as *L'Annunziata* a fresco by *Spinello Aretino*, over one of the doors; *S. Bartolommeo*, a fresco by *Jacopo da Casentino; S. Domenico*, whitewashed frescoes by *Spinello;* the monastery *della Croce*, a *Madonna by *Luca Signorelli*.

In the Strada S. Vito is the *House of Vasari*, in its original condition, containing works by the master.

From Arezzo (r. beautiful retrospect of the town, from which the cathedral rises picturesquely) the line, as well as the highroad, skirts the chain of hills which separate the valleys of the Arno and Chiana from the upper valley of the Tiber. Passing through a tunnel, the train traverses the plain in a straight direction to stat. *Frassineto* and *Castiglionfiorentino*, the latter situated on a mountain ridge; farther on, the dilapidated fortress of *Montecchio* is seen to the l. Somewhat farther Cortona becomes visible to the l. in the distance, loftily situated on an olive-clad eminence. Close to the station of Cortona, to the l. lies *Camuscia*, the inn of which is recommended (obliging landlord). The traveller who makes no stay here is strongly advised, especially if burdened with luggage, not to spend the night at Cortona.

The luxuriant and richly cultivated *Valley of the Chiana*, at a remote period a lake, was until the middle of the last century a noisome swamp. The level was raised and carefully drained, the brooks being so directed as to deposit their alluvial soil in the bottom of the valley. This judicious system was originated by *Torricelli* and *Viviani*, celebrated mathematicians of the school of Galileo, and carried out by the worthy Count *Fossombrone*, who combined the pursuits of a scholar with those of a statesman. The *Chiana*, Lat. *Clanis*, now falls into the Arno, in ancient times into the Tiber.

Cortona *(Albergo d'Europa; Casa Nuti; Trattoria Buffet*, not far from the Piazza; little accommodation here for visitors and therefore better pass the night at Camuscia, see above; omnibus from the station to the town 1 l. each pers.), a small, loftily situated town, above the Valle di Chiana and not far from the Trasimene Lake, commanding a beautiful view of both, is one of the most ancient cities of Italy. It appears that the Etruscans, immigrating from the plain of the Po, wrested the place from the Umbrians, and constituted it their principal stronghold when they proceeded to extend their conquests in Etruria. Cortona was one of the 12 confederate cities of Etruria, and shared the same fate with them, that of being converted into a Roman colony. After various vicissitudes and struggles it came under the dominion of Florence in 1410. Among the artists of which Cortona boasts may be mentioned *Luca Signorelli* (b. 1439, d. at Florence in 1521), and *Pietro Berettini*, surnamed *Pietro da Cortona* (b. 1596, d. at Rome 1669).

The ascent from the inn at Camuscia occupies upwards of $^3/_4$ hr. (pedestrians select the old road which intersects the carriage-road several times); the road passes *S. Spirito* on the r. and leads to the low-lying S. gate of the town; then a long and straight street; to the l. *S. Agostino*, with a picture by *Pietro da Cortona*; farther on, a handsome palazzo of the 16th cent., now the *Guardia Nazionale*; the Piazza with the *Municipio* is then entered.

To the l. lies the small square of the *Palazzo Pretorio*, on which an ancient mazocco. On the first floor of the Palazzo Pretorio the *Accademia Etrusca*, founded in 1726, possesses a

Museum of Etruscan Antiquities (gratuity), the principal ornament of which is an Etruscan *candelabrum *(lampadario)*, circular and intended for 16 lights; on the lower side in the centre a Gorgoneion, around which a combat of wild beasts, then waves with dolphins, finally 8 ithyphallic satyrs alternately with 8 sirens. between each lamp a head of Bacchus. An encaustic painting on lavagna-stone, "Polyhymnia", said to be ancient. Remarkable Etruscan bronzes, a votive hand with numerous symbols, vases, urns, inscriptions etc. The *Ponbuni Library*, in the same building, possesses a fine MS. of Dante.

From the Palazzo Pretorio the street to the l. descends to the
Cathedral, a handsome basilica, ascribed to *Antonio du San Gallo*, altered in the 18th cent. by the Florentine *Galilei*. In the choir a Descent from the Cross and *Institution of the Last Supper, by *Luca Signorelli*. To the l. of the choir a Greek sarcophagus, representing the contest of Dionysius against the Amazons, erroneously represented as the tomb of the ill-fated Consul Flaminius (p. 50). — Opposite to the cathedral is the

Church of the Jesuits (al Gesù), containing two pictures by *Luca Signorelli*, the Conception and Nativity, and three by *Fra Angelico da Fiesole*, the Annunciation and *two "predelle", representing scenes from the life of the Virgin and S. Domenico.

From the Piazza del Municipio the street leads direct to
S. Domenico, dating from the beginning of the 13th cent.; on the l. wall an altar-piece, the Coronation of the Virgin by *Lorenzo di Niccolò* (1440), presented by Cosimo and Lorenzo de Medicis; r. near the high-altar a *Madonna with four saints and angels by *Fra Angelico*.

Somewhat higher in the street is the *Compagnia S. Niccolò*, containing a restored fresco, Madonna and saints, and an *altarpiece, the Body of Christ with angels and saints, by *Luca Signorelli*.

Having explored the town with its precipitous streets, the visitor may ascend to the *church and monastery of *S. Margherita*, a Gothic structure by *Nicola* and *Giovanni Pisano*, commanding a fine *view, especially from under the cypresses in the garden. The *Tomb of the saint is of the 13th cent., the silver front with the golden crown a gift of *Pietro da Cortona*. Among the pictures the following merit inspection: Dead Saviour, by *Luca Signorelli*; S. Catharina, by *Fed. Baroccio*; Conception, with saints. by *Vanni*; Madonna and saints, by *Jacopo da Empoli*. The visitor should not omit to ascend somewhat higher to the dilapidated *Fortezza* (trifle to the porter), from the walls of which the view is completely uninterrupted, except in the rear, where it is bounded only by the mountain-chain, — a most noble prospect.

In returning, the archæologist may inspect the ancient Etruscan *Town Walls*, composed of huge blocks, for the most part well preserved. Even the gates may still be distinguished. Besides these, several less interesting objects: ancient vault beneath the *Palazzo Cecchetti*; near S. Margherita remains of *Roman baths*, erroneously termed a *"Temple of Bacchus"*; outside the gate of S. Agostino an Etruscan tomb, the *"Grotta di Pitagora"*.

The connoisseur of art may (by presenting a visiting-card or passport) succeed in gaining access to the private collection of Sign. *Ulisse Colonnese* in the Palazzo Madama, near the Municipio (p. 48): beautiful half-length picture of St. Stephen and a Nativity by *Luca Signorelli*, a picture of the German school, and two Italian of the 15th cent.

From Cortona to Perugia.

Railway in 1½ hr.; fares 4 l. 80, 3 l. 90 and 3 l. 10 c.

The train leaves Cortona, and in ¼ hr. reaches stat. *Borghetto* and the

Lago Trasimeno, ancient *Lacus Trasimenus*, about 30 M. in circumference, and in some places 8 M. in diameter, surrounded by wooded or olive-clad slopes, which as they recede rise to considerable heights. The lake contains three small islands, *Isola Maggiore* with a monastery, *Isola Minore* near Passignano, and *Isola Polvese* towards the S.; on the W. side an eminence abuts on the lake, bearing the small *Castiglione del Lago*. Its shores abound with wild-fowl and its waters with fish (eels, carp etc.). The brooks which discharge themselves into the lake gradually raise its bed. The greatest depth, formerly 30—40 ft., is now 20 ft. only. A drain (emissarius) in the 15th cent. conducted the water into a tributary of the Tiber. In ancient times the extent of the lake appears to have been less considerable. A project for draining it entirely is at present zealously canvassed.

The reminiscence of the sanguinary victory which (June 23rd, B. C. 217) *Hannibal* here gained over the Roman consul *C. Flaminius* imparts a tinge of gloom to this lovely landscape. It is a matter of no great difficulty to reconcile the descriptions of Livy (22, 4 et seqq.) and Polybius (3, 83 et seqq.) with the present aspect of the lake. In the spring of 217 Hannibal quitted his winter-quarters in Gallia Cisalpina, crossed the Apennines, marched across the plains of the Arnus, notwithstanding an inundation, devastating the country far and wide, and directed his course towards the S., passing the Roman army stationed at Arezzo. The brave and able consul followed incautiously. Hannibal then occupied the heights which surround the defile extending on the N. side of the lake from Borghetto to Passignano, upwards of 5 M. in length. The entrance at Borghetto, as well as the issue at Passignano, are easily secured. Upon a hill in the centre (site of the present Torre) his principal force was posted. A dense fog covered the lake and plain, when in the early morning the consul, ignorant of the plan of his enemy whom he believed to be marching against Rome, entered the fatal defile. When he discovered his error, it was too late: his entire l. flank was exposed, whilst his rear was attacked by the hostile cavalry from

Borghetto. No course remained to him but to force a passage by Passignano, and the vanguard of 6000 men succeeded in effecting their egress (but on the following day were compelled to surrender). The death of the consul rendered the defeat still more disastrous. The Romans lost 15,000 men, whilst the remaining half of the army was effectually dispersed; the Roman supremacy in Italy began to totter. The slaughter continued for three hours. From the Gualandro two small brooks fall into the lake. One of these, crossed by the road, has received its appellation Sanguinetto in reminiscence of the streams of blood which at this spot flowed into the lake.

The line skirts the lake, passes through a tunnel, and at stat. *Passignano* reaches the issue of the defile where the battle took place; it again goes through a short and a long tunnel, and arrives at stat. *Magione*, a borough with ancient watch-tower of the period of Fortebraccio and Sforza. The line once more passes through a long tunnel and reaches stat. *Ellera*. At the left Perugia is visible, picturesquely situated on the heights.

Perugia. Omnibus from the railway-station to the town 1 l., generally well-filled; so no time is to be lost in securing a seat. *Albergo della Posta (Pl. a) or Grande Bretagne, a few paces from the diligence-office, R. 3 l. and upwards, D. 3½, A. ½, L. ½ l.; accommodation not always to be had without previous notice. — *Albergo del Trasimeno (Pl. c), lately removed to Via dei Calderari, Piazza del Sopramuro, of the 2nd cl., R. 2, D. 2½ l.; Corona (Pl. d), not far from the Corso, with moderate accommodation, R. 1½ l. — Trattoria *del Progresso*, Via Nuova 31; several others in the Corso. Cafés: *Baduel (Pl. e), Trasimeno, both in the Corso. — *Giovanni Scalchi* is recommended as a valet-de-place, amateurs however are cautioned against purchasing his "antiquities". Perugia is well adapted for a stay of some duration; apartments moderate, 2 rooms well-situated about 30 l. per month.

Diligences (Office, Corso 38): To *Chiusi* (p. 32) daily at 5 a. m., fare 8 l., coupé 9 l. To *Città di Castello* (p. 57) daily at 8 a. m. To *Gubbio* (p. 79), route of 26 M. through a bleak but not uninteresting hilly district, corriere daily, diligence twice weekly.

Perugia, beautifully situated on the heights (1500 ft.) above the valley of the Tiber, commanding extensive views, capital of the province of Umbria, and residence of the prefect and a military-commandant, is built in an antiquated style, and consists of two distinct portions: the upper part of the town, with numerous palaces of the 14th and 15th centuries, the Corso, cathedral etc., above which rises the fort, destroyed in 1848 and 1859; and the lower town connected by walks with the upper. The town, with a population of 19,000, boasts of a bishop, a university, numerous monasteries and churches and a considerable traffic.

Perusia was one of the 12 Etruscan confederate cities, and not less ancient than Cortona, with which and Arretium it fell into the hands of the Romans, B. C. 310; it subsequently became a municipium. In the war between Octavianus and Antony, who in the summer of 41 occupied Perusia, and after an obstinate struggle was compelled by the former to surrender (bellum Perusinum), the town suffered severely, and was finally reduced to ashes. It was subsequently rebuilt and became a Roman colony under the name of *Augusta Perusia*. In the 6th cent. it was destroyed by the Goth Totila after a siege of 7 years. In the wars of the Lombards, Guelphs and Ghibellini it also suffered greatly; in the 14th cent. it acquired the supremacy over nearly the whole of Umbria, but in 1370 was compelled to surrender to the pope. Renewed struggles followed, owing to the conflicts between the powerful families of Oddi and Baglioni. In 1416 the shrewd and courageous Braccio Fortebraccio of Montone usurped the supreme power, whence new contests arose, until at length Giovanni Paolo Baglioni surrendered to Pope Julius II. Leo X. caused him to be executed at Rome in 1520. In 1450 Paul III. erected the citadel, "*ad coercendam Perusinorum audaciam*", as the inscription, destroyed during the last revolution, recorded. In 1708 the town was captured by the Duke of Savoy, on May 31st, 1849 by the Austrians, and in 1860 by the Piedmontese.

The *Umbrian School of Painting*, whose works are most numerously encountered at Perugia, developed itself under the influence of the new phase of religious life which emanated from Assisi, unaffected by the realistic tendency of the Florentines. Revery, longing and profound devotion are the characteristics in the representation of which they are most successful, and which repeatedly recur. This was the case even with the older masters whose productions were more original, as *Gentile da Fabriano*, *Benedetto Bonfigli*, *Giovanni Santi*, Raphael's father, and *Niccolò Alunno da Foligno*. This bias of art attained its climax in *Pietro Vannucci* of Città della Pieve (p. 57), surnamed *Il Perugino*, who, though a pupil of Bonfigli, was entirely devoted to the Florentine style whilst resident at Florence, but after his removal to Perugia followed the Umbrian tendency, to which he thenceforth systematically adhered. Next to Perugino in importance ranks *Bernardino Pinturicchio* (1454—1513), then the Spaniard *Giovanni*, surnamed *Lo Spagna*; other pupils of the great Umbrian master were *Giannicola*, *Tiberio d'Assisi*, *Adone Doni*, *Eusebio di S. Giorgio*, the two *Alfani* and *Raphael*.

From the Citadel at the end of the Corso, now a heap of ruins, a magnificent prospect is enjoyed, embracing the Umbrian valley (or valley of Foligno) with Assisi, Spello, Foligno, Trevi and numerous other villages, bounded by the principal chain of the Apennines from Gubbio onwards; then the Tiber and a portion of Perugia. By the citadel an ancient gateway with interesting sculptures, bearing the inscription *Colonia Vibia;* underneath, *Augusta Perusia* was formerly inscribed, but removed on the construction of the citadel.

In the Corso the *Palazzo Comunale (Pl. 12), of 1282—1333, an Ital. Gothic structure, marred by modern alterations, with handsome entrance adorned with the arms of the confederate towns. In the group of animals over the principal entrance (No. 118) the griffin represents Perugia, and the wolf overcome by it Siena. Passing through the principal gate, and ascending to the third story, the visitor reaches (l.) the Sala della Prefettura, decorated with damaged frescoes from the history of St. Herculanus and St. Louis of Toulouse, by *Bonfigli*. On the ground-floor is the *Sala del Cambio (exchange, now disused; custodian at No. 108, fee $1/_2$ l., best light in the morning), adorned with frescoes by *Pietro Perugino:* r. sibyls and prophets; above, God the Father; l. heroes, kings and philosophers of antiquity; opposite, the Nativity and Transfiguration. On a pillar to the l. the portrait of Perugino. In the execution of these frescoes, especially the arabesques on the ceiling, *Raphael* is said to have assisted. They were painted in 1500, and Perugino received a remuneration of 350 ducats from the guild of merchants. An altar-piece and frescoes by *Gian. Manni* in the adjoining chapel.

to Rome. PERUGIA. 8. Route. 53

The Corso terminates in the cathedral square. In front of the cathedral a *Fountain, consisting of 3 basins, adorned with a number of biblical and allegorical figures in relief, executed by *Nicola* and *Giovanni da Pisa* in 1277—1280. The statuettes of the central basin are by *Arnolfo di Cambio*.

On the other side of the cathedral is the *Piazza del Papa*, so named from the statue in bronze of Julius III. by *Vincenzio Danti* (1556).

The *Cathedral of S. Lorenzo* (Pl. 11), dating from the close of the 15th cent., is an edifice of imposing, but heavy proportions. The chapel in the r. aisle contains *Baroccio's* masterpiece, a *Descent from the Cross, in 1797 conveyed to Paris but restored in 1815. Painted window above by *Constantino da Rosaro* and *Fra Brunacci*, a Benedictine of Monte Casino (1565). In the l. aisle the *Cappella dell' Anello*, which till 1797 contained the celebrated Sposalizio of *Perugino*, now in the museum of Caen in Normandy. In both the chapels are beautifully carved seats. R. by the high-altar a marble sarcophagus containing the remains of Popes Innocent II., Urban IV. and Martin IV. The winter-choir contains an altar-piece by *Luca Signorelli*: Madonna with SS. John the Baptist, Onuphrius the Hermit, Stephen, and a bishop receiving alms. In the library precious MSS. are preserved, as the Codex of St. Luke of the 16th cent., gold on a purple ground.

Opposite the cathedral, No. 10, is the *Palazzo Conestabile*, with a small gallery containing frescoes by *Perugino* (brought from the Pal. Alfani), S. Rosalia by *Sassoferrato*, and a **Madonna by *Raphael*, a small circular picture of his Perugian period.

From the rear of the cathedral the Via Vecchia descends to the *Arco di Augusto, an ancient town-gate with the inscription *Augusta Perusia*. The foundations date from the Etruscan period, the upper portion from that subsequent to the conflagration. From this point the direction of the walls of the ancient city, which occupied the height where the old part of the present town stands, may be distinctly traced. Considerable portions of the wall are still preserved.

From the Arco di Augusto the visitor proceeds to the l. to the *University* (Pl. 29), founded in 1320, now established in a monastery of Olivetans suppressed by Napoleon (custodian, corridor to the l., No. 19; fee $1/2$—1 l.). It possesses a small *Botanic Garden, Scientific Collections*, a *Museum of Etruscan and Roman Antiquities* and a *Picture Gallery*.

The *Pinacoteca* in the basement-floor, formed (since 1863) from the spoils of suppressed churches and monasteries, is an invaluable aid in the study of the Umbrian School. 1st Room: at the entrance No. 185 and follg., Angels, by *Bonfigli*; 1. 164. St. Sebastian, *Perugino*; 151. Madonna, *School of Siena;* 153. Annunciation, *Sinibaldo Ibi;* frescoes from S. Giuliano and S. Severo, the finest a Pietà, to the l. Miniatures of the 14th and 15th centuries. — 2nd Room: r. 206. Madonna and Saints, *Benozzo Gozzoli;* Madonna and Saints, *Fiorenzo di Lorenzo;* 209., 210., 212., 214., 227., 228., 233., 234. Miracles of St. Bernardino of Siena, *master unknown;* 220. Miracles of St. Nicholas of Bari, *Fiesole;* 221., 222. Annunciation, *same master;* 216., *223., 225. Madonna with saints, *same master;* 236. Madonna, *Raphael (?);* 237. Circumcision, *Perugino;* 247. Adoration, *same master;* unnumbered, The Lord's Supper and Ascension, *same master;* Madonna with saints and "predella", *Domenico Bartoli.* — 3rd Room (corridor), nothing worthy of mention. — 4th Room: Pictures of the school of Siena. — 5th Room (formerly a church) contains the principal works: 1. St. Bernardino of Siena, *Bonfigli;* 2. Ascension, *Perugino;* 4. Madonna and saints, *Boccati da Camerino;* 5. Madonna and saints, *Dom. Alfani;* 8. Adoration of the Magi, *Eusebio da S. Giorgio;* 23. Adoration of the Shepherds, *Perugino;* 25. Madonna, *Spagna;* *30. Altar-piece by *Pinturicchio*, Madonna and saints; 35. Madonna, *Perugino;* °39. Adoration of the Magi, *Ghirlandajo (?);* 41. Baptism of Christ, *Perugino;* 49. Lunette: God the Father and angels, *Spagna;* 51. Annunciation, *Bonfigli;* 59. Madonna, *Alfani;* 75. Annunciation, *Niccolò Alunno.*

The first floor contains the *Antiquarian Museum*. On the staircase and in the passages Etruscan mortuary urns and Lat. inscriptions. Contents of the rooms similar. In the 1st Room the longest Etruscan inscription known, consisting of 45 lines, as yet undeciphered, and ancient Etruscan sculptures. 2nd Room: mediæval coins and other objects. 3rd Room: ancient bronzes, among which the bronze and silver plates, found in 1810, appertenances of a chariot, or as now thought, from a tomb. 4th Room: terracottas and several painted vases. Lid of a sarcophagus: Death seizing his victims. 5th Room: cinerary urns of terracotta with traces of painting. In the centre a sarcophagus of terracotta, with sacrificial procession.

The other scientific collections are of little value. Two of the corridors contain casts of ancient and modern sculptures.

From the Piazza del Papa the visitor soon reaches the chapel *S. Severo* (Pl. 14), formerly a monastery of the order of *Camaldoli*, now a college, containing *Raphael's* first *fresco (greatly damaged), of 1505: God the Father (obliterated) with 3 angels and the Holy Ghost; beneath, the Redeemer and the saints Maurus, Placidus, Benedict, Romuald, Laurentius and Jerome. The painting resembles the upper portion of Raphael's Disputa in the Vatican. Inscription: *Raphael de Urbino Domino Octaviano Stephano Volaterrano Priori Sanctam Trinitatem Angelos astantes Sanctosque pinxit, A. D. M. D. V.* At the sides, lower down, St. Scholastica, St. Jerome, St. John, St. Gregory the Great, Boniface and Martha, by *Pietro Perugino.*

Hence to the *Piazza del Sopramuro*, resting on extensive foundations, between the two hills on which the fortress and the cathedral are situated.

From the Piazza del Sopramuro the visitor proceeds to the Fortezza, and descends hence to the suburb of S. Domenico.

S. Domenico (Pl. 7), with lofty and now partially removed campanile, was erected by *Giovanni Pisano* in 1632 to supersede an older church of 1304, of which the choir with a Gothic window (1411) now alone remains. 4th Chapel with cinquecento decoration. In the l. transept the *Monument (by *Giovanni da Pisa)* of Pope Benedict XI., who, July 6th, 1304, fell a victim to the intrigues of Philip IV., and died after partaking of poisoned figs.

Farther on, near the Porta S. Costanza, outside the Porta S. Pietro, the church of *S. Pietro de' Casinensi* (Pl. 13) is reached, a basilica with 18 antique columns of granite and marble and a number of valuable pictures. In the r. aisle (4th) chapel of St. Joseph: *Monument of the Countess Baldeschi, from drawings by *Fr. Overbeck;* above the sacristy: Saints, copies by *Sassoferrato.* In the Sacristy 5 Saints, by *Perugino* (which formerly surrounded the Ascension by the same master, removed by the French, now at Lyons); Holy Family, *Parmeggianino;* *Jesus and John, copy from *Perugino,* by *Raphael.* The choir-books contain fine miniatures of the 16th cent. In the l. aisle, by the first altar: Pietà, *Perugino.* R. of the 2nd Altar: Adoration of the Magi, by *Adone Doni,* whom Raphael is said to have assisted, and whose portrait is said to be here recognizable. In the *Cappella del Sagramento* frescoes by *Vasari;* Madonna, an altar-piece by *Lo Spagna,* much damaged; Judith, *Sassoferrato.* At the end of the l. aisle: Madonna and saints by *Bonfigli* (1469). *Choir-stalls in walnut, carved by *Stefano da Bergamo* from designs by *Raphael.* A planted terrace is now reached, whence a magnificent *prospect of the valley of Foligno and the surrounding Apennines.

Besides the above (if time permit), the traveller should inspect:

The following churches (most of the paintings with which they were formerly decorated have been removed to the Pinacoteca):

S. Agnese (Pl. 4), with two chapels adorned with paintings by *Perugino* (not easily accessible).

S. Angelo (Pl. 6), a circular structure with 16 antique columns in the interior, resembling S. Stefano Rotondo in Rome, and probably dating from the 16th cent.; fresco of the period of *Giotto.*

Confraternità della Giustizia di S. Bernardino (Pl. 17), with very tasteful façade by *Agostino Fiorentino* (1461). Near it

S. Francesco dei Conventuali (Pl. 9). A wooden receptacle in the sacristy contains the remains of the Condottiere Braccio Fortebraccio, slain at the siege of Aquila, June 5th, 1424, a few months after his rival Sforza had been drowned in the Pescara. Raphael's Entombment of Christ, now in the Borghese Gallery at Rome (p. 149), was originally painted for this church.

Private Collections:

Palazzo Baldeschi (Pl. 21), in the Corso, containing Raphael's *drawing for one of the frescoes of *Pinturicchio* in the library of the cathedral of Siena (see p. 28): Æneas Sylvius as bishop at the betrothal of Frederick III. with Eleonora of Portugal.

Palazzo Donini (Pl. 24), with two drawings by *Perugino*, Madonna by the same etc.

Palazzo Penna (Pl. 27), with an extensive gallery, containing pictures by *Perugino*, *Salvator Rosa*, *Luca Signorelli* and other celebrated masters.

Collection of *Avv. Romualdi* (Via del Bufalo 5, not far from the Albergo della Posta), comprising bronzes, coins, cameos, drawings and pictures by *An. Caracci*, *Perugino* etc., is about to be opened as a museum.

The *Libreria Pubblica* (Pl. 3), containing 30,000 vols. and MSS., such as Stephanus Byzant. of the 5th cent., St. Augustine with illuminations etc.

The *House of Perugino* is in the Via Deliziosa, Nr. 18.

The *Necropolis* of Perugia, discovered in 1840, lies on the new Roman road, near the Ponte S. Giovanni. The *Tomb of the Volumnii, "Grotta de' Volunni"*, by the road, recognised by a group of cypresses, 3 M. from the town, one of the finest, though not most ancient of N. Etruria, was first discovered. It consists of 10 chambers, hewn in the coarse-grained tuffstone of the hill: in front inscriptions in Etruscan and Latin. Here a number of cinerary urns, with portraits and various kinds of decorations, were found. The tomb is well-preserved. The urns, lamps and other curiosities may be inspected at the neighbouring villa of Count Baglioni, where the custodian is to be found.

Those who travel by carriage may combine this visit with their onward journey; otherwise it must be undertaken from Perugia. Pedestrians in going may select the old road, quitting the town by the Porta S. Pietro; in returning, the new road to the Porta Costanza.

From Perugia to Narni by Todi. Distance 49 M.; communication by corriere. Before the opening of the railway between Foligno and Rome this road, being the shortest route between Perugia and Rome, was the scene of animated traffic. Its importance is now merely local, as it is far inferior to that by Foligno and Terni in natural attractions and historical interest.

Perugia is quitted by the *Porta Costanza*; the road to Foligno soon diverges to the l. It descends rapidly into the valley of the Tiber, which it crosses near *Ponte Nuovo*, 7 M. from Perugia. For a distance of about 18 M. the road remains on the l. bank of the Tiber, then ascends to

Todi (*Posta*, at the gate), the ancient Umbrian *Tuder*, a loftily situated town with 4—5000 inhab.; the mountain is so abrupt that the upper part of the town is not accessible to carriages. Its ancient importance is betokened by the fragments of walls and the extensive ruin of a *Temple* or *Basilica*, usually styled a temple of Mars. Although poor in treasures of art, the town possesses several edifices of architectural interest, among which are the *Cathedral* and the *Town Hall* in the piazza. *S. Maria della Consolazione*, in the form of a Greek cross, with lofty dome, is a masterpiece of *Bramante* (dome often ascended for the sake of the splendid panorama). *S. Fortunato*, with handsome portal. Todi was the birthplace of the poet Jacopone da Todi (d. 1306), author of the "Stabat mater dolorosa".

to Rome. CITTÀ DI CASTELLO. 8. Route. 57

From Todi to Narni 23 M., by the villages of *Rosaro*, *Castel Todino* and *San Gemine*. About 1½ M. from the last, on the ancient, now abandoned Via Flaminia, are the interesting ruins of the once prosperous *Carsulae*. From San Gemine (9½) M. from Narni) the road gradually descends to the beautiful valley of the *Nera*. As the river is crossed, a good survey may be obtained of the *bridge of Augustus. Travellers may here alight (comp. p. 67) and ascend in a straight direction by the bridle-path, whilst carriages describe a long circuit to the Porta Ternana.

Narni see p. 66.

From Perugia to the Upper Valley of the Tiber (diligence daily at 8 a. m. to Città di Castello). The road soon crosses the Tiber and ascends on its left bank to *Fratta* or *Umbertide*, a small town 18½ M. from Perugia. In the church of *S. Croce* a Descent from the Cross by *Luca Signorelli*. Valuable collection of majolicas at the house of Sign. *Dom. Mavarelli*. At Fratta the road crosses to the r. bank of the river, and shortly afterwards re-crosses by a ferry to the l. bank, traverses a luxuriantly cultivated district and reaches (13 M.)

Città di Castello, with 6000 inhab., occupying the site of *Tifernum Tiberinum* which was destroyed by Totilas, in the 15th cent. under the dominion of the Vitelli family, subsequently under that of the Church. Raphael resided at the court of the Vitelli, but the pictures by him which were formerly here have been sold, among them the Sposalizio in the Brera at Milan. The *Cathedral (St. Floridus)* is of 1503, from a design by *Bramante*; beautiful carving in the choir. In *S. Cecilia* a Madonna by *Luca Signorelli*. The *Confraternità della S. Trinità* possesses two procession-flags, the designs of which are ascribed to Raphael.

Palazzo Comunale in the Gothic style. Four palaces of the *Vitelli*. *Palazzo Mancini*, with fine paintings, among them a *Nativity by *Luca Signorelli*; a small *Annunciation by *Raphael*.

From Città di Castello 8 M. to *Borgo S. Sepolcro*, formerly pertaining to Tuscany, a small and cheerful town. The churches contain several pictures by *Pietro della Francesca*, who was born here.

Roads lead from Borgo S. Sepolcro to *Arezzo* (p. 45), and across the Central Apennines to *Urbania* and *Urbino*. From Borgo S. Sepolcro the *Source of the Tiber*, near the village of *Le Balze*, may also be visited.

From Perugia to Foligno by Assisi.

Railway to *Assisi* in 1 hr., fares 2 l. 35 c., 1 l. 95 c., 1 l. 55 c.; from *Assisi* to *Spello* 1 l., 75 c. and 60 c.; from *Assisi* to *Foligno* 1 l. 50, 1 l. 15, 95 c.; from *Assisi* to *Spoleto* 4 l. 40, 3 l. 20, 2 l. 40 c. Foligno is unattractive. On the other hand a visit to Assisi (p. 58), for which 3—4 hrs. suffice, should on no account be omitted.

The line runs along the heights on which Perugia is situated, and, beyond stat. *Ponte S. Giovanni*, crosses the Tiber, which in ancient times formed the frontier between Etruria and Umbria; then across the *Chiascio* to stat. *Bastia*, and a short distance farther stat. *Assisi*. The town is picturesquely situated upon the hill. Before ascending to Assisi the magnificent church of *S. Maria degli Angeli* (10 M. walk from the stat.) should be visited; it was erected by *Vignola* on the site of the original oratory of St. Francis, the so-called *Portiuncula*. After the damage occasioned by the earthquake of 1831 the nave and choir of the church were re-erected; the dome, however, had not suffered. Beneath the latter, in front of the oratory, the *Vision of St. Francis,

"Mary with a choir of angels", alleged to have been witnessed by the saint in 1221, a fresco by *Overbeck*, 1829. Farther on, to the r., is the hut in which Francis expired, Oct. 4th, 1226, with inscription and frescoes by *Lo Spagna*, representing the followers of the saint. The other parts modern. A beautiful path leads hence to Assisi in $1/2$ hr. The services of the guides who importune travellers at S. Maria degli Angeli and at Assisi are entirely superfluous.

Assisi *(Leone; Firmina Lepri*, in the Piazza, both hardly recommended as quarters for the night), a small town and episcopal see, the ancient Umbrian *Assisium*, where B. C. 46 the elegiac poet *Propertius*, and in 1698 the opera-writer *Pietro Metastasio* (properly *Trapassi*, d. at Vienna in 1782) were born, stands in a singularly picturesque situation.

It is indebted for its reputation to *St. Francis* who was born here in 1182. He was the son of the merchant Pietro Bernardone, and spent his youth in frivolity. At length, whilst engaged in a campaign against Perugia, he was taken prisoner and attacked by a dangerous illness. Sobered by adversity he soon afterwards (1208) founded the monastic order of *Franciscans*, which speedily found adherents in all the countries of Europe, and was sanctioned in 1210 by Innocent III., and in 1223 by Honorius III. Poverty and self-abnegation formed the essential characteristics of the order, which under different designations (Seraphic Brethren, Minorites, Observantes and Capuchins, who arose in 1526) was soon widely diffused and still exists. St. Francis is said to have been favoured with visions, as that of 1224, when Christ impressed on him the marks of his wounds (stigmata); also the apparition of the crucified seraph, whence his surname *Pater Seraphicus*.

St. Francis expired Oct. 4th, 1226, and in 1228 was canonized by Gregory IX., who appointed the day of his death to be kept sacred to his memory. He was the author of several works, especially of letters which display talent, and was one of the most remarkable characters of the middle ages. Dante (Paradiso 11, 50) says of him that he rose like a sun and illumined everything with his rays.

Having reached the town, the visitor proceeds to the l. to the *Monastery of the Franciscans*, which, reposing on its massive foundations on the verge of the hill, has long attracted the attention. Passing the church, the visitor enters the monastery, now dissolved, and requests one of the monks, left here for that purpose, to act as guide (1 l. or more). The monastery was founded in 1228, it is believed, by the Emp. Frederick II.: with the exception of several frescoes in the refectories, it contains nothing of interest. From the external passage a magnificent *view of the luxuriant valley is enjoyed.

The two *Churches*, erected one above the other, are objects of far greater interest. A third, the *Crypt*, with the tomb of the saint, was added in 1818, when his remains are said to have been re-discovered. The lower church was erected in 1218—32, and consecrated by Innocent IV. The style is Ital. Gothic, the architects *Jacopo d'Alemannia*, also named *Lapo* by the Italians, and the monk *Fra Filippo da Campello*.

The *_Lower Church_, used for divine service, is always accessible; entrance by a side-door on the terrace, in front of which is a vestibule of 1487. The interior is low and obscure. To the r. a tomb, above it a vase of porphyry, said to be that of John de Brienne, King of Jerusalem, who in 1237 entered the order of St. Francis; or that of Hecuba of Lusignan, Queen of Cyprus (d. 1243). Opposite the entrance is the chapel of the Crucifixion. To the r. in the nave the chapel of St. Louis, with altar-piece by _Lo Spagna_ and frescoes by _Adone Doni_ (1560). On the vaulted ceiling *prophets and sibyls, by _Andrea del Ingegno_ of Assisi. The chapel of S. Antonio di Padua, with frescoes by _Giottino_, is entirely modernized. In the chapel of S. Maddalena frescoes by _Buffalmacco_ (1320), representations from the life of the saint. In the S. transept frescoes by _Taddeo Gaddi_ and _Giovanni da Milano_. The high-altar stands on the spot where the remains of St. Francis lay. The four triangles of the vaulting above are decorated with frescoes by _Giotto_: Poverty, Chastity, Obedience, and the praises of St. Francis.

In the N. transept frescoes by _Puccio Capanna_, pupil of Giotto, representing St. Francis receiving the stigmata. The small altar of St. John unfortunately conceals to some extent the * Crucifixion, by _Pietro Cavalini_, painted for Walther de Brienne, Duke of Athens, whilst captain of the Florentines (1342). The figure on the mule, with golden accoutrements, is said to represent Walther. At this point is the entrance to the sacristy, the interior containing handsome cabinets of the 17th cent., in which (before the spoliation of 1797) the treasures of the church were preserved. Among the relics are the "veil of the Virgin", a benediction in the handwriting of St. Francis and the rules of his order, sanctioned by Honorius III., which the holy man always carried with him. Over the door his portrait, said to be by _Giunta da Pisa_, painted soon after his death. Farther on in the church, to the l., is the pulpit, adorned with a Coronation of the Virgin, ascribed to _Fra Martino_, pupil of Simone di Martino. Beneath the music-gallery *St. Francis receiving the stigmata, a fresco by _Giotto_. The last chapel to the N. is dedicated to St. Martin; representations from his life by _Simone di Martino_.

The stained windows of the lower church are by _Angeletto_ and _Pietro da Gubbio_ and _Bonino d'Assisi_, those of the upper church upwards of a century later.

The _Crypt_ was constructed in the Doric style, harmonizing little with the two churches, in 1818, after the relics of the saint had been discovered in a rude stone coffin. It is approached by a double staircase.

The * _Upper Church_, the simpler of the two, is opened on the occasion of great festivals only, but may be visited by the stranger accompanied by the sacristan. It is in the form of a Latin cross, with niches for Gothic windows, transept and tribune. The W. side has a handsome wheel-window and beautiful pediment. The ceiling and walls of the nave are adorned with * frescoes by _Cimabue_ and _Giotto_ (1298) of events from the life of St. Francis; those above are from the Old and New Testament, by _Cimabue_. Frescoes in the transept by _Giunta da Pisa_ (about 1252), injured. *Choir-stalls carved and decorated with figures by _Domenico da S. Severino_ (about 1450). Papal throne, of red marble of Assisi (by _Fuccio_), erected by Gregory IX.

The church of _S. Chiara_, near the gate, a fine Gothic structure by _Fra Filippo da Campello_ (1253, unfortunately altered subsequently), is now undergoing restoration (if closed, visitors go round the church to the l. and knock at the door at the back), contains, beneath the high-altar, the remains of S. Clara, who, inspired with enthusiasm for St. Francis, abandoned her parents and wealth, and died as first abbess of the order of Clarissines which she had founded. A crypt, similar to that in the church of

S. Francesco, is now being constructed about her tomb. On the arch above the high-altar frescoes by *Giottino;* those in the lateral chapel on the r. are attributed to *Giotto*.

The *Cathedral of S. Rufino*, in the upper part of the town, named after the first bishop (240), dates from the first half of the 12th cent., the crypt from 1018. Façade ancient; the interior entirely modern. Entrance r. of the church (5 soldi).

The *Chiesa Nuova* occupies the site of the house in which St. Francis was born.

In the Piazza the beautiful fragment of a *Temple of Minerva*, consisting of 6 columns of travertine, converted into a church of *S. Maria della Minerva*. Ancient inscriptions immured in the vestibule. Adjacent to the church is the entrance to the ancient *Forum*, which corresponded to the present *Piazza*, but lay considerably lower. In the forum a *Basement* for a statue with a long inscription (fee 1/2 l.).

In a ravine of the lofty *Monte Subasio* (3620 ft.), in the rear of Assisi, is situated the hermitage *delle Carcere*, whither St. Francis was wont to retire for devotional exercises.

The drive from Assisi to *Spello* is very beautiful (one-horse carr. 4—5 l.). By train it is reached in 13 min. (express does not stop). To the r. of the road as the town is approached are the ruins of an amphitheatre of the imperial period, but they are not visible from the railway.

Spello, a small town with 2500 inhab., picturesquely situated on a mountain-slope, is the ancient *Hispellum (Colonia Julia Hispellum)*. The *Porta Veneris* by which the town is entered, with its three portrait-statues, as well as portions of the wall, are ancient. In *S. Maria Maggiore*, r. of the entrance, an ancient cippus serves as basin for consecrated water. To the l. the Cap. del Sagramento with *frescoes by *Pinturicchio* (1501), l. Annunciation (with the name and portrait of the painter), opposite the visitor the Adoration, r. Christ in the Temple; on the ceiling, the Sibyls. L. of the high-altar Pietà, r. a Madonna by *Perugino*. Above the altar in the sacristy a Madonna by *Pinturicchio*.

S. Francesco (or *Andrea*), consecrated in 1228 by Gregory IX., contains in the r. transept an altar-piece, Madonna and saints, by *Pinturicchio* (1508); above, a letter to the painter by *G. Baglione*.

Among other antiquities the "House of Propertius" is shown, although it is by no means certain that the poet was born here. In the *Pal. Comunale* and the church-wall of S. Lorenzo, Roman inscriptions. The upper part of the town commands an extensive view of the plain, with Foligno and Assisi. Numerous ruins occasioned by the earthquake of 1831 are still observed.

The line to Foligno crosses the *Topino* and reaches stat. *Foligno* (halt of 25 min., good refreshment-room). About 1/2 M. from the stat. is

Foligno (*Posta; *Albergo di Gius. Barbacci, R. 1½ l.: Croce Bianca; *Trattoria Stella d' Oro. One-horse carr. from the stat. to the town for 1 pers. with luggage 40 c.). near the ancient *Fulginium*, an episcopal residence with 13,000 industrial inhab., situated in a fertile district. In 1281 it was destroyed by Perugia, in 1439 united to the States of the Church, in 1860 again separated from them. The earthquake of 1831 occasioned serious damage; those of 1839, 1853 and 1854 were less injurious.

Foligno also boasts of a school of painting akin to that of Perugia, the most distinguished master of which is *Niccolò Alunno* or *da Foligno*.

Beyond its pleasant and attractive exterior the town possesses little to arrest the traveller, who should therefore, if possible, at once proceed on his journey to Spoleto.

In the Piazza is the cathedral of *S. Feliciano* with Gothic façade of the 15th cent., interior renovated.

S. Anna, or *delle Contesse*, with dome by *Bramante*, formerly contained the celebrated Madonna di Foligno by Raphael, now in the Vatican.

S. Niccolò; in the chapel r. of the high-altar is a fine altarpiece and a Coronation of the Virgin with "predella" by *Niccolò Alunno*. — *S. Maria infra Portas*, with frescoes by the same master.

La Nunziatella, with a fresco by *Perugino*, the Baptism of Christ.

The *Palazzo del Governo* is adorned with frescoes by *Ottaviano Nelli* (in the old chapel). *Palazzo Comunale*, a modern building of the Ionic order.

About 6 M. to the W. is **Bevagna** on the *Clitumnus*, the ancient *Merania* of the Umbri, celebrated for its admirable pastures, with remains of an amphitheatre and other antiquities. From Bevagna (or from Foligno direct 6 M.) the traveller may visit the lofty **Montefalco**, a small town with several churches containing a number of fine paintings; thus, *S. Francesco*, with frescoes from the life of the Saint by *Benozzo Gozzoli* (1422); in the chapel good frescoes by various masters. The churches *dell' Illuminata*, *S. Leonardo* and *S. Fortunato* (3¼ M. from the town, on the way to Trevi) also contain objects of interest; charming views of the plain from the height.

At Foligno the line unites with that from Ancona (see R. 11).

From Foligno to Rome.

Railway. From Foligno to Rome 3 trains daily in 7—8 hrs., fares 19 l. 75, 14 l. 60, 9 l. 75 c. A fourth train runs as far as Narni only, in 3 hrs., fares 7 l. 50, 5 l. 25, 3 l. 75 c.

The railway, as well as the high-road, intersects the luxuriant, well-watered valley of the *Clitumnus*, whose flocks are extolled by Virgil, and proceeds in a straightto direction

Stat. *Trevi*. The small town, the ancient *Trebia*, lies picturesquely on the slope to the l. The church of **La Madonna delle lagrime* possesses one of *Perugino's* finest frescoes, the Adoration of the Magi. The church of *S. Martino*, outside the gate, also contains good pictures by *Tiberio d' Assisi* and *Lo Spagna*.

The small village of *Le Vene*, on the Clitumnus, is next passed. Near it, to the l., a small ancient * *Temple*, usually regarded as that of *Clitumnus* mentioned by Pliny (Epist. 8, 8), but probably not earlier than Constantine the Great, as the Christian emblems, the vine and the cross, on the façade testify. The temple, now church of *S. Salvatore*, lies with its rear towards the road; it may easily be reached on foot from Trevi in 1 hr. Near Le Vene the abundant and clear *Source of the Clitumnus*, beautifully described by Pliny, wells forth from the limestone-rock. On the height to the l. the village of *Campello*. On the way to Spoleto, to the l. in the village of *S. Giacomo*, a church with frescoes by *Lo Spagna*, of 1526; beautiful road through richly cultivated land.

Spoleto *(Posta; Albergo Nuovo;* from the stat. to the town 1/2 M., two-horse carr. 1 l.), the ancient *Spoletium*, said to have been an episcopal residence as early as A. D. 50, now an archiepiscopal see with 11,000 inhab., is an animated town, beautifully situated, and containing some remarkable antiquities.

In B. C. 242 a Roman colony was established here, and in 217 the town vigorously repelled the attack of Hannibal when on his march to Picenum after the battle of the Trasimene Lake, as Livy (22, 9) relates. It subsequently became a Roman municipium, suffered severely during the civil wars of Sulla and Marius, and again at the hands of the Goths, after the fall of the W. Empire. The Lombards here founded a duchy (as in Beneventum) in 570, the first holders of which were *Faroald* and *Ariolf*. After the fall of the Carlovingians *Guido* of Spoleto even attained the dignity of Emperor, as well as his son *Lambert*, who perished while hunting in 898. Innocent III. and Gregory IV. incorporated Spoleto with the States of the Church about 1220. The *Castle* of Spoleto, erected by Theodoric the Great, restored by Narses, and strengthened by 4 towers by Cardinal Albornoz, now a prison, fell into the hands of the Piedmontese Sept. 18th, 1860, after a gallant defence by Major O'Reilly, an Irishman.

The town is built on the slope of a hill, the summit of which is occupied by the old castle. Ascending from the principal street in the lower part of the town, where the hotels are situated, the traveller first reaches a gateway of the Roman period, termed *Porta d'Annibale* or *Porta della Fuga*, in allusion to the above-mentioned occurrence. Beyond it the Piazza is crossed; then an ascent to the l. to the *Palazzo Pubblico*, containing several inscriptions, and a *Madonna with saints by *Lo Spagna*. The street to the l. leads to the loftily situated

Cathedral of S. Maria Assunta, erected by Duke Theodelapius in 617, but frequently restored; on the façade (13th cent.) 5 arches with antique columns, a frieze with griffins and arabesques, at each extremity a stone pulpit; above the entrance a large mosaic by *Solsernus* (1207) of Christ with Mary and John. Interior renovated in 1644. In the choir *frescoes by *Fra Filippo Lippi*, completed after his death by *Fra Diamante* in 1470, Annunciation, Birth of Christ and Death of Mary; in the cupola her Coronation and Assumption (unfortunately damaged). The winter-choir is embellished with carving by *Bramante* and paintings by *Lo Spagna*. At the entrance to the chapel, on the l. of the choir, is the tomb of *Fil. Lippi*, who died here in 1469 of poison administered by the family of Lucrezia Buti, a noble Florentine. Although a monk, he had succeeded in gaining the affections of this lady and abducting her from a convent. The monument was erected by Lorenzo de Medicis, the epitaph is by Poliziano. Opposite is the monument of an Orsini. The Baptistery contains frescoes in the style of *Giulio Romano;* on the *font of travertine, sculptures from the life of Christ. In the adjacent chapel are the remains of some frescoes by *Pinturicchio*. — The Piazza is believed to have been the site of the palace of the Lombard dukes.

The other churches are of inferior interest. *S. Domenico* (disused) contains a copy of Raphael's Transfiguration, attributed to Giulio Romano. **S. Pietro*, outside the Roman gate, is a Norman edifice; façade adorned with sculptures.

Some of the churches contain relics of ancient temples; thus in that *del Crocefisso*, without the town, fragments of a temple of Concordia (?); columns etc. in *S. Andrea* and *S. Giuliano;* remnants of a theatre; a ruin styled "Palace of Theodoric" etc. None of those, however, claim special attention.

No one should omit to visit the *Fortress* or the opposite *Monte Luco*, for the sake of the view. The fortress being a prison and somewhat unattractive, the visitor will probably prefer the latter. A short distance before the entrance to the prison is reached, the path ascends to the r., issuing by a gate which here forms an entrance to the town, where to the l. polygonal foundations, remnants of the ancient castle-wall, are perceived. Without the wall is a profound ravine, spanned by the imposing **Aqueduct delle Torri*, which serves as a bridge, uniting the town with Monte Luco: a brick structure resting on 10 arches, 273 ft. in height, and 231 yds. in length. Its construction is attributed to Theodelapius, 3rd duke of Spoleto (604). A window midway affords a view. To the l. on the height is perceived the monastery of *S. Giuliano;* beneath, *S. Pietro*, above which the Capuchin monastery, shaded by beautiful trees. *Monte Luco* is densely wooded, and possesses a number of hermitages, most of which are converted into country-residences. The road ascends rapidly near the aqueduct. After 10 min. a more unbroken prospect is obtained, embracing the fortress and town, and the spacious valley. — The summit is attained after a fatiguing ascent of 1½ hr. Towards the l. a lofty cross, whence an unimpeded panorama to the N. and E., of the valley of the Clitumnus with Trevi, Foligno, Spello and Assisi; then Perugia and the Central Apennines near Città di Castello and Gubbio. In the other directions the view is intercepted by the mountains in the vicinity. Towards the E. these are overtopped by the rocky peak of the Sibilla, snow-clad until late in the summer. Returning to the r. the traveller passes the poor Capuchin monastery of *S. Maria delle Grazie*, an ancient resort of pilgrims. The monks (at present 12 in number), who live in great poverty, are extremely courteous to strangers, but accept no donations.

Quitting Spoleto, the train ascends during 1 hr. on the slopes of *Monte Somma* (3788 ft.) to the culminating point of the line (2100 ft.), passes through a long tunnel, and reaches the fertile valley of the *Nera*. To the l. lies

Terni *(Europa; Angleterre;* **Tre Colonne)*, the ancient *Interamna*, where (it is believed) the historian Tacitus and the emperors Tacitus and Florianus were born. Remains of an amphitheatre (erroneously styled a *"Temple of the Sun"*) in the grounds of the episcopal palace, Roman inscriptions in the *Palazzo Pubblico*, palaces of the Umbrian nobility etc. are objects of interest. Agreeable promenade on the ramparts, whence the beautiful Nera Valley is surveyed; l. Collescipoli, r. Cesi, opposite the spectator Narni.

From Terni a walk of 1½ hr. to the celebrated ** *Waterfalls (Le Cascate* or *La Caduta delle Marmore)*; one horse carr. 3—4, two-horse 5—6 l. and according to circumstances an additional gratuity. The traveller should not fail to be provided with an abundant supply of the copper-coin of the country. At the different points of view contributions are levied by the custodians (not above 3—4 sous); then gates require opening (1—2 sous), in addition to which a host of beggars and guides sorely try the patience of the visitor. The pedestrian is cautioned against engaging the superfluous services of a guide before Papigno is reached, to which point the high-road is followed.

Descending from the Piazza by the Strada Garibaldi the traveller soon reaches the gate and crosses the Nera. The high-road to Rieti, traversing gardens and olive-plantations, is followed for ¾ hr., the valley of the Nera attained, and a road on the l. entered. The highest eminence above the river is crowned by the ruins of an old castle. The road affords fine views of the mountain-group of Terni, M. Somma, and the rocky heights of the Nera Valley. *Papigno* stands on an isolated rock, surrounded by ravines, in a remarkably picturesque situation on the l. bank of the Nera. The carriage-road leading round Papigno is followed;

at the gate the stranger is subjected to the importunities of guides and donkey-drivers. The services of a guide are by no means necessary, but may be accepted as a protection against farther molestation. Guide $^{1}/_{2}$—1 l.: donkey about the same; a bargain, however, should be made. The carriage-road is followed, which may occasionally be abridged by shorter footpaths; then through the ravine and across the Nera. Beyond the bridge, the garden of the *Villa Graziani (Castelli)* is entered immediately to the r., and an avenue of lemon and orange-trees traversed; the farther end of the garden is shaded by cypresses. Lofty rocks rise above the narrow valley, forming a striking contrast to the luxuriant vegetation of the garden (gardener 10—15 c.). The path skirts the verge of the impetuous Nera, shaded by evergreen oaks. After about 10 min., the broader path terminates, and the moistness of the atmosphere betokens the proximity of the fall. A narrow footpath is followed in a straight direction, finally ascending rapidly. Where it divides, a few paces to the r. lead to a projecting rock, whence the lower fall is surveyed. The ascent to the l. leads to a small arbour, where the finest view of the central fall is obtained (fee 20 c.).

The *Velino*, which here discharges itself into the Nera, is so strongly impregnated with lime that its deposit continually raises its bed. In consequence of this the plain of Rieti (1310 ft.) is frequently exposed to the danger of inundation. In ancient times Marcus Curius Dentatus endeavoured to counteract the evil by the construction of a channel (B. C. 271), which, although altered, is to this day in use. The rising of the bed of the river, however, rendered new measures necessary from time to time. Two other channels were subsequently excavated, the *Cava Beatina* or *Gregoriana* in 1417, and the *Cava Paolina* by Paul III. in 1546; these, however, proving unserviceable, Clement VIII. reopened the original "emissarius" of Dentatus in 1598. In 1787 a new cutting was required, and another has at the present day become necessary. The regulation of the Velino-fall has long formed the subject of vehement discussions between Rieti and Terni, as the unrestrained descent of the water in rainy seasons threatens the valley of Terni with inundation. The height of the upper fall (1200 ft. above the sea-level) is 50 ft., that of the central or principal fall is stated at 5—600 ft., that of the lower, down to its junction with the Nera, 240 ft.; total height 8—900 ft.; according to other measurements, however, only 5—600 ft. in all. In volume of water and beauty of adjuncts these falls cannot easily be surpassed. The footpath continues in the valley of the Nera. Retracing their steps, visitors enter the first path to the l., crossing the Nera by a natural bridge, beneath which the water has hollowed its own channel. Where the path divides, the gradual ascent to the l. is to be selected. The surrounding rocks (in which there is a quarry) have been formed by the incrustations of the Velino. The channel on the r. *(Cava Paolina)* is full in winter only. The division of the cascade is here surveyed; the central fall, in the spray of which beautiful rainbows are occasionally formed, may be approached more nearly. A farther ascent leads to a small pavilion of stone on a projecting rock (fee 10—20 c.), whence a beautiful view of the principal fall and the valley of the Nera. Another point of view is the garden of the first cottage which is reached (20 c.; flowers and petrifactions of the Velino offered, 10—20 c. more); view of Terni. The traveller should now descend immediately to the high-road (having previously ordered his carriage to meet him here). instead of returning to Papigno as the drivers prefer. The entire excursion occupies at least 3—4 hrs.

If time permit, the excursion may be extended (3 M.) to the beautiful *Lake of Piedilugo*. The Velino is crossed, and the lake attained in $1/2$ hr.; its indentations are skirted, and the village of *Piedilugo*, with its ruined castle reached in $1/2$ hr. more. Boats may be hired at the *inn; the opp. bank, where a fine echo may be awakened, is most frequently visited by water.

Cesi, loftily situated, $4^3/_4$ M. to the N. of Terni, possesses remnants of ancient polygonal walls and interesting subterranean grottoes of considerable extent, from which a current of cool air in summer, and of warm in winter issues.

From Terni a pleasant route by Rieti, Aquila, Popoli and Solmona leads to *Naples*. To Rieti 23 M., diligence every alternate day. From Rieti to Rome by the ancient *Via Salara*, diligence three times weekly in 10 hrs. (9 l.). This route is, however, inferior in interest to the following and is seldom selected by tourists.

From Terni to Narni 8 M., one-horse carr. 5 l.

The railway intersects the rich valley of the Nera. R. on the hill *Cesi* (see above), l. *Collescipoli*, then

Narni *(* Posta)*, the ancient Umbrian *Narnia* (originally *Nequinum*), birthplace of the Emperor Nerva, Pope John XIII. (965—72) and of Erasmus of Narni, surnamed Gattamelata, the well-known "condottiere" of the 15th cent. It is picturesquely situated on a lofty rock on the *Nar*, now *Nera* (whence its name), at the point where the river forces its way through a narrow ravine to the Tiber. The old castle is now a prison.

The *Cathedral* of Narni, dedicated to St. Juvenalis the first bishop (369), erected in the 13th cent., is architecturally interesting. The *Monastery of the Zoccolanti* contains the *Coronation of Mary by *Lo Spagna*, one of that master's finest paintings, and long believed to be the work of Raphael.

From Narni to Perugia by Todi see p. 56.

From Narni 6 M. to the ancient and beautifully situated Umbrian mountain-town of *Amelia*, Lat. *Ameria* (inn outside the gate), mentioned by Cicero, with admirably preserved walls in the Cyclopean style and other antiquities. The road, identical with the Via Flaminia, now traverses a well-cultivated district.

7 M. **Otricoli**, a village near the site of the ancient *Otriculum*, the frontier-town of Umbria, where numerous antiquities, among others the celebrated bust of Jupiter in the Vatican, have been discovered. In descending from Otricoli the geologist will observe in the direction of the Tiber the first traces of the volcanic deposits which recur so frequently in the Campagna. The towering summit of Soracte becomes visible to the l.

The road passes the small episcopal town of *Magliano*, said to derive its name from Manlius Torquatus, now belonging to the *Sabina*, and leads to the l. to the Tiber, which is crossed by the handsome *Ponte Felice*, constructed by Augustus, restored in 1589 by Pope Sixtus V., formerly the approach from Umbria to Etruria, now that from the kingdom of Italy to the States of the Church. Custom-house formalities.

A small steamboat runs twice weekly from this point (from Porta della Rosa, 15 M. farther down, when the river is low) to Rome in 8—10 hrs., affording a convenient, although not very comfortable opportunity of becoming acquainted with the banks of the river, which will be found interesting.

The train quits Narni on the r. bank of the Nera, and in a few minutes reaches the *Bridge of Augustus* for the Via Flaminia (p. 77), which led hence to Bevagna (p. 61). The arch on the l. bank is 60 ft. in height, of the other two the buttresses alone remain.

It may be best surveyed from the new bridge which crosses the river a little higher up. Beneath the remaining arch a fine glimpse is obtained of the monastery of *S. Casciano*. By the carriage-road from Narni to the bridge is a drive of 1/2 hr.; the far more picturesque route is on foot, descending by the somewhat precipitous bridle-path in 1/1 hr.

The road continues to follow the magnificent valley of the Nera, with its singularly beautiful plantations of evergreen oaks, passes through two tunnels, and then by a chain-bridge (not far from the influx of the Nera) crosses the *Tiber*, which here forms the boundary between the Kingdom of Italy and the States of the Church.

Stat. **Orte** (passports demanded, restored at Correse, see below), the ancient *Horta*, loftily situated on the bank of the Tiber, contains nothing of interest beyond its picturesque situation. This will be the junction of the line now described with that from Florence by Siena and Orvieto.

The line descends the valley of the Tiber on the r. bank, affording pleasing glimpses of both banks. To the r. the lofty and indented ridge of *Soracte* (p. 69) becomes visible. L., on the other side of the river, lie *S. Vito* and *Otricoli* (see above). R. stat. *Galese*; farther on, high on the l. bank, *Magliano*. The next stat. *Borghetto* is commanded by a ruined castle, on the height to the r. Here the Tiber is crossed by the handsome *Ponte Felice* (see above) which formerly served as a link of communication between Rome and the N.E. provinces. From Borghetto by Cività Castellana by the old high-road to Rome see p. 68.

Beyond Borghetto *Cività Castellana* becomes visible for a short time. The line crosses to the l. bank of the Tiber. Stat. *Stimigliano* and the following stat. *Montorso* are situated in the mountainous district of the *Sabina*, which produces abundant supplies of oil. The country is here extremely attractive, but cannot conveniently be visited by the traveller without letters of introduction, on account of the paucity and poverty of inns (tolerable at *Poggio Mirleto* only). To the r. the Soracte is seen.

At stat. *Passo di Correse* (douane; passports returned) the States of the Church are again entered. The name is a corruption of *Cures*, the ancient Sabine town, birthplace of Numa Pompilius, the ruins of which are in the vicinity.

The train continues its route on the l. bank of the Tiber to stat. *Monte Rotondo;* the town, 2$^1/_3$ M. higher, possesses a castle of the Orsini, now the property of the Piombino family, commanding beautiful views of the Sabine Mts. The village was attacked by Garibaldi on the 26th Oct. 1867; 2 M. distant is Mentana (p. 270), where he was defeated by the Papal and French troops, and compelled to retreat.

The line follows the direction of the ancient *Via Salara* (p. 66; to the r. on the hill the site of the ancient *Antemnae*) and crosses the *Anio* (p. 271); to the l. the Sabine and Alban Mts.; Rome with the dome of St. Peter's becomes visible. A wide circuit round the city is described, near Porta Maggiore (p. 144) the so-called temple of Minerva Medica (p. 144) is passed and the central-station entered near the Thermæ of Diocletian (Pl. I 25). Arrival in Rome see p. 86.

From Borghetto to Rome by Cività Castellana and Rignano.

From Borghetto (p. 67) the road ascends (4$^2/_3$ M.) to the picturesquely situated **Cività Castellana** (*Posta; Speranza*, in the market-place), which may best be visited from this station. Here lay *Falerii* or *Falerium Vetus*, the town of the *Falisci*, conquered by Camillus B. C. 396; Etruscan and Roman antiquities in the environs. A lofty bridge, erected in 1712, carries the road across a ravine, 120 ft. in depth, into the town. The bridge was overthrown by an earthquake a few years ago, and has not yet been completely restored. This necessitates a circuit of 4$^1/_2$ M. The ravine may, however, be crossed on foot by the robust pedestrian (not recommended to ladies). A trifling donation (1$^1/_2$—2 l. for a carriage) obviates the necessity of douane-formalities. Visa of passport procured for 25 c. — The Cathedral of *S. Maria* dates from 1210; the *Citadel*, erected by Alexander VI. in 1500 from a design by *Sangallo*, enlarged by Julius II. and Leo X., was last employed as a state-prison. Cività Castellana contains nothing to arrest the traveller except its picturesque situation. The deep ravines by which it is enclosed testify to vast volcanic convulsions. They contain scanty remnants of ancient walls and numerous Etruscan tombs hewn in the rock, especially near the citadel.

Interesting excursion to the ruins of **Falerii** (pronounced Falleri), 3 M. distant.

Near the citadel the *Ponte del Terreno* is crossed to the l., where tombs honeycomb the rocks on all sides, this being the more direct route to *Falerium Novum* or *Colonia Junonia*, founded by the Romans about 240, situated in the plain, 3 M. to the N. of Cività Castellana. Etruscan and Roman tombs are here seen side by side. The town was nearly in the form of a triangle; the walls are well preserved, protected by strong square towers and penetrated by gates, one of which on the W. *(Porta di Giove)* is still in good condition. Another gate towards the S.E., the *Porta del Bove*, is also worthy of a visit; near it the theatre of Roman construction. Also the piscina and what is regarded as the forum, in the rear of the theatre.

At the Porta di Giove, within the walls, is the *Abbadia di S. Maria* of the 12th cent. In the nave antique columns; in 1829 the roof fell in, but the damage has been repaired. The adjoining building contains inscriptions, statues etc., the result of excavations made here. An amphitheatre has also been recently discovered. One of the men at the farm-buildings may be requested to act as guide. Picturesque views from the walls.

Rome can be reached in one day from Cività Castellana.

This route, corresponding to the ancient Via Flaminia, is 33 M. in length, but nearly 5 M. shorter, and moreover less hilly, than that by Nepi. At the same time it affords a convenient opportunity for visiting Soracte (3—4 hrs. suffice). Those who travel with a vetturino alight 2 M. before Rignano is reached, where the horses may be fed. Travellers in the opposite direction order the carriage to meet them 2 M. beyond Rignano. One-horse carr. from Rignano to Cività (9 M.) 6—7 l.; guides offer their services for the ascent of Soracte, but may well by dispensed with.

The road descends at the E. end of Cività Castellana to the deep valley of the *Treja*, which it gradually again quits. 2 M. from Rignano (7 from Cività) the road ascends to the l. to the Soracte; pedestrians may alight here, whilst those who prefer it continue their route to Rignano and there obtain horses, donkeys or a light conveyance (in which half the distance only can be performed) for the ascent. 1 M. farther is the church *de' Santi Martiri*, with Christian catacombs.

Rignano *(*Posta)*, a small place which boasts of a few Roman relics. Here Cesare and Lucrezia Borgia and their brothers and sisters, children of Cardinal Roderigo Borgia (Alexander VI.) were born. The environs are in many respects interesting to the antiquarian and naturalist.

Soracte, mentioned by Horace (Carm. I. 9: *Vides ut alta stet nive candidum Soracte)* and Virgil (Æn. 7, 785: *Summi deum sancti custos Soractis Apollo)*, is now termed *Monte di S. Oreste,* the word Soracte having been erroneously written S. Oracte and thence corrupted to S. Oreste. It is a limestone-ridge, descending precipitously on both sides. extending 3—4 M. from N. W. to S. E. and culminating in several peaks of different heights. On the central and highest summit (2100 ft.) stands the church of *S. Silvestro*. On the slope which gradually descends towards the S.E. the village of *S. Oreste* is situated. Thus far the road is practicable for carriages, but walking or riding is far preferable. Leaving the miserable village to the r., the path ascends gradually to the l., and in 1/2 hr. the monastery of *S. Silvestro* is reached. founded in 746 by Charleman, son of Charles Martel and brother of Pepin. The monks live in a very humble style; refreshments should be brought for the excursion if required. The summit. with the church and a small disused monastery, may now be attained in a few minutes. In ancient times a celebrated Temple of Apollo occupied this site.

The **view, uninterrupted in every direction, embraces: E. the valley of the Tiber. the Sabina, in the background several snow-clad peaks of the Central Apennines, among them the Leonessa: S. the Volscian and Alban Mts., then the broad Campagna, Rome. the sea: N. the mountains of Tolfa, the Lake of Bracciano, the Ciminian forest. the crater of Baccano and numerous villages.

Pedestrians, returning from the monastery, may descend by a direct path, which, although somewhat precipitous, is considerably shorter than that by S. Oreste.

Beyond Rignano the road ascends slightly. After 4 M. the dome of St. Peter's becomes visible. Midway between Città Castellana and Rome is the osteria of *Castel Nuovo*, where the vetturini usually halt for a few hours to rest their horses. if no stay has been made at Rignano. As the district and the neighbouring village of Castel Nuovo are unattractive, a halt at Rignano is in every respect preferable. Beyond Castel Nuovo the road gradually descends to the valley of the Tiber. Remains of pavement and a few tombs indicate the course of the ancient road. About 16 M. beyond Castel Nuovo, 7 M. from Rome, the road descends to *Prima Porta*, where the ruins of the imperial *Villa of Livia* or *ad Gallinas* is situated. Here in 1863 the beautiful statue of Divus Augustus (in the Vatican) was found. The excavations have since then been continued. One of the rooms with *mural paintings merits a visit. Near Prima Porta lies *Saxa Rubra*, a station on the ancient road; in the plain, on the bank of the river, the defeat of Maxentius took place, A.D. 312. The road hence, remaining in the vicinity of the Tiber, is extremely picturesque. On the opposite bank lies *Castel Giubileo*, the ancient *Fidenae*. The road soon crosses the *Valchetta*, the ancient *Cremera*. which descends from Veii and was the scene of the well-known defeat of the Fabii. 3 M. from Prima Porta is situated a remarkable rock-tomb of the family of the *Nasones*. 2 M.

farther *Ponte Molle* is reached, where the Via Flaminia and Via Cassia unite, see p. 43.

From **Cività Castellana to Rome by Nepi.** Travellers are occasionally compelled to take this longer route, when that above described is under repair. This is in fact the regular post-road, which at Monterosi unites with that from Siena, Orvieto and Viterbo.

From Civita to Nepi, partly through forest, 8 M. A shorter route, for pedestrians or riders only, leads by the interesting *Castel S. Elia*, a resort of pilgrims.

Nepi, the ancient Etruscan *Nepete* or *Nepet*, subsequently *Colonia Nepensis*, is a picturesquely situated little town, residence of a bishop, surrounded by mediæval walls and towers. Venerable *Cathedral*; *Town Hall* with Roman sculptures and inscriptions. In ancient times it was a place of importance, but is now in a decaying condition, principally owing to its destruction by the French in 1799. Falerii is 6 M., Sutri 7 M. distant from Nepi.

The road now traverses a bleak volcanic district, and a short distance before *Monterosi* is reached unites (4²/₃ M.) with the road from Siena to Rome. From Monterosi to Rome see p. 41.

9. From Bologna to Rome by Ancona *(Falconara and Foligno.*

An express-train runs daily from *Bologna* to *Rome* in 17 hrs., halting for 1½ hr. at *Falconara-Ancona*. The other trains are also convenient. Fares 56 l. 40, 42 l. 55, 30 l. 35 c. From *Bologna* to *Ancona* 4 trains daily in 5—7 hrs., fares 22 l. 45, 18 l., 13 l. 50 c.

From the railway-station on the N. side of the city, outside the Porta Galliera, the line runs parallel with the high-road in the direction of the ancient *Via Æmilia*, and as far as Forli traverses fertile plains in nearly a straight direction; in the distance to the r. the spurs of the Apennines. Stat. *Mirandola* and *Quaderna*. Stat. *Castel S. Pietro*, on the *Sillaro*, with a castle erected by the Bolognese in the 13th cent.

Imola *(S. Marco)*, on the *Santerno*, is an ancient town with 10,916 inhab. and seat of a bishop (since 422), 'the Roman *Forum Cornelii*, incorporated with the States of the Church in 1509. birth-place of St. Petrus Chrysologus, Archbishop of Ravenna (d. 449); his tomb is in the cathedral of *S. Cassiano*, where the remains of the saint of that name also repose.

The line crosses the Santerno and soon reaches stat. *Castel Bolognese*, an ancient stronghold of the Bolognese, constructed in 1380. Branch-line hence to *Ravenna*. Then across the river *Senio*, ancient *Sinnus*, to

Faenza *(Corona; Posta)*, a town with 17,486 inhab., on the *Lamone* (ancient *Anemo*), the *Faventia* of the Boii, celebrated for its pottery (whence the term *"faience"*), and containing considerable silk and weaving manufactories. Among the churches the cathedral of *S. Costanzo* deserves mention; it contains a *Holy Family by *Innocenzo da Imola*, and bas-reliefs by *Benedetto da Majano*. The *Capuchin Monastery*, outside the town, possesses an admirable picture by *Guido Reni*, a *Madonna and St. John. In *S. Maglorio* a *Madonna, attributed to *Giorgione*, more probably by *Girolamo da Treviso;* by the latter a fresco (1533). Madonna with saints, in the *Commenda* (in the Borgo), where there is also a *Collection of Pictures* by native masters, such as Bertucci etc.

The *Palazzo Comunale was in the 15th cent. the scene of the murder of Galeotto Manfredi by his jealous wife Francesca Bentivoglio; the grated window in the centre, where the deed was perpetrated, is still shown.

In 1782 the *Canale Zanelli* was constructed from Faenza to the *Po di Primaro* near *S. Alberto*, in order to connect the town with the Adriatic.

A good road leads from Faenza to *Ravenna* (diligence 3 times weekly), and another by Marradi and Borgo S. Lorenzo to *Florence* (corriere daily; diligence 3 times weekly in 12 hrs.; office, Corso 68).

The line intersects the plain in a straight direction, the *Lamone* is crossed, then the *Montone*, which falls into the Adriatic not far from Ravenna.

Forli *(Posta)*, the ancient *Forum Livii*, a well-built town with 17,723 inhab., till 1848 seat of the cardinal-legate.

The **Cathedral of S. Croce* contains a chapel of the Madonna del Fuoco; in the dome *frescoes by *Carlo Cignani:* Assumption of the Virgin. A Ciborium from a design by Michael Angelo, a casket of relics of the 13th cent., and the sculptures of the principal door of the 15th cent. are worthy of notice.

S. Girolamo contains a *Madonna with angels, by *Guido Reni;* in the 1st chapel to the r. frescoes by *Melozzo* and *Palmezzano*. — *S. Mercuriale* possesses a *painting by *Innocenzo da Imola*, sculptures of 1536 and several good pictures by *Marco Palmezzano*, an artist of this town. On a house adjacent to the "spezeria" or shop of the druggist *Morandi* are remains of fine frescoes by *Melozzo da Forli* (about 1470). The *Finacoteca* contains good pictures by *Marco Palmezzano*, *Fra Angelico*, *Lorenzo di Credi* etc. The *Piazza with the *Palazzo Comunale* and other edifices deserves a visit. The Citadel, constructed in 1361, now serves as a prison.

A road leads from Forli on the l. bank of the Ronco to *Ravenna* (about 15 M.); another through the Apennines by *Rocca S. Casciano* and *S. Benedetto* to *Florence*, diligence 3 times weekly, corriere daily at noon.

The line to Rimini crosses the *Ronco* and passes stat. *Forlimpopoli*, the ancient *Forum Popilii;* to the r. on the hill *Bertinoro* with its productive vineyards; then by *Polenta* and across the *Savio (Sapis)* to the town of

Cesena (*Posta or Leone Bianco), with 8000 inhab., charmingly situated. In the *Piazza* is the handsome *Palazzo Pubblico with a statue of Pius VI., who was born at Cesena in 1717. In the interior a *Madonna with saints, by *Francesco Francia*. The *Capuchin Church* possesses a fine picture by *Guercino*. The *Library, founded in 1452 by Domenico Malatesta Novello, contains 4000 MSS.

On an eminence, ¹/₂ M. distant, stands the handsome church of *S. *Maria del Monte*, a work of *Bramante*, and a Benedictine monastery. Productive sulphur-mines in the vicinity, towards the S.

The line crosses the stream *Pisciatello*, which bears the name of *Urgone* in its upper course and is here identical with the celebrated *Rubicon* which Cæsar crossed in his march against Rome. On the road between Cesena and Savignano stands a column bearing a decree of the Roman senate, threatening to punish those who should unbidden trespass beyond the Rubicon. Montesquieu regarded this as genuine, but it is doubtless of modern origin.

Before Rimini is reached, the five-arched *Bridge of Augustus, one of the finest existing ancient works of this description, crosses the *Marecchia*, the ancient *Ariminus*. Here the Via Æmilia united with the Via Flaminia which led to Rome.

Rimini (*Tre Re), the ancient *Ariminum*, a town of the Umbri and a Roman colony, belonged during the exarchate to the Pentapolis Maritima. It is situated on the estuary of the Marecchia and Ausa, possesses 17,000 inhab., fisheries and silk-manufactories, and has recently come into notice as a sea-bathing place. The *Porta Romana, of travertine and adorned with sculptures, erected, as the inscription records, to commemorate the completion of the road by the Emp. Augustus, deserves particular attention. Near the *Cappuccini*, the supposed remains of an amphitheatre. From the stone *Basement* in the market-place Cæsar is said to have harangued the army after the passage of the Rubicon. The old harbour of Rimini at the mouth of the Marecchia, now filled with sand, is employed only by numerous fishing-boats. The following churches are interesting:

*S. Francesco (Duomo, Tempio dei Malatesta), of the 14th cent., in the Ital. Gothic style, restored in 1420 from designs by *Leo Battista Alberti*. The chapels contain several fine sculptures and frescoes.

S. Giuliano, with altar-piece by *Paolo Veronese*, and an ancient picture by *Lattanzio della Marca*. — *S. Girolamo*, with *picture of the saint by *Guercino*. — The *Palazzo del Comune* possesses an altar-piece by *Domenico del Ghirlandajo*, and a Pietà by *Giovanni Bellini* (about 1470). The *Palazzo Diottoleri* also contains several fine pictures. The *Library*, founded in 1617 by the jurist Gambalunga, contains 23,000 vols. and MSS. The dilapidated *Castle of the Malatesta*, now the citadel, still bears traces of the roses and elephants of the family escutcheon. From the history of the Malatestas Dante derived the touching episode of "*Francesca da Rimini*" in the 5th canto of the Inferno.

In the *Castello di S. Leo*, 18 M. to the W. of Rimini, the notorious *Cagliostro* (Giuseppe Balsamo) died in confinement in 1794. From S. Leo a bridle-path, much frequented by fishermen, leads to *Florence* by *Camaldoli* and *Vallombrosa*, traversing picturesque ravines.

A somewhat shorter excursion may be made to the ancient republic of **San Marino**, the smallest in the world, said to have been founded in an inaccessible wilderness by St. Marinus at the time of the persecutions of the Christians under Diocletian. This diminutive state braved all the storms of mediæval warfare and even the ambition of Napoleon. It retained its ancient constitution till 1847, when its senate was converted into a chamber of deputies. The precipitous rock in a bleak district on which the town (1000 inhab.) is situated is reached by one road only from Rimini. The village of *Borgo* at the base is the residence of the wealthier inhabitants. A cavern, through which a perpetual current of cold air passes, is an object of curiosity. The celebrated epigraphist and numismatist *Bartolommeo Borghesi*, born at Savignano in 1781, was from 1821 until his death on April 16th, 1860, a resident at S. Marino, where he arranged and described his admirable collections, and received visits from foreign savants.

Beyond Rimini the line skirts the coast, passes *S. Martino* and *S. Lorenzo*, crosses the streams *Marano* and *Conca* (the Crustumium Rapax of Lucan. Pharsal. II. 406) and reaches stat. *La Cattolica*. Then across the *Tavollo* and the *Foglia* (ancient *Isaurus* or *Pisaurus*) to

Pesaro (**Leone d'Oro*), the ancient *Pisaurum*, once capital of the united "delegations" of Urbino and Pesaro, and formerly appertaining to the Pentapolis Maritima. The palace of the Dukes of Urbino, with a magnificent hall, is now the seat of the authorities.

The Foglia is crossed by a Bridge of Roman origin.

Among the churches may be mentioned: *S. Francesco*, with a *Coronation of the Virgin by *Giovanni Bellini*; *S. Cassiano*, with a St. Barbara by *Simone da Pesaro*; *S. Giovanni de' Riformati*, with a badly restored altar-piece by *Guercino*. In the market-place stands the statue of Urban VIII.

The *Biblioteca Olivieri* contains 13,000 vols. and 600 MSS. Adjacent to it is a small *Museum of Antiquities*. The *Ospizio degli Incurabili* possesses an attractive collection of majolica-vases; in the *Palazzo Astico* are the *Marmora Pisaurensia*, described by Giordani in 1738. The treasures of art of which Pesaro formerly boasted have long since been transferred to Rome and Paris.

Near Pesaro is *Monte S. Bartolo*, where the Roman tragic dramatist L. Attius is said to be interred, and beyond it *L'Imperiale*, once a favourite villa of the dukes, but abandoned since the 18th cent. The handsome staircases, terraces and corridors testify to its ancient splendour. In the vicinity is the church *to Rome.* URBINO. *9. Route.* 75

of the *Girolamitani*, with an unfortunately damaged picture of St. Jerome by *Giovanni Santi*. One of the finest prospects in the environs is obtained from an eminence behind the monastery.

On the r., on the road to Rimini, is situated the *Villa Vittoria*, once the residence of Queen Caroline of England when Princess of Wales. The garden contains the monuments erected by her to the memory of her daughter Charlotte, and her brother the Duke of Brunswick who fell at Waterloo.

An excursion to *Urbino* may most easily be accomplished from Pesaro. Diligence daily at 7 a. m. from Urbino to Pesaro in 5—6 hrs., returning on the arrival of the afternoon trains (fare 2—3 1.). The road leads through the valley of the *Foglia*, which falls into the sea at Pesaro, to *Montecchio*, and then gradually ascends by the brook which falls into the Foglia.

Urbino *(Italia)*, the ancient *Urbinum Metaurense*, deriving its name from the neighbouring Metaurus, lies on an abrupt cliff, surrounded by barren mountains. The town (8000 inhab.) boasts of a university with as many professors as students. Its monuments and historical associations are interesting.

In the 13th cent. the town came into the possession of the *Montefeltro* family, and under *Federigo Montefeltro* and his son *Guidobaldo* in the 15th cent. attained to such prosperity as entirely to eclipse the neighbouring courts of the Malatestas at Rimini and the Sforzas at Pesaro. *Federigo Montefeltro*, who distinguished himself as a condottiere in the feuds of the 15th cent., in 1474 married his daughter to *Giovanni della Rovere*, a nephew of Sixtus IV. and was in consequence created Duke of Urbino. In this capacity he acquired a well-merited reputation as a patron of science and art, and Urbino was styled the "Italian Athens". His example was followed by his son *Guidobaldo I.*, zealously seconded by his duchess, the beautiful and accomplished *Elizabeta Gonzaga*. Guidobaldo was in 1497 expelled by *Caesar Borgia*, but after the death of Alexander VI. returned in triumph to Urbino, where he was visited during three festive days by his relative *Julius II.*, who now became Pope (1503—13), while on his route to Bologna. On this occasion the latter became acquainted with the youthful *Raphael Santi*, who, born March 28th, 1483, at Urbino, at first studied under the guidance of his father, the master *Giovanni Santi*, subsequently under the celebrated *Pietro Vannucci (Perugino)* at Perugia, and in 1504 went to Florence to perfect himself by the study of the works of *Leonardo da Vinci* and *Michael Angelo Buonarotti*. On the death of Duke Guidobaldo in 1508, Julius II. summoned Raphael to Rome to decorate the Stanza della Segnatura with frescoes. Under Julius and his successor Leo X. Raphael acquired the reputation of the greatest painter of the day and died April 6th, 1520. For the development of his genius, however, he was in a great measure indebted to the munificent patronage of the court of Urbino. Here Count *Balthasar Castiglione* wrote his "Cortegiano", the ideal of a courtier; here, also, the erudite *Polydorus Vergilius* resided, and the artist *Federigo Baroccio*, who distinguished himself at Rome as a successful imitator of Raphael, was a native of Urbino (b. 1528), where he died in 1612. In 1626 the duchy was incorporated with the States of the Church, when Urban VIII. persuaded the last and childless Duke *Francesco Maria II.* to abdicate.

The town still contains much that recals its pristine splendour. The *Ducal Palace*, erected by *Luziano di Lauranna* in 1468 by order of Federigo Montefeitro, was at that period regarded as the finest structure of the description in Italy, and is still a most interesting example of the early Renaissance, remarkable for its symmetrical proportions and the rich decoration of its halls, windows, buttresses, chimney pieces (by *Francesco di Giorgio* and *Ambrogio Baroccio*, ancestor of the painter of that name) etc.

On the stair the statue of Duke Frederick. The library of the palace and other collections were transferred to Rome. The corridors contain a considerable collection of well-arranged inscriptions from Rome and the Umbrian municipia, established by the epigraphist *Fabretti*.

The *Cathedral possesses good pictures, by *Federigo Baroccio*, of St. Sebastian and the Eucharist, by *Timoteo della Vite* of St. Martin and Thomas à Becket, with a portrait of the duke.

S. Francesco contains pictures by *Giovanni Santi*, a Madonna with St. John the Baptist, St. Sebastian, St. Jerome and St. Francis, with three kneeling figures of the donors, members of the Ruffi family (not of the family of Raphael, as was formerly believed); St. Rochus and Tobias by *Timoteo della Vite*; also monuments of the princes of Urbino.

S. Francesco di Paola, with two pictures of *Titian*, the Resurrection and Eucharist. — *S. Giuseppe*, with a *Madonna, by *Timoteo della Vite*, and (in the oratario) a copy of Raphael's Sposalizio, by *Andrea Urbani*. — The *Oratorio of the Confraternità di S. Giovanni* is covered with paintings by *Lorenzo da S. Severino* and his brother, of the school of Giotto, History of the Virgin and John the Baptist. — The college near *S. Agata* contains an interesting picture by *Justus van Ghent*, a pupil of Van Eyck, of 1474. — In the church of **S. Bernardino*, 3|4 M. from the town, are the tombs of the Dukes Federigo and Guidobaldo; in the sacristy 13 painted panels, by *Antonio di Ferrieri* (1435), and the Dead Christ by *Giovanni Santi*.

Raphael's House is indicated by an inscription over the door. On one of the walls is seen a Madonna with sleeping Child, long regarded as an early production of Raphael, but ascertained to have been executed by his father *Giovanni Santi*. It is contemplated to erect in his native town a monument worthy of the great master, for which purpose a committee has for some years existed.

In the *Theatre*, formerly celebrated for its decorations by *Girolamo Genga*, the first Italian comedy was performed. This was the Calandra of Cardinal *Bibbiena* (or rather *Bernardo Dirizio* of Bibbiena in the Casentino, b. 1470, d. at Rome 1520), the friend of Pope Leo X. and patron of Raphael.

From the height of the *Fortezza* an interesting *survey of the sterile chain of the Apennines may be made.

From Urbino to *Fossombrone* (p. 78) diligence daily in 3 hrs.

From Pesaro to Ancona the line skirts the coast, occasionally approaching within a few paces of the sea, of which a pleasant view is afforded.

Fano *(*Il Moro; Tre Re)*, the *Fanum Fortunae* of antiquity, a cheerful little town, surrounded by ancient walls and deep fosse, as a watering-place more unpretending than Rimini.

The principal curiosity is the **Triumphal Arch of Augustus*, embellished with columns by Constantine. The harbour, once celebrated, is now insignificant.

Churches: **Cathedral of S. Fortunato*, the four recumbent lions in front of which formerly supported the pillars of the portico. In the interior the chapel of S. Girolamo (the 2nd to the l.) contains a monument of the Rainalducci family; nearly opposite (4th to the r.) is a chapel adorned with 16 frescoes by *Domenichino*, once admirable, now disfigured by restoration. In the chapel of the sacristy a Madonna with two saints, by *Lodovico Caracci*. — *S. Maria Nuova* possesses two fine paintings by *Pietro Perugino*. — *S. Paterniano*, with the Espousals of the

Virgin by *Guercino*. — *S. Pietro*, with frescoes by *Viviani;* in the chapel of the Gabrielli the Annunciation by *Guido Reni*.

The *Collegio Folfi* contains David with the head of Goliath by *Domenichino*, and copies of his frescoes in the cathedral.

From Fano to Gubbio and Foligno see below.

Beyond Fano the line crosses the river *Metaurus*, celebrated as the scene of Hasdrubal's defeat (B. C. 207), then, a short distance before stat. *Marotto*, it crosses the *Cessano*, and reaches

Sinigaglia *(Locanda della Formica)*, the *Sena Gallica* of the ancients, with 10,500 inhab. It was destroyed by Pompey during the Social War between Marius and Sulla, and also suffered frequent devastation during the middle-ages, so that it now presents quite a modern appearance. Pope Pius IX. (Conte Mastai-Ferretti) was born here (May 13th, 1792); also the celebrated singer Angelica Catalani (1784, d. at Paris July 13th, 1849). A fair which has been established for 600 years, is held here from July 30th to August 8th.

Stat. *Case Bruciate*. The train crosses the *Esino* and reaches stat. *Falconara*, where the line branches off to Rome and *Ancona*. For the description of the town and continuation of the journey see R. 11.

From Fano to Foligno and Rome viâ Gubbio.

The high-road which connects *Rome* with the *Valley of the Po* traverses the Umbrian plains of Terni and Spoleto, and then ascends the valley of the Topino and the Chiascio, until it reaches its culminating point on the Apennines. Descending on the E. side of that range it follows the course of the Metaurus to its mouth at Fano, after which it skirts the coast and leads N. to Bologna and the valley of the Po. It is identical with the ancient *Via Flaminia*, constructed B. C. 220 by the Censor C. Flaminius (who subsequently fell at the Battle of the Trasimene Lake, see p. 50), in order to secure the possession of the district of the Po which had been at that time wrested from the Gauls. This road is still one of the most important channels of local traffic in Central Italy, but since the completion of the Apennine Railway from Bologna to Florence, and the recently opened line from Ancona to Rome (R. 11), has been little frequented by tourists. It is, however, replete with natural attractions, and affords the traveller an opportunity of becoming acquainted with several towns which merit a visit on account of their monuments and historical associations. The most interesting points are Urbino, Gubbio, and the route across the Apennines from Fossombrone to La Schieggia.

From *Bologna* to *Fano* railway in $3^{3|_4}$ hrs., fares 17 l. 30, 13 l. 85, 10 l. 40 c. From *Fano* to *Fossato* (54 M.) corriere daily in about 10 hrs. From *Fossato* to *Foligno* railway in 2 hrs., fares 4 l. 60, 3 l. 20, 2 l. 30 c. From *Foligno* to *Rome* railway in 7—8 hrs., fares 19 l. 65, 12 l. 50, 9 l. 70 c. — From Fano diligence twice weekly to Perugia by Schieggia and Gubbio; thence diligence twice daily to Foligno (see p. 57).

The road to Foligno, the ancient *Via Flaminia*, leads on the N. bank of the *Metaurus*, the fertile valley of which is well cultivated, to Fossombrone, 17 M. distant. About 1 M. from the latter, near the church of *S. Martino al Piano*, was once situated the Roman colony of *Forum Sempronii*, of which but scanty remains now exist. After its destruction by the Goths and Lombards, it was superseded by

Fossombrone *(Posta)*, long under the dominion of the Malatesta family, until under Sixtus IV. it accrued to the States of the Church. It is now a prosperous little town with 4500 inhab. and silk-factories, charmingly situated in the valley, which here contracts, and commanded by a castle on the height above. Ancient inscriptions on the cathedral, in the Seminary etc. may be inspected. From Fossombrone to Urbino see p. 76; the road diverges to the r. at *Calmazzo*, 2 M. from Fossombrone. The Via Flaminia here crosses the *Metaurus*, which descends from the valley near *S. Angelo in Vado* from the N., and follows the l. bank of the *Candigliano*, which at this point empties itself into the Metaurus. The valley soon contracts; to the r. rises the hill of *Pietralata*, occasionally named *Monte d'Asdrubale*. Here according to the popular tradition, the memorable Battle of the Metaurus was fought, in which, B. C. 207, Hasdrubal, whilst marching to the aid of his brother Hannibal with 60,000 men, was signally defeated and slain by the consuls Livius Salinator and Claudius Nero. This was the great event which decided the 2nd Punic War in favour of Rome. The valley now becomes still more confined. At the narrowest portion, where the rocky walls approach so near each other as to leave space for the river only, is the celebrated **Furlo Pass* (Furlo from forulus = passage, the ancient *petra intercisa*), a tunnel 18 ft. broad, 15 ft. high and 40 yds. in length. The originator of the work was the Emp. Vespasian, as the inscription preserved at the N. entrance records *(Imp. Caesar. Augustus. Vespasianus. pont. max. trib. pot. VII. imp. XXVIII. cos. VIII. censor. faciund. curavit.).* A short distance beyond it stands the small church *Badia del Furlo*. 9 M. from Fossombrone, at the confluence of the Candigliano and *Burano*, is situated the village of *Acqualanga*. The road crosses the Candigliano and thenceforward follows the l. bank of the Burano. From this point to the lofty *Cagli* about 6 M. At the foot of the hill on which the latter is situated, an antique bridge, consisting of huge masses of rock, crosses a tributary brook.

Cagli *(Posta*, in the Piazza, charges according to bargain), a small town with about 3000 inhab., occupies the site of the ancient borough of *Cales* or *Calle*. S. Domenico contains one of the greatest works of *Giovanni Santi*, Raphael's father, a Madonna with saints, al fresco. The angel on the r. of the Madonna is said to be a portrait of the young Raphael. Likewise a Pietà with St. Jerome and Bonaventura, by the same master. *S. Francesco* and *S. Angelo Minore* also possess pictures worthy of inspection.

From Cagli to *Cantiano* 6 M.; in the church *della Collegiata* a Holy Family by *Perugino*.

Hence to La Schieggia 8 M. The road ascends considerably; culminating point upwards of 2300 ft. **Schieggia** is an insignificant place, deriving its sole importance from the roads which here converge. On *Monte Petrara*, in the vicinity, stand the ruins of the celebrated temple of *Jupiter Apenninus*, whose worship was peculiar to the Umbrians. Several bronzes and inscriptions have been discovered in the environs. The strange-looking *Ponte a Botte* (a cylinder above an arch), which here crosses a ravine, was constructed in 1805. Picturesque oak-plantations in the neighbourhood.

At La Schieggia the road divides: the ancient Via Flaminia descends to Foligno, another to Gubbio and Perugia. Descent from Schieggia to Gubbio 8 M.; from Gubbio a route of 13 M. back to the Via Flaminia (2 M. above Gualdo Tadino, p. 83), so that the digression by Gubbio for those proceeding to Foligno does not amount to more than 6—7 M. Another road leads (8 M.) from Schieggia to *Fossato* (p. 83). A single traveller without luggage may obtain a seat in the post-conveyance from Schieggia to Gubbio.

Gubbio *(Locanda di Spernichia)* is situated at the base of *Monte Calvo*, in a valley surrounded by mountains. The town (6000 inhab.) presents an entirely mediæval aspect, and the proximity of the Apennines imparts to it a more severe character than that of most Italian towns.

The ancient *Iguvium*, mentioned by Cicero and Cæsar, extended farther towards the plain. It was destroyed by the Goths, was in 1155 besieged by the Emp. Frederick I., became an independent state, subsequently belonged to the duchy of Urbino, and with it finally accrued to the States of the Church. A branch of the Umbrian school of painting flourished here, of which the principal representatives were *Sinibaldo Ibi*, *Ottaviano* and *Tommaso Nelli*, and *Nucci*. Majolica-painting also attained a high degree of perfection here.

The **Palazzo del Comune*, an imposing edifice erected in 1332—1340 by *Matteo di Giovanelli* of Gubbio, surnamed *Gattapone*, is at present disused. *View from the tower.

The *Ducal Palace, by *Luciano Lauranna*, the architect of the palace at Urbino, is constructed in a similar style.

The **Cathedral of S. Mariano e Jacopo Martire* contains fine pictures and carving; a Madonna with S. Ubaldo and S. Sebastian by *Sinibaldo Ibi*.

S. Maria Novella, with a Madonna by *Ottaviano Nelli* and frescoes by *Gentile da Fabriano*. The other churches *(S. Pietro, S. Francesco, S. Domenico)* also contain valuable pictures.

The collections of the Marchese *Rangiasci-Brancaleoni* in his palace in the upper part of the town, comprising pictures, antiquities etc. also merit a visit.

Outside the town are numerous ruins, among which a theatre, excavated a few years ago, appears to date from the republican period. Amidst its ruins the *Eugubian Tables were found in 1440, now preserved in the Palazzo Municipale. They are of bronze and bear inscriptions, 4 in Umbrian, 2 in Latin and 1 in Latin and Umbrian, which have long baffled the investigation of the learned. Their language as well as contents have given rise to the most conflicting doubts, which according to the works of *Maffei*, *Lanzi*, *Lepsius*, *Aufrecht* and *Kirchhoff* have not yet been solved. The characters are read from r. to l.

The celebrated miniature-painter *Oderisi*, termed by Dante in his Purgatorio (11,80) "l'onor d'Agobbio" was a native of Gubbio (d. about 1300).

The road to Perugia (23 M.) first traverses the plain of Gubbio and then a bleak, uninteresting hilly district, until it reaches the valley of the Tiber at *Busco*. It then crosses the Tiber near *Felcino*, and ascends to *Perugia*, which it enters by the Porta del Sole. Perugia, and from Perugia to Foligno, see p. 51.

The direct route from Schieggia to Foligno follows the grassy valley of the *Chiascio* as far as the small town of *Sigillo*. Stalactite-cavern in the vicinity. 3 M. farther is *Fossato*, a station on the Rome and Ancona line. Hence to Foligno see p. 83, from Foligno to Rome p. 61.

10. From Trieste to Ancona.

Steamboats of the Austrian Lloyd (Office in the Tergesteo, Via del Teatro) once weekly (1868, Tuesdays at 4 p. m.) on their route to Greece and the Levant; to Ancona average passage 15 hrs. Fares 1st cl. 17, 2nd cl. 12 florins Austr. currency (1 fl. = 2½ fr.); food extra (D. exc. W. 1 fl.). The vessels are clean and well fitted up, the service regular. Embarcation without additional expense at the Molo S. Carlo. — Italian vessels of the *Società Peirano Danovaro et Comp.* leave every Monday at 10 a. m. viâ Venice (where they stop 1½ day) for Ancona, arriving there early on Thursday.

Trieste. **Hotels.** **Hôtel de la Ville*, formerly Hôtel National, R. 1½ fl., L. 40, B. 70, A. 40 kr. (10 kreuzers = 6 of the old currency = 2½ d.), newly fitted up and well managed, with café and reading-room; Grand Hotel; Victoria Hotel; Hôtel de l'Aigle Noir; Hôtel de France, good restaurant, beer; Albergo Daniel (Eliseo), tolerable restaurant, beer.

Cafés. Hôtel de la Ville (see above); Specchi, Piazza Grande; Caffè al vecchio Tommaso, near the Hôtel de la Ville.

Restaurants, see above; also Toni, Zum Tiroler, both in the old town. Solder's Garden below the fort, beautiful view of the town and sea, music 2—3 times weekly.

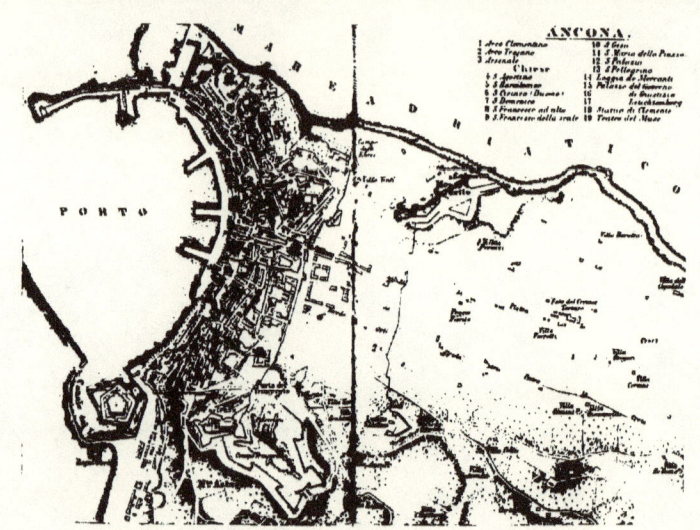

ANCONA. *11. Route.* 81

Carriage from the station to the town, one-horse 50 kr., two-horse 1 fl., at night 20 kr. more; in the town 1'/4 hr. 30—45 kr., 1'/2 hr. 50—80 kr., 3/4 hr. 75 kr. — 1 fl. 10 kr., 1 hr. 1 fl. — 1 fl. 30 kr., every additional 1'/4 hr. 20—30 kr.; luggage 20 kr.; drive in the town for 1—2 pers. usually 30 kr.

Description of the town and its objects of interest see Part I. of this Handbook *(Northern Italy)*.

As the harbour is quitted a retrospect is obtained of the charming situation of Trieste. To the N. appears the château of *Miramar*, once property of the unfortunate Emp. Maximilian of Mexico. To the S.E. the undulating, olive-clad coast of Istria; in the bay *Capo d'Istria* with an extensive house of correction. On an eminence the church of *Pirano*, supported by arches; the town (9000 inhab.) with its saltworks is picturesquely situated in a bay. Here the Venetians conquered the fleet of Frederick I. and took his son Otto prisoner.

The following points now become visible in succession: the lighthouse of *Salvore*; *Umago*; the château of *Daila*, property of the Counts of Grisoni; *Cittanova*; *Parenzo*, with remarkable cathedral, a basilica of 961, a town where 600 years ago the crusaders generally made their first halt; on an island the watchtower and deserted monastery of *S. Niccolò*; *Orsēra*, once an episcopal residence, situated on an eminence. In the distance to the E. rises *Monte Maggiore* (4400 ft.). The vessel gradually leaves the coast behind; *Rovigno*, a place of some importance, is the last point which is faintly distinguished.

Early on the following morning the Italian coast is approached: on the spurs of the Apennines the towns of *Pesaro*, *Fano* and *Sinigaglia* become visible; the vessel soon enters the harbour of Ancona (see below). Landing or embarcation 1 l. for each person with luggage.

11. From Ancona to Rome.

Railway in 13¹/4 hrs.; fares 33 l. 95, 24 l. 55, 16 l. 85 c.; to Foligno (14 l. 20, 9 l. 95 and 7 l. 10 c.) in 5 hrs., where a halt of ¹/2 hr. is made. Passport-formalities see p. 67.

Ancona (*La Pace, near the harbour, table d'hôte 3¹/2 l.; Vittoria, Strada Calamo, with trattoria, R. and L. 2, S. ¹/2 l.; Caffè del Commercio, near the theatre, 1st floor; Caffè Dorico, opp. the Exchange; Birraria Svizzera, in Piazza Cavour), the *Ancon* of the Greeks. i. e. "elbow", from the form of the promontory, whence to the present day an elbow forms part of the armorial bearings of the town, is beautifully situated between the promontories of *Monte Ciriaco* and *Monte Conero* or *M. Guasco*, and possesses an excellent harbour. Population 31,857, among whom 6000 Jews. As Ancona is a free harbour, luggage is examined at the gates on departure from the town; it is also the residence of a military commandant.

BAEDEKER. Italy II. 2nd Edition. 6

Ancona was founded by Doric Greeks from Syracuse, whence termed *Dorica Ancon* by Juvenal (Sat. IV. 40). Subsequently a Roman colony, it was furnished by Trajan with an enlarged quay. In the middle ages it repeatedly recovered from the ravages of the Goths and others, and in 1532 came into the possession of Pope Clement VII. through the instrumentality of Gonzaga. Ancona is also frequently mentioned as a fortress in the annals of modern warfare. Thus in 1796 it was surrendered to the French, in 1799 to the Austrians, in 1805 to the French again; in 1815 it was ceded to the pope, to whom it belonged till 1860. In 1832—38 the citadel was garrisoned by the French (under the Perier ministry), in order to keep in check the Austrians, who were in possession of Bologna and the surrounding provinces. In 1849 the town was the scene of many excesses, and on June 18th was re-captured by the Austrians; on Sept. 20th, 1860. after the Battle of Castelfidardo, it was finally occupied by the Italians.

On the old quay the marble *Triumphal Arch*, erected A. D. 112 by the Roman senate in honour of Trajan on the completion of the new wharf, as the inscription records, is still standing. It is perhaps the finest ancient work of this description which is preserved to us. Traces of the bronze decorations with which it was once embellished are still distinguished.

The new quay, constructed by Pope Clement XII, also boasts of a triumphal arch, from designs by *Vanvitelli*, but far inferior to the above-mentioned. The harbour is defended by several forts.

The *Cathedral of S. Ciriaco*, dedicated to the first bishop of Ancona, stands on a lofty site, once occupied by the Temple of Venus mentioned by Catullus (36, 13) and Juvenal (IV, 40), and contains the magnificent columns which once appertained to the ancient temple. The structure was begun in the 10th cent., the façade is of the 13th. The foremost columns of the beautiful Gothic portico rest on red lions. The octagonal dome is reputed the oldest in Italy. A crypt in the r. transept contains the *Sarcophagus of Titus Gorgonius*, Prætor of Ancona and Christian Antiquities; in the other transepts are the tombs of St. Cyriacus, Marcellinus and Liberius. Within a house in the vicinity, scanty remains of a Roman amphitheatre. The churches of *S. Francesco* and *S. Agostino* possess Gothic vestibules, and that of *S. Maria della Piazza*, built in the Romanesque style, is also well worth notice. The *Loggia de' Mercanti* (Exchange), designed by Tibaldi, has a Moorish aspect. The *Palazzo del Governo* contains a small picture-gallery. In the *Piazza di S. Domenico* stands a marble statue of Pope Clement XII. (Corsini, 1730—40), the especial benefactor of the town. Ancona is celebrated for the beauty of its women.

The train runs on the rails of the Ancona and Bologna line, which with the old high-road skirts the coast (r. a beautiful retrospect of the town and harbour), as far as stat. *Falconara*, situated on an eminence to the l. Here it diverges S.W. into the valley of the *Esino* (Lat. *Æsis*), which it soon crosses at stat. *Chiaravalle*, a small town with 3500 inhab. The following stat. is

Jesi, now one of the most prosperous manufacturing towns of the province, the ancient *Æsis*, where on Dec. 26th, 1194, the Emp. Frederick II., the illustrious son of Henry VI. and Constantia of Sicily, and grandson of Frederick Barbarossa, was born. The cathedral is dedicated to the martyr S. Septimius, who was the first bishop of the place in 308. Jesi was also the birthplace of the composer *G. Spontini* (b. 1778, d. 1851).

The valley gradually contracts, the line crosses the river twice. Stat. *Castel Planio*. Beyond stat. *Serra S. Quirico*, near *Monte Rosso*, the mountains approach so nearly together as barely to leave room for the road, which here passes through a wild ravine, frequently endangered by falling rocks. The railway penetrates Monte Rosso by a long tunnel, crosses the river repeatedly, and at length reaches the pleasant valley of

Fabriano *(Leon d'Oro; Campana)*, a prosperous town with 7500 inhab., celebrated for its paper-manufactories, situated in the vicinity of the ancient *Tuficum* and *Attidium*, towns long since destroyed. The Town Hall contains ancient inscriptions; the *Campanile* opposite bears an absurdly extravagant inscription with regard to the unity of Italy. The churches of *S. Niccolò, S. Benedetto, S. Agostino* and *S. Lucia*, as well as the private houses *Casa Morichi* and *Fornari*, contain pictures of the school of painting which flourished here. *Gentile da Fabriano*, the greatest master of the school, is remarkable for the softness and delicacy of his style. The Marchese *Possenti* possesses a collection of objects in ivory, which well merits a visit.

From Fabriano 10 M. to *Matelica*, a town with 4000 inhab.; the church of S. Francesco contains an altar-piece by Melozzo da Forli, and the Pal. Piersanti a small picture-gallery. From Matelica to Camerino 3 M., to San Severino 12 M.

From Fabriano a good mountain-road (9 M.) leads by the picturesque *La Genga* to the lofty **Sassoferrato**, situated in a fertile valley, consisting of the upper and lower town, with 2000 inhab., and possessing interesting churches and pictures. Here in 1605 *Giambattista Salvi*, surnamed *Sassoferrato*, was born. He afterwards became celebrated as an historical painter under the guidance of Domenichino and Guido Reni at Rome, and was especially noted for the beauty of his Madonnas. He died at Rome in 1685. His works show that he had carefully studied the older masters, especially Raphael. *S. Pietro* contains a Madonna by him. In the vicinity are the ruins of the ancient *Sentinum*, where, B. C. 296, the great decisive battle took place between the Romans and the allied Samnites, Gauls, Umbrians and Etruscans, on which occasion the consul Decius heroically sacrificed himself. The Roman supremacy over the whole of Italy was thus established.

Beyond Fabriano the line skirts the brook *Giano*, leads by a long tunnel through the central chain of the Apennines to *Fossato* (routes to Schieggia and Urbino see p. 79), and enters the broad valley of the *Chiascio*. To the l. on the height the village of *Palazzolo*, r. *Pellegrino*; farther on, l. *Talazzo, S. Facondino*, and stat. *Gualdo Tadino* (to Gubbio see p. 80), a small town with

7000 inhab., near which, about 2 M. from the railway, lie the insignificant ruins of the ancient *Tadinum*. Here in 552 Narses defeated and slew the Ostrogothic king Totilas, in consequence of which he soon afterwards gained possession of Rome. The church of S. Francesco contains an altar-piece by *Niccolò da Foligno*, of 1471. The cathedral possesses a fine rose-window; in the sacristy pictures by *Niccolò da Foligno*.

The line now gradually descends to stat. *Nocera*, an episcopal town, occupying the site of the ancient *Nuceria*, a city of the Umbri. In the vicinity are mineral springs, known since 1510. The narrow *Val Topina* is then entered, the brook crossed several times, a tunnel passed through, and the train descends by *Ponte Centesimo* to

Foligno, see p. 61; hence to Rome see p. 61.

Before the completion of the Ancona and Rome line, the mails were forwarded by the Ancona and Brindisi line as far as *Civitanuova* (in 1½ hr.; 4 l. 75, 3 l. 35, 2 l. 40 c.); thence by corriere to Foligno in about 10 hrs. It is not improbable that this regular communication between Civitanuova, Tolentino and Foligno will still be maintained.

The line from Ancona to Civitanuova penetrates the heights surrounding Ancona by means of a tunnel; 1. the promontory of *Monte Conero*, r. on the height the venerable town of *Osimo*, the ancient *Auximum*, 5 M. distant from the station. To the r. *Castelfidardo* soon becomes visible, where on Sept. 20th, 1860, the papal troops under Lamoricière sustained their well-known total defeat by the Italians under Cialdini.

Then *Loreto* and *Recanati* (described in Part I. of this Handbook). The line crosses the *Potenza*. Stat. *Potenza Picena*, named after a Roman colony once established in the vicinity, the ruins of which have now entirely disappeared. On the hill, 4 M. distant, lies *Montesanto*.

Stat. *Porto Civitanuova*, at the mouth of the *Chienti*; the town 1 M. inland.

The railway is here quitted. The road ascends the fertile valley of the Chienti, affording views of the rocky summits of the Central Apennines, snow-clad until late in summer. The *Sibilla* (6700 ft.) group first becomes visible. The country is admirably cultivated, the villages prosperous, but few antiquities or treasures of art are here encountered.

Macerata *(Pace; Posta)*, a flourishing town with about 20,000 inhab., capital of the province of Macerata, picturesquely situated on the heights between the valleys of the *Chienti* and *Potenza*, possesses a university, an agricultural academy etc.

In the *Cathedral* a Madonna with St. Francis and St. Julian, ascribed to *Perugino*. In *S. Giovanni* an Assumption of the Virgin by *Lanfranco*.

The *Palazzo Municipale* and the *Pal. Compagnoni* contain inscriptions and antiquities from *Helvia Ricina*, a Rom. colony, situated on the l. bank of the Potenza, 3 M. distant. — Macerata also possesses a triumphal arch, the *Porta Pia*.

Without the gate on the road to Fermo, a handsome building for the national game of the pallone; ¾ M. farther the church of the *Madonna della Vergine*, designed by *Bramante*.

The learned *Giovanni Crescimbeni*, founder of the Roman academy of Arcadians, was born here in 1663 (d. at Rome in 1728); likewise in 1552 the zealous missionary *Matteo Ricci* (d. at Pekin in 1609).

A good road leads from Macerata to Fermo (about 6 M.), crossing the *Chienti* and *Tenna*, and skirting the base of *Mont' Olmo*, birthplace (in 1732) of *Luigi Lanzi*, the erudite archæologist and connoisseur of art, who in 1807 was elected president of the Accad. della Crusca at Florence (d. 1810).

6 M. from Macerata (3 M. from Tolentino) is the village of *Urbisaglia*, the Rom. *Urbs Salvia*, with extensive ruins, amphitheatre, walls, baths etc.

The Rom. road continues to traverse a fertile tract on the bank of the *Chienti*, on both sides of which, not far from Tolentino, Joachim Murat, King of Naples, was defeated by the Austrians under Bianchi, May 3rd, 1815.

(12 M.) **Tolentino** (*°Corona*), the ancient *Tolentinum Picenum*, on the *Chienti*, with 4000 inhab., possesses a remarkable Gothic gateway, and was formerly strongly fortified. The town-hall in the Piazza contains a few antiquities. The cathedral of *S. Niccolò di Tolentino* is entered by a Gothic vestibule. In the interior rich carving on the ceiling and frescoes from the life of St. Nicholas, by *Lorenzo* and *Jacopo da San Severino*. The chapel of the saint contains two paintings, the conflagration of St. Mark's at Venice, and the Plague in Sicily, ascribed to *Tintoretto* and *Paolo Veronese* respectively. The environs are picturesque, and command fine views of the mountains.

Here the learned *Francis Philelphus* was born in 1388, one of the first scholars who studied and promoted the dissemination of classical litterature. On Feb. 19th, 1797, a treaty between General Buonaparte and the ambassador of Pope Pius VI. was signed, by which the latter ceded the Romagna with Ancona and Avignon, with the reservation of the legations of Bologna and Ferrara, to the French, as well as a number of works of art and MSS., which were partly restored in 1815.

From Tolentino to San Severino 6 M.; the road traverses the chain of hills which separate the valley of the Chienti from that of the Potenza. **San Severino**, which arose after the destruction of the ancient *Septempeda*, contains 4000 inhab. In the church *del Castello* frescoes by *Diotisalvi d'Angeluzzo*, and altar-piece by *Niccolò da Foligno* (1468); in the sacristy of the *Duomo Nuovo* a Madonna by *Pinturiccho*. *S. Lorenzo* stands on the site of an ancient temple. Inscriptions and antiquities in the townhall, and at the residence of the Conte *Servanze-Collio*.

From San Severino 10 M. to **Camerino** (diligence daily, 1 l.), the ancient *Camerinum Umbrorum*, situated on an eminence at the base of the Apennines. It was once the capital of the Umbrian Camertes, who during the Samnite wars allied themselves with Rome against the Etruscans. It is now the chief town of the province, with 5000 inhab., a university and (as early as 252) an episcopal residence. The cathedral of *S. Sovino* occupies the site of a temple of Jupiter; in front of it stands the bronze *Statue of Pope Sixtus V., of 1587. The painter *Carlo Maratta*, the last of the once celebrated Roman school, was born here in 1625 (d. at Rome in 1713).

From Camerino 6 M. to *La Muccia* on the Roman road; other roads lead to the small town of *Matelica* and to *Fabriano*.

The Roman road proceeds from Tolentino on the l. bank of the Chienti, through a pleasant district and numerous plantations of oaks, to *Belforte*, the post-stations *Vaicimara* and *Ponte della Trare*, and (18 M. from Tolentino)

La Muccia (Leone), the usual halting-place of the vetturini. The mountain slopes are studded with small villages on both sides. At *Getagno* the road begins to ascend, the district becomes barren and bleak (the vetturini here procure the aid of oxen). The passage of the Apennines from La Muccia to Foligno occupies about 6 hrs. by carriage. *Serravalle* lies in a narrow ravine; above it rise the ruins of an old castle. $1^1\vert_2$ M. farther are the sources of the *Chienti* (p. 84). The road now ascends to the grassy table-land of *Colfiorito* (Locanda di Bonelli), 2716 ft. above the sea-level, skirts a small lake, traverses a grove of oaks and descends somewhat abruptly by *Case Nuove* and *Pale* to Foligno. Above Pale towers the lofty *Sasso di Pale*, one of the last spurs of the Apennines. In descending, the road affords a beautiful *view of Foligno and the charming valley of the Clitunno. The road follows the course of the brook, and 1/2 M. from Foligno reaches the *Via Flaminia*, which leads to *Fano* by the Furlo Pass. From Foligno to Rome see p. 61.

12. Rome.

Arrival. Carriages with one horse for 1—2 pers. 80 c., for 3 pers. 1 l., after dark 20 c. additional. Small articles of luggage free, trunk 50 c.; facchino 25—40 c. — The landlords of the hotels and private houses give notice to the police of the arrival of travellers by showing their passports. — Before Rome is quitted, passports must be visé by the traveller's ambassador and by the police; charge for the latter 1 scudo; if the journey be postponed for 6 days, the visa must be renewed (gratis). Other visas are superfluous.

Consulates: English, Palazzo Poli; American, Piazza di Spagna 26.

Money. In Rome francs (lire), soldi and centesimi (1 lira = 20 soldi = 100 c.) are current. The papal silver coins (pieces of 2, 1, 1½ l., 5 soldi) are of the same value as the French and Italian. The copper coins are 5 soldi, 1 soldo, 2 c. Paper money (notes of 5, 10 l. etc.) has a low and very fluctuating rate of exchange; it is better to change gold into paper, as that is received everywhere. Besides these new coins the old pieces of 1 scudo = 10 = paoli = 100 bajocchi are still current. In silver there are also 1 scudo (generally Spanish pieces of 20 reals) = 5 l. 37½ c., ½ scudo (Spanish 10 real-pieces) = 2 l. 68 c., 2 paoli (papetto) = 21½ soldi, 1 paolo = 11 soldi, ½ paolo (grosso) = 5½ soldi. The old copper coins of 1,2, 1, 2 bajocchi are worth the same as the new (½, 1, 2 soldi). The old paper, notes (1, 5, 10 scudi etc.) are of the same value as the new. The equivalent worth in the new coinage is stated on the back of the note.

Bankers. Spada Flamini & Co., *Torlonia's successor*, Via Condotti, Palazzo Torlonia; Kolb (German), P. S. Luigi de' Francesi 64 (entrance in the Pozzo delle Cornacchie 63 A); Theop. Linder (Swiss), 9 Via Condotti. *Money-changers*: Corso 179 and 204, Via Condotti 92 etc.

Hotels. The best are in the *Strangers' Quarter*, between the Porta del Popolo and the Piazza di Spagna: °Isole Britanniche (Pl. a) in the Via Babuino, Piazza del Popolo; Albergo di Russia (Pl. b) in the Via Babuino; Albergo di Londra (Pl. c), a large establishment in the Piazza di Spagna; °Albergo di Europa (Pl. d) in the Piazza di Spagna; Albergo di Brighton (Pl. e), Via S. Sebastiano, below the Pincio; °Albergo d'Inghilterra (Pl. f), Via Bocca di Leone; °Albergo d'America (Pl. g), Via Babuino; Albergo di Washington (Pl. h), corner of the Via Carozza and the Via Bocca di Leone; °Albergo di Roma (Pl. i), Corso 128, newly fitted up, attendance good. In all the above the charges are about the same: R. 3 l. and upwards, table d'hôte 4—6 l., B. (comp. p. 87) 1½, A. 1 l. — Less pretending: Albergo d'Allemagna (Pl. k), Via Condotti 87, 88, especially adapted for families; Albergo di Vittoria (Pl. l); Albergo di Minerva (Pl. m), formerly Palazzo Conti, contiguous to the church of S. Maria sopra Minerva (the hotel is the property of the Jesuits and much frequented by the clergy), R. 2½ l. and upwards, B. 1, A. 1, °D. 4 l.; Albergo di Cesari (Pl. n), Via della Pietra, rooms only, no food or refreshments provided in the house, bargaining necessary. When a prolonged stay is made, an agreement with regard to charges had better be previously made with the landlord. Breakfast and dinner often better and less expensive at a café or restaurant. French spoken at all the hotels.

Private Apartments. The best are in the vicinity of the Piazza di Spagna and the Corso. *Karl Pochalsky*, Via del Corso 455, can be recommended for making arrangements. The most expensive and least sunny are those in the Corso, the Piazza di Spagna and the Via del Babuino. A northern aspect should most sedulously be avoided, and a stipulation made for stove, carpet and service (stufa, tapeti, servizio). Rent of two well-furnished rooms in a good locality 60—100 l. per month; for a suite of 3—5 rooms 100—300 l. Miss Smith, Piazza di Spagna 93, pens. 10 l. and upwards; Madame Tellenbach, Piazza di Spagna 51, pens. from 7 l. Artists generally reside in the V. Felice, Quattro Fontane and that neighbourhood. In the Forum of Trajan apartments with a sunny aspect may be obtained, conveniently situated with regard to the old part of the town. In the Casa Tarpeja or Protestant Hospital on the Capitol, comfortable apartments may also be procured. Those who engage apartments in the Corso should come to an understanding with regard to the windows for the Carnival. — Firewood at Ficchelli's, P. di Spagna 87, 11—12 l. per *mezzo passo*. — Rome possesses no directory; an unknown address may be ascertained at the police office. From the 1st Oct. till 1st April a List of Visitors appears three times weekly. Subscription per month 4 l. 30 c., 7 months 22 l. 60 c., at Filippo Martelli's Via Frattina 139.

Restaurants (Trattorie). Handsomely fitted up: Nazzari, P. di Spagna 81, 82; °Spillmann, V. Condotti, 10 and 12; °Alla Sala delle Colonne, Corso 116 (table d'hôte with half-bottle of wine 3 1/2 l.). Good refreshments may also be procured at the Caffè Roma, see below. Less pretending: °Falcone, P. di S. Eustachio 58, near the Pantheon; Lepre, V. Condotti 80; °Belle Arti, Via in Lucina, between Nos. 403 and 404 in the Corso; Europa, Via Mario de' Fiori; °Carlin, Via Felice 1. For moderate requirements: Torretta, Via della Torretta 1, near the Palazzo Borghese; Tre Ladroni, in the street of that name, No. 47 (between 248 and 249 in the Corso); Tre Re, Via S. Marco. French cuisine: Bédeau, V. Croce; Dufour, V. della Mercede 35; Sauvan, V. S. Sebastianello, Pincio 16; these last also supply families in their own apartments, °D. for 2 pers. 4—6 l. The waiter of a restaurant is named *cameriere*, in an osteria *bottega*. Attempts at imposition may be frustrated if a written account be asked for. The best restaurants contain a *lista* or bill of fare, generally however the waiter enumerates the viands verbally. The following are a few of the average charges: Zuppa 4—6 s., maccaroni 10 s., fritto (also half-portions) 10 s., pork (cinghiale, majale) and other kinds of meat "in umido" (with sauce) 12 s., pudding (dolce paste) 5—10 s., wine 4—5 s. per 1/2 foglietta. The waiter receives a donation of 2—4 s. from each pers.

The **Osterie** (wine-houses, comp. Introd.), where good wine of the country (6—10 s. per foglietta) and occasionally other refreshments (osteria con cucina) may be procured, are numerous, but of a very unpretending description. They may, however, be visited by those who desire an insight into the character of the lower classes. The most popular are those outside the gates, on Monte Testaccio (p. 191) etc., which attract a most motley assemblage of customers on Sundays and holidays. A few of those in the town may be mentioned: Caccia Bove, V. di Caccia Bove 9, near Piazza Colonna; Campanella, in the Marcellus Theatre (No. 35); Palombella, V. della Palombella 2, near the Pantheon. Wine of *Orvieto* 18 s., *Montefiascone* (Est est, comp. p. 37) 30 s., *Aleatico* 25 s. Foreign wines in the first-class restaurants.

Beer (birra), generally brewed and sold by Germans: Via de' due Macelli 74, V. di S. Giuseppe 23 etc. Also sold at the cafés.

Cafés. The best are: Café di Roma, Corso 120; Café Carlo, Corso 427; Café Greco, V. Condotti 86; Café Convertite, corner of Corso and V. delle Convertite; Café Nuovo. Corso 418a; Café Sciarra, Corso 320 (good ices). Other cafés in almost every street; coffee generally good; sent, if desired, to private apartments. "*Café forte*", which is usually placed before the stranger, is distinguished from that usually drunk by being served in better porcelain, and charged for at double the ordinary price. **Charges**: coffee without milk (café nero), with little milk (ombra di latte) or with an excess of milk (molto latte) 2 1/2—3 1/2 s.; mischio and aura (coffee with chocolate) 3 s.; chocolate 6 s. Breakfast at a café

6—8 s.; at an hotel 20—30 s. Bread and butter (pane al burro) 4 s., egg 3 s.; ices (gelato) about 6 p. m., in summer half-frozen (granita) in the morning; 1/2 portion 4, whole portion 8 s. Cool beverages: Limonata and Amarena. — *English Baker*, Via del Babuino 100; *German*, Via S. Claudio 88.

Gratuities. As the demands made on strangers in this respect are generally exorbitant, the following averages should be noticed. In the galleries for 1 pers. 10 soldi, for 2—3 pers. 15 s., for 4 pers. 1 l.; regular frequenters 5 soldi. To servants and others who open doors of houses, churches, gardens etc. 5 s.; if other services are rendered (guidance, explanations, providing light etc.), 1/2—1 l. — At the restaurants the usual fee to the waiter is 2 s.; at the osterie and cafés 1—2 s.

Baths at the hotels. Also in the V. Belsiana 64, V. Babuino 96, V. Ripetta 116. Bath 2 l., gratuity 5 s.

Physicians. Those who are attacked with fever, or other malady occasioned by local causes, are recommended to call in the aid of a skilful Italian medical man. M. Nardini, Pal. Doria on the P. Venezia (hrs. for consultation 3—4) is most successful in all cases of fever. Dr. Erhardt, Mario de Fiori 16; Dr. Taussig, Via del Babuino. *Surgeons:* Feliciani, S. Carlo al Corso 433; Mazzoni (accoucheur and operator) Mario de' Fiori 89. Well known American dentist: Dr. Burridge, Piazza di Spagna 5. — Information on this subject may be obtained of the principal booksellers etc.

Chemists: Sinimberghi, Via Frattina 135; Borioni, Via del Babuino 98; Cesanelli, Via del Marforio 87.

Booksellers. Spithœver, 84 and 85 Piazza di Spagna. English, French, Italian and German books; Monaldini, Piazza di Spagna 79, 80, and Piale, corner of the P. di Spagna and the V. del Babuino, both English books; Merle, Corso 348, for French, Gallarini, Piazza di Monte Citorio 19, for Italian literature. Rare old works may be purchased of Gallarini, Petrucci, Corso 148, and other dealers in second-hand books. — The *Osservatore Romano* is the most widely-circulated newspaper; office, Via dei Crociferi 48, near Fontana Trevi, to the r.

Books may be consulted or read in many of the public and private libraries but are not lent out. Scientific books may be obtained at the Archæological Institute; permission to use them may be procured of the secretaries, Prof. Henzen and Dr. Helbig. English reading-room at Piale's and Monaldini (see above); French circulating library at Merle's. — Bookbinders: Schmidt, Via Marroniti 10; Olivieri, Via Frattina 1.

Teachers of the Italian language: Dubois (speaks English and French), Via Babuino 154; Barghilione, Via Frattina 35; Ambrosi (speaks French and a little German), to be enquired for at the Capitol in the Archæological Institute. For ladies: Mademoiselle Losser, Via Calabraga 22.

With respect to instruction in *archaeology, ancient languages* etc., the secretaries of the Archæological Institution (p. 109) afford information. — *Musical Instruction:* piano, M. Bretschneider, Corso 437; singing, M. Mustafà (of the Sixtine Chapel), Via del Pellegrino 175; Alari, Via Copelle 2; violin, Ramacciotti, Via del Vantaggio 1.

Studios. *Sculptors:* Achtermann, Via de' Cappuccini 1; Galletti, Quattro Fontane 107; Galli, Piazza Pia 89; Giacometti, Piazza Barberini 41; Miss Hosmer, Via Margutta 5; Jerichau, Piazza del Popolo 2; Imhof, Piazza de' Cappuccini 9; Kopf, Vicolo degli Incurabili 9; Mayer, Corso 504; Pettrich, Via Basilio 71; Schöpf, Villa Malta; Schubert, Vicolo del Fiume 67; Steinhäuser, Piazza Barberini 12; Tadolini, Via del Babuino 150A; Tenerani, Quattro Fontane 14; Wolff, Quat. Fontane 151.

Artists: Bühlmann (landscape), Via de' Cappuccini 85; Böcklin (landscape), Via del Babuino 68; Consoni, Vicolo del Vantaggio 7; Corrodi (water-colours), Via dell' Angelo Custode 30; Dreber (landscape),

Passeggiata della Ripetta 35; Feuerbach, Passegg. della Ripetta 70; Hebert, Director of the French Academy, Villa Medici; Gunkel, Vigna del Papa Giulio, outside the Porta del Popolo; Lindemann-Frommel (landscape), Via del Babuino 39; Müller, Piazza Barberini 60; Overbeck, Via Porta Pia 43 (Sundays 11—1); Pasini, Via Sistina 68 (Saturdays 2—4); Podesti, Via di S. Claudio 86; von Rhoden, Via dell' Olmo 18; Riedel, Via Margutta 86; Romako, Villa Malta; Seitz, Via Cappuccini 1; Vanutelli, Via. Margutta 53B; Wittmer, Via delle Quattro Fontane 29.

Colours and Drawing-materials: Dovizielli, Via del Babuino 136 and Piazza di Spagna 43. *Paper:* Ricci, Corso 211, Piazza Colonna; Antonelli, Corso 229, Piazza Sciarra. — *Casts:* Leopoldo and Alessandro Malpieri, Corso 54 and 51. *Engraver:* Odelli, Via Angelo Custode 67. *Antiquities:* Castellani, Via Poli 88; L. Depoletti, Via del Leoncino 14; Martinetti, Via della Fontanella Borghese 36; Guidi, opp. the Thermæ of Caracalla, Via di Porta S. Sebastiano. *Imitations of ancient bronzes:* Hopfgarten, Via due Macelli 83; smaller works, Röhrich, Via Sistina 105. *Gold ornaments:* the celebrated Castellani, Via Poli 88, who also possesses an interesting collection of ancient golden trinkets, and executes imitations from Greek, Etruscan and Byzantine models; Ansorge, Via Condotti 2. *Cameos:* Saulini, Via del Babuino 96. *Mosaics:* Francescangeli, Via del Babuino 133; Gallandt, Piazza di Spagna 7; Barberi, Piazza di Spagna 98; Maglia, Via del Babuino 133. Jewellery, cameos, mosaics etc. may also be purchased at moderate prices in the Stabilimento Piazza Borghese 106. *Roman pearls:* Rey, Via del Babuino 122; Bartolini, Via della Scrofa 113.

Those who are desirous of studying, drawing or copying in Roman museums or private collections must procure a permesso, for which application must be made in writing, accompanied by a recommendation from the ambassador or consul. In the case of the papal museums etc. (Vatican, Lateran, Capitol) the necessary permission is granted by Monsgr. Pacca (maggiordomo of the pope) at his office in the Vatican (in the court of the loggia, under the arcades to the l., 9—1 o'cl.), the written application having been left there a day or two previously. In the case of private galleries application must be made to the proprietor (in French, if the applicant prefer), stating at the same time precisely which picture it is intended to copy, as well as the size and description of the copy. In some collections copies of the original size may not be made. Respecting this and similar regulations, information should be previously obtained from the custodian. The following is a formula of application to the Monsgr. Maggiordomo, and which may be also employed in framing a similar application to a principe or marchese, the address being made conformable to lay instead of clerical rank.

Eccellenza Revma,

Il sottoscritto che si trattiene a Roma con lo scopo di proseguire in questa capitale i suoi studj artistici (storici etc.) *si prende la libertà di rivolgersi con questa a Vra Eccellenza Revma pregando La perchè voglia accordargli il grazioso permesso di far degli studj* (dei disegni, delle notizie etc.) *nel Museo* (nella Galleria) *Vaticano* (Capitolino, Lateranense).

Sperando di essere favorito da Vra Eccellenza Revma e pregando La di gradire anticipatamente i più sinceri suoi ringraziamenti, ha l'onore di protestarsi col più profondo rispetto

Roma li . . . .
A Sua Eccellenza Revma
Monsignor Pacca
Maggiordomo di Sua Santità.

di Vra Eccellenza Revma
Ummo Obbmo Servitore
N. N.

The export of works of art, modern or ancient, is liable to supervision and duty. Smaller objects, which are packed with the traveller's ordinary luggage, usually escape notice; in other cases application is made

90   *Route 12.*   ROME.   *Theatres.*

to the Cav. *Bompiani*, Vicolo Vantaggio 1, who values the objects, and a request (*supplica*, *istanza*) is addressed to the minister of commerce (Via Larga, near Chiesa Nuova) to permit the export. The duty on articles of less value than 500 scudi is 2½ l., on articles of higher value a much heavier tax is generally levied. In order to be spared these vexatious formalities, the traveller may send his acquisition to the cabinet-maker *Teroni* in the Via Felice, who undertakes the packing and the payment of the tax in return for a moderate remuneration. — In the case of antiquities of considerable value, the traveller must communicate with the commendatore *P. E. Visconti*, commissario delle antichità di Roma, Via Belsiana 77, first floor.

Shops. *Photographs* (of statues, pictures, architecture etc.): S p i t h œ - v e r (p. 88); M o n a l d i n i (p. 88); C u c c i o n i, Via dei Condotti 18; S o m m e r & B e h l e s, V. Mario de' Fiori 28 and Corso 196. Less expensive, but occasionally not inferior: B e n c i n i, Ripetta 185. Photographs from drawings, Christian antiquities, ornaments etc.: S i m e l l i, Corso 509 and Via di S. Sebastiano 6. Portraits: A l e s s a n d r i, Corso 12; M a n g, Piazza di Spagna 9; U f e r, Via Felice 114; S o m m e r & B e h l e s (see above). — *Engravings:* at the S t a m p e r i a C a m e r a l e, Via della Stamperia 6, near Fontana Trevi. — *Opticians:* A n s i g l i o n i, Corso 150; S u s - c i p i, Corso 182. — *Watchmakers:* R e i f f e n s t e i n (from Geneva), Corso 233 (Piazza Sciarra); C l a u d i, Corso 345.

Clothing. Materials generally dear and of inferior quality. *Tailors:* S c h r a i d e r, P. di Spagna 29; E v e r t, P. Borghese 77; B r a s s i n i, Corso, adjoining Via Condotti. *Dress-maker:* V. N a n n i, V. dei Serviti 15. — *Shoemakers:* B r ü g n e r, P. Barberini 60; Z i e g l e r, Capo le Case 46; J e s i, Corso 129; B r a s i n i, Corso 137. — *Portmanteaus* etc.: P. di S. Silvestro 61. *Saddler* etc.: E t z o l d, Quattro Fontane 6. — *Milliners:* C l a r i s s e, Corso 166 (the best); B o r s i n i - D u p r è s, Corso 172. Less pretending: G a t t i, Corso 316; Q u a t t r i n i, Via Frattina 91 (straw-hat-warehouse). — *Ladies' dress:* R i p a r i, Corso 156; N a t a l e t t i, Piazza dei Prefetti. — *Roman shawls:* B i a n c h i, P. della Minerva 82 (also other Rom. silk wares); A m a d o r i, Via Condotti 72. — *Gloves:* P. di S. Lorenzo in Lucina 4 A, Via della Vite 10. — *Small wares* etc.: C a g i a t i, Corso 181. — *Lamps* etc.: F a u c i l l o n, Via di Propaganda 25.

Music etc. Instruments: H. S p i t h œ v e r, in the Monastery of S. Carlo al Corso (437), who also possesses an extensive musical lending-library. Italian musical lending-library, Corso 139. — *Strings:* S e r a f i n i, V. Tor Argentina 32 and P. Capranica.

Theatres. The largest is the T e a t r o A p o l l o near the Ponte S. Angelo. T e a t r o A r g e n t i n a, Via di Tor Argentina, not far from S. Andrea della Valle, and T e a t r o V a l l e, in the Sapienza, for operas and dramas. The smaller T. C a p r a n i c a, Piazza Capranica, M e t a s t a s i o, near the Via Scrofa in the Via d'Ascanio, V a l l e t t o (near the Teatro Valle) for operettas and comedies. Summer-performances (about 5 p. m.) in the M a u - s o l e u m o f A u g u s t u s, Via de' Pontefici, in the Ripetta (dramas and comedies). Three different companies: the first during the months of autumn. and winter till Christmas, the second till Lent, the third after Lent. Boxes, as usual in Italy, are generally let permanently, and visits there paid and received. Ladies frequent the boxes only, gentlemen the pit (*platea*). Particulars about prices etc. are published in the hand-bills.

Church Festivals. Details are contained in the *Diario di Roma* (50 c.) and *L'Année Liturgique* (1 l.), published annually. The best work on the ceremonies of the Holy Week and their signification is the: *Manuale delle cerimonie che hanno luogo nella settimana santa e nell' ottava di pasqua al Vaticano* (1½ l., also a French edition). Admission to the Sixtine Chapel, as well as to St. Peter's on great occasions (to the reserved part), is accorded only to gentlemen in uniform or evening-dress, to ladies in black dresses and black veils or black caps. Gentlemen stand; seats are reserved for ladies, but are only to be obtained by card during the Easter festivities, and on account of the great demand should be secured some

Church Festivals. ROME. *12. Route.* 91

time previously by application to a consul or banker. Overcoats are deposited in the cloak-room of the Sixtine Chapel (l\f2 l.). The concourse at Easter is generally immense. The *Pope* officiates in person three times annually: on Christmas-day, Easter-day, and the Festival of St. Peter and St. Paul (June 29th); four times annually he imparts his benediction: on Holy Thursday and Easter-day from the balcony of St. Peter's, on Ascension-day from the Lateran, and on Aug. 15th, the anniversary of the "Assumption of the Virgin", from S. Maria Maggiore. The most celebrated festivities are those of the *Holy Week*, from Palm Sunday to Easter-day, the most important of which take place in the Sixtine Chapel, accompanied by the music (*"lamentations"* etc.) of Palestrina and other old masters. The Pope is also present at a number of other festivals, on which occasions the papal band (*cappella papale*) performs. The following are the principal festivals:

January 1. Cappella Papale in the Sixtine, 10 a. m.
— 5. Cappella Papale in the Sixtine, 3 p. m.
— 6. Epiphany. Cappella Papale in the Sixtine, 10 a. m.; at 4 p. m. procession in Araceli.
— 17. S. Antonio Abbate (Pl. II, 25, near S. Maria Maggiore), benediction of domestic animals.
— 18. Anniversary of foundation of the chair of St. Peter, Cap. Papale in St. Peter's, 10 a. m.
— 21. S. Agnese fuori (p. 136).
February 2. Candlemas. Cap. Papale in St. Peter's, 9 a. m.

On Ash-Wednesday and every Sunday during Lent, Cappella Papale in the Sixtine at 10 a. m. The Lent sermons in Gesù (Pl. II, 16), S. Maria sopra Minerva (Pl. II, 16) and other churches are celebrated. Others are preached in the streets towards evening and in the Colosseum (on Fridays).
March. Every Friday at 12 the Pope repairs to St. Peter's to pray during the confession.
— 7. St. Thomas Aquinas, in S. Maria sopra Minerva (Pl. II, 16).
— 9. S. Francesca Romana (in the Forum).
— 16. Festival in the chapel of the Palazzo Massimi (Pl. II, 17) in commemoration of a resuscitation by S. Filippo Neri.
— 25. Annunciation. Cap. Papale in S. Maria sopra Minerva (Pl. II, 16)

Holy Week.

Palm-Sunday. Cappella Papale in St. Peter's, 9 a. m. Consecration of palms and procession, then mass. At 2 p. m. confession in the Lateran (Pl. II, 30).
Wednesday. Cappella Papale in the Sixtine, 3 p. m. Tenebræ and Miserere.
Holy Thursday. Cappella Papale in the Sixtine, 10 a. m. Towards noon the great benediction "Urbi et Orbi" from the loggia of St. Peter's. Then washing of feet in St. Peter's, immediately after a dinner to twelve pilgrims in the loggia of St. Peter's. Cappella Papale in the Sixtine, 3 p. m. Tenebræ and Miserere (Palestrina).
Good Friday. Cappella Papale in the Sixtine, 9 a. m. (music by Palestrina). At 3 p. m. Tenebræ and Miserere.
Saturday. Cappella Papale in the Sixtine, 9 a. m. Baptism of converted infidels and Jews in the Lateran.
Easter-Sunday. Cappella Papale in St. Peter's, 9 a. m. The pope appears in the church at 10 o'clock and reads mass. The elevation of the host (about 11) is accompanied by the blast of trumpets from the dome. The pope is then carried in procession from the church, and about noon imparts the benediction Urbi et Orbi from the loggia of St. Peter's. After sunset illumination of the dome of St. Peter's, 1 hr. later torches are substituted for the lamps (the so-called cambiamento).
Easter-Monday. Cappella Papale in the Sixtine, 9 a. m. About 8 p. m. "girandola" in S. Pietro in Montorio.

Easter-Tuesday. Cappella Papale in the Sixtine, 9 a. m.
Saturday in Albis. Cappella Papale in the Sixtine, 9 a. m.
April 25. Procession of the clergy from S. Marco (Pl. II, 16) to St. Peter's at 7. 30 a. m.
May 26. S. Filippo Neri. Cappella Papale in the Chiesa Nuova, 10 a. m.
Ascension. Cappella Papale in the Lateran. Great benediction from the loggia.
Whitsunday. Cappella Papale in the Sixtine, 10 a. m.
Trinity. Cappella Papale in the Sixtine, 10 a. m.
Corpus Domini (*Fête de Dieu*). Procession of the Pope and clergy round the piazza of St. Peter's, 8 a. m.
June 1, 17, 21. Cappella Papale in the Sixtine in commemoration of Gregory XVI., and the accession and coronation of Pius IX.
— 24. John the Baptist. Cappella Papale in the Lateran, 10 a. m.
— 28. Eve of St. Peter and St. Paul. Cappella Papale in St. Peter's, 6 p. m.
— 29. Day of St. Peter and St. Paul. — Forenoon, Cappella Papale in St. Peter's. Evening, girandola in S. Pietro in Montorio.
July 14. S. Bonaventura, in S. S. Apostoli.
— 31. S. Ignazio, in Gesù.
Aug. 1. St. Peter in Vinculis, in S. Pietro in Vincoli (Pl. II, 23).
— 5. S. Maria della Neve, in S. Maria Maggiore (Pl. II, 25).
— 15. Assumption of the Virgin. Cappella Papale in S. Maria Maggiore (Pl. II, 25), 9 a. m.; great benediction from the loggia.
Sept. 8. Nativity of the Virgin. Cappella Papale in S. Maria del Popolo (Pl. 1, 18), 10 a. m.
— 14. Elevation of the Cross, in S. Marcello (Pl. II, 16).
Oct. 7. S. Marco, in the church of that saint (Pl. II, 16).
— 18. S. Luca, in the church of that saint (Pl. II, 20).
Nov. 1. All Saints' Day. Cappella Papale in the Sixtine, 10 a. m. and 3 p. m.
— 2. All Souls' Day. Cpapella Papale in the Sixtine, 10 a. m.
— 3. Requiem for former popes. Cappella Papale in the Sixtine, 10 a. m.
— 4. S. Carlo Borromeo. Cappella Papale in S. Carlo, 10 a. m.
— 5. Requiem for deceased cardinals in the Sixtine.
— 7. Requiem for deceased singers of the cappella papale in the Chiesa Nuova (Pl. II, 10).
On the 4 Sundays of Advent Cappella Papale in the Sixtine, 10 a. m.
Dec. 8. Conception. Cappella Papale in the Sixtine, 3 p. m. Procession from Araceli (Pl. II, 20).
— 24. Christmas Eve. Cappella Papale in the Sixtine, 8 p. m. Towards midnight, solemnities in Araceli, about 3 a. m. in S. Maria Maggiore (Pl. II, 25).
— 25. Christmas Day. Cappella Papale in St. Peter's, 9 a. m.; elevation of the host announced by trumpets in the dome.
— 26. St. Stephen's Day. Cappella Papale in the Sixtine, 10 a. m.
— 27. St. John the Evang. Cappella Papale in the Sixtine, 10 a. m.
— 31. Cappella Papale in the Sixtine; after which, about 4 p. m.; grand Te Deum in Gesù (Pl. II, 16).

Popular Festivals (which have lost much of their former interest):

Epiphany (Jan. 6), celebrated in the evening near S. Eustachio (Pl. II, 13): array of booths and prodigious din of toy-trumpets.

The Carnival extends from the 2nd Saturday before Ash-Wednesday to Shrove-Tuesday and consists in a daily (Sundays and Fridays excepted) procession in the *Corso*, accompanied by the throwing of bouquets and comfits, and concluding with a horse-race; the last evening is the Moccoli- (taper) evening. A window in the Corso is the best point of view; most animated scene between Piazza Colonna and S. Carlo; balconies there in great request and dear (as high as 200 l.); single places are let on the balcony of the Café Nuovo, fitted up for the occasion.

The October Festival, formerly celebrated, now comparatively insignificant, takes place during the vintage-season, and consists in singing, dancing and carousals at the osterie at the gates (e. g. on the Testaccio); at the Villa Borghese tombola and dancing.

Street-scenes. The "Spanish Staircase" (Pl. I, 20) is the focus of favourite artists' models, most of whom are Neapolitans. Their costumes are a well-known subject of photographs and pictures.

The *Campagnole* are one of the most singular apparitions in the streets of Rome. They pass a great part of their lives on horseback, whilst tending their herds of oxen, horses etc. Their equipment usually consists of a low felt-hat, wide, grey mantle, leathern leggings and spurs; in their hands "il pungolo", or iron-pointed goad for driving their cattle. The peasants of remote mountain-districts, wearing sandals (whence termed *ciocciari*), and with swathed feet and ankles, also present a most grotesque appearance. The favourite haunts of the country-people are in front of the Pantheon (Pl. II, 16) and the Piazza Montanara (Pl. II, 17) below the Capitol. The *pifferari* (bag-pipers) of the Abruzzi, attired in faded brown cloaks, pointed hats and sandals, and often a sore trial of patience to their auditors, become most conspicuous towards Christmas. They wander from morning to night in pairs, from one image of the Madonna to another, the elder with the bag-pipes, the younger with a species of clarionet or reed-pipe. Whilst the former plays the melody, the latter half sings, half recites a prayer, producing at intervals, by way of variation, the most excruciating tones from his instrument. This is repeated 9 times, and each Madonna is thus greeted 3 times daily. At Christmas the pifferari extract their modest remuneration from the citizens. Between Christmas and New Year's Day they again commence their operations, and after a few days depart with their spoil to their miserable homes, or in some cases to another sphere of action.

Promenades. The most frequented is Monte Pincio (Pl. I, 18), where a military band plays daily one hour before sunset. Of the villas the most popular is the Borghese, to the r. without the Porta del Popolo. With regard to the other villas, information is contained in the paragraph on that head. Within the walls the space from the forum to the Porta S. Sebastiano and on the other side as far as the Lateran and S. Croce. Monte Testaccio (Pl. III, 13). Environs (see R. 13). Points of view on the l. bank: Villa Medici (Pl. I, 18), Basilica of Constantine (Pl. II, 20), Palatine (Pl. II, 21), piazza in front of the Lateran (Pl. II, 30), Monte Testaccio (Pl. III, 13); on the r. bank: S. Pietro in Montorio (Pl. II, 13), Acqua Paola (Pl. II, 12), S. Onofrio (Pl. II, 7). Fine views are in fact commanded by almost every elevated spot.

Fiacres and Omnibuses. Comfortable one-horse conveyances are to be found in every piazza. Tariff: drive in the town for 1—2 pers. 16 s., for 3 pers. 1 l.; per hour (1—3 pers.) 1 l. 70 c.; after sunset per drive, 1—2 pers. 1 l., 3 pers. 1 l. 20 c.; per hour (1—3 pers.) 2 l. 20 c. Two-horse: drive in the town for 1—5 pers. 1 l. 50 c.; per hour (1—5 pers.) 2 l. 20 c.; after sunset per drive, 1—5 pers. 1 l. 70 c.; per hour 2 l. 70 c. Small articles of luggage free, box 50 c. For a drive within 3 M. of the gates one-horse carr. 2 l. 20 c. per hour, after sunset 2 l. 70 c. Two-horse carr. 2 l. 70 c. per hour, after sunset 3 l. 20 c. For longer distances no tariff, bargain with driver necessary; the charges by time within the walls serve, however, as a standard. The charge for a drive on the Corso, in a two-horse carr., during the afternoons of the carnival-week is not fixed by tariff. The driver (vetturino) is bound to furnish the passengers with his number before starting (generally neglected). Each vehicle is provided with a tariffa in Italian and French. Omnibuses: from the Piazza del Popolo (p. 109; Pl. I, 18) to the P. del Gesù (p. 124; Pl. II, 16) and thence to the Vatican (Pl. I, 4), fare 3 s., a line recently opened. From the P. di Venezia omnibus every 1/2 hr. to S. Paolo fuori le Mura (p. 193), fare 6 s. On Sundays and holidays, after 2 p. m., omnibus every 1/2 hr. between Ponte Molle and P. di Popolo (p. 109), fare 7 s. Omnibus from Monte Citorio (p. 117) to the railway-station 1/2 hr. before the departure of each train, also from the railway-station to Monte Citorio $1\frac{1}{2}$ hr. after the arrival of a train.

English Church Service performed by a resident chaplain. *Church* on the l., outside the Porto del Popolo.

Post and Telegraph Office. Post Office (Piazza Madama) open daily from 9 to 5, on Sundays from 9 to 11 o'clock. Letters within the frontier 20 c. Stamped letters are put into the box r. of the yard near the office-window, not into the outside one close by the principal entrance. Poste restante letters are obtained at the section indicated by the initial letter of the addressee's name, which should be written in large and distinct characters.

Telegraph Office (open day and night), Piazza di Monte Citorio 121. Charge for a single telegram (20 words) within the Papal States 1 l., within the kingdom 3 l., to Paris 5 l., to Austria 6 l., to Berlin 6 l., to London 15 l.

Cigars. Travellers may bring 100 across the frontier for their own use. In Rome the *Spaccio Normale*, or government-shop, is the best. *Zigari forti* (1 s.) and *Zigari scelti* ($1\frac{1}{2}$ s.) are the inferior qualities. Genuine cigars are expensive. Cigars and matches are vended in the cafés by the *Zigarraro*.

Vetturini, in the Piazza della Stelletta and Via dell' Orso, in the *Campana*, Via della Campana 20, all in the Via Scrofa; also Monte Citorio 124, whence omnibuses run daily to Tivoli and Subiaco. Written contract necessary (comp. Introd.)

Railways. Lines at present in use to Civita-Vecchia (R. 2), Naples, Frascati (R. 13) and Foligno, and Ancona (R. 11). Time-tables (Guida dei Viaggiatori, 60 c.) at the office, Piazza di Monte Citorio 128 (Pl. I, 16), where every information may be obtained. Omnibuses run thence in connection with the trains to the station (Piazza di Termini, not far from S. Maria Maggiore) (35 c.). — Travellers are recommended to be at the station $1\frac{1}{2}$ hr. before the departure of the train.

Steamboats. The small vessels which ply on the Tiber cannot be relied on for punctuality on account of the frequent variations in the state of the river. Inquiries should be made in the post-office buildings, at the entrance of the Piazza Madama, immediately to the l. on the ground-floor.

Of the steamers from Civita-Vecchia to Naples, Leghorn and Genoa those of the *Messageries Impériales* (Office, Via della Fontanella Borghese 45) are somewhat more expensive, but more comfortable and punctual than those of the other companies (*Valery Frères*, Rosati, Via Condotti 91; *Fraissinet*, Sebasti, P. Nicosia 43; *Italian Co.*, Freeborn, V. Condotti 11). Fares of the latter companies reduced according to bargain. — G o o d s - a g e n t s: *De Antonis*, P. di Pietra 34; *Caldani*, P. di Pietra 38; *Tombini & Pruckmayer*, V. Scrofa 23.

The following are the principal attractions which should be visited by those whose time is limited.

C h u r c h e s: St. Peter's (217), S. Giovanni in Laterano (p. 202), S. Maria Maggiore (p. 140), S. Lorenzo fuori le Mura (p. 142), S. Paolo fuori le Mura (p. 193), Sixtine Chapel (p. 235). S. Agostino (p. 151), S. Clemente (p. 200), S. Croce in Gerusalemme (p. 144), S. Maria degli Angeli (p. 137), S. Maria in Araceli (p. 168), S. Maria sopra Minerva (p. 155), S. Maria della Pace (p. 158), S. Maria del Popolo (p. 110), S. Maria in Trastevere (p. 232), S. Onofrio (p. 223), S. Pietro in Vincoli (p. 146), S. Prassede (p. 141), S. Trinità de' Monti (p. 112).

P a l a c e s: Palazzo della Cancelleria (p. 161), Farnese (p. 162), Giraud (p. 215), di Venezia (p. 122).

R u i n s: Forum (p. 171), Colosseum (p. 177), Imperial Palaces (pp. 185, 188), Cloaca Maxima (p. 186), Thermæ of Titus and Caracalla (p. 180 and 195),

Pantheon (p. 153), Theatre of Marcellus (p. 167), Forum of Trajan (p. 182), the so-called Temple of Neptune (p. 117), Pyramid of Cestius (p. 190). — Catacombs of S. Calisto (p. 250).

Museums of the Vatican (p. 234), Capitol (p. 208), Lateran (p. 204), Villa Ludovisi (p. 127), Albani (p. 129), Borghese (p. 124), Palazzo Spada (p. 163).

Pictures: Raphael's Loggie and Stanze (p. 237). the Farnesina (p. 225), galleries of the Vatican (p. 252) and Capitol (p. 210), of the Palazzo Borghese (p. 148), Barberini (p. 131), Doria (p. 119) and Sciarra (p. 117).

Promenades: Monte Pincio (p. 110), Villa Borghese (p. 124), Pamfili (p. 229). Via Appia (p. 194). Views from the Belvedere of the Villa Medici (p. 112) and from S. Pietro in Montorio (p. 228).

With regard to the visits which may best be combined the plan should be studied and the annexed lists consul.ed.

Collections, Villas etc.

*Albani, Villa (p. 129), antiquities and pictures, Tuesdays, with permission, obtained at the Palazzo Torlonia (p. 122).

*Borghese, Palazzo (p. 148), picture-gallery, daily 9—2 o'clock, Saturdays and Sundays excepted.

*Borghese, Villa (p. 124), garden daily; statues in the casino Saturdays. in winter 1—4, in summer 4—7 o'clock.

*Barberini, Palazzo (p. 131), picture-gallery, Mondays, Tuesdays and Wednesdays 12—5. Thursdays 2—5, Fridays and Saturdays 10—5 o'clock, closed at dusk in winter.

*Capitoline Museum (p. 208), daily 9—4 (fee); Mondays and Thursdays (gratis), in winter 12—3, in summer 3—6 o'clock.

*Colonna, Palazzo (p. 121), picture-gallery daily, Mondays, Thursdays and Saturdays 11—3 o'clock.

Conservatori, Palace of the (p. 209), same time as Capitoline Museum, see above.

*Corsini, Palazzo (p. 226), picture-gallery, daily 9—12 o'clock.

*Doria, Palazzo (p. 119), picture-gallery, Tuesdays and Fridays 10—2 o'clock.

Farnese. Palazzo (p. 162), frescoes by Ann. Caracci, admission not always granted.

*Farnesina, Villa (p. 224), Sundays 10—3 o'clock.

Kircheriano, Museo (p. 118, ladies not admitted), collection of antiquities, Sundays 10—11 o'clock.

Lateran, Collections of the (p. 204), daily 9—4 o'clock.

S. Luca, Accademia di (p. 181), daily 9—5 o'clock.

*Ludovisi, Villa (p. 127), collection of ancient sculptures, Thursdays, in winter only, with permission obtained through ambassador or consul.

Massimo, Villa (p. 207), frescoes, accessible by leaving visiting-card at the Palazzo Massimo (p. 159).

Massimi alle Colonne, Palazzo (p. 159), best time 9—11 a. m.

96   *Route 12.*   ROME.   *Diary.*

Medici, Villa (p. 112), collection of casts, daily, except Saturday, 8—12 o'clock, and afternoon till dusk.
**Palatine, Excavations of the Imperial Palaces* (pp. 185, 188), Thursdays, visiting-card presented at entrance.
**Pamfili, Villa Doria* (p. 229), garden (in the casino a few statues), Mondays and Fridays, two-horse carriages also admitted.
Quirinale, Palazzo Apostolico al (p. 133), daily 9—2 o'clock, afternoon till 2 hrs. before sunset, with permission (separate permission for garden and palace) obtained through ambassador or consul.
Rospigliosi, Palazzo (p. 134), picture-gallery in the casino, Wednesdays and Saturdays 11—3 o'clock.
**Sciarra - Colonna, Palazzo* (p. 117), picture - gallery, Saturday 11—3 o'clock. Generally inaccessible in summer.
Spada alla Regola, Palazzo (p. 163), antiquities and picture-gallery, daily 10—2 o'clock.
** *Vatican Collections* (p. 234), daily 9—3 o'clock, except on Sundays and high festivals; Monday 12—3 (gratis), with the exception of the picture-gallery, which is then closed.

Diary.

(To be compared with the preceding alphabetical list.)

Daily open, except Sunday: In the Vatican: Museum (p. 179) 9—3; Etruscan Museum (p. 250) 9—3, except Monday; Library (p. 254) 12—3; Raphael's Loggie and Stanze (p. 237) 9—3. Sixtine Chapel (p. 235) 9—3. Capitoline Museum (p. 208) and Palace of the Conservatori (p. 209) in winter 9—5, in summer 9—7. Collections of the Lateran (p. 204) 9—3. Academy of S. Luca (p. 181) 10—3. Galleria Corsini (p. 226) 9—3. Galleria Borghese (p. 148) 9—2, except Saturdays. Galleria Colonna (p. 121) 11—3. Galleria Spada (p. 163) 10—3. Galleria Barberini (p. 131) Mon., Tues. and Wed. 11—5, Thurs. 2—5, Frid. and Sat. 10—5. — Villa Borghese (p. 124), except Mondays. Villa Wolkonsky (p. 208).

Mondays: Vatican Collections (p. 234) gratis, 12—3. Capitoline Museum (p. 208) and gallery of the Palace of the Conservatori (p. 209) gratis (the hours vary with the Roman time between 12—3 and 4—7). Villa Pamfili (p. 229).

Tuesdays: Galleria Doria (p. 119) 10—3. Villa Albani (p. 129).

Wednesdays: Casino Rospigliosi (p. 134) 12—3. Villa Torlonia (p. 136).

Thursdays: Capitoline Museum (p. 208) and gallery of the Palace of the Conservatori (p. 209), as on Mondays. Imperial palaces on the Palatine (pp. 185, 188). Villa Ludovisi (p. 127).

Fridays: Galleria Doria (p. 119) 10—8. Gall. Sciarra (p. 117) 12—3 (in summer). Villa Pamfili (p. 229).
Saturdays: Galleria Sciarra (p. 117) 12—3 (in winter). Casino Rospigliosi (p. 135). Antiquities in the Casino of the Villa Borghese (p. 124), hours as on Mondays in the Capitol. Museum.
Sundays: Farnesina (p. 225) 10—3. Museo Kircheriano (p. 118) 10—11. Catacombs of S. Calisto (p. 259) and S. Agnese etc. (p. 260). Overbeck's studios 2—4 (p. 89).

P r e l i m i n a r y D r i v e. The stranger should engage a vehicle for 2—3 hrs. (tariff, p. 93) and drive down the Corso as far as the Piazza di Venezia, through the Via di Marforio to the Forum, past the Colosseum, through the Via di S. Giovanni in Laterano to the Piazza in front of the church, commanding a fine view of the Alban Mts.; then through the Via in Merulana, passing S. Maria Maggiore, through the Via di S. Maria Maggiore, Via di S. Lorenzo in Paneperna, Via Magnanapoli, across the Forum of Trajan through the Via di S. Marco, Via delle Botteghe Oscure, across the Piazza Mattei with handsome fountain, through the Via de' Falegnami, P. S. Carlo, Via de' Pettinari, by Ponte Sisto to Trastevere, through the Longara to the Piazza di S. Pietro, then through Borgo Nuovo across the Piazza Pia, past the Castle of S. Angelo, over the Ponte S. Angelo, through the Via Tordinone etc. in a straight direction back to the Corso.

History of the City of Rome †.

As the more remote history of Italy is involved in much obscurity, so also the origin of the city of Rome is to a great extent a matter of mere conjecture. It was not till a comparatively late period that the well known legend of Romulus and Remus was framed, and the year B. C. 753 fixed as the date of the foundation. In all probability, however, Rome may lay

---

† Works on the history and topography of Rome, especially of the ancient city, are extremely numerous. On the revival of science many scholars devoted themselves with the utmost zeal to antiquarian research: thus Poggio (1440), Flavio Biondo, Lucio Fauno. The most important of the earlier works is that of Nardini ("Roma antica", 1660; 4th ed. by Nibby, 1818). The following are the most eminent Roman writers on the subject of the present century: C. Fea, "Nuova Descrizione di Roma Antica e Moderna", 1820; Canina, "Indicazione Topografica", 3rd ed. 1841; also Nibby, "Roma nell' anno 1838", 3 vols., 1843. — The most exhaustive German work on the subject, and one which has generally formed the basis of all subsequent investigations, is that commenced under Niebuhr's auspices and contributed to, by Platner, Bunsen, Gerhard, Röstell and Urlichs (3 vols., Tübingen 1830—42). Subsequent discoveries have been made by W. A. Becker ("Topographie", Leipzig 1843), L. Preller and other learned archæologists. The article on "Ancient Rome" in Smith's Dict. of Greek and Roman Geography (also pub. separately, 1864) affords a clear and intelligent view of the subject. — Mediæval Rome has been treated of far less frequently. The standard works on the subject are perhaps those of Gregorovius (6 vols., Stuttgart, 1858—65) and Reumont (3 vols., Berlin, 1867), both extensive works of great merit.

claim to far greater antiquity. We are led to this conclusion, not only by a number of ancient traditions, but also by the recent discovery in Latium of relics of the flint-period, an epoch far removed from any written records. The Palatine was regarded by the ancients as the nucleus of the city, around which new quarters grouped themselves by slow degrees. Here Romulus is said to have founded his city, the Roma Quadrata of which Tacitus (Ann. 12, 24) states the supposed extent. Modern excavations have brought to light portions of its wall, as well as a gateway and the street of Victoria which pertained to the most ancient settlement (see pp. 183, 188). After the town of Romulus on the Palatine, a second, inhabited by Sabines, sprang up on the Quirinal, and the two were subsequently united into one community. Whilst each retained its peculiar temples and sanctuaries, the Forum, situated between them, and commanded by the castle and the temple of Jupiter on the capitol, formed the common focus and place of assembly of the entire state, and the Forum and Capitol maintained this importance down to the latest period of ancient Rome. The rapid growth of the city is mainly to be attributed to its situation, the most central in the peninsula, alike adapted for a great commercial town and for the capital of a vast empire. The advantages of its position were thoroughly appreciated by the ancients themselves and are thus enumerated by Livy (5, 54): "flumen opportunum, quo ex mediterraneis locis fruges devehantur, quo maritimi commeatus accipiantur, mare vicinum ad commoditates nec expositum nimia propinquitate ad pericula classium externarum, regionum Italiae medium, ad incrementum urbis natum unice locum." The Tiber was navigable for sea-going ships, as far as Rome, whilst its tributaries, such as the Anio, Nera, Chiana and Topino, contained sufficient water for river vessels, which maintained a busy traffic between Rome and the interior of the peninsula. The state of these rivers has, however, in the course of ages undergone a complete revolution, chiefly due to the gradual levelling of the forests on the mountains, and at the present day the lower part only of the Tiber, from Orte downwards, is navigable.

Whilst the origin of the capital of the world is referred to Romulus, its extension is attributed with something more of certainty to Servius Tullius. Around the twin settlements on the Palatine and Quirinal, extensive suburbs on the Esquiline and Caelius, as well as on the lower ground between the hills, had sprung up; for not only were numerous strangers induced to settle permanently at Rome on account of its commercial advantages, but the inhabitants of conquered Latin towns were frequently transplanted thither. Out of these heterogeneous elements a new civic community was organized towards the close of the period of the kings, and its constitution commemorated by the erection of the Servian wall, considerable remains of which are still extant. This structure, which was strengthened by a moat externally and a rampart within, is of great solidity. It enclosed the Aventine (p. 189), the Caelius, Esquiline, Viminal, Quirinal (p. 132) and Capitol and is computed to have been about 7 M. in circumference. Whilst care was taken thus to protect the city externally, the kings were not less solicitous to embellish the interior with handsome buildings. To that period belongs the Circus in the valley between the Palatine and the Aventine (p. 188), and above all the Cloaca Maxima (p. 186), destined to drain the swampy site of the Forum, and still admired for its massive construction. This vigorous and brilliant development of the city under the kings of the Tarquinian family in the 6th cent. B. C. came to a close with the expulsion of the last king Tarquinius Superbus (509).

During the first century of the republic the united efforts of the citizens were directed to the task of establishing themselves more securely in the enjoyment of their new acquisitions; and in this they succeeded, although not without serious difficulty. It was a hard and bitter period of probation that the nation had to undergo in the first enjoyment of its new liberty, and it was not till the decline of the Etruscan power that Rome began to breathe freely again. After protracted struggles she succeeded in conquering and destroying her formidable rival Veii (396), a victory by which the Roman supremacy was established over the south of Etruria as far as the Ciminian Forest. Shortly afterwards (390) the city, with the exception of the Capitol, was taken and entirely destroyed by the Gauls. Although this catastrophe occasioned only a transient loss of the prestige of Rome, it produced a marked effect on the external features of the city. The work of re-erection was undertaken with great precipitation; the new streets were narrow and crooked, the houses poor and unattractive, and till the time of Augustus, Rome was far from being a handsome city. Her steadily increasing power, however, could not fail in some degree to influence her architecture. During the contests for the supremacy over Italy, the first aqueduct and the first high road were constructed at Rome by Appius Claudius in 312 (Aqua and Via Appia, p. 195); in 272 a second aqueduct (Anio Vetus) was erected. Down to the period of the Punic wars Rome had not extended beyond the walls of Servius Tullius; but, after the overthrow of Carthage had constituted her mistress of the world, the city rapidly increased. The wall was almost everywhere demolished to make room for new buildings, so that even at the time of Augustus it was no longer an easy matter to determine its former position, and new quarters now sprang up in every part. Speculation in houses was extensively carried on, and it was by this means that the Triumvir Crassus, among others, amassed his fortune; for rents were high and the houses of a slight and inexpensive construction. These insulae, or blocks of houses erected for hire, contrasted strikingly with the domus, or palaces of the wealthy, which were fitted up with the utmost magnificence and luxury. Thus, for example, the tribune Clodius, the well-known opponent of Cicero, purchased his house for the sum of 14,800,600 sesterces (i. e. about 130,525 l.). During the last century B. C. the city began to assume an aspect more worthy of its proud dignity as capital of the civilized world. The streets, hitherto unpaved, were now converted into the massive lava-causeways which are still extant on many of the ancient roads (e. g. Via Appia). The highest ambition of the opulent nobles was to perpetuate their names by the erection of sumptuous public buildings. Thus in 184 M. Porcius Cato erected the first court of judicature (Basilica Porcia) in the Forum, and others followed his example. Pompey was the founder of the first theatre in stone (p. 164). Generally, however, the structures of the republic were far inferior to those of the imperial epoch, and owing to this circumstance but few of the former have been preserved (Tabularium of E. C. 78, p. 170; tombs of Bibulus, p. 123, and of Caecilia Metella, p. 265).

The transformation of the republic into a military despotism involved the introduction of a new architectural period also. Usurpers are generally wont to direct their energies to the construction of new buildings, with a view to obscure the lustre of the older edifices, and to obliterate the associations connected with them. Caesar himself had formed the most extensive plans of this nature, but their execution was reserved for his more fortunate nephew. Of all the ruins of ancient Rome those of the buildings of Augustus occupy by far the highest rank, both in number and importance. The points especially worthy of note are the Campus Martius with the Pantheon and the Thermae of Agrippa (p. 154), the Theatre of Marcellus (p. 167) and the Mausoleum (p. 147), the Basilica Julia (p. 173) and the Forum of Augustus with the Temple of Mars (p. 182). No fewer than 82 temples were restored by Augustus ("templorum omnium conditorem ac restitutorem" as he is termed by Livy), who might well boast of having transformed Rome from a town of brick into a city of marble. During the republican period the ordinary volcanic stone of the neighbourhood was the usual building material, but the marble from the quarries of Carrara (discovered about 100 B. C., but not extensively worked till the time of Augustus) and the beautiful travertine from the vicinity of Tivoli were now employed. The administration and police-system of the city were also re-organized by Augustus, who divided Rome into 14 quarters (regiones), adapted to its increased extent. A corps of watchmen (vigiles), who also served as firemen, was appointed to guard the city by night. These and other wise institutions, as well as the magnificence attained by the city

7*

under Augustus, are depicted in glowing terms by his contemporaries. His successors followed his example in the erection of public edifices, each striving to surpass his predecessors. In this respect Nero (54—68) displayed the most unbridled ambition. The conflagration of the year 64, which reduced the greater part of Rome to ashes, having been ignited, it is said, at the emperor's instigation, afforded him an opportunity of rebuilding the whole city in the most modern style and according to a regular plan. For his own use he erected the "golden house", a sumptuous palace with gardens, lakes and pleasure-grounds of every description, occupying an exorbitant area, extending from the Palatine across the valley of the Colosseum and far up the Esquiline (p. 177). These and other works were destroyed by his successors, and well merited their fate: the fragments which still bear the name of Nero at Rome are but insignificant.

The Flavian dynasty, which followed the Julian, has on the other hand perpetuated its memory by a number of most imposing works, above all the Colosseum, which has ever been regarded as the symbol of the power and greatness of Rome, the Baths of Titus on the Esquiline (p. 180), and the Triumphal Arch (p. 176) erected after the destruction of Jerusalem. Under Trajan, architecture received a new impetus and indeed attained the highest development of which the art was capable at Rome. To this the Forum of Trajan, with the column and the reliefs, afterwards employed to decorate Constantine's arch, bear the most eloquent testimony. Under Trajan, indeed, the culminating point both of art and of political greatness was attained. Thenceforward the greatness of the empire began gradually, but steadily to decline. Although under the next emperor Hadrian this downward tendency was apparently arrested, yet the monuments of his reign, such as the temple of Venus and Roma (p. 176) and the castle of S. Angelo (p. 214), begin to exhibit traces of degeneracy. The same remark applies also to the time of the Antonines. They were remarkable for their excellent qualities as sovereigns, and their peaceful reign has frequently been regarded as the period during which mankind in general enjoyed the highest degree of prosperity. Tradition even still associates the hope of the return of the good old times with the equestrian statue of the good Marcus Aurelius. This, however, was but the lull preceding a storm. The great plague under the latter emperor was the first of a series of fearful calamities which devastated the empire. Throughout an entire century civil wars, incursions of barbarians, famine and pestilence succeeded each other without intermission. Although Rome was less affected by these horrors than the provinces, it is computed that the population of the city, which at the beginning of the 2nd cent. was about $1^1/_2$ million, had dwindled to one-half by the time of Diocletian. A constant decline in architectural taste is still observed; but, as building always constituted an important feature in the policy of the emperors, the number and extent of the ruins still preserved is considerable. To this epoch belong the column of Marcus Aurelius (p. 117), the triumphal arch of Septimius Severus (p. 172), the sumptuous Baths of Caracalla (p. 195), the Temple of the Sun of Aurelian (p. 122), and the extensive Thermæ of Diocletian (p. 137).

After the Punic War the walls of the city had been suffered to fall to decay, and during nearly five centuries Rome was destitute of fortification. Under the Emperor Aurelian, however, danger became so imminent that it was deemed necessary again to protect the city by a wall against the attacks of the barbarians. This structure is to a great extent identical with that which is still standing. The latest important ruins of antiquity bear the name of Constantine the Great, viz. the Basilica (p. 175), Baths (pp. 122, 132) and Triumphal Arch (p. 179). The two former were, however, erected by his rival Maxentius. Constantine manifested little partiality for Rome and ancient traditions; the transference of the seat of empire to Byzantium (in 330) marks a decided turning-point in the history of the city, as well as in that of the whole empire. Rome indeed was still great on account of the glorious past and its magnificent monuments, but in many respects it had sunk to the level of a mere provincial town. No new works were henceforth undertaken, whilst the old gradually fell to decay. According to the statistics of this period Rome possessed 37 gates, from which 28 high roads diverged, 19 aqueducts, 3 bridges across the Tiber. There were 423 streets, 1790 palaces and 46,602 dwelling-houses. Among the public structures are mentioned 11 Thermæ, 856 bath-rooms, 1352 fountains in the streets, 423 temples, 36 triumphal arches, 10 basilicas etc. When the grandeur and magnificence suggested by these numbers is considered, it may appear a matter of surprise that comparatively so few relics now remain; but it must be borne in mind that the work of destruction progressed steadily during nearly at housand years, and was not arrested till the era of the Renaissance, but for which even the monuments still extant would ere now have shared the fate of those already buried in oblivion.

CHRONOLOGICAL LIST.

B.C. Rom. Emp.	Popes†.	A.D. Rom. Emp.	Popes.
44 Julius Cæsar murdered.		202	Zephyrinus.
		217 Macrinus.	
28 Cæsar Octavianus Au-		218 Heliogabalus.	Calixtus I.
		222 Alexander	
A.D. gustus.		Severus.	
14 Tiberius.		223	Urban I.
37 Caligula.		230	Pontianus.
41 Claudius.		235 Maximin.	Anterus.
54 Nero.		236	Fabianus.
67	Martyrdom of St. Peter.	238 Gordian I. and II.	
68 Galba.	Linus.		Maximus
69 Otho.			and
Vitellius.			Balbina.
69 Vespasian.		238 Gordian III.	
78,	Cletus or	244 Philip the	
79 Titus.	Anacletus.	Arabian.	
81 Domitian.		249 Decius.	
91	Clement I.	251 Gallus and	Cornelius.
96 Nerva.		Volusianus.	
98 Trajan.		252	Lucius I.
100	Evaristus.	253 Æmilian.	Stephen I.
109	Alexander I.	Valerian.	
117 Hadrian.		257	Sixtus II.
119	Sixtus I.	259	Dionysius.
128	Telesphorus.	263 Galienus.	
138 Antoninus Pius		268 Claudius II.	
139	Hyginus.	269	Felix I.
142	Pius I.	270 Aurelian.	
161 Marcus Aurelius.		275 Tacitus.	
		275 Florian.	Eutychianus.
168	Soter.	276 Probus.	
177	Eleutherius.	282 Carus.	
180 Commodus.		282 Carinus and	
190	Victor I.	Numerian.	
193 Pertinax.		283	Cajus.
Didius Julianus.		284 Diocletian.	
		296	Marcellinus.
193 Septimius Severus.		305 Constantius Chlorus and	
198 Caracalla (Geta).		Maximianus Galerius.	

† The dates of the popes down to Constantine are uncertain, having been handed down by vague tradition only.

A.D.	Rom. Emp.	Popes.	A.D.	Rom. Emp.	Popes.
307	Constantine the Great.		530	Justinian I. (528—565).	Boniface II†.
308	Maximin II.	Marcellus I.	532		John II.
	Licinus.		535		St. Agapitus I.
	Maxentius.		536		St. Silverius.
310		Eusebius.	538		Vigilius.
311		Melchiades.	555		Pelagius I.
314		Sylvester I.	560		John III.
336		Marcus.	574		Benedict I.
337	Constantine II. Constantius. Constans.	Julius I.	578		Pelagius II.
			590		St. Gregory I. the Great.
352		Liberius.	604	Phocas 602.	Sabinianus.
361	Julian.		607	Heraclius 610.	Boniface III.
363	Jovian.		608		S. Boniface IV.
			615		Deusdeditus.
364	Valentinian I. and Valens. } Division of the Empire.		619		Boniface V.
			625		Honorius I.
			640		Severinus. John IV.
			642	Constans II.	Theodorus I.
366		Damasus I.	649		St. Martin I.
367	Gratian.		655		St. Eugene I.
375	Valentinian II.		657	Constantine III (d. 668).	St. Vitalianus.
379	Theodosius.				
383	Arcadius.		672		Adeodatus.
385		Siricius.	676		Donus I.
393	Honorius.		678		St. Agathus.
397		Anastasius I.	682		St. Leo II.
401		Innocent I.	684		St. Benedict II.
402	Theodosius II.		685	Justinian II.	John V.
417		Zosimus.	686		Conon.
418		Boniface I.	687		St. Sergius I.
421	Constantius II.		701		John VI.
422		Cœlestinus I.	705		John VII.
425	Valentinian III		708	Philippicus Bardanes 711. Anastas. II. 713.	Sisinnius.
432		Sixtus III.			
440		Leo I. the Great.			Constantinus.
450	Marcian.		715	Leo the Isaurian 718.	St. Gregory II.
455	Avitus.				
457	Leo and Majorianus.		731		St. Gregory III.
			741	Constantinus Copronymus.	S. Zacharias.
461	Libius Severus.	Hilarius.			
467	Anthemius.	Simplicius.	752		Stephen II.
472	Olybrius.		757		St. Paul I.
473	Glycerius.		768		Stephen III.
474	Zeno.		772		Hadrian I.
475	Romulus Augustulus.		795	Charlemagne.	St. Leo III.
			814	Louis the Pious.	
483		Felix II.			
492		Gelasius.	816		Stephen IV.
496		Anastasius II.	817		St. Paschalis I.
498		Symmachus.	824		Eugene II.
514		Hormisdas.	827		Valentinus.
523		John I.			Gregory IV.
526		Felix III.	843	Lothaire.	

† Thus far all the preceding popes have been canonized.

A.D.	Rom. Emp.	Popes.	A.D.	Rom. Emp.	Popes.
844		Sergius II.	1048		Damasus II.
847		St. Leo IV.	1049		St. Leo IX.
855	Louis II.	Benedict III.	1055		Victor II.
858		St. Nicholas I.	1056	Henry IV.	
867		Hadrian II.	1057		Stephen IX.
872		John VIII.	1058		Nicholas II.
876	Charles the Bald.		1061		Alexander II.
			1073		Gregory VII. Hildebrand.
882		Martin II.			
884	Charles the Fat.	Hadrian III.	1086		Victor III.
			1088		Urban II.
885		Stephen V.	1099		Paschalis II.
887	Arnulf.		1106	Henry V.	
891		Formosus.	1118		Gelasius II.
896		Boniface VI.	1119		Calixtus II.
		Stephen VI.	1124		Honorius II.
897		Romanus I.	1125	Lothaire of Saxony.	
898		Theodorus II.			
		John IX.	1130		Innocent II.
900	Louis the Child.	Benedict IV.	1137	Conrad III. of Hohenstaufen.	
903		Leo V.			
		Christophorus.	1143		Cœlestine II.
904		Sergius III.	1144		Lucius II.
911		Anastasius III.	1145		Eugene III.
912	Conrad I.		1152	Frederick I. Barbarossa.	
913		Landonius.			
914		John X.	1153		Anastasius IV.
919	Henry I. the Fowler.		1154		Hadrian IV.
			1159		Alexander III.
928		Leo VI.	1181		Lucius III.
929		Stephen VII.	1185		Urban III.
931		John XI.	1187		Gregory VIII.
936	Otho I.	Leo VII.	1187		Clement III.
939		Stephen VIII.	1190	Henry VI.	
942		Martin III.	1191		Cœlestine III.
946		Agapetus II.	1197	Otho IV.	
956		John XII.	1198		Innocent III.
964		Leo VIII.	1215	Frederick II.	
		Benedict V.	1216		Honorius III.
955		John XIII.	1227		Gregory IX.
972		Benedict VI.	1241		Cœlestine IV.
974	Otho II.	Donus II.	1243		Innocent IV.
975		Benedict VII.	1250	Interregnum.	
983	Otho III.	John XIV.	1254		Alexander IV.
985		John XV.	1261		Urban IV.
996		Gregory V.	1265		Clement IV.
999		Sylvester II.	1271		Gregory X.
1002	Henry II.		1273	Rudolph of Hapsburg.	
1008		John XVII.			
		John XVIII.	1276		Innocent V.
1009		Sergius IV.			Hadrian V.
1012		Benedict VIII.			John XX. or XXI.
1024	Conrad II.	John XIX.	1277		Nicholas III.
1033		Benedict IX.	1281		Martin IV.
1039	Henry III.		1285		Honorius IV.
1046		Gregory VI.	1288		Nicholas IV.
		Clement II.			

A.D.	Rom. Emp.	Popes.	A.D.	Rom. Emp.	Popes.
1290	Albert I. and Adolph of Nassau.		1523		Clement VII. (Julius Medici).
1294		St. Cœlestine V.	1534		Paul III. (Alexander Farnese).
1294		Boniface VIII.	1550		Julius III. (Joan. Maria de Monte).
1303		Benedict XI.			
1305		Clement V.	1555		Marcellus II.
1309	Henry VII. of Luxembourg.				Paul IV. (Gian Pietro Caraffa of Naples).
1313	Louis of Bavaria and Frederick of Austria.		1558	Ferdinand I.	
			1559		Pius IV. (Joan. Angelus Medici of Milan).
1316		John XXII.			
1334		Benedict XII.	1564	Maximilian II.	
1342		Clement VI.	1565		St. Pius V. (Ghislieri of Piedmont).
1346	Charles IV. of Luxembourg.				
1352		Innocent VI.	1572		Gregory XIII. (Ugo Buoncompagni of Bologna).
1362		Urban V.			
1370		Gregory XI.			
1378	Wenzel.	Urban VI.			
1389		Boniface IX.	1576	Rudolph II.	
1400	Rupert of the Palatinate.		1585		Sixtus V. (Felix Peretti).
1404		Innocent VII.	1590		Urban VII. (Giambattista Castagna of Rome).
1406		Gregory XII.			
1409		Alexander V.			
1410	Sigismund.	John XXIII.			
1417		Martin V.	1590		Gregory XIV. (Nic. Sfondrati of Milan).
1431		Eugene IV.			
1437	Albert II.				
1440	Frederick III.		1591		Innocent IX. (Giannantonio Facchinetti of Bologna).
1447		Nicholas V.			
1455		Calixtus III.			
1458		Pius II. (Æneas Sylvius of Siena).	1592		Clement VIII. (Hippolyt. Aldobrandini of Florence).
1464		Paul II.			
1471		Sixtus IV. (Francis de Rovere of Savona).	1605		Leo XI. (Alexander Medici).
1484		Innocent VIII. (Joann. B. Cibo of Genoa).	1612	Matthias.	Paul V. (Camillo Borghese).
			1619	Ferdinand II.	
1492		Alexander VI. (Roder. Borgia).	1621		Gregory XV. (Alexander Ludovisi).
1493	Maximilian I.				
1503			1623		Urban VIII. (Maffeo Barberini).
		Pius III. (Francis Piccolomini of Siena).			
1503		Julius II. (Julian della Rovere).	1637	Ferdinand III.	
			1644		Innocent X. (Giambattista Pamfili).
1513		Leo X. (John de' Medici).	1655		Alexander VII. (Fabio Chigi of Siena).
1519	Charles V.				
1522		Hadrian VI. (of Utrecht).	1658	Leopold I.	

A.D.	Rom. Emp.	Popes.	A.D.	Rom. Emp.	Popes.
1667		Clement IX. (Giul. Rospigliosi).	1758		Clement XIII. (Carlo Rezzonico of Venice).
1670		Clement X. (Emilio Altieri).	1765	Joseph II.	
1676		Innocent XI. (Benedetto Odescalchi).	1769		Clement XIV. (Giov.Ant. Ganganelli of Rimini).
1689		Alexander VIII. (Pietro Ottobuoni).	1775		Pius VI. (Giov. AngeloBraschi).
1690	Joseph I.		1790	Leopold II.	
1691		Innocent XII. (Ant. Pignatelli).	1792	Francis II.	
			1800		Pius VII. (Gregor Barnaba Chiaramonti of Cesena).
1700		Clement XI. (Giov. Franc. Albani).	1823		Leo XII. (Annib. della Genga of Spoleto).
1711	Charles VI.				
1721		Innocent XIII. (Mich. Ang. de Conti).	1829		Pius VIII. (Franc. Xav. Castiglione of Cingoli).
1724		Benedict XIII. (Vinc. Maria Orsini).	1831		Gregory XVI. (Mauro Capellari of Belluno).
1730		Clement XII. (Lorenzo Corsini).	1846		Pius IX. (Giovanni Maria Mastai-Feretti of Sinigaglia, born 13. May, 1792, Cardinal 1839, Pope 16. June 1846).
1740		Benedict XIV. (Prosp. Lambertini).			
1741	Charles VII. of Bavaria.				
1745	Francis I.				

Rome is situated (41° 5′ 54″ N. lat., 12° 29″ E. longit.,
meridian of Greenwich) in an undulating volcanic plain, which
extends from Capo Linaro, S. of Civita Vecchia, to the Promontorio Circeo, a distance of about 85 M., and between the Apennines and the sea, a width of 25 M. The city is built on both
sides of the Tiber, the largest river in the Italian peninsula,
14 M. from its influx into the Mediterranean. The prospect from
one of the hills of Rome — and no city is more replete with
ever-varying and delightful views — is bounded towards the E.
by the unbroken chain of the Apennines, which rise at a distance
of 10 to 20 M. In the extreme N. towers the indented ridge
of Soracte, occupying an isolated position in the plain, and separated by the Tiber from the principal range of the Apennines.
Farther E., and still more distant, is the Leonessa group, which
approaches the Central Apennines. Considerably nearer lies the
range of the Sabine Mts. The summit at the angle which they
form by their abutment on the Campagna is M. Gennaro, the

Lucretilis of Horace; the village at the base is Monticelli. Farther off, on the slope of the hill, lies Tivoli, recognised by its villas and olive-gardens. More towards the S., on the last visible spur of the Sabine Mts., Palestrina, the Præneste of antiquity, is situated. A depression, 4 M. in width only, separates the Apennines from the volcanic Alban Mts., above which a few peaks of the distant Volscian Mts. appear. On the E. spur of the Alban Mts. lies the village of Colonna. The following villages are Rocca Priora and Monte Porzio; then the town of Frascati below the ancient Tusculum. The highest peak of the Alban Mts. is M. Cavo, once surmounted by a temple of the Alban Jupiter, now by a Passionist monastery. On it lies the village of Rocca di Papa, loftily and picturesquely situated, beneath which, towards the plain, is the town of Marino. The village, with the castle farther to the W. on the hill, is Castel Gandolfo; the mountain then gradually sinks to the level of the plain. Towards the W. the sea is visible from a few of the highest points only. On the N. the eye rests on the Janiculus, a volcanic chain of hills approaching close to the river, beyond which the horizon is bounded by mountains also of volcanic formation: towards the sea, to the l., the mountains of Tolfa, then the heights around the lake of Bracciano with the peak of Rocca Romana, the Ciminian Forest (now usually termed the mountains of Viterbo); the nearest point to the r. is the crater of Baccano, with the wooded height of M. Musino. The plain, enclosed by this spacious amphitheatre of mountains, and intersected by the Tiber and the Anio, which descends from Tivoli and falls into the former 1½ M. above Rome, contains a sprinkling of farms and villages, but is far more replete with witnesses of its former greatness and present desolation in the innumerable and extensive ruins covering it in every direction.

The wall by which Rome of the present day is surrounded is about 12 M. in length, constructed of brick, and on the exterior about 50 ft. in height. The greater portion of it dates from 271—274, having been begun by the Emp. Aurelian and completed by Probus, and subsequently restored by Honorius, Theodoric, Belisarius and several popes. The city is entered by 12 gates (several of earlier date are now walled up). Of these the most important is the Porta del Popolo, whence the grand route to N. and E. Italy issues and crosses the Tiber by the Ponte Molle, 1½ M. from the city. Receding from the river, follow: Porta Salara, Porta Pia, Porta S. Lorenzo (road to Tivoli), Porta Maggiore (to Palestrina), Porta S. Giovanni (to Frascati and Albano), Porta S. Sebastiano (Via Appia), Porta S. Paolo (to Ostia). Then on the r. bank of the Tiber: Porta Portese (to Porto), Porta S. Pancrazio, Porta Cavaleggieri and Porta Angelica.

The Tiber reaches Rome after a course of about 220 M., and intersects the city from N. to S. The water is turbid (the "flavus Tiberis" of Horace) and rises to a considerable height after continued rain. The navigation of the river, by means of which the commerce of imperial Rome was carried on in both directions, with transmarine nations as well as with the Italian provinces, is now comparatively insignificant. The Tiber enters the city not far from the base of M. Pincio and describes three curves within its precincts: the first towards the S. W., skirting the quarter of the Vatican, the second to the S. E., bounding the Campus Martius and terminating at the island and the Capitol. and the third to the S. W., quitting the city by the Aventine.

On the r. bank of the Tiber lies the more modern and smaller portion of the city. This part is divided into two halves, on the N. the Borgo around the Vatican and St. Peter's, encircled with a wall by Leo IV. in 852 and constituted a separate town; on the S., lying on the river and the slopes of the Janiculus, Trastevere, which from a very remote period has formed a tête-de-pont of Rome against Etruria, and was under Augustus a densely-populated suburb. These two portions are connected by the long Via della Longara, constructed by Sixtus V. The banks of the Tiber are connected by means of 5 bridges: Ponte S. Angelo near the castle of that name, below which the new suspension-bridge Ponte Leonino crosses from the Longara; then from Trastevere the Ponte Sisto; another traverses the island, from Trastevere to the island termed Ponte S. Bartolommeo, thence to the l. bank Ponte de' Quattro Capi; finally, below the island, the Ponte Rotto.

The more ancient portion of the city, properly so called, lies on the l. bank, partly in the plain which extends along the river, the ancient Campus Martius, and partly on the surrounding hills. Modern Rome is principally confined to the plain, whilst the heights on which the ancient city stood are now to a great extent uninhabited. These are the far-famed Seven Hills of Rome. The least extensive, but historically most important, is the Capitoline, 151 ft. above the sea-level, in the vicinity of the Tiber and the island; at the present day it forms in some degree the barrier between ancient and modern Rome. It consists of a narrow ridge extending from S.W. to N.E., culminating in two summits, separated by a depression: on the S. W. point, towards the river, stands the Palazzo Caffarelli, on that to the N. E., towards the Quirinal, the church of S. Maria in Araceli. Contiguous to the Capitoline, in a N. E. direction, and separated from it by a depression which the structures of Trajan considerably widened, extends the long Quirinal (148 ft.). On the N. a valley, in which the Piazza Barberini is situated, separates the Quirinal from the Pincio (165 ft.), which, as its ancient appellation "collis hortorum" indicates, was occupied by gardens, and not regarded as a portion of the city. E. of the Quirinal, but considerably less extensive, rises the Viminal (160 ft.). Both of these may be regarded as buttresses of the third and more important height, the Esquiline (177 ft.), which, forming the common basis of these two, extends from the Pincio on the N. to the Cælius. Its distinguishing feature with regard to modern Rome is the conspicuous church of S. Maria Maggiore, with regard to ancient Rome, S. Pietro in Vincoli and the ruins oft the Thermæ of Titus, where it approaches the Quirinal, Palatine and Cælius. S. E. of the Capitoline, in the form of an irregular quadrangle, rises the isolated Palatine(160 ft.), with the ruins of the palaces of the emperors, and on the low ground between these hills lies the ancient Forum. Farther S., close to the river, separated from the Palatine by the depression in which the Circus Maximus extended, is the Aventine (146 ft.), with the churches of S. Sabina. S. Balbina etc. Finally, E. of the latter, the long-extended Cælius, with S. Gregorio and S. Stefano Rotondo; in the low ground between the Cælius, Palatine and Esquiline is situated the Colosseum; farther E., by the city-wall, between the Cælius and Esquiline, the Lateran.

By far the greater portion of the area enclosed by the walls, inhabited during the imperial period by $1^{1}/_{2}$—2 millions of souls, is now untenanted. On the Palatine, Aventine, Cælius, Esquiline and the entire region immediately within the walls, once densely-peopled streets are now superseded by the bleak walls of vineyards. The modern city is divided into two halves by the Corso or principal street, which runs from N. to S., from the Porta del Popolo to the Piazza di Venezia in the vicinity of the Capitoline. The E. half, at the base and on the ridge of the Pincio and Quirinal, presents a modern aspect, and is the principal resort of strangers. The W. half, on the bank of the Tiber, consists of narrow and dirty streets, occupied by the humbler classes.

According to the Annuario Pontifico (Rom. government-almanac) of Easter, 1867, the population of Rome amounted to 215,573 souls, of whom 6227 were clergymen, 4945 nuns, 4650 Jews, 457 Protestants and 7360 soldiers. To these numbers must be added the numerous and ever-varying influx of visitors, of whom upwards of 25,000 congregate in the city at Easter.

An intimate acquaintance with the most interesting points in Rome cannot be acquired during a brief visit. The appended description is, however, so arranged as to enable even those whose stay does not exceed a week or a fortnight to visit the most celebrated places in the most convenient manner possible. Rome is especially adapted for a winter-residence (October to May), on account of the mildness of the climate, as well as for the attractions of its church-festivals at Christmas and Easter and the Carnival. In summer the heat and malaria banish great numbers of the inhabitants, whilst in winter thousands of visitors from all countries flock to the city. The *Artists' Association* (German), in which non-professional men are also readily received (in the building adjoining the Fontana Trevi; entrance, Via della Stamperia 4; subscription 8 l. per month, or 30 l. annually on payment of 10 l. entrance-money), is a favourite rallying-point for artists, the *Archaeological Institution*, Monte Caprino 130—132, for the scientific. With the exception of the theatres, Rome affords little opportunity for modern gaieties, a deficiency for which, however, its monuments of antiquity and treasures of art, ancient and modern, abundantly compensate.

I. *Strangers' Quarter and Corso.*

From the N., not far from the Tiber. the city is entered by the *Porta del Popolo*, constructed in 1561 by *Vignola*, the inner portion embellished by Bernini on the occasion of the entry of Queen Christina of Sweden, and deriving its appellation from the neighbouring church of that name. At the gate is the handsome *Piazza del Popolo (Pl. I, 18), in the centre of which rises an *Obelisk* between four water-spouting lionesses, which, after the defeat of Antony, Augustus caused to be brought from Heliopolis, placed in the Circus Maximus (p. 188) and dedicated to the Sun. It was removed to its present position by order of Sixtus V. To the r. of the gate is the church of *S. Maria del Popolo* (see below), opposite to it the *Barracks of the Gendarmi Pontifici*. Towards the W. the Piazza is bounded by an arched wall with Neptune and Tritons, opposite to which is a similar structure with Minerva and river-gods. On each side of the latter is an approach to the *Pincio* (p. 110); adjacent to it on the r. is the hotel Isole Britanniche. Three streets diverge from the piazza on the S.: r. the *Via di Ripetta*, parallel with the river, prolonged by the V. Scrofa which leads direct to the post-office (p. 153); in the centre the *Corso* (p. 115); l. the *V. del Babuino*, leading stands *Piazza di Spagna* (p. 113). Between the two latter streets to the the church of *S. Maria in Monte Santo*, to the r. adjoining it, that of *S. Maria de' Miracoli*, both dating from the latter half of the 17th cent., with domes and vestibules, designed by Rinaldi, completed by Bernini and Fontana. Without the gate, to the r. is the *Villa Borghese* (p. 124), to the l. the **English**

Church, a yellowish grey building with three doors sheltered by roofs.

*S. Maria del Popolo (Pl. I, 18), said to have been founded by Paschalis II. in 1099 on the site of the tombs of the Domitii, the burial-place of Nero which was haunted by evil spirits, was under Sixtus IV. in 1477 re-erected by *Baccio Pintelli*, the interior subsequently decorated by *Bernini* in the baroque style. It consists of nave, aisles, transept and octagonal dome, and contains numerous works of art, especially handsome monuments of the 15th cent.

The 1st Chapel in the r. aisle, formerly *della Rorere*, now *Venuti*, was painted by *Pinturicchio;* °altar-piece, Adoration of the Infant Christ; in the °lunettes°, life of St. Jerome; l. tomb of Cardinal della Rovere. r. that of Cardinal di Castro. In the 2nd Chapel: Assumption of Mary, altar-piece by *C. Maratta*. 3rd Chapel, painted by *Pinturicchio:* above the altar, Madonna with four angels, l. Assumption of the Virgin, in the lunettes, scenes from the life of Mary, in the predelle representations of martyrs in grisaille; r. tomb of Giov. della Rovere (d. 1483); l. recumbent bronze figure of a bishop. In the 4th Chapel marble-sculptures of the end of the 15th cent. above the altar: St. Catharine between St. Antony of Padua and St. Vincent; r. tomb of Marcantonio Albertoni (d. 1485), l. that of the Cardinal of Lisbon (d. 1508). In the r. transept, on the r., tomb of Cardinal Podocatharus of Cyprus. Near it is a door leading into a passage at the end of which is the sacristy, containing the former °canopy of the high-altar of the close of the 15th cent., with an ancient Madonna (of the Sienese school) and two beautiful tombs, l. that of Archbishop Rocca (d. 1482), r. of Bishop Goniel. — In the 1st Chapel in the l. aisle, l. and r. of the altar, two ciboria of the 15th cent., l. tomb of Card. Ant. Pallavicino (erected 1507). By a pillar near it the baroque monument of a Princess Chigi, by *Posi* (1771). The 2nd Chapel was constructed under the direction of Raphael by *Agostino Chigi* in honour of St. Mary of Loreto; on the vaulting of the dome eight °mosaics by *Aloisio della Pace* (1516), from Raphael's cartoons, the Creation of the heavenly bodies: the sun, the moon, Mercury, Venus, Mars, Jupiter, Saturn, who, conducted by angels, perform the circuit of the universe; in the lantern an emblem of God the Father, surrounded by angels; altar-piece, Nativity of the Virgin, by *Sebastiano del Piombo*, the other pictures by *Salviati*. Bronze relief at the altar, Christ and the Samaritan woman, by *Lorenzetto;* in the niches 4 statues of prophets: at the altar, l. Jonah, r. Habakuk; at the entrance, l. Daniel, r. Elijah. Beneath are °Jonah and Elijah by *Lorenzetto*, designed by *Raphael;* the others by *Bernini*. In the l. transept the tomb of Cardinal Bernardino Lonati (15th cent.). In the choir (not accessible during service; sacristan usually shows it and opens the chapels; 1/2 l.) °ceiling-frescoes by *Pinturicchio:* Madonna, the 4 Evangelists and the 4 Fathers of the church, Gregory, Ambrose, Jerome and Augustine. Beneath are the °tombs of the cardinals Girolamo Basso and Ascanio Sforza by *Andrea Sansovino*, erected by order of Julius II. The same pope is said to have caused the two fine painted-glass windows to be executed by *Claudius* and *William of Marseilles*.

The church gives a title to a cardinal. In the adjacent Augustine monastery Luther resided during his visit to Rome.

Ascending the ***Pincio** (Pl. I, 18) the visitor encounters in the first circular space two columns *(columnae rostratae)*, adorned with the prows of ships, from the temple of Venus and Roma (p. 176); in the niches 3 marble statues, and above them captive

Dacians, imitations of antiques. Beyond these, farther up, a large relief.

The projecting terrace at the summit commands a magnificent *View of modern Rome. Beyond the Piazza del Popolo with the building above described, on the opposite bank of the Tiber, rises the huge pile of St. Peter's, contiguous to which is the Vatican to the r., in the vicinity the citywall. Of the chain of hills which here bound the horizon, the point planted with cypresses to the r., where the Villa Mellini is situated, is Monte Mario. L. of St. Peter's close to the Tiber, which, however, is not visible from this point, is the round castle of S. Angelo, so called from the bronze angel by which it is surmounted. The pine-grove on the height to the l. of the castle belongs to the Villa Doria-Pamfili. Farther to the l., on the height, the façade of the Acqua Paola, decorated with a cross. Between the spectator and the river a labyrinth of houses and churches. The following points will serve as landmarks. The two nearest churches are: that with the two towers to the r., S. Giacomo in the Corso, that with the dome to the l., S. Carlo in the Corso; between the two appears the flat dome of the Pantheon, beyond which a part of the Campagna is visible. To the l. of this, on the height in the extreme distance, rises the long, undecorated side of a church, behind which a tower appears: the church is S. Maria in Araceli, and the tower appertains to the senatorial palace on the Capitoline. On the r. side of the Capitoline lies the Palazzo Caffarelli (residence of the Prussian ambassador), in front of which the upper portion of the column of M. Aurelius in the Piazza Colonna is visible. Adjacent to the Capitoline on the l. is the bright-looking Villa Mills (now belonging to a nunnery), shaded by cypresses, on the Palatine. Farther l. a low brick-built tower on the Quirinal, the so-called Torre di Nerone. To the extreme l. and less distant, the spacious papal palace on the Quirinal.

The Pincio, the *collis hortorum* or "hill of gardens" of the ancients, probably derived its name of *Mons Pincius* from the estates of the Pincii situated here in the latest period of the empire. Here were once the celebrated gardens of Lucullus, and at a later date Messalina, the wife of Claudius, celebrated her orgies here. It is now a favourite promenade; a military band plays daily an hour before sunset, attracting a considerable audience of all classes in carriages and on foot. The walks are shaded by plantations and groups of trees and adorned with busts of celebrated Italians. To the r., at the foot of the lofty wall which serves to support the hill, lies the Villa Borghese (p. 124), with its extensive and shady grounds. The dilapidated grey building on Monte Mario, below the Villa Mellini, is the Villa Madama. On the E. side a large portion of the city-wall is visible. The public grounds are adjoined by the garden of the Villa Medici.

Following the carriage-road, and passing a large antique granite basin, the visitor reaches an obelisk, which Hadrian erected to the memory of Antinous in Egypt. It was subsequently brought to Rome and erected here in 1822. (Refreshments in the neighbouring building.) Proceeding in this direction, the footpath (above) and carriage-road (below) command an ever-varying *prospect. The public grounds are closed by a gate, to the l. before reaching which the visitor will observe the white Villa

Medici with its two corner-turrets, now the seat of the Académie Française; in front of it is a fountain, shaded by evergreen-oaks, whence a celebrated view of St. Peter's is obtained, especially striking towards evening or by moonlight.

The **Villa Medici** (Pl. I, 18) was erected in 1540 by *Annibale Lippi* for Cardinal Ricci da Montepulciano, then (about 1600) in possession of Cardinal Alessandro de' Medici and subsequently of the grand-dukes of Tuscany, until in 1801 the French transferred thither the seat of their academy of art, founded by Louis XIV. Entrance to the garden, to which visitors are readily admitted, by the gate to the r., or by the staircase to the r. in the house. On the tastefully decorated garden-side of the villa ancient reliefs have been built into the walls. The r. wing contains a collection of casts (open daily, except Sundays, 8—12, and in the afternoon till near sunset), comprising many from statues etc. not preserved at Rome, e. g. from the Parthenon of Athens, museum of the Louvre etc., which are valuable in the history of art. Adjoining the wing is a terrace, by the frontwall of which stand casts of the Niobides; entrance by the sidedoor, opposite the museum of casts, which if closed will be opened by the porter (5 s.). Skirting the balustrade, and traversing the oak-grove in a straight direction, the visitor ascends 60 steps to the *Belvedere, whence a charming *panorama is enjoyed. To the l. of the villa are grounds with pleasant, shady walks, and a few ancient statues, among others a colossal Roma in a sitting posture.

The avenue ends in the *Piazza Trinità;* l. the church of *SS. Trinità de' Monti*. The obelisk in front of it, a conspicuous object from most points of view, is an ancient imitation of that in the Piazza del Popolo, and once stood in the gardens of Sallust.

SS. Trinità de' Monti (Pl. I, 20), erected by Charles VIII. of France in 1495, plundered during the French Revolution, was restored in 1817 at the cost of Louis XVIII.

Left, 1st Chapel: Cast of the Descent from the Cross, by *Achtermann*. 2nd Chapel: on the l. an altar-piece al fresco, Descent from the Cross, by *Daniel da Volterra*, master-piece of the artist. 3rd Chapel: Madonna, altar-piece by *Veit*. 4th Chapel: St. Joseph by *Langlois*. 6th Chapel: Christ, the wise and foolish Virgins, and Return of the Prodigal, an altar-piece by *Seitz*. - Right, 3rd Chapel: Assumption of the Virgin, *Dan. da Volterra*. 5th Chapel: Presentation in the Temple, Adoration of the Magi, Adoration of the Shepherds, a work of the school of Sodoma (?). 6th Chapel: Resurrection, Ascension, Descent of the Holy Ghost, school of Perugino. — In the transept paintings by *Perino del Vaga* and *F. Zuccaro*.

The church is open on Sundays before 9 a. m., and in the evening during Vespers ($1/2$ hr. before Ave Maria), when the nuns usually perform choral service with organ-accompaniment.

When the church is closed, visitors ascend the side-staircase on the l. and ring at a door protected by a roof.

The convent connected with the church has since 1827 been tenanted by the Dames du Sacré Cœur (instructresses of girls).

The piazza is quitted to the l. by the broad *Via Sistina*, prolonged by the *Via Felice* and *Via delle Quattro Fontane*, which descends in 5 min. to the Piazza Barberini (p. 127) and leads in 20 min. over the Quirinal and Viminal to S. Maria Maggiore on the Esquiline (p. 140). To the r. is the small *Via Gregoriana*, leading to the transverse Via Capo le Case. Between the Via Sistina and Via Gregoriana is situated the **Casa Zuccari**, once the property of the family of the artists of that name (on the ground-floor paintings by Federigo Zuccaro), at the beginning of the present century in possession of the Prussian consul Bartholdy (whence "*Casa Bartholdy*"), who caused one of the apartments to be adorned with *frescoes from the history of Joseph by the most celebrated German artists then at Rome. (At present accessible on Sundays 11 — 12 o'clock. The house being a private dwelling, the hour is liable to variation. Porter $1/_2$—1 l.)

On the long window-wall: 1. Joseph sold, *Overbeck*; r. Joseph and Potiphar's wife, *Veit*. On the short window-wall: Recognition of the brethren, *Cornelius*. In the lunette above: the Seven lean Years, *Overbeck*. On the second long wall: l. Joseph's interpretation of the dreams in prison; r. the Brethren bringing Jacob the bloody coat, both by *W. Schadow*. On the second short wall: Joseph's interpretation of Pharaoh's dream, *Cornelius*; in the lunette above, the Seven Years of Plenty, *Veit*.

The long "**Spanish Staircase**" (Pl. I, 20) descends from S. Trinità by 125 steps. It was constructed by Specchi and de Sanctis in 1721—25, and was until within the last few years a favourite resort of beggars, who are now more equally distributed throughout the city. The present fraternity with their picturesque costumes who frequent this locality, especially towards evening, afford favourite models for artists.

The long **Piazza di Spagna** (Pl. I, 17), the central point of the strangers' quarter, is surrounded by hotels and attractive shops.

In the centre of the piazza is *La Barcaccia* (barque), a tasteless fountain by Bernini. To the l. is the *Column of the Immacolata* (Pl. I, 20, *1*), erected by Pius IX. in commemoration of the doctrine of the immaculate conception of the Virgin, promulgated for the first time in 1854; on the summit of the cipolline column stands the bronze statue of Mary; beneath are Moses, David, Isaiah and Ezekiel.

Beyond is the **Collegio di Propaganda Fide** (Pl. I, 19, *16*), founded in 1662 by Gregory XV. and extended by his successor Urban VIII. (whence "*Collegium Urbanum*"), an establishment for the propagation of the Rom. Catholic faith, in which pupils of many different nationalities are educated as missionaries. The printing-office of the college was formerly celebrated as the richest in type for foreign languages. A public festivity is celebrated here at the beginning of every year, when short speeches in the different languages taught are delivered by the pupils; permessi may be obtained through an ambassador or consul, or on personal application. Adjacent, to the l., is the *Piazza Mignanelli*, where (No. 22) the Spaccio Normale (p. 94) is situated; to the r. the palace of the Spanish ambassador, whence the piazza derives its name.

Immediately opposite the Spanish Stairs is the *Via de' Condotti*, containing numerous emporiums of jewellery, mosaics, antiquities, photographs etc. It terminates in the Corso, opposite the spacious *Palazzo Ruspoli* (p. 116).

From the Piazza di Spagna the Via del Babuino leads N. to the Piazza del Popolo (p. 109), opposite to which street, to the l. of the Propaganda, is the *Via de' due Macelli*, and to the r. the *Via di Propaganda*. If the latter be followed, the church of **S. Andrea delle Fratte** (Pl. I, 19) is reached at the corner of the next transverse street, the *Via di Capo le Case*. It was erected under Leo X. by *La Guerra*, the unsightly dome and campanile by *Borromini;* the façade was added in 1826 by *Valadier* in consequence of a bequest by Cardinal Consalvi.

The pictures of the interior are mediocre works of the 17th cent.; the two angels by the tribune by *Bernini*, originally destined for the bridge of S. Angelo. In the 2nd Chapel on the r. is (on the r. side) the monument of a Lady Falconet by *Miss Hossmer;* on the last pillar to the r., in front of the aisle, the monument of the artist R. Schadow by *E. Wolff*. In the 3rd Chapel to the l., by the wall r., is the tomb of the accomplished Swiss artist Angelica Kauffmann. The eminent archæologist Zoëga is erroneously said to be interred in this church.

At the extremity of the *Via di S. Andrea delle Fratte* the narrow *Via di Nazareno* is entered to the l. On the l. is the *Collegio Nazareno* (in the court several ancient statues), founded by Card. Tonti (1622) for the education of destitute boys. Opposite is the *Pal. del Bufalo*. Then to the l. the *Via dell' Angelo Custode* (in which, immediately to the r., is the small church of *SS. Angeli Custodi*) and *Via del Tritone* lead direct to the Piazza Barberini (p. 127).

To the r. is the *Via della Stamperia*, so called from the papal *Printing-office* situated in it (r.). Adjacent to the latter is the extensive papal *Engraving Institute* with warehouse. No. 4 is the entrance to the German *Artists' Association* (p. 109).

The visitor now reaches the ***Fontana di Trevi** (Pl. I, 19) (derived from "trivio", there having been three outlets for the water). which vies in magnificence with Acqua Paola. The ancient *Aqua Virgo*, now *Acqua Vergine*, repaired by Nicholas V. in 1450, and subsequently by Pius IV., Pius V. and Gregory XIII., which issues here, was conducted by M. Agrippa, B. C. 27, to supply his baths at the Pantheon (p. 154) from the Campagna, chiefly by a subterranean channel 14 M. in length. It enters the city by the Pincio, not far from the Porta del Popolo. Tradition ascribes the name to the fact of a girl having pointed out the spring to a thirsty soldier. The Fontana Trevi in its present form, erected near the Palazzo Poli, was completed from a design by *Niccolò Salvi*; in the central niche Neptune by *Pietro Bracci*, at the sides Health (l.) and Fertility (r.); in front of these the large stone basin. On quitting Rome the superstitious partake of the water of this fountain and throw a coin into the basin, in the pious belief that their return is thus ensured. Opposite is the church *SS. Vincenzo ed Anastasio*, erected in its present form, with unsightly façade, by the well-known Card. Mazzarini.

The Via di S. Vincenzo terminates in the Via della Dataria (l.), which leads to the Quirinal (p. 133). From the Fontana Trevi the busy *Via delle Muratte* leads to the l. to the Corso.

The Corso.

The **Corso** leads from the Piazza del Popolo, which it quits between the Via di Ripetta and Via del Babuino, to the Piazza di Venezia, once from the Capitol the ancient *Via Flaminia*, now the principal street of Rome, with numerous shops and enlivened, especially towards evening, by crowds of carriages and pedestrians. Here the Carnival is celebrated and the street throughout its entire length is thickly strewn with sand for the horse-races. From the Piazza del Popolo to the Via Condotti is a distance of 750 yds., thence to the Piazza Colonna (p. 117) 520, and thence to the Piazza di Venezia 610 yds., i. e. a total distance of 1880 yds., or upwards of a mile. From either side diverge numerous streets and lanes, which to the r. lead to the crowded purlieus on the bank of the Tiber, and to the l. to the now partially uninhabited hills of the city.

The first part of the street as far as the Piazza S. Carlo is less frequented than the other portions. R. between the 1st and 2nd transverse streets is *Pal. Rondinini* (Pl. I, 17, 18); in the court an unfinished Pietà by *Michael Angelo*. After the third transverse street is passed, to the r. stands the church of *S. Giacomo in Augusta* or *degli Incurabili*, with façade by C. Maderno. It belongs to the adjoining surgical hospital, which extends as far as the Via Ripetta and accommodates 340 patients; founded 1338, enlarged 1600. Nearly opposite, on the l., is the small Augustine church of *Gesù e Maria*, with façade by Rinaldi. In the Via de' Pontefici, the third transverse street from this point to the r., is situated the Mausoleum of Augustus (p. 147). The *Piazza S. Carlo* is next reached. Here to the r. is **S. Carlo al Corso**, the national church of the Lombards and the resort of the fashionable world: the tasteless façade was constructed in the 17th cent. by *Longhi*, afterwards by *Pietro da Cortona*. The ceiling-paintings of the interior are by *Giacinto Brandi*. At the high-altar is one of the finest works of *Carlo Maratta:* the Virgin recommending St. Charles Borromæus to Christ (the heart of the saint is preserved under the altar).

On the opposite side, the *Café* and *Albergo di Roma*. Immediately beyond, the *Via de' Condotti* diverges to the l. to the P. di Spagna (p. 113); its prolongation to the r., the *Via della Fontanella*, leads to the Palazzo Borghese (p. 148) and the bridge of S. Angelo (p. 214). On the r. the spacious *Palazzo Ruspoli* (Pl. I, 16), built in 1586 by Amanati, in which the Café Nuovo is established.

To the l. the *Via Borgognona* and *Via Frattina* diverge to the P. di Spagna. Opposite the latter street is the *Piazza di S. Lorenzo in Lucina* (Pl. I, 16) with (l.) **S. Lorenzo in Lucina**, an ancient but frequently restored church; the campanile, with new roof, now alone remains of the original structure. It has since 1606, with the contiguous monastery, belonged to the Minorites, who have given it its present form. The portico is supported by four columns; at the door two half-immured mediæval lions. In the interior by the 2nd pillar to the r., the tomb of Nic. Poussin (d. 1660), erected by Chateaubriand; above the high-altar a Crucifixion by *Guido Reni*.

Farther on to the r., somewhat removed from the street and concealed by other houses, is the uncompleted *Pal. Fiano* (in which the Trattoria delle belle Arti). In front of it in the Corso (see inscription on opposite house, No. 167, which records that Alex. VII. levelled and widened the Corso in order to afford space for the horse-races) a triumphal arch of M. Aurelius stood until 1665; some of the reliefs are now preserved in the palace of the Conservatori (p. 209).

R. *Pal. Teodoli* (385); opposite to it the *Via delle Convertite* leads to the *Piazza di S. Silvestro* with the old church of *S. Silvestro in Capite*.

R. *Pal. Verospi* (374); then, at the corner of the Piazza Colonna, the extensive **Pal. Chigi** (Pl. I, 16), commenced in 1526 by *Giac. della Porta*, completed by *C. Maderno*.

On the first floor are a few antiquities (Venus by Menophantus, Mercury with new head, Apollo) and a small picture-gallery of no great value, comprising a few works of *Caracci*, *Domenichino*, *Albani*, *Dosso Dossi* (St. Bartholomew with the apostle John and others in a landscape) and two ascribed to *Titian*. The study of the prince (not always accessible) contains a fine marble vase with a relief: Eros tormenting Psyche. — The *Bibliotheca Chisiana* contains valuable MSS.

The handsome ***Piazza Colonna** (Pl. I, 16) is bounded on the r. by the Pal. Chigi, opposite to which is the *Pal. Terrajuoli* (with the *Café Colonna*): in the Corso is situated the *Pal. Piombino*, opposite to it the *Guard-house* and the *Military Casino*, formerly the post-office; the ancient Ionic columns of the front were found at Veii (p. 297). In the centre of the piazza stands the **Column of Marcus Aurelius*, adorned, like that of Trajan, with reliefs from the wars of the emperor against the Marcomanni and other German tribes on the Danube. It consists of 26 blocks, besides the basement and capital, and is approached by steps. Sixtus V. caused it to be restored in 1589 and ascribed it, according to the then prevalent opinion, to Antoninus Pius, by whose name it is still frequently designated. On the summit a statue of St. Paul.

Adjacent to the Piazza Colonna (to the r., past the Milit. Casino) is the *Piazza di Monte Citorio*, on the r. side of which stands the spacious *Police-office* (Pl. I, 16, *14*), containing the passport-office (l. on the ground floor), courts of justice and police-courts. The design of the building by Bernini, afterwards modified by C. Fontana. On the first floor, in a niche in front of the staircase, a group, Apollo and Marsyas, of the 16th cent. On the opposite side of the Piazza the *Railway*, and to the l. on the S. side the *Telegraph* offices; the corner adjoining the latter is the point of departure and arrival of the vetturini. The *Obelisk* in the centre of the Piazza was brought by Augustus, like that in the P. del Popolo (p. 109), to Rome, where it served as the indicator of a sun-dial. It stood till the 9th cent., was afterwards overthrown, and under Pius VI. restored and erected here. The elevation of the Piazza towards the N. is due to the unexcavated ruins of a vast ancient edifice, perhaps the amphitheatre of Statilius Taurus, erected under Augustus.

The next lateral street to the r., the *Via di Pietra* (descending from Monte Citorio and turning to the l.), leads from the Corso by the Locanda Cesāri to the *Piazza di Pietra*. Here is situated the ***Dogana di Terra**; immured in the façade are 11 Corinthian columns of a temple, which once possessed 15 in its length and 8 in its breadth. The style is mediocre, not earlier than the 2nd cent. The edifice is sometimes, though on insufficient authority, termed a *Temple of Neptune*.

The *Via de' Pastini* leads hence to the Pantheon (p. 153). From the Corso, opposite the Via di Pietra, the *Via delle Muratte* leads to the Fontana Trevi (p. 114).

Then the oblong *Piazza Sciarra*, with the café of that name, and opposite to it the ***Palazzo Sciarra-Colonna** (Pl. I, 16), the handsomest palace in the Corso, erected in the 17th cent. by *Flaminio Ponzio*, with portal of more recent date. It contains a small but choice *Picture Gallery, inherited to a great extent from the Barberini collection (open on Saturdays 10—3 o'clock; ½ l.).

1st Room: 2. Ecce Homo, Cav. d'Arpino; 3. St. Barbara, Pietro da Cortona; 4. Madonna with St. Lawrence and St. John, School of Perugino; 5. Beheading of John the Baptist, Valentin; 10. Transfiguration, copy from Raphael by C. Saraceni; 12. Madonna, Gior. Bellini; 13. Holy Family, Innoc. da Imola; 15. Triumph of Rome, Valentin; 16. Christ and the Samaritan woman, Garofalo; Madonna, Titian; 21. Portrait of Card. Barberini, Maratta. — 2nd R.: Battle, Borgognone; 8., 9. Landscapes, Locatelli; 17. Landscape, Claude Lorrain; 18. Landscape and sunset, C. Lorrain; 26. Ceremonies in the Gesù church, figures by A. Sacchi, architecture by Gagliardi; 36. Landscape with St. Matthew, N. Poussin; 50. Landscape, Locatelli. — 3rd R.: 8. Caritas, Elisabetta Sirani; 9. Boar-hunt, Garofalo; 11. Holy Family, And. del Sarto; 17. "Old and New Testament", allegory by Gaudenzio Ferrari, believed rather to represent a vision of the heavenly Jerusalem; 25. Moses with the tables of the Law, Guido Reni; 26. The Vestal Claudia, drawing up the Tiber the boat containing the image of Cybele, Garofalo; 33. The Fornarina, copy from Raphael by Giul. Romano; 36. Holy Family with angels, L. Cranach (1504). — 4th R.: 4. "Et in Arcadia ego", Schidone; 5. St. John, Guercino; 6. "Violin-player" (1518, perhaps the improvisatore Andrea Marone), Raphael; 7. St. Mark, Guercino; 8. Herodias with the head of the Baptist, Giorgione (?); 12. "Matrimonial affection", Ag. Caracci; 13. Vulcan's forge, Breughel; 16. The Players (usually kept under glass in the 1st Room), one of the finest works of Caravaggio; 18. Ulysses in the lower regions, Breughel; 19., 32. Magdalene, Guido Reni; 20. Landscape with Madonna, Breughel; 22. Scenes from the life of Christ, School of Giotto; 24. Portrait, Titian; 25. "Vanity and Modesty", Luini; 26. St. Sebastian, Perugino (?); 29. "Bella di Tiziano", portrait by Titian; 30. St. Jerome, Guercino; 31. Death of Mary, old Dutch School.

The Via del Caravita, the first side-street to the r., leads to the Piazza di S. Ignazio, on the principal side of which is the Jesuit church of **S. Ignazio** (Pl. II, 16), with façade by Algardi (1685). Interior overladen; paintings on the vaulting, dome and tribune and the picture over the high-altar by the Padre Pozzi, by whom the chapel of St. Lod. Gonzaga, in the aisle to the r., was also designed. (The perspective of the paintings on the ceiling and dome is correctly seen from a circular stone in the centre of the nave.) Adjacent is the **Collegio Romano** (Pl. II, 16) (from S. Ignazio the Via di S. Ignazio to the l., or from the Corso the side-street to the r., leads to the Piazza del Coll. Romano, in which is the principal entrance), a much-frequented Jesuit establishment, where the higher branches of classics, mathematics, philosophy etc. are taught and degrees conferred. The building, erected by B. Amanati, contains the lecture-rooms, apartments of the Jesuit professors, library and the ***Museo Kircheriano**, founded by the erudite Athanasius Kircher, born 1601, in 1618 a Jesuit and teacher at Würzburg, subsequently professor of mathematics in the Coll. Romano, celebrated for his mathematical and scientific discoveries (d. 1680). The museum is accessible (not to ladies) on Sundays, 10—11 o'clock (director Padre Tongiorgi). Entrance in the farther (r.) corner of the court, whence a staircase ascends to the 3rd floor.

In the corridor, opp. the entrance: mosaic with Egyptian representations, found on the Aventine. **1st Room**: model of ancient columbaria, with numerous cinerary urns, inscriptions etc. — 2nd R.: *antique bronze seat, inlaid with silver. In the 1st cabinet on the l., oriental ornaments in silver, in the 2nd gladiator's weapons in bronze. The door to the l. leads to the **3rd R.**: In the glass-cases in the centre a valuable *collection of ancient Roman (cast) coins, some unstamped ("æs rude"). In front of the window of the shorter wall the *Ficoronian Cista (in a glass-case; name derived from former proprietor), discovered near Palestrina in 1744, a cylindrical vessel with admirably engraved designs (arrival of the Argonauts in Bithynia, victory of Polydeuces over king Amycus). The feet and figures on the lid are of inferior workmanship; on the latter the inscription: -Novios Plautios Romai med (Romæ me) fecid". It dates from the 5th cent. of the city. The silver goblets in the cabinet by the l. wall are also interesting (l. by the window); they were found at the mineral spring of Vicarello (Lago di Bracciano), and bear a description of the stations on the route from Cadiz to Rome. — Another door leads from the 2nd R. into the **4th R.**, or gallery. To the l. an interesting collection of masks; to the r. several cabinets, containing terracottas, glasses etc. At the end a number of ancient statuettes. At the farther extremity, to the l., is the entrance to the **5th R.**, containing Christian antiquities; to the r. by the door a caricature of the Christians, found on the Palatine: a man with the head of an ass affixed to a cross, two men at the side, with the words: Ἀλεξαμενος σεβετε θεον (Alexamenos prays to God); beyond it on the r., an image of Christ of the 5th cent. (?).

In the Corso, beyond the Piazza Sciarra, to the r. is the *Palazzo Simonetti*, in which the bank is established. Opposite is the church of **S. Marcello** (Pl. II, 16), in the small *Piazza di S. Marcello*, mentioned as early as 499. The interior of the present structure was designed by *Giac. Sansovino*, the poor façade by *Carlo Fontana*.

The 4th Chapel contains paintings by *Perino del Vaga*, completed after his death by *Dan. da Volterra* and *Pellegrino da Modena*, and the monument (by *Rinaldi*) of the celebrated Card. Consalvi, minister of Pius VII, whose memoirs, written with great fidelity, have lately been published. Paintings of the tribune by *Giov. Battista da Novara*, those of the 2nd Chap. to the l. by *Fed. Zucchero*.

The church and the adjoining monastery are the property of the Servi di Maria, or Servites.

On the r. the small church of *S. Maria in Via Lata*, mentioned as early as the 7th cent., in its present form of the 17th; façade by *Pietro da Cortona;* from the vestibule a stair ascends to an ancient chamber in which tradition alleges St. Paul and St. Luke to have taught.

Contiguous to this church is the

*Palazzo Doria (Pl. II, 16) (formerly *Pamfili*), an extensive pile of buildings, and one of the most magnificent palaces in Rome; façade towards the Corso by *Valvasori*, that towards the Coll. Romano by *P. da Cortona*, and that of the adjoining palace towards the Piazza di Venezia, by *P. Amati*. From the Corso (No. 305) the handsome court, surrounded by arcades, is entered. To the l. is the approach to the stair ascending to the *Picture Gallery* on the 1st floor (Tuesdays and Fridays 10—2 o'clock; catalogues in each room; ½ l.). This, the most extensive of Roman collections, comprises many admirable, as well as numerous mediocre works.

1st Room, also copying-room, to which the finest pictures in the collection are frequently brought. Antiquities: four Sarcophagi with the hunt of Meleager, history of Marsyas, Diana and Endymion and procession of Bacchus. Two fine circular altars, archaic statue of the bearded Dionysus and a number of statuettes. Pictures: Landscapes imitated from Poussin; *Madonna, *Mariotto Albertinelli*. — 2nd R.; ancient busts, a centaur of pietradura and rosso antico (modernized); 5. Circumcision, *Giov. Bellini* (?); 7. Madonna with saints, *Basaiti*; 15. St. Antony, *School of Mantegna*; 35. Birth of St. John, *Pisanello*; 21. Sposalizio, *Pisanello*; 23. St. Silvester before Maximin II., *Peselino*; *28. Annunciation, *Fil. Lippi*; 29. Leo IV. appeasing a dragon, *Peselino*; 33. St. Agnes, *Guercino*; 37. Magdalene, copy from *Titian* (original in the Pitti at Florence); 39. Boy playing with lion, *Titian*. — 3rd R. (sleeping-apartment): 9. Madonna, *Sassoferrato*. — 4th R.: *16., 32. Landscapes, *Brill*; 34. St. John, *Caravaggio*. Antique bronzes etc. in frames. Near the window a bronze jar with curious chasing (comparatively late); a recumbent river-god, of pietradura. — 5th R.: *17. Money-changer disputing, *Quintin Messys*; 25. St. Joseph, *Guercino*; 27. Landscape, *Domenichino*. In the centre: Jacob struggling with the Angel, marble group of the school of Bernini. — 6th R.: 5. Holy Family, *S. Botticelli* (?); 13. Madonna, *Maratta*; *30. Portrait of a boy, *Spanish School*. The contiguous raised passage-cabinet contains several small Dutch pictures and female portrait-busts by Algardi. — 7th R.: 3, 8. Landscapes, *Salv. Rosa*; 19. Slaughter of the Innocents, *Mazzolino*. — 8th R.: 17. Madonna, *Lod. Caracci*; 22. St. Sebastian, by the same. In the corner *marble head of Serapis. — 9th R.: several interesting ancient portraits. — 10th R.: pictures of food etc. The galleries are now entered; to the l. is the 1st Gallery: 3. Magdalene, *An. Caracci*; 8. Heads, *Quintin Messys*; 9. Holy Family, *Sassoferrato*; 14. Portrait, *Titian*; 15. Holy Family, *A. del Sarto*; 16. Creation of the animals etc., *Breughel*; 20. The three Periods of Life, *Titian* (?); 25. Landscape with the flight to Egypt, *Cl. Lorrain*; 26. Mary visiting Elisabeth, *Garofalo*; 38. Copy of the Aldobrandine Nuptials (ancient panel-painting in the library of the Vatican, p. 255), *Poussin*; 45. Madonna, *Guido Reni*; 50. Holy Family, a copy from *Raphael* by *G. Romano*. — 2nd Gallery: *6. Madonna, *Fr. Francia*; *14. "Bartolus and Baldus", portraits by *Raphael*; 13. Christ in the Temple, *Mazzolino*; *17. Portrait, *Titian*; 21 Portrait, *Van Dyck* (?); 22. Sleeping girl, *C. Saraceni*; 24. Heads, *Giorgione*; 26. Sacrifice of Isaac, *Gerbrand van den Eckhout* (erron. attrib. to Titian); *40. Herodias with the head of the Baptist, *Pordenone*; 50. Portrait of a monk, *Rubens*; *53. Johanna of Arragon, after *Raphael*, school of *Leonardo*; 56. Magdalene, copy from *Titian*; 61. Adoration of the Child, *Ortolano*; *69. Unfinished allegorical painting, *Correggio*; 78. Holy Family, older *Dutch School*; beneath it a female *portrait, ascribed to *Holbein*; 80. Portraits, *Titian*. Between the windows: 25. Madonna, *G. Bellini*. — 3rd Gallery: 1, 6, 18, 28. Landscapes with historical accessories by *An. Carracci*; 5. Landscape with Mercury's theft of the cattle, *Claude Lorrain*; 11. Portrait of Macchiavelli, *Bronzino*; *12. "The Mill", *Cl. Lorrain*; *23. Landscape with temple of Apollo, by the same (two of the most admirable landscapes of this master); 21. St. Catharine, *Garofalo*; 26. Portrait, *Mazzolino*; 27. Portrait, *Giorgione* (? *A. del Sarto*); 31. Holy Family, *Fra Bartolommeo*; 33. Landscape with Diana hunting, *Cl. Lorrain*. Adjoining No. 38 two small pictures of the old Dutch school. Adjacent is a small Corner-cabinet: 1. Portrait, *Lucas v. Leyden* (?); *2. Portrait of Andrea Doria, *Seb. del Piombo*; 3. Gianetto Doria, *Bronzino*; *5. Innocent X., *Velasquez*; *6. Entombment, *Rogier v. d. Weyde*. The 4th Gallery contains statues of no great value, most of them greatly modernized.

On the l. side of the Corso, opposite the Pal. Doria, is the *Pal. Salviati*, the side-street bounding which, as well as the preceding and the following, lead to the *Piazza di SS. Apostoli*, with the church of that name, where to the r. the *Pal. Colonna* is situated; on the narrow side is the adjoining *Pal. Valentini* with a few antiquities (the pictures it formerly contained have been sold and are now in England); on the second longer side of the piazza is the *Pal. Ruffo* to the l., and the *Pal. Odescalchi*, façade of the latter by Bernini.

*SS. Apostoli (Pl. II, 19), originally founded by Pelagius I. in honour of St. Philip and St. James, was re-erected under Clement XI. in 1702. The vestibule by *Baccio Pintelli* is all that remains of earlier date; in it to the l. monument of the engraver Giov. Volpato by *Canova* (1807), r. an ancient *eagle with chaplet of oak-leaves, from the Forum of Trajan.

In the r. aisle, 3rd Chapel: St. Antony by *Luti*. In the l. aisle, 2nd Chapel: Descent from the Cross by *Franc. Manno*. At the extremity, to the l. over the entrance into the sacristy: Monument of Clement XIV. by *Canova*, on the pedestal Charity and Temperance. In the tribune, with altar-piece by *Muratori* (said to be the largest in Rome), are the monuments erected by Sixtus IV. to his two nephews, the Cardinals Riario, to the l. that of Pietro R. (d. 1474) and that of Alexander R. behind the altar and partially concealed by the organ. On the vaulted ceiling of the tribune, Fall of the Angels, a fresco by *Giov. Odassi*, in the baroque style but of striking effect. The former church was decorated by *Melozzo da Forli*; a fine fragment of these frescoes is now in the Quirinal (p. 133), others in the sacristy of St. Peter's (p. 221).

In the adjoining monastery, the passage nearest to the church contains a monument by *Mich. Angelo* and the tomb of Card. Bessarion.

*Palazzo Colonna (Pl. II. 19), commenced by Martin V., subsequently greatly extended and altered, is now almost entirely let to the French ambassador; a number of rooms on the ground floor, containing interesting frescoes, are therefore inaccessible. In the l. wing is the approach to the *Picture Gallery*, situated on the first floor (daily 11—3, except Sundays and holidays). A large hall containing family-portraits is first entered, and thence three ante-rooms adorned with Gobelins, in the second of which are four ancient draped statues; in the third a small ancient statue of a girl, erroneously termed a Niobe. In the gallery itself the pictures are not numbered, but are furnished with the names of the artists.

1st Room: On the wall of the entrance: Madonna, *Fil. Lippi*; same by *Luca Longhi* and *S. Botticelli*. L. wall: Madonna (much damaged), *Luini*; Portrait, *Giov. Santi* (father of Raphael); Crucifixion, *Jacopo d'Avanzo*; two Landscapes, *Albano;* Madonna, *Giulio Romano;* same, *Gentile da Fabriano*. Wall of the outlet: Holy Family, *Parmeggianino;* same, *Innoc. da Imola;* *two Madonnas surrounded by smaller circular pictures (erroneously attrib. to Van Eyck), of the later Dutch school. — 2nd R.: Throne-room with fine old carpet. — 3rd R.: Ceiling-painting by *Battoni* and *Luti* (in honour of Martin V.). Entrance-wall: St. Bernhard, *Giov. Bellini;* Onuphrius Panvinius, *Titian;* Poggio Bracciolini, *Girolamo Trevisani;* Holy Family, *Bronzino*. L. wall: Rape of Europa, *Albano;* Madonna, *Domenico Pulego;* Beaneater, *Ann. Caracci*; ᶜSt. Jerome, *Spagna*; Madonna with saints, *Paris Bordone*. Wall of the outlet: Lor. Colonna, *Holbein* (?); Portrait of a man, P. *Veronese*; Holy Family, *Bonifazio*. Window-wall: Cain and Abel, *l. Mola*; Madonna, *Sassoferrato*. — 4th R.: *Eleven landscapes by *G. Poussin*, some of that artist's finest works, all well worthy of careful examination, although not all favourably hung. Entrance - wall: Architectural picture, *Canaletto*; Landscape, *Crescenzo d'Onofrio*; opp. to these, Landscape, by *Claude Lorrain* (?); Chase and cavalry skirmish, *Wouvermans* (?); Metamorphosis of Daphne, *N. Poussin*; a large cabinet with ivory carving by *Franc.* and *Dom. Reinhard*. — *N.* Gallery with ceiling-paintings by *Coli* and *Gherardi* (Battle of Lepanto, Oct. 8th, 1571, which Marcantonio Colonna at the head of the papal army assisted in gaining). On the walls mirrors painted with flowers (by *Mario de' Fiori*) and genii (by *G. Maratta*). Statues here of no great value, most of them modernized. Reliefs built into the wall under the windows (r.): Head of Minerva; Wounded man, borne away by his friends; Selene in the chariot (archaic style). L. wall: Assumption of the Virgin, *Rubens*; ᶜFed. Colonna, *Sustermanns*; Christ in the lower regions, *Crist. Allori*; Adam and Eve, *Salviati*; ᶜDon Carlo Colonna, equestrian portrait, *Van Dyck*; Martyrdom of Emmerentia, *Guercino*; Family-portrait of the Colonnas, *S. Gaetano*. R. wall: Double portrait, *Tintoretto*; Pastoral scene, *N. Poussin*; Madonna rescuing a child from a demon, *Niccolo d'Alunno*. — VI. In the raised room, from r. to l.: Card. Pomp. Colonna, *Lor. Lotto*; Vittoria Colonna, *Muziano*; Portrait, *Moroni*; Hylas, *Tintoretto*; Rape of the Sabine women, *Ghirlandajo*; Madonna with St. Peter etc., *Palma Vecchio*; Holy Family, *Titian* (or Palma?); Lucrezia Colonna, *Van Dyck*; Portrait, *Moroni da Brescia*; Pompeo Colonna, *Ag. Caracci*; Giac. Sciarra Colonna, *Giorgione*; Franc. Colonna, *Pourbus*. In the centre a column of red marble with representations from a campaign in relief (Renaissance).

The beautiful *Garden of this palace (entered through the palace, or from Monte Cavallo, Via del Quirinale 12) contains several antiquities, fragments of a colossal architrave, said to have belonged to Aurelian's temple of the sun, and considerable portions of the brick-walls of the Thermæ of Constantine which once extended over the entire Piazza of Monte Cavallo.

At the extremity of the Corso, on the r., with portal towards the Piazza di Venezia, is the *Pal. Bonaparte*, formerly *Rinuccini*. erected by de' Rossi, where Madame Lætitia, mother of Napoleon, died, Feb. 2nd 1806. The Corso terminates with the *Piazza di Venezia*, which derives its appellation from the *Palazzo di Venezia (Pl. II. 16), one of the most imposing of modern Rome. It was built by *Bernardo di Lorenzo* for the Borgias in 1455, presented in 1560 by Pius IV. to the Republic of Venice, with which it subsequently came into the possession of Austria, and is now the residence of the Austrian ambassador. The extensive court with arcades is, with the exception of a small portion, uncompleted, so also a second court to the l. of the other.

Opposite the side-entrance of the above is the **Pal. Torlonia**, formerly *Bolognetti*, erected about 1650 by *C. Fontana*, occupying the block as far as Piazza SS. Apostoli, the property of the banker Prince Torlonia, Duke of Bracciano. It is lavishly decorated, and contains among other works of art Canova's Raving Hercules, but is not accessible to the public. L. on the ground-floor permessi for the Villa Albani may be procured.

From the Piazza Venezia the visitor proceeds in a straight direction through the narrow *Ripresa dei Barberi*, so named because the "Barbary" horses, which were formerly employed in the races of the Carnival, were here caught. Here to the l. (No. 174) is the *Pal. Nipoti*, inhabited by the dowager Queen of Naples until her death. The first transverse street to the l. leads to the Forum of Trajan (p. 182). To the r. the *Via S. Marco*, passing under an arch of the passage which leads from the Pal. di Venezia to S. Maria di Araceli, brings the visitor to the *Piazza di San Marco*. Here to the r. is **S. Marco** (Pl. II. 16), incorporated with the Pal. di Venezia, a church of very ancient origin (said to date from the Emp. Constantine), re-erected in 833 by Gregory IV., adorned in 1455 by *Bernardo di Lorenzo* with fine vestibule and probably with the ceiling of the nave, and finally embellished according to modern taste in 1744 by Card. Quirini.

Roman and ancient Christian sarcophagi and inscriptions are built into the walls of the vestibule. St. Mark in relief, above the handsome inner principal portal. The interior is approached by a descent of several steps. With the exception of the tribune and the beautiful ceiling, all the older portions have been disfigured by restorations. The tribune with handsome pavement (opus Alexandrinum) lies a few steps higher than the front part of the church. The mosaics (in the centre Christ, l. the saints Mark, Agapetus and Agnes. r. Felicianus and Mark escorting Gregory IV.) date from the period of the greatest decline of this art (about 833). In the r. aisle, 1st Chapel: altar-piece by *Palma Giovine*, the Resurrection. 3rd Chapel: Adoration of the Magi, *Maratta*. At the extremity by the tribune: "Pope Mark, an admirable ancient picture. In the l. aisle, 2nd Chapel: altar-relief. Greg. Barbadigo distributing alms, by *Ant. d'Este*. 4th Chapel: St. Michael, *Mola*.

In the Piazza, to the l. in front of the church, is the so-called *Madonna Lucrezia*, the mutilated marble bust of a colossal female statue, which carried on conversations with the Abate Luigi near the Pal. Vidoni (p. 159), similar to those of Pasquin with the Marforio.

The Via di S. Marco terminates in the *Via Araceli*, which to the l. leads to the Piazza Araceli (p. 168) and the Capitol, and to the r. to the Piazza del Gesù (p. 124).

From the Piazza Venezia the Ripresa de' Barberi and its continuation the *Via di Marforio* lead by the N.E. slope of the Capitoline to the Forum and the Arch of Severus (p. 172). The name is derived from Forum Martis (i. e. the forum of Augustus). The celebrated statue of Marforio which formerly stood in this street, opposite the Carcer Mamertinus, is now in the Capitoline museum (p. 210). Beyond the second transverse street, the *Via della Pedacchia*, which connects the Piazza Araceli with the Forum of Trajan, is situated on the l. the (long since built over) *Monument of C. Publicius Bibulus*, to whom the ground was granted by the senate as a burial-place for himself and his family in recognition of his merits ("honoris virtutisque causa", as the inscription records), dating from the latter years of the republic. This point must accordingly have lain without the walls of Servius, which extended immediately beneath the Capitol.

From the Piazza Venezia the broad *Via del Gesù* leads to the r., past the Pal. di Venezia: on the r. are Pal. Bonaparte (p. 122), Doria (p. 119) and Grazioli. Then *Pal. Altieri* with extensive façade, erected in 1670, bounding the N. side of the small *Piazza del Gesù*. By the palace the Via del Gesù ascends to the Piazza della Minerva (p. 155), a walk of 5 min. Opposite to the church, adjoining which is the cloister of the Jesuits where their general resides, the busy *Via de' Cesarini* leads to the r. to S. Andrea della Valle (p. 159) and to the bridge of S. Angelo *(Via Papale)*.

*Gesù (Pl. II, 16), principal church of the Jesuits, is one of the most sumptuous in Rome. It was built by *Vignola* and *Giac. della Porta* by order of Card. Alessandro Farnese. 1568—75.

In the nave *ceiling-painting by *Baciccio*, by whom the dome and tribune were also painted, one of the best and most life-like of the baroque works of that period. The walls were covered with valuable marble at the cost of the Principe Aless. Torlonia in 1860. On the high-altar with its 4 columns of giallo antico: Christ in the Temple, by *Capalti*; on the l. the monument of Card. Bellarmino with figures of Religion and Faith, in relief; on the r. the monum. of P. Pignatelli, with Love and Hope. In the transept to the l.: *Altar of St. Ignatius with a picture by *Pozzi*, beneath which a silvered relief of St. Ignatius is said to be concealed. The silver statue of the saint, by *Le Gros*, which was formerly here, is said to have been removed on the suppression of the order in the previous century. The columns are of lapis lazuli and gilded bronze; on the architrave above are two statues: God the Father, by *B. Ludovisi*, and Christ, by *L. Ottoni*, behind which, encircled by a halo of rays, is the emblematic Dove. Between these the globe of the earth, consisting of a single block of lapis lazuli (said to be the largest in existence). Beneath the altar, in a sarcophagus of gilded bronze, repose the remains of the saint. On the r. and l. are groups in marble; on the r. the Christian Religion, at the sight of which heretics shrink, by *Le Gros*; on the l. Faith with the Cup and Host, which a heathen king is in the act of adoring, by *Théodon*. Opposite, in the transept, on the r. the altar of St. Francis Xavier.

The church presents the most imposing spectacle during the "Quarant'ore" (two last days of the Carnival), when it is brilliantly illuminated in the evening. During Advent and Lent (generally at other seasons also) sermons are preached here at 11 a. m., often by the most talented members of the order.

Following the Via di Araceli, to the l. of the Piazza di Gesù, and passing the cloister, the visitor reaches (in 5 min.) the *Piazza di Araceli*, in front of the Capitol (p. 168).

Villa Borghese.

The *Villa Borghese (Pl. 1, 21), immediately to the r. without the Porta del Popolo, founded by Card. Scipio Borghese, nephew of Pius V., subsequently enlarged by the Giustiniani gardens and the so-called villa of Raphael, which with a large portion of the plantations was destroyed during the siege of 1849, is accessible daily, Mondays excepted; the *Casino* with the collection of antiquities on Saturdays only, 1—4 o'clock in winter, 4—7 in summer. The beautiful and extensive grounds are justly in high repute as a promenade, and are in October the scene of popular festivities, the Tombola, races etc. The gardens contain a number of ancient statues and inscriptions.

On entering, the visitor should select the 'footpath which skirts the carriage-road on the r., and leads to an Egyptian gateway (8 min.); thence in a straight direction, passing a grotto with antique fragmen:s (l.); then to the l., either in a straight direction, in which case the closed private gardens of the prince lie on the l., as far as an artificial ruin of a temple, and then to the r.; or the first footpath to the r. may be selected, leading by an avenue of evergreen oaks to a small temple, and thence to the l., by a similar avenue, to a circular space with a fountain (10 min.). From this point the carriage-road leads to the Casino, which is also connected with the same spot by beautiful, shady footpaths.

If from the Egyptian gate, instead of the path to the l., a straight direction be pursued, the remains of Raphael's villa will be reached (on the l.) in 3 min., and in 3 min. more an arch with a statue of Apollo, whence the road diverges to the l. and leads to the Casino.

The *Casino* formerly contained one of the most valuable private collections in existence, which at the instance of Napoleon I. was transferred to the Louvre. In consequence, however, of recent excavations, especially near Monte Calvi in the Sabina, Prince Borghese has again established a *Museum* which contains several objects of great interest. (Custodian ¹/₂ l.)

I. Vestibule: Two candelabra; on the narrow walls two reliefs from the triumphal arch of Claudius in the Corso near the Pal. Sciarra, which was removed in 1527. Several sarcophagi, to the l. by the wall of the egress one with a harbour, lighthouse and ships. — II. Saloon with ceiling-painting by *Mario Rossi*. On the floor mosaics, discovered in 1835 near the Tenuta di Torre Nuova, with gladiator and wild beast combats. L. wall: 4. Dancing Faun, beneath it a Bacchan. relief. Long wall: 7. Tiberius; 8. Meleager; 9. Augustus; above, a raised relief of a galloping rider (M. Curtius?); *10. Priestess; 11. Bacchus and Ampelus. R. wall: 14. Hadrian; 16. Anton. Pius; colossal busts. Entrance-wall: 18. Diana. — III. (1st Room to the r.): in the centre, *Juno Pronuba, found near Monte Calvi. Left wall: 3. Urania; 4. Ceres; 5. Venus Genetrix. Opp. the entrance: 8. Relief: Sacrificial prayer (of Hesiod?) to Eros; 11. Relief of the Rape of Cassandra. R. wall: 16. Statue with drapery. Entrance-wall: 20. Greek relief from a tomb. — IV. In the centre: Amazon on horseback contending with a warrior. Entrance-wall: 2. Pan; 4. Sarcophagus with the achievements of Hercules; on the cover: Reception of the Amazons by Priam; 6. Head of Hercules; 7. Pygmæa. L. wall: 9. Statue of Hercules. Wall of the egress: 15. Hercules in female attire; 17. Sarcophagus with the exploits of Hercules. Window-wall: 21. Venus; 23. Three-sided ara with Mercury, Spes and Bacchus. — V. Room: In the centre, Apollo. L. wall: 3. Scipio Africanus; 4. Daphne metamorphosed into a laurel. Following wall: 7 head of a Maïnade; 8. Melpomene; 9. Genre-group; 10. Clio. R. wall: *13. Statue of Anacreon in a sitting posture, perhaps a copy from a celebrated work of *Cresilas* at Athens; 14. Lucilla, wife of L. Verus. Entrance-wall: 16. Erato; 17. Polyhymnia. — VI. R.: Gallery with modern busts of emperors in porphyry. In the centre a porphyry bath, said to have appertained to the mausoleum of Hadrian; 22. Bacchus; *28. Statue of a Satyr in basalt; 32. Bronze statue of a boy. (By the second door of the entrance-wall the upper story is reached.) — VII. R., with columns of giallo antico and porphyry, on the floor ancient mosaics. L. wall: *2. Boy with bird; 3. Bacchus; *4. Captive boy. Wall of the egress: 7. Recumbent Hermaphrodite; 9. Sappho (doubtful); 10. Tiberius. Entrance-wall: *13. Roman portrait-bust (said to be Domitius Corbulo); *14. Head of a youth; 15. Boy with Hydria; 16. Female bust. — VII. R.: In the centre: *Portrait-statue of a Greek poet, perhaps Alcæus. L. wall: 2. Athene; 4. Apollo (archaic style). Following wall: 6. Figure from a tomb; 7. Candelabrum with Hecate. R. wall: 8. Danaide; 10. Leda; 15. Æsculapius and Telesphorus. — IX. R.: In the centre: *Boy on a dolphin; 3. Isis; 4. Paris; 8. Ceres, the white extremities new; 10. Gipsy woman; 13. Venus; 14. Female figure (archaic); *16. Bacchante; 18. Satyr; 19. Hadrian; 20. Satyr. — X. R.: *1. Dancing Satyr, erroneously restored (he originally played on the flute); 2. Ceres; 3. Mercury with a lyre; 4. Dancing Satyr; 3. Satyr reposing, after Praxiteles; 9. Pluto with Cerberus; 14. Periander; 19. Dionysius enthroned. The beautiful ceiling-paintings in this room by *Conca* should not fail to be inspected.

On the upper floor a large saloon (fee ½ l.) contains three early works of *Bernini*: Æneas carrying Anchises; Apollo and Daphne; David with the sling. The ceiling-paintings are by *Lanfranco*, the 5 *Landscapes on the l. wall by *Phil. Hackert*. In one of the following rooms the recumbent statue of Pauline Borghese, sister of Napoleon I., as Venus, by *Canova*. Other apartments contain modern sculptures and numerous pictures, which with a few exceptions (e. g. Portrait of Paul V. by *Caravaggio* in the 2nd room) are of little value. The balcony commands a fine view of the gardens and the city.

II. The Hills of Rome.

Quirinal. Viminal. Esquiline.

The following description comprises the E. part of Rome which extends over the three long, parallel hills of the Quirinal, Viminal and Esquiline, and adjoins the Corso and Strangers' Quarter, but is almost entirely occupied by vineyards and gardens, especially towards the walls.

From the Piazza della Trinità on the Pincio, running in a S. E. direction as far as the church (visible thence) of S. Maria Maggiore on the Esquiline, a street, 1 M. in length, bearing the different names of *Via Sistina*, *Via Felice* and *Via delle Quattro Fontane*, intersects this quarter of the city. It is termed Via Sistina as far as the first transverse street (Via di Porta Pinciana), Via Felice thence to the Piazza Barberini, and Via delle Quattro Fontane in the remaining portion. From the Pincio to the Piazza Barberini is a descent of ¼ M., and thence to the summit of the Quirinal an ascent of ¼ M., where this line of streets is intersected by a street (Via del Quirinale and Via di Porta Pia) which extends in a straight direction along almost the entire ridge from the Piazza di Monte Cavallo to the Porta Pia. From the Quirinal the street then descends, traverses the Viminal, and finally ascends the Esquiline near S. Maria Maggiore. The first portion of this street, into which several lateral streets lead, presents a busy scene, and is frequented by a considerable number of strangers; the part beyond the Quirinal, on the other hand, is comparatively deserted, and partly uninhabited.

After the Piazza della Trinità is quitted, the first transverse street reached is the *Via di Capo le Case*, which descends; its prolongation to the l. is the *Via di Porta Pinciana*, which ascends to the gate of that name (closed in 1803), and in which (l.) the *Villa Malta*, once property of King Louis I. of Bavaria, is situated.

The Via Felice now descends, passing *S. Francesca* on the l. and *S. Ildefonso* on the r., to the extensive *Piazza Barberini*. In the centre the *Fontana del Tritone*, by Bernini, a Triton blowing on a conch. On the r. one side of the Palazzo Barberini (p. 131) adjoins the Piazza. As the Piazza is ascended the *Via di S. Niccolò di Tolentino* leads to the r. past the palace to the church of that name, then again to the r., under the name *Via di S. Susanna*, to the Fontana and Piazza di Termini (p. 135); to the l. the *Via di S. Basilio* leads to the Villa Ludovisi (6 min.), and through the Porta Salara to the Villa Albani (1 M.).

The avenue to the l. at the extremity of the Piazza ascends to (on the r.) **S. Maria della Concezione** (Pl. I, 23), or *dei Cappuccini*, which, with the contiguous cloister, belongs to the Capuchins. It was founded in 1624 by Card. Barberini.

In the interior, over the door, a copy of *Giotto's* Navicella (in the vestibule of St. Peter's, p. 218) by *Beretta*. In the 1st Chapel (r.) *St. Michael, a celebrated picture by *Guido Reni*; in the 3rd, mutilated frescoes by *Domenichino*. At the high-altar a copy of an Ascension by *Lanfranco*, now destroyed. Beneath a stone in front of the steps to the choir reposes the founder of the church, Card. Barberini ("hic jacet pulvis cinis et nihil"); on the l. the tomb of Alex. Sobiesky, son of John III. of Poland, who died in 1714. The last chapel contains (l.) an altar piece by *Sacchi*; in the first, one by *Pietro da Cortona*.

Beneath the church are four mortuary-chapels, decorated in a ghastly manner with the bones of the dead. Each of these contains a tomb with earth from Jerusalem. In case of a new interment the bones which have longest remained undisturbed, are employed in the manner alluded to. On All Souls' Day (Nov. 2nd) these vaults are lighted up and visited by numbers of people.

The *Via di S. Isidoro* ascends hence to the church of *S. Isidoro*, founded in 1622.

If the Via di S. Basilio be ascended in a straight direction for 5 min. (the first part only is inhabited), it will lead the visitor to the entrance, on the r., of the

Villa Ludovisi (Pl. I, 23), erected during the first half of the 17th cent. by Card. Ludovisi, nephew of Gregory XV., and subsequently inherited by the princes of Piombino (accessible on Thursdays in winter; permessi obtained through ambassador or consul). The grounds were laid out by Le Nôtre.

From the gateway (5—10 s. on leaving) the visitor proceeds to the r. to the *first Casino*, containing valuable ancient sculptures. Catalogues may be purchased of the custodian (1/2 l.).

1st Room: 1., 3., 7., 42., 46., 48. Statues; 20. Female head, very ancient; 18. Candelabrum in the form of a twisted tree; 15. Sitting statue of a Roman, by *Zenon*; 25. Female draped figure; 37. Tragic mask, mouth of a fountain in rosso antico. — 2nd R.: *28. Group of a barbarian who having killed his wife plunges the sword into his own breast, Pergamenian school. R. of the entrance: *55. Warrior reposing (Mars?), probably destined originally to decorate the approach to a door; 51. Statue of Athene from Antioch; 46. Bust, name unknown; *45. Head of a Medusa, of the noblest type; 43. Rape of Proserpine, by Bernini; 42. Judgment of Paris, the r. side restored according to Raphael's plan; **41. "Juno Ludovisi", the most celebrated and one of the most beautiful heads of Juno; 30. Mercury, in the same position as the so-called Germanicus in Paris. L. of the entrance: *1. Mars reposing, probably of the school of Lysippus; *7. Theseus and Æthra (or Telemachus and Penelope, commonly called Orestes and Electra), by *Menelaos*, pupil of Stephanos; *9. Youthful Satyr; 14. Dionysus with a satyr; 15. Head of Juno.

To the l. of the gateway, by a wall with a hedge, and then past a mound with pavilion, a path (4 min.) leads to the *second Casino* (dell' Aurora) (fee 5 s.), where on the ground-floor is a ceiling-fresco of *Aurora by *Guercino*, on the first floor *Fama by the same. The staircase (containing among other curiosities an interesting ancient relief of two Cupids dragging a quiver) ascends hence to the upper balconies, whence a magnificent *view of Rome and the mountains is enjoyed.

Several paths lead from the Casino to the city-wall, which is skirted by beautiful avenues of cypresses and other evergreens. Ancient sculptures are distributed in different parts of the grounds; e. g. by the city-wall a sarcophagus with representation of a battle, possibly that of Alex. Severus against Artaxerxes, A. D. 232.

From the Villa Ludovisi to the *Porta Salara* by the *Via di Porta Salara* (Pl. I, 27) is a walk of 8 min., bounded on the l. by the walls of the villa, on the r. by vineyards. Here in ancient times lay the magnificent *Gardens of Sallust*, the historian, subsequently the property of the emperors. They also comprised a circus, occupying the hollow between the Pincio and Quirinal which are united farther up by the gate. Where the view is unintercepted to the r., considerable remains of the enclosing walls are observed on the Quirinal opposite. A road to the r. near the gate leads (in 3 min.) to the Via di Porta Pia.

The Via Salara leads from the gate, skirting the Tiber within a short distance of its bank, to the Sabina. According to Pliny, it derives its name from the fact that the peasantry were in the habit of transporting salt by this route from the ancient works at Ostia. — 8 min. walk beyond the gate lies (on the r.) the

*__Villa Albani__ (see map p. 262: Tuesdays, with permission obtained by sending visiting-card with request to the office, Pal. Torlonia, Piazza Venezia 135, p. 122, ground-floor l.), founded in 1760 by Card. Aless. Albani and decorated with admirable works of art; the building by *C. Marchionne*. Napoleon I. transferred 294 of the finest statues to Paris, which on their restoration in 1815 were sold there by Card. Giuseppe Albani, in order to avoid the onerous expenses of transport. Some of them are now in the Glyptothek at Munich. In 1834 the Counts of Castelbarco became proprietors of the villa, and caused the arrangement of the statues to be altered. The villa has recently been purchased by Prince Torlonia.

Three paths enclosed by hedges diverge from the entrance; that in the centre leads first to a circular space with column in the middle, then to a fountain whence a comprehensive view is obtained: 1. the Casino with the galleries on either side; opposite is a small building with cypresses on one side, the so-called Billiard-room; on the r. the building in the crescent is the "Café". The finest *view from the terrace is obtained near the side-staircase, farther to the r., whence, to the r. of the cypresses, S. Agnese and S. Costanza appear in the centre, above which rises Monte Gennaro, with Monticelli at its base. (Most favourable light towards evening.)

1. *Casino*. Vestibule. In the 6 niches: Tiberius, L. Verus, Trajan, M. Aurelius, Antoninus Pius, Hadrian; in the centre a female portrait-statue sitting (Faustina); circular Ara with Bacchus, Ceres, Proserpine and 3 Horæ, another with female torch-bearer and the Seasons; sitting female figure (perhaps the elder Agrippina). By the pillars on the l. and r. are statues: on the 1st to the r. Hermes; 5th l. female, r. male double statue; 7th r. Euripides. Now to the l.: *a*. The small Atrio della Cariatide, containing two canephori, found between Frascati and Monte Porzio (baskets new). In the centre a Caryatide, found in 1766 near the Cæcilia Metella, by the Athenians *Criton* and *Nicolaus* (the names engraved on it); on the pedestal ᵉCapaneus struck by lightning; busts of Titus and Vespasian. *b*. Gallery, containing statues: the third to the r. Scipio Africanus, the third to the l. Epicurus.

In the small central space in the corridor is the approach to the Staircase on the l.; in front of the stairs, l. Roma sitting on trophies (in relief). Behind the stair (generally closed) two reliefs of butchers' shops, one of them inscribed with verses from the Æneid. On the staircase reliefs: on the first landing, r. Death of the Children of Niobe, l. beneath, Philoctetes in Lemnos (?); on the third landing, above, two dancing Bacchantes. Upper floor (when closed, visitors ring, ¹/₂ l.): I. Room: ᵃLarge marble basin with Bacchanalian festivities, among the figures is Hercules (most of the heads new). L. of the door: Statue of a youth by *Stephanos*, pupil of Pasiteles. Opposite: Cupid bending his bow, probably a copy from Lysippus. — II. Saloon: (on the ceiling Apollo, Mnemosyne and the Muses painted by *Raph. Mengs*). In the niches of the entrance-wall ᵃPallas and Zeus. Reliefs (over the door): Apollo, Diana, Leto in front of the temple of Delphi (ancient victory-relief). Then to the r., youth with his horse, from a tomb near Tivoli; l. Anton. Pius with Pax and Roma. The eight fragments of mosaic at the sides of this door, and that of the balcony, and in the 4 corners are for the greater part ancient. By the l.

wall: 1. Two women sacrificing, r. Dancing Bacchantes. By the window-wall: Hercules and the Hesperides; Dædalus and Icarus (these reliefs belong to the eight in the P. Spada, see p. 163). Beautiful view from the balcony of the Alban and Sabine Mts. — III. In the first room to the r. of the saloon, over the chimney-piece: *Mercury conducting Eurydice back from the infernal regions. By the entrance-wall, Theophrastus; window-wall, 1. Hippocrates; wall of the egress, *Socrates. — IV. 2nd R.: Picture Gallery. On the wall of the egress: 1. *picture in 5 compartments by *Pietro Perugino:* Joseph and Mary adoring the Infant Christ, Crucifixion, Saints (of 1491). R. wall: 2. *Sketches in colours for the frescoes from the history of Psyche in the Pal. del Te at Mantua, by *Giulio Romano* (one of these is lately removed): 58. a lunette by *Cotignola:* Dead Christ with mourning angels. Wall of the entrance: 9. Madonna, *Salaino;* 8. Madonna, *Camuccini*, copy from Raphael; 58. Paul III., copy from *Titian.* — V. 3rd R.: Cartoons of *Domenichino.* — VI. First room to the 1. of the saloon: over the chimney-piece the celebrated *Relief of Antinous, from the Villa of Hadrian, the only object in the collection which was brought back from Paris. — VII. 2nd Room from the entrance on the l.: flute-playing Pan; ancient Greek relief from a tomb. L. wall: *Greek relief in the best style, a group of combatants, found in 1764 near S. Vito. Beneath it, Procession of Hermes, Athene, Apollo and Artemis (archaic style). By the window to the l. ancient statue of Pallas, found near Orta. Wall of the egress, on the l.: Greek tomb-relief (greatly modernized). — VIII. 3rd (corner) Room, with a few cartoons by *Domenichino.* L. wall: Madonna with saints by *Niccolò Alunno*, 1475. — IX. 4th R.: In front of the window: Æsop, perhaps after *Lysippus*, the head of beautiful workmanship. In the niche in the entrance-wall Apollo Sauroctonus, after *Praxiteles.* Adjacent to the r. a small statue of Diogenes. Opposite, Farnese Hercules in bronze. — X. L. by the door: A Cardinal, *Domenichino*, and opposite another by an unknown artist. On the l. wall: Fornarina, copy from *Raphael.* — XI. Room with Gobelins. Returning to the circular saloon the visitor now descends to the lower corridor. Here at the extremity to the l., corresponding to the Atrio della Cariatide, is the: 1. Atrio della Giunone, containing two canephori, as in the corresponding room. In the centre a figure said to represent Juno. II. Gallery, in the centre: marble vase with six dancing Bacchantes. In the first niche a *Bacchante with Nebris, in the second a *Satyr with the young Bacchus. Some of the statues by the pillars are fine, but arbitrarily named. III. Stanza della Colonna (antique columns of variegated alabaster, found at the Marmorata). On the l. a *sarcophagus with the Nuptials of Peleus and Thetis. Above, four sarcophagus-reliefs: on the l. Hippolytus and Phædra. Over the egress: Rape of Proserpine. On the r. Bacchanalian procession. Over the entrance: Death of Alcestis. — IV. Small room: Bearded Bacchus. — V. Stanza delle Terracotte. By the l. wall to the entrance, 156. Greek tomb-relief; 157. Greek votive relief. Beyond the door: 166. Love-sick Polyphemus and Cupid. Diogenes and Alexander. Opp. the entrance, 173. Dædalus and Icarus, in rosso antico. Beneath, 172. ancient landscape-picture. On the r. wall, 177. Mask of a river-god; 1. 163. Bacchus pardoning the captive Indians, formerly in Winckelmann's possession. r. 167. Greek votive relief. Contiguous to it, and on the entrance-wall several fine reliefs in terracotta. — VI. R.: Marble basin with the 12 exploits of Hercules, found in 1762 on the Via Appia. In the window to the l., Leda with the swan. VII. R.: Above the entrance-door, Bacchanalian procession of children, from Hadrian's Villa; 1. statue of a recumbent river-god. VIII. R.: Apollo on the tripod. Reliefs in the first window to the l.: The god of sleep.

Hence by an avenue of oaks with columns from tombs (cippi), to the

2. *Bigliardo* (generally closed; if desired the wife of the custodian, to be found here or at the café, will open it; 1/2 l.). In a niche in front: Theseus with the Minotaur, found in 1740 near Genzano; beneath, a frieze with playing Cupids. In a niche of the vestibule: *Greek relief, probably Hercules, Theseus and Peirithous in the lower regions. The window commands a fine view of the garden and environs.

3. **Café.** In the semi-circular hall, on the r. a statue of the orator Hortensius; 1. 1. bust of Alcibiades (?); 1. 2. Statue of Mars; 5. Statue of Chrysippus; 3. Apollo reposing; 5. Karyatide. In the centre an Anteroom is entered to the l. Here in the department on the r.: in front of the middle-window Iris; 1. Theseus with Æthra, a sarcophagus-relief. In the department on the l.: In front of the middle-window Marsyas bound to the tree; on the l. a relief of Venus and Cupid. Also several statues of comic actors. In the Saloon, in the niche to the l. of the door, Libera with a fawn. Beneath, mosaic with meeting of 7 physicians. Corresponding to the latter, to the r. of the door, mosaic of the liberation of Hesione by Hercules. R. of the balcony-door, Ibis of rosso antico; Atlas, bearer of the universe; l. boy with comic mask; colossal head of Serapis, of green basalt. The balcony commands a pleasing view. Visitors now return to the semicircular hall. Here to the l. on the first pillar which stands alone, a statuette of Neptune. Near it a Caryatide, r. on the 3rd pillar mask of Poseidon. Nearly opp., to the l., ancient Greek *Portrait-head (styled Pericles, perhaps rather Pisistratus); l. female statue (called Sappho, possibly Ceres); r., the last small statue, Isocrates.

Before the hall of the Café is entered, a stair to the l. descends to a lower part of the garden. On the basement of the building several fragments of sculpture are walled in, and a few Egyptian statues arranged in a hall. In the centre: Ptolemæus Philadelphus, of grey granite; r. the lionheaded goddess Pascht; l. statue of a king, in black granite; several sphynxes. On a fountain in front of the hall: reclining Amphitrite; l. and r. two colossal *Tritons.

Numerous antique statues are distributed throughout the garden, among which the colossal busts of Titus on the l. and Trajan on the r., below the terrace in front of the Casino, deserve mention.

The visitor may now return by the avenue of evergreen oaks, which is entered by an arch at the extremity of the l. gallery of the Casino. In the centre of the avenue a colossal bust of the German savant Winckelmann, the intimate friend of Card. Albani, the founder of the villa, by *E. Wolff.*

As the Via delle Quattro Fontane is ascended from the Piazza Barberini, on the l. is situated the

*Palazzo Barberini (Pl. I, 22), begun by *Maderno* under Urban VIII., completed by *Bernini*, recently improved in appearance by the removal of several houses, which formerly partially concealed it. A portion of the extensive edifice is let to the French garrison. The principal staircase is to the l. under the arcades; built into it is a Greek *tomb-relief; on the landing of the first floor, a *lion in high-relief, from Tivoli. A number of mediocre ancient sculptures are distributed throughout the courts and other parts of the building. The principal saloon of the palace contains frescoes by *Pietro da Cortona;* in the private apartments of the prince are a number of interesting oil-paintings. At the r. extremity of the arcades a winding staircase ascends to the picture-gallery (Mon., Tues., Wed. 12—5, Thurs. 2—5, Frid., Sat. 10—5 o'clock; in winter closed at dusk).

1st Room: 9. Pietà, *Caravaggio;* 15. Magdalene, *Pomarancio;* 19. Betrothal of St. Catharine, *Parmeggianino.* — 2nd R.: 30. Madonna, after *Raphael;*

35. A Cardinal, attrib. to *Titian*; 49. Madonna, *Innoc. da Imola*; *58. Madonna, *Gior. Bellini*; 63. Portrait of his daughter, *Mengs*. — 3rd R.: 73. Portrait, *Titian* (?); 76. Quay, *Cl. Lorrain*; 78. Portrait, *Bronzino*; *79. Christ among the doctors, painted in 5 days in 1506, by *Dürer*; *82. Portrait of the so-called Fornarina, so frequently copied, unfortunately marred by restoration, *Raphael*; 83. Lucrezia Cenci, stepmother of Beatrice, *Gaetani*; 84. Anna Colonna, *Spanish School*; *85. Beatrice Cenci, *Guido Reni*; 86. Death of Germanicus, *N. Poussin*; 88. Wharf, *Claude Lorrain*; 90. Holy Family, *And. del Sarto*; 93. Annunciation, *S. Botticelli*.

The *Library* of the palace (Thursdays 9—2 o'clock) contains 7000 MSS., among which are those of numerous Greek and Latin authors, of Dante etc. Librarian, the Abbé *Pieralesi*.

The Via delle Quattro Fontane now leads to the summit of the Quirinal, on which a street nearly 1 M. in length extends from the Piazza di Monte Cavallo to the Porta Pia. At the four corners formed by the intersection of these two main-streets, are four fountains erected by Sixtus V., who caused the construction of the former street, whence its appellation.

The *Via del Quirinale* is now entered to the r. At the corner on the l. is the small and unattractive church of *S. Carlo*. Farther on, to the l. *S. Andrea*, by Bernini, with the *Noviciate of the Jesuits*. To the r. some buildings connected with the papal palace are passed, and in 4 min. the visitor reaches the **Piazza di Monte Cavallo** (Pl. II, 19) (named from the two statues), with the *Obelisk* which once stood in front of the mausoleum of Augustus and was erected here in 1787, a *Fountain* with ancient granite basin, and the two admirable colossal **Horse Tamers* in marble, once an ornament of the Thermæ of Constantine in the vicinity. They are frequently mentioned in history, and have never been covered or required excavation. The inscriptions on the pedestals: *Opus Phidiae* and *Opus Praxitelis* (which during the dark ages were believed to be the names of two philosophers, who, having divined the thoughts of Tiberius, were honoured by the erection of these statues in recognition of their wisdom) are purely apocryphal, the groups being works of the imperial age.

Opposite the Apostolic Palace stands the *Pal. of the Consulta*, erected under Clement XII. by del Fuga, where the tribunal of that name, charged with the internal administration of the Papal States, is established. Farther on, to the l., is the Pal. Rospigliosi (p. 134). The gate on the r. enters the garden of the Pal. Colonna (p. 122).

The piazza commands a fine view. In consequence of the construction of new streets at the railway-station the piazza has been extended, the houses in some places removed for the convenience of carriages, and steps constructed for foot-passengers. The new *Via della Dataria*, passes the *Pal. della Dataria*, erected by Paul V., on the r., and descends in a straight direction to the Corso, whilst the first transverse street to the l. *(Via di S. Vincenzo)* leads to the Fontana Trevi (p. 114).

During recent excavations extensive fragments of the walls of the Thermæ of Constantine were discovered, and beneath them older walls of solid blocks, which appear to have belonged to those of Servius Tullius.

The *Palazzo Apostolico al Quirinale (Pl. I, 19), begun under Gregory XIII. by *Flaminio Ponzio*, continued under Sixtus V. and Clement VIII. by *Fontana*, and completed under Paul V. by *Maderno*, has frequently been occupied by the popes in summer on account of its lofty and salubrious situation (Pius IX. resides in summer at the Castel Gandolfo in the Alban Mts.). Here the last conclaves of the cardinals were held, and the name of the newly elected pope proclaimed from the balcony of the façade towards Monte Cavallo. Here Pius VII. expired in 1823. The apartments are shown daily 9—12 o'clock, and from 2 until two hours before sunset (1 l.). Permessi (one for the palace, another for the garden) are procured through an ambassador or consul. The custodian lives in the court below the passage to the second court; door with bell on the r. The palace is entered by the portal in the Via del Quirinale.

In the court, to the r. under the arcades, the staircase ascends; on the landing is immured: *Christ with angels, fresco by *Melozzo da Forli*, transferred hither in 1711 from the old church of SS. Apostoli. The stair then ascends to the r. to the *Sala Regia*, decorated with frescoes by *Lanfranco* and *Saraceni*, where the custodian is generally to be found.

Adjacent is the *Cappella Paolina*, erected by Carlo Maderno, not at present shown. It is decorated with gilded cornicings and copies (in grisaille) of Raphael's Apostles in S. Vincenzo ed Anastasio alle tre Fontane. On the r. are situated a suite of the pope's private apartments. In the 4th a Madonna, perhaps by *Lor. Lotto*, and a Last Supper by *F. Baroccio*. The 5th, 8th and 9th contain interesting Gobelins. In the 10th, mosaics on the floor from Hadrian's villa. In the 14th, a °Ceiling-painting by *F. Overbeck* (1859), to commemorate the flight of Pius IX. in 1848: Christ eluding the pursuit of the Jews who endeavoured to cast him over a precipice (Luke 4, 28, 29). In the 15th views from the Vatican. Towards the garden the *Royal Guest-chamber*, which has been occupied by Napoleon I., Francis I. of Austria and in 1861 by Francis II. of Naples. In the 17th apartment, pictures. On the r. wall: *Peter (completed by *Raphael*) and °Paul, *Fra Bartolommeo*; St. George, *Pordenone*; window-wall: St. Bernhard, *Seb. del Piombo*; St. Cecilia, *Vanni*. In the Audience-saloon (19th apartment) the frieze consists of a cast of the °Triumphal Procession of Alex. the Great, a work by *Thorwaldsen*, ordered by Napoleon I. for the decoration of this saloon. After 1815 the original became the property of the Marchese Sommariva and is now in the Villa Carlotta near Cadenabbia on the Lake of Como, formerly a residence of that nobleman. Another chamber contains: John in the wilderness, a copy from *Raphael*. In the small chapel dell' Annunziata an *Annunciation, altar-piece by *Guido Reni*. In the apartment adjoining the *Sala del Consistorio* °Views of the interior of the ancient basilicas of St. Peter, St. Paul, S. Maria Maggiore and S. Giovanni in Laterano. In the Sala itself: Madonna, a colossal figure by *C. Maratta*;

*Madonna with St. Peter and St. Paul, surrounded by cardinals, by an unknown master of the 15th cent.

The garden was tastefully laid out by C. Maderno. The long passage to the r. in the court in front of the staircase is entered, and access obtained by the first door to the l. ($^1/_2$ l.). The terrace by the palace affords a pleasant view. At the opposite extremity a hot-house and an aviary, containing many rare and beautiful plants and trees. The walls are adorned with a few antiques.

*Palazzo Rospigliosi (Pl. II, 19), begun in 1603 by Card. Scipio Borghese, nephew of Paul V., on the ruins of the Thermæ of Constantine, afterwards the property of the princes Rospigliosi of Pistoja, relations of Clement IX. Here are preserved frescoes from the Thermæ, a beautiful *Cl. Lorrain* (temple of Venus) and other treasures of art, accessible only by special permission of the prince. The *Casino*, however, is open on Wednesdays and Saturdays 11—3 o'clock ($^1/_2$ l.). Under the arcades on the l. adjoining the palace the visitor turns to the l. and knocks at the door which is approached by steps (5 s.). Several well-executed small statues in the garden. By the external wall of the casino are placed ancient sarcophagus-reliefs (Hunt of Meleager, Rape of Proserpine etc.). By the door to the r. the visitor enters the

Hall. *Ceiling-painting by *Guido Reni:* Aurora strewing flowers before the chariot of the god of the sun, who is surrounded by dancing Horæ, the master's finest work. Opp. the entrance is placed a mirror, in which the painting may be conveniently inspected. On the frieze landscapes by *Paul Brill*, and on the narrow sides, Triumph of Fauna and Cupid (from Petrarch's poems), by *Tempesta.* R. wall: Statue of Athene Tritogencia with a Triton; *Portrait, *Van Dyck.* By the door to the room on the r.: Vanità, *Venet. School* (perhaps *Lor. Lotto*). By the long wall a bronze steed from the Thermæ of Constantine.

In the room to the r., opp. the entrance, the Fall of man, *Domenichino.* On the r. wall: *Portrait, *Dutch School;* Venus and Cupid, *Domenichino;* *Holy Family, *Luca Signorelli.* On the entrance-wall: Samson, *L. Caracci* (?). In the room to the l., entrance-wall: Pietà, *Passignani;* Portrait of *N. Poussin*, said to have been painted by himself; l. wall: Bearing the Cross, *Dan. da Volterra.* In the corner a bronze bust of Sept. Severus. On these two and the following wall: Christ and the Apostles, 13 pictures, attributed to *Rubens*, probably only partially the work of that master.

A short distance farther in the Via del Quirinale, to the r., is the church of **S. Silvestro a Monte Cavallo** (Pl. II, 19), erected at the close of the 16th cent., and with the adjacent monastery in possession of the fraternity of St. Vincent of Paula since 1770.

In the dome four oval frescoes by *Domenichino:* David dancing before the Ark, Solomon and the Queen of Sheba, Judith, Esther and Ahasuerus. In the second chapel to the l., two landscapes by *Caravaggio* and his assistant *Maturino:* "Betrothal of the Infant Christ with St. Catharine", and Christ appearing as the gardener to Mary Magdalene.

Beyond this the *Vicolo delle tre Cannelle* diverges to the r. and a short distance farther the *Via Magnanapoli* descends r. to the Forum of Trajan.

At the corner of the Via Magnanapoli and the Via del Quirinale is the *Palace of Card. Antonelli*. — Opposite is the small church of *S. Caterina di Siena* of the 17th cent. Behind it, in the adjoining monastery, rises the *Torre delle Milizie*, erected about 1200 by the sons of Petrus Alexius, commonly called *Torre di Nerone*, because Nero is said to have witnessed the conflagration of Rome from this point. Another similar and contemporaneous tower is the *Torre dei Conti*, near the Forum of Augustus, to which the Via del Grillo descends directly (p. 182). It was erected under Innocent III. (Conti) by Marchionne of Arezzo, but a considerable portion was removed in the 17th cent.

Turning to the l. from the Via del Quirinale the visitor reaches S. Maria Maggiore (p. 140).

From the Quattro Fontane the *Via di Porta Pia* leads to the *Porta Pia* (3/4 M.). The corner house on the r. is *Pal. Albani*, erected by Domen. Fontana, subsequently the property of Card. Albani, now that of Queen Christina of Spain.

In the Via di Porta Pia on the r. are the two uninteresting churches of *S. Teresa* and *S. Cajo*. About 1/4 M. farther, on the r., somewhat removed from the street, is **S. Bernardo** (Pl. I, 22), a circular edifice which originally formed one of the corners of the Thermæ of Diocletian, converted by Catherine Sforza, Countess of S. Fiora, into a church. The vaulting is ancient, but like the Pantheon was once open. In the subterranean chambers under this building a large quantity of lead was found.

On the opposite side (l.) of the street is the ancient church of *S. Susanna*, modified to its present form in 1600 by *C. Maderno* at the instance of Card. Rusticucci. Paintings on the lateral walls from the history of Susanna, by *Baldassare Croce;* those of the tribune by *Cesare Nebbia*.

To the r. extends the **Piazza di Termini** (Pl. I, 25) with the railway-station and the Thermæ of Diocletian (p. 137). At the corner is the *Fontanone dell' Acqua Felice*, erected by Domen. Fontana under Sixtus V., with a badly-executed copy of the Moses of Michael Angelo by *Prospero Bresciano*, who is said to have died of vexation on account of his failure; at the sides Aaron and Gideon by *Giov. Batt. della Porta* and *Flam. Vacca;* in front four modern lions. The *Acqua Felice* was conducted hither in 1583 from Colonna in the Alban Mts., a distance of 22 M., by order of Sixtus V.

To the l. the *Via di S. Susanna* descends to the *Via di S. Nicola di Tolentino*, which leads to the Piazza Barberini.

At the corner to the l. stands the church of **S. Maria della Vittoria** (Pl. I, 23), so-called from an image of the Virgin, believed to have been instrumental in gaining the victory for the imperial troops at the battle of the "White Mountain" near Prague, which was brought here and in 1833 burned. With the exception of the façade the church was designed by *C. Maderno*.

In the 2nd Chapel on the r., an altar-piece (Mary gives the Infant Christ to St. Francis) and frescoes by *Domenichino*. In the l. transept the notorious group of St. Theresa by *Bernini*. In the 3rd Chapel on the l., the Trinity by *Guercino*, and a Crucifixion attrib. to *Guido Reni*.

The street becomes deserted; about 4 min. before the gate is reached a street to the l. diverges to the Porta Salara and the *Via del Macao* to the r., terminating in the vicinity of the railway-station. Farther on, to the l. is the *Villa Bonaparte*, on the r. the *Villa Torlonia*.

The *Porta Pia*, commenced by Pius IV. from the design of Michael Angelo in 1564, is undergoing restoration by order of Pius IX. On the external side 2 statues, St. Agnes and St. Alexander by *Amatori*. To the r. of it is the old *Porta Nomentana*, closed since 1564, which led to Nomentum.

From the gate an unimpeded view is obtained to the l. of the Villa Albani and the Sabine Mts. R. the entrance to the *Villa Patrizi*, with pleasant garden and beautiful view (permessi at the Pal. Patrizi, P. S. Luigi de' Francesi, p. 153). $1/4$ M. farther, on the r., the **Villa Torlonia** (see map p. 262; accessible on Wednesdays 11—4 o'clock, except in summer when the prince resides here; permessi obtained at the Pal. Torlonia, Piazza di Venezia), with pleasant gardens and artificial ruins. This road, the ancient *Via Nomentana*, commanding uninterrupted views from various points, leads to ($1^1/4$ M. from the gate) ***S. Agnese fuori le Mura**, on the l., which still presents many of the characteristics of an early Christian basilica. Constantine founded a church over the tomb of St. Agnes, which Honorius I. (625—38) re-erected. It was altered in 1490 by Innocent VIII., and restored by Pius IX. in 1856.

The gate leads into a court, where through the large window to the r. a view is obtained of the fresco, which was painted in commemoration of the escape of Pius IX. on April 15th, 1855. The floor of a room adjoining the church, to which his Holiness had retired after mass, gave way, and he was precipitated into the cellar beneath, but fortunately was extricated unhurt. On the farther side of the court, on the r., is the entrance to the church, to which a staircase with 45 marble steps descends (on the walls of the stair are numerous ancient Christian inscriptions from the catacombs).

The church is divided into nave and aisles by 16 columns of breccia, porta santa and pavonazetto, which support arches; above these a gallery with smaller columns. The *Tabernacle* of 1614 is borne by 4 fine columns of porphyry; beneath is the statue of St. Agnes, of alabaster; on the highaltar a restored antique. In the tribune *mosaics of the 7th cent. (St. Agnes between the Popes Honorius I. and Symmachus) and an ancient episcopal chair. To the r. in the 2nd Chapel a beautiful altar, inlaid with mosaic; above it a *relief of St. Stephen and St. Lawrence, of 1490. In the l. aisle is an entrance to the catacombs (p. 260). Over the altar of the chapel a fine old fresco: Madonna and Child.

Beneath the gateway which is entered from the street, on the r.. is the approach to the apartments of the canons (visitors ring when the porter is not visible; 5 s.). In the passage of the first floor are remains of frescoes of 1344, among them an *Annunciation. An apartment fitted up for the reception of the Pope contains a head of Christ in marble, formerly in the church, a mediocre work of the 16th cent., erroneously attributed to Michael Angelo. The same porter keeps the keys of the neighbouring church ($^1/_2$ l.) of

S. Costanza, originally erected as a monument by Constantine to his daughter Constantia, re-erected in 1256. The dome is supported by 24 clustered columns in granite. In the vaulting of the entrance are ancient *mosaics of the 4th cent. with genii gathering grapes. The porphyry sarcophagus of the saint, which formerly stood in one of the niches (now in the museum of the Vatican, Sala a Croce Greca) is similarly adorned; the mosaics of the niches are of later date.

With regard to the catacombs which may here be visited, see p. 260.

Route from S. Agnese to the Campagna see p. 270.

We now return to the Piazza di Termini. To the l. by the Fontana an establishment for poor children, and an asylum for the deaf and dumb. Opposite is the **Railway Station**, whence a new street is now being constructed to the Via delle Quattro Fontane, in consequence of which the piazza will be considerabl enlarged. Opposite the station are the **Thermæ of Diocletian** (Pl. 1, 25), once the most extensive in Rome, constructed by Maximian and Diocletian at the commencement of the 4th cent., by means, it is said, of the compulsory services of Christians, who imprinted the sign of the cross on the bricks.

Within these is situated the church of ***S. Maria degli Angeli**, converted from a large vaulted hall into a church by *Michael Angelo* at the desire of Pius IV. The present transept was then the nave, the principal portal was in the narrow end on the r., and the high-altar placed on the l. In 1749 *Vanvitelli* entirely disfigured the church by these inconsistent alterations.

A small rotunda is first entered. The first tomb on the r. is that of the painter Carlo Maratta (d. 1713). In the Chapel Angels of Peace and Justice, by *Pettrich*. The first tomb on the l. is that of Salvator Rosa (d. 1673). In the Chapel, Christ appearing to Mary Magdalene, altar-piece by *Arrigo Fiamingo*.

The great transept is now entered. The chapel on the l. in the passage contains the °Delivery of the Keys, altar-piece by *Muziano*; to the r. in the niche, St. Bruno, a colossal statue by *Houdon*. The transept (formerly nave) is 290 ft. long, 93 ft. high and 89 ft. wide. Of the 16 columns 8 are of oriental granite. — Most of the large pictures here and in the tribune were brought from St. Peter's, where they were replaced by copies in mosaic. In the r. half (on the pavement the meridian of Rome, laid down in 1703): on the r., Crucifixion of St. Peter by *Ricciolini*; Fall of Simon Magus, after *F. Vanni* (original in St. Peter's); on the l., °St. Jerome among the hermits, *Muziano* (landscape by *Brill*); Miracles of St. Peter, *Baglioni*. On the narrow end: chapel of B. Niccolò Albergati. In the l. half: on the l., Mass of St. Basil with the Emperor Valens, *Subleyras*; Fall of Simon Magus, *Pomp. Battoni*; on the r., Immaculate Conception, *P. Bianchi*; Resuscitation of Tabitha, *P. Costanzi*. On the narrow end: chapel of St. Bruno.

In the tribune (undergoing restoration; one of the monks may be requested to act as guide here and in the monastery): r. Mary's first visit to the Temple, *Romanelli*; °Martyrdom of St. Sebastian (fresco), *Domenichino*; l. Death of Ananias and Sapphira, *Pomarancio*; Baptism of Christ, *Maratta*. The choir contains two monuments (l. Pius IV., r. Ant. Serbelloni), designed by *Michael Angelo*.

A door to the r. leads hence into the first court of the adjacent *Carthusian Monastery*, from which the *second court, embellished with 100 columns and designed by *Mich. Angelo*, is entered. The beautiful cypresses in the centre are also said to have been planted by the great master. Permission to inspect the other chambers of the Thermæ, which are employed as military magazines, must be obtained from the commandant, Piazza Colonna. They contain nothing to interest the traveller, and were moreover greatly damaged by a fire in 1864. The most interesting portions, to the summit of which the visitor may ascend (comprehensive survey), appertain to the monastery, to the prior of which application should be made (letter of introduction desirable). The principal structure of the Thermæ was enclosed by a wall, which is partially concealed in adjoining buildings, as in the prison at the corner of the V. Strozzi and Piazza di Termini, and partially exposed to view, as in the garden of the monastery of S. Bernardo. The corners on this side consisted of two circular buildings, one of which, the present church of S. Bernardo (p. 135), still exists. The other belongs to the prison.

Within the precincts of the railway-station the **Wall of Servius**, intersected by the railway, may be seen. A "lasciapassare" should be procured from the inspector of the station (capostazione); best time 9—11 a. m. Other antiquities are also preserved here. Above is a sitting statue of Roma, beneath which lie several small ancient chambers.

In a line with the railway-station the *Via Strozzi* descends to the r. into the Via delle Quattro Fontane, not far from S. Pudenziana (see below).

Ascending by the station to the l., the road to the r. leads to *Porta S. Lorenzo* (15 min.). Proceeding thence in a straight direction between two pines and then through a gateway, the traveller reaches (in 10 min.) the *Campo di Macao* or *Campo*

Militare, the camp of the Prætorians of imperial Rome. It was originally established by Tiberius, but destroyed by Constantine so far as it lay without the town-wall, from which it projects in a quadrangular form. On the narrow end to the l. and the long side, traces of gates are still distinguished; the wall was skirted by a passage, beneath which small chambers are situated. It has again been devoted to military purposes, and the large, newly-erected barracks impart unwonted life to the place. Popular recreations, horse-races, rope-dancing etc. occasionally take place here.

From the Quattro Fontane to S. Maria Maggiore is a walk of 10 min. The Quirinal is first descended; to the l. is a newly constructed street to the railway-station. The Viminal, here of insignificant elevation, is now traversed. In the valley between the Viminal and Esquiline, in the street to the r., is situated

S. Pudenziana (Pl. II, 25; open till 9 a. m.; custodian to be found in the adjacent monastery, Via Quattro Fontane 81), traditionally the most ancient church in Rome, erected on the spot where S. Pudens, who entertained St. Peter, with his daughters Praxedis and Pudentiana is said to have lived. The church is first mentioned in 499, and has since been frequently renewed; the last complete restoration was in 1598. The portal supported by columns on the façade is ancient.

In the pillars of the aisle in the interior the marble columns, which originally supported the wall are still to be seen. The mosaics in the tribune (4th cent.), Christ with S. Praxedis and S. Pudentiana and the Apostles, above them the emblems of the Evangelists on either side of the cross, are considered as the oldest Christian remains in Rome, but have been greatly modernized. The dome above the high-altar was painted by *Pomarancio*. The aisles contain remnants of an ancient mosaic pavement. In the l. aisle the *Cappella Gaetani*, on the altar of which an Adoration of the Magi, marble-relief by *Olivieri*. At the extremity of this aisle an altar with relics of the table at which Peter is said first to have read mass. Above it Christ and Peter, a group in marble by *G. B. della Porta*.

Beneath the church are ancient vaults of a good period of architecture, to which the custodian conducts visitors if desired.

The Esquiline is now ascended, whence the back of S. Maria Maggiore is visible; a second main street intersecting the hills here diverges. From the Forum of Trajan it ascends the Quirinal under the name of *Via Magnanapoli*; to the l. diverges the Via del Quirinale (p. 132); in a straight direction the church of S. *Domenico e Sisto*, erected about 1640, the cloister attached to which is now employed as barracks, is passed on the r., and the *Villa Aldobrandini*, which after passing through numerous hands is now in possession of Prince Borghese, on the l. (access seldom granted; beautiful grounds and a few ancient sculptures). In the *Via Mazzarina*, the next lateral street to the l., is situated on the r., opposite the Villa Aldobrandini, the church of *S. Agata alla Suburra*, originally erected in the 5th cent., now remarkable only as containing the tomb of Johannes Lascaris, author of the first modern Greek grammar. In a straight direction the *Via di S. Lorenzo in Paneperna* ascends the Viminal, the elevation of which between the Quirinal and Esquiline is here most marked. On the highest point, on the l., stands the church of **S. Lorenzo in Paneperna** (Pl. II, 22), the spot where St. Lawrence is said to have suffered martyrdom. It is ancient, but greatly restored. The street then again descends. and ascends the Esquiline under the name of *Via di S. Maria Maggiore*.

In front of the choir of the church, which is now approached, one of the two *Obelisks* from the mausoleum of Augustus stands; the other is on Monte Cavallo (p. 132). The piazza in front of the church is embellished with a handsome *Column* from the basilica of Constantine, placed here and furnished with a bronze figure of the Virgin by Paul V.

****S. Maria Maggiore** (Pl. II, 25) is also termed *Basilica Liberiana*, and *S. Maria ad Nives*, because, according to the legend, erected by Pope Liberius (352—366) in consequence of simultaneous dreams of the Pope and the Roman Patrician Johannes, on the spot where on the following day (Aug. 5th) they found a miraculous deposit of snow. In 432 it was entirely altered by Sixtus III., enlarged by Nicholas IV. in 1292 by the addition of the tribune with its mosaics, and restored by Gregory XIII. in 1575 according to the taste of that period; the campanile was renewed in 1376. The dimensions of the interior are 120 yds. in length and 50 yds. in width.

The five arches of the *Façade* by Fuga (1743) correspond to the five entrances of the church, the last of which to the r. (Porta Santa) is closed. The vestibule contains the statue of Philip IV. of Spain on the r.; on the l. is the approach to the loggia with the mosaics of the original façade of the 13th cent. (The door is opened by a verger.) Above in the centre Christ: on the l. the Virgin, St. Paul and St. James; on the r. John, Peter and Andrew. Beneath, on the l. dream of Pope Liberius and the Patrician Johannes; on the r. meeting of the two, and the tracing of the site of the church on the newly-fallen snow.

The interior is a basilica with nave and two aisles. The architrave, adorned with mosaic, is supported by two Ionic columns, above which, and on the triumphal arch, are mosaics of the 5th cent. (restored in 1825), those on the arch representing New Testament events, those on the walls. events from the history of the patriarchs and prophets. In front of the triumphal arch is the high-altar, consisting of an ancient sarcophagus of porphyry, said to have been the tomb of the Patrician Johannes, and containing the remains of St. Matthew and other relics; the canopy is borne by four columns of porphyry. In the apse of the tribune are 'mosaics by *Jacopo da Turrita* (1295): Coronation of the Virgin, with saints, near whom are Pope Nicholas IV. and Card. Jac. Colonna.

At the beginning of the nave are the tombs of Nicholas IV. (d. 1292) on the l. and Clement IX. (1669) on the r., erected by Sixtus V. and Clement X. respectively. First chapel in the r. aisle: Baptistery with fine ancient font of porphyry. Farther on is the Cap. del Crocefisso with 10 columns of porphyry, containing five boards from the manger (whence termed *Cappella del Presepe*) of the Infant Christ. In the r. transept is the sumptuous °*Sixtine Chapel* (which the custodian opens if desired), constructed by *Fontana*; the altar in the r. niche is an ancient Christian °sarcophagus; opp. to it, on the l., an altar-piece (St. Jerome), *Ribera*; on the r. the monument of Sixtus V., the statue of the Pope by *Valsoldo*; on the l. Pius V. by *Leonardo da Sarazana*; in the "Confessio" in front of the altar a statue of S. Gaetano, by *Bernini*, and an altar-relief of the Holy Family, by *Cecchino da Pietrasanta* (1480). At the extremity of the r. aisle the Gothic monument of Card. Consalvi (Gunsalvus, d. 1299) by *Giov. Cosmas*. In the l. aisle, 1st Chapel (of the Cesi): Martyrdom of St. Catharine, altar-piece by *Girol. da Sermoneta*; on the r. and l. two bronze statues to the memory of cardinals of the family. 2nd Chapel (of the Pallavicini-Sforza), said to have been designed by Mich. Angelo: Assumption of Mary, altar-piece by *Gir. Sermoneta*. In the l. transept, opp. the Sixtine Chapel, is the *Borghese Chapel*, constructed by *Flaminio Ponzio* in 1611, and also furnished with a dome. Over the altar, which is sumptuously decorated with lapis lazuli and agate, an ancient and miraculous picture of the Virgin, painted (almost black) according to tradition by St. Luke, which was carried by Gregory I. as early as 590 in solemn procession through the city and again by the clergy in the war of 1860. The frescoes in the large arches are by *Guido Reni*, *Lanfranco*, *Cigoli* etc. The monuments of the Popes (l.) Paul V. (Camillo Borghese, d. 1621) and (r.) Clement VIII. (Aldobrandini, d. 1605) are by pupils of Bernini. The crypt contains tombs of the Borghese family.

To the l. in the *Piazza di S. Maria Mggyiore* is the church of *S. Antonio Abbate*, with portal of the 13th cent. The interior is uninteresting. S. Antonio is the tutelary saint of animals, and in front of the church from Jan. 17th to Jan. 23rd domestic animals of every description are blessed and sprinkled with holy water. On Jan. 23rd the Pope and many of the higher classes send their horses here for that purpose.

To the r. in the Piazza is a side-entrance to

*__S. Prassede__ (Pl. I, 25), dedicated in 882 by Paschalis I. to St. Praxedis, daughter of St. Pudens with whom Peter lodged at Rome, and sister of S. Pudentiana. It was restored by Nicholas V. about 1450, again in 1832, and is now undergoing repair. The church is generally entered by the side-door.

The nave is separated from the two aisles by 16 columns of granite. The °mosaics (9th cent.) deserve special inspection. On the triumphal arch the new Jerusalem guarded by angels, Christ in the centre, towards whom the saved are hastening; on the arch of the tribune the Lamb, at the sides the 7 candlesticks and the symbols of the evangelists; lower down the 24 elders; on the vaulting Christ surrounded with saints (among them Peter, Paul, Praxedis and Pudentiana). On either side of the tribune are galleries. The 3rd chapel in the r. aisle is the *Chapel of the Column* (ladies admitted on the Sundays of Lent only; the sacristan opens the door when desired). At the entrance are two columns of black granite with ancient entablature. The interior is entirely covered with mosaics on gold ground (about the 10th cent.), whence the chapel is sometimes termed *Orto del Paradiso*. On the vaulting a medallion with head of Christ, supported by four angels. Above the altar a Madonna between the saints Praxedis and Pudentiana. To the r. in a niche, the column at which Christ is said to have been scourged. The 4th chapel contains the tomb of Card. Cetti (d. 1474). At the extremity of the r. aisle the *Cap. del Crocifisso* contains the tomb of a French cardinal (d. 1286). In the l. aisle by the entrance-wall is a stone-slab, on which St. Praxedis is said to have slept. The *Cap. di S. Carlo Borromeo* (the 2nd) contains a chair and table used by the saint. *Cap. Agiati* (3rd) contains paintings by the *Cav. d'Arpino*. The marble spout of a fountain in the nave indicates the spot where St. Praxedis collected the blood of the martyrs.

The Confessio (keys kept by the sacristan) contains ancient sarcophagi with the bones of the sainted sisters Praxedis and Pudentiana on the r. and those of martyrs on the l. The altar is decorated with fine mosaic of the 13th cent. Above it an ancient fresco of the Madonna between the sister saints. The entrance to the catacombs was formerly here.

Several streets run E. and S.E. towards the walls from the Piazza S. Maria Maggiore. That to the l. passing S. Antonio soon divides again, and to the l. in 10 min. leads to the

Porta di S. Lorenzo (Pl. II, 32), constructed by Honorius against an arch, over which according to the inscription the three aqueducts Marcia, Tepula, Julia passed. The latter stands on its original site, whilst the arch of the gateway occupies considerably higher ground. It derives its appellation from the basilica situated without the gate, and stands on the site of the ancient Porta Tiburtina, which led to Tivoli (Tibur). The road (*Via Tiburtina*) is enclosed by walls, and does not afford views of the Sabine Mts. until the church is reached, $3/4$ M. from the gate.

*S. Lorenzo fuori le Mura (see map, p. 262) occupies the spot where Constantine first founded a church on the burial-place of St. Lawrence and St. Cyriaca, which however soon fell to decay. In 578 Pelagius II. again found the remains of St. Lawrence and erected a church, which Honorius III. restored. Under Nicholas V. and Innocent X., and finally under Pius IX. in 1864, the church has undergone extensive alterations, and is now at least partially freed from the patchwork by which it was formerly disfigured. In the piazza in front of the church is a column with a bronze statue of St. Lawrence. The front has been recently embellished with mosaics representing the founders and patrons of the church: Pelagius II., the Emp. Constantine, Honorius III., Pius IX., Sixtus III. and Hadrian I. The vestibule is supported by 6 ancient columns, above which an architrave with mosaic (S. Lorenzo and Honorius III.), and contains old, disfigured frescoes, two tombs in the form of temples, and two rude sarcophagi. The door-posts rest on lions.

The interior consists of two parts. The first and more modern, which to a great extent dates from Honorius III., consists of nave and two aisles, separated by 22 antique columns of granite and cipolline of unequal thickness, and plain entablature, above which an undecorated wall and open roof rise. On the capital of the 8th column on the r. are a frog and a lizard, supposed on doubtful grounds to have been brought from the colonnade of the Octavia, where two sculptors Batrachos (frog) and Sauros (lizard) are said to have adopted this method of perpetuating their names. The pavement, opus Alexandrinum, dates from the 12th cent. To the r. of the entrance a mediæval canopy, under which is an ancient *sarcophagus with representation of a wedding, in which in 1256 the remains of Card. Fieschi, nephew of Innocent IV., were placed. In the nave are the two elevated *ambones, that to the r. for the gospel, near which is a wreathed candelabrum for the Easter candle, that to the l. for the epistle (12th cent.). On the triumphal arch are modern mosaics of the Madonna and saints. At the extremity of the l. aisle a staircase descends to a chapel and the catacombs. By the Confessio 7 steps descend into the second part of the church, the edifice of Pelagius II., the pavement of which is considerably lower than that of the upper church. The entrance was formerly on the opposite side. 12 magnificent fluted columns of pavonazetto with Corinthian capitals (those of the two first are formed of trophies, in front of them are mediæval lions) support the entablature which consists of antique fragments and bears a gallery with graceful smaller columns. On the triumphal arch, of which this is the original front, are restored mosaics of the time of Pelagius II.: Christ, r. St. Peter, St. Lawrence, St. Pelagius; l. St. Paul, St. Stephen, Hippolytus. The canopy with modern dome dates from 1148. By the farther wall is the handsome episcopal throne. — The space below contains nothing of interest; it was formed in the course of the restoration of 1864.

The handsome old **Court of the Monastery* (usually closed; application may be made to one of the monks in the church) contains numerous fragments of sculptures and inscriptions immured in its walls; in the corner to the r. of the principal entrance is the lid of a sarcophagus adorned with the triumphal procession of Cybele. The church is adjoined by an extensive churchyard, consecrated in 1837, considerably enlarged in 1854, from the upper part of which there is a beautiful view of the mountains and Campagna.

Where the Via di Porta S. Lorenzo diverges to the l., the *Via di Eusebio* proceeds in a straight direction. Immediately to the r. it is joined by the *Via di S. Vito*, where the church of that name lies (Pl. II, 28), and the *Arch*, erected in 262 in honour of the Emp. Gallienus by a certain M. Aurelius Victor, "on account of his bravery, surpassed only by his piety", is situated. The architecture is simple and in the degraded style of the age.

Farther on in the principal street, on the r., is *S. Giuliano;* on the l., standing back from the street, the church of *S. Eusebio* (Pl. II, 28), re-erected in the last century, with the exception of the campanile. The ceiling-painting, the glory of St. Eusebius, is one of the earliest works of *Raphael Mengs;* the high altar-piece by *Bald. Croce.*

The street now divides: to the l. diverges the *Via di S. Bibiana*, to the r. the *Via di S. Croce*, between which the *Via di Porta Maggiore* pursues a straight direction. Between the first and last of these are seen considerable remains of a water-tower of the *Aqua Julia* or *Claudia*, in the niches of which the so-called trophies of Marius, now on the balustrade of the Capitol, were formerly placed (p. 169). The ruin is termed *Trofei di Mario*.

To the l. in 5 min. the traveller reaches **S. Bibiana** (Pl. II, 31), consecrated as early as 470, re-constructed in 1625 by Bernini; to the l. by the entrance the stump of a column, at which the saint is said to have been scourged to death. The church is open to the public on Dec. 2nd, the anniversary of the Saint.

The interior contains eight antique columns; above these are frescoes from the life of the saint, on the r. by *Ciampelli*, l. by *Pietro da Cortona*, now defaced. The statue of St. Bibiana at the high-altar is by *Bernini*.

Opposite to the church, to the r. in the *Vigna Magnani* is the so-called **Temple of Minerva Medica** (Pl. II, 32), the picturesque ruin of an unknown ancient edifice, a decagon with deep niches in the walls, formerly covered with marble beneath and stucco above. It must have appertained to some sumptuous establishment, as a number of ancient statues have been found in the vicinity. One of these, the Minerva Giustiniani of the Braccio Nuovo in the Vatican (p. 243), has given rise to the otherwise unfounded appellation of "Temple of Minerva". In the middle ages the ruin was termed *Le Terme di Galluccio*, a name conjectured to be a corruption of "Gaius and Lucius Cæsar", but without the slightest historical authority. The arch has fallen in since 1828.

The Via di Porta Maggiore leads in 18 min. from the church of S. Maria to the ***Porta Maggiore** (Pl. II, 35), formed by two arches of the Aqua Claudia, over which by means of a second conduit the Anio Novus flowed. The inscriptions record the construction of the aqueduct, 45 M. in length, by the Emp. Claudius, A. D. 50, and its restoration by Vespasian and Titus. The gate derives its appellation from its imposing dimensions. Two roads diverged hence: to the l. through the now closed arch the *Via Labicana*, to the r. the *Via Praenestina*. Between the two, in front of the gate, during the removal in 1838 of the more recent fortifications of Honorius, the **Monument of the Baker Eurysaces*, erected in the form of a baker's oven towards the close of the republic, was discovered. Hence to the Campagna see p. 269.

From the Porta Maggiore a road leads to (5 min.) S. Croce, passing under the arch of the Claudian aqueduct and skirting the wall on the inside. From S. Maria Maggiore to this church by the Via di S. Croce is a walk of 20 min.

***S. Croce in Gerusalemme** (Pl. II, 36), once termed *Basilica Sessoriana*, because the *Sessorium*, probably an ancient court of judicature, once stood here, is said to have been erected by St. Helena in honour of the cross found by her. As early as 433 it served as a place of meeting for a council, under Lucius II. in

S. Croce in Gerusalemme. ROME. *S. Martino ai Monti.* 145

1144 it was re-constructed, and under Benedict XIV. in 1743 entirely modernized. (Façade by *Gregorini*.)

The nave of the church was originally borne by 12 antique columns of granite, of which 8 only are now visible. An ancient sarcophagus of basalt beneath the high-altar contains the relics of St. Anastasius and Cæsarius. In the tribune are modernized *frescoes by *Pinturicchio*, the Finding of the Cross. The church contains numerous relics, among them the "Inscription on the Cross".

To the l. of the tribune a stair descends to the lower church, where on the l. is an altar adorned with a relief in marble (Pietà); at the sides are statues of Peter and Paul of the 12th cent. On the r. the chapel of St. Helena. On the vaulting mosaics attributed to Bald. Peruzzi, representing the 4 evangelists. In the centre Christ. In the arch over the entrance, on the l. St. Helena, r. St. Sylvester; over the altar on the l. St. Peter, on the r. St. Paul. The altar-statue of St. Helena is ancient, but greatly restored. (A monk may be requested to open the door of the chapel.)

The monastery belongs to the Cistercians. The *Library*, although despoiled of many of its treasures, is still of great value.

Adjacent to S. Croce in the direction of the Lateran, in the vineyard of the monastery, is situated the *Amphitheatrum Castrense (Pl. II, 36) of which a portion of 16 arches only, which has been united with the city-wall, now exists. The structure is of brick, of which the Corinthian capitals and other decorations also consist. Date of erection uncertain. — On the other side of S. Croce is an apse with arched windows and the beginning of the contiguous walls, which are conjectured to have formed part of a *Temple of Venus and Cupid*, or a *Nymphaeum* of Alexander Severus, or a *Sessorium* or hall of assize.

From S. Croce to the Lateran is a walk of 5 min.

From S. Maria Maggiore the *Via in Merulana* leads to the r. to the Lateran (in 15 min.). The first transverse street to the r. is the *Via di S. Prassede* with the church of that name (see p. 141). which under different names leads through a comparatively well-peopled quarter to the Forum. The *Via di S. Vito* to the l. leads to the arch of Gallienus (p. 143).

The second side-street to the r. leads to

S. Martino ai Monti (Pl. II, 26), also termed *SS. Silvestro e Martino*, erected by Symmachus about 500, renewed by Sergius II. in 847 and by Leo IV., and modernized in 1770.

The interior contains 24 antique columns, the r. aisle six *frescoes with representations from the life of Elijah by *G. Poussin*. In the l. aisle six smaller *frescoes. Also two pictures representing the interior of the old Lateran and Church of St. Peter. The presbyterium is 11 steps higher; beneath it the lower church. From the latter a large, ancient vault is entered, probably once belonging to Thermæ, but at an early period converted into a church. The vaulting bears traces of very ancient painting.

The *Via di S. Pietro in Vincoli* is now reached, leading to the r. to the church of that name, whilst its prolongation, the

Via delle Sette Sale skirts the vineyards of the Esquiline and terminates near S. Clemente (p. 200).

If the latter be selected, the entrance to the so-called *Sette Sale* (Pl. II, 26) is reached immediately to the r., in the Vigna, No. 10. These seven, or rather nine chambers, running parallel with each other, appear to have served as reservoirs for the Thermæ of Titus. In the vicinity the celebrated group of the Laocoon (p. 246) was found. Other and still more imposing ruins in the vigna probably formed part of the same bath-establishment.

*S. Pietro in Vincoli (Pl. II, 23), not far from the Thermæ of Titus (open before 11 a. m. and after 3 p. m.; when closed, visitors ring at the door to the r. adjoining the church), was founded by Eudoxia, wife of Valentinian III., about 442, as a receptacle for the chains of St. Peter which had been presented by her to Pope Leo I., whence also termed *Basilica Eudoxiana*, restored by Pelagius I. and Hadrian I. The vestibule was subsequently added by Baccio Pintelli; the whole is now modernized.

The nave and aisles are separated by 20 antique Doric columns. To the l. of the high-altar is the monument of Pietro and Antonio Pollajuolo (d. 1498). The l. aisle contains the monument of the erudite Card. Nicolaus Cusanus (from Cues on the Moselle). Above it a relief: Peter with keys and chains, on the l. the donor (Nic. Cusanus). r. an angel. On the 2nd altar to the l. a mosaic of the 7th cent. with St. Sebastian. At the extremity of the r. aisle the monument of Pope Julius II. with the *°Statue of Moses, by *Michael Angelo*, one of his most famous works. The monument was originally destined for St. Peter's, and intended to be a most imposing work, consisting of upwards of 30 statues. (The Uffizi at Florence contain M. Angelo's designs for this work, drawn by his own hand.) Owing to various adverse circumstances the portion which is here preserved was alone completed. (Two statues destined for this monument are at the Louvre.) The statues of Moses, Rachel and Leah (as symbols, on the l. of meditative, on the r. of active life) alone are the work of the great master, of the remainder the grouping only was from his design. The figure of the pope (who is moreover not interred here) by *Maso del Bosco* is a failure; the prophet and the sibyl at the side are by *Raf. da Montelupo*.

Adjacent is the entrance to the sacristy. A cabinet here with *°bronze doors (by the *Pollajuoli*, 1477) contains the chains of St. Peter, which are exhibited to the pious on Aug. 1st. The Speranza by *Guido Reni* which was formerly here, was sold and sent to England some years ago. The *court of the adjacent cloister of the canonici regolari, with a fountain by *Antonio da San Gallo*, is now entered, after inspecting which visitors may retrace their steps.

The piazza in front of the church is adorned by a handsome palm-tree. To the l. (where the street divides, to the l. again) the Thermæ of Titus (p. 180) are reached in 5 min. The street in a straight direction descends to the Basilica of Constantine (p. 175), whence the above church is usually visited. On the r. lies the church of *S. Francesco di Paola* with the monastery. In front of it a picturesque view is obtained.

III. Rome on the Tiber.

That portion of the city which extends W. from the Corso as far as the river, in the most ancient times uninhabited, subsequently converted into magnificent grounds by the emperors *(Campus Martius)*, is now densely peopled. The character of this quarter is essentially mediæval: it consists of a network of narrow and dirty streets and lanes, enlivened by the busy traffic of the humbler classes, and rarely intersected by great thoroughfares. The topography is occasionally puzzling, and the aspect of these purlieus unattractive; but they are nevertheless replete with the most interesting churches and palaces, and are strongly recommended to the notice of those who desire acquaintance with mediæval Rome and an insight into the characteristic peculiarities of the citizens. The following description commences with the N. side.

From the Piazza del Popolo the broad *Via di Ripetta* skirts the bank of the river and the small harbour, where its name is changed to *Via della Scrofa*, and in 16 min. leads to the Piazza S. Luigi de' Francesi (where the post-office is situated), near which on the r. the Piazza Navona and on the l. the piazza of the Pantheon are situated.

After 4 min. a modern building with numerous windows is seen on the r. It was erected by Gregory XVI., and contains a number of studios and a collection of casts belonging to the academy of St. Luca (p. 181). The gate of this edifice leads to a quiet quay, planted with trees, where the barges and steamboats which ascend the river lie. Pleasing view of the opposite bank.

Proceeding hence to the l., in the 3rd transverse street, the Via de' Pontefici 57 (r.) the traveller reaches the entrance to the

Mausoleum of Augustus (Pl. I, 17; fee ½ l.), erected by that emperor as a burial-place for himself and his family, and in which most of his successors down to Nerva were interred. On a huge basement, which contained the mortuary-chambers, arose a mound of earth in the form of terraces, embellished with cypresses and on the summit a statue of the emperor, and environed with a park. In the middle ages it was employed by the Colonnas as a fortress. At the present day a small day-theatre, occasionally also used as a circus, is fitted up within the precincts of the basement. A few only of the tomb-chambers are still preserved.

To the l. in the Via di Ripetta the traveller next reaches the church of *SS. Rocco e Martino* (Pl. I, 14), erected in 1657 by *de Rossi*, the façade with its two pairs of Corinthian columns in

1834. Immediately beyond it, on the r., is the *Harbour of the Ripetta*, constructed by Clement XI. in 1707. The height attained by the water during inundations is indicated on the two columns on the arched wall. Ferry 6 soldi. Bathing-establishment on the opp. bank in summer. On the l. the small church of *S. Girolamo degli Schiavoni* (Pl. I, 14). Farther on, to the l., a bath-establishment, not recommended.

The Via della Scrofa, as the street is now termed, is soon intersected (about 9 min. from the Piazza del Popolo) by a main street, which quitting the Corso opposite the Via Condotti leads to the Ponte S. Angelo under different names, and forms the most direct communication between the strangers' quarter (Piazza di Spagna) and the Vatican. The church of S. Trinità de' Monti is visible the greater part of the way, forming the termination of the street. From the Corso to the Piazza Borghese with the celebrated palace of that name (4 min.) it is termed *Via della Fontanella Borghese;* thence to the Via della Scrofa, *Via del Clementino*, in which on the l. is the *Caserma de' Vigili* or guard-house of the firemen, and the adjacent back-buildings of the *Palazzo di Firenze*, formerly the residence of the Tuscan ambassador.

The *Palazzo Borghese (Pl. I, 16), begun by order of Card. Deza in 1590 by the architect *Mart. Longhi the Elder*, came through Paul V., who caused it to be completed by *Flam. Ponzio*, into the possession of the Borghese family. The principal façade (with respect to the construction of the court) towards the street bears the inscription: *Bonitatem et disciplinam et scientiam docem(us);* the more imposing lateral façade is towards the Piazza Borghese. The *Court on the basement and first floor is surrounded by arcades, consisting of arches resting on clustered columns. Beneath these are three ancient colossal statues (two Muses and an Apollo Musagetes); at the extremity of the r. passage a fragment of the statue of an Amazon, in the centre of that to the l. the entrance to the **Picture Gallery (open daily 9—2 o'clock, Sat. and Sun. excepted; fee ½ l.). It is arranged according to the schools, and contains many admirable works. Catalogues in each room. The apartments are artistically decorated.

1st Room: works principally of the school of Leonardo. °Decorations, in grisaille and gold, by *Carlo Villani.* °1. Madonna, *Sandro Botticelli;* 2. Madonna, *Lorenzo di Credi*; 4. Portrait, attrib. to the same master; 8. Vanità, same; °17. Ecce Homo, same; 26. Madonna, same; 27., 28. Petrarch and Laura (?); 30. Ecce Homo, *Perugino* (?); 32. St. Agatha, *Sch. of Leonardo;* °33. Christ when a boy, *Leonardo da Vinci* (?); 34. Madonna, *Perugino* (a copy); °35. Raphael when a boy, after Passavant, *Timoteo della Vite* (?); 43. Madonna, *Fr. Francia* (?); 45. St. Catharine, after *Raphael*; 48. St. Sebastian, *Perugino;* 49., 57. History of Joseph, *Pinturicchio;* °54. Holy Family, one of the finest works of *Lorenzo di Credi;* 56. Leda and the swan, - copy of the celebrated picture, *Leonardo;* 61. St. Antony, *Fr. Francia* (?);

*65. Madonna, Sch. of Leonardo; 67. Adoration of the Child, Ortolano; *69. Holy Family, Pollajuolo. — 2nd R.: numerous pictures by Garofalo, of which the finest only are enumerated. 3. Portrait, copy from Perugino; 5. Madonna with St. Joseph and St. Michael, Garofalo; 6. Madonna with two saints, Fr. Francia; *8. Christ mourned over by his friends, Garofalo; *17. Portrait of Julius II., an admirable copy from Raphael; *23. Madonna with St. Joseph and St. Elizabeth (Mad. col divino amore), Raphael (original at Naples); *25. Portrait of Cæsar Borgia (?), Raphael; 35. Madonna, Andrea del Sarto; **37. Entombment (1507), Raphael, his last work before going to Rome, ordered by Atalanta Baglioni for her chapel in S. Francesco de' Conventuali at Perugia, afterwards purchased by Paul V. The predella which belongs to it (Faith, Hope and Charity) is in the Vatican Gallery. 38. Madonna di Casa d'Alba, a copy, Raphael; 39. Holy Family, Fra Bartolommeo; 42. Madonna, Fr. Francia; 43. Madonna, Sodoma; *50. St. Stephen, Fr. Francia; 58. Adoration of the Magi, Mazzolino; *64. Portrait of the socalled Fornarina, a good copy of the original of Raphael in the Pal. Barberini, perhaps by Giulio Romano; 68. John in the wilderness, after Raphael. — 3rd R.: 1. Christ bearing the Cross, Andrea Solario; *2. Portrait, Parmeggianino; 5. Christ risen, Aless. Allori, attrib. to Mich. Angelo; 11. The Sorceress Circe, Dosso Dossi; 13. Mater Dolorosa, Solario (?); 15. Madonna, Scarsellino; 22. Holy Family, Sch. of Raphael; *24. Madonna with angels, Andrea del Sarto; 22. Madonna, by the same; 35. Venus with two Cupids, And. del Sarto; 37. Portrait, unknown; **40. Danae, one of the finest easel-pieces of Correggio; 42. Portrait of Cosimo de' Medici, Bronzino; '46. St. Magdalene, after Correggio's original at Dresden; 47. Holy Family, Pomarancio; *48. Scourging of Christ, Sebast. del Piombo (the same piece is in Pietro in Montorio as a fresco); 49. Mary Magdalene, And. del Sarto. — 4th R.: this and the following rooms principally contain works of the Bolognese school (that of the Caracci) and the "naturalists" (Caravaggio etc.). 1. Entombment, Ann. Caracci; *2. Cumæan Sibyl, Domenichino; 4. Head, Lod. Caracci; 10. Rape of Europa, Cav. d'Arpino; 14. Entombment. Sch. of the Caracci; *15. Sibyl, Guido Cagnacci; 20. St. Joseph, Guido Reni; 27. St. Francis, Cigoli; 29. St. Dominicus, Ann. Caracci; 33. Martyrdom of St. Ignatius, Luca Giordano; 36. Madonna, Carlo Dolce; 37. Mater Dolorosa, by the same; 38., 41. Annunciation, Furino; 39. Neptune, Ribera; 40. St. Jerome, by the same; 42. Head of Christ, Carlo Dolce; 43. Madonna, Sassoferrato. — 5th R.: *11., 12., 13., 14. Four Seasons, landscapes with mythological accessories, Franc. Albani; *15. Diana and her Nymphs practising with their bows, Domenichino; 21. Liberation of Peter, Francesco Mola; 22. Psyche borne aloft by nymphs, copy from a picture in the Farnesina; 25. Christ bewailed by angels, Fed. Zuccari; 26. Madonna with St. Anna and the Child Jesus, Caravaggio; 27. Venus, Varotari (il Padovanino); 20. Battle, Cav. d'Arpino; 29. Landscape, Sch. of Poussin. — 6th R.: 1. Mater Dolorosa, Guercino; 2. Female half-figure, by the same; *3. Portrait of Orazio Giustiniani, Andrea Sacchi; 5. Return of the Prodigal, Guercino; 7. Portrait of Gius. Ghislieri, Piet. da Cortona; *10. St. Stanislaus with the Child Jesus, Ribera; 12. Joseph interpreting the dreams in prison, Valentin; *13. Three periods of life, Giorgione; 16, 17. Landscapes, Franc. Grimaldi; 18. Madonna, Sassoferrato; 22. Flight of Æneas from Troy, Baroccio; 24., 25. Landscapes in the style of Poussin. — 7th R.: the lower part of the wall is principally decorated with mirrors, on which Cupids (by Giroferri) and wreaths of flowers (by Mario de' Fiori) are painted. The niches in the upper part of the walls are occupied by 16 ancient portrait-busts, some of them greatly restored. In the centre a table of irregular mosaic composed of stones of every variety, some of them extremely rare. — 8th R.: containing a number of small objects of art and curiosities, which do not always correspond to the numbers. Entrance-wall: Orpheus with the animals in a landscape, Brill (?): 86. Mater Dolorosa, Marcello Provenzali; *90. Female head, a drawing of the Sch. of Leonardo. Window-wall: By this and the wall of the egress are 12 small bronze antiquities. 38. Landscape, Franc. Viola. Wall opp. window: 4. Madonna, Giulio Clodi; 91. The Graces, Vanni; *88. View of the Villa Borghese of the 17th cent. Opposite the

150 *Palazzo Borghese.*   ROME.   *Palazzo Galizin.*

door of egress the visitor obtains a view of the banks of the Tiber beyond the fountain below. To the l. a passage adorned with landscape-frescoes leads to the 9th R., where several frescoes are collected which have been removed from the place of their original destination. The most important are °three from the so-called Villa of Raphael, which formerly stood within the grounds of the Villa Borghese and was removed in 1849 (p. 124), 1. Nuptials of Alexander and Roxana from an extant drawing by Raphael, which was based on the description of a work of Ætion (Lucian, Herod. 5). A similar picture by Sodoma is in the Farnesina. 2. Nuptials of Vertumnus and Pomona. 3. The so-called "Bersaglio de' Dei" (shooting-contest of the gods), from a drawing in the Brera at Milan bearing the name of Mich. Angelo. The three were probably executed by Raphael's pupils. Some of the other paintings are from the Villa Lante. The balcony reached from this room affords a pleasing view of the Tiber and its banks as far as Monte Mario. Returning to the mirror-room and selecting the door to the l. in the opp. wall, the visitor enters the 10th R., principally containing, like the following room, works of the Venetian school: 1. °Portrait, *Moroni;* °2. Cupid equipped by Venus (erroneously called "the Graces"), *Titian;* 4. Judith, said to have the features of Titian's wife, *Sch. of Titian* or *Giorgione;* 6. Cupid and Psyche, *Sch. of Ferrara;* °9. Portrait, *Pordenone;* °13. David with the head of Goliath, *Giorgione;* 14. John the Baptist preaching repentance, *Paolo Veronese;* 16. St. Dominicus. *Titian;* 19. Portrait, *Giac. Bassano;* °°21. "Amor sagro e profano" (Earthly and heavenly love), one of the greatest works of *Titian;* 22. Concert, *Leonello Spada;* °30. Madonna, an early work of *Gior. Bellini;* 34. St. Cosmas and St. Damianus, *Venet. Sch.;* 35. Family scene, probably the nativity of the Virgin, *Venet. Sch.* — 11th R.: 1. Madonna with Adam and St. Augustine, *Lor. Lotto* (1508); 2. St. Antony about to preach to the fish, *Paolo Veronese* (?); 3. Madonna, *Titian* (?); 9. Portrait, *Moroni;* 11. Venus and Cupid on dolphins (unfinished), *Luc. Cambiaso;* 14. Last Supper, *And. Schiavone;* 15. Christ among his disciples and the sons of Zebedee with their mother, *Bonifazio;* 16. Return of the Prodigal, by the same; 17. Samson, *Titian;* 18. Christ and the adulteress, *Bonifazio;* 19. Madonna with saints etc., *Palma Vecchio* (?); 20. Venus and Cupid, *Paolo Veronese;* 23. Portrait, *Schidone;* 24. Madonna, by the same; 25. Portrait of himself, *Titian* (a copy); °27. Portrait, *Giov. Bellini;* 31. Madonna and St. Peter, by the same; °32. Holy Family, *Palma Vecchio;* 33. Family-portrait, *Licinio da Pordenone;* 39. Portrait, *Giov. Bellini.* — 12th R.: Dutch and German masters. 1. Crucifixion, *Van Dyck* (?); °7. Entombment, by the same; °8. Genre picture, *D. Teniers;* 9. Genre picture, *A. Brower;* 15. Mary's visit to Elisabeth, *Brabant Sch.;* 19. Portrait (said to be of Louis VI. of Bavaria), *Dürer* (?); 20. Portrait, *Holbein;* 21. Landscape and accessories, *Wouverman* (?); 22. Cattle-piece, *Potter* (?); 23. Quay, *Backhuyzen;* 26. Crossing the ice, in different shades of brown, perhaps by *Berghem;* 24. Portrait, *Holbein* (?); 27. Portrait, *Van Dyck;* °35. Portrait, *Lucas van Leyden* (?); 37. Portrait, *German School;* 41. Lot and his daughters, *Gherardo delle Notti;* 44. Venus and Cupid, *Lucas Cranach.* In a small cabinet (which the custodian does not open unless desired) are a number of less important Italian pictures of the 14th and 15th cent.

From the Via della Scrofa to the Ponte S. Angelo is a walk of 10 min. by a street separated from the river by a single row of houses only, and of which the name frequently changes.

It soon reaches the *Piazza Nicosia*, where in the corner to the l. the recently erected *Pal. Galizin*, built to some extent on the plan of the Pal. Giraud near St. Peter's (p. 215), is situated. Farther on in the *Via della Tinta*, on the l., is the small church of *S. Lucia*, mentioned as early as the 9th cent. In the Via di Monte Brianzo, dell' Orso and dell' Arco di Parma there are no buildings worthy of note.

From the last mentioned the Vicolo of the same name diverges, in which the *Pal. Lancelotti*, erected under Sixtus V. by Franc. da Volterra, subsequently by C. Maderno, is situated. The portal was designed by Domenichino; the court contains ancient statues and reliefs.

The *Via di Tordinone* or *Tor di Nona*, so termed from the prison-tower once situated here, is now pursued. To the l. the Vicolo de' Marchegiani diverges to the church of *S. Maria di Loreto* (comp. p. 183) with the adjacent court of a monastery, erected by Ursini in 1450, entirely reconstructed under Pius IX. in 1862. At the extremity of the Via Tordinone, on the r., is the *Theatre of Apollo* (p. 90), restored by Valladier in 1830.

The street terminates in the *Piazza di Ponte S. Angelo*, whence three others diverge. The Via in Panico leads with its prolongations to the Piazza Navona (p. 156), the Via del Banco di S. Spirito in the centre to the Piazza Farnese (p. 161) and the Via Paola to the Ponte Leonino and to the Via Giulia which skirts the bank of the Tiber. The place of execution, now near Ponte Rotto (p. 231), was formerly here.

———

If the Via della Scrofa be followed, passing the Pal. Galizin on the r., the 4th transverse street on the r. (at the l. corner, Via della Scrofa 70, is the palace of the general-vicar, where permessi for the catacombs are obtained, 11—12 a. m.) leads to the *Piazza di S. Agostino*.

*S. Agostino (Pl. I, 13), erected by *Baccio Pintelli* in 1483 at the instance of Card. d'Éstouteville, protector of the Augustine order, on the site of a former oratorium, was the first Roman church with a dome. The façade and spacious staircase are said to have been constructed of the stones of the Colosseum. The interior, in the form of a Latin cross, was lately restored and adorned with frescoes by *Gagliardi*.

On the entrance-wall a Madonna and Child, by *Jacopo Tatti*, pupil of *Sansovino*, surrounded by numerous votive offerings. In the 1st Chapel on the r. St. Catharine by *Venusti*; in the 2nd *Nucci's* copy of the lost Madonna della Rosa of *Raphael*; in the 4th °Christ delivering the keys to Peter, group by *Cotignola*. By the 5th Chapel is the monument (the second to the l.) of the erudite Onofrio Panvinio (d. 1568). The r. transept contains the chapel of St. Augustine with an altar-piece by *Guercino*: St. Augustine between John the Baptist and Paul the Hermit. High-altar decorated by *Bernini*; the image of the Madonna is said to have been brought from the church of St. Sophia at Constantinople and painted by St. Luke. In the chapel on the l. of this, the remains of St. Monica, mother of Augustine, are preserved; altar-piece by *Gottardi*.

The 2nd Chapel in the l. aisle contains a °group in marble (St. Anna, Mary and Jesus) by *Andrea Sansovino* (1512). In the 4th, St. Apollonia, altar-piece by *Muziano*. In the nave, on the 3rd pillar to the l., *Raphael's Prophet Isaiah, holding a scroll with the words from Is. XXVI, 2., painted in 1512, but unfortunately retouched by *Dan. da Volterra*. In the execution of this work the great master is said to have been influenced by that of M. Angelo in the Sixtine Chapel.

The neighbouring monastery contains the *Bibliotheca Angelica* (entrance on the r. of the church), comprising 90,000 vols. and 30,000 MSS., of which complete catalogues have been formed. Admission daily, Thursdays and holidays excepted, $7\frac{1}{2}$—$11\frac{3}{4}$ a. m.

Proceeding from the Piazza di S. Agostino in a straight direction under the archway, the traveller reaches the *Piazza S. Apollinare*, then the *Piazza Tor Sanguigna* and *Via de' Coronari* (continuing to follow the narrow street in a straight direction), leading to the Via in Panico and the Ponte S. Angelo (8 min.). This is the nearest way from the Piazza Colonna to the Vatican.

In the Piazza S. Apollinare is situated the *Seminario Romano* (Pl. I, 13), a species of grammar-school, with the church of *S. Apollinare*, the present form of which was imparted to it by Fuga under Benedict XIV. To the l. over the altar in the inner vestibule is a Madonna by *Perugino*. Opposite the church is the *Pal. Altemps* of the 16th cent., possessing a handsome double court with arcades, the lateral colonnades of which are closed with masonry, and containing a few ancient statues and other relics.

From the Piazza S. Apollinare the Via Agonale leads S. to the Piazza Navona (p. 156); from Tor Sanguigna, S. Maria dell' Anima (p. 157) and della Pace (p. 158) are reached to the l.

In the direction of the Vatican (3 min.) the Pal. Lancelotti (p. 151) lies on the r.; a short distance farther is the side-entrance to S. Maria di Loreto (p. 151).

The Via della Scrofa leads to the small, but much frequented and busy *Piazza di S. Luigi de' Francesi*. Here on the r. is situated **S. Luigi de' Francesi** (Pl. II, 13), consecrated in 1589, having superseded a succession of earlier churches. Façade by *Giac. della Porta*. It is one of the better structures of its period; the interior also is decorated with taste and judgment.

R. aisle, 1st Chapel: St. John, altar-piece by *G. B. Naldini*. 2nd Chapel: frescoes from the life of St. Cecilia, one of the most admirable works of *Domenichino*; on the r. the saint distributes clothing to the poor, in the lunette above she and her betrothed are crowned by an angel; on the l. the saint suffers martyrdom with the blessing of the Pope, above she is urged to participate in a heathen sacrifice; on the ceiling, admission of the saint into heaven; altar-piece, a copy of *Raphael's* St. Cecilia (in Bologna) by *Guido Reni*. 4th Chapel, of St. Dionysius: altar-piece by *Giac. del Conte;* frescoes on the r. by *Girolamo Sicciolante (da Sermoneta*), on the l. by *Pellegrino da Bologna*. 5th Chapel, del Crocifisso: on the l. monument of the painter Guérin, on the r. that of Agincourt (d. 1814), the writer on art.

Over the high-altar: °Assumption of Mary, by *Franc. Bassano*. L. aisle, 1st Chapel: St. Sebastian, altar-piece by *Massei;* on the r. and l. modern frescoes; by the first pillar on the r. the monument of Claude Lorrain, erected in 1836. 3rd Chapel, of St. Louis: altar-piece by *Plantilla Bricci*, who is said to have designed the architecture also; picture on the l. by *Gimignani*. 5th Chapel, of St. Matthew: altar-piece and pictures on r. and l. by *Caravaggio*, l. the evangelist's vocation to the apostleship, r. his death.

Opposite the church is the *Palazzo Patrizi* (Pl. II, 13), where permission to visit the Villa Patrizi (p. 136) is obtained, adjoining which at the extremity of the piazza is situated the *Post Office* in the Pal. Madama (Pl. II, 13), the principal façade of which looks towards the piazza of that name (p. 156).

By the post-office, in a straight direction, the Via delle Poste descends. On the l., opposite the post-office, in the small *Piazza S. Eustachio* is the *Palazzo Giustiniani* (Pl. II, 13), erected by Giov. Fontana. It formerly contained a valuable collection of pictures and sculptures; most of the former are now in Berlin, the latter partly in the Vatican and partly in possession of Prince Torlonia; the reliefs immured in the court and passages of the ground-floor now alone remain. On the opposite side is the *Pal. Maccarini*, designed by Giul. Romano, on the r. is the back of the

Università della Sapienza (Pl. II, 13, 25), founded in 1303 by Boniface VIII. and after a rapid decline re-established by Eugene IV. (Entrance Via della Sapienza 71.) It attained to its greatest prosperity under Leo X., in whose honour on the Friday of the Carnival mass is celebrated and a panegyric pronounced in the church. Additional grants were accorded to the university by Leo XII. and Gregory XVI., and it now possesses five faculties (theology, philosophy, law, medicine, philology) and a staff of 42 professors and lecturers. The present edifice was designed by *Giac. della Porta*, the church (S. Ivo) by *Borromini* in the form of a bee, in honour of Urban VIII., in whose armorial bearings that insect figures, and provided with a baroque spiral tower.

The street to the l., like the two preceding cross-lanes, leads to the **Piazza della Rotonda** (Pl. II, 16). Above the large fountain erected by Lunghi under Gregory XIII., Clement XI. caused the upper extremity of a broken obelisk to be placed. This piazza generally presents a busy scene, and affords the stranger opportunities of observing the characteristics of the peasantry.

Here is situated the church of *S. Maria Rotonda*, or the ****Pantheon** (Pl. II, 16), the only entirely preserved ancient edifice in Rome. The statues, however, and architectural decorations have been added by modern taste, notwithstanding which the huge circular structure with its vast colonnade presents a strikingly imposing aspect. The walls, constructed of admirable brickwork, were originally covered with marble and stucco. The ground in the vicinity has gradually been so much raised that the pavement of the temple, which was formerly approached by an ascent of five steps, now lies below the level of the piazza.

The portico consists of 16 Corinthian columns of granite, upwards of 36 ft. in height; the tympanum formerly contained reliefs, and the roof was embellished by statues. Eight of the columns are in front; the others form three colonnades, originally vaulted over, terminating in niches, in which the colossal statues of Augustus and his son-in-law M. Agrippa stood. The latter, according to the inscription on the frieze (M. Agrippa L. F. Cos. tertium fecit), caused the edifice to be erected B. C. 27. The central colonnade leads to the entrance, still closed by an ancient door strongly secured by bronze plates, in order to diminish the weight of which the upper portion is replaced by a railing. The interior, illuminated solely by the aperture in the centre of the dome, produces so beautiful an effect that even in ancient times it gave rise to the belief that the temple derived its appellation of *Pantheon* (to this day not satisfactorily explained) from its resemblance to the vault of heaven. The seven large niches in the interior contained statues of Mars, Venus, Caesar etc. The fretted ceiling of the vault, which consists of concrete, was decorated with stucco; the entire roof was covered with gilded bronze tiles, which the Emp. Constans II. caused to be removed to Constantinople in 655; under Gregory III. they were replaced by lead. (For the ascent of the dome a permesso from the maggiordomo of the pope is necessary.)

The temple was connected with the *Thermae of Agrippa*, the ruins of which lie in the rear, and was once believed to have originally appertained to them, and to have been converted into a temple at a subsequent period. The name *Pantheum* was however used as early as the year 59 A. D. It was restored by Domitian, Trajan, Septim. Severus and Caracalla; the names of the two last are inscribed on the architrave of the portico.

In 610 the Pantheon was consecrated by Pope Boniface IV. as a Christian church, under the name of *S. Maria ad Martyres*. In commemoration of this event the festival of All Saints was instituted and celebrated on May 13th, subsequently on Nov. 1st. A palace, a cathedral-chapter and a cardinal's title were afterwards attached to the church of *S. Maria Rotonda*, or *La Rotonda* as it is commonly termed. Under Urban VIII. (Barberini) the two campanili were erected by Bernini, the "ass's ears" of the architect as they have been derisively named. The same pope removed the brazen tubes, on which the roof rested, from the portico and caused them to be converted into columns for the canopy of the high-altar, and cannons for the defence of the castle of S. Angelo. This Vandalism gave rise to the complaint of Pasquin: "*Quod non fecerunt barbari, fecerunt Barberini.*" Pius IX. has caused the church to be judiciously restored.

In the first Chap. l. by the high-altar stands the simple monument of Card. Consalvi (1757—1824), state-secretary of Pius VII., by *Thorwaldsen*.

On the 3rd altar on the l. is *Raphael's Tomb* (b. Apr. 6th, 1483; d. Apr. 6th, 1520). The inscription on the wall with the graceful epigram:

*Ille hic est Raphael, timuit quo sospite vinci
Rerum magna parens, et moriente mori.*

is by Card. *Bembo*.

A lengthy inscription beside it announces that Raphael's remains were placed in a new sarcophagus in 1833.

The Pantheon also is the last resting-place of other celebrated artists: Ann. Caracci, Tadd. Zucchero, Bald. Peruzzi, Perino del Vaga and Giov. da Udine.

A visit to the interior by moonlight should on no account be omitted, but the sacristan must be informed some time previously, as admittance is then obtained in the evening by the door at the back of the sacristy, Via della Palombella 10.

From the Piazza of the Pantheon the *Via de' Pastini* leads to the Piazza di Pietra (p. 117); or the ascent to the l. at the beginning of the street, leading to the *Piazza Capranica*, with the small theatre of that name, and Monte Citorio (p. 117), may be preferred; the *Via del Seminario* leads to S. Ignazio (p. 118).

Descending to the l. by the Pantheon, the Via della Minerva leads to the *Piazza della Minerva*, where the church of *S. Maria sopra Minerva* lies on the l., and the Hôtel de la Minerve (p. 86) opposite the traveller. In the centre stands an elephant in marble; on its back a small obelisk has been placed (by *Bernini*), which, with that in the Piazza della Rotonda (p. 153), is said once to have been erected in front of a temple of Isis formerly situated here.

S. Maria sopra Minerva (Pl. II, 16) was erected by the Dominicans in 1370 in the Ital. Gothic style, on the ruins of a temple of Minerva founded by Pompey. In 1848—1855 it was restored and re-decorated, and contains valuable works of art.

By the entrance-wall, on the r., the tomb of the Florentine knight Diotisalvi (d. 1482); in the l. aisle, on the l.,·that of the Florentine Franc. Tornabuoni, by *Mino da Fiesole*; above it the monument of Card. Giac. Tebaldi (d. 1466). To the r. of the altar in the 3rd Chapel, °St. Sebastian, by *Mino da Fiesole*. On the altar: head of Christ, by *Perugino*. In the 5th Chapel is (r.) the monument of the Princess Lante, by *Tenerani*. In the r. aisle, by the pillar between the 4th and 5th chapels is an outlet with an ancient sarcophagus (Hercules taming the lion). In the 5th Chapel, the °Annunciation, a picture on a golden ground (in the foreground Card. Giov. a Torrecremata recommends to the Virgin three poor girls), painted to commemorate the institution of the charitable institution of S. Annunziata, erroneously attrib. to *Fiesole*; on the l. the tomb. of Urban VII. (d. 1590), by *Ambrogio Buonvicino*. The 6th Chapel (Aldobrandini) contains paintings by *Alberti*, over the altar the Last Supper by *Baroccio*; monuments of the parents of Clement VIII. by *Gioc. della Porta*. In the transept a small chapel on the r. is first observed, containing a wooden crucifix attrib. to *Giotto;* then the °Caraffa Chapel, painted by *Filippino Lippi;* on the r. Thomas Aquinas, surrounded by allegorical figures; on the wall at the back the Assumption of the Virgin; altar-fresco, the Annunciation with a portrait of the donor Card. Caraffa; sibyls on the vaulting by *Rafaellino del Garbo;* on the l. the monument of Paul IV., designed by *Pirro Ligorio*, executed by *Giac.* and *Tom. Casignola*. By the wall, adjacent to the latter, the tomb of Bishop Guiliel. Durantus (d. 1296) with a Madonna in mosaic by *Giov. Cosma*. The first chapel by the choir contains an altar-piece by *C. Maratta*. The second is the Cappella del Rosario; altar-piece groundlessly attributed to *Fiesole;* on the r. the tomb of Card. Capranica (about 1470). The choir contains the large monuments of the two Medicis, (l.) Leo X. and (r.) Clement VII., designed by *Ant. da San Gallo*, that of Leo executed by *Raf. da Monte Lupo*, that of Clement by *Giov. di Baccio Bigio*; on the pavement the tombstone of the celebrated scholar Pietro Bembo (d. 1547). In front of the high-altar is *Mich. Angelo's* °°Christ with the Cross (1527), unfortunately marred by bronze drapery. On the l. by the choir is a passage to the Via S. Ignazio; on the wall the tombstone (first on the l.) of Fra Beato Angelico da Fiesole, who died in the neighbouring monastery in 1455, with his portrait and the inscription: *Hic jacet Venerabilis pictor Frater Johannes de Florentia Ordinis praedicatorum 14 LV.* In the l. transept is the Chapel of S. Domenico, with 8 black columns, and the monument of Benedict XIII. by *P. Bracci*. Contiguous, to the r., is the entrance to the sacristy and the library.

The principal of the order resides in the adjoining Dominican monastery, which contains the *Bibliotheca Casanatensis* (entrance to the l. by the church, first door to the r. beyond the court), the most extensive in Rome after that of the Vatican, comprising 120,000 vols. and 4500 MSS., accessible daily 8—11 and $1^1/_2 - 3^1/_2$ o'clock. (The afternoon hours vary according to the time of sunset.)

From the Piazza della Minerva, passing to the l. by the church, the *Via del Piè di Marmo* leads in a straight direction to the Piazza del Coll. Romano (p. 118); from the Piè di Marmo the Via del Gesù diverges to the r., leading in 3 M. to the Piazza del Gesù (p. 124).

From the Piazza S. Luigi de' Francesi (Pl. II, 13) a short street between the church and the post-office (or through the buildings of the latter and turning to the r.) leads to the *Piazza Madama*, where to the l. the traveller perceives the façade of the **Palazzo Madama** (Pl. II, 13), so called from Margaret of Parma, daughter of Charles V., by whom it was once occupied. Previously and subsequently it was in possession of the Medicis, afterwards Grand-dukes of Tuscany, who in 1642 caused it to be altered (by *Marorelli*) to its present form. The offices of the minister of finance and the postal authorities are now established here; one entrance is from the Piazza di S. Luigi, the other from the P. Madama. On the balcony facing the latter, on Saturdays at noon, the winning numbers of the Lotto are drawn, a proceeding which attracts a crowd of spectators. A short sidestreet leads hence to the

*Piazza Navona (Pl. II, 13), the largest in Rome after that of St. Peter, where, as its form still indicates, the *Circus* or *Stadium of Domitian* was formerly situated. The appellation is said to be derived from the contests, agones (corrupted to Navone, Navona), which took place here. Of the three *Fountains* that on

S. Agnese. ROME. *S. Maria dell' Anima.* 157

the N. is unattractive; not far from it is a trough consisting of a large ancient basin of Pentelic marble; the largest in the centre was erected by *Bernini* under Innocent X.; at the corners of the mass of rock, the different parts of which represent the four quarters of the globe, are placed the gods of the four largest (?) rivers, the Danube, Ganges, Nile and Rio della Plata, executed by pupils of Bernini; the whole is surmounted by an obelisk, formerly in the Circus of Maxentius, and originally erected in honour of Domitian. The other fountain is adorned with masks, Tritons and the statue of a Moor by Bernini. The piazza has been employed as a market-place since 1447, and is resorted to by the usual busy concourse of peasants, market-women, hawkers etc., presenting a peculiar phase of Roman life. The singular custom formerly prevailed here of (annually in August) laying the piazza under water for the amusement of the people, by preventing the escape of the water from the fountains.

On the W. side stands the church of **S. Agnese** (Pl. II, 13), the interior of which is in the form of a Greek cross; campanile by *C. Rinaldi*, façade by *Borromini*. In order not to be distressed by the aspect of the latter, the Nile on the great fountain veils his head, as Bernini used to maintain.

Over the principal door is the monument of Innocent X. by *Maini;* to the l. in the chapel of the transept, is a statue of St. Sebastian, into which an ancient statue has been converted by Maini. Beneath the dome are eight columns of "cognatello". The old church was in the side-vaults of the Circus where the saint suffered martyrdom. Two chapels with ancient vaulting still remain.

To the l. by the church is the *Pal. Pamfili* (Pl. II, 13), also erected by Rinaldi, now the property of Prince Doria. Opposite to it is the dilapidated national church of the Spaniards, *S. Giacomò dei Spagnuoli*, of the 15th cent.

The *Via di S. Agnese*, to the r. by the church, leads to the *Via dell' Anima* on the r., where on the l. side ***S. Maria dell' Anima** (Pl. II, 13) is situated (open till 8½ a. m., on holidays till noon. When closed, visitors go round the church by the Vicolo dell' Anima on the r. and ring at the first large door on the l., the entrance to the Austrian Hospice. Immediately opposite to this is S. Maria della Pace). The name is derived from a small marble-group in the tympanum of the portal: a Madonna invoked by two souls in purgatory. It is the German national church, connected with the Hospice, and was completed in 1514. Façade by *Giuliano da Sangallo;* according to some *Bramante* designed part of the architecture of the interior.

The central window of the entrance-wall formerly contained stained glass by *William of Marseilles*, now modern. In the r. aisle, 1st Chapel: *St. Benno receiving from a fisherman the keys of the cathedral at Misnia (Saxony), which had been recovered from the stomach of a fish, altar-piece by Carlo Saraceni.* 2nd Chapel: Holy Family, altar-piece by *Gimig-*

nani; monument and bust of Card. Slusius. 4th Chapel: altered copy of *Michael Angelo's* Pietà in St. Peter's, by *Nanni di Baccio Bigio*. In the l. aisle, 1st Chapel: *Martyrdom of St. Lambert, *C. Saraceni*. 3rd Chapel: frescoes from the life of St. Barbara. *Mich. Coxcie;* the altar-piece (Entombment) and frescoes by *Salviati*.

In the **Choir**: over the high-altar, Holy Family with saints, by *G. Romano*, damaged by inundations; on the r., *monument of Hadrian VI. of Utrecht (preceptor of Charles V., d. 1523), designed by *Baldassare Peruzzi*, executed by *Michelangiolo Sanese* and *Niccolò Tribolo;* opp. to it that of a Duke of Cleve-Julich-Berg (d. 1575) by *Egidius of Rivière* and *Nicolaus of Arras*.

***S. Maria della Pace** (Pl. II, 13), erected by Sixtus IV. (1484) and Innocent VIII., was restored by Alexander VII., and provided by *Pietro da Cortona* with a façade and semi-circular portico. The church consists of nave alone, and terminates in an octagon with a dome.

Over the 1st Chapel on the r. are ***Raphael's* Sibyls, painted in 1514 by order of Agostino Chigi who erected the chapel, skilfully freed from "restorations" by *Palmaroli* in 1816; seen best 10—11 a. m. Prophets in the lunette above by *Tim. della Vite*. At the sides of the 1st Chapel on the l. monuments of the Ponzetti family. In the 2nd Chapel on the l., fresco altar-piece by *B. Peruzzi:* Madonna between St. Brigitta and St. Catharine, in front the kneeling donor Card. Ponzetti. To the l. beneath the dome, entrance to the sacristy and court (see below). Over the first altar on the l., Adoration of the Shepherds by *Sermoneta*. The second altar, with handsome marble-work partially gilded, is of the 16th cent. The high-altar is adorned with an ancient and greatly revered Madonna. Over the adjacent altar to the r., Baptism of Christ, *Sermoneta*. Over the niche, Mary's first visit to the Temple, *Bald. Peruzzi*.

It is the custom for newly-married couples to attend their first mass in this church. — The *court of the monastery, with arcades constructed by *Bramante* by order of Card. Caraffa in 1504, merits a visit; entrance through the church, or Arco della Pace 5.

From the portal of the church the *Via della Pace* and the *Via in Parione* lead in a straight direction to the animated *Via del Governo Vecchio*. The latter with its prolongations under different names forms the most direct and frequented route between the Piazza del Gesù and the Vatican (distance from Gesù to the Ponte S. Angelo 18 min. walk).

From the Piazza del Gesù the *Via de' Cesarini* is followed, leading to the *Piazza delle Stimate* on the r., with the church of that name (Pl. II, 16) and the opposite *Pal. Strozzi* (Pl. II, 16) (the prolongation of the street leads to the Piazza della Minerva, p. 155); the *Piazza Strozzi*, named after the palace, is then entered on the r., then the *Via di Tor Argentina*, which to the r. leads to the Pantheon; on the l. is the *Teatro Argentina*. The *Via del Sudario* now leads direct to the church of Andrea della Valle, which is already visible.

The corner-house (No. 13) before the church is reached is the **Palazzo Vidoni** (Pl. II, 13), formerly *Caffarelli* and *Stoppani*, originally constructed from designs by Raphael: on the staircase a few ancient statues (L. Verus, Minerva, Diana). In one of the rooms is preserved the celebrated *Calendarium Praenestinum* of Verrius Flaccus, five months of a Roman calendar found by Card. Stoppani at Præneste. This palace was once occupied by Charles V. (access not easily obtained). — On the side of the palace towards the church is the so-called *Abbate Luigi*, a mutilated ancient statue (see p. 123).

*S. Andrea della Valle (Pl. II, 13), begun by *P. Olivieri* in 1591 on the site of several earlier churches, was completed by *C. Maderno;* façade from drawings by *Rainaldi*. The interior is of symmetrical proportions, but unfortunately partially whitewashed.

On the r. the 2nd Chapel (Strozzi) contains copies in bronze of the Pietà (in St. Peter's), and the Rachel and Leah (in S. Pietro in Vinc.) of *Michael Angelo*. On the l. the 1st Chapel (Barberini) is adorned with several marble statues by *Mocchi* (St. Martha), *P. Bernini* (John the Bapt.), *Stati da Bracciano* (M. Magdalene) and *Amb. Buonvicino* (St. John). At the extremity of the nave are the monuments of (l.) Pius II. and (r.) Pius IV. by *Nic. della Guardia* and *Pietro Paolo da Todi*. In the dome: Glory of Paradise, by *Lanfranco;* beneath, the *Evangelists by *Domenichino*, one of his finest works. By the same master, *paintings on the vaulting of the apse. In the girding-arch: John the Bapt., St. John and St. Andrew pointing to Christ ("this is the Lamb . . ."); in the vaulting itself, on the l. the Scourging of St. Andrew; then the Vocation of Peter and Andrew by Christ; on the r., St. Andrew beholds and adores the cross to which he is about to be affixed; beneath, 6 allegorical female figures; the lower, and extensive frescoes by *Calabrese* (martyrdom of the saint) are of no great value.

The *Via de' Massimi* is now followed, reaching after a few paces, on the r. No. 17, the

Palazzo Massimi alle Colonne (Pl. II, 13, *11*), a fine structure by *Baldassare Peruzzi*. The outline of the façade forms an arch; the glimpse obtained of the double court is strikingly picturesque.

A room on the first floor contains the celebrated statue of the *Discus-thrower, a copy of the bronze statue of *Myron*, found on the Esquiline in 1761, one of the most interesting antiques in Rome and far better preserved than the inaccurately restored duplicate in the Vatican. Visitors are not always admitted; the most favourable time is 9—11 a. m.; the staircase to the r. in the colonnade in the court is ascended to the first floor and a servant (1 l.) in the anteroom applied to; a permesso for the Villa Massimo (p. 207) may at the same time be asked for. The passages and saloons of the palace contain several other ancient statues, inscriptions etc. On the second-floor the chapel of *S. Filippo Neri*, who is said to have resuscitated a child of the family; open on March 16th.

Within the buildings connected with this palace the Germans *Pannartz* and *Schweinheim* established the first printing-office in Rome in 1485, where Apuleius, Augustinus de Civitate Dei and other works were published, furnished with the name of the printers and the addition of: *In aedibus Petri de Maximis*. The Massimi family claims descent from the ancient Maximi, and their armorial bearings have the motto *"Cunctando restituit"*.

To the l. the *Via de' Baullari* leads to the Pal. Farnese (p. 162), which is visible from here. The small *Piazza S. Pantaleo* is next reached, with the small church of that name on the r. In a straight direction is seen the spacious

Palazzo Braschi (Pl. II, 13, 17), erected by *Morelli* at the close of the last century, and now much neglected. It contains a fine *marble staircase and a few ancient statues; concerts occasionally given in the large hall in winter. The rear of the building adjoins the Piazza Navona (p. 156).

Passing the palace the traveller reaches the *Piazza di Pasquino*, which derives its appellation from an ancient group of statuary placed at the obtuse corner of the Pal. Braschi. This was an admirable, now unfortunately greatly mutilated work of the beginning of the imperial age, and was so named from the tailor Pasquino who lived in the vicinity and was notorious for his lampooning propensities. It became the custom to affix all kinds of satires and ebullitions of malice to these statues (the answers to which used to be attached to the Marforio, p. 210), and to refer them to the slanderous tailor, whose name is perpetuated in the term "pasquinade". The group represents Menelaus with the body of Patroclus, at the moment when in the tumult of the battle he looks round for help. Duplicates of the group are in the Loggia de' Lanzi and Palazzo Pitti at Florence, fragments in the Vatican.

The Via del Governo now continues to be followed. After 3 M. the Via in Parione diverges to the r. to the church S. Maria della Pace. Then on the r. the *Pal. del Governo Vecchio*, which was long the seat of the tribunals of justice and police. No. 124 on the opposite side is a small, tastefully constructed house in the style of Bramante. The *Via della Chiesa Nuova* diverges to the l. and leads to the piazza of that name, with the

Chiesa Nuova (Pl. II, 10) *(S. Maria e S. Gregorio in Vallicella)*, erected by S. Filippo Neri for the order of Philippines founded by him, and completed in 1605. Architecture by *Giov. Matteo da Città di Castello*, interior by *Martino Lunghi*, façade by *Rughesi*.

The interior, dark and unfavourable for pictures, is richly decorated. The ceiling of the nave, the dome and the tribune were painted by *Pietro da Cortona*. On the r., 1st Chapel: Crucifixion, *Scip. di Gaetano*; 3rd Chapel, dell' Ascensione: altar-piece by *Muziano*. On the l., 2nd Chapel: Adoration of the Magi, *Ces. Nebbia*; 3rd Chapel: Nativity, *Durante Alberti*. 4th Chapel: Visit of Elisabeth, *Baroccio*. In the transept, on the l., Presentation in the Temple, *Baroccio*; Peter and Paul. statues in marble by *Valsoldo*. Here, too, by the tribune is the small and sumptuous chapel of S. Filippo Neri, beneath the altar of which his remains repose. Above is the portrait of the saint in mosaic, after the original of *Guido Reni* which is preserved in the adjoining monastery. In the transept, Coronation of the Virgin, *Cav. d'Arpino*; John the Bapt. and St. John, statues in marble by *Flaminio Vacca*. Over the high-altar, with its four columns of porta santa, a Madonna by *Rubens*; on the r. *SS. Gregory, Maurus and Papia, on the l. *SS. Nereus and Achilleus, also by *Rubens*.

Pal. della Cancelleria. ROME. *S. Lorenzo in Damaso.* 161

In the Sacristy (entered from the l. transept), constructed by *Marrucelli*; on the vaulting: Angel with instruments of torture, by *Pietro da Cortona*. Colossal statue of the saint by *Algardi*.
The adjoining monastery, erected by *Borromini*. is of irregular form, but remarkable for the massiveness of its construction. It contains an apartment once occupied by the saint with various relics. — The valuable *Library* founded by S. Filippo Neri and gradually enriched by rare MSS. is not generally accessible to the public.

From the Piazza della Chiesa Nuova the *Via de' Filippini* leads to the r. to the *Piazza dell' Orologio*, whence to the l. the *Via dei Banchi Nuovi* diverges to the *Via del Banco di S. Spirito* (the *Bank* is at the corner on the l.). which last leads to the Ponte S. Angelo.

The Via de' Baullari, opposite the Pal. Massimi. leads to several interesting palaces in the best style of the Renaissance. Somewhat removed from the street, immediately on the r.. is a small but tastefully constructed edifice, the * *Palazzetto Farnese*, the architect of which is said to have been *Baldassare Peruzzi*.

The next street to the r. leads to the piazza named after the ***Palazzo della Cancelleria** (Pl. II, 13), designed by *Bramante* and one of the finest structures in Rome. Within its precincts is the church of S. Lorenzo, originally erected near the theatre of Pompey. The elegant façade (with portal subsequently added by *Dom. Fontana)* consists of blocks of travertine from the Colosseum. The columns of the double *court, surrounded by arcades, are ancient; the graceful capitals are decorated with roses, that flower being prominent in the armorial bearings of the founder Card. Riario. In this palace in 1848 Pius IX. convoked the parliament which was to deliberate on the reforms to be undertaken in the States of the Church. On Nov. 15th of that year the minister Count Rossi was murdered on the first landing of the staircase.

To the r. of the palace (entrance to the r. from the court) is situated the church of **S. Lorenzo in Damaso** (Pl. II. 13), which has the above-mentioned façade in common with the palace. It was also designed by *Bramante* (originally erected by Damasus I.) and is enclosed by arcades on three sides. The pictures were destroyed during the revolution of the previous century, and the architecture alone continues to be an object of interest. At the extremity of the r. aisle is the monument of the ill-fated Count Rossi. by *Tenerani*.

The Piazza della Cancelleria is adjoined by the *Piazza di Campo di Fiori*, a focus of commercial traffic, and the latter by the *Piazza Farnese*, adorned with two fountains. Here is situated the

Palazzo Farnese (Pl. II. 14), one of the finest in Rome, begun by Paul III. (Alex. Farnese, 1534—45) when cardinal, from designs by Anton. da *Sangallo*, continued under the direction of *Michael Angelo*, and completed by the construction of the loggia at the back towards the Tiber by *Giac. della Porta*. The building materials were taken partly from the Colosseum and partly from the theatre of Marcellus. This palace was inherited by the kings of Naples, and since 1862 has been tenanted by the ex-king Francis II. The threefold *colonnade of the entrance was designed by *Sangallo*, the two lower halls of the court by *Mich. Angelo*, after the model of the theatre of Marcellus. The court contains two ancient sarcophagi. The celebrated antiquities once in this palace are now partly in the Museum of Naples (Farnese Bull, Hercules, Flora) and partly in England. The remainder are in a room on the 1st floor; among them a sarcophagus, with relief representing a battle between Amazons. Permission to inspect the frescoes is not always granted. Inquiry should be made of the porter; the most favourable hour for admittance is 4 p. m.

The *Gallery* on the 1st floor is embellished with *frescoes by *Annibale Caracci*, his finest work, consisting of mythological representations with rich architectural painting.

Principal Subjects: 1. Triumph of Bacchus and Ariadne; 2. Pan, offering goats' wool to Diana; 3. Mercury with a trumpet bringing the apple to Paris; 4. Aurora in her chariot embraces Cephalus who has been carried off by her; 5. Galatea surrounded by nymphs and Tritons (these two are by *Lodovico Caracci* from the designs of his brother *Annibale*); 6. Polyphemus playing on the syrinx in order to win the affection of Galatea; 7. Polyphemus hurling a mass of rock after Acis who escapes with Galatea; 8. Apollo abducts Hyacinthus; 9. Ganymedes carried off by Jupiter's eagle; 10. Juno encircled with the cestus of Venus approaches Jupiter; 11. Luna embracing the sleeping Endymion; 12. Hercules and Omphale, the latter with the club and lion's skin; 13. Anchises removing the cothurnus of Venus. — In the round reliefs: Leander and Hero; Pan pursuing the nymph Syrinx; Salmacis embracing Hermaphroditus; Cupid seizing a Faun; Apollo flaying Marsyas; Boreas carrying off Orithyia; Eurydice conducted back from the infernal regions; Rape of Europa. — On the narrow ends of the saloon: Perseus petrifies Phineus and his companion with the head of the Medusa; Perseus hastening on Pegasus to liberate Andromeda (said to have been almost entirely executed by *Domenichino*). — Over the niches and windows are eight smaller paintings: Arion on the dolphin; Prometheus educating man; Hercules slaying the dragon which guards the apples of the Hesperides; Hercules delivering Prometheus on Caucasus; Icarus precipitated into the sea; Callisto bathing; the same nymph metamorphosed into a bear; Apollo receiving the lyre from Mercury. — Over the principal door, a girl caressing a unicorn, the emblem of the Farnese family, executed by *Domenichino* from *A*. Caracci's designs. Other apartments which are not accessible contain several works of *A. Caracci*, *Daniel da Volterra*, *Salviati*, *Vasari* and the two *Zuccari*.

From the Piazza Farnese a street *(Via di Monserrato, Via de' Banchi Vecchi)* leading to the Ponte S. Angelo contains several churches. The third on the l., *S. Maria di Monserrato*, is the national Spanish church, connected with a hospice, erected in

1495 by *Sangallo*; the first chapel on the r. contains an altarpiece by *Ann. Caracci*.

The Vicolo de' Venti, to the l. opposite, leads to the *Piazza di Capo di Ferro*. No. 13 on the r. is the

*Palazzo Spada alla Regola (Pl. II, 14), erected about 1540 by Card. Capodiferro under Paul III. in imitation of a house built by Raphael for himself, and since the time of Urban VIII. (1640) in possession of the Spada family. It contains an interesting collection of *antiquities (on the ground-floor) and pictures (1st floor), to which access is most easily obtained between 10 and 12 o'clock (custodian 1/2 l. for 1 pers., more for a party; exorbitant demands occasionally made).

Antiquities: In the 1st Room by the long wall: sitting °statue of Aristotle, with the inscription: *APIΣT* . . . . . on the basis, formerly erroneously interpreted as Aristides, copy from a celebrated Greek work; r. arm and l. leg new. — In the 2nd R. eight fine °reliefs, found in 1620 in S. Agnese fuori le Mura, where they formed part of the pavement with their faces towards the ground. Entrance-wall: r. Dædalus and Pasiphaë, l. Paris as cowherd. Window-wall: Wounded Adonis; Ulysses and Diomedes carrying off the Palladium. Narrow end: Endymion; Perseus and Andromeda, casts from the originals in the Capitoline museum. L. wall: Paris taking leave of Œnone; Hypsipyle finds Opheltes who had been entrusted to her killed by a snake; Amphion and Zethus; Bellerophon watering Pegasus. Besides these, busts, small statues etc.

In the upper story a *Colossal Statue of Pompey*, found under Julius III. (1550) in digging the foundations of a house in the *Vicolo de' Leutari*. The upper portion was in the ground of one proprietor whilst the legs were in that of another. As both parties laid claim to the statue the judge directed that it should be divided! The pope, however, prevented this by purchasing the statue for 500 scudi and presenting it to Card. Capodiferro. The head, although of a detached block, belongs to the original. The work is mediocre.

The Picture Gallery (provided with catalogues) is reached beyond several rooms containing frescoes of little value. 1st Room: 3. Madonna, *Bolognese Sch.*; 7, 12. Portraits, *French Sch.*; 10. Card. Patrizi, *Canuccini*; 22. Portrait. *Caravaggio*; 40. Julius III., *Sc. Gaetano*; 56. Madonna, *Sch. of Francia*. — 2nd R.: 1. Astronomer, *Seb. del Piombo*; 9. Landscape, *Breughel*; 10. Judith, *Guido Reni*; 12. Landscape, *G. Poussin*; 18. Visitation of Elisabeth (greatly damaged), *And. del Sarto*; 45. Christ and the scribes. *Leonardo da Vinci* (a copy from the original in England). — 3rd R.: 2. St. Anna and the Virgin, *Caravaggio*; 4. John the Bapt., *G. Romano* (?); 15. Landscape, *Breughel*; 24. Dido's death, *Guercino*; 26. Design of the ceiling-painting in Gesù, *Baciccio*; 29. Landscape, *Salvator Rosa*; 31. Portrait, *Titian*; °Portrait, *Moroni*; 48.. 49. God the Father, and Bearing the Cross, *Marco Palmezzano*; 51. Card. Paolo Spada, *Titian* (?); 60., 70. Landscapes, *Salv. Rosa*; 63. Abduction of Helen, *Guido Reni*; 67. Cavalry-skirmish, *Borgognone*. — 4th R.: 4. Card. Bernardo Spada, *Guido Reni*; 9. Paul III., after *Titian*; 10. Portrait (1511), *German Sch.*; 15. Laughing angel's head, *Caravaggio*; 18. Portrait, *German Sch.*; 26. Christ in the garden, *Ger. Honthorst*; 31. Card. Fabricius Spada, *Maratta*; 30. St. Cecilia, *Caravaggio*; 44. Madonna, *And. del Sarto* (?); 54. Portrait, *French. Sch.*

Proceeding in the same direction from the Piazza Capo di Ferro the traveller reaches the *Piazza de' Pellegrini*; on the l. is the rear of the *Monte di Pietà*, formerly *Pal. Santacroce* (Pl. II, 14), which a money-lending establishment, instituted in 1539, has occupied since 1604. On the r. the church *S. Trinità de' Pellegrini*, erected in 1614: high-altar adorned with the Trinity by *Guido Reni*. The neighbouring hospital is destined principally for the accommodation of pilgrims.

Hence to the r. the *Via de' Pettinari* leads to the Ponte Sisto (p. 227), the street to the l. to the Via de' Giubbonari (see below). At the extremity on the r. is the small church of *S. Salvatore in Onda* (Pl. II, 14), re-erected in 1684, on the l. the *Fontanone di Ponte Sisto*, constructed by Giov. Fontana under Paul V.

In a straight direction from the fountain, near the river, runs the *Via del Fontanone*, prolonged by the *Via Giulia*, constructed by Julius II., and leading (in 12 min.) to the Ponte S. Angelo. To the l. in the latter street, opposite the garden of the Pal. Farnese. lies the small church of *S. Maria della Morte* or *dell' Orazione*, erected by Fuga about the middle of the previous century and belonging to a burial-society. Then to the l. *Pal. Falconieri*, built by Borromini, where the picture-gallery of Card. Fesch was formerly established; farther on. on the same side the *Carceri Nuovi*, a prison founded by Innocent X.; then (No. 66) the *Pal. Sacchetti* (Pl. II, 10), originally erected by Antonio da San Gallo as his private residence; in the court are some interesting antiques. At the end of the street, l. **S. Giovanni de' Fiorentini** (Pl. II, 10), the stately national church of the Florentines, designed by *Sansovino* and *Giac. della Porta*, and begun at the commencement of the 16th cent. *Michael Angelo*, although an old man, took an active part in its erection; the façade was added by *Aless. Galilei* in 1725. It contains nothing worthy of mention except a picture (St. Cosmas and St. Damianus at the stake) by *Salvator Rosa* in the chapel of the r. transept.

By the church an iron-bridge (1 soldo), constructed in 1863, crosses the river to the Longara (p. 223). The Via Paola leads from the church to the Ponte S. Angelo.

In the Piazza di Campo di Fiori, towards S. Andrea della Valle, once lay the *Theatre of Pompey*. In the court of the *Pal. Righetti*, Piazza del Biscione 95, the bronze statue of Hercules (p. 248) and substructures of the theatre were discovered.

From the Piazza di Campo di Fiori the animated *Via de' Giubbonari* leads to the Capitol and the S. quarters of the city. After 2 min. it expands into the *Piazza S. Carlo a Catinari*. On the l. the church of **S. Carlo a Catinari** (Pl. II, 14), erected by S. Carlo Borromeo at the beginning of the 17th cent. The form is that of a Greek cross: beneath the dome, paintings by *Domenichino*.

In the 1st Chapel on the r., Annunciation, by *Lanfranco*. In the transept to the r., Death of St. Anna, *Andrea Sacchi*. Over the high-altar,

Card. Borromeo in the procession of the plague at Milan. *P. da Cortona;* tribune decorated by *Lanfranco;* the other paintings are of little value.

Opposite is the *Pal. Santacroce,* facing the Piazza Branca (r.). The court contains a few ancient reliefs.

The street now divides: to the l. the *Via de' Falegnami* leads to the *Piazza Mattei* or *Tartaruga,* named after the graceful *Fontana delle Tartarughe* (tortoises), erected by Giac. della Porta in 1585 and embellished with the figures of four youths.

Immediately to the r., Piazza Mattei 10 (another entrance, Piazza Costaguti 16), is the

Palazzo Costaguti, erected about 1590 by *Carlo Lombardi.* Of the ceiling-paintings on the 1st floor access to the following only (porter ½ l.) is permitted: 1. Hercules bending his bow against Nessus, *Franc. Albani;* 2. Apollo in the quadriga, to which Truth raises herself, discovered by Time, *Domenichino* (greatly retouched); *3. Armida with Rinaldo in the dragon-chariot, admirably coloured, by *Guercino.* Those which are not visible are by the *Cav. d' Arpino* and other good masters. One wing of the palace (formerly *Boccapaduli)* was long the residence of Poussin, and still contains works by him, but is not now accessible.

Adjoining the piazza on the l. is the

Palazzo Mattei (Pl. II, 17, 27), originally an aggregate of separate buildings which occupied the block between the Via di S. Caterina de' Funari and Via Paganica. Of these the handsomest is the present so-called palace (principal entrance V. di S. Caterina de' Funari 32, side-entrance No. 31), erected in 1616 by *Carlo Maderno,* and one of his finest productions. In the passages of the entrances, the arcades and the lateral walls of the court a great number of ancient reliefs are immured: among those in the court, r. Mars with Rhea Silvia and Apollo with the Muses; l. the Calydonian hunt and Rape of Proserpine; in the portico, Sacrifice of Mithras, Apollo with the Muses, Bacchanalian procession, all from sarcophagi. The statues in the court and niches on the stairs, some of them greatly modernized, are of no great value. The decorations of the ceiling on the staircases, in stucco, are well executed.

The picture-gallery is now greatly reduced in extent; the frescoes do not merit special mention.

Then in the V. di S. Caterina de' Funari, on the l., the church of *S. Caterina de' Funari* (Pl. II, 17), erected in 1564 by Giac. della Porta, with a singular-looking tower, situated within the area of the ancient *Circus Flaminius.* The interior contains a few unimportant pictures by Nanni, Venusti, Muziano and Agresti. The adjoining convent of Augustine nuns is an educational establishment for girls.

The street terminates in the *Via Delfini*, which to the l. leads to the Via di Araceli (p. 124), and to the r. to the *Piazza di Campitelli*, beyond the next corner. Here on the r. stands **S. Maria in Campitelli** (Pl. II. 17), erected by *Rinaldi* under Alexander VII. for the more worthy reception of a miraculous image of the Virgin, to which the cessation of the plague in 1656 was ascribed; a smaller church of the same name, mentioned in the 13th cent., formerly stood on this site. The architecture of the interior has an imposing effect. Beneath the canopy over the high-altar is placed the miraculous Madonna. In the 2nd Chapel on the r., the Effusion of the Holy Ghost, by *Luca Giordano;* in the 1st Chapel on the l. two monuments resting on lions of rosso antico. In the r. transept the tomb of Cardinal Pacca by *Pettrich*. — Opposite the church is the *Pal. Pacca*.

The street in a straight direction from the piazza leads to the Via Tor de' Specchi at the foot of the Capitoline. that to the l. to the Piazza Araceli (p. 168), r. to Piazza Montanara (p. 167).

From the Piazza di S. Carlo a Catinari the Via del Pianto leads to the r. to the *Piazza Giudea* or *di S. Maria del Pianto*, called after a church of that name. Adjoining this piazza on the r. is the *Piazza Cenci*, where on the l. in the corner, the *Synagogue* and on the r. the

Palazzo Cenci-Bolognetti (Pl. II. 17) are situated. In the latter once resided the ill-fated Beatrice Cenci, executed for the murder of her father, a man of execrable fame. Her portrait, which is of questionable authenticity, is preserved in the Pal. Barberini, and is a favourite subject for reproduction with the Roman artists.

From the Piazza Giudea the *Pescheria* (fish-market), which presents an animated scene on Friday mornings, leads to the Colonnade of Octavia. Between the Pescheria and the Tiber lies the **Ghetto** (Pl. II. 17), the quarter allotted by Paul IV. to the Jews, who in ancient and mediæval times occupied a quarter in Trastevere, formerly closed by a gate. It consists of several streets parallel with the river and connected by narrow lanes. The same pope enacted that the Jews should wear yellow head-gear and pay unusually heavy taxes; amongst other oppressive exactions they were compelled to provide the prizes for the horse-races at the Carnival. The traveller may explore these purlieus for the sake of observing the marked oriental type of their occupants, who with their characteristic industry seek to counteract the disadvantages of their social position. The *Via de' Fiumari*, the nearest to the river, leads to the *Ponte de' Quattro Capi* (see p. 231).

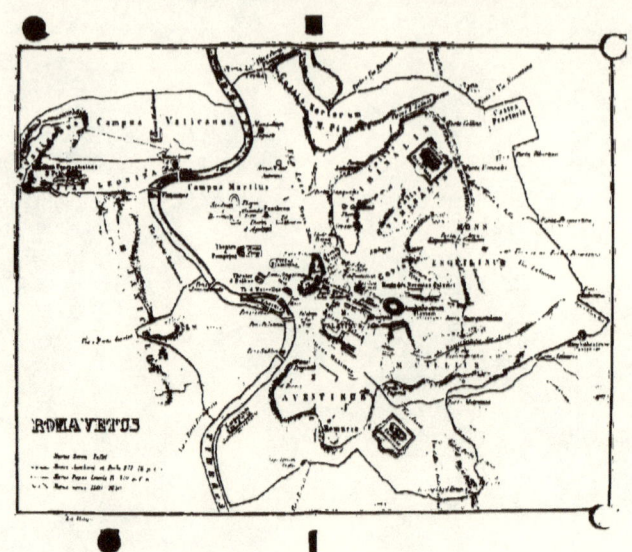

Near the Pescheria are situated the interesting remains of the **Colonnade of Octavia**, erected by Augustus on the site of a similar structure of Metellus (B. C. 149) and dedicated to his sister. Under Titus it was destroyed by a conflagration which raged in this quarter of the city, and was subsequently restored by Sept. Severus and Caracalla in 209, as the inscription records. The colonnade enclosed an oblong space, within which temples of Jupiter Stator and Juno stood. Some obstructive buildings have lately been removed from the ruins.

Proceeding in the direction of the Pescheria from the colonnade the street reaches the **Theatre of Marcellus** (Pl. II, 17, 5), commenced by Cæsar, completed B. C. 13 by Augustus and named after his nephew. Of the external wall of the space for the spectators twelve arches are still standing, now occupied by smiths and other artizans as workshops. The lower story, partly filled up, is in the Doric, the second in the Ionic style, above which, as in the case of the Colosseum, a third probably rose of the Corinthian order. It is said to have accommodated 20,000 spectators. The stage lay towards the Tiber. In the 11th cent. the theatre was employed by Pierleone as a fortress. His descendants yielded possession to the Savelli, whose palace (opposite the Ponte Quattro Capi) stands on a lofty mound of debris within the theatre. In 1712 it was purchased by the Orsini; in 1816—1823 the historian Niebuhr, when Prussian ambassador, resided here.

The external wall adjoins the small and busy *Piazza Montanara*, a frequent resort of the peasantry of the Campagna. To the l. a street leads to the Piazza Araceli, to the r. the animated *Via della Bocca della Verità* to the piazza of that name (p. 186). Immediately to the r. in the latter street, standing back, is the church of *S. Niccolò in Carcere*, recently restored, containing ancient columns in the interior and on the external walls which appear to have belonged to three different temples, among them those of *Spes* and *Juno Sospita*. Visitors may descend and examine the foundations of this temple; fee to the sacristan, who carries a light, $1/2$ l.

IV. Ancient Rome.

This portion of the description comprises the S. part of the city, commencing with the Capitoline and extending E. as far as the Lateran: i. e. the hills of the Capitoline, Palatine, Aventine, Cælius and the S. slope of the Esquiline. The ruins and reminiscences of classical antiquity impart to this the (now almost entirely deserted) principal quarter of the Republican and Imperial city its characteristic aspect. At the same time, however, a number of ancient churches, extremely interesting to students of

Christian architecture, as well as the imposing collections of the Capitol and Lateran, attract numerous visitors. The description begins with the Capitol.

From the *Piazza Araceli* (Pl. II, 17) three approaches lead to the Capitoline Hill: 1. the lofty flight of steps (124 in number), constructed in 1348 (principal entrance generally closed, see below), to the church of *S. Maria in Araceli*, whence the appellation of the piazza below. To the r. the Via de' tre Pile ascends to the *Pal. Caffarelli*, erected in the 16th cent. by Ascanio Caffarelli, a former page of Charles V., now the residence of the Prussian ambassador and occasionally of members of the royal family of Prussia. In the garden ancient substructures of massive blocks have recently been excavated, appertaining perhaps to the temple of Jupiter.

S. Maria in Araceli (Pl. II, 20). The usual entrance is from the piazza of the Capitoline by the stair to the l. (in the rear of the Capitoline museum), and then to the l. from the first landing. Over the door here an ancient Madonna The church probably occupies the site of a temple of Juno Moneta, and is mentioned as early as 935. Façade unfinished. The interior is disfigured by modern additions. The nave is supported by 22 ancient columns, most of them of granite; on the 3rd to the l. the inscription: *A cubiculo Augustorum*. The church derives its appellation from a legend that Augustus erected an altar here to Christ, with the inscription: *Ara primogeniti Dei*, which is pointed out in the l. transept beneath the altar (restored in 1835) of St. Helena with its circular canopy, where this saint is said to be interred.

By the wall of the principal entrance, to the l., is the tomb of the astronomer Lodovico Grato (1531), figure of Christ said to be by *And. Sansovino*; on the r. the monument of Card. Lebretto (1465) with partially preserved painting. In the r. aisle, 1st Chapel: *frescoes from 'the life of St. Bernhard of Siena, by *Pinturicchio*, restored by *Camuccini*. Frescoes on the ceiling attrib. to *Franc. da Città di Castello* and *L. Signorelli*. The 5th Chapel (of St. Matthew) contains good pictures by *Muziano*. In the 2nd Chapel of the l. aisle a manger (presepe) is fitted up at Christmas, i. e. a gorgeous representation of life-size of the Nativity, with the richly decorated image of the Infant Christ (*il santo bambino*), which constitutes the principal ornament of the church. It is believed to protect those in imminent danger, is frequently invoked and revered, and is conveyed to the houses of those who are dangerously ill, on which occasions passers-by kneel on its approach. During the week after Christmas, 3—4 o'clock daily, a number of children from 5 to 10 years of age address their petitions to the bambino. In the transept, on the r. and l. by the pillars of the nave are two "ambos from the former choir, by *Laurentius* and *Jacobus Cosmas*. The Chapel on the r. belongs to the Savelli; on the r. and l. monuments of the family of the 13th cent. (of the parents and a brother of Honorius IV.). Besides the canopy already alluded to, the l. transept contains the monument of Matthæus of Aquasparta (d. 1302), the principal of the Dominican order mentioned by Dante. In the choir, to the l., the monument of Giov. Batt. Savelli (d. 1498). Over the high-altar, prior to 1565, was the Madonna di Foligno of Raphael, ordered for this

Piazza del Campidoglio. ROME. *Pal. del Senatore.* 169

church but now in the Vatican Gallery. The donor, Sigismondo Conti da Foligno, is interred in the choir. The present altar-piece is an ancient picture of the Madonna, attrib. to St. Luke.

The adjacent cloister (reached by the continuation of the staircase from the piazza of the Capitoline) has since 1251 belonged to the Frati minori Osservanti di S. Francesco. It is at present partially occupied by soldiers. In the passage beyond the second of the two handsome courts a broad staircase to the r. ascends to a chapel and corridor, both commanding magnificent *views of Rome, especially of the Quirinal, Esquiline, Cælius, Palatine and Forum. The library, established in 1732, is accessible by special permission only.

The central asphalt-stairs lead to the celebrated **Piazza del Campidoglio (Pl. II, 20), or square of the Capitol. The design of the whole is due to *Michael Angelo*, and its execution was begun in 1536 by Paul III.; the palaces of the Conservatori and Senators were already in existence, but their façades were altered. At the foot of the steps *(Cordonnata)* which lead to the Capitol are two handsome, water-spouting Egyptian lions in basalt: above, the celebrated groups of Castor and Pollux, said once to have adorned the theatre of Pompey. At the sides of the balustrade are the so-called *Trophies of Marius*, from the water-tower of that name of the Acqua Julia near S. Maria Maggiore (p. 144), and the statues of the Emp. Constantine and his son Constans from the Thermæ of Constantine on the Quirinal; on the r. the first ancient milestone of the Via Appia (on the l. a modern counterpart).

In the centre of the piazza stands the admirable bronze *Equestrian Statue of Marcus Aurelius* (161—181), once gilded and originally placed in the forum near the arch of Sept. Severus; in 1187 it was erected near the Lateran, and, as the inscription records, transferred hither in 1538. For its excellent state of preservation it has been indebted to the popular belief that it was a statue of Constantine, the first Christian emperor. Beyond it is situated the **Pal. del Senatore**, re-erected by Boniface IX. on the site of the ancient Tabularium, and provided by *Michael Angelo* with its handsome flights of steps, under whose directions, it is believed, the façade was constructed by *Giac. della Porta*; the river-gods are those of the (r.) Tiber and (l.) Nile: in the centre a fountain, above which a sitting statue of Rome. The palace contains a spacious hall for the solemn meetings of the senate, the offices of the civic administration, an observatory and dwelling-apartments. The campanile was erected by Gregory XIII. to replace a former structure, which like the four corner-towers (one of them towards the forum, on the l., is still recognised) probably belonged to the edifice of Boniface. The roof, embellished by a standing Roma, commands a fine view, but the ascent has of late years been prohibited. The great bell is employed to convoke the senators, to announce the approach of the Carnival, and the death of a pope.

The two palaces at the sides were erected in the 17th cent. by Giac. del Duca with some deviations from the plans of Mich. Angelo; on the r. the *Pal. of the Conservatori* (p. 209) (with guard-house below), and on the opposite side the *Capitoline Museum* (p. 210). The staircases with three-arched halls at the sides of these palaces were erected by *Vignola*; that to the l. by the museum leads to the church of S. Maria in Araceli and the contiguous Franciscan monastery; that to the r., on the opposite side, to *Monte Caprino*, where the Archæological Institution (p. 109) and the Protestant hospital are situated. Descent to the Forum on either side of the Senatorial Palace.

The **Capitol**, 151 ft. above the sea-level, formed the central and principal point of ancient Rome. The depression between its two culminating points, i. e. the present piazza of the Capitol, was occupied by the asylum which, according to tradition, Romulus opened for the reception of the exiles of the neighbouring tribes. On the height to the l., on the site of S. Maria in Araceli, stood the *Temple of Juno Moneta* and the *Arx*, or citadel in the strict sense, a term commonly employed to designate the entire hill.

On the height to the r., the **Tarpeian Rock,** best seen from the garden of the Casa Tarpeia (custodian, Monte Caprino 130) or from the Via Tor de' Specchi (between Nos. 37 and 38), lay the *Temple of Jupiter Capitolinus.* The precipitousness of the ground has however been greatly diminished since ancient times; moreover the precise situation of the rock from which the condemned were hurled is still involved in some doubt, so that a visit to this spot may well be omitted.

Of the buildings which in ancient times covered the Capitol some imposing remains alone are preserved where the Senatorial Pal. stands (entrance by the r. small wall, visitors ring at the first door); if the custodian is not at hand he may generally be found in the upper story, where the offices of the civic administration are established. This edifice was the **Tabularium*, erected B. C. 78 by the consul A. Lutatius Catulus for the reception of the state archives, and resting on the massive substructures which surround the hill. It consisted of a five-fold series of vaults, the last of which towards the Forum was an open hall, long employed as a salt magazine, with half-pillars in the Doric style, as seen from without. The blocks of stone have been much corroded by the action of the salt. From this point there is a beautiful view of the Forum, enabling the spectator distinctly to trace its form and situation. The custodian points out an ancient staircase which descended hence to the Forum, where, to the l. of the

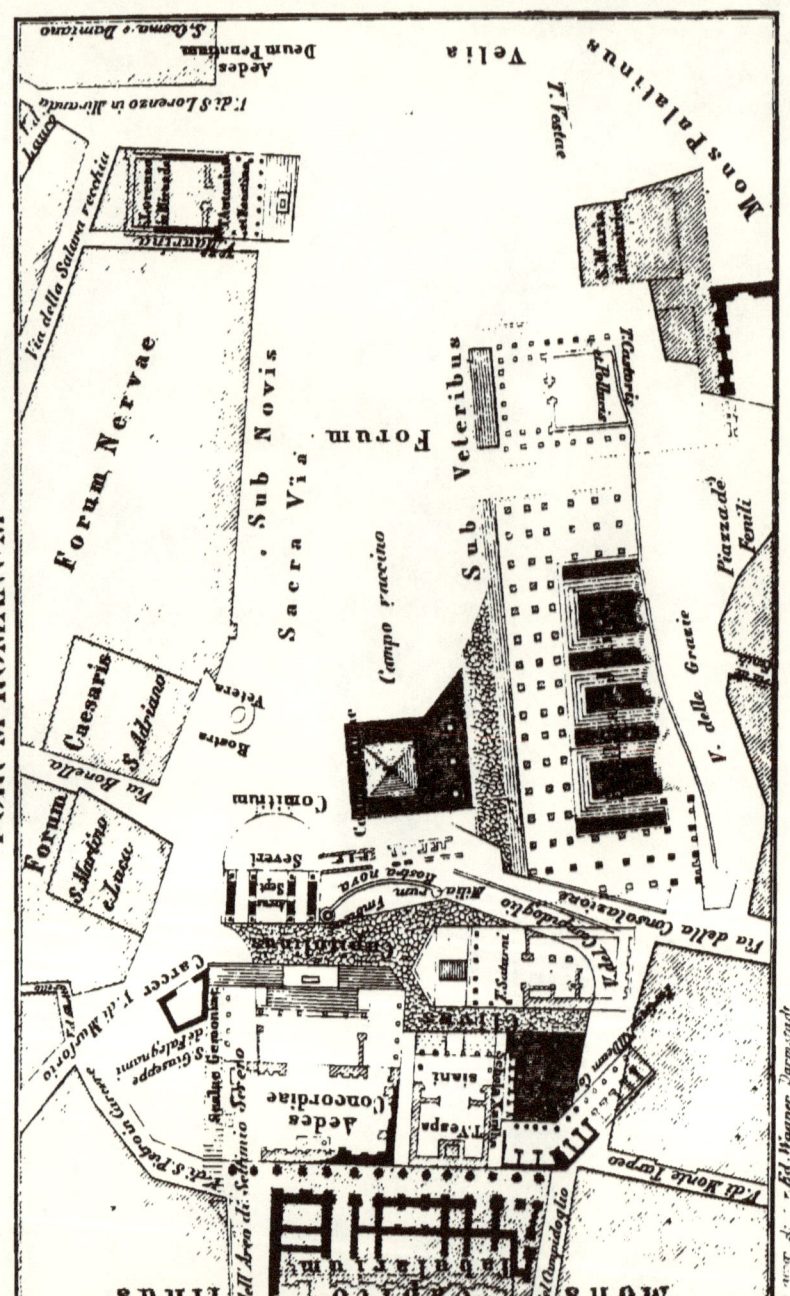

Forum Romanum. ROME. *Temple of Saturn.* 171

temple of Vespasian, the archway where it issued is recognised. A few architectural fragments from the neighbouring temples and other buildings are here preserved.

Descending from the piazza of the Capitol on the r. by the Senatorial Palace, the traveller enjoys from the lower extremity a good *survey of the Forum. The excavated portions consist of two different divisions. The larger to the l. beneath contains among other relics the temple of Saturn, to which the 8 unfluted columns belong, the 3 columns of the temple of Vespasian, the arch of Septim. Severus, and immediately below in the corner the colonnade of the 12 gods. The second division comprises the column of Phocas and 3 columns of the temple of Castor. Beyond these, to the l., is the temple of Faustina now converted into a church, then the huge arch of the basilica of Constantine, the Colosseum, the arch of Titus, and to the r. the gardens of the Palatine.

Here on the S. W. depression of the hill *(Clivus Capitolinus)* the *Sacra Via* descended to the **Forum Romanum, which extended as far as the temple of Faustina. It formed the focus of political and civic life, the scene of popular assemblies, judicial transactions, commercial negociations and public amusements. Near the temple of Faustina stood an archway, the *Arcus Fabianus*. dedicated in B. C. 123 to Fabius Maximus. conqueror of the Allobrogi. This formed the S. boundary of the forum, which was about 650 ft. in length. As this limited space became more and more inadequate to the requirements of the vast city, the entire business of which was here concentrated, attempts were made to remedy the difficulty by the construction of basilicas and secondary fora. Few spots in the world have a history like this, which has witnessed the legal and political development of every possible phase of public life. Under the emperors it soon came to be regarded as a venerable antiquity and an appropriate site for honorary statues and triumphal arches. To this period most of the extant ruins belong. whether of edifices then erected or restored only. In the middle ages it experienced many a severe blow during the contests of the great, and at length, as its present appellation *Campo Vaccino* indicates, became a pasture for cattle. The present excavations were begun about 60 years ago. and will, it is hoped, if continued, lead to new and interesting discoveries.

Descending by the steps on the r., or by the carriage-road. the traveller then enters the street to the r.; the entrance is by the door at the corner (Via della Consolazione); if closed, application may be made to a stone-mason in the vicinity (5 s.).

The first edifice, of which on a basement 15 ft. in height 8 granite columns are still standing, is the *Temple of Saturn, originally consecrated under the consuls Sempronius and Minucius, B. C. 491, and restored by Munatius Plancus about 44 B. C., where from the most ancient times the Ærarium Publicum (treasury of state) was established. The inscription: *Senatus populusque Romanus incendio consumptum restituit* refers to a later restoration undertaken hastily and without taste.

Below the Tabularium, of the upper gallery of which one arch only now stands, in the angle formed with it by the street, lies the *Schola Xantha* with the **Colonnade of the Twelve Gods** *(deorum consentium)*, whose images Vettius Agorius Prætextatus, the præfectus urbi and one of the principal champions of expiring paganism, erected here, A. D. 367. The entire structure was destined for the accommodation of the public scribes and notaries; the name Schola Xantha is derived from a certain Fabius Xanthus who had previously restored it. In 1858 the ruin was considerably modernized.

To the r. of the latter the Tabularium is adjoined by the *Ruin of the Three Columns* or ***Temple of Vespasian**, erected under Titus, restored by Sept. Severus. The inscription ran thus: *"Divo Vespasiano Augusto Senatus populusque romanus imperator Caesar Severus et Antoninus Pii Felices Augusti restituerunt."* Of this a portion of the last word only is preserved. The columns and entablature bear testimony to the superiority of the workmanship.

Farther on, to the r., also adjoining the Tabularium in the rear, is the **Temple of Concordia**, founded B. C. 388 by M. Furius Camillus, re-constructed and enlarged by Tiberius. B. C. 7. It was dedicated to Concord to commemorate the termination of the protracted struggle between patricians and plebeians. The smaller projecting rectangle of the raised substructure was the temple itself, whilst the larger edifice behind, extending on both sides of the temple (ascent to Araceli on one side) was the senatorial assembly-hall, the threshold of which is still recognised.

In front of the temple of Concordia, on the opposite side of the street (clivus Capitolinus), rises the ***Triumphal Arch of Septimius Severus** with three passages. It was erected in honour of that emperor and his sons Caracalla and Geta (Caracalla afterwards caused the name of his brother whom he had murdered to be obliterated), A. D. 203, to commemorate his victories over the Parthians, Arabians and Adiabeni, and was surmounted by a brazen chariot with six horses, on which Severus, crowned by Victory, stood. Above the arch are figures of Victory, at the sides crowded representations from the wars of the emperor, on the bases of the columns captive barbarians, all betokening the degraded condition of the sculpture of that period. In the middle ages the arch was temporarily converted by the ruling powers into a species of castle, and deeply imbedded until extricated by Pius VII. in 1803.

The arched wall by the arch of Severus is the remains of the imperial **Rostra** or orator's tribune. At its extremity was the *Umbilicus urbis Romae*, or ideal central point of the city and empire, the remnants of which are recognisable. At the other extremity, below the street are a few traces of the *Miliareum Aureum* or central milestone of the roads diverging from Rome.

From this region of the excavations a passage leads from the arch of Severus beneath the modern street to the second division. It is generally closed on holidays, but if notice is given on entering the excavations it will be opened (5 s.).

To the l. the *Column of Phocas, erected in 608 by the exarch Smaragdus in honour of the tyrant Phocas of the E. Roman empire, and taken by him from a more ancient edifice. Beside it are basements which were employed for similar honorary columns and fragments of other structures.

On the opposite side is the now partially excavated **Basilica Julia,** commenced by Cæsar and completed by Augustus, a magnificent edifice consisting of five contiguous halls. These basilicæ, the first of which (Basilica Porcia) Cato the Censor erected on the opposite side near *S. Adriano*, served to draw off a portion of the traffic from the limited space of the forum and were employed as courts of justice, commercial meeting-places etc. Several of these lay on each side of the forum.

Beneath the Basilica runs an antique and still partially visible channel by which the water from the Forum was conducted to the Cloaca Maxima (p. 186).

By the Basilica Julia, in the direction of the Palatine, are the three columns of Parian marble from the *Temple of Castor and Pollux, erected after the decisive victory over the Latins at Lake Regillus (B. C. 496) and subsequently re-erected by Tiberius. They are the most perfect of all that have been preserved. To the r. by this temple once stood the ancient *Regia*, or royal palace, subsequently the official residence of the pontifex maximus, the site of the present church of *S. Maria Liberatrice;* behind it was the *Temple of Vesta*. Cæsar's remains were burned by the people in front of the Regia.

We now return to the excavated portions of the forum. Passing to the l. of the arch of Severus, the traveller reaches the small church of *S. Giuseppe de' Falegnami* to the l. at the entrance of the *Via di Marforio*, by the steps ascending to Araceli. Beneath it (entrance adjoining the stairs, 1/2 l.) is the *Carcer Mamertinus, one of the most ancient structures in Rome. It was originally the excavation of a well (*Tullianum*, whence traditionally attributed to Servius Tullius), and subsequently served as a prison, where Jugurtha and Catiline's accomplices perished. It consists of two chambers, one beneath the other, of very ancient construction; the vaulting of the lower is formed by the oblique arrangement of the coping-stones. It contains a spring, which, according to the legend, St. Peter, who was imprisoned here under Nero, miraculously caused to flow in order to baptize his jailers. The building is therefore termed *S. Pietro in Carcere.*

Nearly opposite stands the church of *SS. Luca e Martino*, erected on the site of an ancient building. Passing it the Via Bonella leads to the academy of *S.* Luca (p. 181) and the Forum of Augustus (p. 182). Then the church of *S. Adriano* with its unadorned façade, like the former of little interest and also occupying the site of an ancient edifice, perhaps the *Curia Hostilia*, which was subsequently re-erected under the name of *Curia Julia* by Cæsar and Augustus, and employed as an assembly-hall by the senate.

The route is now continued on the l. side of the forum, where humble workshops now occupy the site of sumptuous palaces and temples. Of the *Temple of Faustina, within which the church of *S. Lorenzo in Miranda* has been erected, the portico (with 10 columns of cipollino, 6 of which form the façade) and a portion of the cella are still standing. It was dedicated by Antoninus in 141 to his wife, the elder Faustina, and re-dedicated to that emperor himself after his death. The first line of the inscription *Divo Antonino et divae Faustinae ex S. C.* was then added.

Adjacent is the church of *SS. Cosma e Damiano, erected by Felix IV., having been incorporated with an ancient circular temple (possibly of the Penates), to the portico of which the two cipolline columns half projecting from the ground to the r. of the church, in front of the Oratorium della Via Crucis, probably belonged. The level of the pavement was so much raised by Urban VIII. on account of the humidity of the soil, that an upper and lower church were thus formed. The entrance with the columns of porphyry and bronze doors is ancient. Behind this church the remains of an ancient plan of Rome, now in the Capitoline Museum, were found (p. 211), fragments of which were also discovered in 1867 and 68. Entrance to the excavations in the *Via Alessandrina*, last door r. near the Basilica of Constantine.

The church is entered by the rotunda. On the triumphal arch and in the tribune are interesting *mosaics of the 6th cent. (largely restored about 1660; access most easily obtained towards evening); on the triumphal arch the Lamb with the Book and seven seals, according to Revelations IV.; adjoining these the seven candlesticks, four angels and the symbols of the evangelists. In the tribune: Christ to whom the saints Cosmas and Damianus are conducted by Peter and Paul; on the l. side St. Felix with the church, on the r. St. Theodorus. Beneath, Christ as the Lamb, towards whom the twelve lambs (apostles) turn.

The lower church (entrance to the l. in the tribune; the sacristan acts as guide, 1'₂ l.) is unattractive. It contains the tomb of the saints Cosmas, Damianus and Felix, an ancient altar, and somewhat lower a spring. said to have been called forth by St. Felix. Near it a niche with remains of paintings of the 10th cent.

The three colossal arches of the *Basilica of Constantine are next reached. They were long believed to appertain to Vespasian's temple of Peace. which however was entirely burned down under Commodus. Nearly on the same spot Maxentius erected a basilica, which was subsequently altered by his conqueror Constantine. The entrance originally faced the Colosseum, afterwards the Via Sacra. It was a basilica of three halls with vaulting of vast span, which has served as a model for modern architects, in the construction, for example, of that of St. Peter's. which is of equal width. The only column of the interior which has been preserved now stands in front of S. Maria Maggiore. The traveller should on no account fail to ascend to the summit of the ruin in order to enjoy the magnificent **panorama of ancient Rome. The route is as follows. The first arch is passed through, and the street followed in a straight direction (which in 5 min. ascends to S. Pietro in Vincoli) for about 150 paces, then in the street to the r. (Via del Coliseo) is r. No. 61, an institution for poor girls (visitors ring; 1 l.), from the garden of which the stair ascends. The aperture by the staircase affords the best view of the Colosseum, to the l. of which are the Thermæ of Titus on the Esquiline; to the r. the circular S. Stefano; nearer, S. Giovanni e Paolo with the new dome, both on the Cælius. Beyond the Colosseum the Alban, and to the l. the Sabine Mts. To the S. the Palatine with the ruins of the imperial palaces and two monasteries, and the opposite bank of the Tiber with the Villa Pamfili. Towards the W. the Capitol, to the r. of which, between the domes of two churches, Trajan's column is visible; above the latter M. Mario; farther to the r. the Torre di Nerone and the Quirinal. Towards the N. the church of S. Pietro in Vincoli with its magnificent palm, and S. Maria Maggiore, recognised by its two domes and Romanesque tower, both on the Esquiline.

Towards the close of the forum rises the height anciently termed *Velia*, where, adjoining the basilica of Constantine and partially occupying the site of a temple of Venus and Roma (see below), the church of *S. Francesca Romana* with adjoining cloister (now barracks) is situated.

S. Francesca Romana (Pl. II, 23), or *S. Maria Nuova*, stands on the site of an older church of Nicholas I. founded about 860; it was re-erected about 1216 under Honorius III. after a conflagration, and was finally modernized by *Carlo Lombardo* in 1615.

On the r., 2nd Chapel: (r.) monument of Card. Vulcani (d. 1322) and that of the papal commandant and general Antonio Rido (d. 1475). 3rd

Chapel: Miracles of St. Benedict, altar-piece by *Subleyras*. In the tribune mosaics of the 12 cent.: in the centre Madonna, l. SS. John and James, r. Peter and Andrew. Over the high-altar an ancient Madonna, traditionally attrib. to St. Luke, which is said alone to have escaped destruction in the conflagration. To the r. of the apse: monument of Gregory XI., who transferred the papal residence from Avignon to Rome (d. 1378), with relief by *Olivieri*. Here on the r., immured in the wall, are two stones on which Peter and Paul are said to have knelt when they prayed for the punishment of Simon Magus. On the l. wall, to the l.: Madonna with four saints, by *Sinibaldo*, pupil of Perugino, 1524. Beneath the tribune, Confessio (closed; the sacristan escorts visitors with a light, if desired) with the tomb of the saint, and over the altar a marble relief by Bernini. The sacristan now conducts the visitor into a court behind the church, where there is a good view of the well-preserved western apse of the Temple of Venus and Roma (fee 1/2 l.).

On the summit of the Velia, by the Palatine, rises the *Triumphal Arch of Titus, erected in commemoration of his victory over the Jews, and dedicated to him under his successor Domitian in 81, as the inscription towards the Colosseum records: *Senatus populusque Romanus divo Tito divi Vespasiani filio Vespasiano Augusto*. The arch is embellished with fine reliefs. On the exterior, on the same side as the inscription, a representation of a sacrificial procession on the frieze. Within, Titus crowned by Victory in a quadriga driven by Roma; opposite, the triumphal procession with the captive Jews, table with the show-bread and candelabrum with seven branches. In the middle ages the arch was converted into a small fortress, crowned with pinnacles and adjoined by new walls. When these were removed under Pius VII., the arch lost its support, and it became necessary to reconstruct it. as the inscription on the other side informs us.

The street now descends, passing a number of nameless ruins on both sides, to the Colosseum. On the l. the double apsis of the **Temple of Venus and Roma,** erected by Hadrian in 135 and restored by Maxentius in 307. This was the largest and one of the most sumptuous temples in Rome, with ten columns at the ends and twenty on each side. It is evident that there must have been two temples under the same roof, with entrances from the Colosseum and Capitol and adjacent cellæ, so that there was a niche on each side of the central wall for the image of a god. One half is now within the precincts of the monastery of S. Francesca Romana (p. 175), the other towards the Colosseum is open.

On the descent hence to the Colosseum the remains of an extensive square *Basis* of masonry are seen to the l. below. Here once stood the gilded bronze *Colossal Statue of Nero*, as god of the sun, surrounded with rays, and 110 ft. in height, executed by Zenodorus by order of the emperor himself, when after the conflagration (A. D. 64) he founded his golden palace with lavish splendour. The latter fell to decay soon after the emperor's death (in 68), and the statue was removed thence under Hadrian to the above-mentioned basement. In the space occupied by an artificial lake in the gardens of Nero, Vespasian founded the *Amphitheatrum Flavium*, which was completed by Titus in the year 80, and usually (since the 8th cent.) named after the former colossal statue of Nero the

****Colosseum** (Pl. II, 24), Ital. *Il Coliseo*, the largest theatre and one of the most imposing structures in the world. On its completion it was inaugurated by gladiatorial combats continued during 100 days, in which 5000 wild animals were killed and naval contests represented. 87,000 spectators could be accommodated within its walls.

It was restored by Alex. Severus, as it had suffered from a conflagration under Macrinus. In 248 the Emp. Philip here celebrated the 1000th anniversary of the founding of Rome with magnificent games. In 405 gladiator-combats were abolished by Honorius as inconsistent with the spirit of Christianity, but wild-beast fights continued down to the time of Theodoric the Great. In the middle ages the Colosseum was employed by the Roman barons, especially the Frangipani, as a stronghold. In 1312 the Annibaldi were compelled to surrender it to the Emperor Henry VII., who presented it to the Roman senate and people. In 1332 the Roman nobility again introduced bull-fights. After this period, however, the destruction of the Colosseum began, and the stupendous pile began to be regarded as a species of quarry. In the 15th cent. Paul II. here procured the materials for the construction of the Pal. di S. Marco (di Venezia), Card. Riario for the Cancelleria, and Paul III. (1534—49) for the Pal. Farnese. Benedict XIV. (1740—58) was the first to protect the edifice from farther demolition by consecrating the interior to the Passion of Christ, on account of the frequency with which the blood of martyrs had there flowed, and erecting small chapels within it, where sermons are still preached on Fridays by a Capuchin. The following popes, especially Pius VII. and Leo XII., have averted the imminent danger of the fall of the ruins by the erection of huge buttresses. The stairs in the interior were restored by Pius IX.

The Colosseum is constructed of blocks of travertine (bricks have also been employed in the interior), which were originally held together by iron cramps. The numerous holes hewn in the stone were made in the middle ages, for the purpose of extracting the then very valuable iron. The external circumference of the elliptical structure measures 1790 ft., or upwards of one-third of a mile, the long diameter 620 ft., the shorter 525 ft., height 190 ft. Above the arena rise the rows of seats intersected by steps and passages, most of which are now in ruins and only partially accessible.

On the exterior the preserved N.E. portion (towards the Esquiline) consists of 4 stories; the 3 first are formed by arcades, the pillars of which are embellished with half-columns of the Doric, Ionic and Corinthian order in the 1st, 2nd and 3rd stories respectively. A wall with windows between Corinthian pilasters constitutes the 4th story. Statues were placed in the arcades of the 2nd and 3rd stories, as appears from the representations on ancient coins. At the extremities of the diameters are the 4 triple main-entrances, those towards the Esquiline and Cælius for the emperor, the others for the solemn procession before the commencement of the games, and the introduction of the animals and machinery. Towards the Esquiline are seen traces of the stucco-decorations which were restored under Pius VII. and once served as models for Giov. da Udine, the pupil of Raphael. The arcades of the lowest story served as entrances for the spectators, and were furnished with numbers up to LXXX. (Nos. XXIII. to LIV. still exist), in order to indicate the stairs to the different places. Below on the exterior are two rows of arcades, then a massive substructure for the seats. Every fourth arch contains a staircase. A portion of the rows of seats is still distinguishable, the foremost of which, the *Podium*, was destined for the emperor, the senators and the Vestal Virgins; the emperor occupied a raised seat (Pulvinar), the others seats of honour. Above the Podium rose 3 other classes of seats, the first of which was allotted to the knights. In the last division were the humbler spectators, in a colonnade, on the roof of which sailors of the imperial fleet were stationed for the purpose of stretching sail-cloth over the entire amphitheatre to avert the burning rays of the sun. Apertures are still seen in the external coping, and beneath them corbels, for the support of the masts to which the necessary ropes were attached. Beneath the amphitheatre were chambers and dens for the wild beasts, and an apparatus by means of which the arena could be laid under water, all of which it has been necessary to fill up, the level of the ground being so low as to endanger the ruins.

Although one-third of the gigantic structure alone remains, the ruins still produce an overwhelming effect. An architect of the previous century estimated the value of the materials still extant at $11/2$ million scudi, which according to the present value of money would be equivalent to at least half a million pounds sterling. Thus the Colosseum has ever been a symbol of the greatness of Rome and gave rise in the 8th cent. to a prophetic saying of the Anglo-Saxon pilgrims of that age:

"While stands the Colosseum, Rome shall stand,
When falls the Colosseum, Rome shall fall,
And when Rome falls — the World!"

Those who desire to explore the ruins are strongly recommended to ascend to the upper stories (the custodian is to be found by knocking at a door to the l. in the passage of the egress towards the Lateran, 5—10 soldi; his farther services may be declined). A steep wooden staircase of 56 steps ascends to the first story. Of the three arcades the inner should be selected and followed to the l. for the sake of the survey thus afforded of the interior. Over the entrance towards the Palatine the modern staircase of 48 steps ascends to the 2nd, and then to the l. direct to a projection in the 3rd story. The *view from the restored balustrade to the r. in the 4th story, to which another flight of 55 steps ascends, is still more extensive. It embraces the Cælius with S. Stefano Rotondo and S. Giovanni e Paolo; farther off, the Aventine with S. Balbina, in the background S. Paolo fuori le Mura; nearer, to the r., the Pyramid of Cestius; to the r. the Palatine, to which the arches of the Aqua Claudia approach.

An indescribable impression is produced by the moonlight-effects in the Colosseum, or when illuminated by torches or Bengal lights, a scene which may occasionally be witnessed on winter-evenings, and is strongly recommended to the traveller's notice if an opportunity presents itself. A permesso from the office of the commandant (Piazza Colonna) must be procured. The custodian (who precedes visitors with a torch) is generally to be found at the entrance from the Piazza of the Capitol. The Flora found among the ruins of the Colosseum comprises 420 species, which have been collected by an English botanist.

Retracing his steps and quitting the Colosseum by the same gate, the traveller perceives on the l. in front of the edifice the so-called *Meta Sudans*, the partially restored fragment of a magnificent fountain erected by Domitian. Farther on, to the l. between the Cælius and Palatine, rising above the *Via Triumphalis* which here united with the Via Sacra, stands the

*Triumphal Arch of Constantine (Pl. II, 24) the best-preserved of these structures, erected after the victory over Maxentius at Saxa Rubra, near the Ponte Molle, in 311, when Constantine declared himself in favour of Christianity. The inscription is as follows: *Imp. Caes. Fl. Constantino Maximo pio felici Augusto Senatus Populusque Romanus, quod instinctu divinitatis mentis magnitudine cum exercitu suo tam de tyranno quam de omni ejus factione uno tempore justis rem publicam ultus est armis arcum triumphis insignem dicavit.* The arch has three passages, and is adorned with admirable sculptures from a triumphal arch of Trajan, which stood at the entrance of Trajan's Forum. The age of Constantine would have been incapable of such workmanship. The following are from the arch of Trajan: the captive Dacians above (7 ancient; one entirely, and the heads and hands of the others are new); the reliefs (facing the Colosseum), to the l.: Trajan's entry into Rome, to the r. of which: 2. Prolongation of the Via Appia; 3. Trajan causing poor children to be educated; 4. Trajan condemning a barbarian; on the other side, to the l.: 5. Trajan crowning the Parthian king Parthamaspates; 6. Soldiers conducting two barbarians into Trajan's presence; 7. Trajan addressing the army; 8. Trajan sacrificing; the 8 medallions beneath these reliefs represent sacrifices and hunting-scenes; on the narrow sides two battles with the Dacians; beneath the central arch, the vanquished imploring pardon, and Trajan crowned by Victory. The contrast between the condition of art in Trajan's and that in Constantine's age is exhibited by the smaller reliefs inserted between the medallions, representing the warlike and peaceful achievements of Constantine. In 1804 Pius VII. caused the ground to be lowered to its original level.

On the opposite side, a few hundred paces from the Colosseum (in the Via Labicana, 1st door l.. fee $1/2$ l.; the Via della Polveriera here ascends to the l. between walls in 5 min. to S. Pietro in Vincoli, p. 146), are situated on the Esquiline the

*Thermæ of Titus (Pl. II, 26) ($1/2$ l.), where Mæcenas once possessed a villa, afterwards incorporated with the golden palace of Nero. On the site of the latter in the year 80 Titus hastily erected his sumptuous Thermæ, which were greatly altered and enlarged by Domitian, Trajan and others. The ruins occupy an extensive space and are scattered over several vineyards. The smaller portion only is accessible which was excavated in 1813. The earlier structure of Nero is easily distinguished from that of Titus. The long vaulted parallel passages first entered belong to the Thermæ. They form together a semicircular substructure, the object of which is not clearly ascertained. Most of the chambers beneath, which were filled up by Titus in the construction of his baths, and re-excavated at the beginning of the 16th cent., belonged to the golden palace of Nero. A series of 7 rooms is first entered here; to the l., near that in the centre, are remains of a spring. Traces of the beautiful paintings, which before the discovery of Pompeii were the sole specimens of ancient decoration of this description, and served as models for Giov. da Udine and Raphael in the decoration of the loggie, are still perceived. Colonnades appear to have existed on both sides of these rooms. A passage leads hence to a bath-room. To the l., at a right angle to this suite, are a number of small and unadorned rooms, probably the dwellings of the slaves; and again to the l., opposite the first suite, a passage once lighted from above, the vaulting of which was adorned with beautiful frescoes still partially visible.

Fora of the Emperors. Academy of S. Luca.

On the route returning hence to the forum, in the plain to the N.E. of the forum of the republic, were situated the *Fora of the Emperors*, erected by their founders rather as monuments and ornaments to the city than for practical purposes. The chief edifice in these fora was always a temple. The Forum Julium, the first of the kind, was begun by Cæsar and completed by Augustus; the second was constructed by Augustus; the Temple of Peace (p. 175) of Vespasian is often mentioned as a third, another was founded by Domitian, and finally, the most magnificent of all these structures, the Forum of Trajan. They are here enumerated in order from the Temple of Peace, which probably lay on the site of the basilica of Constantine, to the Forum of Trajan, as they all adjoined each other within this area.

Adjacent to the Temple of Peace lay the forum founded by Domitian and completed by Nerva, whence called the **Forum of Nerva,** sometimes also *Forum Transitorium* from being intersected by a principal street. Here stood a temple of Minerva, taken down by Paul V. in order to decorate the Fontana Paolina on the Janiculus with the marble, and a small temple of Janus. Remains of the external walls exist in the so-called *Colonacce,* two half-buried Corinthian columns, with entablature richly decorated with reliefs (branches of art, weaving etc., which were specially protected by the goddess); above them an attic with a Minerva. Passing through the l. arch of the basilica of Constantine, and ascending the street (V. Alessandrina) on the l., the traveller reaches this ruin at the corner of the second cross-street to the r., and will here be enabled to form an idea of the grandeur of the original structure. The following cross-street is the *Via Bonella.*

Near the Forum, Via Bonella 44, is the

Accademia di S. Luca, a school of art founded in 1595, the first director of which was *Federigo Zuccaro.* Open daily 9—5 o'clock. Visitors ring or knock at the principal door.

Immured in the passage of the staircase a few casts from Trajan's Column (disfigured with whitewash). On the first landing, entrance to the collection of the competitive works of the pupils (usually closed; the custodian of the gallery opens the door if requested). 1st Room: Discus-thrower reposing, in plaster, *Kessels.* 2nd R.: r. of the door, Christ on the Mt. of Olives, drawing by *Seitz.* 3rd R.: Reliefs by *Thorwaldsen* and *Canova.* In the back part of the saloon the casts of the *Æginetan* sculptures are at present placed. 4th R.: Ganymede giving water to the eagle, *Thorwaldsen.*

Another stair ascends to the

Picture Gallery (1½ l.). A small ante-chamber (with engravings etc.) leads to the 1st saloon, lighted from above. Entrance-wall: Landscape, *Berghem;* Wharf, *Tempesta;* Madonna and Descent from the Cross, old Dutch Sch.; Venus crowned by graces. *Rubens;* Madonna. *Van Dyck;* St. Jerome, *Titian;* Wharf, *Jos. Vernet;* narrow wall: two Landscapes, *G. Poussin.* Second wall: Scribe disputing, *Ribera;* Venus, *P. Veronese;* Portrait, *Van Dyck* (?); Portrait, *Titian;* Vanity, by the same; Coast Landscape, *Claude Lorrain;* Wharf, *Jos. Vernet.* The saloon is adjoined on one side by a small room, principally containing portraits of artists; among them, on the pillar, Virginie Lebrun; by the window-wall marble busts of Thorwaldsen and Piranesi; on the other side is the 2nd saloon. On the entrance-pillars: Architectural design, *Canaletto;* Trumpeter in a rustic tavern, *Palomedes.* L. wall: Discovery of the guilt of Calisto, *Titian* (usually covered); *Boy as garland-bearer, fresco by *Raphael;* Lucrezia, *Guido Cagnacci.* Narrow wall: St. Andrew, *Bronzino;* Portrait, *Venet. Sch.;* Cupid. *Guido Reni;* St. Luke painting the Madonna, beside him Raphael observing him. *Raphael* (only partly executed by him; original an altar-piece in S. Martino); Portrait. *Tintoretto;* Tribute-money, after *Titian.* R. wall: Bacchanalian dance, *Poussin;* Galatea, copy by *Giulio Romano* from Raphael; Wharf, *J. Vernet.*

Round the upper part of this saloon is a double row of portraits of artists.

Access to the collection of casts for the purposes of study requires the permission of the director.

The Via Bonella is terminated by an ancient wall with a gateway.

In front of the latter, to the l., are three beautiful and lofty *Corinthian columns with entablature, which belonged to one of the sides of the *Temple of Mars Ultor* in the **Forum of Augustus** (Pl. II, 20). The forum was enclosed by a lofty *wall of peperine (grey volcanic rock), of which a considerable part is seen near the temple, and especially at the arch *(Arco de' Pantani)*. This wall was adjoined by the back of the temple which Augustus, when engaged in war against Cæsar's murderers, vowed to erect.

Between this and the ancient republican forum lay the *Forum of Caesar* with a temple of Venus Genetrix. Scanty remnants of the external wall of tuffstone are seen to the l. in the court of No. 18 Vicolo del Ghettarello, which diverges to the r. from the Via di Marforio between Nos. 47 and 46.'

The traveller now ascends to the l. through the Arco de' Pantani by the huge wall which now forms part of a nunnery, and a short distance farther descends to the l. by the *Salita del Grillo* (in the court of No. 6, walls of Trajan's forum, see below) to the busy *Via Campo Carleo*, the prolongation of the Via Alessandrina, whence immediately to the r. the *Piazza della Colonna Trajana* is entered.

The Forum of Augustus was adjoined by the *Forum of Trajan** (Pl. II, 19), an aggregate of magnificent edifices, designed by the architect Apollodorus of Damascus (111 — 114). In the portion excavated in 1812 (keys kept by a barber, P. della Colonna Trajana 68) four rows of columns, the foundations of which were then discovered, are first encountered (fragments of columns were also found here, but it is not certain whether they belong to those which stood on the spot), being part of the five-halled *Basilica Ulpia*, which lay with its sides towards the end of the present piazza. Between this Basilica and the Forum of Augustus lay the *Forum Trajani*, of the S.E. semicircular wall of which a portion is still seen in the court of No. 6 Via della Salita del Grillo, two stories in height; the chambers of the lower were probably shops. In the centre of this Forum rose Trajan's equestrian statue. On the other side of the basilica stands **Trajan's Column**, 117 (or incl. pedestal and statue 149) ft. in height; diameter 11. at the top 10 ft.; entirely covered with admirable reliefs from Trajan's war with the Dacians (which can be more conveniently examined on the cast in the Lateran), comprising, besides animals, machines etc., upwards of 2500 human figures, each averaging

S. Maria di Loreto. ROME. *Palatine Hill.* 183

2 ft. in height. Beneath it Trajan was interred, on the summit was placed his statue (now that of St. Peter); in the interior a stair of 184 steps ascends. The height of the column at the same time indicates how much of the Quirinal and Capitoline must have been levelled in order to make room for these buildings. Moreover to this forum belonged a temple, dedicated to Trajan by Hadrian, a library and a triumphal arch of Trajan, all situated on the other side of the column. Some of the reliefs from the last mentioned were taken to adorn the arch of Constantine (p. 179).

On the N. side of the piazza are two churches, that on the r. *del Nome di Maria*, erected in 1683 after the liberation of Vienna from the Turks, restored in 1862; that on the l. *S. Maria di Loreto*, erected by *Sangallo* in 1507; in the 2nd chapel a statue of St. Susanna by *Fiammingo*, high altar-piece of the school of Perugino.

Three connecting streets lead hence to the *Piazza SS. Apostoli* (p. 121). Ascending to the r. the Via Magnanapoli leads in 16 min. in a straight direction to S. Maria Maggiore (p. 140); to the l. it leads to the Piazza di Monte Cavallo (p. 132). The street to the l. leads to the Piazza S. Marco, or if it be quitted by the first street to the r., the Piazza di Venezia (p. 122) is reached.

The Palatine.
Velabrum and Forum Boarium.

The **Palatine Hill**, in the form of an irregular square, rises on the N.W. side of the forum. In ancient times it was bounded on the N. towards the Capitol by the Velabrum and Forum Boarium (p. 186), on the W. towards the Aventine by the Circus Maximus (p. 188), and on the S. towards the Cælius by the Via Triumphalis and Via Appia (now Via di S. Gregorio). The Palatine is the site of the most ancient city, the *Roma Quadrata*, of the enclosure of which traces still remain (p. 184), and on this hill tradition places the dwellings of the ancient heroes Evander, Faustulus and Romulus. At a later period the most illustrious men of Rome generally resided here, such as the Gracchi, Cicero, Mark Antony etc., until at length the entire area was taken possession of by the emperors. The Palatine retained its magnificence down to a comparatively late period, and was the residence of Byzantine generals and German kings, but finally fell entirely to ruin. The entrance is from the Forum opposite the basilica of Constantine, by the post of the sentinel. The area is at present occupied by two monasteries, several vineyards and the *Farnese Gardens*, purchased in 1861 by Napoleon III. from the ex-king Francis II. It is therefore impossible to visit all the extant ruins in consecutive order.

The most *interesting are those excavated by order of the Emperor of the French, under the direction of the architect Cav. Pietro Rosa, in the extensive Farnese Gardens (accessible on Thursdays by entering name in the visitors' book, no fee). Notwithstanding the difficulty of the task (the debris being in places 20 ft. in depth), these excavations have already led to important discoveries, and although the names of many of the extricated ruins are involved in obscurity, they suffice to convey an idea of the striking grandeur and magnificence of the whole. Cav. Rosa, on whose views the following description is based, has drawn a map of the ruins which is photographically reproduced and hung up in the museum (it may be purchased for $3^1/_2$ l. at Merle's, Corso 348). The first stair leads to a small space, where on the l. the *Temple of Jupiter Stator* and the *Porta Mugionis*, one of the gates of the ancient "square city", are situated, and on the r. the dwellings of Caesar, Cicero and Clodius, as has been assumed. All the principal points are furnished with tickets with the most important quotations referring to the localities. To the r. is situated the small *Museum*, where Cav. Rosa has formed a collection of the most interesting objects which have come to light in the course of the excavations, either in the original or in casts.

In the centre, near the entrance, a boy from the group of a Dea Kurotrophos; statue of Venus Genetrix; l. cast of a Cupid (the original in Paris); r. torso of the well-known satyr attributed to Praxiteles; l. head of a barbarian. By the l. wall, lamps etc.; specimens of the different kinds of stones found in the ruins. By the r. wall, coins, glasses, articles in ivory, fragments, seals.

The *Clivus Victoriae* descends hence to the r., and leads through the Porta Romana to the Forum. Subsequently, as the imperial palace continued to extend its boundaries, the street was entirely built over. At the summit the beginning of the bridge should be observed, which Caligula caused to be thrown across the Forum to the Capitol, in order that he might thus be better enabled to commune with the Capitoline Jupiter, whose image on earth he pretended to be. The small stair is now ascended, to the l., to this bridge and the palace of Tiberius *(Domus Tiberiana)*, of which a number of chambers and passages have been excavated, apparently belonging to a dwelling-house. The slope of the hill, affording a succession of admirable views, is next skirted. In the foreground the spectator surveys the slopes of the Palatine: in front of the temple of the Dioscuri, the church of *S. Maria Liberatrice* with the extensive adjacent walls occupies the site of the temple of Vesta and the Regia; the ancient circular church of *S. Teodoro* farther off likewise rests on a similar foundation (temple of Romulus?). The fragments to the l. of "opus reticulatum" belong to structures of a more ancient period. Visitors now ascend an eminence commanding an extensive view of Trastevere and the Aventine. The *Auguratorium*, the lofty square substructure where the auspices were consulted, and other unimportant ruins are then passed, and the excavations on the S. slopes reached. Here stood the *Temple of Jupiter Victor*, consecrated B. C. 295, the substructure of which is still preserved; it was approached by a grand flight of steps from the Circus Maximus. The latter, extending between the Aventine and Palatine, with the white tombstones of the Jewish burial-ground, is well surveyed from this point. To the r. by the wall of the *Villa Mills*, now a nunnery of the order of Francis de Sales, was the once celebrated *Palatine Library*. Below it through the fallen ceiling are seen massive ancient foundations of peperine blocks.

The **Palatium** or imperial residence is next visited. It exhibits the proportions and arrangements of an ordinary Roman dwelling which, with the omission of the accessory apartments, are here reproduced on a large scale. It is entered in the rear. The first apartment is the *Triclinium* or dining-room. Then the *Peristylium*, a spacious and magnificent court once surrounded by arcades, the centre of which was doubtless occupied by a fountain. A stair descends hence to the subterranean chambers, with traces of stuccos and painting; blocks of tuffstone are here also observed, probably appertaining to an earlier structure, over which the more recent was erected. To the l. of the Triclinium is the *Nymphaeum*. In front of the peristyle lies the *Tablinum*, the apartment where in ordinary habitations the portraits, archives etc. of the family were preserved. L. of this is the *Basilica Jovis*, where the emperor administered justice; r. the *Lararium*, or private chapel, for the Lares, the gods of the household and hearth. From this point the slight remains of the *Temple of Jupiter Stator* near the *Porta Mugionis* may be visited. They are reached by descending the street to the r., part of which is ancient. The underground apartments, entered on the l., are the so-called *Bagni di Livia*; steps lead from them up to the plateau where the residence of the director is situated. Beautiful *view of the city and the Sabine Mts.; Palestrina may be distinguished in the distance between the Colosseum and the Lateran.

From the *Monastery of S. Bonaventura* (approached by the street in the valley, adjoining the arch of Titus) the Cælius and the Colosseum may be well surveyed. The palms of the monastery-garden are celebrated.

Quitting the Forum, skirting the slope of the Palatine past the church of S. Maria Liberatrice, which stands on the site of the temple of Vesta, and traversing the Via di S. Teodoro, the traveller first reaches (l.) the church of *S. Teodoro*, lying low and somewhat removed from the street. It is mentioned for the first time under Gregory the Great, and probably occupies the site of an ancient temple. In the interior (open on Fridays from an early hour till 9 o'clock) an early Christian mosaic. A little beyond it the street divides: to the r. it descends to the ancient *Velabrum*, a quarter or street which extended through the *Vicus Tuscus* to the Forum and was prolonged through the Forum Boarium to the river; in a straight direction it leads to the *Janus Quadrifrons*, an edifice with four arched passages, dating from the later imperial age, destination unknown, possibly a species of exchange; above it once rose a second story.

To the r. of this is **S. Giorgio in Velabro**, founded in the 4th cent., re-erected in the 7th, and often restored subsequently. The portico, according to the metrical inscription, dates from the 13th cent. The interior consists of a three-halled basilica with 16 ancient columns. The frescoes of Giotto, with which it was once adorned, have disappeared. (The church is rarely open; visitors knock at the door by the church to the l. behind the arch.)

Adjacent to the church is the small *Arcus Argentarius*, decorated with worthless sculptures, which, according to the inscription, was erected by the money-changers and merchants of the *Forum Boarium* (cattle-market) in honour of Septimius Severus and his family. This forum must therefore have reached from this point as far as the Tiber, an extensive space and the scene of the busiest commercial traffic.

Proceeding through the low archway of brick, opposite the above arch, and passing the mill, the traveller arrives at the ***Cloaca Maxima**, one of the most ancient structures in Rome, founded under the Tarquinii for the drainage of the Forum and the adjacent low ground. It is the earliest known application of the arch-principle in Rome, and has defied the storms of more than 2000 years; two-thirds of the depth are now filled up. A basin was formed here, into which, in order to facilitate the flow, springs were conducted. In the mill (5 soldi) the continuation of the cloaca towards the Forum is seen, and from the Ponte Rotto its influx into the Tiber. It is constructed of peperine with occasional layers of travertine; at the influx, of peperine alone.

Continuing to follow the street beyond the Janus and turning to the l., the traveller reaches the *Piazza della Bocca della Verità*, which occupies a portion of the ancient Forum Boarium, with a fountain in the centre. Here to the l., at the foot of the Aventine, stands the church of **S. Maria in Cosmedin**, or *Bocca della Verità*, so called from the ancient mouth of a fountain to the l. in the portico, into which, according to the belief of the middle ages, the ancient Romans inserted their right hands when binding themselves by an oath. It occupies the site of an ancient temple, 10 columns of which are immured in the walls (3 on the l. side, the others in the anterior wall), probably the *Temple of the Three Deities* (Ceres, Liber and Libera), which was founded in consequence of a vow during a famine, B. C. 497, or according to others a *Temple of Fortune*. The nave is also supported by 10 ancient columns. The church, which is said to date from the 3rd cent., was re-constructed by Hadrian I. in the 8th (from which period the beautiful campanile dates), and was subsequently often restored. The beautiful opus Alexandrinum of the *pavement in the interior merits inspection. In the nave remnants of the ancient choir are preserved, on the r. and l. two handsome ambos and a candelabrum for the ceremonies of Easter. Canopy of the high-altar by *Deodatus* (13th cent.). In the apse a handsome episcopal throne of the same period and an ancient Madonna.

Opposite the church, on the Tiber, stands the small and tolerably well preserved circular *Temple of Hercules Victor (?) (now *S. Maria del Sole*), formerly regarded as a **Temple of Vesta**, consisting of 20 Corinthian columns (one of those next to the river is wanting), insufficiently covered by a wooden roof.

A short distance hence up the stream, immediately to the r., is a second small and well preserved *Temple (converted in 880 into the church of *S. Maria Egiziaca*), with 4 Ionic columns at each end, and 7 on one side; the once open portico has been closed by a wall. It has been known by a variety of different appellations (e. g. Temple of Fortuna Virilis), but was probably dedicated to Pudicitia Patricia. The interior contains nothing worthy of note. On the other side of the transverse street is situated the picturesque mediæval *House of Crescentius (10th cent.), commonly known as the *Casa di Rienzi* or *di Pilato*, constructed principally of ancient fragments. The long inscription which it bears has given rise to a great variety of interpretations.

Here the *Ponte Rotto* crosses to Trastevere (p. 231), where in ancient times the *Pons Æmilius* stood, having been constructed B. C. 181. After frequent restoration the two arches (5 in all) nearest the l. bank fell, and the bridge was never reconstructed, whence its present appellation. Within the last few years, however, an iron chain-bridge has been thrown across the gap (1 soldo), whence a picturesque view is enjoyed: on the r. the island of the Tiber, in form resembling a ship; l. the Aventine; beneath, the influx of the Cloaca Maxima, and extensive embankments which protect the banks against the violence of the current.

From the Piazza Bocca della Verità the busy Via della Bocca della Verità leads to the Piazza Montanara and the Theatre of Marcellus (p. 167); in the opposite direction the Via della Salara to the Porta S. Paolo and the Aventine (p. 189).

If. in proceeding from the Forum through the Via di S. Teodoro, the Janus Quadrifrons be left on the r., the traveller soon reaches to the l. in the Via de' Fenili, No. 1, the entrance to the *Papal Excavations on the Palatine* (admission free; this vigna was purchased by the Emperor of Russia and presented to the city), which have been undertaken principally in the slopes of the hill. To the l. an altar with ancient inscription *(sei deo sei deirae sacrum etc.)*; beyond it ancient foundations of tuff-blocks without mortar, which pertained to the walls of the most ancient Rome, the *Roma Quadrata*, are recognised beneath the more recent structures of the republican and imperial ages. In this direction the *Porta Romana* may be reached, one of the three gates of this original city, whence the Clivus Victoriæ ascended. To the r. of the entrance, beyond the spacious play-ground, a series of chambers are encountered which appear to have been occupied by the imperial pages. The walls are painted and covered with various scrawled names etc.; thus, "Corinthus exit de pædagogio"; an ass in a mill with the remark "labora aselle quomodo ego laboravi et proderit tibi"; a caricature on the Christians is now in the Kircherianum (p. 119). — Above are the Farnese Gardens and the handsome cypresses of the *Villa Mills* (convent of the Salesian nuns). A path winding upwards through a kitchen-garden leads to other *Ruins of the Imperial Palaces*, in which the Pope has lately caused excavations to be made. The visitor is conducted through a number of underground apartments, the use of which is uncertain, containing antiquities found here; among them the *half-draped figure of a woman, sitting (fce 1/2 l.). The vigna is then ascended and a terrace reached, whence a magnificent *prospect. Beyond the vigna, towards the nunnery, lay a Stadium; in the direction of the Cœlius three arches of the *Aqua Claudia* are seen, which supplied the Palatine with water.

Farther on in the Via de' Fenili, at the corner, is the church of *S. Anastasia*, mentioned as early as 449, frequently restored, finally in the style of the previous century. On the side towards the Palatine the different periods of the construction are distinguished. By the buttresses of the interior the ancient columns are still standing. In the l. aisle the monument of Card. Angelo Mai. Beneath the church are substructures belonging to the Circus Maximus, and still earlier remains of the walls of Roma Quadrata.

The *Via de' Cerchi* is followed to the l., running between the Palatine and Aventine, where, as its name suggests, the **Circus Maximus** was situated, which was originally instituted by the kings, subsequently extended by Cæsar and furnished with stone seats, and finally more highly decorated by the emperors. The limits were in the direction of the Forum Boarium; in the centre ran a wall (spina) longitudinally, which, connecting the metæ (goals), bounded the course of the racers. With a few trifling exceptions the walls of the circus have entirely disappeared; its form is best distinguished from a higher point, as from the Palatine. Within its precincts, at the base of the Aventine, the Jewish burial-ground is situated.

The Via de' Cerchi soon after divides, leading to the l. to the Via di S. Gregorio (p. 198), and to the r. to the Via di Porta S. Sebastiano (p. 194).

The Aventine.
Monte Testaccio. S. Paolo fuori.

The **Aventine,** anciently the principal residence of the Roman Plebs and subsequently densely peopled, is now entirely deserted, being occupied by monasteries and vineyards only. At its base lies the *Porta S. Paolo*, leading to the celebrated Basilica of that name, adjoining which is the Pyramid of Cestius with the Protestant Burial-ground and the enigmatical Monte Testaccio. The main street skirts the base of the hill close to the river, whilst others rapidly ascend the hill. The principal route is described first.

It commences at the Via della Salara from the Piazza della Bocca della Verità (p. 186) and passes S. Maria in Cosmedin; by the church a street diverges to the l., leading (to the r. where it divides) in 10 min. to S. Prisca (p. 192). 2 min. farther, at the small chapel of St. Anna, the street ascends in 5 min. to the three adjacent churches (p. 191).

The main street then continues between houses and walls of no interest and (as the *Via della Marmorata*) reaches the Tiber in 6 min. from the Piazza Bocca della Verità, skirting the river for about 2 min. To the r. a pleasing retrospect of the Ponte Rotto and the Capitol. The large building on the opposite bank is the *Hospital of S. Michele*, in front of it the small harbour where the steamboats to Ostia and Porto lie. The *Marmorata* is next reached, the landing-place and depôt of the unwrought marble of Carrara. In 1867 and 1868 excavations were made near the river, and the ancient quay discovered.

After following the foot-path by the river for 8 min., two raised landing-places with inclined planes to facilitate the removal of heavy weights are reached. Rings for mooring vessels are still visible. Numerous blocks of wrought and unwrought marble were found in the vicinity, some of a rare description and great value; many still bear the marks of the quarry, numbers, addresses and other inscriptions.

From the Marmorata the street proceeds between walls and through an archway of brick *(Arco di S. Lazaro)*. After 6 min. the street from the three churches on the Aventine descends from the l. Opposite, on the r., the large gateway (No. 21) leads to the *Prati del Popolo Romano*, which enclose the Protestant cemetery and Monte Testaccio. On the l. a powder-magazine is passed, the Pyramid of Cestius and the old burial-ground being left to the l., and in 3 min. the gate of the **Protestant Cemetery** (Pl. III, 16) (custodian present from 7 a. m. to $4^1/_4$ p. m.; $^1/_2$ l.). The smaller and older burying-ground for non-Romanists, laid out at the beginning of the century, adjoining the pyramid and surrounded by a ditch, is now disused (the custodian unlocks the gate if desired). Here is the grave of the painter *J. A. Carstens* (d. 1798).

In 1825 the present area, since doubled in extent, was set apart for this purpose. It is a retired spot, rising gently towards the city-wall, affording pleasing views and shaded by lofty cypresses, where numerous strangers, English, American, German, Russian etc. are interred. Amongst many illustrious names the eye will fall with interest upon that of the poet *Shelley* (d. 1822), "cor cordium"; his heart was alone buried; his remains were burned in the bay of Spezia, where they were washed on shore.

The *Pyramid of Cestius, originally situated in the Via Ostiensis, was enclosed by Aurelian within the city-wall. It is the tomb of Caius Cestius, who died within the last thirty years before Christ, and, according to the inscriptions on the E. and W. sides ("C. Cestius L. F. Pob. Epulo. Pr. Tr. Pl. VII. vir Epulonum"), was prætor, tribune of the people and member of the college of Septemviri Epulonum, or priests whose office was to conduct the solemn sacrificial banquets. The inscription on the W. side beneath records that the monument was erected in 330 days under the supervision of L. Pontius Mela and the freedman Pothus. Alexander VII. caused the somewhat deeply imbedded monument to be extricated in 1663, on which occasion, besides the two columns of white marble, the colossal bronze foot, now in the Capitoline Museum, was found. According to the inscription on the basement it appears to have belonged to a colossal statue of Cestius.

The Egyptian pyramidal form was not unfrequently employed by the Romans in the construction of their tombs. That of Cestius is constructed of brick and covered with marble blocks; height 110 ft., width of each side of the base 87 ft. The interior (16 ft. in length, 13 ft. in width) was originally accessible by ladders only, the present entrance having been made by order of Alexander VII. (key kept by the custodian of the Protestant cemetery). The vaulting exhibits traces of painting.

Traversing the meadows, the traveller next proceeds to **Monte Testaccio** (Pl. III, 13), the summit of which is indicated by a wooden cross. It commands a magnificent **panorama: N. the city, beyond it the mountains surrounding the crater of Baccano, then the isolated Soracte with its five peaks. E. the Sabine Mts., in the background the imposing Leonessa, in the nearer chain M. Gennaro, at its base Monticelli, farther to the r. Tivoli. Beyond this chain the summits of M. Velino above the Lago Fucino are visible. S. of Tivoli appears Palestrina. After a depression, above which some of the Volscian Mts. rise, follow the Alban Mts.: on the buttress farthest E. is Colonna, beyond it Frascati, higher up Rocca di Papa, M. Cavo with its monastery, below it Marino, finally to the r. Castel Gandolfo. The most conspicuous objects in the broad Campagna are the long rows of arches of the Aqua Claudia and the Acq. Felice towards the S., and the tombs of the Via Appia with that of Cæcilia Metella.

M. Testaccio, 160 ft. in height, is, as its name signifies, entirely composed of the remains of broken pottery. When and how this hill was formed is still an unsolved mystery. The popular belief was that the vessels in which subjugated nations paid their tribute-money were here broken, whilst the learned have assumed that potteries once existed in the vicinity, and that the broken fragments together with other rubbish were here collected to be used for building purposes. Others have connected this remarkable hill with the Neronian conflagration, or with the magazines situated here on the Tiber near the harbour (emporium). It existed prior to the Aurelian wall, and remnants of temples found there date from the first centuries of the Christian era. It is now honey-combed with cellars, in some of which wine is purveyed, attracting pleasure-seeking crowds on holidays.

A visit to the three adjacent churches on the Aventine may conveniently be accomplished in going or returning from S. Paolo. On the route from the city thither the traveller first reaches

*S. Sabina (Pl. III, 18), erected under Celestine I. by Petrus, an Illyrian priest, in 425, restored in the 13th, 15th and 16th centuries, and since the time of Innocent III. appertaining to the Dominicans. It is usually entered by a side-door; if closed, visitors ring at the door to the l. and proceed through the monastery to the former portico, now closed, and the principal portal with handsome carved doors, probably of the 12th cent. The interior, with its 24 Corinthian columns of Parian marble and open roof, has well preserved the character of an ancient basilica. It probably occupies the site of an ancient temple.

On the entrance-wall, over the door, an inscription with the name of the founder, on the l. a figure emblematical of the Ecclesia ex Circumcisione (Jewish Christians), on the r. that of the Eccl. ex Gentibus (Pagan Christians).

On the pavement in the centre of the nave is the tomb of Munio da Zamora, principal of the Dominican order (d. 1300), adorned with mosaic. In the chapel of St. Dominicus, at the extremity of the r. aisle, the °Madonna del Rosario (l.) and St. Catharine (r.), altar-piece, one of the finest works of *Sassoferrato*. Other paintings (by *Zuccari* and others) of no great value.

The handsome court of the adjoining monastery is embellished with upwards of 100 small columns. The garden commands a fine *view of Rome with the Tiber in the foreground.

S. Alessio (Pl. III, 18) (when closed, visitors ring at the door to the l. beneath the portico) is an ancient church of uncertain date. It is known, however, that it was re-consecrated by Honorius III. after the recovery of the relics of the saint in 1217. In 1426 it came into the possession of the order of St. Jerome, to which with the neighbouring monastery it still belongs. The interior was modernized in 1750, and has been recently re-modernized.

The l. aisle contains a well and a wooden staircase belonging to the house of the parents of the saint, which formerly stood by the side of the church. Two small columns adorned with mosaic in the choir are, according to the inscription, the remnants of a work of 19 columns by Jac. Cosmas.

A small piazza is next reached. The green door on the r. side contains the celebrated key-hole through which St. Peter's is seen at the extremity of the principal avenue of the garden. Visitors ring in order to obtain access to the church of

S. Maria Aventina, or *del Priorato* (Pl. III, 18). The adjacent monastery is a priory of the Maltese order. The church, founded at a very remote period, was restored by Pius V. and altered to its present unsightly form by Piranesi in 1765. On the r. of the entrance an ancient sarcophagus, on which Homer, Pythagoras and the Muses are represented; the remains of a Bishop Spinelli was afterwards placed in it. Also the tombs of several members of the Maltese order (Caraffa, Caracciolo, Seripando etc.) of the 15th cent. Fine view of the opposite bank of the Tiber from the garden.

Beyond S. Maria in Cosmedin the *Via di S. Sabina* and afterwards (l.) the *V. di S. Prisca* traverse the Aventine, terminating opposite the Porta di S. Paolo. Midway stands the church of *S. Prisca* (Pl. III, 21). usually closed, founded at a very remote period, but in the 17th cent. entirely modernized. The ancient columns have been incorporated with the modern masonry.

The *Vigna Maccarani*, opposite the church (the vigna is traversed in a straight direction as far as the extremity, whence the main path to the l. is followed), contains a fragment of the venerable *Servian Wall*, excavated on the slope of the Aventine. It consists of large blocks of tuffstone; the arch seen here belongs to a much later period. In the latter period of the republic the wall, as the ruins betoken, was disused and entirely built over. Another, but more imperfect fragment may be seen in the vigna on the other side of the street, below S. Saba.

Below S. Prisca, towards the gate, the street ascends to *S. Saba* (Pl. III, 28), a church of great antiquity but almost entirely re-erected in 1465. To the l. in the portico an ancient sarcophagus with representation of a wedding and Juno Pronuba. The interior contains 14 columns, some of granite, others of marble. with mutilated capitals; the walls of the nave bear traces of painting.

About $1^1/_2$ M. from the *Porta S. Paolo* (Pl. III, 16), the ancient *Porta Ostiensis*, is situated the celebrated church of *S. Paolo fuori le Mura*, with an important Benedictine Abbey. About midway on the unattractive route a small chapel on the l. indicates the spot where, according to the legend, St. Peter and St. Paul took leave of each other on their last journey. (Omnibus in the afternoon every half-hour from the corner of the Pal. Venezia, at the back of Gesù, 6 soldi; fiacres $1^1/_2$—2 l.)

**S. Paolo fuori le Mura, founded in 388 by Theodosius and Valentinian II. on the site of a small church of Constantine, renewed and embellished by numerous popes, especially Leo III., was, prior to the conflagration of the night of July 15th, 1823, the finest and most remarkable church in Rome. It was a five-halled basilica, with roof of open-work; 80 columns of pavonazzetto and Parian marble, adorned with busts of the popes, supported the architrave. It moreover contained numerous ancient mosaics and frescoes, and in the Confessio the sarcophagus of St. Paul, who, according to tradition, was interred by a certain Lucina on her property. The front towards the Tiber was approached by a colonnade, and in the middle ages an arcaded passage connected it with the city.

Immediately after the fire, Leo XII. commenced the restoration, which was presided over by Belli, afterwards by Poletti. In 1840 Gregory XVI. consecrated the transept, and in 1854 Pius IX. the entire church. Unfortunately the ancient basilica has been superseded by a modern, and in many respects unsightly fabric. The dimensions, however, of the interior (386 ft. in length) are imposing. The principal portal towards the Tiber is still unfinished; the present entrance is from the road on the opposite side.

The small space first entered contains a colossal statue of Gregory XVI., and a few frescoes and ancient mosaics rescued from the fire. To the l. is the entrance to the Sacristy, which contains several good oil-paintings. Over the door the Scourging of Christ (attrib. to *Signorelli*), on the r. a Madonna with SS. Benedict, Paul, Peter and Justina. Then 4 single figures of the same saints. In a straight direction from the entrance-hall several chapels are reached, containing a few ancient but greatly restored frescoes. To the l. in the last is the entrance to the court of the monastery, to the r. that of the church, the transept of which is first entered. We begin, however, with the nave, which with the four aisles is borne by columns of granite from the Simplon. The two yellowish columns of oriental alabaster at the entrance, as well as the four of the canopy of the highaltar, were presented by the Viceroy of Egypt to Gregory XVI. Above the columns of the nave and aisles. and in the transept, a long series of portrait-medallions of all the popes in mosaic (each 5 ft. in diameter) have been placed. Between the windows in the upper part of the nave are representations from the life of St. Paul by *Gagliardi*, *Podesti*, *Consoni*, *Balbi* etc. The windows of the external aisles are in process of being filled with stained glass (St. Peter, St. John etc.). On the sides of the approach to the transept are the colossal statues of St. Peter and St. Paul: the *Confessio*, or shrine, is richly decorated with rosso and verde from the lately re-discovered ancient quarries in Greece.

On the triumphal arch *mosaics of the 5th cent. (constructed at the instance of Galla Placidia, sister of Honorius and Arcadius): Christ with the 24 elders of revelation. On the side towards the transept: Christ in the centre, l. Paul, r. Peter. Beneath the triumphal arch is the high-altar with *canopy by Arnolfus and his assistant Petrus (1285). — Transept: in the tribune *mosaics of the commencement of the 13th cent., Christ in the centre, on the r. SS. Peter and Andrew, on the l. Paul and Luke. Under these are the 12 Apostles and two angels. Beneath, the modern episcopal throne. To the l. by the apse the (1st) *Chapel of St. Stephen*, with statue of the saint by *Rinaldi*, and two pictures (Stoning of St. Stephen. by *Podesti*, and the Council of high-priests, by *Coghetti*). (2nd) *Cappella del Crocifisso:* in front of the mosaic beneath, Ignatius Loyola and his adherents pronouncing the vows of their new order, April 22nd. 1541. On the r. the (1st) *Cap. del Coro*, designed by *C. Maderno*, spared by the fire. (2nd) *Cap. di S. Benedetto*, with his statue by *Tenerani*. By the narrow walls of the transept: l. altar with the Conversion of St. Paul by *Camuccini* and the statues of St. Romuald by *Stocchi*, and St. Gregory by *Laboureur;* r. altar with the Assumption of the Virgin by *Podesti*, and statues of SS. Benedict and Theresa by *Baini* and *Tenerani*.

The *Monastery* of the church has since 1442 belonged to the Benedictines. It possesses a beautiful * *Court* of the 13th cent. (entrance see p. 193; visitors apply for the key in the sacristy; 1/2 l.), containing numerous ancient and early Christian inscriptions from the neighbouring, now inaccessible catacombs, and a few fragments of ancient and mediæval sculptures, among which a large sarcophagus with the history of Apollo and Marsyas. The monastery is richly endowed, but the situation is so unhealthy that it is deserted during the summer. The principal festivals of the church are on Jan. 25th, June 30th and Dec. 28th. Opposite the church a poor osteria; the taverns, however, on the road 1/2 M. farther are favourite popular resorts. Visit to the Tre Fontane see p. 262.

The Via Appia within the City.
Thermae of Caracalla. Tomb of the Scipios. Columbaria.

From the Arch of Constantine the Via di S. Gregorio between the Palatine and Cælius is followed. After 5 min. S. Gregorio (p. 198) lies on the l.; then the Via de' Cerchi (p. 188) diverges to the r. and skirts the Palatine. A short distance farther the street proceeds in a direct line over the Aventine, below S. Saba, to the Porta S. Paolo. The *Via di Porta S. Sebastiano* is now entered to the l. Here was anciently situated the Capuan Gate

(*Porta Capena*), whence the **Via Appia** issued. At the extremity of a rope-walk a street ascends on the r. to the church of *S. Balbina* (Pl. III. 23), situated on the slope of the Aventine, an edifice of considerable antiquity, with open roof, but modernized and destitute of ornament (visitors ring at the gate on the r. of the church). The adjacent building is fitted up as a Reformatory for youthful criminals. The old tower (ascended by an uncomfortable staircase) commands a fine *view.

From the street a view is obtained of the Cælius with the Villa Mattei (p. 199) and S. Stefano Rotondo (p. 199) to the l. The *Via delle Mole di S. Sisto*, diverging to the l., leads thither. The turbid streamlet *Marrana* is now crossed. Immediately to the r. the Via Antonina leads to the ruins of the *Thermæ of Caracalla (or *Antoninianae*) (Pl. III. 23), 4 min. from the Arch of Constantine (visitors ring at the gate to the l., 1/2 l.; the custodian has a collection of antiquities at high prices). They were commenced in 212 by Caracalla, extended by Heliogabalus, and completed by Alex. Severus: 1600 bathers could be accommodated at once. The magnificence of the establishment was extraordinary. A number of statues (among them the Farnese Bull, Hercules and Flora at Naples), mosaics etc. have been found here. Bare as the walls now are, and notwithstanding the destruction of the roof, the technical perfection of the structure is still apparent. The entire establishment was quadrangular in form, and surrounded by a wall, with porticoes, race-course etc. The destination of all the chambers cannot now be precisely ascertained. The most important only are here enumerated. A spacious oblong is first entered, once surrounded by columns (peristyle); scanty remnants of mosaic pavement. To the l. a large saloon is reached, which appears to have been fitted up as the *Calidarium* or hot-air bath. By one of the pillars on the r. a new stair has been constructed, ascending by 98 steps to the roof, whence a magnificent *panorama of the Campagna and of ancient Rome. From the calidarium a second peristyle is entered, corresponding to the former and containing remnants of mosaic-pavement. The semicircular *Exedra* now leads hence to the *Tepidarium* or warm bath, situated in the centre, adjacent to the calidarium. L. of this is the *Frigidarium* or cold bath, a large round space, the vaulting of which has fallen in. A small stair by the wall here affords a survey of a part of the grounds which surrounded the baths. In this direction the stadium was situated. Other remains of the thermæ are scattered over the neighbouring vineyards.

The main street is now regained. L. the public arboretum; some distance farther, r. the church of **SS. Nereo ed Achilleo** (Pl. III. 26), standing on the site of a temple of Isis, founded at an early period, restored by Leo III., and almost entirely reconstructed by Card. Baronius at the close of the 16th cent.

The interior exhibits the characteristics of an ancient basilica. At the extremity of the nave is an ambo on the l., supposed to be of great age, transferred hither from S. Silvestro in Capite; opposite is a marble candelabrum for the Easter-candles, of the 15th cent. Above the arch of the tribune are fragments of a mosaic of the time of Leo III., largely supplemented by painting: Christ between Moses and Elias, in front the kneeling Apostles, r. the Annunciation, l. the Madonna.

The opposite church of *S. Sisto*, restored by Benedict XIII., contains nothing worthy of note. Adjoining it is the collection of the antiquity-vendor *Guidi*, who has commenced to excavate the Thermæ of Caracalla opposite; the remains of an ancient dwelling-house with numerous paintings have already been discovered.

Then to the l. the *Via della Ferratella* diverges to the Lateran, passing a small temple of the Lares.

Somewhat farther, on the r., **S. Cesareo**, a small but remarkable church, mentioned before the time of Gregory the Great, finally restored by Clement VII.

In the centre of the anterior portion of the church are two altars dating from the close of the 16th cent.; at the farther extremity, to the l., the old pulpit with sculptures: Christ as the Lamb, the symbols of the Apostles, and sphynxes; opposite, a modern candelabrum with ancient basis. The inlaid screen of the presbyterium and the decorations of the high-altar are mediæval. The tribune contains an ancient episcopal throne.

The piazza in front of the church is adorned with an ancient column. Here the *Via di Porta Latina*, the ancient *Via Latina*, which traversed the valley of the Sacco and terminated at Capua, diverges to the l. The old *Porta Latina* is now closed. Near it to the l. (5 min. walk from S. Cesareo), beyond the former monastery, is the church of *S. Giovanni a Porta Latina* (Pl. III, 29), erected by Celestine III. in 1190, and effectually modernized by restorations in 1566, 1633, and finally by Card. Rasponi in 1686. The 4 antique columns in the portico and 10 in the interior are now the only objects of interest it possesses.

To the r., nearer the gate, an octagonal chapel of the 16th cent., on the spot where the saint suffered martyrdom. The adjoining vigna (formerly Vigna Sassi) (key kept by custodian of the church) contains (immediately to the l.) a columbarium (see p. 197), interesting on account of its decorations in stucco and colours, the so-called *Tomb of the Freedmen of Octavia*. A stair, partly modern, descends to a niche decorated with plaster, below which is a cinerary urn with shells and mosaic. Beneath is the vaulted tomb; r. an apsis with painted vine-wreaths and Victories. Here and by the wall are several ædiculæ, or cinerary urns in the form of temples, with inscriptions and representations.

The vigna commands a pleasing view of the city. It may be traversed and quitted by an egress to the Via di Porta S. Sebastiano. At the outlet is the tomb of the Scipios (see below).

Those who approach by the Via di Porta S. Sebastiano reach on the l. by the cypress, No. 13 in the *Vigna Sassi*, the celebrated *Tomb of the Scipios, discovered in 1780 (1/2 l.). A model only of the ancient sarcophagus of peperine-stone, which Pius VII. caused to be removed with the fragments of the others to the Vatican (see p. 245), is now here. In this sarcophagus reposed L. Cornelius Scipio Barbatus, Consul B. C. 297, the eldest member of the family here buried. The Venetian Quirini interred at Padua the bones of the hero which had been found in a good state of preservation; in consequence of this pious act they are withdrawn from the gaze of the curious. Here, too, were interred the son of the latter, Consul in 259, many of the younger Scipios, the poet Ennius, as well as members of other families and freedmen. The tomb was originally above the surface of the earth, with lofty threshold; the interior was supported by walls hewn in the solid tuffstone-rock. It was probably injured, or at least altered during the imperial age, when freedmen were interred here. Over the entrance-arch in the interior traces of a cornice are observed, and above are Doric half-columns.

The adjacent Vigna Codini, No. 14, contains three admirably preserved *Columbaria. These were tombs capable of containing a large number of cinerary urns, and derive their appellation from their resemblance to pigeon-holes (columbaria). They were usually constructed by several persons in common, or as a matter of speculation, and the single recesses could be purchased, sold or inherited. The names of the deceased were inscribed on marble tablets over the niches, on which their mode of acquisition of the spot was occasionally also recorded. Two of these structures are very similar: a steep stair descends into a square vault, supported by a central buttress, which as well as the external walls contains a number of niches. The third, discovered in 1853, consists of three vaulted passages, in the niches of which ædiculæ and small, sarcophagus-like monuments are immured. The adjoining dark passages were destined for the interment of slaves.

The gate is 25 min. walk from the arch of Constantine. Immediately before it is the **Arch of Drusus**; for it is probable that this now much mutilated monument is the arch erected in honour of Claudius Drusus Germanicus, B. C. 8. It is constructed of travertine-blocks, partially covered with marble, and still possesses two marble columns on the side towards the gate. It terminated in a pediment, until Caracalla conducted over it an aqueduct to supply his baths with water, the brick remains of which greatly detract from the effect.

The marble blocks of the *Porta S. Sebastiano*, formerly *Porta Appia*, appear to have been taken from ancient buildings; it is surmounted by mediæval towers and pinnacles. With regard to the Via Appia without the city see p. 264.

The Caelius.

This once densely peopled hill is now deserted like the Palatine and Aventine.

If from the arch of Constantine the Via di S. Gregorio be followed, or the public grounds above it to the l., the *Piazza di S. Gregorio* will be reached. Here to the r. is situated

S. Gregorio *(al Monte Celio)* (Pl. III, 24), on the site of the house of Gregory the Great's father, originally founded by that pope himself and dedicated to St. Andrew. In 1633 it was restored by Card. Borghese, who caused the stair, colonnade, portico and façade to be constructed by *Giov. Batt. Soria*. The reconstruction of the church was commenced in 1725.

In the entrance-court, decorated with pilasters etc. of the Ionic order, beneath the portico: l. monument of the Guidiccioni of 1643, but with sculptures of the 15th cent.; r. monument of the two brothers Bonsi of the close of the 15th cent. Over the high-altar: St. Andrew, altar-piece by *Balestra*. At the extremity of the r. aisle: *St. Gregory*, altar-piece by *S. Badalocchi*. Beneath it a *predella: the Archangel Michael with the apostles and other saints, attrib. to *L. Signorelli*. Here to the r. is a small chamber preserved from the house of St. Gregory, containing a handsome ancient *seat of marble and relics of the saint. Opposite, from the l. aisle, the Cap. Salviati is entered. In front of the altar on the r. an ancient and highly revered Madonna, which is said to have addressed St. Gregory; l. a. *ciborium of the 15th cent., disfigured by re-gilding. The sacristan, if desired (½ l.), now conducts visitors to three *chapels lying somewhat removed from the rest of the church, and connected by a colonnade. To the r., Chapel of St. Silvia, mother of Gregory, with her statue by *Cordieri*: above it in the vaulting of the niche, a fresco by *Guido Reni*, greatly damaged. In the centre the Chapel of St. Andrew: over the altar: Madonna with SS. Andrew and Gregory, painting in oils by *Roncalli*; on the r. Martyrdom of St. Andrew (a copy in the Lateran, p. 207), *Domenichino;* l. *St. Andrew, on the way to the place of execution, beholds the cross, *Guido Reni*, two pictures which formerly enjoyed the highest celebrity. To the l. the Chapel of St. Barbara with a sitting statue of St. Gregory in marble, said to have been begun by *Michael Angelo*, completed by *Cordieri*. In the centre a marble table with antique feet, at which St. Gregory is said to have entertained 12 poor persons daily. According to the legend an angel one day appeared, so as to form a thirteenth!

An ascent to the r., between fragments of ancient walls, is now made to

S. Giovanni e Paolo (Pl. II, 24), which has existed since the 5th cent. The portico, mosaic-pavement in the interior, and architecture of the apse are of the 12th cent. The church contains little that is worthy of mention. A marble slab, railed in, is shown on which the saint was beheaded.

The adjoining cloister is the property of the Passionists. Beneath it are spacious ancient vaults. Visitors ring at the door on the r. in front of the colonnade of the church, and are escorted by a monk. The vaults, which are only partially freed from rubbish, were formerly believed to be substructures of the Temple of

Claudius; it is now supposed that they were connected with the Colosseum and served as dens for the wild beasts etc. By the upper door of the cloister gentlemen may obtain admittance into the *garden, whence there is a beautiful prospect of the Forum, Colosseum, Lateran, S. Stefano Rotondo etc. (5—10 soldi).

The street enclosed by walls is now ascended farther to the *Arch of Dolabella and Silanus*. erected A. D. 8. of travertine. through which an aqueduct appears to have passed.

Somewhat farther. on the r.. the portal. embellished with mosaic, of a former hospital. which belonged to the insignificant church of *S. Tommaso in Formis* (Pl. III, 24) situated behind it. The interesting mosaic. representing Christ between a Christian and a Moor, was executed in the 13th cent. by two masters of the Cosmas family.

To the l. is the descent to the Colosseum, r. is the *Piazza della Navicella*, so called from the small marble ship which Leo X. caused to be made from the model of the ancient original formerly in the portico of the church. The church of **S. Maria in Domnica,** or *della Navicella* (visitors knock). one of the most ancient deaconries of Rome, was re-erected by Paschalis I. in 817, to which period the columns of the nave and the tribune belong: the portico was erected by Leo X. from designs, it is said. by *Raphael*.

The nave rests on 18 beautiful columns of granite; above, beneath the ceiling, a frieze painted by *Giulio Romano* and *Perino del Vaga* (in grisaille; genii and lions in arabesque), afterwards retouched. The arch of the tribune rests on two columns of porphyry; the mosaics date from the 9th cent.. but were considerably restored under Clement XI.; above the arch Christ between two angels and the apostles. beneath are two saints; in the vaulting Madonna and Child imparting blessings, on either side angels, Paschalis I. kissing her foot. beneath all the figures flowers spring forth.

(No. 4. adjoining, is the entrance to the once celebrated *Villa Mattei* with a few antiquities; charming grounds and views. Permesso obtained of Cav. Forti. Longara 47, about 1 p. m.)

Opposite is **S. Stefano Rotondo** (Pl. III, 27) (visitors proceed to the r. in the *Via di S. Stefano*, through the first green door on the r.. and ring to the r. under the portico).

It is interesting on account of its construction, and. although greatly diminished in extent. is the largest circular church. It was erected at the close of the 5th cent. by Simplicius, and subsequently gorgeously decorated with marble and mosaics. It then fell to decay and was restored by Nicholas V. In the original edifice the present external wall formed the central row of columns, whilst another wall. decorated with pilasters. 32 ft. distant, now perceived at a considerable height around the church, formed the circumference. Nicholas V. excluded the external wall and closed the intervals between the central columns with masonry, with the exception of a few receding chapels. The roof is rudely constructed of wood. The old entrance was on the E., the present portico was erected by Nicholas; here to the r. is the ancient episcopal throne, from which Gregory the Great delivered one of his homilies.

To the l. of the entrance an altar-niche with mosaic of the 7th cent.; farther on, to the l., a chapel with (l.) a well-executed monument of the beginning of the 16th cent. Most of the 56 columns are of granite, a few of marble. The lateral walls bear frescoes of fearful scenes of martyrdom by *Tempesta* and *Pomarancio* (much retouched). In the centre a canopy of wood.

If the Via di S. Stefano be farther pursued, it leads by the extensive fragments of masonry of an ancient aqueduct in 5 min. to the vicinity of the Lateran (p. 202).

S. Clemente. The Lateran.

From the Colosseum three streets run in a N.E. direction, to the l. the Via Labicana to the Thermæ of Titus (p. 180), r. the Via de' Quattro Santi to the church of that name, uniting with the following near the Lateran, and finally between these two the Via di S. Giovanni in Laterano, 12 min. walk, to the Piazza of the Lateran and the Porta S. Giovanni.

If the latter be selected it leads in 5 min. to a small piazza, where on the l. is situated

S. Clemente (Pl. II, 27) (side-entrance from the street usually open; if not, visitors ring at the principal door under the portico), which in its original form is one of the best-preserved basilicas of Rome, and has been invested with additional attractions owing to important excavations recently undertaken. Beneath the present church the original structure, which St. Jerome mentions in 392 as occupying this site, has thus been brought to light. Hadrian I. decorated it with paintings, still partially preserved. After it had been almost entirely destroyed in 1084 on the entry of Robert Guiscard, Paschalis II. erected in 1108 on its ruins the present (upper) church, for which he made use of all the available portions (e. g. the choir) of the lower. It was afterwards frequently restored; finally by Clement XI. with considerable taste, but unfortunately he added the unsuitable ceiling.

An entrance-court surrounded by a colonnade is first traversed, and the church entered thence. The nave contains the *screen of the choir and the ambos from the lower church, with the monogram of Pope John VIII. (key kept by the sacristan). The canopy with 4 columns of pavonazzetto dates from the time of Paschalis II.; in the tribune an ancient episcopal throne, restored in 1108. Mosaics of the tribune of the 12th cent. On the arch in the centre: Bust of Christ with the symbols of the 4 evangelists, l. SS. Paul and Lawrence, beneath them Isaiah, lower down the city of Bethlehem, r. SS. Peter and Clement, beneath them Jeremiah, lower down the city of Jerusalem. On the vaulting: Christ on the Cross, with John and Mary surrounded by luxuriant wreaths, beneath which the 13 lambs. On the wall of the apse Christ and the apostles. The restoration of these consisted of painting only. On the walls by the tribune monuments of the close of the 15th cent. In the chapel at the extremity of the r. aisle a statue of John the Bapt. by Donatello's brother *Simone*. L. of the principal entrance the Cappella della Passione with *frescoes by *Masaccio*, unfortunately retouched, one of the finest extant works of this master. On the arch over the entrance the Annunciation. To the l. by the entrance St. Christophorus. On the wall behind the altar a Crucifixion, on the l. scenes from the life of St. Catharine: above, she refuses to worship a heathen idol; she teaches the king's daughters in prison; below, she disputes before Maxentius with the doctors; an angel breaks the wheels on which she was to be broken; her execution. The paintings on the windowwall, greatly damaged, probably referred to St. Clement.

The greater part of the Lower Church has been excavated within the last few years; the sacristan attends visitors (½ l., in addition to which a donation is requested for the prosecution of the works). It was a more extensive, and likewise three-halled basilica, and appears to have been erected in the 4th cent.

On the wall of the r. aisle *frescoes of Christ's Resurrection, Descent to Hell, Crucifixion, the Marriage at Cana and Assumption of the Virgin; on a throne above, the Saviour borne by four angels. on the r. St. Leo with the inscription: *S. Dom. Leo P. P. RO.*, probably dating from the time of Hadrian I.

Beneath this church ancient chambers and substructures of tuffstone have been discovered, the latter probably of the republican period. The descent into these chambers is at the end of the r. aisle, where a Mithras-altar has been found. S. Clemente gives a title to a cardinal and belongs to Irish Dominicans.

A transverse street opposite to S. Clemente leads to the Via de' Quattro Coronati, and to the (on the l. side) church of

SS. Quattro Coronati (Pl. II, 27), dedicated to the saints Severus, Severianus, Carpophorus and Victorinus, who suffered martyrdom under Domitian for refusing to make images of heathen gods. The date of the foundation is very remote; the materials were probably partially derived from some ancient structure. After its destruction by Robert Guiscard it was rebuilt by Paschalis II. in 1111, restored under Martin V. by Card. Alph. Carillo, and subsequently partially modernized.

The church now possesses two entrance-courts (when closed, visitors apply for admission to the r. under the entrance of the first court, ½ l.). On the r., beneath the hall in front of the entrance to the second court, is the *Cap. di S. Silvestro*, consecrated under Innocent IV. in 1246, containing interesting, although somewhat unattractive ancient paintings from the life of Constantine and a still more remote period. The second court still contains ancient columns and traces of the entablature. The tribune is decorated with baroque frescoes by *Giov. da S. Giovanni*.

The adjacent nunnery comprises an establishment for the education of orphans.

To the r., farther on in the Via di S. Giovanni, is the *Villa Campana*, which formerly contained a valuable collection of antiquities, now in Paris and St. Petersburg.

To the r. at the entrance of the spacious and quiet *Piazza di S. Giovanni in Laterano* is situated a large hospital for women, accommodating about 600 patients. The Via in Merulana then diverges to the l. to S. Maria Maggiore (p. 140). Opposite is the octagonal baptistery of *S. Giovanni in Fonte;* farther on, the church, and before it the palace with the museum. In the centre is the *Obelisk* erected here in 1588 by Sixtus V., once placed by King Tuthmosis in front of the temple of the sun at Heliopolis, and brought to Rome by Constantine.

The gate to the l. opposite the projecting palace is the entrance to the *Villa Massimo* (p. 207). Facing the spectator is the *Scala Santa*, 28 marble steps from the palace of Pilate at Jerusalem, brought to Rome in 326 by the Empress Helena, and which may only be ascended on the knees. The two adjoining flights are for the descent. The chapel at the summit contains a picture of the Saviour, traditionally attributed to St. Luke. Beneath are two groups in marble by *Giacometti*, Christ and Judas, and Christ before Pontius Pilate.

In the corner to the l. the street diverges to the Villa Wolkonsky (p. 208). The *Piazza di Porta S. Giovanni* is now entered, where, especially in front of the church and to the r. by the city-wall, a charming prospect of the mountains and Campagna is enjoyed. To the l. by the Scala Santa is a tribune erected by Benedict XIV. with copies of the ancient mosaics in the triclinium of Leo III. — Beyond this a survey is obtained of the row of arches of the Aqua Claudia. An avenue leads hence in 5 min. to S. Croce (p. 144). The *Porta S. Giovanni*, named after the church, was erected in 1574 (hence to the Campagna see p. 268), superseding the ancient and now closed *Porta Asinaria* (a short distance to the r.).

*S. Giovanni in Laterano (Pl. III, 30), *"omnium urbis et orbis ecclesiarum mater et caput"*, was after the time of Constantine the Great the principal church of Rome. It was overthrown by an earthquake in 896, re-erected by Sergius III. (904—911) and dedicated to John the Baptist. In 1308 it was burned down, but was restored by Clement V. and decorated by Giotto: again altered under Martin V. (1430), Eugene IV. and Alexander VI., and finally modernized under Pius IV. (1560), by the alterations of Borromini (1650) and the façade of Galilei (1734).

The *Façade* by *Aless. Galilei* is one of the best of this description in Rome. From the central upper loggia the Pope pronounces his benediction on Ascension-day. To the l. in the portico is an ancient statue of Constantine the Great, found in the Thermæ of that emperor. Of the 5 entrances the *Porta Santa* on the r. is closed; that in the centre possesses two bronze doors with garlands and other decorations. The portico is 31 ft. in depth and 164 ft. in width; the church 384 ft. in length.

The interior consists of nave and double aisles; the nave is supported by 12 pillars, the work of *Borromini*, by which the ancient columns are partially enclosed; in the niches the 12 apostles, of the school of *Bernini*, above them reliefs by *Algardi*. Over these are the pictures of 12 prophets;; the ceiling from designs by *Michael Angelo*. To the r. and l. at the extremity of the nave are the only two ancient granite columns now visible. Beneath in front of the Confessio, is the ⁕monument in bronze of Pope Martin V. (d. 1431), by *Simone*, brother of Donatello. In the centre of the transept, which is raised by two steps, is the ⁕Canopy (about 1390), a beautiful work lately restored, with greatly retouched paintings by *Barna da Siena*, containing numerous relics, especially the heads of the apostles Peter and Paul. Beneath it is the high-altar (*altare papale*), at which the pope alone reads mass, containing a wooden table from the catacombs which is said to have been employed as an altar by St. Peter. The transept was restored under Clement VIII. by *Giac. della Porta* (1606) and adorned with frescoes. Here to the l. is the great *Altar of the Sacrament* with four ancient columns of gilded bronze, once appertaining to the original basilica. The (generally closed) chapel of the choir, to the l. by the tribune, contains a portrait of Martin V. by *Scip. Gaetano*, and an altarpiece by the *Cav. d'Arpino*. The tribune is embellished with mosaics by *Jacopo da Turrita* (1290): the Saviour enveloped in clouds; beneath, at the sides of a cross, l. the Virgin, at whose feet Nicholas IV. kneels, St. Peter and St. Paul, r. John the Bapt., St. John, St. Andrew and other saints. To the r. in the transept two fine columns of giallo antico. An egress here leads to the piazza of the Lateran. The passage ("*Portico Leonino*", because constructed by Leo I.), entered to the r. behind the tribune, is embellished on either side by mosaic tablets, the subjects of which relate to the construction of the church; farther on, r. the kneeling figure of a pope (10th cent.); to the l. in the centre an altar with ancient crucifix, on either side statues of Peter and Paul (10th cent.). Farther on. r. the entrance to the Sacristy, the inner bronze doors of which date from 1196. In the first chapel on the l. an Annunciation by *Seb. del Piombo* (?); in the last chamber, the cartoon of a Madonna by *Raphael*. On the l. at the extremity of the passage is a handsome marble sanctuarium (about 1500): near it the *Tabula Magna Lateranensis*, or list of relics. Objects of interest in the aisles: at the back of the first pillar on the r. in the nave, ⁕Boniface VIII. between two cardinals announcing the first jubilee (1300), by *Giotto*. The 2nd chapel on the r. belongs to the Torlonia family and is richly decorated with marble and gilding; over the altar. Descent from the Cross by *Tenerani* (a custodian opens this and other closed chapels, 1½ l.). The 3rd chapel belongs to the Massimi, constructed by *Giac. della Porta*, with the Crucifixion, an altar-piece by *Sermoneta*. Farther on in the r. aisle, the monument of Card. Guissano (d. 1287). The 1st ⁕chapel on the l., that of And. Corsini, designed by *Galilei* in 1734. contains ancient columns and a large vessel of porphyry from the portico of the Pantheon, in front of the bronze figure of Clement XII. (Corsini, d. 1740); the walls sumptuously inlaid with precious stones. Beneath the chapel is the burial-vault of the Corsini, with a ⁕Pietà by *Bernini*. In course of the excavation of the latter the antiques, now in the Pal. Corsini, were found.

The sacristan conducts visitors to the l. from the last chapel into the interesting * *Court of the Monastery* (12th cent.) with numerous small columns, spiral and decorated with mosaic. Various fragments from the old church are placed in the passages. Visitors return through the church and quit it by the egress to the r. in the transept, leading to the portico; this front dates from the time of Sixtus V. The hall to the r. beneath contains a statue of Henry IV. of France, by *Nic. Cordieri*.

The door of the court is now entered to the l., the steps in the court to the r. are descended, and a door on the l. between two immured columns of porphyry, with antique architrave, leads to the octagonal *Baptistery (or *S. Giovanni in Fonte*), where according to tradition Constantine the Great was baptized. It assumed its present form by slow degrees, finally under Gregory XIII. and Urban VIII. The Borgia Chapel is first entered, where over the door to the Baptistery a Crucifixion, a relief in marble, is perceived, date 1494. The Baptistery contains 8 large columns of porphyry, with ancient architrave of marble, alleged to have been presented by Constantine. In the centre a font of green basalt. Frescoes by A. Sacchi, Maratta etc. On the r. an oratorium of St. John with bronze doors of 1196; statue of the saint by *Landini*. Adjoining this door is the entrance to the Oratorio di S. Venanzio, with ancient mosaics of the 8th cent. On the l. the oratorium of John the Bapt. with bronze statue of the saint by *L. Valadico* (after Donatello), between two columns of serpentine. The bronze doors, presented by a Bishop Hilarius, are said to have belonged to the Thermæ of Caracalla.

The residence of the popes from the time of Constantine until the migration to Avignon adjoined the Church of S. Giovanni. Under Clement V. the palace was burned down and not re-erected till 1588 under Clement V., from designs of *Dom. Fontana*. As it remained unoccupied, it was converted by Innocent XII. into an orphan-asylum in 1693. In 1843 Gregory XVI. here established a collection of the heathen and Christian antiquities for which the Vatican and Capitoline museums no longer afforded space. This **Museum Gregorianum Lateranense** has since then steadily increased in extent and importance. On the basement-floor are 16 rooms containing ancient sculptures; the first floor is principally occupied by Christian antiquities.

The collections are accessible daily 9—4 o'clock. The entrance is by the portal in the piazza with the obelisk; visitors ring on the r. in the passage when the custodian is not on the spot. There are neither catalogues nor numbers, but the custodian (1 l.) is well-informed.

The inspection begins on the r. under the arcades of the entrance-wing.

1st Room: principally sculptures, formerly preserved in the Appartamenti Borgia of the Vatican. Entrance-wall: relief of the Abduction of Helen; tomb-relief (warrior's farewell); priest of the oracle of Dodona. L. wall:

two pugilists, termed Dares and Entellus (in relief); bust of M. Aurelius; Trajan accompanied by senators (relief from Trajan's Forum); in front of the latter a statuette of Nemesis. R. wall: sarcophagus-reliefs of Mars and Rhea Silvia, Diana and Endymion; Adonis; Diana and Endymion. In the centre a mosaic with pugilists, from the Thermæ of Caracalla (see 1st floor p. 207). — 2nd R.: interesting architectural fragments, especially from the Forum of Trajan. Fragments of a *frieze in the centre of the walls of the entrance, the egress and. that on the r. merit inspection. — 3rd R.: by the entrance-wall a statue of Æsculapius. R. wall: *Antinous, found at Palestrina. Wall of egress: child's sarcophagus with scenes of pugilism. In the window several well-wrought feet of tables. — 4th R.: on the entrance-wall *Medea with the daughters of Peleus, a Greek relief. On the board above (numbered 762) a beautiful small head of a female satyr. Statue of Germanicus. R. wall: *statue of Mars. Wall of egress: copy of the reposing satyr of Praxiteles. On a cippus: *bust of the youthful Tiberius. In the first window: basis of a column from the Basilica Julia. In the centre a beautiful basin of lumachella (a species of shell-marble).

The passage is now crossed to the

5th Room. R. wall: Roman portrait-bust; statue of Priapus; a Muse; statue of Priapus; *cinerary urn with representation of a cock-fight. In the centre: sacrifice of Mithras (found near the Scala Santa); stag of basalt; a cow. — 6th R.: collection of sculptures from Cervetri, the ancient Cære, probably found among the ruins of a theatre. Entrance wall: l. circular altar with Pan and two dancing women. Then a colossal portrait-head (perhaps Augustus); r. statue of an emperor, head new. R. wall: draped statue; colossal sitting statues of Tiberius and Claudius, between them the younger Agrippina; toga-statue (perhaps the elder Drusus). Wall of egress: statue of an emperor; bust of Caligula. In the adjacent window: relief with representation of the deities of three Etruscan cities (Tarquinii, Vetulonia and Volci). On the pillar between the windows: female portrait-statue (perhaps Drusilla). In the centre: two sleeping figures (from a fountain); altar with representation of sacrifice. — 7th R., r. wall: *dancing Satyr, found near S. Lucia in Selce, possibly from a group by Myron; Marsyas endeavouring to collect flutes thrown away by Athene. By the door: (r.) head of Paris (?); (l.) barbarian monarch. L. wall: Apollo. Opp. the entrance:**Sophocles, one of the most beautiful ancient portrait-statues preserved to us, found at Terracina in 1838. The desire to exhibit this statue in an appropriate locality contributed in a great measure to the foundation of the Lateran museum. — 8th R., entrance-wall: l. *relief of a poet, with masks, and a Muse; r. sarcophagus with the Calydonian hunt. L. wall: Hercules shooting. In the centre: *statue of Poseidon, found at Porto. — 9th R., containing numerous architectural fragments brought to light by the excavations in the Forum and the Via Appia. Entrance-wall: sarcophagus-relief with masked Cupids bearing garlands. Wall of egress, to the l. by the door: small head of Victory. In the centre: *triangular ara with Bacchanalian dances. — 10th R., chiefly sculptures from the tombs of the Haterii, on the Via Labicana near Centocelle, found in 1848. Entrance-wall: small and female portrait-busts; between them relief of a large tomb, with powerful lifting-machine; adjoining R. wall: relief of the laying out of a dead woman, surrounded by mourners. Wall of egress: relief with representation of Roman buildings, to the r. apparently the Colosseum, the others not clearly ascertained. Above it a relief with Mercury (broken), Proserpine, Pluto and Ceres. In the centre: Cupid on a dolphin.

A second passage is now crossed to the

11th Room: The sculptures were principally found in the tombs on the Via Latina (p. 268). Entrance-wall: l. sleeping nymph, from a fountain; r. Bacchanalian sarcophagus; then statues of Liber and Libera. R. wall: several statues of the bearded Bacchus; sarcophagus with the Seasons;

206   *Lateran.*   ROME.   *Christian Museum.*

Ephesian Diana; Sarcophagus with Adonis. Wall of egress: sarcophagus; Greek tomb-relief (farewell-scene). In the centre: large sarcophagus with triumphal procession of Bacchus. — 12th R., entrance-wall: 1. youthful Hercules; r. °sarcophagus with the history of Orestes (death of Ægistheus etc.). R. wall: large sarcophagus with Cupids bearing garlands. Then a head of Augustus. °Boy with a bunch of grapes. In the corner Satyrs. Wall of egress: °sarcophagus with the destruction of the Children of Niobe, found in the Vigna Lozzano Argoli in 1839. — 13th R., entrance-wall: relief of a Titan fighting; °portrait-statue of C. Lælius Saturninus (of Parian marble). Wall of egress: relief, Pylades supporting the exhausted Orestes. In the centre: oval sarcophagus of P. Cæcilius Vallianus, with the representation of a funeral-banquet. Then a three-sided candelabrum-stand with Pluto, Neptune and Persephone. — 14th R., entrance-wall: r. a small group in relief, possibly Orpheus and Eurydice. L. wall: unfinished statue of porphyry. Opp. the entrance: statue of a captive barbarian, unfinished. interesting on account of the visible marks of measurement made by the sculptor. Beneath. sarcophagus of L. Annius Octavius with representation of the preparation of bread; adjacent is the inscription: *Erasi, effugi, spes et fortuna valete, Nil mihi robiscum est, ludificate alios*. The two antique columns of pavonazzetto were found in the Marmorata. By the door of egress, casts of the statues of Sophocles (7th R.) and the Æschines at Naples, interesting for comparison. — 15th R. and the following are devoted to the yield of the new excavations at Ostia. In the glass cabinets under the windows are lamps, terracottas, fragments of glass, ivory-articles etc. On the pillar, mosaic from a niche, with Silvanus; on each side fragments of slabs of terracotta. Wall of egress: r. Sarcophagus with Tritons and Nereids. Then l. a °small female head, probably of a nymph. Above, to the r. by the door, head of Atthis. — 16th R.: r. lead pipes from ancient aqueducts. Pictures from a tomb near Ostia with representations of the lower regions.

The *Christian Museum was founded by Pius IX. and arranged by the *Padre Marchi* and the *Cavaliere de' Rossi*. Entrance in the rear, to the r. in the court (½ l.). In the first hall a statue of Christ by *Sosnowsky;* in the wall 3 mosaics, that in the centre of Christ. Peter and Paul from the lower church of St. Peter, the two others from the catacombs.

In the large corridor of the staircase a collection of ancient Christian sarcophagi, chiefly of the 4th and 5th centuries, with representations from the Old and New Testament. R. by the narrow wall: two statues of the Good Shepherd; large Sarcophagus with reliefs of the Creation, Miracle of the loaves, Raising of Lazarus, Adoration of the Magi, Daniel among the lions, Moses striking the rock for water etc. On the staircase: (l.) 1. Miracle of Jonah; 2. Christ's entry into Jerusalem. At the top (l.) 4. The Good Shepherd among vines, with genii gathering grapes. Farther on, a °canopy with two columns of pavonazzetto and an interesting sarcophagus. Above, on the wall of the staircase, the manger and adoration of the Magi. Beneath, translation of Elijah. Above, on the narrow wall, °sitting statue of St. Hippolytus, upper part modern, from the catacombs near S. Lorenzo fuori le Mura; on the chair a Greek inscription recording the saint's achievements and an Easter-table. The door on the l. leads to the upper arcades, the opp. door to the rooms with the collection of pictures (see below). The posterior walls of the three open arcades exhibit a systematically arranged (by the Cav. de' Rossi) selection of ancient Christian °inscriptions, an invaluable aid in the study of Christian antiquity. They are distributed with respect to the arches thus: 1st—3rd. Elegies on martyrs etc. of the age of Damasus I. (366—384); 4th—7th. Dated inscriptions (238—557); 8th, 9th. Inscriptions of doctrinal importance; 10th. Popes, presbyters, deacons; 11th, 12th. Other illustrious personages; 13th. Relations, friends etc.; 14th—16th. Symbolic and other records; 17th. Simple epitaphs from various catacombs.

The Collection of Pictures (entrance see above) comprises in 2 rooms copies of pictures from the catacombs of S. Calisto, SS. Nereo ed Achilleo, S. Sebastiano etc. The 3rd contains frescoes (of the 12th cent.), transferred hither from S. Agnese fuori le Mura. The visitor now enters to the r. the properly so called

Picture Gallery. 1st Room, by the entrance-wall: ancient *mosaic, pavement of an unswept dining-room (asaroton), by *Heraclitus*, found on the Aventine in 1833. Above it, Stoning of Stephen, cartoon by *Giulio Romano*. L. wall: Christ and Thomas, cartoon by *Camuccini*. Between the windows: Descent from the Cross, rough sketch in colours by *Dan. da Volterra* (the finished fresco is in S. Trinità de' Monti, p. 112). The door in the r. wall enters the — 2nd R., entrance-wall: Annunciation, *Car. d'Arpino*. R. wall: George IV. of England, *Laurence*. In the r. corner is the door to a stair ascending to the gallery of the adjoining saloon, on the floor of which is the extensive *mosaic with 28 pugilists, found in the Thermæ of Caracalla in 1824. It bears obvious indications of the decline of art in the age of its production. The door in the l. wall of the 1st R. enters the — 3rd R., entrance-wall: *Madonna with the saints Lawrence, John the Bapt., Peter, Francis, Antonius the Abbot and Dominicus, by *Marco Palmezzano* of Forli (1557). In the corner: Madonna with saints, by *C. Crivelli*, altar-piece of 1481. L. wall: "St. Thomas receiving the girdle from the Virgin, with predella, by *Benozzo Gozzoli* (erroneously attributed to *Fiesole*). Wall of egress: Madonna with John the Bapt. and St. Jerome, *Palmezzano* (1510). — 4th R., entrance-wall: Portrait, *Van Dyck* (?); *Madonna, *C. Crivelli* (1482); Madonna, master unknown; Sixtus V., *Sassoferrato*. L. wall: two modern Gobelins from the pictures of Fra Bartolommeo in the Quirinal. Wall of egress: Christ with the tribute money. — 5th R., r. wall: Entombment, *Venet. School.* Opp. the entrance: Holy Family, *And. del Sarto*. L. wall: Assumption of the Virgin, *Cola della Matrice* (1515). — 6th R., entrance-wall: Baptism of Christ, *Cesare da Sesto* (?). L. wall: St. Agnes, *Luca Signorelli*; Annunciation. *Fr. Francia*; SS. Lawrence and Benedict, *Luca Signorelli*. Wall of egress: Coronation of Mary, *Fra Filippo Lippi*. Window-wall: St. Jerome, tempera-picture by *Gior. Santi*, Raphael's father. — 7th R. l.: altar-piece by *Antonio da Murano* (1464). — 8th R., containing a large copy in oils of a fresco by *Domenichino* of the Martyrdom of St. Andrew, original in S. Gregorio (p. 198). — 9th R.: a number of casts by *Pettrich* from subjects derived from the life of the N. American Indians.

Several apartments on the 3rd floor of the palace contain a *cast of Trajan's column, to which the custodian (usually engaged except at an early hour in the morning) conducts visitors when requested.

Villa Massimo (Pl. II, 30). Permesso obtained at the Pal. Massimi alle Colonne (Pl. II, 13; p. 159), on leaving a visiting-card. Visitors ring at the entrance in the Piazza of the Lateran; if the custodian does not appear, enquiry may be made at the café near the entrance.

The grounds are neither extensive nor particularly interesting, the antiquities of little value; the casino, however, the ground-floor of which Prince Camillo Massimo caused to be decorated with frescoes from the great Italian poets by German artists, merits a visit.

The antechamber contains a few mediocre ancient statues and chests with beautiful carving (Renaissance). The Central Room is now entered, adorned with representations from Ariosto by *Schnorr*, completed in 1827. Ceiling-painting: Nuptials of Ruggiero and Bradamante and celebration of victory. Entrance-wall: the Emp. Charles hastens to protect Paris against Agramant. In the lunette above: Archangel Michael, l. victorious combat of Rinaldo, r. Roland's contest with Agramant. L. wall, to the l.: the sorceress Melissa causes Bradamante to behold her posterity, r. baptism of Ruggiero. In the lunette above: Melissa triumphing, beside her the magician Atlas, Ruggiero's foster-father, and Alcina, l. Marfisa, r. Bradamante. R. wall: *Angelica and Medoro. In the foreground: Roland on the l., sad and mournful, r. in a state of frenzy. In the lunette above: St. John with Astolph, who brings back from the moon Roland's lost reason, l. Bradamante, r. Zerbino. Window-wall, between the windows: Saracen heroes. Above, l.: Dudo conquers the Saracens by sea, r. conquest of Biserta. The room on the r. contains representations from Dante. Pictures on the walls by *Koch*. Entrance-wall: Dante threatened by a lion, leopard and she-wolf, finds Virgil his guide; r. Tartarus, with Minos, the judge of the infernal regions, surrounded by the damned. Opp. the entrance: gate of purgatory, guarded by an angel. In the foreground: *boat with souls about to do penance, conducted by an angel. On the window-wall: purgatory with those undergoing penance for the seven mortal sins. On the ceiling: representations from Paradise by *Ph. Veit*. Room on the l. with pictures from Tasso by *Overbeck* and *Führich*. Ceiling-painting: *Jerusalem delivered. Window-wall: Call of Godfrey de Bouillon by the archangel Gabriel. Above: Sofronia and Olindo at the stake, delivered by Clorinda. Opp. the entrance: Godfrey chosen as commander; preparations for the siege of Jerusalem; Pierre of Amiens encourages the warriors. On the extreme r. the portraits of Prince Massimo and the artist (Overbeck) are introduced. Above: *Erminia coming to the shepherds, all these by *Overbeck*. L. wall: r. meeting of Rinaldo and Armida. In the centre: Tancred in the enchanted wood, these two last by *Führich*; l. death of Gildippe and Odoardo. Above: Rinaldo and Armida on the enchanted island. Entrance-wall: Godfrey de Bouillon at the Holy Sepulchre. Above: baptism of Clorinda by Tancred, her death. The *predelle, in grisaille, which run beneath the pictures, also represent scenes from "Jerusalem Delivered". From the central room a flower-garden, commanding a beautiful view, is entered.

Villa Wolkonsky (Pl. II, 33), accessible daily; the street to the l. by the building adjoining the Scala Santa, pursuing a straight direction beyond the 3rd arch of the aqueduct, leads to the entrance-gate ($^1/_2$ l.). The tastefully laid out grounds are intersected by the Aqua Claudia, on and near which various antique fragments are immured. Several Roman tombs of the period of the first empire have lately been excavated here. Fine *view of the Campagna and mountains, especially towards sunset, from the roof of the small casino, to which the gardener conducts the visitor if desired (fee $^1/_2$ l.).

Collections of the Capitol.

With regard to the buildings see p. 170. The objects of interest here are preserved in the two lateral palaces, that of the Conservatori (r. in ascending) and the Capitoline museum (l.). Both collections, with the exception of a small portion of the palace of the Conservatori, are open (gratis) on Mondays and Thursdays, in winter 12—3, in summer 3—6 o'clock; on payment of a fee (5 s. on the ground-floor, $^1/_2$ l. on the upper floor), daily 9—4.

Palace of the Conservatori.

On the r. of the central door is the entrance to the 7 rooms of the *Protomotheca*, founded by Pius VII., a collection of the busts of celebrated Italians. In the 1st Room a few foreigners, among them N. Poussin, Raf. Mengs and Winckelmann. 2nd R.: musicians and statesmen. 3rd R. (large saloon): poets, scholars, artists. 4th R.: artists of the 14—16th cent. 5th R.: artists since the 17th cent. 6th R.: modern poets and scholars. 7th R.: monument of Canova.

The principal door enters the court, where r. by the door is a statue of Cæsar, 1. Augustus. By the r. wall of the court: hand and limbs of a colossal figure in marble, 1. colossal head in marble, high-relief of a province on the pedestal. Adjacent is the cinerary urn of Agrippina, wife of Germanicus, which in the middle-ages was employed as a measure for corn; inscription: *Ossa Agrippinae M. Agrippae f. divi Augusti neptis uxoris Germanici Caesaris Matris C. Caesaris Aug. Germanici principis*. In the centre of the hall opp. the entrance: statue of Roma; at the sides statues of barbarians in grey marble. L. in the corner: colossal bronze head, r. *horse torn by a lion. By the entrance-wall farther on, to the l., opp. the stair, a modern columna rostrata with the genuine fragment of an inscription composed in honour of C. Duilius, the victor at Mylæ, B. C. 260. and renewed under Tiberius. In niches on the landing of the staircase, 1. Thalia, r. Urania. Here in the small court four *reliefs are immured from a triumphal arch of M. Aurelius, found at S. Martina in the Forum: r. sacrifice in front of the Capitoline temple; on the long wall, entry of the emp., passing the temple of Jupiter Tonans, pardon of conquered enemies, and his reception by Roma at the triumphal gate. In the passage above, two reliefs from the triumphal arch of M. Aurelius (in the Corso near Pal. Fiano), which was removed under Alex. VII. in 1653: 1. apotheosis of Faustina, r. sacrifice in front of her temple (still standing). Visitors now ring at the door opposite the stair (¹/₂ l.) and enter the large saloon decorated with frescoes by the *Caval. d'Arpino*: combat of the Horatii and Curiatii and other scenes from the period of the kings. By the entrance-wall: marble statue of Leo X., by *Giac. del Duca*; on the r. wall, r.: that of Urban VII. by *Bernini*. Wall of egress: bronze statue of Innocent X. by *Algardi*. — 2nd R. (r.): pictures by *Laureti*, monuments of the generals Marcantonio Colonna (by the entrance-wall), r. Alex. Farnese, 1. Rospigliosi, Aldobrandini, Barberini. — 3rd R.: scenes from the Cymbrian war; celebrated bronzes. In the centre: so-called *Capitoline Wolf*, with Romulus and Remus, in the early Etruscan style, perhaps that erected B. C. 296 by the Ædiles Cneius and Quintus Ogulnius. An injury on the r. hind-leg is alleged to have been occasioned by the lightning, by which according to Cicero the group was struck during the consulship of Manlius and Cotta, B. C. 65; the twins are modern. Wall of egress: 1. bust of Michael Angelo, said to have been executed by himself, r. expressive *head, supposed to represent L. Junius Brutus, who expelled the kings and became first consul; the eyes renewed. Entrance-wall: *boy extracting a thorn from his foot. — 4th R.: fragments of the *Fasti Consulares*, lists of the Rom. consuls, found in the 16th cent. (smaller fragments in 1818) near the temple of the Dioscuri, and probably once immured in the Regia. — 5th R.: several small antiques. Entrance-wall: female head in bronze, serving as a jug; two ducks. Wall of egress: head of Medusa by *Bernini*. — 6th R., senatorial hall: paintings on the frieze from the life of Scipio Africanus, attrib. to *Ann. Caracci*; on the walls tapestry, woven in S. Michele. — 7th R.: *Sodoma's* frescoes from the first and second Punic wars. The cabinets contain Rom. weights and measures. Adjacent, on the r., is a small chapel with an *altar-fresco (Madonna), probably by *Pinturicchio*.

Visitors now retrace their steps through the 1st R. to the passage. By the narrow entrance-wall to the *Museo Etrusco* (the custodian unlocks the door if desired, fee ¹/₂ l.) is an interesting collection of vases, terracottas and bronzes from Etruria and Latium, presented to the city by *A. Castel-*

lani in 1866. The door to the l. at the extremity leads to two rooms with lists of modern Rom. magistrates; thence a passage is entered. and a court, to the l. in which is a door with the inscription *Galleria de' Quadri*, leading to the

Collection of Pictures (established by Benedict XIV.). Visitors ring and ascend a stair in a straight direction to the 1st R. (a written catalogue may be obtained from the custodian 1/2 l.).

1st Room, r. wall: 2. Redeemed spirit (unfinished), *Guido Reni*; 8. Landscape with M. Magdalene, *Caracci*; 9. M. Magdalene, *Albano*; 13. John the Baptist. *Guercino*; 14. Flora. *N. Poussin*; 16. M. Magdalene, *Guido Reni*; 20. Cumaean Sibyl, *Domenichino*. Narrow wall: 26. M. Magdalene, *Tintoretto*; 27. Presentation in the Temple, *Fra Bartolommeo*; 30. Holy Family, *Garofalo*; 34. Persian Sibyl. *Guercino*. L. window-wall: 42. Good Samaritan, *Palma Vecchio* (?); 49. Landscape with St. Sebastian. *Domenichino*; 52. Madonna and saints, *S. Botticelli* (?); *61. Portrait of himself, *Guido Reni*. Entrance-wall: 76. Apollo, *Polid. Caravaggio*; 78. Madonna and saints, *Fr. Francia*, 1513; 80. Portrait, *Velasquez*; 87. St. Augustine, *Giov. Bellini*; *89. Romulus and Remus, *Rubens*. — 2nd R., r.: *100. Two portraits. *Van Dyck*; 104. Adoration of the Shepherds, *Mazzolino*; 105. Portrait, *Titian*; 106. Two portraits, *Van Dyck*; *116. St. Sebastian, *Guido Reni*; 117. Cleopatra and Octavian, *Guercino*; *119. St. Sebastian, *Lod. Caracci*; *132. Portrait, *Giov. Bellini*; *134. Portrait of Michael Angelo, perhaps by *Marco Venusti*; 128. Fortune-telling gipsy, *Caravaggio*; 136. Petrarch, *Giov. Bellini* (?); 137. Landscape. *Domenichino*; 139. St. Bernhard, *Giov. Bellini* (?). Narrowwall: 142. Nativity of the Virgin. *Albano*; *143. S. Petronella raised from her tomb and shown to her bridegroom, *Guercino*; 145. Holy Family. *Giorgione* (?). L. wall: 157. Judith. *G. Romano*; 199. Death and Assumption of the Virgin. *Cola della Matrice*. Entrance-wall: Virgin and angels, *Paolo Veronese*; *224. Rape of Europa, *Paolo Veronese*.

Capitoline Museum,

commenced under Innocent X., extended under Clement XII., Benedict XIV., Clement XIII. and Pius VI. The works carried off by the French were restored with few exceptions to Pius VII. The collection is considerably less extensive than that of the Vatican, but is replete with admirable works. (The catalogue, last published in 1843, is now out of print. Gratuity on the groundfloor 5 soldi, on the upper 1/2 l.)

Above the fountain in the centre of the court is the *Marforio (supposed to be derived from "Forum Martis"), a colossal river-god holding a shell, representing probably the Rhine or Danube. erected in the middle ages in the Via di Marforio opp. the Carcer Mamertinus, where it was employed as a vehicle for the sarcastic answers to the interrogatories of Pasquino (see p. 160). At the sides two Satyrs from the Forum of Trajan [and several sarcophagi and busts. L. of the entrance in the lower hall: 3. Colossal Minerva; 4. Leg of Hercules with the Hydra, pertaining to No. 30; 6. Sarcophagus with Bacchanalian representation. On the l. at the extremity is the entrance to the

Room of the Bronzes. In the centre an unfortunately mutilated horse of admirable workmanship, excavated in 1849 in the Vicolo delle Palme in Trastevere. By the entrance-wall: bronze implements, tripod, measures. balance etc. Wall of egress: 5. Three-fold Hecate; 2. Vase found near Porto d'Anzio, presented by King Mithridates to a gymnasium. Long wall: "1. Boy employed in sacrifices (Camillus"); 8. Remains of a bull found at the same time as the horse. In the adjoining room: 47. Ephesian Diana, on the walls inscriptions; in the 3rd E. inscriptions and two sarcophagi with representations of the Calydonian and another hunt. Returning to the hall. l. on the narrow side: 9. Province in high-relief. Farther on, to the l., several mediocre female draped statues.

R. of the principal entrance: r. 19. Diana; 20. Young Hercules; 21. Luna; 24. Mercury; l. 23. Cyclopean Polyphemus with one of his victims; l. 26. Hadrian as a priest; r. 27. Sarcophagus with the Calydonian hunt; r. 28. Jupiter; r. 29. Colossal Mars; 30. Hercules with the Hydra. Contiguous, to the r.. is the entrance to three rooms containing inscriptions and several interesting sarcophagi.

In the **first** an ara, which stood in the market-place of Albano till 1743, with archaic representation of the exploits of Hercules; also a few insignificant busts. In the **second**, r. a °sarcophagus with battle between the Romans and Gauls; the commander of the latter commits suicide (perhaps Anerostus, defeated B. C. 225 near Pisa); l. cippus of T. Statilius Aper; at his feet a wild boar (aper). In the **third** a large °sarcophagus (formerly regarded as that of Alex. Severus and his mother Mammaea), with scenes from the life of Achilles: Achilles among the daughters of Lycomedes, l. farewell of Deidamia, r. arming of Achilles; on the back: Priam begging for the body of Hector (found with the Portland Vase of the British Museum near Porta Maggiore). L. of the door: sitting statue of Pluto. By the r. wall ancient mosaic: Hercules attired as a woman, spinning; Cupid chaining a lion.

In the walls of the staircase are immured the fragments of the marble *Plan of Rome*, an important topographic relic, executed under Sept. Severus, found in the 16th cent. in SS. Cosma e Damiano. Portions of the pieces found have been lost, but supplemented from the extant drawings (these portions are indicated by asterisks). On the landing of the stair two female statues, groundlessly designated as Pudicitia and Juno Lanuvina. Visitors ring on reaching the top, and are first ushered into the

I. Room of the Dying Gladiator, containing the finest statues in the museum. In the centre: 1. **Dying Gladiator, representing a mortally wounded Gaul; a Greek work of the Pergamenian school, found in the Gardens of Sallust together with the group of barbarians now in the Villa Ludovisi (p. 128). It is a work of profound interest and unrivalled excellence. The right arm is a restoration by Mich. Angelo. The visitor will readily recal the exquisite lines by Byron: Childe Harold. Canto IV., 140. — 2. (r. of the door) Apollo with lyre. R. wall: 3. Faustina. traces of gilding on the head; *4. Head of Dionysius, erroneously taken for a woman's (Ariadne's); 5. Amazon; 6. Alex. the Great; 7. Demeter. Wall opp. the entrance: 9. Head of M. Jun. Brutus. the "tu quoque Brute" of Caesar; 10. Priestess of Isis; 8. Flora from the villa of Hadrian. L. wall: *13. Antinous from Hadrian's villa; °15. Satyr of Praxiteles. the best of the extant copies; 16. Female statue bearing a vessel. Entrance-wall: 17. Zeno, found in 1701 in a villa of Antoninus Pius at Civita Lavinia.

II. Stanza del Fauno. On the walls reliefs, inscriptions etc., among which the *Lex Regia* of Vespasian (black tablet on the wall r.), whence Cola di Rienzi "the last of the Tribunes" once demonstrated to the people the might and liberty of ancient Rome. In the centre the *Satyr (Fauno)* of rosso antico, raising a bunch of grapes to his mouth, from Hadrian's villa, placed on a remarkable *Altar*, dedicated to Serapis. Window-wall: 6. Colossal head of Bacchus. Wall of egress: 10. Head of Mercury (?); 13. Sarcophagus with relief of Diana and Endymion; *12. Head of Juno Sospita; 15. Boy with mask of Silenus. R. wall: 16. Small Minerva; 18. Mars; 20. Isis. Entrance-wall: Statue of Hercules; 21. Boy struggling with a goose, excavated near the Lateran in 1741; *26. Sarcophagus with battle of Amazons, on the corner (25) the °head of Ariadne crowned with ivy.

III. Large Saloon. In the centre: Jupiter of black marble (nero antico), found at Porto d'Anzio. On an altar with Mercury, Apollo and Diana: 2. and 4. °Two Centaurs of bigio morato, by *Aristeas* and *Papias*, found in Hadrian's villa in 1736; 3. Colossal statue of the youthful Hercules. found on the Aventine; it stands on a beautiful altar of Jupiter, embellished with representations of his birth, education etc.; 5. Æsculapius, of nero antico, on an altar representing a sacrifice. Window-wall: 6. Hygeia; 8. Apollo with lyre; 9. M. Aurelius; 10. Amazon; 11. Mars and Venus, found near Ostia; 13. Athene. Wall of egress: 14. Satyr; 15. Apollo; 16. Minerva; 17. Colossal bust of Trajan with civic crown. R. wall: 21. Hadrian as Mars found near Ceprano; 23. Gilded statue of Hercules, found in the Forum Boarium. The two columns adjoining the niche were found near the tomb of Cæcilia Metella. 25. Amazon; 26. Apollo; 27. Mercury; 28. Old woman, probably from a group of the Children of Niobe; 30. Ceres (?). Entrance-wall: 31. Colossal bust of Anton. Pius; 33. Hunter with a hare; 34. Harpocrates, god of silence, from Hadrian's villa.

IV. **Room of the Philosophers.** On the wall valuable *Reliefs*, five from the frieze of a temple of Neptune, death of Meleager; sacrificial implements; an Archaic Bacchanalian relief by Callimachus etc. In the centre the sitting consular *statue of M. Claudius Marcellus (?), conqueror of Syracuse, B. C. 212, from the Giustiniani collection, formerly in the Museo Chiaramonti. Also 93 *busts of celebrated characters of antiquity, to some of which arbitrary names are affixed. 1. Virgil (?); 4., *5., 6. Socrates; 9. Aristides the orator; 10. Seneca (?); 13. Lysias (?); 16. Marcus Agrippa; 19. Theophrastus; 20. Marcus Aurelius; 21. Diogenes the Cynic; 22. Sophocles (not Archimedes); 23. Thales; 24. Æsculapius; 25. Theon; 27. Pythagoras; 28. Alexander the Gr. (?); 30. Aristophanes (?); 31. Demosthenes; 33., 34. Sophocles; 35. Alcibiades (? certainly not Perseus); 37. Hippocrates; 38. Aratus (?); 39., 40. Democritus of Abdera; 41., 42., 43. Euripides; 44., 45., *46. Homer; 47. Epimenides; 48. Cn. Domitius Corbulo, general under Claudius and Nero; *49. Scipio Africanus, recognisable by the wound on his head which he received when a youth at the battle of Ticinus, whilst saving his father's life; 52. Cato the Censor; 54. Sappho (?); 55. Cleopatra (?); *59. Arminius, erroneously named Cecrops; 60. Thucydides (?); 61. Æschines, 62., 64. Epicurus; 63. Epicurus and Metrodorus; 68., 69. Masinissa; 70. Antisthenes; 72, 73. Julian the Apostate; 75. Cicero; 76. Terence, according to others C. Asinius Pollio; *82. Æschylus (?). The names of the busts by the window-wall are unknown.

V. **Room of the Busts of the Emperors.** Reliefs by the entrance-wall: over the door, Mercury, Hercules, Graces, Nymphs carrying off Hylas; *2. Endymion asleep, beside him the watchful dog; *3. Perseus liberates Andromeda (these two belong to the eight reliefs in the Pal. Spada, p. 163). 4. (above the door of egress): sarcophagus-reliefs, Muses. Then more reliefs; triumph of the youthful Bacchus, circus-games, Bacchanalia, Calydonian hunt. The collection of the emperors' busts is one of the most complete in existence; the names are for the most part verified by coins. In the centre: *Sitting female statue, believed to be Agrippina, daughter of M. Agrippa, wife of Germanicus and mother of Caligula. The numbering of the busts commences in the upper row, 1. of the entrance-door. 1. Julius Cæsar; 2. Augustus; 3. Marcellus, nephew of the latter (?); 4., 5. Tiberius; 6. Drusus the elder; 7. Drusus, son of Tiberius; 8. Antonia, wife of the elder Drusus, mother of Germanicus and Claudius; 9. Germanicus; 14. Agrippina, his wife; *11. Caligula, in basalt; 12. Claudius, son of Drusus; 13. Messalina, fifth wife of Claudius; 10. Agrippina the younger, daughter of Germanicus, mother of Nero; 16. Nero; 17. Poppæa (?), Nero's second wife; 18. Galba; 19. Otho; 20. Vitellius (?); 21. Vespasian; 22. Titus; 23. Julia, his daughter; 24. Domitian; 25. Nerva (modern?); 27. Trajan; 28. Plotina, his wife; 29. Martiana, his sister; 30. Matilda, their daughter; 31., 32. Hadrian; 33. Sabina, his wife; 34. Ælius Cæsar, his adopted son; 35. Antoninus Pius; 36. Faustina the elder, his wife; 37. M. Aurelius as a boy; 38. M. Aurelius, more advanced in life; 39. Faustina the younger, daughter of Antoninus, wife of Aurelius; 41. Lucius Verus; 43. Commodus; 45. Pertinax; 50., 51. Septim. Severus; 53. Caracalla; 57. Heliogabalus; 60. Alex. Severus; *62. Maximin; 64. Gordian Afr.: 65. Gordian; 76. Gallienus; 80. Diocletian (?); 82. Julian the Apostate. — Visitors now enter the

VI. Corridor, where on the narrow side, to the l., No. 76. a beautiful marble vase on archaic *puteal with the 12 gods: Jupiter, Juno, Minerva, Hercules, Apollo, Diana, Mars, Venus, Vesta, Mercury, Neptune and Vulcan. Then, the back of the visitor being turned to the window: l. *73. Head of Silenus; l. 72. Trajan: l. *71. Pallas, found at Velletri, exactly corresponding to the statue in the Braccio Nuovo of the Vatican; l. 70. M. Aurelius, as a boy; r. *69. Bust of Caligula; l. 66. Augustus; l. 64. Jupiter, on a cippus with relief: Claudia Quinta drawing a boat containing the image of the Magna Mater up the Tiber; r. 56. Female draped statue. (The door opposite leads to the Venus-room.) L. 55. Head of Apollo; r. 59. Antinous; l. 53. Psyche; r. *48. Sarcophagus with representation of the birth and education of Bacchus; r. 44. Selene; l. 43. Head of Ariadne. Here and in the following compartments, on the r., are immured the inscriptions from the columbarium of Livia (found in 1726 near the church of Domine quo Vadis). R. 40. Niobide; l. 39. Venus; r. 38. Juno; l. 37. Marble vessel with Bacchanalian representations; r. 36. Copy of the discus-thrower of Myron (Pal. Massimi alle Colonne, p. 159), incorrectly restored as a warrior; l. 33. Flute-playing Satyr; r. 32. Muse; l. 29. octagonal cinerary urn with Cupids in the attitudes of celebrated statues; r. 28. Sarcophagus with the rape of Proserpine; r. 26. The child Hercules with the snakes; l. 22. Archaic relief, a lute-player (?); l. 20. Old woman intoxicated; r. 16. Sitting draped statue. Opp. the entrance into the Room of the Doves: l. *13. Cupid bending his bow; r. 12. Flute-playing Satyr; l. 9. Recumbent lion; r. 5. Silenus; r. 3. Septim. Severus; l. 2. Faustina: l. 1. M. Aurelius.

VII. Room of the Doves, so called from the *mosaic on the r. wall: *Doves on a fountain-basin*, found in Hadrian's Villa near Tibur, copy of a celebrated work, mentioned by Pliny, by *Sosus* of Pergamum. Beneath, a sarcophagus: Prometheus forming man, whom Minerva inspires with life. Farther on, a mosaic and several masks. Under them: *69. Sarcophagus with Selene and Endymion. The busts 54., 55., 56., 58., 61 on the narrow wall are particularly good. In the 2nd window by the l. wall, the *Ilian Tablet*, a small relief of palombino, a soft species of marble, with the destruction of Troy and flight of Æneas in the centre, and many other representations from the legends of the Trojan war. explained by Greek inscriptions, probably designed for purposes of instruction, found near Bovillae. In the centre: girl protecting a dove, instead of the snake it was most probably a dog or some animal of the kind in the original mosaic.

VIII. On the gallery is situated the *Venus Room*, which is shown to visitors before leaving (fee 5 soldi; closed on Mondays and Thursdays), containing the **Capitoline Venus**, universally acknowledged to be the workmanship of a Greek chisel, a supposed copy from *Praxiteles*, found almost uninjured immured in a house of the Suburra. L., Leda with the swan, a mediocre work; r. *Cupid and Psyche, found on the Aventine.

V. *Quarters of the City on the Right Bank.*

On the r. bank of the Tiber are situated two distinct quarters: towards the N. that of the Vatican; farther S., Trastevere.

On the Vatican Hill the ancient Etruscan city Vaticum is said once to have stood, whence the name is derived. Under the emperors gardens and monumental tombs were situated here, and the circus of Caligula and Nero, which was subsequently superseded by the church of St. Peter. In order to protect the latter Leo IV. (852) erected a wall round this portion of the city, the *Civitas Leonina*, which with its vast church and the neighbouring palace is surpassed in celebrity by no other spot in the world.

The river is crossed by the five arches of the **Ponte S. Angelo**, erected by Hadrian in order to connect his tomb with the city, A. D. 136, and named after him *Pons Ælius*. The bridge commands a pleasing view of the Pincio with the Villa Medici.

At the approach to the bridge Clement VII. replaced two former chapels by statues of Peter by *Lorenzetto*, and Paul by *Paolo Romano*. The 10 colossal statues of angels, formerly much admired, were executed from *Bernini's* designs in 1688, and testify to the low ebb of plastic taste at that period. One angel (fourth on the r., with the cross) is erroneously ascribed to Bernini himself; the two executed by him for this bridge are now in S. Andrea delle Fratte (p. 114).

From the bridge to St. Peter's is a walk of 8 min. The bridge leads direct to the **Castello S. Angelo** (Pl. I, 10), the huge monumental tomb erected by Hadrian for himself and family (*Moles Hadriani*), after the example of the mausoleum of Augustus, the tomb of Cæcilia Metella etc. It was completed in 140 by Antoninus Pius. On a square substructure arose a cylinder of travertine, externally covered with marble, of which no trace now remains: on the verge of the summit stood numerous statues in marble. The cylinder was probably surmounted by another of smaller dimensions, on which a colossal statue of Hadrian was placed. The head in the Sala Rotonda of the Vatican is supposed to have appertained to the latter. According to others the pine-apple in the Giardino della Pigna of the Vatican (p. 244) formed the culminating-point of the structure. The ancient entrance is seen in the court opposite the bridge. A passage gradually ascended thence, winding round the building in the interior, and then diverging to the central tomb-chamber, which is now reached partly by other approaches. This was the last resting-place of Hadrian and his family; the niches for the reception of the urns are still seen, but are now empty. A sarcophagus of porphyry is said to have been found here, the cover of which is employed as a font in S. Peter's. Many of the following emperors also reposed here, but when the Goths under Vitiges besieged Rome the tomb was converted into a fortress, and the statues on the summit hurled down on the besiegers. Gregory the Great, whilst conducting a procession to the Castello S. Angelo to pray for the cessation of the plague then raging, beheld the Archangel Michael sheathing his sword, in commemoration of which Boniface IV. erected a chapel on the summit, *S. Angelo inter Nubes*, afterwards superseded by the marble statue of an angel by *Montelupo*, and in 1740 by the present bronze statue by *Verschaffelt*. Subsequently to 923 the edifice was always employed by the party in power as a stronghold to intimidate their adversaries, and on the possession of which the subsistence of their sway depended. Since the time of Innocent III. it has been in the power of the popes, and here in 1527 Clement VII. underwent the fearful siege, on which occasion Benvenuto Cellini asserted he had thence shot the Constable Bourbon. The outworks were constructed by Urban V., and about 1500 the covered passage which leads hither from the Vatican was added. In 1822 the interior was freed from rubbish. The fort has lately been strengthened and is now strongly garrisoned (entrance immediately to the r. by the sentinel). Permission to visit it must be obtained at the office of the commandant, P. Colonna side-building; a sergeant (1½ l.) acts as guide. The visitor perceives several gloomy dungeons in which Beatrice Cenci, Cellini, Cagliostro and others are said to have been incarcerated: a passage with 80 large boilers in which the oil thrown on besiegers was formerly heated; former apartments of the popes; a saloon with frescoes by Raphael's pupil *Perino del Vaga*. The view from the summit is remarkably fine. The Girandola (p. 92) was formerly burned here.

The Castle of S. Angelo is adjoined by the *Piazza Pia*, whence four streets diverge to the W.: 1. by the river the *Borgo S. Spirito*, r. *Borgo S. Angelo*; between the latter and the city-wall lies a quarter consisting of small and dirty dwellings. In the centre, from the two sides of the fountain erected, like the two adjacent façades, by Pius IX., the *Borgo Vecchio* (l.) and *Borgo Nuovo* (r.) lead to the *Piazza Rusticucci*. The ordinary route to the Vatican is by the Borgo Nuovo.

To the r. in this street is the church of *S. Maria Traspontina* (Pl. I, 7), erected in 1566; farther on, to the r., in the *Piazza Scossa Cavalli*, is the handsome **Pal. Giraud*, erected in 1506 by Bramante for Card. Adriano da Corneto, now the property of Prince Torlonia, who in an adjacent building possesses a valuable collection of antiquities (the so-called Vesta Giustiniani, not accessible). By the small fountain in the piazza is the insignificant church of *S. Giacomo* (Pl. I, 7). In a straight direction the Piazza Rusticucci is reached, forming (246 ft. in length) a species of entrance-court to St. Peter's.

The Borgo S. Spirito, issuing from the Piazza Pia, terminates under the colonnades of the piazza of St. Peter. To the l. in this street, by the river, is the spacious *Ospedale di S. Spirito* (Pl. I, 7), established by Innocent III., and comprising a hospital, lunatic-asylum, foundling-institution and a valuable medical library. The three first-mentioned are capable of accommodating 1000, 500 and 3000 persons respectively. The military hospital is opposite.

Farther on, l. the church of *S. Spirito in Sassia* (Pl. 1, 7), erected by Antonio da S. Gallo under Paul III., the façade by Mascherino under Sixtus V. It pertains to the adjoining hospital and possesses nothing remarkable except a bronze ciborium on the high-altar.

Then follows on the l. the *Porta S. Spirito*, from which the Via della Longara leads to Trastevere (p. 227).

A short distance from the colonnades, on the l. the small church of *S. Michele in Sassia*, erected in the previous century, last resting-place of the artist Raphael Mengs.

The ****Piazza di S. Pietro** is a square with a crescent in front which is enclosed by the imposing colonnades of Bernini. Its length as far as the portico of the church is 1034 ft., greatest breadth 588 ft. The colonnades, erected by Alexander VII., consist of four series of columns in each, of the Doric order. Three covered passages are formed by 284 columns and 88 buttresses, on the roofs of which are placed 126 statues of saints in the style of Bernini. The cost of the construction amounted to 850,000 scudi; the pavement, laid down under Benedict XIII., alone cost 88.000 scudi. The whole presents a strikingly imposing aspect, and forms an appropriate approach to the largest church in the world. The great *Obelisk* in the centre of the piazza, brought to Rome by Caligula and placed in the Vatican Circus, is the sole monument of the description which has never been overthrown.

Under Sixtus V. in 1586 this huge monument, estimated by Fontana to weigh nearly one million pounds, was removed by means of rollers from its original position, and on Sept. 10th erected under the superintendence of Domenico Fontana on its present site. Representations of this extremely difficult undertaking are frequently seen. It is related that Fontana in the construction of his machines had omitted to make allowance for the tension of the ropes produced by the enormous weight, and that at the critical moment, although the bystanders were prohibited under pain of death from shouting, one of the 800 workmen, the sailor Bresca di S. Remo, exclaimed: "Acqua alle funi!" (water on the ropes), thus solving the difficulty. As a reward his relations (of Bordighera near S. Remo) were granted the privilege, still enjoyed by them, of providing the palm-branches on Palm-Sunday for St. Peter's, which are then prepared and plaited by the nuns of S. Antonio Abbate.

On the pavement around the obelisk is placed an indicator of the points of the compass. At the sides are two handsome *Fountains*, 43 ft. in height, that next to the Vatican erected by Maderno, the other under Innocent XI. On both sides, between the obelisk and the fountains, round slabs of stone indicate the centres of the radii of the colonnades, of which each series of columns appears thence as one. At the sides of the steps leading to the portico of St. Peter's (see p. 218), the statues of St. Peter and St. Paul, executed by Mino del Regno under Pius II., formerly stood. They are now at the entrance to the Sacristy (p. 221), and have been replaced by Pius IX. by works of De Fabris and Tadolini. To the r. at the extremity of the colonnades is the entrance to the Vatican (see p. 234), passing the Swiss guard and ascending the broad staircase on the r.

**S. Pietro in Vaticano.

St. Peter's, like S. Giovanni in Laterano, S. Paolo, S. Croce, S. Agnese and S. Lorenzo, is said to have been founded by the Emp. Constantine at the request of Pope Silvester I. It was erected in the form of a basilica with nave, double aisles and transept, on the site of the circus of Nero, where St. Peter suffered martyrdom, and contained the brazen sarcophagus of the apostle. It was approached by an entrance-court with colonnades, and surrounded with smaller churches, chapels and monasteries. The interior was sumptuously decorated with gold, mosaics and marble. At Christmas, in the year 800, Charlemagne received the Roman imperial crown from the hands of Leo III., and numerous emperors and popes were subsequently crowned here. In the course of time the edifice had at length become so damaged that Nicholas V. determined on its reconstruction, and in 1450 commenced the posterior tribune, from the design of the Florentine *Bernardino Rossellini*. Half-a-century later, in 1506, Julius II. recommenced the tardy operations, and entrusted the execution of his plan to the eminent *Bramante (Donato Lazzari* from Urbino). His design was a Greek cross, surmounted by a dome in the centre over the tomb of St. Peter. Under Leo X. *Raphael* deviated from this design by substituting a Latin for a Greek cross, having with *Giuliano da San Gallo* and *Fra Giocondo da Verona* succeeded to the supervision of the works after the death of Bramante in 1514. From 1518 to his death (1520) Raphael was sole director. Different designs were again made by *Baldassare Peruzzi* (to 1536) and *Antonio da San Gallo* (to 1546), under whom the work progressed slowly. *Michael Angelo* (to 1564) returned to the Greek cross of Bramante; the great dome was now to be surrounded by four smaller ones and a portico with pointed pediment; he erected the drum and left a precise model of the dome, in accordance with which (after the interval during which *Barozzi da Vignola*, till 1573, and *Pirro Ligorio* had conducted the work) *Giac. della Porta* (to 1604) and *Domenico Fontana* executed the work in 22 months with the aid of 600 workmen. The formidable difficulties which the construction presented and the beauty of the outlines render it a marvel of architectural skill. The façade only was now wanting, when Paul V. directed the architect *Carlo Fontana* (to 1629) to prolong the nave towards the front, and thus complete the Latin cross. *Bernini* finally erected one (l.) of the two projected campanili, which however was afterwards removed, as the substructure appeared inadequate to the weight. Under Alex. VII. Bernini added the great colonnades at the sides of the façade, in order to enhance its effect. The new church was then consecrated by Pope Urban VIII., Nov. 18th, 1626, on the 1300th anniversary of the day on which St. Silvester is said to have consecrated the original edifice. The interior was filled by Bernini with the sculptures of his contemporaries, the buttresses covered with marble of different colours, and niches, which destroyed the massive effect, formed in the principal pillars. At the end of the 17th cent. the building-expenses of St. Peter's amounted to upwards of 47 million scudi (about $9^1/_2$ million pounds) and the present annual cost of its maintenance is 6000 pounds. The new sacristy was erected by Pius VI. at a cost of 900,000 sc. (about 180,000 pounds).

The result of these various vicissitudes is that S. Peter's is the largest and most imposing, although not the most beautiful church in the world; its area amounts to 199,936 sq. ft., whilst that of the cathedral at Milan is 110,808, St. Paul's at London 103,620, St. Sophia at Constantinople 90,864, and the cathedral of Cologne 69,400 sq. ft. Length externally 613, internally 592 ft.; height of nave near the entrance 152, width 87 ft. Width of each aisle 33, total width 197 ft. Breadth of transept 208 ft. Height of dome from the pavement to the lantern 405, to the cross on the summit 448 ft.; diameter 139 ft., i. e. 3 ft. less than that of the Pantheon, which doubtless served Michael Angelo as a model. The church contains 290 windows, 390 statues, 46 altars and 748 columns.

The *Façade* of St. Peter's by *Carlo Maderno*, with 8 columns, 4 pilasters and 6 semi-pilasters of the Corinthian order, is 357 ft. long and 144 ft. in height. It is surmounted by a balustrade nearly 6 ft. in height, with statues of the Saviour and apostles, 18 ft. in height. The inscription runs thus:

In. Honorem. Principis. Apost. Paulus. V. Burghesius. Romanus. Pont. Max. A. MDCXII. Pont. VII.

Over the central of the 5 entrances is the *Loggia* in which the new pope is crowned, and whence he imparts his benediction at Easter to the concourse assembled in the piazza.

The *Portico*, the ceiling of which is magnificently decorated with stucco, is 224 ft. in length, 40 in width and 64 in height. At the extremities equestrian statues, r. Constantine the Great by *Bernini*, l. Charlemagne by *Cornacchini*. At the entrances are antique columns of pavonazzetto and African marble. Over the interior of the central external entrance *St. Peter on the sea, termed *"La Navicella"*, a mosaic after *Giotto*, formerly in the entrance-court of the earlier church, unfortunately considerably altered by *Marcello Provenzale* and *Fr. Beretta*. A copy of the original is preserved in S. Maria della Concezione in the Piazza Barberini (p. 127). Of the 5 doors of the church that on the extreme r. is termed *Porta Santa*, indicated by a cross, and is only opened during the year of jubilee (the last was in 1825). The great central entrance with the brazen doors, which Eugene IV. caused to be made in 1447 by *Ant. Filarete* and *Sim. Donatello* after the model of those of S. Giovanni at Florence, is only opened during the highest festivals; the two doors at the sides are those generally employed.

The portico unfortunately greatly diminishes the effect of the whole, and, even when the spectator is not in the immediate vicinity, conceals a considerable part of the cylinder of the dome. The effect which Michael Angelo intended the latter to produce cannot be appreciated except from a distance.

Interior. On the pavement of the nave, immediately within the principal entrance, is a round slab of porphyry on which the emperors were formerly crowned, and beyond it stones on which are inscribed the length of St. Paul's in London, of the cathedral of Milan etc. On each side, as far as the dome, are four pillars with Corinthian pilasters; above these a sumptuous entablature, which bears the arches extending from pillar to pillar and the gorgeously fretted and gilded °vaulting of the ceiling. The niches of the pillars here and in the other parts of the church contain baroque statues of the founders of various orders. The pavement, like the walls, consists entirely of marble, inlaid from designs by *G. della Porta* and *Bernini*. By the fourth pillar to the r. is the sitting statue of St. Peter in bronze, on a throne of white marble beneath a canopy, a work of the 5th cent., brought by Paul V. from the monastery of S. Martino. The r. foot is almost destroyed by frequent contact with the lips of devotees; in front of it two large candelabra.

The dome rests on four huge buttresses, the niches of which beneath are occupied by statues, 16 ft. in height, of (r.) St. Longinus by *Bernini* and St. Helena by *Bolgi*, (l.) St. Veronica by *Mocchi* and St. Andrew by *Duquesnoy*; above them are the four loggie of Bernini, whence the greatest relics are exhibited on high festivals, on which occasions the loggie may be entered by none but the canons of St. Peter's. Above these are 4 mosaics of the evangelists after the *Cav. d'Arpino*, of colossal dimensions. The pen of St. Luke is 7 ft. in length. The frieze bears the inscription in mosaic:

Tu es Petrus et super hanc petram aedificabo ecclesiam meam et tibi dabo claves regni caelorum.

The 16 ribs of the vaulting of the dome are decorated with gilded stucco; between them are 4 series of mosaics. In the lowest the Saviour, the Virgin and the Apostles. At the elevation of the lantern, God the Father, by *Marcello Provenzale* after the *Cav. d'Arpino*.

Beneath the dome rises the *Canopy*, 92 ft., with the cross 95 ft. in height, borne by four richly gilded spiral columns, constructed in 1633 under Pope Urban VIII., from designs by *Bernini*, of the metal taken from the Pantheon (p. 154). Under the canopy is the high-altar, consecrated in 1594, where the pope only reads mass on high festivals. It stands immediately over the *Tomb of St. Peter*. The *Confessio*, constructed by *C. Maderno* under Paul V., is surrounded by 89 ever-burning lamps. The descent is by a double marble stair. Doors of gilded bronze, dating from the earlier church, close the niche which contains the sarcophagus of the apostle. Between the stairs the statue of Pius VI. in the attitude of prayer, by *Canova*.

Beyond the dome the nave is continued and terminates in the tribune, containing the tasteless bronze *Cathedra Petri* of Bernini, which enclosed the ancient wooden episcopal chair of St. Peter. On the r. is the monument of Urban VIII. (d. 1644) by *Bernini*; l. that of Paul III. (d. 1549) by *Gugl. della Porta*, probably under the supervision of Michael Angelo. Above is the figure of the pope pronouncing his benediction; beneath on the r. Prudence, on the l. Justice; the figure of the latter, owing to its extreme voluptuousness, is now draped with bronze. Two other figures belonging to the group are now in the Pal. Farnese. Beneath the two founders of orders here and the two next in the nave, Pius IX. caused the names to be engraved of the bishops and prelates who, Dec. 8th, 1854, accepted the new dogma of the immaculate conception of the Virgin.

The visitor, having traversed the nave and surveyed the stupendous dimensions of the fabric, now proceeds to examine the aisles and transepts. St. Peter's possesses few pictures; those formerly here are replaced by copies in mosaic.

In the **right aisle** the (1st) *Chapel della Pietà* contains an admirable early work of *Michael Angelo*: ⁂Mary with the dead body of Christ on her knees. Adjacent, to the r. beneath the arch, is the monument of Leo XII., erected by Gregory XVI., by *De Fabris*; l. cenotaph and bronze relief-portrait of Christina of Sweden, daughter of Gustavus Adolphus and a convert to the Romish faith. The 2nd altar is adorned with the Martyrdom of St. Sebastian after *Domenichino*. Beneath the next arches the monuments of (r.) Innocent XII. by *Fil. Volte*, and (l.) the Landgravine Mathilde of Tuscany (d. 1115) by *Bernini*, executed by order of Urban VII. who had transferred her remains from Mantua hither. On the r. the (3rd) *Chapel of the Holy Sacrament*, closed by an iron gate, contains an altar-piece by *Pietro da Cortona*; r. the finely-executed monument of Sixtus IV. (d. 1484) by *Ant. Pollajuolo* (1493). Here Julius II. (like Sixtus, of the della Rovere family), who was the first to prosecute the construction of the church after

Nicholas V.. is also interred. Under the next arch, r. the monument of Gregory XIII., the rectifier of the calendar (d. 1585), by *Camillo Rusconi*; l. the unadorned sarcophagus of Gregory XIV. Opposite, over the altar by the principal buttress, is the Communion of St. Jerome, after *Domenichino* (original in the Vatican). R. the *Gregorian Chapel*, erected under Gregory XIII. from the design of *Michael Angelo*, at a cost of 80.000 scudi; here to the r. is the *monument of Gregory XVI. (d. 1846), by *Amici* (1854); beneath it is the tomb of St. Gregory of Nazians (d. 390). Under the following arch, r. the tomb of Benedict XIV.; l. altar with the mass of St. Basilius, after *Subleyras*. The Right Transept contains by the tribune three altars with pictures by *Caroselli*, *Valentin* and *Poussin*, representing the Martyrdom of St. Erasmus. The prolongation of the r. aisle is now entered. Beneath the arch: r. *monument of Clement XIII. (Rezzonico of Venice, d. 1760) by *Canova*; the figure of the pope and the two lions are worthy of inspection; l. altar of the Navicella, with Christ and Peter on the sea, after *Lanfranco*. Then the *Chapel of the Archangel Michael*, on the r. the *Archangel, after *Guido Reni*; in a straight direction, Burial of St. Petronella, after *Guercino*. Under the (l.) following arch: r. monument of Clement X.; Raising of Tabitha by Peter, after *Costanzi*. The principal tribune is now passed, and the l. aisle entered. Here, immediately on the r., is the monument of Alexander VIII. (Ottoboni of Venice, d. 1691) by *Arrigo di S. Martino*; l. Healing of the lame man by Peter and John, after *Mancini*; farther on, r. the altar of Leo I. with marble relief by *Algardi* (about 1650), the Conversion of Attila. Facing the visitor is the *Cappella della Colonna*, containing a highly-revered Madonna from a pillar of the older church. Beneath the altar an ancient Christian sarcophagus (on the front Christ and the apostles), containing the remains of Leo II. (d. 683), Leo III. (d. 816) and Leo IV. (d. 855). Turning hence to the l. the visitor first perceives on the r., over the small door (of egress), the unattractive monument of Alex. VII. (d. 1667) by *Bernini*. Opposite is an altar with an oil-painting (on slate) by *Fr. Vanni*, Punishment of Simon Magus. The Left Transept, with tribune and 3 altars, is next entered. It contains confessionals for 11 different languages, as is indicated by the inscriptions. By the pillar of S. Veronica, beneath the statue of S. Juliana, is an elevated seat, whence on high festivals the grand-penitentiary dispenses absolution. Over the first altar on the r. St. Thomas, by *Camuccini*; in front of that in the centre, the tomb of the great composer Palestrina (1520—1592), whose works are still performed in St. Peter's; altar-piece, Crucifixion of Peter, after *Guido Reni*; l. St. Francis, after *Domenichino*. The portal to the r. under the following arch leads to the Sacristy; above it the monument of Pius VIII. by *Tenerani*. From this point the effect of the dome, tribune and transept collectively may best be appreciated. Then the *Clementine Chapel*, erected by Clement VIII. (1592—1605); beneath the altar on the r. reposes Gregory I., the Great (590—604); altar-piece after *Andr. Sacchi*; facing the visitor the *monument of Pius VII. (d. 1823), by *Thorwaldsen*, erected by Card. Consalvi; l. Death of Ananias and Sapphira, after *Roncalli*. The visitor now turns to the l. and perceives beneath the arch on the l. the mosaic copy of Raphael's Transfiguration, four times the size of the original. Opposite, to the r. the Left Aisle is entered. Here under the arch on the r. the monument of Leo XI. (d. 1605) by *Algardi*, with a relief of the recantation of Henry IV. of France; l. monument of Innocent XI. (d. 1689) by *C. Maratta*, with relief of the delivery of Vienna by King John Sobieski. The great chapel of the choir, gorgeously decorated by *della Porta* with stucco and gilding, contains the tombstone of Clement XI. (d. 1721) and two organs. Here on Sundays ceremonies accompanied by beautiful musical performances frequently take place; ladies only admitted when provided with black dress and veil, gentlemen also in black (evening-dress). Beneath the arch, to the r. over the door, is the temporary resting-place of each pope during the interval between his decease and the erection of his monument; l. the *monument of Innocent VIII. (d. 1492), by *Ant.* and *Piet. Pollajuolo*. Then on the r. an altar with Mary's first visit to the Temple, after *Romanelli*; adjoining this to the l. is a point whence the entire depth of the church may be surveyed, as far as the chapel of St. Michael. Under the arch, to the r. over the door which leads to the dome, the eye of the English traveller will rest with deep interest upon the monument of Maria Clementina Sobieski (d. 1735 at Rome), wife of Charles Edward the young Pretender, and to the l. the tomb of the last of the Stuarts, by *Canova* (1819), with busts of "James III." and his sons Charles Edward, and Henry, better known as Cardinal York. In the last chapel on the r. is a font consisting of the cover of a sarcophagus from the mausoleum of Hadrian. Over the altar, Baptism of Christ, after *Maratta*.

The *Sacristy* (entrance by the grey marble portal on the l. immediately before the transept is reached; it may most conveniently be visited, at the same time as the grottoes, 9—11 a. m.), erected in 1775 by Pius VI. from designs of *C. Marchionne*, consists of 3 chapels in a corridor adorned with ancient columns and inscriptions. At the entrance the statues of (r.) St. Peter and (l.) St. Paul, of the 15th cent., which formerly stood in the Piazza of St. Peter. The central chapel, *Sagrestia Comune*, is octagonal and embellished with 8 columns of bigio from the villa of Hadrian at Tibur. A guide ($^1/_2$ l.) is here found to show the others. L. the *Sagrestia dei Canonici*. with the Cap. dei Canonici. altar-piece by *Franc. Penni* (Madonna with the saints Anna, Peter and Paul), opposite to which a *Madonna and Child by *Giulio Romano*. Adjacent is the *Stanza Capitolare*, containing 3 *pictures from the former Confessio, by *Giotto* (Christ with a cardinal, Crucifixion of Peter, Execution of Paul), and *fragments of the frescoes by *Melozzo da Forli* from the former dome of SS. Apostoli (angels with musical instruments and several heads of apostles). On the r. the *Sagrestia de' Benefiziati*, with altar-piece by *Muziano*, the Delivery of the Keys. Contiguous is the *Treasury* of St. Peter's, containing jewels, candelabra by *Benvenuto Cellini* and *Michael Angelo*, the dalmatica borne by Charlemagne at his coronation etc. Over the sacristy are the *Archives of St. Peter's* with ancient MSS., e. g. Life of St. George, with miniatures by *Giotto;* also a few classic authors. The treasury and archives are not always accessible.

The *Sagre Grotte Vaticane* also merit a visit (9—11 a. m., except on holidays; the sacristan, to be found in the sacristy, conducts visitors, 1 l. Ladies require a permission from the general vicar, Via della Scrofa 70). They consist of passages with chapels and altars beneath the pavement of the present church; entrance by the pillar of St. Veronica, beneath the dome. The *Grotte Nuove*, a circular passage with 4 altars, constructed by Paul V., in the centre of which the tomb of the apostle is situated, are distinguished from the *Grotte Vecchie* appertaining to the ancient basilica. The former are entered first, and a portion of them traversed to the r. Here, among the objects of interest are: r. statue of St. James, l. a marble cross from the pediment of the ancient church; r. in the chapel of the Madonna della Bocciata an altar-piece by *Simone di Martino*, about 1340:

in the corridor r. a *mosaic from the tomb of the Emp. Otho II. At the entrance of the chapel *delle Partorienti* are the statues of the two apostles James; a *relief of Boniface VIII. by *Andrea Pisano*. By the chapel of *St. Andrew* is the entrance to the three halls of the *Grotte Vecchie*, 57 ft. in width and 142 ft. in length, with numerous tombs of popes and princes from the earlier church: Nicholas I., Gregory V., the Emp. Otho II., Hadrian IV. (granite sarcophagus), Pius II. (Æn. Sil. Piccolomini), Pius III., Boniface VIII., Nicholas V. (founder of the new church of St. Peter and the Vatican Library), and Paul II. by *Mino da Fiesole*. From the Grotte Vecchie the remaining portion of the Grotte Nuove is entered. Here are preserved numerous reliefs of the 15th cent. from the tombs of the popes, among them a Madonna with St. Peter and St. Paul by *Mino da Fiesole*. Reliefs from the tomb of Paul II., Hope, Faith, Charity and the Last Judgment. On the l. side, by the sides of the entrance to the shrine, marble *reliefs, representing the martyrdom of Peter and Paul, from the tombstone of Sixtus IV. Opp. the entrance of the shrine the large *sarcophagus of the prefect Junius Bassus (d. 359), with admirable sculptures from the Old and New Testament, found here in 1595. The Confessio, or Shrine of St. Peter and St. Paul, situated in the centre of the circular passage, is sumptuously decorated with gold, jewels etc. Over the altar, consecrated in 1122, are two ancient pictures of St. Peter and St. Paul. The sarcophagus of St. Peter (formerly in the catacombs on the Via Appia, then in the Lateran) has been preserved here since the 15th cent.

For the ascent of the *Dome* (7—11 a. m.) a permesso, which generally admits 6 pers., must be obtained (at present with some difficulty) through a consul or ambassador. The custodian (beneath the monument of Maria Clementina Sobieski, first door to the l. in the l. aisle) at the entrance gives the necessary permission for the guide on the roof ($^{1}/_{2}$ l.), which is reached by eight flights of broad steps (142 in all). The walls bear memorial-tablets of royal personages who have performed the ascent. On the roof a number of domes and small structures are seen, some of which serve as dwellings for the workmen and custodians. One of the octagonal chambers in the pillars which support the dome contains a *model of the church by *Michael Angelo* and his predecessor *Ant. da S. Gallo*, for admission to which a separate permission must be obtained through an ambassador or consul; here, too, a model of the ancient throne of St. Peter is preserved. The dome rises 300 ft. above the roof, and is $613^{1}/_{2}$ ft. in circumference. The huge hoops of iron are here seen, by which the dome was strengthened in the 17th cent., being then considered in a dangerous condition. The gallery within the dome affords a striking view of the interior. Commodious stairs ascend between the external and internal walls of the dome to the *Lantern*, whence a view of the entire church and its environs, and in favourable weather of the Campagna from the mountains to the distant sea, is obtained. A narrow iron staircase, admitting one person only at a time, ascends to the copper ball on the summit, which can contain 16 persons, but affords no view.

The coronation of the new pope, as well as the canonization of a new saint, always takes place at St. Peter's. At Christmas, Easter, and on the festival of SS. Peter and Paul (June 29th) the pope here celebrates high mass in person. The most important of the other festivities have already been enumerated (p. 90), the remainder will be found in the Roman calendar. On Easter-day and June 28th the dome, the façade and the colonnades are illuminated in the evening by 4400 lamps, by which the lines of the architecture are thrown into singularly prominent relief; $1^1/_4$ hr. after sunset this illumination is exchanged with great rapidity by 400 workmen for a blaze of torch-light.

Ascending by St. Peter's, to the l. beyond the colonnades, the visitor reaches (on the l. before the sacristy is reached) the **Cimeterio dei Tedeschi**, the most ancient Christian burial-ground, instituted by Constantine, and filled with earth from Mt. Calvary. In 1779 it was granted to the Germans by Pius VI. Near it is the church of *S. Maria della Pietà in Campo Santo*.

The cemetery being quitted by the egress on the r., the circuit of St. Peter's may be performed by passing the sacristy, through the gate in a straight direction, and across three courts of the Vatican to the *Cortile di S. Damaso* (p. 235). A distinct conception of the vast proportions of the church will thus be acquired.

In the second street ascending to the l. behind the colonnades is situated (l.) the *Palace of the SS. Ufficio*, or seat of the Inquisition, now converted into barracks. That body was constituted in 1536 by Paul III. by the advice of Card. Caraffa, afterwards Paul IV., and this edifice allotted to it by Paul V.

The Longara.

The Borgo is connected with Trastevere by the *Via della Longara*, $3/_4$ M. in length, constructed by Sixtus V. The Borgo is quitted by the *Porta di S. Spirito*, begun by Ant. da San Gallo. Near the gate the steep Salita di San Onofrio ascends to the r. (then to the l. where the street divides) in 5 min. to

*S. Onofrio (Pl. II. 7), on the slope of the Janiculus, erected in 1439 by Nicolo da Forca Palena in honour of the Egyptian hermit Honophrius; adjoining it is a monastery of the order of St. Jerome. The church and cloister are approached by a hall borne by 8 columns, where in the lunettes and protected by glass are frescoes from the life of St. Jerome by *Domenichino*. If the church is closed, visitors ring at the door of the monastery (r.). through which access may be obtained.

The 1st Chapel on the l., restored by Pius IX., contains the tomb of the poet Torquato Tasso (by *de Fabris*, 1857), who died in this monastery in 1595. In the 3rd chapel the tombstone of the linguist Card. Mezzofanti (d. 1849). — The 2nd chapel on the r. contains a Madonna, altar-piece by *Ann. Caracci*. At the extremity of the r. wall: monument of Archbp. Sacchi (d. 1302); in the lunette a Madonna by *Pinturicchio*. The tribune contains restored frescoes, the upper attributed to *Pinturicchio*, the lower to *Bald. Peruzzi*.

Ladies are not admitted to the monastery. A passage on the first floor contains a **Madonna with the donor, a fresco by *Leonardo da Vinci*. The cell is still shown in which Tasso resided, when about to receive the laurel on the Capitol, and died April 25th, 1595. It contains his bust in wax, taken from the cast of his face, his autograph etc. In the garden (ladies may enter by a side-door) of the monastery, near some cypresses, are the remains of an oak (destroyed by lightning in 1842), under which Tasso was in the habit of sitting. Admirable *view of the city and retrospect of St. Peter's.

Those desirous of proceeding hence to Trastevere may in descending select the shorter and steeper road to the r.

To the r. in the Longara is the extensive lunatic-asylum erected by Pius IX., with long inscription.

Farther on, l. the new chain-bridge (1 soldo), on the opposite bank *S. Giovanni dei Fiorentini* (Pl. II, 10). R. the extensive *Pal. Salviati* with handsome court; the pictures formerly here are now for the most part in the Borghese Gallery, Prince Borghese having inherited the palace and sold it to the government, which has established the civic archives in the building. The adjacent garden, skirted by the street, was converted by Gregory XVI. in 1837 into a *Botanical Garden* (visitors ring at the small door on the r.) which belongs to the Sapienza (see p. 153). About 10 min. walk from the Porta S. Spirito is situated the small church of *S. Giovanni alla Lungara*, said to have been founded by Leo IV., altered in the 17th cent. The adjoining convent is tenanted by nuns who have been reclaimed from a career of vice.

About 5 min. farther, l. opposite the Pal. Corsini, is the

*Villa Farnesina (Pl. II, 11) (Sundays 10—3, 1/2 l.), erected in 1506 by *Bald. Peruzzi* for Agostino Chigi, from 1580 until lately the property of the Farnese family, now that of the ex-king of Naples. This small palace is one of the most pleasing renaissance-edifices in Rome, simple and of symmetrical proportions. Owing to the work of restoration now in progress the upper story

Villa Farnesina.   ROME.   *Raphael's Frescoes.*   225

with the celebrated frescoes, especially the Nuptials of Alexander and Roxana, is inaccessible. The principal space on the basement-floor was originally an open hall, but is now closed with large windows in order to protect the paintings. The ceiling was designed by *Raphael* (1518—1520) and decorated by his pupils *G. Romano* and *Franc. Penni* with **12 representations from the myth of Psyche, numbered in order, beginning at the narrow wall to the l. and continued on the wall opposite the entrance.

Raphael adhered to the charming fable of Apuleius which may be briefly related as follows. A king had three daughters, the youngest of whom, Psyche, excites the jealousy of Venus by her beauty. The goddess accordingly directs her son Cupid to punish the princess by inspiring her with love for an unworthy individual (1). Cupid himself becomes enamoured of her, shows her to the Graces (2) and carries her off. He visits her by night only, warning her not to indulge in curiosity as to his appearance. Psyche, however, instigated by her envious sisters, disobeys the injunction. She lights a lamp, a drop of heated oil from which awakes her sleeping lover. Cupid upbraids her for her mistrust and leaves her in anger. Psyche wanders about filled with despair. Meanwhile Venus has been informed of her son's attachment, imprisons him, and requests Juno and Ceres to aid her in seeking for Psyche, which both goddesses decline to do (3). She then drives in her dove-chariot to Jupiter (4) and begs him to grant her the assistance of Mercury (5). Her request is complied with, and Mercury flies forth to search for Psyche (6). Venus torments her in every conceivable manner and imposes impossible tasks on her, which, however, with the help of friends she is enabled to perform. At length she is desired to bring a casket from the infernal regions (7), and even this, to the astonishment of Venus, she succeeds in accomplishing (8). Cupid, having at length escaped from his captivity, begs Jupiter to grant him Psyche; Jupiter kisses him (9) and commands Mercury to summon the gods to deliberate on the matter (ceiling-painting on the r.). The messenger of the gods then conducts Psyche to Olympus (10), she becomes immortal, and the gods celebrate the nuptial-banquet (ceiling-painting on the l.). In this pleasing fable Psyche evidently represents the human soul purified by passions and misfortunes, and thus fitted for the enjoyment of true and celestial happiness.

The garlands which surround the different paintings are by *Gior. da Udine*. The frescoes, having suffered from exposure to the atmosphere, were retouched by *Maratta*. The blue ground, which was originally of a much warmer tint, as is apparent from the few portions still unfaded, was most seriously injured. The whole nevertheless produces a charming and brilliant effect owing to the indestructible beauty of the designs. The felicity with which the scenes have been adapted to the unfavourable spaces is also remarkable.

The *ceiling of the adjoining Loggia towards the garden, which was likewise formerly exposed to the external atmosphere, was decorated and painted by *Baldassare Peruzzi* (representations of Perseus and Diana). The lunettes contain scenes from the Metamorphosis, the first Roman work of *Seb. del Piombo*. The colossal head in the lunette on the l. lateral wall is said to have been drawn by *Michael Angelo* in charcoal, whilst in vain seeking Dan. da Volterra who was also here engaged. On the entrance-wall Raphael in 1514 painted with his own hand the **Galatea, borne across the sea in a conch, surrounded by Nymphs, Tritons and Cupids, one of the most charming works of the master. The Polyphemus adjoining, to the l., was painted by *Seb. del Piombo*, but was afterwards almost entirely obliterated and badly restored. The landscapes are erroneously attributed to G. Poussin. The restorations which the two rooms have recently undergone have only been partially successful.

Opposite is the ***Palazzo Corsini** (Pl. II, 11), formerly the property of the Riarii, purchased by Clement XII. for his nephew Card. Neri Corsini in 1729, altered by *Fuga*, and in the 17th cent. the residence of Queen Christina of Sweden, who died here, April 19th, 1689. A double staircase ascends from the principal portal to the 1st floor, where the *Picture-Gallery* is situated (9—12 o'clock daily, 1/2 l.; the custodians are well-informed and obliging). Among a large number of mediocre and inferior works are a few pictures of rare merit. Catalogues in each room.

1st Room. 1., 5. Landscapes, *Bloemen (Orizzonte)*; 2., 4. Landscapes, *Lovatelli*. This room also generally contains a small Holy Family by *Battoni*. By one of the walls a well-preserved ancient sarcophagus with seagods, from Porto d'Anzio. — 2nd R.: 4. Holy Family, *Bassano*; 12. Madonna in a glory, *Eliz. Sirani*; 15. Landscape, *G. Poussin* (?); 17., 19. Landscapes wtih cattle. *Berghem*; 20. Pietà, *Lod. Caracci*. On the walls a number of ancient heads. some of which merit examination. — 3rd R.: °4., 5. Wharf, *Peters*; 17. Madonna, *Cararaggio*; °23. Evening Landscape, *Both*; 43. Martyrdom of two saints, *Saracent*;*44. Julius II., after *Raphael*; 50. Philip II. of Spain, *Titian*; 55. Kitchen-scenes, *Dutch School*; 61. Holy Family, *Vasari*; 84. Cavalry skirmish, *Borgognone*; 88. Ecce Homo, *C. Dolce*. — 4th R.: °11. Herodias, *Guido Reni*; 16. Madonna, by the same; 22. Christ and Mary Magdalene. *Baroccio*; 27. Heads as studics, *Lod. Caracci*; 40. Portrait of his daughter, *Maratta*; 41. Female portrait, after *Raphael*, copy of that in the Tribune at Florence; 43. Madonna, *Maratta*; 44. Hare, *A. Dürer*; 47. Landscape with the judgment of Paris, designed by Raphael, *Poelemburg* (?); also 11 small pictures from military life by *Callot*. This room likewise contains an ancient marble chair with reliefs, found near the Lateran. On a table stands the "Corsinian vase in silver, with representation of the atonement of Orestes in chased work. Two emblematical marble statuettes, Hunting and Fishing, by *Tenerani*. — 5th R., where Christina of Sweden is said to have expired. Decorations of the ceiling of the school of the Zuccheri. 2. Holy Family, *Perino del Vaga*; °14. Annunciation, *Maratta*; 20. Polyphemus and Ulysses, *Lanfranco*; 23. Madonna, *Franc. Albano*; 44. Holy Family, designed by Michael Angelo, *Marc. Venusti*. — 6th R.: containing an interesting collection of portraits, most of which are worthy of notice. 19. Male portrait, *Holbein*, much retouched; °20. Mons. Giberti, *G. Romano*; °22. Old woman, *Rembrandt* (?); 23. Male portrait, *Giorgione*; 26. Portrait, *Span. Sch.*; °32. Portrait, *Van Dyck*; °34. Nativity of Mary, after Dürer's woodcut; °43. Cardinal, *Germ. Sch.* (erroneously attrib. to Dürer); 47. Portrait of himself, *Rubens*; 50. Card. Alex. Farnese, *Titian* (?). — 7th R.: °11. Madonna, *Murillo*; °13. Landscape, *G. Poussin*; 21. Christ as a boy in the Temple, *L. Giordano*; °22., °23., *24. Descent of the Holy Ghost, Last Judgment, Ascension, *Fiesole*; 31., 32. Landscapes, *N. Poussin*. — 8th R.: 6. Landscape, *Claude Lorrain* (?); °7. Landscape, *G. Poussin*; 10. History of Niobe, design in the form of a frieze, *Polidoro da Cararaggio*; 11. Holy Family, *N. Poussin*; 12. St. George, *Erc. Grandi*; 13. La Contemplazione, *Guido Reni*; °15., 21., 23. Landscapes, *G. Poussin*; 24. St. Jerôme, *Guercino*; 25. St. Jerome, *Ribera*. This room also contains two marble busts, portraits of members of the Corsini family. The adjoining cabinet contains pictures of the older Florentine and Sienese schools, most of them of little value and badly preserved. 23. Madonna, *Gher. Sternina*; 26. Madonna, *Spagna*. — 9th R.: 2. Interior of a stable, *Teniers*; 8. Pietà, *Lod. Caracci*, sketch of No. 20 in the 2nd R.; Innocent X., *Velasquez* (see Pal. Doria, p. 120); °28., 29. Battles, *Salv. Rosa*; 30. Female heads, *Giorgione*; 36. Portrait, master unknown; 49. Madonna, *Gherardesca da Siena*. In the adjoining private apartment, opened by the custodian if requested: ancient mosaic of two unmanageable oxen with a plough and their driver; two ancient portrait-statues; also a bronze relief of the Rape of Europa, attributed to *Benvenuto Cellini*.

The *Library* of this palace (entrance from the street by the last door on the r.), founded by Card. Neri Corsini, one of the most extensive in Rome, is open daily (Wednesdays excepted) in winter 8—12 o'clock, in summer in the afternoon. In 8 rooms are preserved a number of MSS. and printed works of great value; then a *Collection of Engravings*, one of the largest in the world.

The spacious and beautiful *Garden extends behind the palace on the slopes of the Janiculus. From the height a beautiful *view of Rome.

A short way beyond these palaces the Via della Longara is terminated by the *Porta Settimiana* (Pl. II, 11), a gate in the older wall of Trastevere, preserving by its name a reminiscence of the gardens of Septim. Severus which were situated in the vicinity.

Trastevere.

This quarter of the city is inhabited almost exclusively by the working classes, among whom numerous well-built and handsome individuals of both sexes are encountered. The inhabitants of Trastevere maintain that they are the most direct descendants of the ancient Romans, and their character differs in many respects from that of the citizens of other quarters.

Trastevere is connected with the city by three bridges, the most N. of which is the *P.nte Sisto* (Pl. II, 11), constructed by Sixtus IV. in 1474 and named after him. It occupies the site of the *Pons Aurelius*, destroyed in the 8th cent., and commands an interesting view.

To the r. the *Via di Ponte Sisto* leads in 3 min. to the Porta Settimiana (see above), outside of which the broad *Via delle Fornaci* ascends to the l. After this street has been followed for 5 min. to the point where the ascent becomes more rapid, a newly made carriage-road winds up to S. Pietro in Montorio, the Acqua Paola, Porta S. Pancrazio and Villa Pamfili. After an ascent of 3 min. more, by a direct foot-path, the traveller arrives at

S. Pietro in Montorio (Pl. II, 12), erected in 1500 by Ferdinand and Isabella of Spain, from designs by *Baccio Pintelli*, on the spot where St. Peter is said to have suffered martyrdom. The campanile and tribune were almost entirely destroyed during the siege of 1849.

The 1st *Chapel on the r. was decorated by *Seb. del Piombo* with frescoes from Michael Angelo's drawings: Scourging of Christ, adjoining which are St. Peter on the l. and St. Francis on the r.; on the ceiling the Transfiguration; on the exterior of the arch a prophet and sibyl. The 2nd Chapel (Coronation of Mary on the arch) was painted by pupils of Perugino. The altar-piece of the 5th Chapel, Paul healing Ananias, is by *Vasari*. The high-altar was once adorned by Raphael's Transfiguration. The last chapel on the l. contains an altar-piece by *Dan. da Volterra* (?), Baptism of Christ:

in the 4th an Entombment by a Dutch master; the 3rd was painted by pupils of Perugino; in the 2nd are sculptures of the school of Bernini; in the 1st St. Francis by *G. de' Vecchi*. By the wall near the door, the tomb of St. Julian, archbp. of Ragusa, by *G. A. Dosio*, 1510.

In the court of the monastery rises the *Tempietto, a small circular structure with 16 Doric columns, erected in 1502 from *Bramante's* designs, on the spot where the cross of St. Peter is supposed to have stood. The interior contains two chapels and a statue of St. Peter.

The piazza in front of the church (185 ft.) commands a magnificent **view of Rome and the environs, which may be admirably surveyed from this point. The more important places are here enumerated in order from r. to l., except where the contrary is stated. S. the Tiber, crossed by the iron-bridge of the railway to Civita Vecchia; beyond it the extensive basilica of S. Paolo fuori le mura. Then a portion of the city-wall, in front of which the green Monte Testaccio, the cypresses and tombstones of the Protestant burial-ground, and the pyramid of Cestius. Nearer rises the Aventine, its base washed by the Tiber (not at this point visible), with the three churches of S. Maria del Priorato, S. Alessio and S. Sabina. Beyond, the Alban Mts. with M. Cavo on the r. and Frascati l. (comp. p. 106); in the foreground on this side of the river is the hospital of S. Michele, and in the immediate vicinity the extensive new tobacco-manufactory. On the Cælius, Villa Mattei and S. Stefano Rotondo, above which, on the extreme spur of the Alban Mts., Colonna; between this and the Sabine Mts. near Palestrina, the more distant Volscian Mts. Then the Palatine with the ruins of the palaces of the emperors and the beautiful cypresses of the former Villa Mills, above which rise the statues on the façade of the Lateran. Next, the Colosseum, the three huge arches of the basilica of Constantine: then the Capitol with the Pal. Caffarelli, the tower of the senatorial palace, a portion of the façade of the Capitoline Museum and the church of Araceli; the two domes and campanile above these belong to S. Maria Maggiore on the Esquiline. Farther on, near the cypresses, the spacious papal palace on the Quirinal, in front of which, near a bright-looking dome, rises Trajan's column; more towards the foreground the church del Gesù with its dome, beyond which is the M. Gennaro. Then on the Pincio, the most N. of the Roman hills, the bright Villa Medici, and to the r. of it S. Trinità de' Monti, rising with its two towers above the Piazza di Spagna; then the Villa Ludovisi. Nearer, not far from the Tiber, rises Pal. Farnese with the open loggia. To the r. of it the spiral tower of the Sapienza, farther r. a portion of the dome of the Pantheon, concealed by the dome-church of S. Andrea della Valle, to the r. of which the column of M. Aurelius in the Piazza Colonna is visible. Again to the l. on the height is the

Passeggiata of the Pincio with the two dome-churches of the Piazza del Popolo. Then near the river the Chiesa Nuova, beyond it the indented ridge of Soracte. On this side of the Tiber the castle of S. Angelo, beyond it the heights of Baccano. By the chainbridge stands S. Giovanni de' Fiorentini. Farther off, M. Mario with the Villa Mellini; finally at the extreme angle to the l. rises the dome of St. Peter's. In Trastevere, at the base of the hill, is situated the church of S. Maria in Trastevere, the bright campanile to the l. of which belongs to S. Cecilia.

Descending from S. Pietro in Montorio in a straight direction, passing through the Vicolo della Frusta on the r., and entering the Via de' Fenili on the l., the traveller reaches the *Piazza di S. Maria* (p. 232).

The street which continues to ascend the hill leads in 2 min. to the *Acqua Paola (Piazza del Fontanone)*. The steep road (formerly for carriages, now only used by foot-passengers) leads from the foot of the hill, passing several mills driven by the aqueduct, which it then reaches to the l. (5 min.).

This aqueduct is the ancient *Aqua Trajana*, 35 M. in length, supplied by the Lago di Bracciano (p. 300). It had fallen to decay, but was restored by Fontana and Maderno in 1611 under Paul V., who caused the great fountain to be decorated with the divided columns from the temple of Minerva in Trajan's forum; the massive basin was added under Innocent XII. The view is much more obstructed by the surrounding buildings than that from S. Pietro below, but is worthy of notice on account of the various objects more distinctly seen hence (thus the Pantheon).

The main road, continuing to ascend, reaches after 5 min. the *Porta di S. Pancrazio*, on the summit of the Janiculus, adjacent to the ancient *Porta Aurelia*. It was taken by storm by the French under Oudinot in 1849, and renewed in 1857 by Pius IX. The surrounding walls and gardeners' dwellings had suffered serious damage on that occasion. In a straight direction the entrance to the Villa Pamfili (see below) is reached hence in 3 min.

From this gate to the Porta Portese (p. 234; vice versâ not recommended) is a pleasant walk of $1/2$ hr. The walls, restored in 1849, are skirted on the exterior for 12 min., then a descent, and a crescent is reached, affording a charming *view of the Campagna and the deserted S. quarters of the city. From a second crescent lower down the view extends over the modern city as far as the Pincio. The road leads hence to the gate in 10 min.

The *Villa Doria Pamfili (Pl. II, 9), accessible on Mondays and Fridays to pedestrians and *two-horse* carriages (5 soldi as the grounds are quitted; carriages more in proportion), is situated 3 min. walk from the Porta S. Pancrazio on the summit of the

Janiculus, commanding an extensive and uninterrupted prospect. The undulating grounds were skilfully laid out by *Algardi*, by order of Prince Camillo Pamfili, nephew of Innocent X. The present proprietor is Prince Doria. This is the most extensive and delightful of the Roman villas, and is termed by the Italians *Belrespiro*. Considerable damage was occasioned by the siege of 1849.

From the entrance the carriage-road passes under a triumphal arch and leads in 8 min. to the entrance of the Casino. Here to the r. is a terrace affording a beautiful *view of (r.) the Campagna, l. M. Mario and St. Peter's, between which Soracte bounds the horizon.

Visitors ring at the door to the l. (1/2 l. on leaving) in order to obtain access to the * *Casino* (built by *Algardi*). The external walls are adorned with reliefs (some of them ancient) and statues.

The vestibule contains several fine female statues. In the rooms a few antiques: in the 1st, r. Cybele, riding on a lion; in the 3rd a female statue, in style resembling the Æthra (or Penelope or Electra) in the Villa Ludovisi. The balcony of this room affords a pleasant survey of the flower-garden. In the circular billiard-room the statue of an Amazon etc.

The rooms of the 1st floor contain views of Venice by *Heintius*, of the 17th cent. The staircase ascends to the platform of the villa, where a fine *panorama is enjoyed of the grounds and environs. The sea is said to be visible in clear weather.

From the Casino the visitor proceeds to inspect the * *Columbaria* (r., among the trees), discovered in 1838, and situated on the ancient *Via Aurelia*. One of them is well-preserved and contains some interesting painting.

The stair by the Casino descends to the flower-garden, where the camellias are especially fine; permission to visit it must be obtained of the Principe.

The road by which the Casino has been reached turns to the l. skirting a meadow, carpeted in spring with anemones. In its centre stands an ara, with representations of the gods and Ant. Pius sacrificing to the Penates. After 5 min., where it inclines to the r., a beautiful *view is obtained of the Alban Mts. and the Campagna; it then proceeds in numerous windings, at first skirting a grove of pines, to a pond with swans (10 min.), and along the bank to the fountain by which it is supplied (5 min.). The Casino may hence be regained either by the direct footpath or by the carriage-road, which in 4 min. leads to the hot-houses (r.) and the pheasantry (l.) containing beautiful silver-pheasants. On the road-side (l.), 50 paces farther, a monument was erected in 1851 by Prince Doria to the memory of the French who fell and were interred here.

The island in the Tiber *(Isola Tiberina* or *di S. Bartolommeo)* was once traversed by the *Pons Sublicius*, the most ancient means of communication between Rome and its suburb on the Janiculus. At the present day it is crossed from the Piazza Montanara (p. 167) by the *Ponte de' Quattro Capi* (Pl. II, 17), so named from the four-headed figures on the balustrades, constructed B. C. 62 by L. Fabricius, as the inscription records. Pleasing view.

Immediately to the r. on the island is the church of *S. Giovanni Colabita* (Pl. II, 17), appertaining to the Brothers of Charity, as well as the neighbouring monastery and hospital. Farther on, to the l. in the small piazza, perhaps occupying the site of an ancient temple of Æsculapius, is situated the church of **S. Bartolommeo** (Pl. II. 18), erected about the year 1000 by the Emperor Otho III. in honour of St. Adalbert of Gnesen, and erroneously named S. Bartolommeo. The emperor had desired the Beneventans to send to him the relics of that saint, but received those of St. Paulinus of Nola in their stead. The present church is uninteresting; façade by *Lunghi* in 1625. The interior contains 14 ancient columns; in the choir are remains of an early mosaic; in the centre of the steps leading to the presbyterium is the mouth of a former fountain of the 12th cent., of the sculptures on which the figure of Christ with a book in the hand is still distinguished.

In the small garden of the monastery (entrance to the r. by the church) a portion of the ancient enclosure of travertine is seen, which imparted the appearance of a ship to the island. An obelisk represented the mast. The figure of a snake hewn on the bow of the ship is a reminiscence of the story that the Romans, when sorely afflicted by the plague, sent for Æsculapius from Epidaurus B. C. 293, and that a snake, a reptile sacred to the god, concealed itself in the vessel and escaped on reaching the harbour to this island, which was dedicated to Æsculapius in consequence.

The island is connected with Trastevere by the ancient *Pons Cestius (Gratianus)*, now **Ponte S. Bartolommeo** (Pl. II, 18), erected under Augustus, and, according to the lengthy inscription, restored by the Emperors Valentinian and Gratian. Pleasing view to the l. The establishment of the wooden mills in the river in the direction of Ponte Sisto dates from the siege of Belisarius, when the Goths destroyed the aqueducts, thus rendering the mills on the Janiculus useless. In a straight direction the Via della Longara leads to the vicinity of the

Ponte Rotto (Pl. II, 18), probably the ancient *Pons Æmilius*, built B. C. 181, which after frequent destruction from inundations was not again restored after 1554. A chain-bridge (1 soldo) now supplies the place of the missing arches.

From this point to the l. to S. Cecilia (see p. 233). To the r. the traveller follows the *Via della Lungarina* and its straight prolongation the *Via della Lungaretta*. After 6 min. a small piazza is reached, to the l. in which is the side-entrance to **S. Crisogono**, said to have been founded by Sylvester I., frequently restored (for the last time in 1626). It is interesting on account of its ancient columns, especially the two of porphyry supporting the triumphal arch, which are the largest in Rome. The ceiling-paintings of the transept are by *Arpino*. In 1866 and 67 an *excubitorium* of the VII. cohort of the *vigiles* (a station of the Roman firemen) was excavated near the Piazza di S. Crisogono; a small court-yard with a well in the centre and several rooms are visible. On the walls are numerous inscriptions of the 3rd cent.

Immediately beyond the church in the principal street is a gaudily-painted building, the hospital (for cutaneous diseases) of *S. Gallicano*.

After 9 min. the *Piazza di S. Maria* is reached, with a fountain and the church of

*S. Maria in Trastevere (Pl. II, 12), said to have been founded by Calixtus I. under Alex. Severus, on the spot where a spring of oil miraculously welled forth at the time of the birth of Christ. It is mentioned for the first time in 449, was re-erected by Innocent II. (1140), and consecrated by Innocent III. in 1198. The present portico was constructed by *C. Fontana* under Clement XI. in 1702. The edifice is now undergoing repair. In front are mosaics of Mary and the Child, on either side the small figure of a bishop (Innocent II. and Eugene III.) and 10 virgins, eight of whom have burning lamps and crowns, two are not thus provided, a work of the 12th, greatly restored in the 14th cent. The portico contains the remains of two Annunciations, one stated to be by *Cavallini*, and numerous inscriptions; by the lateral wall on the r. is a Christian sarcophagus with representation of Jonah.

The interior possesses 22 ancient columns of unequal sizes, some of the Ionic capitals of which are decorated with heathen gods, as Jupiter, Harpocrates with his finger on his mouth. The ceiling, decorated with richly-gilded stucco by *Domenichino*. The oil-painting on copper in the centre, a Madonna surrounded by angels, is by the same master. The chapels contain little to detain the traveller. On the last pillar (r.) of the nave [are two ancient mosaics of skilful workmanship, one of which represents aquatic birds. The transept lies 7 steps higher; by the latter an inscription *Fons olei*, indicating the alleged site of the spring of oil. In the transept on the l. are the tombs of two Armelini and an ancient Christian relief of the annunciation to the shepherds. Opposite is an altar erected to St. Philip and St. James by Card. Philip of Alençon, r. his tomb (d. 1397); l. tomb of Card. Stefaneschi (d. 1417) with recumbent statue by *Paolo Romano*. The mosaics of the arch, restored by *Camuccini*, are in the form of a cross: Alpha and Omega, below the symbols of the Evangelists; r. and l. Isaiah and Jeremiah. On the vaulting Christ and the Virgin on thrones, l. St. Calixtus, St. Lawrence, Innocent II., r. St. Peter, St. Cornelius, Julius, Calepodius; beneath, the 13 lambs and representations from the life of Mary, after Vasari by *Cavallini*; in the centre of the wall a mosaic bust of Mary with St. Peter, St. Paul and the donor Stefaneschi.

The Via del Cimiterio and Via de' Fenili lead hence direct to S. Pietro in Montorio (p. 227). The *Via di S. Francesco* descends to the l. to the piazza of that name, in which the church and monastery of *S. Francesco a Ripa* are situated. St. Francis resided in the latter for some time. The church was built in 1231, modernized in the 17th cent. The last chapel on the l. contains the recumbent statue of St. Lodovica Albertoni by *Bernini*.

From the Ponte Rotto the *Via de' Vascellari* to the l., and then the *Via di S. Cecilia* to the r. lead to

S. Cecilia in Trastevere (Pl. II, 15), originally the dwelling-house of the saint, founded by Paschalis I., entirely reconstructed by Card. Franc. Acquaviva in 1725. It is approached by a spacious anterior court, adorned with an ancient vase, and a portico resting on 4 columns of African marble and red granite.

The columns which formerly supported the nave were in 1822 replaced by buttresses. The beautiful high-altar of pavonazzetto was constructed by *Arnolfo di Lapo* in 1283; adjacent is an ancient candelabrum for the Easter-candle; beneath the high-altar the *statue of the martyred S. Cecilia by *Stef. Maderno*. The tribune contains ancient *mosaics (9th cent.): the Saviour on a throne with the Gospel, r. St. Paul, St. Agatha and Paschalis; l. St. Peter, St. Cecilia and her husband St. Valerianus. In the 1st Chapel on the r. an ancient picture of Christ on the Cross; the 2nd Chapel, somewhat receding from the church, is said to have been the bath-room of St. Cecilia, the pipes of which are still seen in the wall. In the last chapel on the r. of the altar: Madonna with Saints, a relief of the 15th cent.; on the r. wall are preserved the remains of mosaics of the 12th cent. detached from the façade of the church. Descent to the lower church by the tribune. The neighbouring convent belongs to Benedictine nuns.

In the direction of the gate, the next transverse street to the r. leads to *S. Maria dell' Orto*, designed by G. Romano in 1512; façade 1762. The interior is overladen with stucco and gilding. Adjacent is the new tobacco-manufactory of the government, erected in 1763. The street to the l. leads to S. Francesco.

The transverse street to the l. from S. Cecilia leads to the *Ripa Grande* with the harbour for the river-vessels; pleasing view of the Marmorata and Aventine. To the r. stands the extensive **Ospizio di S. Michele**, founded in 1689 by Tommaso Odescalchi. After his death it was extended by Innocent XII. and combined with other establishments, now comprising a work-house, reformatory, house of correction, and hospice for the poor. Invalids of both sexes are here provided for, other indigent persons are furnished with work. Poor and orphaned children are instructed in various trades and arts; boys are afterwards discharged with a donation of 30, girls with 100, and if they become nuns with 200 scudi. The establishment possesses several churches, spacious work-rooms and apartments for the sick; the revenues exceed 50,000 scudi annually.

At the end of the Ripa Grande is the *Dogana*, passing which (on the r.) the traveller reaches the *Porta Portese*, whence the road to Porto (p. 304) leaves the town.

The Vatican.

This, the most extensive palace in the world, was originally a dwelling-house for the popes, erected by Symmachus near the anterior court of the old church of St. Peter, and subsequently gradually extended. Charlemagne when in Rome is believed to have resided here. This building having fallen to decay during the tumults of the following centuries, Eugene III. erected a palace near St. Peter's, which was greatly enlarged by Nicholas III. The Vatican did not, however, become the usual residence of the popes until after their return from Avignon, when the Lateran was deserted. After the death of Gregory XI. the first conclave was held in the Vatican in 1378, which resulted in the schism. In 1410 John XXIII. constructed the covered passage to the castle of S. Angelo. In 1450 Nicholas V., in order to elevate the Vatican to the rank of the greatest of all palaces, determined to unite in it all the government-offices and residences of the cardinals. The small portion completed by him, afterwards occupied by Alexander VI. and named Tor di Borgia, was extended by subsequent popes. In 1473 the *Sixtine Chapel* was erected by Sixtus IV., and about 1490 the *Belvedere* or garden-house by Innocent VIII. Bramante, under Julius II., united the latter with the palace by means of a great court, which under Sixtus was divided by the erection of the library into two parts, the anterior court and the Giardino della Pigna. The *Loggie* round the Cortile di S. Damaso were also constructed by Bramante. In 1534 Paul III. founded the *Pauline Chapel*, Sixtus V. the *Library* and the present residence of the popes, which last was completed by Clement VIII. (1592—1605). Urban VIII. erected the *Scala Regia* from Bernini's design, Pius VII. the *Braccio Nuovo* for the sculptures, Gregory XVI. the *Etruscan Museum*, and Pius IX. has closed the fourth side of the Cortile di S. Damaso by covering and reconstructing the great staircase which leads from the arcades of the piazza into the court. Thus the palace now possesses 20 courts, and is said to comprise 11.000 halls, chapels, saloons and private apartments.

The works of art in the Vatican are accessible daily, except on Sundays and high festivals; on Mondays 12—3 o'clock gratis, with the exception of the picture-gallery which is then closed. On other days all the collections may be visited 9—3 o'clock ($1/_2$ l., frequent visitors 5 soldi). On Holy Thursday all the collections are open to the public during the whole day. Artists and scientific men who desire to sketch or take notes in the museums and library must address a written request for permission to the maggiordomo (best through the medium of their consul or ambassador) (p. 89).

Those who desire to see the statues of the Vatican (or Capitol) by *torch-light may apply at M. Spithœver's (see p. 88), where parties are formed for this purpose (18—20 scudi for 13 pers.).

The principal approach to the Vatican is at the extremity of the r. colonnade of the Piazza of St. Peter, ascending immediately beyond the Swiss guard by the staircase, originally open, but

The Vatican. ROME. *Sala Regia.* 235

covered by Pius IX. This leads to the *Cortile di S. Damaso*, a court which derives its appellation from the fountain of St. Damasus erected by Innocent X. It is enclosed on three sides by the Loggie of *Bramante*, formerly open, but now closed with windows for the protection of the frescoes. On the r. is the wing occupied by the Pope; on the l. a door with the inscription *Adito alla Biblioteca ed al Museo* leads to the stair which ascends to the Loggie of Giov. da Udine (extensively but judiciously retouched) on the first floor, and those of Raphael on the second (p. 237). The first door to the l. in the loggie of the first floor leads to the Sala Ducale and the Sistina. By the door at the extremity facing the visitor the Galleria Lapidaria (p. 243) and the Museum of Statues (p. 242) are entered.

Sala Ducale. Sala Regia. **Cappella Sistina. Cappella Paolina.

The Sala Ducale, constructed by *Bernini*, is decorated on the ceiling with frescoes, and beneath them with landscapes by *Brill*. The opposite door leads to the

Sala Regia. [This hall forms the vestibule of the Sixtine Chapel, and on the occasion of ecclesiastical festivals in the latter is approached by the *Scala Regia*, the magnificent staircase ascending at the end of the corridor to which the arcades of the Piazza of St. Peter lead to the r. (by the equestrian statue of Constantine, by Bernini). The Scala was constructed by *Ant. da San Gallo*, and restored by *Bernini* under Alexander VII. The round vaulting is supported by Roman columns.] The Sala Regia, originally destined for the reception of the ambassadors of foreign powers, was designed by *Ant. da Sangallo;* cornicings of the ceiling by *Perino del Vaga*, over the doors by *Dan. da Volterra*.

The mediocre frescoes of *Vasari, Salviati* and the *Zuccari*, according to the titles inscribed beneath, represent (on the window-wall, r.) scenes from the Night of St. Bartholomew (the inscription *Strages Hugenottorum* etc., which was once under them, has been obliterated). On the wall opposite the entrance (in which the door leads to the Sixtine), the alliance of the Spanish and Venetians with Paul V., battle of Lepanto in 1571; on the narrow wall, Gregory VII. acquitting Henry VI. (door to the Pauline), conquest of Tunis; on the entrance-wall, Gregory XI. returning from Avignon, Alex. III. absolving Fred. Barbarossa.

The **Sixtine Chapel was erected under Sixtus IV. by *Baccio Pintelli* in 1473: length 125 ft., width 43 ft., 16 windows on each side above. Beautifully decorated marble screens enclose the space allotted to religious solemnities. The lower part of the walls was formerly on festive occasions hung with Raphael's tapestry; the upper part (with the exception of the wall of the altar) is decorated with interesting frescoes by Florentine masters of the 15th cent.

They represent parallel scenes from the life of Christ (r.) and Moses (l.), beginning at the altar and meeting on the entrance-wall. Left: 1. (by the altar) Moses with his wife Zipporah journeying to Egypt, Zipporah circumcises her son, attributed to *Luca Signorelli*; 2. Moses kills the Egyptian, drives the shepherds from the well, kneels before the burning bush, *Sandro Botticelli*; 3. Pharaoh's destruction in the Red Sea, *Cosimo Rosselli*; 4. Moses receives the Law on Mt. Sinai, Adoration of the calf, by the same; 5. Destruction of the company of Korah and that of the sons of Aaron, *S. Botticelli*; 6. Death of Moses, *L. Signorelli*. Adjoining the latter, on the entrance-wall: Contest of the Archangel Michael for the body of Moses, by *Salviati*, now entirely repainted. Right: 1. Baptism of Christ, *Perugino*; 2. Christ's Temptation, *S. Botticelli*; *3. Vocation of Peter and Andrew, *Dom. Ghirlandajo*; 4. Sermon on the Mount, Cure of the lepers, *C. Rosselli*. Then on the entrance-wall: Resurrection of Christ, originally by *D. Ghirlandajo*, renewed by *Arrigo Fiamingo*. — On the pillars between the windows 28 popes by *S. Botticelli*, not easily distinguishable.

The **Ceiling**, decorated with perhaps the most magnificent example of the pictorial art ever produced, was painted by *Mich. Angelo* in 22 months (1508—11). The fundamental idea of the work is the preparation of the world for the Advent of Christ. In the centre of the ceiling are seen the Creation, Fall and Deluge with the sacrifice and mockery of Noah; around are the figures of the prophets and sibyls, who predicted and proclaimed the Messiah's Advent, and the ancestors of Christ who expected him. These the principal pictures are combined by a felicitous architectural arrangement so as to form an exquisite whole, enlivened moreover by numerous accessory figures, relief-medallions, children as bearers of entablature etc., and worthy of the most minute and repeated inspection. In the centre of the ceiling (seen from the altar) are the following 9 sections: 1. God the Father separates light from darkness; 2. Creation of the sun and moon; 3. Separation of the land from the sea; 4. Adam inspired with life; 5. Creation of Eve, who turns towards the Lord in an attitude of adoration; 6. The Fall and Banishment from Paradise; 7. Noah's thankoffering after the deluge; 8. The Deluge (this [was painted by Mich. Angelo first, and, as it afterwards appeared, with figures of too small proportions); 9. Noah's intoxication and the derision of his sons.

On the lower part of the vaulting are the **Prophets and Sibyls** in earnest contemplation, surrounded by angels and genii.

To the l. of the altar: 1. Jeremiah, in a profound revery; 2. Persian Sibyl, writing; 3. Ezekiel with half-opened scroll; 4. Erythræan Sibyl, sitting by an open book; 5. Joel, reading a scroll; 6. (over the door) Zacharias, turning the leaves of a book; 7. Delphian Sibyl, with open scroll; 8. Isaiah, his arm resting on a book, absorbed by divine inspiration; 9. Cumæan Sibyl, opening a book; 10. Daniel, writing; 11. Libyan Sibyl, grasping an open book; 12. (above the Last Judgment) Jonah sitting beneath the gourd.

In the pointed arches and lunettes of the vaulting are the ancestors of the Saviour in calm expectation. In the 4 corner-arches: on the altar-wall, r. the Israelites in the wilderness with the brazen serpent, l. king Artaxerxes, Esther and Haman. On the entrance-wall, l. David and Goliath, r. Judith. Nearly 30 years later than this ceiling Michael Angelo painted on the altar-wall the **Last Judgment**, 60 ft. in width, completed under Paul III. in 1541. Careful and protracted study alone will enable the spectator to appreciate the details of this vast composition, which is unfortunately blackened by the smoke of centuries, unfavourably lighted and partially concealed. To penetrate into the religious views and artistic designs of the talented master is a still more arduous task. On the right of the figure of Christ as Judge hover the saints drawn back by devils and supported by angels, on his left the sinners in vain strive to ascend; above are two groups of angels with the Cross, the column at which Christ was scourged, and the other instruments of his sufferings; in the centre Christ and the Virgin, surrounded by apostles and saints; beneath the rising dead is hell, according to Dante's conception, with the boatman Charon and the judge Minos, whose face is a portrait of Biagio of Cesena, master of the ceremonies of Paul III., who had censured the picture on account of the nudity of the figures. Paul IV., who contemplated the destruction of the picture on this account, was persuaded to cause some of the figures to be partially draped by *Dan. da Volterra.* Clement XII. caused this process to be extended to the other figures by *Stef. Pozzi*, whereby, as may be imagined, the picture was far from being improved.

Most of the solemnities in which the Pope participates in person, especially those of the *Holy Week*, take place in the Sixtine Chapel (see p. 91).

From the Sala Regia a door to the l. enters the **Pauline Chapel**, designed in 1540 by *Antonio da Sangallo*, and named after Paul III., who was then on the throne. Here also are two frescoes painted by *Michael Angelo* when at a very advanced age: l. the Conversion of St. Paul, r. the Crucifixion of St. Peter; the other pictures are by *Sabbatini* and *F. Zuccaro*, the statues in the corners by *P. Bresciano*. The chapel is employed on the first Sunday in Advent for the exposition of the host during 40 hrs., when, as well as on Holy Thursday, it is brilliantly illuminated.

Raphael's **Loggie and ***Stanze.* **Cappella Niccolina (di S. Lorenzo).*

The same staircase which ascends to the loggie of the first floor also leads to the **Loggie of Raphael** on the second, but this approach can be used on Mondays only. On other days the court below is crossed, a door entered on the l. of the fountain, and beyond the door of the mosaic-manufactory the stair is ascended in a straight direction. On the first floor the Museum or the Sixtine may also be reached to the r.; on the second floor a bell must be rung in order to procure admission to Raphael's Loggie and Stanze ("Ingresso alle Sale e Loggie di Raffaele"); the third story contains the picture-gallery.

The **second story of the loggie, protected since 1813 by glass-windows, was adorned from Raphael's designs and under his supervision by *Giulio Romano* and *Giovanni da Udine.* The decorations consist of stucco-work (in which the influence of the specimens of this work found shortly before in the Thermæ of Titus is recognisable), of ornamental painting, and of pictures on the vaulting composed by Raphael. (The first ceiling was painted by *G. Romano*, the others by other pupils of Raphael, *Franc. Penni*, *Perino del Vaga*, *Polid. da Caravaggio* etc.) Each of the 13 sections of the vaulting contains 4 quadrangular frescoes, which are together known as "*Raphael's Bible*", and display a rare fertility of invention and gracefulness of treatment.

The representations of the 12 first vaults are from the Old, those of the 13th from the New Testament. The subjects (beginning to the r. of the stair) are as follows: I. (over the door) 1. Separation of light from darkness; 2. Separation of land from sea; 3. Creation of the sun and moon; 4. Creation of the animals. II. 1. Creation of Eve; 1. The Fall; 2. Banishment from Paradise; 3. Adam and Eve working. III. 1. Noah building the ark: 2. Deluge; 3. Egress from the ark; 4. Noah's sacrifice. IV. 1. Abraham and Melchisedek; 3. God promises Abraham posterity; 2. Abraham and the three angels; 4. Lot's flight from Sodom. V. 1. God appears to Isaac; 3. Abimelech sees Isaac caressing Rebecca; 2. Isaac blesses Jacob; 4. Esau and Isaac. VI. 1. Jacob's vision of the ladder; 2. Jacob and Rachel at the well; ·3. Jacob upbraids Laban for having given him Leah: 4. Jacob on his journey. VII. 1. Joseph relates his dream to his brethren; 2. Joseph is sold; 3. Joseph and Potiphar's wife; 4. Joseph interprets Pharaoh's dream. VIII. 1. Finding of Moses; 2. Moses at the burning bush; 3. Destruction of Pharaoh in the Red Sea; 4. Moses strikes the rock for water. IX. 1. Moses receiving the tables of the Law; 2. Adoration of the golden calf, Moses breaks the tables; 3. Moses kneels before the pillar of cloud: 4. Moses shows the tables of the Law to the people. X. 1. The Israelites crossing the Jordan; 2. Fall of Jericho; 3. Josuah bids the sun stand still during the battle with the Ammonites; 4. Joshua and Eleazar distribute Palestine among the 12 tribes. XI. 1. Samuel anoints David; 2. David and Goliath; 4. David's triumph over the Syrians; 3. David sees Bathsheba. XII. 1. Zadok anoints Solomon; 2. Solomon's Judgment; 4. The Queen of Sheba; 3. Building of the Temple. XIII. 1. Adoration of the shepherds; 2. The wise men from the East; 3. Baptism of Christ; 4. Last Supper. — Of the stucco-decorations the charming small reliefs in the arches of the windows of the first section may be regarded as a good specimen. Here to the l. above, Raphael is first perceived, sitting and drawing, beneath is a grinder of the colours. Lower down a number of the pupils busied in executing the master's designs, and below them Fama who proclaims the celebrity of the work. On the r. an old bricklayer is seen at work, and a similar figure in the r. curve of the 2nd window, both apparently portraits. The whole taken collectively affords a charming picture of the life and habits of the artists during the execution of the work. — The two other arcades of this story, decorated in stucco by *Marco da Faenza* and *Paul Schor*, and painted by artists of the 16th and 17th centuries, are far inferior to these loggie.

**Stanze of Raphael. By an ante-chamber to the l. at the extremity of Raphael's Loggie is the entrance to the saloon and three apartments *(stanze)* which were decorated with frescoes by *Raphael* under Julius II. and Leo X. (1508—1520). For each of the paintings the master received 1200 ducats. When entered from the loggie the order is as follows: Sala di Constantino, Stanza d'Eliodoro, Camera della Segnatura, Stanza dell' Incendio. They were seriously injured during the plundering of Rome in 1527, but were restored by Carlo Maratta under Clement XI. They are here enumerated chronologically.

I. *Stanza della Segnatura*, so named from a judicial assembly of that designation which is held here. Its decoration was undertaken at the instance of Julius II. by Raphael in 1508, at the age of 25, and completed in 1511. The sections of the vaulting of the apartment had already been arranged by *Sodoma*. On the 4 circular and quadrangular spaces Raphael painted allegorical figures and Biblical and mythological scenes, which in connection with the paintings in the large lunettes are symbolical of the four principal spheres of intellectual life.

I. **Ceiling-paintings.** 1. *Theology (divinarum rerum notitia)*, a figure among clouds, in the left hand a book, with the right pointing downwards to the heavenly vision in the Disputa beneath; adjacent, the Fall of man; 2. *Poetry (numine afflatur)*, crowned with laurels, seated on a marble throne with book and lyre; adjoining it, the Flaying of Marsyas; 3. *Philosophy (causarum cognitio)*, with diadem, two books (natural and moral science) and a robe emblematical of the four elements; adjoining it, the Study of the heavenly bodies; 4. *Justice (jus suum unicuique tribuens)*, with crown, sword and balance; adjacent, Solomon's Judgment.

II. **Frescoes on the walls.** Beneath Theology: 1. The *Disputa*, so-called from the picture having been regarded as the representation of a dispute respecting the sacrament (Disputa del Sagramento). It is divided into two sections: in the centre of the upper, Christ between Mary and John the Bapt., above him a glory of angels, and God the Father imparting a blessing with his right hand; beneath Christ the dove, surrounded by 4 small angels who hold the 4 Gospels. Then on either side of Christ: l. St. Peter, Adam, St. John, David, St. Stephen and a saint half concealed by a cloud; r. St. Paul, Abraham, St. James, Moses, St. Lawrence. St. George; above both series hover three angels. Beneath, to the r. of the altar on which the monstrance is placed: Petrus Lombardus (?) with raised right hand, turning towards St. Ambrose who is seated beside him and looking upwards; in the background between the two a white-robed monk. Farther to the r. is seated St. Augustine, dictating to a youth, behind him a black monk, perhaps Thomas Aquinas. Then Pope Anacletus with the martyr's palm; Card. Bonaventura, reading. Adjacent, more towards the front, Pope Innocent III., in the background Dante; in the foreground an anciently attired figure of unknown import; the black-hooded monk, to the r. of Dante in the background, is Savonarola. The import of most of the figures on the l. of the altar is less apparent: first is perceived a white-robed monk (St. Bernhard?), turning to the sitting St. Jerome with the lion; at his feet lies his translation of the Bible and cardinal's hat; beside him sits Gregory I. The remaining figures cannot now be interpreted: the Dominican to the l. at the extremity has been thought to represent Fiesole, the old man with a book, leaning on the balustrade, Bramante.

In the socle beneath the picture (added by *Perino del Vaga* under Paul III.), from l. to r.: Heathen sacrifice; St. Augustine finding a child attempting to exhaust the sea; the Cumæan Sibyl showing the Madonna to Augustus; allegorical figure of the apprehension of divine things.

Beneath Poetry: 2. The *Parnassus* (r. of the Disputa). In the centre above, Apollo in a grove of laurels, with a violin (perhaps in honour of Giac. Sansecondo, a celebrated violinist of that period), and the Muses. The interpretation of the poets who environ this group is somewhat uncertain: l. Homer, Dante, Virgil, beneath them the sitting female figure of Sappho, beside her Petrarch and perhaps Corinna, Alcæus and Anacreon; r. Tebaldeo (?), Boccaccio, the fifth Sannazaro, in front the seated figure of Pindar (?), and Horace (?) approaching. Under these in grisaille: l. Alexander causes the poems of Homer to be placed in the grave of Achilles; r. Augustus prevents the burning of Virgil's Æneid.

Beneath Philosophy: 3. The so-called *School of Athens*, a representation of the different branches and upholders of ancient philosophy, but the meaning of the figures taken singly is in many cases doubtful. The scene is a beautiful vaulted hall (said to have been designed by Bramante); in front of it a stage approached by steps serves to unite the expressive and life-like groups of which the assembly is composed. The niches in front of the building contain statues of Apollo and Minerva. In the centre of the foreground are the two chief representatives of ancient philosophy: l. Plato with upraised right hand, in his left his Timæus; r. Aristotle, holding his Ethics and pointing forwards. Around them are grouped a circle of attentive hearers. The group farther l. shows Socrates conversing with his pupils, among whom is a young warrior, probably Alcibiades. Lying on the steps in the centre is Diogenes; the groups to the r. on the platform and steps are perhaps the advocates of the Epicurean and Sceptic doctrines. The old man seated in the group to the l. in the foreground, showing a boy a tablet with the principles of musical rythm, is Pythagoras; looking over his book is the Oriental Averroes (?); seated beside him to the l. with ink and pen, Empedocles; r. Anaxagoras, turning towards him; the white-robed youth behind him bears the features of Francesco della Rovere, Duke of Urbino. The last sitting figure on the r. in this group is supposed to represent Heraclitus; it is wanting in the cartoon at Milan. The wreathed figure l. of Empedocles is said to be Democritus. In the group r., in the foreground, the figure stooping to the earth and engaged in geometrical demonstration is regarded as Archimedes (bearing the features of Bramante); the youth standing with half-raised hands is said to be the portrait of Federigo II. of Mantua. The bearded man with a globe, farther r., is Zoroaster; another, crowned and also with a globe, is Ptolemæus. The two last heads to the r. in the foreground are portraits of Raphael and his master Perugino.

In the socle beneath the picture, in different shades of brown, by *Perino del Vaga* (from l. to r.): Allegorical figure of Philosophy; Magicians conversing about the heavenly bodies; Siege of Syracuse; Death of Archimedes.

Beneath Justice: 4. Over the window the three cardinal virtues: Prudence with double visage looking to the future and the past, r. Moderation, l. Strength. Beneath, at the sides of the window, the administration of ecclesiastical and secular law; r. Gregory IX. (with the features of Julius II.) presenting the Decretals to a jurist (surrounded by numerous portraits; to the l. in front Card. de Medicis, afterwards Leo X.). In the socle beneath (by *Perino del Vaga*): Moses brings the tables of the Law to the Israelites; l. Justinian entrusts the Roman Code to Tribonian. In the socle beneath: Solon's address to the Athenian people (?).

The door adjoining the "School of Athens" leads to the following apartment, which derives its appellation from one of the pictures it contains.

II. *Stanza d'Eliodoro*, painted in 1511—1514, represents the triumph and divine protection of the church, with reference to the age of the warlike Julius II. and the elevation of Leo X. On the ceiling 4 paintings from the old Covenant: Jehovah appears to Noah, Jacob's Vision, Moses at the burning bush, Sacrifice of Isaac. On the walls 4 large paintings:

1. Beneath Moses at the burning bush: *Miraculous Expulsion of Heliodorus* from the Temple at Jerusalem by a heavenly horseman (Maccab. II, 3), being an allusion to the deliverance of the States of the Church from their enemies. On the right Heliodorus lies on the ground; one of his companions attempts to defend himself, a second shouts, a third strives to secure his booty; in the background the high-priest Onias praying; l. in the foreground women and children, Pope Julius II. on his throne (the hindmost of the two chair-bearers is the celebrated engraver Marcantonio Raimondi). The entire composition is remarkable for its admirable vigour of expression.

2. Beneath the Sacrifice of Isaac: *The Mass of Bolsena:* an unbelieving priest is convinced of the doctrine of transubstantiation by the bleeding host, a miracle said to have taken place at Bolsena in 1263; beneath are women and children; opposite the priest, Julius II. kneels with calm equanimity; the wrathful cardinal is Riario (founder of the Cancelleria). This painting, an allusion to the conviction of doubters in the infallibility of the Church, is probably the most perfect of Raphael's frescoes with respect to execution.

3. Under Noah: *Attila warded off from Rome by Leo I.*, in allusion to the expulsion of the French from Italy after the battle of Novara in 1513. The pope with the features of Leo X. is seated on a white mule, around him cardinals and attendants on horseback, above him St. Peter and St. Paul

The Vatican.   ROME.   *Raphael's Stanze.*   241

enveloped in a brilliant light and distinctly beheld by Attila and his Huns, struck with terror at the apparition. To the r. of this:
4. Beneath Jacob's Vision: *The Liberation of Peter*, in three sections. Over the window Peter in the dungeon sleeping between the watchmen and awakened by the angel; r. he is conducted away, l. the watchmen awake. On the socle under the pictures, eleven Caryatides and four statues are painted in grisaille. They are symbolical of a life of peace, and distinctly characterized by the inventive fertility of Raphael, notwithstanding considerable restoration. The paintings in different shades of brown between these, of similar import with the large figures, have been still more extensively retouched.

These two apartments were painted by Raphael unaided, and his progressive freedom and decision of touch may be distinctly observed. In the two following rooms he painted the conflagration of the Borgo only (with the exception of a few figures on the l.): the other pictures were executed from his designs, those of the first room under his personal supervision, those of the second after his death.

III. *Stanza dell' Incendio*, beyond the Stanza della Segnatura, is entered by the door on the r. adjoining the Disputa. The ceiling-paintings are by *Perugino*, those on the walls, representing scenes from the reigns of Leo III. and Leo IV., were executed in 1517.

Over the window: 1. *Oath of Leo III.*, sworn by him in presence of Charlemagne (with the gold chain, his back turned to the spectator), in order to exculpate himself from the accusations brought against him, by *Perino del Vaga*. R. of this, on the entrance-wall: 4. *Victory of Leo IV. over the Saracens at Ostia*, executed by *Giov. da Udine*. The pope has the features of Leo X., accompanied by Card. Julius de Medici (Clement VII.), Card. Bibiena and others. On the socle beneath: Ferdinand the Catholic, and the Emp. Lothaire. 3. *Incendio del Borgo*, conflagration of the Borgo, whence the name of the room; Leo IV. appears in the background on the loggia of the old church of St. Peter, near which the fire raged, and by his blessing arrests the progress of the flames. In the foreground are admirable lifelike groups of terrified people escaping or praying. Underneath: Godfrey de Bouillon and Aistulf. 4. *Coronation of Charlemagne in the former Church of St. Peter*. Leo III. has the features of Leo X., the emperor those of Francis I. of France. Beneath: Charlemagne.

From this room a door (generally open on Mondays) to the r., near the 4th picture, leads to a saloon beyond, recently painted by *Podesti* by order of Pius IX., to commemorate the institution and promulgation of the new dogma of the immaculate conception of the Virgin.

IV. *Sala di Constantino*. The pictures of this saloon were executed under Clement VII. by *Giulio Romano*, aided by *Franc. Penni* and *Raf. del Colle*. Raphael probably caused the two allegorical figures of Justitia and Comitas to be painted under his own supervision. They are in oil, whilst the others are al fresco. He also left a cartoon of the Battle of Constantine, and a drawing of Constantine's address to his army. The rest of the composition is probably due to G. Romano.

On the long wall: 1. *Battle of Constantine* against Maxentius at Ponte Molle, the emperor advancing victoriously, behind him flags with the cross, Maxentius sinking in the river, flight and defeat on all sides, painted by G. Romano. This fine composition is full of expression and vigour, but the colouring is less successful. On the l. side of the picture Silvester I. between Faith and Religion; r. Urban I. between *Justice and Charity. 2. *Baptism of Constantine* by Silvester I. (with features of Clement VII.) in the baptistery of the Lateran, by Franc. Penni. L. of this: Damasus I. between Prudence and Peace; r. Leo I. between Innocence and Truth. 3. (on the window-wall) *Rome presented by Constantine to Silvester I.*, by Raf. del Colle; 1. Silvester I. with Fortitude, r. Gregory VII. (?) with Power (?). 4. *Constantine's Address* to his warriors respecting the victorious omen of the cross, by G. Romano, who added the dwarf (perhaps Gradasso Berettai of Norcia, dwarf-chamberlain of Card. Hippol. de Medici) and several other figures. On the l. Peter between the Church and Eternity, r. Clement I. between Moderation and *Urbanity. The socles contain scenes from the life of Constantine, from G. Romano's designs. The ceiling (completed under Sixtus V.) bears an allegory of the victory of Christianity over paganism. On the other wall landscapes of Italy with corresponding allegorical figures in the lunettes.

One of the custodians of this saloon, when desired ($1/2$ l.), shows the neighbouring *Cappella di Niccolò V., erected by Nicholas V. and decorated by *Fra Angelico da Fiesole* in 1447 with frescoes from the life of the saints Lawrence and Stephen. They are one of the last and finest works of that master, but were buried in oblivion until restored under Gregory XIII. and Pius VII.

The upper series represents scenes from the life of St. Stephen: 1. (r. of the door) Stephen consecrated deacon by Peter; 2. He distributes alms as deacon; 3. He preaches; 4. He is brought before the council at Jerusalem; 5. He is dragged away to his martyrdom; 6. His death by stoning. Beneath, in the same order, scenes from the life of St. Lawrence: 1. He is consecrated deacon by Sixtus II.; 2. Sixtus (with the features of Nicholas V. ?) gives him treasures for distribution among the poor; 3. Distribution of the same; 4. The saint is condemned by the emperor; 5. His martyrdom. Also on the wall below: l. St. Bonaventura, r. St. Johannes Chrysostomus. In the vaulting: l. St. Augustine, r. St. Gregory. On the lower part of the r. wall: l. St. Athanasius, r. St. Thomas Aquinas. On the vaulting: l. St. Leo, r. Ambrose. On the ceiling the 4 evangelists.

Museum of Statues.

Galleria Lapidaria. Museo Chiaramonti. Braccio Nuovo. Museo Pio-Clementino. Museo Gregoriano.

The Vatican Collection of antiquities, the finest in the world, was commenced by the Popes Julius II., Leo X., Clement VII. and Paul III. in the *Belvedere*, erected by *Bramante* under Julius II., and commanding a magnificent view of Rome. Here, for example, were preserved the Torso of Hercules, the Apollo Belvedere and Laocoon. Clement XIV. (Ganganelli, d. 1774) determined to institute a more extensive collection, in consequence of which the *Museo Pio-Clementino* arose under him and his successor Pius VI. For the arrangement of the museum we are indebted to the celebrated E. Q. Visconti. It was despoiled of its costliest treasures by the French in 1797, most of which, however, were restored in 1816 to Pius VII. after the Treaty of Paris. Pius VII. extended the collection by the addition of the *Museo Chiaramonti* and (in 1821) the *Braccio Nuovo*; Gregory XVI. added the *Egyptian* and *Etruscan Museums*. Admission see p. 234. Complete French and Italian catalogues may be purchased at the door for 4 l.

The entrance is in the Cortile di S. Damaso (Pl. I, 4), in the l. wing, by a door with the inscription: *Adito alla Biblioteca ed al Museo;* the stair is then ascended, and the door of the museum reached at the extremity of the loggia on the first floor.

The museum commences with a corridor 27 ft. in width and 2131 ft. in length, the first half of which, the *Galleria Lapidaria*, is a collection, begun by Clement XIV. and Pius VI., and extended by Pius VII., of 3000 heathen (r. and l. at the commencement) and ancient Christian (beginning with the 7th window on the l.) inscriptions of all kinds, which, according to a Latin superscription by the last collector, were immured in the walls by the learned *Gaetano Marini*; it also contains ancient cippi, sarcophagi and statues. The last and smaller door on the l. at the extremity of this gallery is the entrance to the library (p. 293). The second half of the corridor, separated from the first by an iron gate, contains the Museo Chiaramonti.

The visitor should first proceed to the *left* to the *Braccio Nuovo, constructed by *Raph. Stern* under Paul VII. in 1821; it is 225 ft. in length, adorned with 14 ancient columns of cipollino and giallo antico, alabaster and Egyptian granite, and lighted from above. It contains 40 statues and about 80 busts, of which the following are especially worthy of inspection.

Right: No. *5. Caryatide, probably one of those executed by Diogenes for the Pantheon, restored by Thorwaldsen; 8. Commodus in hunting-custume with spear; 9. Barbarian head; 11. Silenus with the infant Bacchus; 14. Augustus, found in 1863 near Prima Porta in the villa of Livia, one of the best statues of the emperor, bearing distinct traces of painting. In front of it, on the ground, a mosaic from Tor-Marancio, Ulysses with the Sirens and Scylla; 17. Æsculapius: 20. So-called Nerva (head modern); *23. So-called Pudicitia, from the Villa Mattei, head and r. hand new: 26. Titus, found with the statue of his daughter Julia (No. 111., opposite) near the Lateran in 1828; 27. Medusa (also Nos. 40., 92., 110.; the latter of plaster) from Hadrian's temple of Venus and Roma; 32., 33. Satyrs sitting; 38. Ganymedes (?), found at Ostia, attrib. to Phædimus, fountain-figure; 39. (in the centre) beautiful black vase of basalt, with masks etc.; 41. Satyr, playing on the flute; 44. Wounded Amazon; 47. Caryatide; 48. Trajan; *50. Diana beholding the sleeping Endymion; 53. Euripides; 60. So-called Sulla; *62. Demosthenes. found near the ancient Tusculum. Standing alone: *67. Apoxyomenos (scraper), an athlete cleaning his right arm with a scraping-iron, after Lysippus, found in the Vicolo delle Palme in Trastevere in 1849. Near it, to the l.: *71. Mourning Amazon, apparently a copy from an older work of the best period, arms and feet restored by Thorwaldsen; 81. Hadrian; 83. Juno, erroneously restored as Ceres (head new); 86. Fortuna with cornucopia and helm, from Ostia; *89. So-called Hesiod; 92. Venus, risen from the sea: *94. Spes, erroneously restored as Proserpine; 96. Mark Antony; 97., 99., 101., 103., 105. Athletes; 106. Bust of the triumvir Lepidus. On the ground in this semicircle (behind the Nile) a mosaic with the Ephesian Diana, from Poggio Mirteto. *109. Colossal group of the Nile, surrounded by 16 playing children, emblematic of the 16 yds. which the river rises: at the back and sides of the plinth a humorous representation of a battle between crocodiles and hippopotami, found near S. Maria sopra Minerva in the time of Leo X.; 111. Julia, daughter of Titus (see No. 26.); 112. Head of Juno (so-called Juno Pentini); *114. So-called Minerva Medica, or Pallas Giustiniani (the family to whom it formerly belonged), of Parian marble; 117. Claudius; 118. Barbarian head; *120. Satyr reposing, probably after a celebrated work of Praxiteles; 123. L. Verus; *126. Athlete, erroneously restored with a discus, subsequently recognised as a copy of the Doryphoros (spear-bearer) of Polycletes; 129. Domitian, from the Pal. Giustiniani; *132. Mercury, restored by Canova.

*Museo Chiaramonti.

This collection comprises 30 sections, containing upwards of 700 sculptures in marble, many of them small and fragmentary. Especially worthy of notice: Section I. r. No. 2. Sitting Apollo; 6. Autumn, from a sarcophagus, found at Ostia; 1. 13. Winter, from the sarcophagus of P. Ælius Verus. II. r. 14. Euterpe; 16. Erato. IV. r. 62. Sleep; 63. Minerva; 1. 107. supposed to be Julius Cæsar. VI. r. 120. So-called Vestal Virgin from Hadrian's villa; 121. Clio; 122. Diana. VII. r. 130. Relief, badly executed, a pleasing representation of the sun and moon as the leaders of souls; 144. Bearded Dionysus. VIII. r. °176. Daughter of Niobe, found at Tivoli, of superior Greek workmanship; l. 179. Sarcophagus of C. Julius Euhodus and Metilia Acte, with representation of the myth of Alcestis; 181. Hecate; °182. Ara of Pentelic marble, with Venus and Bacchanalian representations. IX. r. 183. Greek equestrian relief; 197. Head of Roma (eyes renewed), found at the ancient Laurentum; 1. °229. Two heads of Silenus as a double statue; 230. Large cippus, Night with Death and Sleep (?). X. r. 241. Nymph nursing the infant Jupiter: l. 244. Colossal mask of Oceanus, used once as mouth of a fountain; 245. Polyhymnia. XI. r. 255. Jupiter Serapis; 259., 263. Beautiful unknown portrait-heads; l. 285. Apollo with a hind, in imitation of the ancient style; 287. Sleeping fisher-boy. XII. r. 294. Hercules, found 1802, restored by Canova. XIII. r. 300. Fragment of a shield with 4 Amazons, copy of the shield of Athene Parthenos by Phidias; l. 338. Boys fighting. XIV. r. 352. Venus Anadyomene; 353. Venus. XV. r. 360. Ancient relief of three dancing women; 369. Unknown portrait-head; °372. Greek relief with fragment of a rider; l. 392. Hadrian. XVI. r. 400. Tiberius, sitting, found at Veii in 1811; r. 401. Augustus, also found at Veii. XVII. r. °417. Bust of the youthful Augustus; 419. A. Head of Vulcan, found in 1861 on the erection of the column of the Immacolata in the Piazza di Spagna: 420. Demosthenes; l. 441. Alcibiades (?). XX. r. 493. Portrait-statue of a boy; °494. Tiberius, colossal sitting statue, found at Piperno in 1796; °495. The so-called bow-bending Cupid; l. 497. Representation of a mill; 498. Penelope (?). XXI. r. 500. A., 512. A. So-called Varro; °513. A. Head of Venus in Greek marble, found in the Thermæ of Diocletian. XXII. r. 544. Silenus; l. 547. Isis. XXIII. r. 550. Square marble slab with shield of Medusa in the centre: 563. Unknown portrait-bust. XXIV. r. 587. The elder Faustina as Ceres; 588. Dionysus and a satyr; 589. Mercury; l. 591. Claudius. XXV. l. °606. A. Head of Neptune in Pentelic marble from Ostia. XXVI. r. 636. Hercules with Telephus. XXVII. r. °644. Dancing women; 652. A. Head of a Centaur; 655. Narcissus (erroneously restored). XXIX. r. 693. Wreathed head of the youthful Bacchus; 698. Cicero, from Roma Vecchia; 701. Ulysses handing the goblet to Polyphemus; l. 709. Sarcophagus with Bacchanalian representations. XXX. r. 732. Hercules reclining.

By the door to the l. at the extremity, the *Giardino della Pigna* is entered (visitors ring; alleged difficulties are generally overcome by a gratuity of 1/2 l.). Here numerous fragments of statues and reliefs are preserved. On the r. the colossal *Pinecone* from the mausoleum of Hadrian, now the Castle of S. Angelo, the summit of which it is said once to have formed. In the centre is the basement of the column erected to Anton. Pius, which stood near Monte Citorio; it is adorned with the Apotheosis of Antoninus and Faustina and processions of warriors. L., a colossal portrait-head in marble. With the consent of the custodian (1/2 — 1 l.) "*Il Boscareccio*", or the larger *Garden of the Vatican*, may be visited hence. It extends from the Belvedere to the walls of the Leonine city, and is beautifully laid out in the Italian style. To the l. of the entrance, at the base of an eminence planted with trees, stands the *Casino of Pius IV.*, built by *Pirro Ligorio* in 1560, a garden-house sumptuously decorated with sculptures, mosaics and pictures, where the Pope occasionally grants an audience to ladies.

At the extremity of the Museo Chiaramonti a short stair (at the end of which to the l. is the entrance to the Egypt. Museum) leads to the

Museo Pio-Clementino, the real nucleus of the Vatican collection, containing a number of the most celebrated antiques. Respecting its foundation, see p. 242.

The museum comprises 11 departments. The *Vestibule of the Belvedere*, divided by two arches into three halls, is first entered.

In the centre of the first is the celebrated "Torso of Hercules, executed, according to the inscription, by Apollonius of Athens, who probably lived in the 1st cent. B. C.; it was found in the 16th cent. near the theatre of Pompey (Campo de' Fiori). Opp. the window is the 'Sarcophagus of L. Corn. Scipio Barbatus. great-grandfather of the illustrious Africanus, and consul B. C. 298, of peperine-stone, with a very remarkable inscription in Saturnine verses, which record his liberality and achievements; it was found in 1780 in the tomb of the Scipios on the Via Appia (*Vigna Sassi*, see p. 197), at the same time as that of his son L. Corn. Scipio, consul B. C. 259, and that of P. Corn. Scipio (son of Africanus), flamen dialis, all of whose inscriptions are immured around. The bust on the sarcophagus has been groundlessly regarded as that of the poet Ennius. In the *Round Vestibule* a Basin of marble (pavonazzetto), on the balcony to the r. an ancient Wind-indicator, found in 1779 near the Colosseum. Beneath No. 7. is a cippus with relief of a Diadumenos, or youth placing a bandage round his head, which conveys an idea of the celebrated statue of Polycletes of the same name. From this point a remarkably fine "view of Rome with the Alban and Sabine Mts. is enjoyed. A ship in bronze below the balcony contains a fountain. In the adjoining cabinet facing the visitor is a "Statue of Meleager, a good work of the imperial period, found about 1500 outside the Porta Portese. L. a colossal bust of Trajan; above it a late relief, characteristic of the decline of art.

To the l. in the central hall is the entrance to the

Cortile di Belvedere, an octagonal court constructed by *Bramante*. It is surrounded by arcades, separated by four apartments in which several of the most important works in the collection are placed. In the court a fountain with ancient embouchure, above the arcades eight ancient colossal masks, by the walls four sarcophagi and sixteen statues.

In the hall on the r.: 27., 28. Reliefs with Satyrs and griffins, pressing grapes, once forming a trapezophorus (support of a table). 28. Large sarcophagus with dancing satyrs and Bacchantes, found in 1777 whilst the foundations for the sacristy of St. Peter's were being laid. 30. Sleeping nymphs, figures belonging to a fountain. Two baths of black and green basalt. Then to the r. the

Gabinetto di Canova. Perseus by *Canova;* the pugilists Kreugas and Damoxenus, by the same. In the small niches: 34. Mercury; 35. Minerva. In the following hall: r. 37. Sarcophagus with Bacchus and Ariadne in Naxos; r. 38. Relief of Diana and Ceres contending with the Titans and

Giants, found in the Villa Mattei; 1. 44. So-called Ara Casali, the origin of Rome; 49. Sarcophagus with battle of Amazons, Achilles and Penthesilea.

Second Cabinet (dell' Antinoo). °53. Mercury, admirably executed, once erroneously regarded as an Antinous; 1. 55. Relief of a procession of priests of Isis; r. 61. Sarcophagus with Nereids with the arms of Achilles; r. 64., 65. at the sides of the entrance to the Sala degli Animali, two *Molossian hounds.

Third Cabinet. **Laocoon with his two sons entwined by the snakes, by the three Rhodians *Agesander, Polydorus* and *Athenodorus,* once placed according to Pliny, in the palace of Titus, discovered under Julius II. in 1506 near the Sette Sale, and termed by Mich. Angelo a "marvel of art". The work is admirably preserved, with the exception of the three upraised arms which have been incorrectly restored by *Giov. da Montorsoli.* In the delicacy of the workmanship, the dramatic suspense of the moment and the profoundly expressive attitudes of the heads, especially that of the father, it is the grandest representative of the Rhodian school of art.

In the hall: r. 79. Raised relief of Hercules with Telephus, and Bacchus leaning on a Satyr; 80. Sarcophagus with weapon-bearing Cupids; 81. Rom. sacrificial procession after a victory. In the niche: °85. Hygeia; 88. Roma, accompanying a victorious emperor, probably appertaining to a triumphal arch.

Fourth Cabinet. Right, **91. Apollo Belvedere, found at the end of the 15th cent. near Porta d'Anzio, the ancient Antium. According to the most recent interpretation the god, whose left hand has been restored, originally held in it not the bow, but the ægis (as has been discovered from comparison with a bronze), with which he is supposed to be in the act of striking terror into the Celts who have dared to attack his sanctuary of Delphi. The statue is of Carrara marble. (Comp. Childe Harold's Pil. IV, 161). L. relief: Women leading a bull to the sacrifice.

The court is now crossed to the opposite entrance of the

Sala degli Animali, containing a number of animal-pieces in white and coloured marble, most of them modern; the greater part of the floor is covered with ancient mosaics. 1. 194. Pig and litter; 202. Colossal camel's head as the aperture of a fountain; 208. Hercules with Geryon; 210. Diana, badly restored; 213. Hercules and Cerberus; 220. Bacchanalian genius on a lion; 228. Triton carrying off a nymph. Beneath, on an oval sarcophagus-cover, triumphal procession of Bacchus; 232. Minotaur; r. 107. Stag attacked by a hound; 116. Two playing greyhounds; 124. Sacrifice of Mithras; 134. Hercules with the slain Nemean lion; 137. Hercules slaying Diomedes; 138. Centaur with a Cupid on his back. (Adjacent is the entrance to the Galleria delle Statue.) 139. Commodus on horseback (Bernini's model for the statue of Constantine in the Portico of St. Peter's); 151. Sacrificed sheep on the altar; 153. Small group of a shepherd resting, with goats; (in the window) Relief of cow and calf; 173. Stag seized by a hound.

Galleria delle Statue, converted from a summer-house of Innocent VIII. into the present hall by Clement XIV. and Pius VI. The lunettes still contain the remains of paintings by *Pinturicchio.* The statues have been admirably arranged by *Ennio Quir. Visconti.* — R. of the entrance, No. 248. Clod. Albinus, the opponent of Septim. Severus. The statue stands on an interesting cippus of travertine, found in 1777 not far from the mausoleum of Augustus near S. Carlo al Corso, which marked the spot where the body of Caius, son of Germanicus, was burned. °250. Eros of *Praxiteles* (termed *Il Genio del Vaticano),* found near Centocelle on the Via Labicana; on the back are the traces of wings; above it, 249. Relief, attrib. to *Mich. Angelo:* Cosimo I. aiding Pisa; 251. Athlete; °253. Triton, upper part only, found near Tivoli; 255. Paris, copied from a fine original; 256. Youthful

Hercules; 257. Diana (relief); 258. Bacchus; 259. Figure with male torso, probably Apollo, incorrectly restored as Pallas (so-called Minerva Pacifera) with the olive-branch; 260. Greek tomb-relief; *261. Mourning Penelope, an imitation of the more ancient style, on the pedestal a relief of Bacchus and Ariadne; 263. Relief of Victoria in a quadriga; 264. Apollo Sauroctonos, lying in wait for a lizard, in bronze, after *Praxiteles*; *265. Amazon, from the Villa Mattei; 267. Drunken satyr; 268. Juno, from the Thermæ of Otricoli; 269. Relief, Jason and Medea (?); 270. Urania, from Tivoli; *271. and 390. (one on each side of the arch which leads into the following room of the busts) Posidippus and Menander, two admirable portrait-statues of these comic dramatists, in Pentelic marble, perhaps original works of *Cephisodotus*, son of Praxiteles, from the theatre at Athens, found at Rome under Sixtus V. near S. Lorenzo in Paneperna, where they were long revered as saints. The numbers between these statues are found in the

Hall of the Busts. 276. Augustus with wreath of ears of corn; *277. Saturn; 280. M. Agrippa; 283. Apollo; 289. Julia Mammæa. mother of Alex. Severus; *293. Head of Menelaus, from the group of Menelaus with the body of Patroclus (or Ajax with the body of Achilles), found in 1772 in the Villa of Hadrian, a copy of the Pasquino group (see p. 160); at the same time the *bones of the body in the window to the l. were also found; 299. Zeus Serapis, of basalt; 304. Caracalla; 306. Augustus; 308. Nero as Apollo Citharœdus; 309. Ant. Pius; 311. Otho; 315., 316., 320. Heads of Satyrs. In the central niche: *325. Zeus, formerly in the Pal. Verospi; 344. Hercules; 350. Praying woman, so-called Pietà; 351. Interesting sarcophagus with representation of Prometheus and the Fates, possibly Christian; 357. Antinous; 363. Juno; 368. Commodus; *375. Isis; 376. Head of Pallas from the castle of St. Angelo; 382., 384. Anatomical representations in marble; 386. Greek portrait-head, subject unknown; *388. Rom. man and woman, tomb-relief (Niebuhr's favourite group, imitated on his tomb at Bonn by Rauch).

The Galleria delle Statue is now re-entered and Menander passed:

392. Septim. Severus; 393. Girl at a spring, erroneously regarded as a Dido or Penelope; 394. Neptune Verospi; 395. Apollo Citharœdus, archaic; 396. Wounded Adonis (the hand of which there are traces on the figure was probably that of a Cupid dressing the wound); 397. Reclining Bacchus from the Villa of Hadrian; 398. Macrinus, successor of Caracalla. In front of it, in the centre, a large alabaster basin, found near SS. Apostoli; 399. Æsculapius and Hygeia, from Palestrina; 400. Euterpe; 401. Mutilated pair from the group of Niobe, a son and a daughter, found like the Florentine statues near Porta S. Paolo; *405. Danaide; 406. Copy of the Satyr of Praxiteles. In the window-niche: 422. Giustinian fountain-enclosure with Bacchanalian procession, modern copy from the original in Spain. (Adjacent is the entrance to the Gabinetto delle Maschere.) In the centre: 462. Cinerary urn of oriental alabaster, found with the inscriptions Nos. 248., 408., 410., 417., 420., which once contained the remains of a member of the imperial Julian family. On the narrow side: *414. Sleeping Ariadne, formerly taken for Cleopatra, found under Julius II.; beneath it, *Sarcophagus with battle of the giants. At the sides, *412., 413. The Barberini Candelabra, the largest and finest extant, found in Hadrian's villa, on each three reliefs, (l.) Jupiter, Juno, Mercury, and (r.) Mars, Minerva, Spes; 416. Relief of the forsaken Ariadne, similar in expression to the large statue; 417. Mercury; 420. Lucius Verus.

Gabinetto delle Maschere, adjoining the window-niche, closed, application must be made for admittance to the custodian (1/2 l.); on Mondays access is denied. The cabinet derives its appellation from the *Mosaic on the floor, adorned with *masks* etc., found in 1780 in Hadrian's villa. Here to the r., *427. Dancing woman, of Pentelic marble, found at Naples; 428. Relief of the apotheosis of Hadrian; 429. Stooping Venus, in the bath; *431. Torch-bearing Diana. Wall opp. entrance: 432., 434. and on the opp. side 441., 444. Reliefs of the exploits of Hercules; 433. Satyr of rosso antico, copy in the Capitoline; 435. Worshipper of Mithras. Window-wall: 438.

Minerva, from Hadrian's villa; 439. Bathing-chair, of rosso antico, formerly in the court of the Lateran. In the window: 440. Relief of Bacchanalian procession. Entrance-wall: 442. Ganymedes; 443. Apollo. Fine view from the window of M. Mario and Soracte to the l., and the Sabine Mts. to the r.

Sala delle Muse (entered from the central passage of the Sala degli Animali), a magnificent octagonal saloon with cupola, and adorned with 16 columns of Carrara marble, containing many remarkably fine Greek portrait heads. In the ante-room: 489. Relief (above, on the r.), Dance of the Corybantes; r. 490. Statue of Diogenes; r. 491. Silenus; r. 492. Sophocles, the only portrait accredited by an inscription (unfortunately mutilated); 1. (above) 493. Relief of the birth of Bacchus; 1. 494. Greek portrait-figure; 495. Bacchus in female attire; 496. Hesiod. In the saloon: (r.) 498. Epicurus; 499. Melpomene, Muse of tragedy. The statues of the Muses preserved here were found with the Apollo in 1774 in the villa of Hadrian at Tivoli, with the exception of Nos. 504., 520. — 500. The Stoic Zeno; 502. Thalia, Muse of comedy; 503. The orator Æschines; 504. Urania, Muse of astronomy; 505. Demosthenes; 506. Clio. Muse of history; 507. The Cynic Antisthenes; 508. Polyhymnia, Muse of higher lyric poetry; 509. The Epicurean Metrodorus. Opp. to this, 1. 510. Alcibiades; 511. Terpsichore, Muse of dancing; 512. Sleeping Epimenides; 514. Calliope, Muse of epic poetry; 515. Socrates: °516. Apollo Musagetes, in long robe, with an air of poetic rapture, standing on an altar with representation of the Lares; 517. Themistocles (?); 518. Erato, Muse of erotic poetry; 519. Zeno the Eleatic; 520. Euterpe, Muse of music; 521. Euripides. In the approach to the next room: r. °523. Aspasia; 524. Sappho (doubtful); °525. Pericles; 1. 528. Bias the misanthrope of the seven wise men; 530. Lycurgus; 531. Periander of Corinth.

Sala Rotonda, erected under Pius VI. by *Simonetti* after the model of the Pantheon, contains an admirable °Mosaic, found in 1780 in the Thermæ at Otricoli, with Nereids, Tritons, Centaurs and masks. In the centre a magnificent basin of porphyry from the Baths of Diocletian. On either side of the entrance. 536., 537. Comedy and Tragedy, from Hadrian's villa. In the saloon, r. 539. °°Bust of Zeus from Otricoli, the finest and most celebrated extant; 540. Antinous as Bacchus (drapery modern, probably originally of metal), from Hadrian's Prænestine villa; 541. Faustina, wife of Ant. Pius; 542. Genius of Augustus; 543. Hadrian from that emperor's mausoleum (S. Angelo); °544. Hercules, colossal statue in gilded bronze (12 ft. in height), found in 1864 immured in the foundations of the Pal. Righetti, near the theatre of Pompey; 545. Bust of Antinous; 546. Ant. Pius; 547. Sea-god, found near Pozzuoli; 548. Nerva, on the pedestal a fine, but not easily interpreted relief; 549. Jupiter Serapis; °550. So-called Barberine Juno; 551. Claudius; 552. Juno Sospita, from Lanuvium, a reproduction during the period of the Antonines of an ancient Latin image; 553. Plotina, wife of Trajan; 554. Julia Domna, wife of Septim. Severus; °555. Statue restored as Ceres; 556. Pertinax.

Sala a Croce Greca, constructed by *Simonetti*, in the form of a Greek cross, as its name signifies. On the floor are three ancient mosaics. In the centre a head of Pallas, found in 1741 in the Villa Ruffinella, near Frascati. By the stair, between the two sphynxes, a °Flower-basket from Roma Vecchia. R. of the entrance: 559. Augustus; 564. Lucius Verus; 566. Large sarcophagus in porphyry, of Constantia, daughter of Constantine the Great, from her tomb, subsequently church of S. Costanza near S. Agnese; it is adorned with vintage-scenes, in allusion to the Vineyard of the Lord (the vaulting of the tomb is adorned with mosaics of similar style and import); 567. Priestess of Ceres; 569. Clio; 570. The elder Faustina; °574. Venus, perhaps a copy of the Cnidian Venus of Praxiteles, drapery of metal modern; 578. 579. Egyptian Sphynxes; 1. 581. Trajan; 582. Apollo Citharœdus, restored as a Muse; 589. Sarcophagus of St. Helena, mother of Constantine, from her tomb near Torre Pignattara, transferred to the Lateran by Hadrian IV., and hither by Pius VI.; 592. Augustus. By the stair: r. 600. Recumbent river-god, said to have been restored by Mich. Angelo (opp. is an entrance to the Egyptian Museum). The stair (with 20 antique columns from Præneste) is now ascended, leading to the r. to the

Sala della Biga, a circular hall with cupola, named after the admirable (No. 623.) *Biga, or two-horse chariot, here preserved. The body of the chariot, richly adorned with leaves, which for centuries was employed as an episcopal throne in S. Marco, and a portion of the r. horse are alone ancient. *608. Bearded Bacchus, inscribed "Sardanapallos"; *610. Bacchus as a woman; 611. Combatant, in the head resembling Alcibiades, in position a figure of the group of Harmodius and Aristogiton; 612. Draped statue, from the Palazzo Giustiniani in Venice; 614. Apollo Citharœdus; *615. Discobolus, of the Attic school, perhaps after Alkamenes; 616. Portrait-statue of Phocion (?), Epaminondas, or Aristomenes; *618. Discobolus of *Myron*, the original was of bronze; head modern and inaccurately replaced; it should have been turned to the side, as the excellent copy in the Pal. Massimi (p. 159) shows; 619. Chariot-driver: 621. Sarcophagus relief, race of Pelops and Œnomaus; 622. Small Diana. If this saloon is quitted on the r., the visitor proceeds in a straight direction from the stair to the

Galleria dei Candelabri, a corridor, 300 ft. in length, in six departments, containing chiefly small and fragmentary sculptures. I. On the r. and l. of the entrance: 2., 66. Birds' nests and children; r. *19. Boy stooping over dice or something similar; r. 31., l. 35. Candelabra from Otricoli, the former with Satyr, Silenus and Bacchante, the latter with Apollo, Marsyas and the Scythian; l. 45. Head of young Satyr; l. 52. Sleeping Satyr, of green basalt. II. On the r., 74. Pan extracting a thorn from the foot of a Satyr; 81. Ephesian Diana, from the villa of Hadrian; 82. Sarcophagus, with the murder of Ægistheus and Clytemnestra by Orestes; r. 93., l. 97. Candelabra, from S. Costanza; l. *104. Ganymede with the eagle; l. 112. Sarcophagus-relief of Protesilaus and Laodamia; 117., 118. Boy with hydria, fountain-figure; 119. Ganymedes, carried off by the eagle. III. On the r., 131. Mosaic with dead fish, dates etc.; 134. Sophocles, sitting; l. 141., 153. Bacchus with the panther. IV. On the r. 157., and l. 219. Candelabra from S. Costanza; r. 168. Roman matron, draped statue; r. 173. Sarcophagus: Ariadne discovered by Bacchus; r. 177. Old fisherman; r. 184. Goddess of Antioch; 187. Candelabrum with Hercules' theft of the tripod (Hercules, Apollo, Dionysus); 190. Candelabrum with Bacchanalian dance, from Naples, a cast from the original in Paris; l. 194. Boy with a goose; 200. Antique Apollo (inaccurately restored); l. 204. Sarcophagus with the children of Niobe; 208. Marcellus (?), nephew of Augustus; 210. Marble vessel with Bacchanalian dancers. V. On the r., *222. Female runner, from the villa of Hadrian; r. 234. Candelabrum, with Minerva, Jupiter, Venus and Apollo, from Otricoli: l. 240. Negro-boy with bath-apparatus. VI. On the r. 253. Sarcophagus with Luna and Endymion; r. 257. Ganymedes; l. 264. Daughter of Niobe; l. 269. Sarcophagus with the rape of the daughters of Leucippus by the Dioscuri; upon it: Statue of a fighting Gaul.

This gallery is adjoined by that in which some of the tapestry of Raphael is preserved, accessible on Mondays gratis; on other days application must be made to one of the custodians.

The *Tapestry of Raphael ("*Gli Arazzi*") because manufactured at Arras in France) was executed from cartoons drawn by *Raphael* in 1515 and 1516, seven of which were purchased in Flanders by Charles I. of England, and preserved in Hampton Court Palace (now in the Kensington Museum). These designs, derived from the history of the New Testament, are among the most admirable works of the great master. Each piece of tapestry, wrought with great skill in wool, silk and gold, when complete cost about 700 pounds. They were originally destined for the lower and unpainted portion of the walls in the Sixtine Chapel.

They are now greatly damaged and faded, especially in the flesh-tints.

The designs on the socle in bronze-colour partly represent scenes from the life of Leo X. whilst still Card. de Medici. The decorations and arabesques which surround the principal designs are chiefly by Raphael's pupil *Giov. da Undine*. During the siege of Rome in 1527 the tapestry was seriously injured and carried off, but was restored to Julius III. in 1533. In 1798 it fell into the hands of the French, and was sold to Genoese Jews, from whom it was repurchased by Pius VII. in 1808. It is preserved in two different rooms. (I). In the passage adjoining the gallery of the candelabra, and on Mondays accessible to the public, hang: *1. Punishment of Ananias; *2. Peter receiving the keys; *3. The people of Lystra wish to offer sacrifice to Paul and Barnabas; *4. Paul preaching at Athens; 5. Christ appearing to Mary Magdalene; 6. The supper of Emmaus; 7. Presentation of Christ in the Temple; 8. Adoration of the shepherds; 9. Ascension; 10. Adoration of the Magi; 11. Resurrection of Christ; 12. Effusion of the Holy Ghost (the three last badly executed). Opp. to them: 13. Religion between Justice and Mercy; *14. Stoning of Stephen. Those indicated by an asterisk only are from the cartoons of Raphael, the others were probably designed by Dutch masters for the carpet manufacturers. (II). The remaining portions of the tapestry are in a closed room, to which the custodian conducts visitors from the Stanze. *1. Paul in prison at Philippi; *2. Paul heals the lame man in the Temple; *3. Massacre of the Innocents, in 3 parts; *4. Peter's miraculous draught of fishes; *5. Conversion of Paul; *6. The sorcerer Elymas struck with blindness. (The lower part of the tapestry is lost.)

The gallery of the tapestry is adjoined by the *Galleria Geografica*, a passage 500 ft. in length, with maps designed by the Dominican *Ignazio Dante*, and executed by his brother *Antonio* under Gregory XIII. in 1580; the ceiling-paintings are by *Tempesta* and others (1/2 l.).

The ***Museo Gregoriano** of the *Etruscan Antiquities*, founded by Gregory XVI. in 1836, occupies 12 rooms, also on the upper story. A stair is ascended from the entrance to the gallery of the candelabra, and the door reached to the r. (visitors knock, 1/2 l.; on Mondays inaccessible). The museum comprises a number of antiquities excavated principally in 1828—36 in the Etruscan cities Vulci, Toscanella, Chiusi etc.: statues, paintings, vases, golden ornaments, and various domestic utensils of bronze, extremely interesting as forming a link in the history of Italian art, and affording some insight into the habits of the still enigmatical Etruscans. Of the numerous and chiefly small objects the following deserve special attention:

(To the l. by the loggia in the space before the door is a relief of Medea; r. by the door another with a contest of Hercules.)

1st Room: Three sarcophagi of terra cotta with life-size figures of the deceased on the covers. On the walls numerous portrait-heads in terracotta, of peculiar formation. Then the 2,nd R. is entered to the r. Of the sarcophagi one of the larger on the l. is of travertine, adorned with an almost flat relief of a chariot with a bearded man and musicians, on which traces of painting are visible; numerous smaller cinerary urns, some of them of alabaster with mythological reliefs, from Chiusi and Volterra. — 3rd R.: In the centre a large sarcophagus of tuffstone with recumbent figure and reliefs of the murder of Clytemnestra, sacrifice of Iphigeneia,

Eteocles and Polynices, Telephus and Orestes. In the corners are small and strange-looking cinerary urns in the form of houses, perhaps Celtic, found beneath the lava between Albano and Marino. — 4th R.: containing terracottas. *Mercury; on either side fragments of female figures with rich drapery, from Tivoli. R., beneath, a relief in stucco of Venus and Adonis, Cupid dressing the wound of the latter; l. a relief of Jupiter, Neptune and Hercules; on the walls reliefs, cinerary urns, architectural fragments. By the window small terracottas.

The four following rooms contain the *Collection of Vases*. These painted vessels were partly imported from Greece, partly manufactured in Etruria itself, where Vulci, Chiusi, Volterra, Bomarzo etc. are proved to have excelled in this branch of art. The Etruscans imitated the earlier Greek vases with black, as well as the later with red figures, often without a just appreciation of the subjects, and with an obvious preference for tragic scenes, especially murders. An exhaustive examination of the details will be undertaken by the scientific only; the most interesting objects only need be here enumerated. — 5th R.: By the walls a great number of vases with the same decorations from Vulci; on the column towards the window a large *vase with whitish ground and coloured designs, representing the delivery of the infant Bacchus to Silenus; by the window l. a humorous representation of Jupiter and Mercury's visit to Alcmene; in cabinets objects in crystal from Palestrina. — 6th R.: In the centre four remarkably fine vases, on the first, with three handles, a poet and six muses. Towards the posterior wall: *Achilles and Ajax playing at dice (with the name of the manufacturer *Exekias*). In the centre a vessel of great antiquity, with representations of animals. On the second to the l. near the window-wall is *Hector's Death. The sixth by the entrance-wall represents two men with oil-vessels and the inscriptions: "O Father Zeus, would that I were rich" and: "It is already full and even runs over". Over the doors are mosaics from Hadrian's villa. By the second window two basins with ancient Latin inscriptions. — 7th R.: Arched corridor. In the first niche a large vase of S. Italy. In the second *Minerva and Hercules, from Vulci. To the r. and l. of these, imitations of the prize-vases of the Panathenæan games at Athens, with Athene between two fighting-cocks. Then the sixth: *Hector bidding farewell to Priam and Hecuba. The third niche contains a vase of S. Italy; to the l. of it *Achilles and Briseis. — 8th R.: containing an extensive collection of graceful and delicately painted goblets, placed on appropriate stands. The cabinet contains small vases, some of them of irregular form. On the wall above are copies of paintings in a tomb at Vulci, showing that Etruscan art was at this period completely Hellenized. Beneath, as the imperfectly interpreted inscriptions appear to indicate, is an historical scene, an adventure of Mastarna (Serv. Tullius) and Cælius Viberna, besides mythological representations (Cassandra, Achilles slaying the victim for the funeral-sacrifice of Patroclus).

Visitors now return to the sixth room, in order thence to reach the 9th Room on the r., where bronzes of every description, domestic implements, weapons, ornaments, jewellery etc. are arranged. By the wall to the r. the statue of a warrior, with Umbrian inscription, found at Todi in 1835; opposite, a bed, and boy with a bulla sitting. On the wall as far as the window, helmets, shields, mirrors with engraved designs. By the r. window a cista of bronze from Vulci, with Amazon battles in embossed work, which when found contained articles of the female toilet. — Then by a door on the r. to the 10th R., or corridor, where water-pipes, boy with a bird in bronze etc. are preserved. — 11th R.: containing all kinds of vases, as well as copies of tomb-paintings from Corneto and Vulci, invaluable in the study of early Italian art. The most ancient grade is represented by the paintings on the narrow sides of the saloon (excepting the scene over the door), which resemble early Greek designs, but are ruder and more destitute of expression. The next grade is exemplified by the designs on the long walls, where the progress is traced which the Etruscans had made in the art of drawing and in their ideas of the human figure, under the influence of the Greeks; at the same time Etruscan peculiarities, especially in the heads, are observable. These paintings, like the preceding, also represent games and dances performed in honour of the dead. The third and fully developed period is represented by the picture, over the door, of Pluto and Proserpine, which may probably be regarded as coæval with those in the 8th room. The visitor now returns to the 9th R., where immediately to the r. by the window is a glass cabinet with votive objects, found in the mineral springs of Vicarello, near the Lago di Bracciano: golden ornaments, silver goblets, polished stones. In front of the 2nd window a cabinet with objects excavated at Pompeii in presence of Pius IX.; among them an *equestrian relief in marble. The turning glass-cabinet in the centre contains °golden ornaments; in the upper section are arranged those found in 1836 in a tomb at Cervetri, in the lower similar objects from other tombs. These show to how great skill and taste in workmanship of this kind the magnificence-loving Etruscans had attained, and the chains, wreaths, rings etc. afford models which are rarely equalled by Roman jewellers of the present day (see Castellani, p. 90). By the 3rd window is a second, but less perfect cista, adorned with engraving. By the wall a large arm in bronze, numerous mirrors with designs, a restored biga, behind it a male bust; in the cabinet small bronzes. By the fourth wall: candelabra, kettles, shields; in the centre a brazier with tongs and poker. — In the 12th R., on the l., is an imitation of an Etruscan tomb, with three burial recesses, vases etc.; at the entrance two lions from Vulci. The cabinet in the centre contains bronzes from Veii; by the window small ornaments and objects of glass. Also several Chinese curiosities.

The **Egyptian Museum** [entrance by the door to the l. by the approach to the Belvedere (Torso); accessible gratis on Mondays 12—3 o'clock] is below the Etruscan, in the so-called *Torre de' Venti*. Pius VII. purchased the nucleus of the collection from Andrea Gaddi and greatly extended it; so also Gregory XVI. The grotesque and, as it were, petrified specimens of Egyptian art may be cursorily examined by the traveller, for the sake of comparing them with those of the Hellenic and Italian, but the museum contains few objects of great interest.

1st Room: Coptic inscriptions, hieroglyphics, cuneiform characters. By the entrance-wall a small reproduction of the Nile in the Braccio Nuovo (p. 243). Model of a pyramid. 2nd R.: MSS. on Papyrus. 3rd R.: Idols and ornaments; scarabees (stones cut in the shape of beetles); in the cabinet l. of the window Egyptian silver coins. 4th R.: Several mummies of animals; bronzes of animals (ibis, cats etc.). 5th R.: Scarabees. 6th R.: Eight statues of the goddess Pascht (Isis), from the ruins of Carnac, ten mummies and two coffins of stone. 7th R.: Small idols and vases of alabaster. 8th R.: The objects collected here are from Hadrian's villa at Tibur, of Roman workmanship in the Egyptian style: Opp. the entrance: °Colossal statue of Antinous, the favourite of Hadrian, in white marble. On the r. the Nile, in black marble. 9th R.: °Egyptian colossal statues: (1) Mother of Rhamses (Sesostris), of black granite, between (2) two lions of basalt, from the Thermæ of Agrippa, which formerly long adorned the Fontana di Termini; (3) by the entrance-wall, in the centre: Ptolemy Philadelphus, to the l. of him, his Queen Arsinoe, of red granite (from the gardens of Sallust). 10th R.: Two coffins of mummies of green basalt, and four of painted wood. (Egress into the Sala a Croce Greca.)

**Picture Gallery. *Library. *Mosaic Manufactory*.

The ****Picture Gallery** (the lower court is crossed, and on its farther side a door to the extreme l. entered; three stairs are then ascended, and the loggia entered to the l., where visitors ring at a door on the l. side) was founded by Pius VII., who here collected the pictures restored by the French in 1815, most of which had been taken from the churches, and added a few more (access daily, except Mondays, 9—3 o'clock; ½ l.).

1st Room on the l.: St. Jerome, coloured sketch by *Leonardo da Vinci*; *4. Annunciation, Adoration of the Magi, Presentation in the Temple, *Raphael*, predella to the Coronation of Mary (No. 27) in the 3rd R.; 12. Christ and Thomas, *Guercino*; *5. The dead Christ and M. Magdalene who anoints his wounds, *Andrea Mantegna*; 7. Madonna with St. Jerome, *Franc. Francia*. On the window-wall: 6. Scenes from the life of St. Nicholas of Bari, *Fra Angelico da Fiesole*; 14. The Prodigal, *Murillo*; 3. Miracles of St. Hyacinth, *Benozzo Gozzoli (?)*; (without No.) Adoration of the shepherds, *Murillo*; 14. Return of the Prodigal, by the same; 15. Nuptials of the infant Christ with St. Catharine, also by *Murillo* (these three Murillos were presented to Pius IX. by Queen Isabella); 2. The saints Benedict, Scholastica and Placidus, *Perugino*; *8. Faith, Hope and Charity, *Raphael*, predella of the Entombment in the Pal. Borghese; 10. Madonna, St. Joseph and St. Catharine, *Garofalo*. — 2nd R.: On the entrance-wall: r. 17. Communion of St. Jerome, *Domenichino*. Wall of egress: **18. The Transfiguration of *Raphael*, his last great work, painted for Card. Giulio de' Medici (afterwards Clement VII.), till 1797 in S. Pietro in Montorio. The upper part is by Raphael's own hand: Christ hovering between Moses and Elias; Peter, James and John lying on the ground, dazzled by the light. The lower half, where the other disciples are begged to heal the possessed boy, was partly executed by Raphael's pupils. The figures above, to the l., in an attitude of adoration are St. Lawrence and St. Julian. On the narrow-wall: **19. Madonna of Foligno, painted by *Raphael* in 1512; in the background the town of Foligno, into which a bomb falls; r. beneath, St. Jerome recommends to the notice of the Madonna Sigismondo Conti, secretary of Julius II., who ordered the painting for S. Maria in Araceli, whence it was transferred to S. Anna delle Contesse in Foligno; to the l. St. Francis and John the Baptist. The transference (undertaken at Paris) of the picture from wood to canvas has rendered retouching necessary. — 3rd R.: On the entrance-wall: 20. Madonna and Saints, *Titian*; St. Margaret of Cortona, *Guercino*. R. long-wall: 21. Doge of Venice, *Titian*; 22. M. Magdalene, *Guercino*; 23. Coronation of the Virgin, painted by *Bern. Pinturicchio* for the church delle Fratte at Perugia; beneath are the Apostles, St. Francis, St. Bonaventura and 3 Franciscans; 24. Resurrection, *Perugino*; the sleeping youth r. in the foreground is said to have the features of Raphael; 25. Assumption of the Virgin, designed by *Raphael* for the monastery of S. Maria di Monte Luco near Perugia, the upper half painted by *G. Romano*, the lower by *Franc. Penni (il Fattore)*; 26. Adoration of the infant Christ, *School of Perugino*; Joseph's head is said to be by Raphael, other figures by Spagna (formerly in La Spineta near Todi); *27. Coronation of the Virgin, painted by *Raphael* in 1502 in Perugino's school, for S. Francesco at Perugia; *28. Madonna on a throne with Laurentius, Ludovicus, Herculanus and Constantius, the guardian saints of Perugia, by *Perugino*; 29. Madonna, *Sassoferrato*. Narrow wall: 30. Entombment, *Caravaggio*. On the window-wall: Two large paintings in several compartments by *Niccolò Alunno*, Crucifixion of Christ and Coronation of the Virgin. Between these: *31. Fresco from the former library of the Vatican, *Melozzo da Forli*, representing Sixtus IV. the donor, with Card. Giul. della Rovere (Julius II.) and his nephew Pietro Riario; before him kneels Platina, prefect of the library. — 4th R.: Entrance-wall: 32. Martyrdom of Processus and Martinianus, *Valentin*; 33. Crucifixion of St. Peter, *Guido Reni*; 34. Martyrdom of St. Erasmus, *N. Poussin*. R. wall: 35. Annunciation, *F. Baroccio*. Window-wall: Madonna with the saints Jerome and Bartholomew, *Moretto da Brescia*; 38. Vision of St. Helena, *Paolo Veronese*. L. wall: 39. Madonna; beneath, St. Thomas and St. Jerome, *Guido Reni*; 41. Christ in a glory, *Correggio (?)*; 42. St. Romuald, *A. Sacchi*.

*Library (visitors knock at the last small door on the l. in the Galleria Lapidaria; open daily 12—13 o'clock, Sundays and high festivals excepted; 1/2—1 l.). At a very early period the popes began to collect documents which gradually formed the *Archives*, mentioned for the first time under Damasus I., and preserved in the Lateran. After various losses, caused especially by the migration to Avignon, and frequent change of locality, the library is now finally established in the Vatican in 11 rooms, in addition to the great library-hall. Over the door is the inscription: *Paulli Papae V. Archivium*. The Archives comprise a number of the most interesting and important documents, especially of the middle ages, registers of the papal acts, letters of the popes from Innocent III. to Sixtus V. in 2016 vols., correspondence with nuncios and foreign nations etc.

Besides this collection of documents the popes possessed their private libraries. The *Public Library* was first instituted by Nicholas V., and then consisted of 9000 vols.; Giov. Tortelli was the first librarian.

The library was neglected and dispersed by his successors. Sixtus IV. was the first to revive the institution: he appointed a locality under the Sixtine Chapel for the collection, Platina (1475) as its director, and definite revenues for its maintenance. Thus endowed, it increased steadily, and the allotted space became more and more inadequate to its requirements, until in 1588 Sixtus V. caused the present magnificent edifice to be erected by Dom. Fontana, intersecting the great court of Bramante. To this ever-increasing collection several considerable libraries have been added by purchase or donation, some of which are numbered and preserved separately. In 1623 the Elector Maximilian presented to the Pope the *Bibliotheca Palatina* of Heidelberg, when the town was taken in the Thirty Years' War; in 1657 the Bibl. Urbinas, founded by Duke Federigo da Montefeltro, in 1690 the B. Reginensis, once the property of Queen Christina of Sweden, in 1746 the B. Ottoboniana, purchased by Alex. VIII. (Ottobuoni), were added. Most of the MSS. carried off by the French were restored in 1814.

The Vatican Library now possesses nearly 24,000 MSS., of which about 17,000 are Latin, 3450 Greek and 2000 Oriental. Of the latter a printed catalogue has been published (1756—59), continued by A. Mai. Besides these, about 50,000 printed books. The principal director is a cardinal, at present *Tosti*, who in ordinary business is represented by two custodians, the Monsignori *di San Marzano* and *Martinucci*; besides these there are 7 scrittori and several subordinate officials (scopatori). The advantage of using the library is greatly circumscribed by numerous holidays, for it is not available on more than 200 days in the year, as well as by the short space allowed for work daily (9—12 o'clock). Permission to use it is best obtained by applying to the embassy, stating the branch of study contemplated.

An *Antechamber* is first entered, containing framed papyrus-scrolls and a facsimile of the two columns from the Triopium of Herodes Atticus on the Via Appia, with an imitation of the ancient Italian characters, the originals of which are in Naples. Here and in the following reading-room are suspended the portraits of the cardinal-librarians. The *Great Hall*, 226 ft. long, 49 ft. wide, 29 ft. high, supported by 6 buttresses, constructed by Fontana and paved with marble by Pius IX., is now entered. The paintings (of the 17th cent.) are gaudy and unattractive. By the walls and round the pillars are 46 small cabinets containing the MSS., the most celebrated of which are preserved in two glass-cases in the r. wing of the hall. In the 1st are the MSS. of the Greek New Testament (5th cent.), of Virgil (5th cent.), and Terence (the so-called "Bembinus", of the 4th cent.); also autographs of Petrarch and Tasso. In the 2nd the celebrated palimpsest of the Republic of Cicero, Dante with miniatures by *Giulio Clovio*, the ritual of Card. Ottobuoni, breviary of King Matthias Corvinus etc. Between the pillars are placed a number of gifts presented to the popes: a cross of malachite from Prince Demidoff; malachite vase, presented by the Emp. Nicholas to Gregory XVI.; the font of Sèvres porcelain, in which the imperial prince was baptized, presented by Napoleon III. to Pius IX.; vase of Scottish granite, gift of the Duke of Northumberland to Card. Antonelli; two vases of Berlin porcelain, presented by Fred. William IV. Behind a railing two candelabra, presented by Napoleon I. to Pius VII. To the r. at the extremity of the hall is the door to the Archives. Adjacent to this hall, and parallel with the Galler. Lapidaria and the Mus. Chiaramonti, are extensive corridors on the r. and l., to the latter of which visitors are generally first conducted. The two first rooms contain the MSS. of the Palatine and Urbino libraries. In the first, over the entrance, is represented the Interior of SS. Apostoli; in the second, over the entrance, the Erection of the Vatican Obelisk by Fontana (see p. 216); over the egress, St. Peter's according to Mich. Angelo's design. In the third room, quattro-centists and oriental MSS.; by the sides of the egress, two ancient portrait-statues, 1. the orator Aristides, r. supposed Hippolytus. Then the *Museum of Christian Antiquities*. The first room contains curiosities from the catacombs: lamps, glasses, bottles, gems, statuettes, pictures, altar-pieces, crosses etc., the most interesting of which are preserved under glass. To the r. in the first cabinet are several fine diptychs and triptychs in ivory, of which the first on the l. is especially remarkable. The second room, the *Stanza de' Papiri*, adorned with paintings by *Raph. Mengs*, is occupied by documents on papyrus from the 5th—8th cent. The glass-cabinets of the third room contain a large number of small pictures of the 13th—15th cent., unfortunately not distinctly visible. On the entrance-wall on the r. a Russian calender in the form of a cross with miniatures, of the 17th cent.; l. a large cross of rock-crystal, on which the Passion is represented, by *Valerio Vicentino*, presented by Pius IX. To the r. is the entrance to a collection of *Ancient Pictures*. On the floor, ancient mosaics. On the r. wall: Phaedra and Scylla; above, Ulysses and Circe; then the so-called *Aldobrandine Nuptials, one of the finest ancient pictures extant, found in Rome in 1606; above it, Ulysses encountering the Laestrygones; l. *Canace and an unknown female figure; above, Ulysses in the infernal regions; then Cupid in a two-horse chariot; above them, the Spies of Ulysses among the Laestrygones. On the narrow-wall: Myrrha and Pasiphae. These six mythological figures of women celebrated for their unfortuntate love-affairs, are from Torre di Marancio. The representations from the Odyssey were found on the Esquiline. In the following cabinet, a collection of *Ancient Tile-stamps*, and an ancient bronze chair. Returning to the third room: r. in the window, oriental gold and silver plate, a gift from Siam to Pius IX., with his photograph. The door leads hence to the former *Chapel of Pius V.*, with a carved prie-Dieu of Pius IX. (now occupied by the *Collection of Coins*, extensively pillaged in 1797 and 1849), and the conspicuous portrait on glass of Pius IX.

The visitor is conducted hence to the *Appartamenti Borgia*, occupied by the printed books. (Permission to visit these rooms is obtained, sometimes with difficulty, of Monsig. Martinucci, who lives above the library.) Several undecorated rooms are traversed, and the *apartments embellished with paintings by *Pinturicchio*, which are among the finest works of the kind, entered. The subjects are partly allegorical (1st room, arts and sciences), partly from the history of Christ and the saints. The last large saloon is adorned with paintings and stucco-work by *Giov. da Udine* and *Perino del Vaga*, now sadly marred by restoration. The rooms on the r. of the great hall, also occupied by MSS., are less interesting.

In the 1st Room: MSS. of the Vatican library, in the 2nd those of the Reginensis (over the entrance, the Harbour of Ostia). 3rd R.: Bibliot. Ottoboniana. Here and in the following rooms are unpleasing frescoes from the life of Pius VI. and VII. Several cabinets in the last room contain beautiful ancient and modern ornaments etc.; e. g. in the 2nd cabinet r. oriental bronzes, and articles in gold, hair found in an ancient tomb etc. To the l., by the closed door of egress, is a bronze head of Augustus, the finest extant portrait-bust of that emperor.

The *Studio del Mosaico*, or papal manufactory of mosaic, is beneath the gallery of the inscriptions; entrance in the l. angle of the farther side of the Cortile di S. Damaso. Permessi obtained through a consul or ambassador. Numerous hands are here employed in copying celebrated pictures for churches etc. The material used is a kind of coloured glass, of which there are no fewer than 10,000 different shades. The papal *Armoury* and *Mint (La Zecca)* near the Vatican also contain a few objects of interest, e. g. all the papal coins from the time of Hadrian I., and most of the dies since Martin V.

The Catacombs.

Ancient and Christian Rome are apparently separated by a wide chasm, if the modern aspect of the city alone be regarded. The most ancient churches having disappeared, or being concealed beneath a modern garb, the earliest Christian monuments of any importance are several centuries later than the last Roman structures. This interval is filled up in a significant manner by means of the Catacombs, or burial-places of the early Christian centuries, which have recently been rendered specially interesting by a series of important investigations. Access permitted only in the company of a guide, from whom the most necessary information may be obtained. Permessi gratis at the office of the cardinal-vicar, Via della Scrofa 70 (Pl. I, 13), on personal application (best time 11—12 a. m.); a certain day (generally Sunday) and hour are fixed, to which visitors must adhere (gratuity 1/2 l. for 1 pers., 1—2 each for a party). A wax-taper (cerino) should not be forgotten. The scientific may apply for information on abstruse matters to the *Cav. de' Rossi*, or to his Eminence Card. *Reisach*, a well-known and erudite investigator of the catacombs.

The name "Catacombs" is modern, having been extended from those under S. Sebastiano, to which the topographical designation *"ad catacumbas"* was anciently applied, to the others also. The early Christians designated their burial-places by the Greek name *Cœmeteria*, i. e. resting or sleeping-place, probably with reference to the hope of the resurrection. The Roman law, frequently renewed during the empire, prohibiting the interment of the dead, or even their ashes, within the precincts of the city, was of course binding on the Christians also. We accordingly find their burying-places situated between the 1st and 3rd milestones beyond the Aurelian wall, to which Rome had extended long before the construction of the wall itself. A desire to inter the dead instead of destroying them by fire, as well as the example of Jewish custom, gave rise to the excavation of subterranean passages, in the lateral walls of which apertures were made for the reception of the corpses. The formerly prevalent idea that the early Christians employed ancient sand-pits (arenaria) for this purpose, and extended them according to requirement, as well as the belief that the different catacombs were all connected, has been entirely refuted by modern investigation. These subterranean passages are proved to have been excavated almost exclusively for the purposes of Christian interment, in the soft strata of tufa (tufo granolare), of which most of the hills in the environs of Rome consist, and which can be but little used for building purposes. In a few exceptional cases only have the hard tuffstone, employed in building, and the puzzolana, which when mingled with lime yields the celebrated Roman cement, been penetrated. It is moreover ascertained that several of these "cemeteries" were kept within the limits prescribed by the Roman law with regard to excavations, and therefore enjoyed its protection. The Romans distinguished between family-tombs and those of more extended societies (collegia). In both cases the purchase of a definite area was necessary, within which every tomb was sacred and inviolable above and beneath the surface. So also the catacombs are partly family-tombs, and partly those of societies formed by the Christians for the establishment of common burial-places. The approaches to these vaults were everywhere wide and conspicuous, without the slightest indication of attempt at concealment. An ecclesiastical supervision of cemeteries is mentioned for the first time about the year 200, and appears gradually to have extended over all the Christian burial-places, the different districts of which were distributed among the deacons. In the 3rd cent. the safety of the catacombs was frequently endangered, for to them, as well as to the devout who assembled to celebrate divine service at the tombs of the martyrs, the persecutions of the Christians extended. Thus a considerable number of cases are recorded in which the Christians suffered martyrdom in their subterranean places of refuge, and from that period date the occasionally perceptible precautionary measures, as narrow staircases, concealed entrances etc. In the 4th cent., however, peace was restored to the Church and security to the catacombs by Constantine the Great's edict of Milan. Throughout this century interments were here customary, but became rarer towards the commencement of the 5th, and were soon entirely discontinued. The catacombs, however, as well as the tombs of the martyrs, still enjoyed the veneration of pilgrims and the devout. As early as 370 Pope Damasus caused numerous restorations to be made, and the most important tombs to be furnished with metrical inscriptions; apertures for light were constructed, to facilitate the access of visitors, and the walls at a comparatively late period decorated with paintings, which differ materially from those of the earliest Christians in subject and treatment. But at the same time, during frequent devastations undergone by the city, the catacombs were also pillaged and injured. The last extensive restorations were undertaken by John III. in 560—573. In the 8th cent. it became customary to open the tombs of the martyrs and distribute their remains among the different basilicas of the city, and in the 9th the catacombs gradually fell into oblivion, those under S. Sebastiano alone remaining accessible to the visits of pilgrims. Traces of renewed visits to a few of the catacombs are not again perceptible till the close of the 15th cent., and in the 16th *Bosio* undertook comprehensive scientific investigations, which, although never discontinued, have only within the last thirty years led to important results under the directions of *P. Marchi*, and especially those of the *Cav. de' Rossi*. The latter has begun to publish the result of his indefatigable labours in a collection of ancient Christian inscriptions, in a work entitled "*Roma Sotterranea*" (1st vol. 1864, 2nd vol. 1868), and in the "*Bullettino di Archeologia Cristiana*".

The *Arrangement of the Catacombs* was originally extremely simple. Narrow passages, 3 ft. in width, and subsequently even less, were excavated and furnished with recesses in the sides, of the length of the body to be interred. The latter were then closed with tablets of marble, and occasionally of terracotta, which at first recorded only the name of the deceased, with the addition "*in pace*". By degrees these localities were extended; the passages became narrower and higher, or rose in different stages one above another. Catacombs originally distinct were connected by means of new excavations, and the complicated progress of these alterations and extensions is to this day perceptible to the eye of the observant. These operations were carried out by a regular society of *Fossores* (or diggers), who ceased to exist only when the use of the catacombs was discontinued. Altered times and circumstances naturally exercised a corresponding influence on the aspect of the catacombs. They originally differed little from similar heathen localities, and the use of sarcophagi and interment in the rock without other receptacle were equally customary. Occasionally larger spaces are found excavated in the walls of the passages, probably as family-tombs, or for the reception of martyrs, or for certain members of the ecclesiastical community, an example of the last case being preserved in the catacombs of Calixtus, destined for the remains of the popes. Finally chambers are also seen which served for the celebration of divine worship. The opinion is erroneous that this was the original object of the catacombs (divine service being doubtless performed in private houses in the city), although it is well ascertained that the Christians occasionally assembled at the graves of the martyrs for the purposes of prayer and the celebration of the communion. In order to obtain sufficient space for this, two corresponding excavations were usually made on each side of the passage, the two being employed as a single chapel. The tomb of a martyr was then generally used as a tribune, in front of which an altar (often portable) was erected. Light and air were in many cases admitted from above by means of "luminaria". Thus these chapels, concealing or in immediate proximity to the tombs of the martyrs, formed as it were rallying-points throughout the entire system, and, as they continued to be objects of veneration long after the catacombs were disused as burial-places, they were at a later period often rendered accessible by stairs constructed for the use of visitors.

The *Decoration* of the catacombs is one of their most interesting features. Christian art in its origin could of course be but an application of ancient precepts to new subjects. The paintings and sculptures of the catacombs are therefore in no respect different in style from their contemporaries, and with them shared in the precipitate and almost total degradation of art. But, on the other hand, a peculiar significance in the choice and treatment of the subjects is observable from the earliest period. Comparatively few merely historical paintings are found, which have no other object in view than the representation of some simple fact from Jewish or Christian lore. Occasionally a Madonna and Child are observed, most frequently with the Magi (varying in number), who present their offerings, as in the catacombs of St. Calixtus, Domitilla and Priscilla; also a few representations of martyrdoms etc. The great majority, however, of the paintings represent events symbolical of the doctrines and hopes of Christianity. That of most frequent recurrence is the Resurrection, typified either by the raising of Lazarus, who appears at a door enveloped in his grave-clothes, whilst Christ (beardless) [with a wand stands before it, or by the history of Jonah sitting under the gourd, then swallowed, and finally rejected by the whale. The Good Shepherd also frequently appears, with the recovered sheep on his shoulders. sometimes surrounded by lambs, to whom the apostles preach and whose postures are expressively indicative of the different spirit in which they receive the word (e. g. catacombs of St. Calixtus). Daniel among the lions is another favourite subject, represented with hands raised in prayer, an attitude in which the deceased are themselves often depicted. This is doubtless in allusion to the frequently cherished hope that the deceased, especially the martyrs, would intercede for their bereaved friends. Moreover, in addition to the words "(Requiescat) in Pace", the exclamations not unfrequently occur: "Pray for thy husband, for thy son" etc. Finally a number of the principal representations, which recur often and in similar style, are connected with the sacraments of baptism and the communion. Here also the same symbolical mode of representation is employed. For, besides the simple ceremony of baptism, Moses is very frequently seen in the act of striking the rock, whilst the name of Peter is sometimes attached to his figure, whereby the apostle is doubtless designated as the new Moses of a new community. Or the baptism takes place in the water flowing from the rock; or the water is full of fish, which, by a species of acrostic, formed an important Christian symbol, the Greek *ἰχϑύς* (fish) consisting of the initial letters of: *Ἰησοῦς Χριστὸς Θεοῦ Υἱὸς Σωτήρ* (Jesus Christ the Saviour, Son of God). The communion is generally depicted as an assembly of persons (usually 7) around a table, on which, besides the bread, a fish also lies, again containing an allusion to Christ. Combined with this a reference to the miracle of the loaves also frequently appears (baskets with loaves standing on the ground), an event which in other cases is expressly represented. These subjects and many others, especially the traditions of the Old Testament, in which a typical reference to New Testament history could be discerned, recur continually in the paintings of the catacombs and in the sculptures on the ancient Christian sarcophagi. The numerous inscriptions corresponding to these were, as is already mentioned, of a very simple description till the middle of the 3rd cent., after which they become more detailed and contain more elaborate ejaculations of grief and hope.

The catacombs extend around the city in a wide circle, the majority however are concentrated between the Via Salara, Nomentana, Latina, Appia and Ostiensis. The number of cemeteries, exclusive of the smaller, was 26, which, however, at the present day are only partially accessible. The most important are here enumerated, and among these the highest interest attaches to the

*Catacombs of Calixtus on the Via Appia, 1¼ M. beyond the Porta S. Sebastiano (Pl. III, 28). On entering the vigna in which they are situated, the visitor perceives at a short distance a small brick structure with three apses. This was discovered by the Cav. de' Rossi to be the ancient *Oratorium S. Callixti in Arenariis*, and he accordingly induced Pius IX. to purchase the ground, where his investigations were speedily rewarded by the most important discoveries. The present entrance to the catacombs immediately adjoins this building. A passage with tombs is traversed, and a *chamber *(camera papale, cubiculum pontificum)* of considerable dimensions is soon reached on the l., containing the tombs of popes on the l., and of Anteros, Lucius, Fabianus and Eutychianus on the r.; in the central wall that of Sixtus II. (d. 258 as a martyr in the catacombs). In front of the latter is a long metrical inscription in honour of those here interred, composed by Pope Damasus about the close of the 4th cent., and engraved in the elegant and decorated characters which Furius Dionysius Philocalus, the secretary of that pope, invented specially for this purpose. On both sides of the entrance externally a great number of inscriptions have been scratched by devout visitors of the 4th—6th cent. A *chamber, open above, is next entered, which once contained the *Tomb of St. Cecilia*. Her remains now repose in the church of S. Cecilia in Trastevere. Here on the wall are several Byzantine paintings of the 7th—8th cent.: St. Cecilia, St. Urban and a head of Christ. The walls of the aperture for light bear traces of other frescoes. On St. Cecilia's day (Nov. 22nd) mass is here celebrated, on which occasion the chapel and the adjoining chambers are illuminated and open to the public. On the sides of the passages near these chapels are several tombs adorned with the symbolical representations of the communion, baptism etc. above alluded to. Then the tomb-chamber of Pope Eusebius, with an ancient copy of an inscription by Damasus, and another with two sarcophagi in which the remains of the deceased are still seen, one of them preserved and resembling a mummy, the other almost entirely destroyed. Finally the tomb of Pope Cornelius may be mentioned, appertaining originally to a distinct cemetery (that of Lucina).

The **Catacombs of SS. Nereus and Achilleus**, or of **Domitilla**, on the Via Ardeatina, near the catacombs of Calixtus, perhaps the earliest excavations of the description, have recently derived new interest from the discovery of a handsome and evidently public entrance of substantial brick-masonry. The architecture and internal decorations apparently date from the commencement of the 3rd cent. The whole is an extended family-tomb, subsequently placed in connection with other catacombs.

The **Catacombs of St. Prætextatus** on the Via Appia, opposite those of Calixtus, contain important paintings and monuments (tomb of St. Januarius), but are not always accessible on account of the excavations which are at present zealously prosecuted.

The **Catacombs of St. Priscilla**, 2 M. beyond the Porta Salara (Pl. I, 27), of very early construction, contain interesting paintings, among them a *Madonna and Child, probably of the beginning of the 2nd cent. They are also interesting in other respects, and well-preserved.

The **Catacombs of S. Agnese**, outside the Porta Pia, on the l. side of the Via Nomentana (p. 270), $1/4$ M. beyond the church of S. Agnese fuori, are interesting in their construction. One of the chambers furnished with several seats, was, according to the most recent assumptions, probably employed for purposes of instruction. Several others contain mural paintings deviating from the usual style: Christ between two packets of scrolls, the men in the fiery furnace etc. Then in the sides of the passage two corresponding recesses which served as a place for divine worship, in one of them a seat for the bishop and benches for the clergy. Another chapel contains a Madonna of the latter part of the 3rd cent. An ancient sand-pit connected with these catacombs distinctly proves by its character that the burial places and arenaria originally possessed nothing in common.

The **Catacombs of S. Sebastiano**, beneath the church of that name (p. 265), are those which alone have never been consigned to oblivion, and are now accessible without permesso.

The **Catacombs of S. Alessandro**, situated on the Via Nomentana, 7 M. from the Porta Pia (Pl. I, 30), are beyond the circle of the Roman catacombs, and probably appertained to the small town of Nomentum (now Mentana). They have been discovered within the last few years only. Their chief interest arises from the ruins which they comprise of an originally half-subterranean oratorium, the traces of which are still distinctly recognised. They are believed to date from the 5th cent. The apsis contains the episcopal throne, in front of it the altar, beneath which, as an inscription records, the tomb of Pope Alexander once lay. This space is separated from the rest of the church by marble barriers; the adjacent ambos are probably of somewhat later date. This oratory is adjoined by chapels with the tombs of martyrs, and with these other passages with tombs are connected, some of which are in a more undisturbed state of preservation than those in the other catacombs. The construction appears to betoken haste and poverty, the remains of earlier structures having been almost exclusively employed throughout.

The **Jewish Catacombs**, in the *Vigna Randinini*, to the l. of the Via Appia, $^1/_2$ M. from the Porta S. Sebastiano (Pl. III, 28), are more spacious than the Christian, and in some respects different. The tombs generally bear Jewish symbols (the seven-branched candelabrum etc.). About 200 Greek and Latin inscriptions have been found here, as well as a sarcophagus. These catacombs are believed to date from the middle of the 3rd cent.

The **Catacombs of Mithras**, on the Via Appia (p. 264), owe their origin to the mysteries of Mithras, an oriental (Persian) worship of the sun introduced at Rome about one century before Christ, which subsequently became more prevalent and was officially organized by Alex. Severus. Fantastic ceremonies and mysterious doctrines invested it with great attraction, and several Christian features appear to have been eventually incorporated with it, so that the symbols and arrangements here observed are not unfrequently analogous to those of the Christian catacombs.

13. Environs of Rome.

The extensive Campagna di Roma, bounded on the N. by the Ciminian Forest, on the W. by the sea, and on the E. by the Apennine chain of the Sabina, presents an ample field for a number of the most interesting excursions. The mountains with their picturesque contours, and the wild and deserted plain, everywhere replete with imposing ruins, especially those of ancient times, possess attractions of the highest order, which a year of study could hardly exhaust. — The Campagna, once covered by the sea, owes its origin to powerful volcanic agency; lava and peperine are frequently encountered, and the red volcanic tuff is everywhere predominant. A great number of ancient craters may be distinguished, the most important of which are the lakes of the Alban Mts., the lake of Bracciano, the lake of Vico in the Ciminian Forest, and the crater of Baccano. The historical associations connected with this plain are, however, of still higher interest than its natural attractions. The narrow strip of land which stretches between the Alban Mts. and the Tiber towards the sea is the ancient Latium, which victoriously asserted its superiority over the Etruscans on the N., the Sabines on the E., and the Volscians on the S., subsequently effected the union of the Italian peninsula, and finally acquired supremacy over the whole world. Once a densely peopled land, with numerous and prosperous towns, it is now a vast and dreary waste, of which a comparatively small part is traversed by the ploughshare. In May, when the malaria begins to prevail, herdsmen and cattle retire to the mountains, whilst the few who are compelled to remain behind are doomed to a miserable existence and continual attacks of fever. The cause of this change dates from the remote period of the last centuries of the republic, when the independent agricultural population was gradually superseded by proprietors of large estates and pastures. This system inevitably entailed the ruin of the country, for a dense population and high degree of culture alone can avert the malaria, which is produced by defective drainage and the evaporation of the stagnant water in undulating and furrowed volcanic soil. In the middle ages the evil increased. The papal government has repeatedly endeavoured to promote the revival of agriculture, but such attempts cannot be otherwise than fruitless as long as the land is occupied by farms and pastures on a large scale. An entire revolution in the present system, energetically and comprehensively carried out, will alone avail to restore the prosperity of the land.

Excursions in the Campagna may be performed by carriage, on horseback, or on foot, each mode possessing its peculiar advantages. The traveller is particularly cautioned against the hazard of taking cold, owing to the abrupt change of temperature which usually occurs about sunset. Lying or sitting on the ground in winter, when the soil is extremely cold in comparison with the hot sunshine, is also to be avoided. In crossing the fields care should be taken not to encounter one of the formidable herds of cattle, especially in spring; the same remark sometimes applies to the dogs by which they are watched, when the herdsman is absent. Predatory assaults on travellers are of rare occurrence. The longer excursions (p. 273), which require a whole day at least, are enumerated in their geographical order. Those whose residence in Rome is sufficiently prolonged should undertake the excursions in the plain during the winter, and those among the mountains in the warmer season.

The excursions first described are those in the immediate environs, which occupy a few hours only, and will be found invigorating after a morning spent in a church or museum. As far as the gates, and about 3/4 M. beyond, the roads are enclosed by lofty walls, and are consequently tedious and uninteresting. A carriage should therefore be taken as far as the gates at least (80 c.; beyond the gates according to agreement). The city should, if possible, be regained about sunset. The gates are closed at 8 p. m.

The principal points of interest only can be here pointed out. Those who desire to extend their expeditions beyond these limits will find a sufficient indication of the routes among the longer excursions (p. 273). The Cavaliere *Pietro Rosa*, superintendent of the French excavations on the Palatine (p. 184), and at present the most learned investigator of the Campagna, usually forms scientific parties in spring for the purpose of visiting historically interesting localities, as Veii (p. 297), Fidenæ (p. 271), Hadrian's Villa (p. 284) etc., and kindly permits strangers introduced to him to participate in the excursions.

A. Short Excursions in the Campagna.

The excursions are enumerated according to the order of the gates from S. to N.

Beyond Porta S. Paolo (Pl. II, 16).

Tre Fontane. The route as far as the gate, the Protestant Cemetery, the Pyramid of Cestius, and the Church of S. Paolo

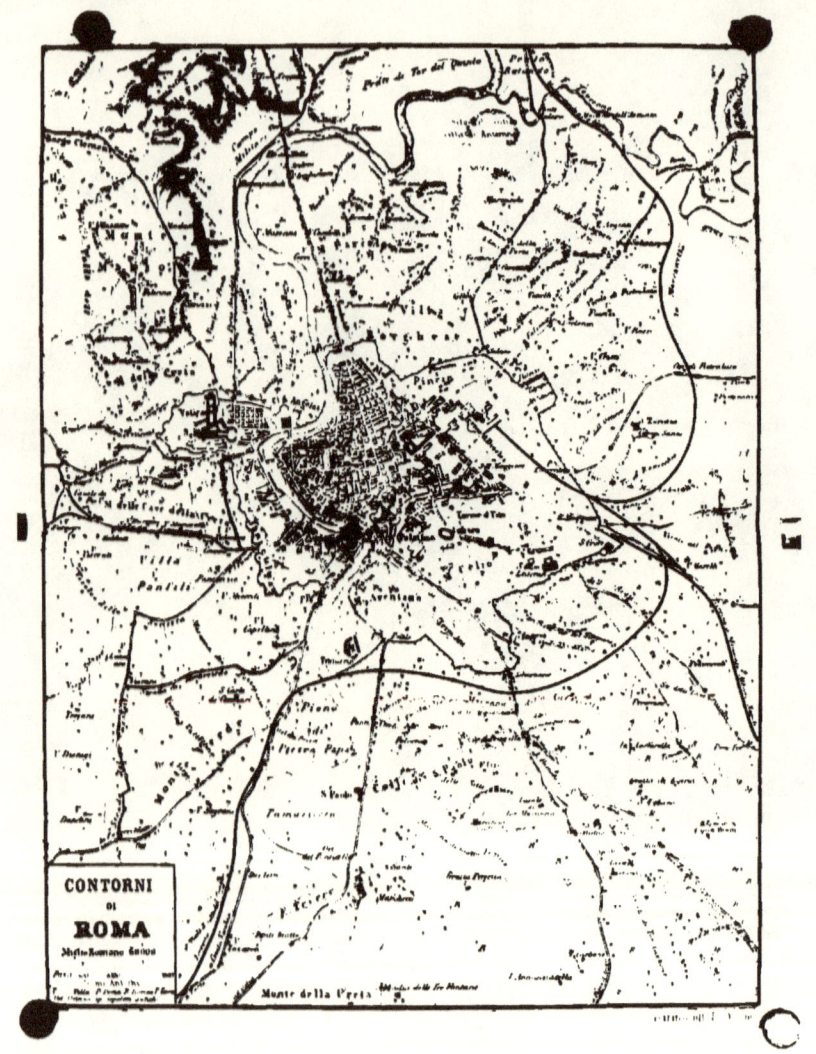

uori le Mura is described at pp. 190 and 194, and may conveniently be combined with this excursion. Those who desire to proceed to the church direct may avail themselves of the omnibus thither, which starts every $1/_2$ hr. from the Piazza di Venezia, at the back of Gesù (6 soldi), a drive of 23 min.

Opposite S. Paolo a pleasant route of 2 M. diverges to S. Sebastiano on the Via Appia (p. 264), and intersects the Via Ardeatina.

The present route proceeds in a straight direction, and 7 min. beyond the church divides at the *Osteria del Ponticello;* r. the ancient *Via Ostiensis* diverges to *Ostia* (p. 302), l. the *Via Ardeatina Nuova*. The latter leads in $1/_2$ hr. to the **Abbey delle tre Fontane** *(ad aquas Salvias)*, almost entirely abandoned on account of the unhealthiness of the situation. A monk who generally remains here till the evening will be found to act as guide. The appellation is derived from three springs which are said to have welled forth when the apostle Paul was here executed, and his head was observed to make three distinct leaps. The three churches are approached by an archway bearing traces of painting, which is believed to have pertained to an earlier church of John the Baptist. *SS. *Vincenzo ed Anastasio*, the largest of the churches, a basilica in the ancient style, was founded by Honorius I., restored in 1221 by Honorius III., as the inscription to the l. of the choir records, and has retained much of its antique peculiarities, especially the marble windows over the nave. The portico contains traces of paintings, among them the portrait of Honorius III. The pillars are embellished with the figures of the 12 apostles, from Raphael's designs or Marcantonio's engravings, recently badly restored. R. of this is the second church, the circular *S. Maria Scala Cœli*, so called because the "vision" of a heavenly ladder here appeared to St. Bernhard (to whom Innocent III. had presented the monastery), on which angels conducted to heaven those whom his prayers had released from purgatory. Its present form dates from the close of the 16th cent. The tribune contains good mosaics by *F. Zuccaro:* the saints Zeno, Bernhard, Vincent the deacon and Vinc. Anastasius, revered by Clement VIII. and Card. Aldobrandini, the finisher of the church. The third church, *S. Paolo alle tre Fontane*, stands on the spot where the apostle is said to have been beheaded, and contains the three springs already mentioned; on the r. is the column of white marble to which St. Paul is said to have been bound at the time of his execution. The present edifice dates from 1599.

Beyond Porta S. Sebastiano (Pl. III, 28).

The route by the Via di Porta S. Sebastiano as far as the gate, and the ruins and edifices situated near it, are described at p. 194.

Via Appia. The military road, constructed B. C. 212 by the censor Appius Claudius Cæcus, led by the ancient *Porta Capena*, near S. Gregorio, to Capua, whence it was subsequently extended to Beneventum and Brundisium. In 1850—53 it was excavated by order of Pius IX., under the superintendence of the minister of commerce Jacobini and the architect Canina, as far as the 11th milestone, and to this day verifies its ancient appellation of the "queen of roads". It affords perhaps the finest of all the excursions in the Campagna. Shortly after the city is quitted, a most magnificent prospect is enjoyed, embracing the Campagna, the ruins of the aqueducts, and the mountains, whilst on either side of the road numerous ancient tombs are situated. But few of the latter are preserved: the remnants of the others have been carefully restored by Canina, so as at least to convey an idea of their architecture and decoration. Pedestrians are recommended to take a carriage (1^1/$_2$—2 l. for one-horse) as far as the tomb of Cæcilia Metella (p. 265), and proceed thence on foot at least as far as Casale Rotondo (p. 266), an excursion of 4—5 hrs. With this a visit to the ruins in the Caffarella valley (p. 267) may most suitably be combined by the pedestrian, thus considerably abridging the first and uninteresting portion of the route.

From the gate the descent is by the ancient *Clivus Martis*, intersected after 4 min. by the railway to Civita Vecchia. About 3 min. farther the brook *Almo* is crossed, where ruins of tombs are observed on the r. and l. After 5 min. more the Via Ardeatina diverges to the r.; on the l. stands the small church of **Domine Quo Vadis,** so named from the legend that St. Peter, fleeing from the death of a martyr, here met his Master and enquired of him: "Domine quo vadis?" to which he received the answer: "Venio iterum crucifigi"; whereupon the apostle, ashamed of his weakness, returned. A footprint which Christ is said to have impressed on the marble is shown here.

A short distance beyond the church a field-road diverges to the l., by a small circular chapel, to the Caffarella Valley (p. 267). The high road now ascends, being enclosed for the next ^{1}/$_2$ M. by unsightly walls. To the r., 1^1/$_4$ M. from the gate, is the entrance to the *Catacombs of St. Calixtus* (p. 259), furnished with an inscription and shaded with cypresses. A carriage-road soon afterwards diverges to the l., leading by S. Urbano (p. 267) and the baths of Acqua Santa to (3 M.) the so-called ruins of Roma Vecchia (p. 266), on the high road to Albano (Via Appia Nuova). Then, ^{1}/$_4$ M. from the catacombs, the church of **S. Sebastiano,** which from a very early period belonged to the seven churches frequented by pilgrims, being erected over the catacombs where the remains of so many martyrs reposed. Mention of it is first made under Gregory the Great. The form was originally that of a basilica, but in 1612 it was altered by Flaminio Ponzio and Giov. Vasanzio. The portico is supported by six ancient columns of granite. The first chapel on the r. contains a "footprint of Christ" in stone; the last on the r. was designed by C. Maratta. Over the high altar a painting by Innocenzo Tacconi, pupil of Ann. Caracci. The second chapel on the l. contains a good statue of S. Sebastian, designed by Bernini and executed by Giorgini. A stair on the l. by the egress descends to the catacombs (1 l.), which however are uninteresting compared with those of Calixtus.

A short distance farther, on the opposite side of the road, lies the *Circus of Maxentius, constructed in 311. It is sufficiently excavated and well-preserved to admit of the arrangement of the structure, which was destined for chariot-races, being observed. Length 1482 ft., breadth 244 ft. Facing the Via Appia was once an extensive colonnade, behind it a grand entrance, opposite to which was another in the semicircle which terminated the structure (on the above-mentioned road, which to the l. leads to S. Urbano). At the sides were other gates, of which the first on the r. is supposed to be the *Porta Libitina* by which the dead were carried out. On either side of the first-mentioned main entrance were the *carceres*, or barriers. The chariots starting hence had seven times to perform the circuit of the course, which was formed by the seats of the spectators and the *Spina*, a wall erected longitudinally in the centre of the arena, and embellished with statues and obelisks (one of these now stands in the Piazza Navona, p. 156). At the extremities of this wall stood the *metae*, or goals. The direction of the spina was somewhat oblique, with a view to equalize the disadvantages of those starting in different positions; for the same reason the carceres are in a curved line. The spectators sat on 10 rows of steps around, on which about 18,000 could be accommodated. — The ruins of a circular building by the circus, on the Via Appia, are supposed to be a temple of Romulus, the son of Maxentius, who died at an early age, and to whose honour the circus was perhaps also constructed.

The traveller now ascends in 5 min. to the *Tomb of Cæcilia Metella, which forms so conspicuous an object in the views of Rome and the Campagna, a circular structure, upwards of 60 ft. in diameter, on a square basement, both of which were originally covered with travertine. The frieze above is adorned with wreaths of flowers and skulls of oxen, from which latter the tomb derives its appellation of *Capo di Bove*. On a marble tablet facing the road is inscribed: *Caeciliae Q. Cretici Filiae Metellae Crassi*, i. e. to the manes of the daughter of Metellus Creticus, wife of the triumvir Crassus, who was here interred. The interior, now almost entirely filled up, contained the tomb-chamber of the deceased. In the 13th cent. the Gaetani converted the edifice into the tower of a stronghold, and furnished it with pinnacles. To this extensive castle, which subsequently passed through various hands, and was destroyed under Sixtus V., belong the picturesque ruins of a palace adjacent to the tower, and a church opposite.

As far as this vicinity extends a lava-stream which once descended from the Alban Mts. and yielded paving material for the ancient road. The more interesting portion of the Via now begins. the ancient pavement is in most places visible, on both sides continuous rows of tombs skirt the road, most of them, however, in a ruined state, and the view becomes more extensive at every step. On the l. the adjacent arches of the Aqua Marcia and Claudia are perceived, the latter now partially converted into the modern Acqua Felice (comp. p. 269). The road gradually ceases to be bordered by houses, and $2^1/_4$ M. from the city-gate the entrance to the excavated portion of the Via Appia, flanked beyond this point by a dense succession of tombs, is attained. Many of the latter contain reliefs and inscriptions worthy of note. The scenery continues to be of the most sublime description. On the l., $1^1/_4$ M. from the entrance, a "casale" has been built within the walls of an ancient church, the so-called *S. Maria Nuova*. Beyond it lie the extensive ruins known as *Roma Vecchia*, which appear to have belonged to a spacious villa of the Quintilii. Several of the chambers were employed as baths.

A large tomb on the l., over which a small farm is now established, $3/_4$ M. from Roma Vecchia, is termed *Casale Rotondo*. It lies by the 6th milestone, and, according to Canina, was erected for Messala Corvinus, a statesman and poet of considerable reputation under Augustus. This assumption, however. is not borne out by sufficiently strong evidence. It may be ascended for the sake of the fine view it commands. The lofty structure on the l., 7 min. farther, on the same side, is an ancient tomb on which the Arabians and Normans subsequently erected a tower, named *Tor di Selce* (tower of basalt).

The prolongation of the Via Appia hence to Albano ($7^1/_2$ M.) is less interesting. Among the tombs may be mentioned, on the l., 2 M. beyond Tor di Selce. the circular *Torraccio* or *Palombaro*, name of deceased unknown. At the 11th milestone the road is intersected by the railway, a short distance beyond which is the Osteria delle Frattochie; hence to Albano see p. 279. Pedestrians who wish to avoid traversing the same ground twice may by crossing the fields to the l. from Tor di Selce (or by a field-road 1 M. farther, leading to the Via Appia Nuova). and intersecting the Via Appia Nuova (at a point about 6 M. from the city-gate), reach stat. *Ciampino* (p. 279) in $^1/_2$ hr., and return by one of the trains from Albano or Frascati (for 1 l. 60, 1 l. and 70 c.).

Temple of the Deus Rediculus. Grotto of Egeria. S. Urbano. At the small chapel beyond the church of Domine quo Vadis the field-road to the l. is taken, leading during 10 min. between hedges. When the open field is reached, the road descending to the l. to the mill is followed. Near the latter is situated the so-called *Temple of the Deus Rediculus*, a Roman tomb of Hadrian's time, on an ancient road which formerly issued from the now closed Porta Latina. The architecture is tasteful; the brick ornaments, Corinthian pilasters (on the S. lateral wall half-columns) and cornicing should be noticed.

Returning hence to the road, the traveller may next ascend the valley of the *Almo* or *Caffarella*. The carriage-road is followed in a straight direction; after 5 min. a gate (cancello) is passed through, immediately beyond which a road diverges to the Tenuta on the l.; 2 min. farther, after a second cancello is passed, the carriage-road, which should be quitted in order to follow the path by the brook, ascends to the r. to S. Urbano. This leads to the so-called **Grotto of Egeria**, which was here sought for, owing to an erroneous interpretation of a passage of Juvenal. It is a Nymphæum, originally covered with marble, and was the shrine of the brook Almo which flows past it, erected at a somewhat late period. A niche in the posterior wall contains the mutilated statue of the river-god; the niches in the lateral walls were also once occupied by statues.

The footpath now passes a small, but formerly more extensive wood on the hill, where, according to the account of the ciceroni, Numa is said to have held his interviews with the nymph Egeria, and ascends to **S. Urbano**, a Roman tomb of the time of the Antonines, long regarded as a temple of Bacchus, an object recognised from a distance by its red brick walls. It appears to have been converted into a church in the 11th cent., from which period the paintings date. The edifice was provided with a portico borne by four Corinthian columns, which was probably walled up during the restoration in 1634, on which occasion the flying buttresses were also added. The interior (5 soldi) is adorned with paintings between the Corinthian pilasters, restored under Urban VIII., but interesting on account of their origin. They were executed, according to an inscription on the Crucifixion over the door, by a certain Bonizo in the year 1011. On the posterior wall is Christ on a throne imparting blessings; also scenes from the lives of Christ, St. Urban and St. Cecilia. A stair, now walled up, is said to lead to the catacombs. From the small wood on the neighbouring hill there is a magnificent prospect of the Campagna and Alban Mts.

The path, partially shaded by trees, and commanding charming views, leads from S. Urbano in 2 min. to the high road, which to the r. leads to the Via Appia, above the catacombs of Calixtus, in 9 min. '(p. 264). Or if the high road be followed to the l., it leads in 2 min. to the Circus of Maxentius, which may be traversed, and the traveller thus reaches the Via Appia below the Tomb of Cæcilia Metella. Those who prefer it may drive as far as S. Urbano, and thence descend to the Grotto of Egeria.

In the other direction the pedestrian may cross the valley of the Almo, leaping a few small ditches, and traverse the fields so as to reach the Via Appia Nuova ($^1/_4$ hr.). The tombs on the Via Latina, a visit to which may be conveniently combined with this, lie near the 2nd milestone, near which the pedestrian arrives; the direction to be followed inclines towards the city.

Beyond Porta S. Giovanni (Pl. II, 33).

Tombs on the Via Latina. The ancient Via Latina diverged from the Via Appia outside the Porta Capena; the now closed Porta Latina in the wall of Aurelian was destined for its point of issue. Like the Via Appia and the other roads emerging from Rome, it was bordered by tombs on both sides, several of which, especially interesting on account of their decorations, were excavated in 1862. The route thither is in a straight direction by the Via Appia Nuova leading to Albano, issuing from the Porta S. Giovanni and commanding beautiful views. At the Trattoria of Baldinotti the road to the l. leads to Frascati (p. 274). The high road is followed as far as the second milestone of the present route, immediately beyond which it is quitted by a road leading to the l. to the ancient Via Latina, passing the remnants of the ancient road, where two interesting *Tombs* are situated (which may be reached by carriage). The custodian ($^1/_2$ l., for a party 1—1$^1/_2$ l.) is to be found on the spot in winter. That on the r., with the two recently restored Roman pilasters, consisted of an anterior court and subterranean tomb, over which the now re-erected sacellum with two columns arose. The interior of the chamber is decorated with interesting reliefs in stucco, sea-monsters, nymphs and genii. The other tomb, beneath a shed opposite, contains in its single chamber landscapes and mythological paintings, framed in *stucco ornaments, the subjects of which are principally derived from the Trojan traditions. According to the inscriptions, both date from the close of the 2nd cent. The third tomb is devoid of interest. A few paces beyond this point, a charming view is obtained. In the immediate vicinity the foundations of a basilica, dedicated to St. Stephen in the 5th cent., have been excavated. From this point it is a walk of 10 minutes only, across the fields, to the Porta Furba, so that these excursions may be conveniently combined. Travellers by carriage should direct the driver to proceed thither.

About 3/4 M. farther on the Via Appia Nuova a road diverges to the cold mineral-baths of *Acqua Santa*, and passing the circus of Maxentius and S. Urbano, leads to the Via Appia near the catacombs of Calixtus (see p. 264).

Porta Furba. This excursion of 2—3 hrs. is pleasanter than many others, as the view is for short distances only obstructed by walls (carriage thither from the gate and back, 2—4 l.). From Porta S. Giovanni a straight direction is followed for 5 min.; at the Osteria the road to Frascati is entered to the l., which after a short distance is crossed by the railway to Civita Vecchia. To the l. the continuous series of arches of the *Acqua Felice* is kept in view, and in front of it the *Aqua Claudia* and *Marcia*, running one above the other, occasionally appear. The *Acqua Felice*, completed by Sixtus V. in 1585, and subsequently frequently restored, extends from the base of the Alban Mts. near Colonna, 11 M. in length ($^2/_3$rds subterraneous), and terminates at the Fontana di Termini (Pl. I, 22). The *Aqua Marcia*, constructed by the Prætor Q. Martius Rex, B. C. 146, extends as far as the Sabine Mts., 56 M. in length; its water was considered the purest in Rome. Over it here flows the *Aqua Claudia*, erected A. D. 50 by the Emp. Claudius, extending from the vicinity of Subiaco, a distance of 58$^1/_2$ M. — To the r. a view of the Via Appia with the tomb of Cæcilia Metella. 2 M. from the gate the "*Porta Furba*" is reached, being an arch of the Acqua Felice, beneath which the road leads. An exquisite *prospect is here enjoyed of the Campagna and the Alban Mts., beyond which rise the more distant Sabine Mts. Below runs the railway to Naples and Frascati. About 2 min. from the Porta Furba, the *Osteria del Pino stands by the pine on the r.

Beyond Porta Maggiore (Pl. II, 35).

Two high roads issue hence: r. the Via Labicana, l. the Via Prænestina. On the ancient *Via Labicana* which leads to Palestrina (comp. p. 290), 3 M. distant, are situated the remains of the octagonal *Monument of the Empress Helena*, whose sarcophagus found here is now preserved in the Vatican. The structure is termed **Torre Pignattara** from the earthenware vessels (pignatte) immured in the vaulting on account of their lighter weight, as was customary during the period of the empire. It contains little to arrest the traveller's attention.

Tor de' Schiavi. Outside the Porta Maggiore the ancient *Via Prænestina* is followed to the l., a quiet and lonely route, but, as the city is left behind, commanding beautiful views of the mountains. About 1 M. from the gate the vineyard-walls cease. Numerous ruins of tombs on the r. indicate the direction of the ancient route, in order to attain which the field may be crossed, as it affords a more unobstructed view than the lower level of the road. About 2 M. from the city-gate the ruins termed *Tor de' Schiavi* are attained. They probably belonged to an extensive villa of the Gordians. First, to the l. of the road, is a hexagonal structure, almost entirely fallen to decay. A column in the centre and the additional erection on the summit, both mediæval, impart a grotesque aspect to the place. Farther on is a circular building with niches and dome, used in the middle ages as a church, whence the now nearly obliterated frescoes; beneath (entrance in the rear) is a vault supported by strong pillars in the centre. Both of these buildings are conjectured to have been pertinents of a bath-establishment. Among the extensive ruins on the r. of the road are a few columbaria.

The road proceeds hence to (12 M.) Gabii and (23 M.) Palestrina (comp. p. 290).

3 M. from the city-gate the road, diverging to the l. (ancient *Via Collatina)* and skirting the *Acqua Vergine*, leads to *Lunghezza*, the ancient *Collatia*, 10 M. distant, a tenuta (or farm) of the Duca Strozzi, on the *Anio*, forming a charmingly shaded oasis in the Campagna. On this road, 5 M. from Rome, lies the *Tenuta Cervara* with the celebrated *Grottoes of Cervara*.

Beyond Porta S. Lorenzo (Pl. II, 31).

The road issuing from this gate leads to the church of the same name (p. 142), and thence to Tivoli (p. 293).

Beyond Porta Pia (Pl. I, 30).

The road issuing hence, the ancient *Via Nomentana*, passes the Villa Torlonia and the church of S. Agnese with the adjoining catacombs (p. 260). 2 M. from the gate it crosses the *Anio* by an ancient, but frequently restored bridge *(Ponte Nomentuno)*, surmounted by a tower. This road is also bordered with ancient tombs. 3 M. from the gate, on the r., is the picturesque and conspicuous *Casale dei Pazzi*. Beyond it is a hill on the l., conjectured to be the *Mons Sacer* celebrated for the secession of the Plebs. 6 M. farther are the catacombs of Alexander (p. 260).

A short distance beyond the catacombs, a road to the r. diverges to Palombara, situated at the foot of M. Gennaro, 21 M. from Rome. The road to the l. leads to *Mentana*, a village belonging to the Borghese family, in the vicinity of the ancient *Nomentum*, 15 M. from Rome, celebrated in recent times as the scene of a battle between the Garibaldians and the French and Papal troops, Nov. 3rd, 1867. The district is in many places extremely bleak, but affords beautiful views of the slopes of the Sabine Mts. From Mentana to Monte Rotondo 2 M., at the base of which the railway-station is situated (p. 68).

Beyond Porta Salara (Pl. I, 27).

The *Via Salara*, a road of very ancient construction, quits Rome by the bank of the Tiber, and then turns towards the district of the Sabines. It passes the Villa Albani (p. 129), and reaches the *Anio* about $2^1/_4$ M. from the city-gate. On the hill to the l., in the angle which the Anio forms at its junction with the Tiber, once lay *Antemnae*, destroyed by Romulus. The summit commands a noble prospect. A visit to this point is best combined with that to Acqua Acetosa (see below). The *Ponte Salaro* over the Anio, with its 2 arches, was destroyed by Totilas and subsequently renewed by Narses, but during the invasion of Garibaldi in 1867 it was again blown up; the ancient foundation of tuffstone may be distinguished from the superstructure of travertine. Beyond the bridge an ancient tomb, built over in the middle ages, now serves as an Osteria. 5 M. from the gate is the *Villa Spada*. From this point to the height on the r. extended the ancient *Fidenae*, once allied with Veii against Rome, and only subdued with its confederate after protracted struggles. Few traces of the city are now recognisable. The fortress lay on the hill close to the river, which is now occupied by *Castel Giubileo* (6 M. from Rome). The summit affords a beautiful and extensive *view. The castle was erected by Boniface VIII. in 1300, and is said to derive its name from a family to whom it once belonged.

The road continues to skirt the river in the plain. 11 M. from Rome the *Scannabechi* is reached, recognised as the ancient *Allia*, on which the Romans were signally defeated by the Gauls, B.C. 399. 2 M. farther is the railway-station of Monte Rotondo.

Beyond Porta del Popolo (Pl. I, 15).

Acqua Acetosa. The uninteresting route as far as Ponte Molle, a distance of $1^1/_2$ M. (p. 43), enclosed by houses and walls, should be performed by carriage (omnibus on Sundays from the Piazza del Popolo 7 soldi; carriage $1-1^1/_2$ l.).

Immediately to the r. outside the gate is the entrance to the *Villa Borghese* (p. 124). After $^1/_2$ M. the *Casino di Papa Giulio* is reached on the r., whence a field-road, passing the *Villa di Papa Giulio*, erected by Vignola for Julius III. (on the ground-floor are *two rooms with richly decorated ceilings, well worthy of a visit; $^1/_2$ l.), formerly celebrated for its splendour, but now deserted, leads to Acqua Acetosa ($1^1/_2$ M.).

Farther on, following the high road, is *S. Andrea* on the r., founded by Julius III. in 1527 in commemoration of his deliverance out of the hands of the Germans, erected by Vignola in the finest style of the Renaissance. Shortly before the bridge is reached is a second chapel of St. Andrew on the r. (comp. p. 43).

Beyond the Ponte Molle is a popular osteria. The present route, one of the most charming in the Roman Campagna, turns to the r. immediately before the bridge and skirts the river for $1/2$ hr., commanding fine views and leading to the *Acqua Acetosa*, a highly-prized mineral-spring, enclosed by a building erected by Bernini, under Alexander VI.

A more direct route (2 M.) leads hence to the city between fences and garden-walls, passing the Villa di Papa Giulio (see above).

A more attractive, but longer return-route is by the height of *Antemnae* and the *Via Salara* ($4^{1}/_{2}$ M.), see p. 271. A field-road is followed, which often entirely disappears, leading at first to the l. in the plain by the river, then ascending the hill, where it runs at a considerable height above the Anio, and reaches the bridge of the Via Salara (comp. p. 271).

Beyond the Ponte Molle the Via Cassia (p. 298) diverges to the l., and the Via Flaminia to the r. in the vicinity of the river. By the latter an attractive excursion may be made to Prima Porta (p. 70), 7 M. from Rome. One-horse carriage 5—7 l. About 2 M. from the Ponte Molle the tuffstone hills begin to rise. In the first of them is an interesting rock-tomb of the *Nasones*, containing greatly damaged stucco-decorations. A *magnificent view from the top. If the valley, which stretches to the l. on this side of the same hill, be followed for about 2 M., the traveller arrives at the so-called *Val di Pussino*, named after a painter of that name, with a picturesquely situated tenuta. On the r. of the road are the ruins of an ancient tomb, termed *Tor di Quinto*.

Immediately to the l. of the bridge a carriage road, at first skirting the river, leads to Porta Angelica; after $3/_{4}$ M. a road thence ascends to the r. to the Villa Madama (p. 273).

Beyond Porta Angelica (Pl. I, 8).

Monte Mario. Two principal routes issue from this gate: r. that in the plain, finally skirting the river, to Ponte Molle, 2 M., unattractive; l. that to M. Mario. This mountain is the N. eminence of the range of hills which form the *Janiculus*; in ancient times it was termed *Clivus Cinnae*, in the middle ages *Monte Malo*; its present name is derived from Mario Mellini, the proprietor in the time of Sixtus IV. of the villa mentioned below. After passing several osterie, which are in October much frequented by the inhabitants for purposes of amusement, the base of the hill is reached (1 M.); the carriage-road ascends by long windings, which may be avoided by means of steep footpaths. A fine view is obtained from the road on the summit, but is far surpassed by that from the villa. The road passes (l.) the church of S. *Maria del Rosario*, and beyond it (r.) the chapel of *S. Croce di M. Mario*, then (by a pine-tree) reaches the entrance to the **Villa Mellini** (permessi obtained of Avv. Corsetti. Piazza Navona 79; visitors, however, are sometimes admitted without this formality; $1/2$—1 l.). Traversing an avenue of oaks, the visitor arrives at the avenue passing the villa and extending along the verge of the hill to its culminating point. The view is unbounded on all sides, embracing Rome, the Campagna, and the mountains as far as the sea. Near the villa is an *Osteria commanding a fine view.

Villa Madama. The above-mentioned carriage-road to Ponte Molle is followed for $1 1/2$ M., when a road to the l. leads direct to the villa. It was erected by *G. Romano* from *Raphael's* designs for Card. Giulio de' Medici (afterwards Clement VII.). It subsequently came into the possession of the Farnese family, then into that of the kings of Naples; it was formerly in a dilapidated condition, but is now at least preserved from ruin. It contains a fine loggia with frescoes by *G. Romano* and *Giov. da Udine* ($1/2$ l.). Beautiful view.

B. Longer Excursions from Rome to the Mountains and the Sea.

The Alban Mountains.

The railways to Frascati and Albano render the Alban Mts. so easily accessible from Rome, that even those whose time is circumscribed may contrive within a single day to obtain a glimpse at some of the most interesting points. Rome should, if possible, be quitted in the evening, in order that the excursion may be commenced at an early hour on the following morning.

Time necessary for Frascati, the villas and Tusculum $1 3/4$—2 hrs., thence to Rocca di Papa (p. 277) 1 hr. (guide necessary, 1 l.), ascent of Monte Cavo $3/4$ hr., descent 20 min., to Nemi $1 3/4$ hr., Genzano $1/2$ hr., Ariccia $1/2$ hr., Albano $1 1/4$ hr., i. e. 7—8 hrs. (without halt), which may be somewhat diminished if the route from Rocca di Papa direct to Albano by Palazzuola (p. 278) be taken. In the reverse direction, beginning with Albano, the excursion occupies about the same time. If the excursion be made by Genzano and Nemi, Castel Gandolfo (p. 280) should be first visited. Those whose time permits will of course find it far more enjoyable to devote several days to a tour among these mountains. The only good inns are at Frascati and Albano, but the smaller villages afford accommodation for the night in case of necessity. For a stay of several days Albano is recommended, as a number of the most beautiful excursions are thence most conveniently accomplished.

A donkey is perhaps the best and most comfortable mode of locomotion, to be obtained at Ariccia and Frascati; charge, with guide, 4—5 l. daily; guide alone 2—$2 1/2$ l. A precise programme of the excursion should be agreed upon with the guides, as they are apt to abridge the journey to the traveller's disadvantage. A supply of provisions for the expedition will also be found desirable. Carriages may be hired at Frascati and Albano, but the most interesting routes are only accessible to pedestrians and riders.

For a visit to the Alban Mts. the stations of Marino (p. 277) and Città Lavinia (p. 282) are also available.

Frascati.

Railway in 1/2 hr., fares 2 l. 45, 1 l. 55 and 1 l. 5 c.; 3—4 trains daily. Comp. remark p. 279. Journey to stat. *Ciampino* see p. 279. Here the main-line to Albano and Naples proceeds to the r. The train to Frascati gradually ascends, passes through a tunnel, and stops at the station, 1 M. distant from the town. Omnibus thither 5 soldi. Frascati with its villas does not become visible until the last winding of the road is reached. The pedestrian may reach the town more expeditiously by ascending the hill to the l.

Vetturini also convey passengers to Frascati twice daily from the Tre Re near S. Marco (Pl. II, 16) in 2^1/$_2$ hrs., fare 2—3 l., but this mode of travelling cannot be recommended. One-horse carriage about 15 l. and gratuity.

Guides and *Proprietors of Donkeys* proffer their services on the arrival of the stranger. For Tusculum and the villas guide (necessary only when time is limited) 1^1/$_2$ l., donkey about the same. The route is to the villas Aldobrandini (see below) and Ruffinella (p. 275), returning by the monastery of Camaldoli (p. 276) and the villas Mondragone (p. 275) and Taverna (p. 275). The traveller desirous of immediately continuing his route to Albano may proceed from Tusculum (guide necessary as far as Nemi or Palazzuola, about 1^1/$_2$ l.) by a forest-road to Rocca di Papa (p. 277), without returning to Frascati. A visit from Frascati to Tusculum and the villas and back requires 2^1/$_2$—3 hrs.

Frascati (**Albergo di Londra* in the piazza, charges according to agreement: *Trattoria Campagna*, adjacent to the hotel) with its charming villas, in a healthy and invigorating situation on the slope of the mountains, is a favourite summer-resort. Apartments may be hired at several of the villas (*Villa Piccolomini, V. Falconieri, V. Muti* etc.). The town itself, uninteresting and of comparatively modern origin, arose, after the ancient Tusculum had been destroyed by the Romans in 1191, on the ruins of an ancient villa, overgrown with underwood *(frasche)*, whence its appellation. The older cathedral of *S. Rocco* was erected in 1309, that of *S. Pietro* in 1700 under Innocent XII. The latter contains, l. of the high-altar, a memorial-tablet of Charles Edward the young Pretender, grandson of James II., who died at Frascati Jan. 31st, 1788. The *Church of the Capuchins* above the town possesses a few pictures. A circular tomb below the Villa Piccolomini is erroneously called that of Lucullus.

The shaded and well-watered villas, always accessible to the public, constitute the great charm of Frascati. *Villa Piccolomini*, above the town, was once the residence of the erudite Cardinal Baronius. The magnificent **Villa Aldobrandini*, now the property of the Borghese, was erected for Cardinal Pietro Aldobrandini.

nephew of Clement VIII., from the designs of *Giac. della Porta*. It contains paintings by the *Cavaliere d'Arpino*. The grounds are adorned with cascades and beautiful oaks, and the views are charming. *V. Montalto*, erected by the Peretti, came into the possession of the Propaganda in 1835. *Villa Ruffinella (or *Tusculana)*, of the 16th cent., formerly the property of Lucian Buonaparte, subsequently of Maria Christina, Queen of Sardinia, now belongs to King Victor Emmanuel. Here in November, 1818, Lucian was attacked and plundered by robbers, an event admirably described in Washington Irving's "Adventure of the Artist". The celebrated villa of Cicero is generally believed to have occupied this site. Inscriptions and antiquities found in the neighbourhood are shown. *Villa Conti*, outside the Porta S. Pietro, the property of the Duca Marino Torlonia, brother of the banker, possesses fine fountains and beautiful points of view. *Villa Taverna*, on the route to Camaldoli, and the neighbouring *Villa Mondragone*, erected by Cardinal Altemps under Gregory XIII., both the property of the Borghese, are surrounded by delightful gardens and points of view. The latter is now fitted up by the Jesuits as an educational establishment. *Villa Falconieri*, the oldest in Frascati, founded about 1550 by Cardinal Ruffini, erected by *Borromini*, possesses pictures by *C. Maratta* etc., and stands in shady gardens.

A shaded road, partly ancient, leads above the villas Mondragone and Ruffinelli in $1/2$ hr. to

Tusculum, a town of great antiquity, the foundation of which is traditionally ascribed to Telemachus, son of Ulysses, the birth-place of the elder Cato and a favourite residence of Cicero. The castle on the summit of the hill was in the middle ages occupied by a warlike race of counts, who were generally in league with the emperors against the Romans. The latter were signally defeated under Frederick I., May 30th, 1167, in retaliation for which they took possession of, and entirely dismantled the castle under Celestine III. in 1191. Nothing therefore now remains of the ancient Tusculum but a heap of ruins. In ascending from Villa Ruffinella, the traveller soon obtains a view of the *Amphitheatre*, outside the town walls. It is 225 ft. in length, 160 ft. in breadth, termed by the guides *Scuola di Cicerone*, and excavated, as an inscription records, in presence of Maria Christina, dowager Queen of Sardinia, on the occasion of the arrival of Gregory XVI., Oct. 7th, 1839. Then the so-called *Villa of Cicero*, excavated in 1861 by Prince Aldobrandini. On the r. is the ancient *Forum* and the *Theatre*, excavated by Lucian Buonaparte, and remarkably well preserved; adjacent is a small miniature-theatre. In the rear is situated a *Reservoir (piscina)* in 4 compartments. Here the guides are generally desirous of returning, but the castle, which is easily accessible to donkeys, should by all means be ascended. The ancient

*Castle (arx) stands on an artificially hewn rock, 200 ft. above the town. Two gateways and the direction of the walls are still distinguishable. The *view from the summit is splendid. On the r. Camaldoli and Monte Porzio, farther distant the Sabine Mts., with Tivoli and Monticelli, then Soracte and the Ciminian Mts., towards the sea the broad Campagna with its aqueducts, Rome and the dome of St. Peter's, l. the Alban Mount (M. Cavo), Castel Gandolfo, Marino and Grotta Ferrata. Descending and turning to the r., the traveller will perceive a fragment of the ancient wall, and adjoining it a *Reservoir of very early and peculiar construction, formed of massive blocks, and vaulted in an almost pointed arch. On the return-route the monastery of *Camaldoli*, founded by Paul V., as well as the villas Mondragone, Taverna and Falconieri (p. 275), may be visited.

Grotta Ferrata, 3 M. from Frascati, is reached by two routes, by the carriage-road to Marino, or by a shorter path through the woods, leading to the l. below Villa Conti, outside Porta S. Pietro. This Greek monastery of the Basilians was founded by St. Nilus under Otho III. in 1002. In the 15th cent. it was the property of Cardinal Giuliano della Rovere, afterwards Pope Julius II., who fortified it with moats and towers. Of the old *Church* the vestibule alone remains, containing (r.) a beautiful statue of the Madonna. The *Portal*, with arabesques and a Greek inscription, dates from the 11th cent.; over the door mosaics of the Saviour, Madonna and St. Basilius. The present church, re-erected by Cardinal Guadagni in 1754, contains nothing worthy of mention.

From the r. aisle the *Chapel of St. Nilus* is entered, decorated with *frescoes from the life of the saint by *Domenichino*, in 1610, when 28 years of age. At the entrance of the chapel, on the l., is represented the meeting of the saint with Otho III.; the attendant in green, holding the emperor's horse, is Domenichino himself; to the r. of the horse, Guido Reni is also represented in a green costume, and behind him Guercino. The boy in front of the horse, with blue cap and white feather, bears the features of a girl of Frascati to whom the artist was attached. On the r. St. Bartholomew arrests the fall of a column, thus saving the lives of the surrounding workmen. At the altar on the l.: St. Nilus heals a boy possessed by an evil spirit with oil from a lamp of the Madonna. R.: Madonna presenting a golden apple to St. Nilus and St. Bartholomew. In the lunette: Death of St. Nilus. Outside the chapel: St. Nilus calming a storm by which the harvest is endangered; the saint kneeling before the cross. On the ceiling: Annunciation. The frescoes were restored in 1819 by *V. Camuccini*, at the cost of Cardinal Consalvi, who died, of poison it was believed, as abbot of Grotta Ferrata in 1824. A monument of the cardinal and several ancient sculptures are shown in the handsome

Abbey. The small Madonna over the altar is by *Ann. Caracci;* a bust of Domenichino is by *Teresa Benincampi*, a pupil of Canova. Fairs held here on March 28th and Sept. 8th are visited by numerous strangers from Rome for the sake of seeing the national costumes of the Alban Mts.

Marino, a small town celebrated for its excellent wine, is picturesquely situated on an eminence of the Alban Mts., 1630 ft. in height, occupying the site of the ancient *Castrimoenium*. In the middle ages it was a stronghold of the Orsini, who here defended themselves against their enemies, especially the Colonna, until the latter under Martin V. in 1424 captured Marino, which they still possess. It contains a *Corso*, the principal street, a *Fountain*, and a *Cathedral* dedicated to St. Barnabas. The church of *S. Trinità*, l. of the Corso, possesses a picture representing the Trinity by *Guido Reni*. In the church of the *Madonna delle Grazie*, St. Rochus by *Domenichino*. In the *Cathedral* a badly-preserved St. Bartholomew by *Guercino*. The town is reached by a beautiful route of 4 M. from Grotta Ferrata. The station on the Rome and Naples line is situated in the Campagna, 3 M. distant (3 trains daily: fares 2 l. 5, 1 l. 30 and 90 c.). From Marino a shady road, commanding extensive views, leads through the well-wooded valley *(Parco di Colonna)* of the ancient *Aqua Ferentina*, often mentioned as a rallying-point of the Latins, to the Alban lake and by Castel Gandolfo to (3 M.) Albano.

Field and forest-paths (guide necessary, 1—1½ l.) lead from Tusculum in 1½ hr. to *Rocca di Papa*, and thence in ³/₄ hr. to the summit of *Monte Cavo* (descent in 20 min.). The distance hither from Albano by Palazzuola (p. 278) is about the same.

Rocca di Papa, situated on the verge of the great crater of Campo d'Annibale (see below), in the midst of beautiful forest-scenery, is a small town with 2500 inhab., well adapted for a summer-residence on account of its altitude. It contains no inn. The two *Trattorie* are scarcely tolerable. Apartments, however (even for one night), may be heard of at the *Caffè del Genio*, in the upper part of the town.

From the Caffè the narrow Via di Monte Cavo ascends to the r.; at its extremity the turn to the l. is taken, and after a few minutes a footpath ascended on the r. Here to the l. is situated the great crater of *Campo d' Annibale*, a name derived from the unfounded tradition that Hannibal once pitched his camp here during his campaign against Rome. It is more probable that the Romans were encamped here at that period, to repel the attacks of the Carthaginians.

The wooded summit of **Monte Cavo** is soon attained by means of the well-preserved and shady *Via Triumphalis*, an ancient road, paved with basalt, by which the generals to whom the senate refused a triumph at Rome, ascended this height and celebrated one on their own responsibility. From two open spaces, about three-quarters of the way up, a better *view than from the top is obtained of Marino on the r., the Lago d'Albano, Ariccia with the viaduct, Genzano, the Lago di Nemi, and Nemi itself.

On the summit of the mountain, the *Mons Albanus* of antiquity, nearly 3000 ft. above the sea-level, stood the venerable sanctuary of the Latin League, the *Temple of Jupiter Latiaris*, where the sacrificial festival of the *Feriae Latinae* was annually celebrated. Its ruins, 240 ft. in length, 120 ft. in breadth, with columns of white and yellow marble, were in a state of tolerable preservation till 1783, when Cardinal York, "the last of the Stuarts", converted them into a Passionist monastery. A portion only of the ancient foundations is preserved on the S. E. side of the garden-wall. The **view from several different points is incomparable. It embraces the sea, the coast from Terracina to Civita Vecchia, the Volscian and Sabine Mts., Rome and the Campagna with a number of towns and villages, and below the spectator the beautiful Alban Mts. (comp. p. 276). The distant view, generally obscured by mist, is seen to the best advantage immediately before sunrise, after sunset, or after a passing shower has cleared the atmosphere. No refreshments are to be had on the summit. The inhospitality of the monastery is frequently complained of. In case of necessity, rough accommodation for the night may be obtained if well paid for.

Returning to the Campo d'Annibale, the traveller then passes above Rocca di Papa, and soon reaches the chapel of the *Madonna del Tufo* in the midst of wood, whence a fine view of the Alban Lake and the plain is enjoyed. From Monte Cavo to Albano 2, to Nemi (with guide) by a beautiful forest-road in 1½ hr.

Palazzuola and the **Alban Lake**. The latter, about 6 M. in circumference, is the crater of an extinct volcano, presenting a somewhat sombre and melancholy aspect, although its banks are well cultivated. It is fed by abundant subterraneous springs, and drained by an outlet of very ancient construction below Caste Gandolfo (p. 281).

On the E. bank of the lake stands the Franciscan monastery of *Palazzuola*, dating from the 13th cent. The garden contains a remarkable rock-tomb in the Etruscan style, respecting which little is known.

Above the monastery, on the narrow ridge between the base of Monte Cavo and the Alban Lake, once lay in a prolonged line, as its name indicates, the city of **Alba Longa**, of which no traces now remain. It may be observed, however, how the rocks towards Palazzuola have been hewn perpendicularly, in order to render the town more impregnable. The foundation of Alba Longa belongs to a pre-historic period, although tradition has attributed it to Ascanius, the son of Æneas. It was the ancient capital of the Latin League, which here possessed its political and religious centre. At an early period, however, it was destroyed by its younger rival on the banks of the Tiber, after which the ancient festivals of the League on the Alban Mt. alone continued to exist.

From Palazzuola by the lake and the Capuchin monastery to Albano is a beautiful walk of $2^1/_2$ M. From Albano to the station 3 M. (omnibus see below).

Albano.

Railway in $3/_4$—$1^1/_4$ hr.; four trains daily; fares 3 l. 30, 2 l. 5, 1 l. 40 c. Travellers are recommended to be at the station $1/_2$ hr. before the advertised time of starting.

Soon after quitting the city the train diverges from the line to Civita Vecchia; l. is the Porta S. Lorenzo (p. 142), r. the row of arches of the Acqua Felice (p. 269), then the tombs of the Via Appia (p. 264). To the l. the Sabine and Alban Mts.; at the foot of the latter Frascati is a conspicuous object. At stat. *Ciampino* the line to Frascati diverges to the l., whilst the S. line approaches the Alban Mts. Stat. *Marino* lies on the nearest chain of hills on the l.; above it, on the mountain-ridge, *Rocca*, adjoining which on the r. rises Monte Cavo (p. 278) with the white monastery-walls. A cutting is then passed through, and to the l. on the olive-clad hill appears Castel Gandolfo (p. 280), immediately beyond which Albano and Ariccia, connected by a viaduct 400 ft. in length, are visible in the distance. These two towns possess stat. *La Cecina* in common, in a lonely and unattractive situation.

An omnibus, with 16 places (8 interior, 4 cabriolet, 4 outside; view from latter alone) at $1/_2$ l. each, runs from the station to the town of Albano, $2^1/_2$ M. distant. A seat should be speedily secured, as the demand is generally great. The ascent (which is performed almost as expeditiously by the pedestrian) is picturesque, although the distant views are for the most part excluded. The ruins of *Castello Savelli* soon appear on the r., *La Turri*, or *Torretta*, on the l. A magnificent view of Ariccia is then obtained, with the ancient castle (p. 281) on the r. and the imposing viaduct (p. 281) on the l., and farther to the l. Albano; to the r. by the entrance to the town stands Villa Loncampa. The omnibus stops near the Hôtel de l'Europe.

Those who are desirous of combining a visit to the *Via Appia* (p. 264) with an excursion to Albano are recommended to engage a carriage for the entire route (one-horse 15—20, two-horse 20—25 l. and gratuity); the last portion of the route, however, is uninteresting. — *Vetturini* also convey passengers to Albano twice daily from the Teatro Argentina (Pl. II, 13) in $2^1/_2$ hrs., fare $2^1/_2$ l., but these conveyances are neither very clean nor comfortable.

The high road, the *Via Appia Nuova*, quits Rome by the Porta S. Giovanni (Pl. II, 33); the ancient Via Appia (p. 264) is somewhat longer. The two unite at the *Fratocchie*, at the 11th milestone (of the new road). On the l. side of the road Clodius once possessed a villa; to the r. in the valley lay *Bovillae*, a colony of Alba Longa, with a sanctuary of the Gens Julia, where the remains of a theatre and circus may still be traced. Remnants of walls and tombs are seen on both sides of the road. A large square structure, about 30 ft. in height, with three niches, was long erroneously regarded as the tomb of Clodius. As the height is ascended, a fine survey of the Campagna, the sea and Rome may be enjoyed. Near the gate of Albano, at the 14th milestone, is seen the shell of a large tomb, supposed to be that of Pompey. To the l. the road traverses the so-called *Lower Gallery* to *Castel Gandolfo*; r. lies Villa Altieri.

Albano (*Europa* or *Posta* in the town, R. 2 l., A. 1/2 l., good "vino del paese" 15 soldi, a café on the ground-floor; *Hôtel de Russie* at the Porta Romana, pension 6 l.; in both of these the charges are by no means fixed), a small town and episcopal residence in a lofty and healthy situation, and a favourite resort of Romans and strangers between the months of June and October, occupies the site of the ruins of the villa of Pompey and the extensive grounds of the *Albanum* of Domitian. Between S. Paolo and the Capuchin monastery lay an *Amphitheatre*, the scanty remains of which are seen from the road. The church of *S. Maria della Rotonda* stands on the foundations of an ancient circular temple. The ruins in the street of Gesù e Maria are supposed to be the remains of baths. The Via Appia intersects Albano in a straight direction. Immediately beyond the town, l. of the ancient road (r. of the new) stands a *Tomb* in the Etruscan style, consisting of a massive cube, 49 ft. in width, 24 ft. in height, surrounded by 4 (of which 2 only are standing) obtuse cones; in the centre a fifth. It was formerly believed to be the tomb of the Horatii and Curiatii, and now, with no better foundation, regarded as that of Aruns, a son of Porsena, who was killed near Ariccia.

Albano is mentioned as early as 460 as the seat of a bishop, then again in the 11th cent. in the contests of the popes with Rome. In the 13th cent. it belonged to the Savelli, from whom in 1697 it came into the possession of the papal government. Albano is recommended as a summer-residence on account of the charming excursions which the environs afford, but in the hottest season is not altogether exempt from fever. The picturesque costume of the Albanian peasant-women (on Sundays) is celebrated. The wine of Albano enjoyed a high reputation in ancient times, and is mentioned by Horace.

From Albano by Palazzuola to Monte Cavo 2 hrs. (see p. 278); if a visit to the emissarius (see below) beneath Castel Gandolfo be paid, 2 hrs. additional are required. To the N.W. of Albano, 3/4 M. distant (the road to the r. leads to Palazzuola, whereas the shady road to l. by the lake, the *Galleria di Sopra* or "upper gallery", is now followed; lower gallery see below) is situated

Castel Gandolfo, the property of the Savelli in the middle ages, since 1596 that of the Pope. Here Urban VIII. erected from designs of *Carlo Maderno* the extensive *Palace*, which is occupied by the popes (by Pius IX. also) as a summer residence.

Its sole attraction is the charming situation. The path to the emissarius descends shortly before the village is reached; the custodian, however, must be first summoned from the latter. The descent occupies nearly $^1/_4$ hr. The **Emissarius**, or tunnel by which the Alban Lake is drained, is a vast and imposing work. According to tradition it was made by the Romans B. C. 397, during the siege of Veii, when the lake rose to an unusual height, but it is probably of still more remote origin. It is hewn in the solid rock; at the entrance is a large structure of massive blocks, resembling a nymphæum. The channel itself is 5—10 ft. in height, and issues $^3/_4$ M. below Albano by the village of *La Mola*, where the water is employed as a motive power for mills, thence descending to the Tiber. The custodian floats lighted pieces of candle on boards down the stream, in order to impress visitors with an idea of its great length (fee for one person 1 l., for a party more in proportion).

From Castel Gandolfo the so-called *Lower Gallery* leads to Albano in $^1/_2$ hr. From the Emissarius to Marino 3 M.

Ariccia (Lat. *Aricia*), the first station on the Via Appia according to Horace (Sat. I, 5), $^3/_4$ M. to the W. of Albano, is separated from it by a valley, which is crossed by an imposing *Viaduct, erected by Pius IX. in 1846—63, 400 paces in length and 192 ft. in height, and consisting of 3 superincumbent series of arcades of 6, 12 and 18 arches respectively. To the l. a view of the Chigi park (see below), r. the extensive plain as far as the sea. To the l. at the extremity of the bridge is the *Palazzo Chigi*, erected by Bernini, with a *park containing fine old timber, and kept as much as possible in a natural condition. Permission to visit it should be applied for at the Palazzo Chigi at Rome (p. 116), but access is occasionally obtained without this formality (fee $^1/_2$—1 l.).

The ancient town of *Aricia*, a member of the Latin League, lay towards the S., in the *Valle Aricciana*, an extinct crater below the modern town, which occupies the site of the former Arx or citadel. At the base of the hill the ancient Via Appia, supported by massive substructures which are still visible, runs as far as the vicinity of Genzano. A circuit of $^1/_2$ hr. by the valley, instead of the direct route from Albano to Ariccia, is interesting. Ariccia was purchased in 1661 from the Savelli, its mediæval proprietors, by the Chigi, who are the lords of the soil to this day. It is a favourite summer resort on account of the proximity of the woods. Ariccia and Genzano are celebrated for the beauty of their women.

Genzano. The ancient Via Appia (see above) may be followed from Albano through the valley of Ariccia, but the route to Genzano (3 M., from Ariccia about 2 M.) by the *Via Appia*

Nuova, traversing the mountain-ridge and passing through Ariccia is preferable. This road is picturesque and shaded, and crosses 4 viaducts which command beautiful views. Near Genzano it divides, descending l. to a Capuchin monastery and the Lake of Nemi, r. to the town, whilst the avenue in a straight direction leads to the *Palazzo Cesarini*, whence a view of the charming lake is obtained. The opposite garden is well worthy of a visit, if time permit (permission readily granted on personal application at the dwelling-house near it).

Genzano, with a population of 6000, produces excellent wine, but contains nothing worthy of note beyond its situation. It attracts numbers of visitors in summer, but possesses no good inns: the atmosphere moreover is occasionally productive of intermittent fever. In the piazza, opp. the fountain, there is a good wine-house.

At Genzano, on the 8th day after Corpus Christi, the celebrated *Infiorata di Genzano*, or flower-festival, is celebrated, and is accompanied by a procession, fireworks and popular amusements. These festivities now again take place after an intermission of some years.

From Genzano a visit may be paid to **Città Lavinia** (3 M.), the ancient *Lanuvium*, celebrated for its worship of Juno Sospita, situated on a W. spur of the Alban Mts. At the W. end of the town are a few remnants of the ancient walls; in the piazza a sarcophagus and several fragments from tombs and villas in the neighbourhood. The town, now a poor and insignificant place, commands fine views of the Campagna towards the sea. Below it, about 1/2 hr. distant, is a railway-station; three trains daily, fares 4 l. 45, 3 l. 55 and 2 l. 15 c.

By the high road Velletri is 9 M. distant. It may, however, be reached by a nearer and more picturesque route in 1 1/2 hr. (with guide). Velletri (*Gallo*, with trattoria), the ancient *Velitrae*, a town of the Volsci which became subject to Rome in 338, celebrated for its wines, is picturesquely situated on an eminence of *Monte Artemisio*. The town, which consists of narrow and crooked streets, contains 12,000 inhab., and is the residence of the Bishop of Ostia (p. 303). The loggia of the *Palazzo Lancelotti* commands an extensive *view. — The railway-station (p. 295) is 1/2 M. from the town; four trains daily, fares 5 l. 65, 4 l. 50, 2 l. 75 c.

Nemi and the **Lago di Nemi**. The former is reached from Genzano in 1/2 hr. A road thither, partly ancient, descends to the Capuchin monastery and skirts the lake. The high road, however, skirting the upper verge of the lake, is preferable. — The *Lago di Nemi* is an extinct crater, about 3 M. in circumference, and like the Alban lake, which lies about 100 ft. lower, of considerable depth (300 ft.). Its outlet is also formed by an artificial emissarius. The precipitous lava-walls of the crater, 300 ft. in height, are admirably cultivated. In ancient times it was termed *Lacus Nemorensis*, and occasionally the "mirror of Diana", from a temple, the substructures of which have been discovered below Nemi, and from a grove sacred to the goddess, whence the present appellation is derived. Diana was worshipped here with barbarous customs; her priest was always a runaway slave, who obtained his office by killing his predecessor in single combat. Tiberius (or Trajan) constructed a magnificent vessel on this lake, a beam of which is preserved in the Museo Kircheriano at Rome (see p. 119). The water is beautifully clear, and rarely ruffled by wind; the whole presents an exquisite picture, the gem of the Alban Mts.

Nemi is a small mediæval town with an ancient fort. The verandah of the inn commands a delightful *view of the lake and the castle of Genzano, beyond them a venerable watch-tower, then the extensive plain and the sea. Nemi would be a most suitable spot for passing a night, but the accommodation at the inn is very limited, and not of a comfortable description. — From Nemi to Monte Cavo (p. 277) guide (1—1½ l.) necessary on account of the intricacy of the numerous forest-paths (1½ hr.); to Albano somewhat farther.

The Sabine Mountains.

The chain of the Apennines, which descend abruptly and bound the Roman plain on the E., termed Sabine Mts. from their ancient inhabitants, are replete with the highest interest for lovers of the picturesque. The formation is limestone, differing entirely from that of the volcanic Alban Mts.; the altitude considerably greater, attaining to 5000 ft. Owing to the want of railway-communication, the characteristics of city-life, which produce an unpleasing impression at Frascati and Albano, are here entirely absent, excepting at Tivoli. Attempts at extortion are, however, not unknown, and the traveller should be on his guard here, as well as in other parts of Italy. As a rule the inns are good and inexpensive, and instead of the usual distasteful bargaining, it may suffice for the stranger to remark that he expects the "*prezzi soliti degli amici di casa*" (usual charge "en bloc" for board and lodging 4—5 l., and ½ l. as gratuity). Those whose time is short must be satisfied with a visit to Tivoli; but, if possible, 4 days at least should be devoted to the Sabine Mts., and may best be employed as follows: 1st day by Frascati to Palestrina, 2nd to Olevano, 3rd to Subiaco, 4th to Tivoli, 5th back to Rome. The entire expedition may be accomplished by carriage, but some of the excursions at least should be undertaken on foot or on a donkey. The public conveyances cannot be recommended when ladies are of the party, in which case a private vehicle should be hired. Best summer-quarters at Tivoli; Subiaco and Olevano also agreeable.

Tivoli.

Distance 16⅓ M. One-horse carr. 15—20 l., two-horse 25 l., fee 2—3 l. During Easter the prices are rather higher. The carriages at the hotels are more expensive (30—40 l.), but generally drive more rapidly, an advantage which will be highly appreciated on the dusty and shadeless high road. *Vetturini* convey passengers to Tivoli twice daily (5 a. m. and at noon), returning from Tivoli at noon, in 4—5 hrs., fare 2½ l.; not to be recommended. Those who wish to visit Hadrian' villa (p. 284), the grottoes, cascades and Villa d'Este, and return to Rome in the evening should start at daybreak. — A railway from Ciampino (p. 279), near Frascati, to Tivoli, passing the recently erected baths of the Albula, has for some years been projected, but not yet commenced.

Tibur with its shady valleys and murmuring cascades was the most popular summer-resort of the ancient Romans, as Horace among others testifies, and to this day attracts a multitude of visitors during the season. A fine day in April or May, when the vegetation and blossoms are in their freshest beauty, is the most favourable period for this excursion.

Rome is quitted by the Porta S. Lorenzo (Pl. II, 31), immediately beyond which is the church of that name on the r.; the road then descends into a ravine, and at the *Osteria di Pietralata* crosses the Ancona railway. Fine retrospect of Rome and St. Peter's. The route, generally identical with the ancient *Via Tiburtina*, crosses the *Anio*, here called *Teverone*, by the *Ponte Mammolo* at the 4th milestone. The river, formerly navigable, rises in the mountains near Filettino, passes Subiaco, Vicovaro, and Tivoli, where it forms the celebrated cascade, and falls into the Tiber at Ponte Salaro near Rome (p. 271). The bridge derives its name from Mammæa, mother of Alexander Severus. To the r. an undulating district with ancient towers. At the (7 M.)

Osteria del Fornaccio a road diverges to the l. to the picturesquely situated village of *Monticelli* with castle and cloister. A few min. later the road reaches at the *Osteria delle Capannacce* its culminating point between the Ponte Mammolo and Ponte Lucano (see below). Farther on, l., *Castel Arcione*, an ancient stronghold of robbers. Beyond it is the calciferous *Lago de' Tartari*, now dried up. Then, somewhat farther, a sulphureous odour betrays the proximity of the *Aquae Albulae*, baths greatly frequented in ancient times, now less popular (bath-house erected in 1862). A channel constructed by Card. Ippolito d'Este conducts the water from the three small sulphureous lakes to the Tiber. In the vicinity are the quarries of travertine *(lapis Tiburtinus)* which have yielded the material for the structures of ancient, as well as modern Rome, for both, the Colosseum and St. Peter's. About 1 1/2 M. farther the Anio is crossed by the *Ponte Lucano;* near it is the well-preserved *Tomb of the Plautii*, dating from the early empire, similar to that of Cæcilia Metella (p. 265).

Immediately beyond the river the road again divides; l. ascending to the town through olive-plantations, a considerably shorter route for the pedestrian; r. to the villa of Hadrian, 1 M. distant, now the property of the Braschi family at Rome, from whom permission to visit it must be obtained (fee for 1 pers. 1/2—1 l.; at the gate a few soldi); an additional fee (1—2 l.). however, is sometimes as efficacious as a permesso.

The *Villa of Hadrian stands on the slope of the heights of Tivoli (whence it is 1/2 hr. walk), and with its pertinents once occupied an area of several square miles. The emperor here laid out magnificent grounds, without rival in the Roman empire, containing palaces, theatres, a circus, academies etc., where he might repose after the labours of government. These sumptuous structures stood till the 6th cent., when they were destroyed by the

Goth Totila. Innumerable works of ancient art, subsequently extricated from the ruins, now adorn churches and museums. Of the buildings themselves extensive remains still exist, to which various names are applied by the guides.

The oldest edifice, the *Palace of Hadrian*, appears to have stood on the highest ground, in the rear of the Hippodrome and Academy. A *Theatre*, with adjacent halls and saloons, belonged to it. The *Thermae* were reached hence by the *Canopus*, a structure fitted up in the Egyptian style, containing a number of statues etc. now in the Vatican. To the E. flows the river *Alpheus*. A large space above the Canopus is termed the *Hippodrome* or race-course, which however shows traces of aqueducts. N. of the palace are situated the so-called *Elysium* and *Tartarus*. A subterranean passage leads E. to the river *Peneus*, and beyond it to the *Vale of Tempe*. On the W. are extensive ruins supposed to be the *Prytaneum*, adjacent to which is the *Scuola*, a circular structure with niches for statues, the *Stoa Pœcile*; then a stadium with colonnade and other remains. By the present entrance are two more *Theatres*, and other ruins, commonly called a *Nymphaeum* and *Palaestra*. The real names and destinations of these, as well as the other remains, are far from being ascertained with precision.

Tivoli (**Locanda della Regina*, in the town; *Sibylla*, charmingly situated by the temples, R. 1½—2 l.; in both an agreement necessary. Parties from Rome, who spend a single day here, generally bring their provisions, procure wine from the Sibylla, and enjoy a delightful picnic-repast beneath the temple in sight of the cascade), the *Tibur* of antiquity, existed, according to later tradition, as a colony of the Siculi long before the foundation of Rome. In B. C. 380 Camillus subjugated Tibur and Præneste, after which it formed a member of the league of the Latin towns allied with Rome. Hercules and Vesta were here especially revered. During the reign of Augustus the emperor himself and many of the Roman nobles (e. g. Mæcenas) founded beautiful villas here; under Hadrian the splendour of the place attained its climax; it was devastated in the wars with the Goths, and finally during the middle ages participated in the fate of Rome. In 1460 Pius II. founded the citadel on the ruins of the amphitheatre. The Tivoli of the present day (7000 inhab.), with its narrow streets, offers few attractions besides its magnificent situation. It is moreover regarded as windy and humid, especially in spring.

Among the finest relics of antiquity are the **Two Temples*, adjacent to the Sibylla inn. One, a circular edifice, surrounded by an open hall of 18 (10 now remain) columns of the Corinthian order, situated above the waterfall, is termed the **Temple of the Sibyl*, by others that of *Vesta* or of *Hercules Saxanus*. In the middle ages it was employed as a church. The door and windows contract at the top. Immediately adjacent is another temple of oblong shape, with 4 Ionic columns in front, now a church of St. George, believed by some to have been dedicated to *Tiburtus*, by others to the *Sibyl*.

The terrace of the temple of the Sibyl commands an admirable *View of the Falls. At the church of S. Giorgio, by the Sibylla, is an iron gate (attendant 2 soldi) admitting to the Grotto of Neptune, formerly the channel of the main branch of the Anio (donkeys for the excursion to the falls 1—1½ l.; guides, who moreover are superfluous, receive about the same, although their first demand is 3—4 l.). The excellent path, affording picturesque glimpses of the great fall, was constructed by the French general Miollis. In 1826 a serious inundation carried away a portion of the village, in consequence of which, in order to prevent the recurrence of a similar disaster, a new course was constructed for the Anio by means of two shafts (885 ft. and 980 ft.) penetrating the limestone-rock of *Mte. Catillo*. In 1834, in the presence of Gregory XVI., the water of the Anio was admitted to its new channel by the engineer *Folchi*, and a *New Waterfall, 320 ft. in height and of the most imposing description, thus formed. Two ancient bridges and several tombs were discovered on that occasion. The Grotto of Neptune thereby lost the greater portion of its water, although the fall is still remarkably fine. Quitting this grotto, the visitor next ascends to the *Sirens' Grotto*, where the surface of the water is seen from above. The path then ascends by an ancient wall, conjectured to pertain to a *Villa of Vopiscus*, to the principal stream by *Monte Catillo*, the tunnel of which (372 paces in length) may be traversed, as far as the influx of the river. Visitors usually quit the ravine for the high road, leading by an avenue of fine olive-trees to a * Circular Terrace, where an admirable survey of the *Great Fall* is enjoyed. A path on the r. bank, skirting the mountain, leads to the hermitage of S. Antonio, commanding a view of *Le Cascatelle, the small waterfalls formed by a branch of the Anio, which here turns mills and the works of an iron-manufactory established by Lucian Buonaparte in the extensive ruins of the erroneously so-called *Villa of Maecenas*. The terrace of these works (entrance by the lower gateway; fee ½ l.) commands an exquisite view of the valley and the Campagna. Other relics of antiquity are seen near the small church of *S. Maria di Quintiliolo* (probably remains of a villa of Quintilius Varus). A *"Villa of Horace"* (who never possessed one at Tibur) is also pointed out by the guides. From S. Maria the valley is crossed by the *Ponte dell' Acquoria*, and the hill of Tibur (Clivus Tiburtinus) again ascended to the halls of the so-called *Villa of Maecenas*, and an ancient circular building known by the singular appellation of *Templo della Tosse* ("temple of the cough"; probably a tomb of the *Turcia* or *Tuscia* family). Traces of ancient villas are frequent on the neighbouring slopes. On those below the Greek college, supposed to have been the site of a *Villa of Cassius*, various works of art, some of which are now in the hall of the Muses in the Vatican (p. 248), were discovered.

*Villa d' Este, at the entrance to the town, near Porta S. Croce (entrance r. of S. Francesco), erected by *Pirro Ligorio* in 1549 for Card. Ippolito d' Este, was presented by the Duke of Modena to Monsig. Hohenlohe. Though sadly neglected, it still retains traces of its former splendour: in the casino, frescoes by *Federigo Zuccari* and *Muziano* (damaged); in the garden, terraces, grottoes with cascade, densely shaded avenues, lofty cypresses, magnificent groups of trees of the most varied hues, and charming points of view.

Villa Braschi, founded by Pius VI., and the *Terrace* of the *Jesuits' College* by Porta S. Croce also afford magnificent views of the Campagna and Rome.

The most beautiful excursions may be made from Tivoli to the Sabine Mts. Those most recommended are to Subiaco in the upper valley of the Anio, to Licenza, to the Sabinum of Horace, to Ampiglione (ancient Empulum), S. Angelo, Monticelli, Palombara and Monte Gennaro; also to Palestrina (beautiful, but fatiguing) by Gericomio, S. Gregorio, Casape and Poli (7 hrs.), or by a nearer carriage-road by Passerano and Zagarolo (15 M.).

Subiaco.

A vetturino conveys passengers 3 times weekly from Subiaco to Tivoli (24 M.) in 5 hrs., fare 4 l., returning to Subiaco on the following day; other conveyances are also frequently to be met with. The road traverses the valley of the Anio. A shorter route for pedestrians, about 18 M., in some places remarkably interesting, but fatiguing, leads through the valley of the aqueduct, and by Gerano (about $^2/_3$rds of the way), as far as which it is a carriage-road. The traveller is recommended to avail himself of a carriage for this portion (5—8 l.), as from Gerano to Subiaco (3 hrs. walk) is the most arduous part of the journey. Guide from Gerano necessary, 1^1|$_2$ l.; donkey, the same.

Pedestrians quit Tivoli by the Porta S. Giovanni and keep to the l. by the slopes of *M. Ripoli* and *M. Spaccato*. 1 M. from the gate a road diverges to the l. to *Ampiglione (Empulum)*. The arches of the venerable *Aqua Marcia*, and shortly afterwards remnants of the *Aqua Claudia* and the *Anio Vetus* become visible. About 4 M. from the town are (l.) the ruins of the ancient *Empulum*, 1 M. farther those of *Sassula*, beyond which a lonely district is traversed. Below *Siciliano* the road turns to the r. to *Gerano*, a village with poor osteria.

The path now ascends the heights, whence a fine view of the mountains and valleys as far as Olevano (p. 292) is disclosed. The villages to the l. are *Canterano* and *Rocca Canterano*, r. *Rocca S. Stefano* and *Civitella*. After frequent ascents and descents on the mountain-slopes, and a succession of pleasing views of the valleys in the vicinity, beyond the last defile the valley of the Anio and Subiaco below suddenly come into view.

The Carriage-road leaves Tivoli by the Porta S. Angelo, and continues along the r. bank of the Anio. R. beyond the first mile are seen a few arches of the *Aqua Claudia*. After 3 M. a road diverges l. to the lofty *S. Paolo*, whence *Monte Gennaro* may be ascended. Farther on are the ruins of the old castle of *Saccomuro*, then to the r. the loftily situated village of *Castello Madama*. About 7½ M. from Tivoli, *Vicovaro*, the ancient *Varia* is attained, possessing interesting walls of travertine-blocks, and the octagonal, late-Gothic chapel of *S. Giacomo* (containing a miracle working image of the Madonna), designed in the 16th cent. by *Simone*, a pupil of *Brunellesco*. Beyond Vicovaro the road divides, leading l. to the village of *Licenza*, celebrated on account of the Villa of Horace, r. by the river to Subiaco. *Cantalupo* (the *Mandela* of Horace), situated on a rock, is left on the r.

1½ M. from Vicovaro the monastery of *S. Cosimato* is passed, and soon afterwards the *Licenza*, an affluent of the Anio, crossed. On the l. bank of the river opens the valley of *Sambuci*, through which Siciliano and the above-described pedestrian-route from Tivoli to Subiaco are reached. Above the valley, 2500 ft. higher than the river, lies the village of *Saracinesco*, which soon becomes visible. It is said to have been founded by the Saracens; the costume of the inhabitants is curious. At the *Osteria della Ferrata*, mid-way between Tivoli and Subiaco, the road again divides, l. the Via Valeria to *Arsoli* and the *Lago di Fucino* (see Bædeker's Southern Italy), r. the *Via Sublacensis* to Subiaco. About half-way to the latter is situated *Roviano*, opposite to which is *Anticoli* on the l. bank.

Beyond Roviano the valley of the Anio becomes wilder and more picturesque. Farther on, l. is *Agosta*, beyond it *Cerbara* on a lofty rock, r. *Canterano* and *Rocca Canterano*. Subiaco, charmingly situated in the midst of wood and rock-scenery, now soon becomes visible.

Subiaco (*La Pernice, recommended for a prolonged stay, pension 4 l.; *Europa*), the capital of the Comarca with 6000 inhabitants, the *Sublaqueum* of antiquity, in the territory of the Æqui, sprang up on the grounds of an extensive villa of Nero, embellished by three artificial lakes ("*Simbruina stagna*" of Tacitus, Ann. 14, 22; whence the name), which were destroyed by an inundation in 1305. On the l. side of the Anio, opposite the monastery of S. Scolastica, walls and terraces are seen of the time of Nero, who, according to Tacitus, narrowly escaped being struck by lightning whilst supping here.

The present town has a mediæval aspect, and is commanded by a castle in which the popes formerly frequently resided. The environs are delightful, and the far-famed *monasteries (12—3 p. m. not accessible) extremely interesting. Guide desirable, although not absolutely necessary. The road on the r. bank of the Anio leads in 10 min. to the bridge. Above it lies the chapel of St. Placida; ¼ hr. walk higher are the monasteries of S. Scolastica; thence an ascent of 20 min. to S. Benedetto (see below). When time is limited, it is advisable to visit S. Benedetto first, and S. Scolastica on the return-route. Returning again to the bridge, and crossing to the l. bank of the Anio, the traveller may then ascend the road to the r. as far as the rear of the castle, whence a road descends to the town. The entire excursion requires about 3 hrs., and affords a continued succession of beautiful views.

Subiaco having fallen to decay at the commencement of the middle ages, *St. Benedict*, born at Nursia in Umbria in 480, retired to this solitary spot, took up his abode in one of the grottoes, now converted into chapels *(il Sagro Speco)*, as a hermit, and in 530, on a precipitous eminence on the farther side of the town, founded the first monastery, *S. Scolastica*, which was confirmed in its possessions by Gregory I. and his successors. In the 7th cent. it was destroyed, in 705 rebuilt, now entirely modern. In 1052 a *second* monastery was erected, and finally a *third* added in 1235 by the abbot Landus. The first (entrance to the r. in the passage of the monastery, after the anterior court has been passed) possesses a few antiquities; by the fountain a sarcophagus with Bacchanalian representations, handsome columns etc., probably found on the erection of the building. The monastery formerly possessed a library containing valuable MSS. Here in 1465 the German printers Arnold Pannartz and Conrad Schweinheim printed the first book published in Italy, an edition of Lactantius, of which a copy is still preserved here. They subsequently practised their art at Rome in the Palazzo Massimi (see p. 159). The second monastery, dating from 1052, is one of the earliest specimens in Italy of the pointed style. The court contains a quaint relief and two mediæval inscriptions. The third, of 1235, contains an arcaded court decorated with mosaic. The *Church of S. Scolastica*, originally founded by Benedict VII. in 975, was entirely renovated in the 18th cent., and now contains nothing worthy of note, excepting the fine carved choir-stalls.

S. Benedetto, or *Il Sagro Speco*, lies ¼ hr. higher, built against the rock, overtopped by a huge mass of stone, and shaded by oaks. The first corridor entered contains representations from the lives of St. Benedict and his sister St. Scholastica, painted in 1466. Visitors descend thence to two chapels, the pictures of which (Madonna, Slaughter of the Innocents etc.) were executed in 1219 by the otherwise unknown master *Conxolus* (earlier than Cimabue). The grotto of St. Benedict contains his statue by *Bernini*. The walls are decorated with venerable paintings. The garden of the monastery abounds with beautiful roses. They were, according to tradition, originally thorns, cultivated by St. Benedict for the mortification of the flesh, but converted by St. Francis into roses, when he visited the monastery in 1223.

Palestrina.

22 M. from Rome. Vetturino 3 times weekly from the Tre Re, near S. Marco, to Palestrina and Olevano, returning to Rome on the following day. A preferable route, however, is by railway to Frascati, and thence (12 M.) by carriage, on a donkey, or on foot to Palestrina. *Valmontone* (stat. on the line to Naples) is only 4 M. distant from Palestrina, but the insecurity of this neighbourhood has frequently been complained of.

The road from Frascati to Palestrina, especially the first half, is beautiful, but destitute of shade. First an ascent from the station to Frascati (p. 274), then to the l. the road from Rome is immediately entered. R. a glimpse of the Villa Mondragone; then the ruined vaults of an ancient villa, said to have belonged to Cato. After $1^1/_2$ M. the road passes the olive-clad hill on which *Monte Porzio* is picturesquely situated; $1^1/_2$ M. farther it reaches *Monte Compatri*, with a château of the Borghese, the ancient *Labicum*. The village is not entered, but the somewhat rough road descends by a spring as far as an image of the Madonna, where it divides. That to the r. is selected, leading in 1 hr. to the *Osteria S. Cesareo*, where the road from Rome is reached (*Via Labicana*, *Strada di Palestrina*). At S. Cesareo the latter divides, the road r. diverges to *Lugnano*, the main road l. leads to Palestrina, $4^1/_2$ M. distant.

The situation of the town on the mountain slope is strikingly picturesque, but the streets are narrow, precipitous and dirty. On arriving, the traveller is recommended at once to direct a boy to conduct him to the house of the widow *Arpina Bernardini*, where unpretending, but good accommodation may be obtained (pension 4 l. per diem). *Arena* in the Corso is reputed inferior and dearer.

From Rome to Palestrina two routes lead from the Porta Maggiore, the ancient *Via Praenestina*, and the modern and more convenient *Via Labicana*. The former, starting from the Porta Maggiore, anciently *Porta Praenestina*, proceeds l. between vineyards, past ($1/_2$ hr.) the ruins of *Tor de' Schiavi*, probably a villa of the Gordians (p. 270), to the mediæval *Tor tre Teste*, $3^1/_2$ M. from Rome; then across the 7 arches of the *Ponte di Nono*, an early Roman structure of lapis gabinus, to the *Osteria dell' Osa* on the brook Osa, which descends from the lake near the ancient Gabii, situated near the conspicuous tower of *Castiglione*. Lake *Regillus* (now dried up), celebrated for the battle of the Romans against the Latins, B. C. 496, must have lain in the broad plain between Gabii and the small town of *Colonna* (near the Casale di Pantano, it is thought), which rises on the slope to the r., towards Frascati. A short distance farther, towards the mountains, lies the village of *Compatri*.

The other route to Palestrina, the *Via Labicana* (p. 269) or road to *Labicum*, at first skirts the railway, then leads in a nearly direct line towards Palestrina as far as *S. Cesareo*, where it diverges to the r. and follows a S. direction through the valley of the Sacco. On issuing from the Porta Maggiore the road is parallel for a short distance with the *Aqua Claudia*;

after 2 M. the *Torre Pignattara* (p. 269), tomb of the Empress Helena, is reached, where near the Vigna del Grande ¡catacombs have been recently discovered. 4¹/₂ M. from Rome the arches of the aqueduct of Alex. Severus, the *Aqua Alexandrina*, become visible. 9 M. from Rome is the *Osteria del Finocchio*, beyond which the *Casale Pantano* lies, the supposed site of Lake Regillus. About 3 M. farther is *Colonna*, situated on an eminence. The road then gradually rises to the above-mentioned Osteria di S. Cesareo.

Palestrina, the *Praeneste* of antiquity, one of the most ancient towns of Italy, was captured by Camillus B. C. 380, and was thenceforth subject to Rome. In the civil wars it was the principal armoury of the younger Marius, and after a long siege was taken and entirely destroyed by Sulla, who subsequently rebuilt it in a magnificent style as a Roman colony. Under the emperors it was a favourite resort of the Romans on account of its refreshing atmosphere, and is extolled by Horace (Carm. III, 4, 22) together with Tibur and Baiæ. A celebrated *Temple of Fortune* and an *Oracle* ("sortes Prænestinæ", Cic. Div. II, 41) attracted numerous visitors. In the middle ages Palestrina was long the source of sanguinary conflicts between the powerful Colonnas and the popes, the result of which was the total destruction of the town in 1436. The territory was purchased in 1630 by the Barberini, who are still the lords of the soil.

The small and insignificant town of Palestrina is almost entirely erected on the ruins of the temple of Fortuna, which, rising on vast terraces and surrounded by a semicircular colonnade, occupied the site of the Palazzo Barberini. The substructures of the latter are exclusively ancient. On entering the town, the visitor perceives the lowest of these terraces constructed of brick. The detailed plan of the building cannot now be ascertained with accuracy. The arcades with 4 Corinthian half-columns in the piazza near the cathedral, now converted into a wine-cellar, appear to have pertained to the second terrace. In the Barberini garden (in the Corso), the *Grottini*, or interior of these substructures, are accessible, less conveniently however in spring than in autumn, on account of the water which settles there. From the Corso the visitor ascends to the *Palazzo Barberini* (fee ¹/₂—1 l.), which merits inspection. It contains a large antique mosaic, representing landscapes of the Nile, with numerous animals and figures in Egyptian and Greek costumes. This relic was found near the cathedral, and was probably manufactured under Domitian. The garden of the palace contains statues and inscriptions. The ancient *Walls of Palestrina, of which various fragments are visible, exhibit four different systems of building, from the Cyclopean mode of heaping huge blocks of stone together, to the brick-masonry of the empire. Two walls of communication, of which that to the N. is the best preserved, connected the town with the citadel *(Arx)* on the summit of the hill, now *Castel S. Pietro*, consisting of a few poor houses. A somewhat fatiguing path ascends from the Palazzo Barberini in 1½ hr., for which, however, the noble prospect from the summit (2460 ft.) amply compensates. The spacious Campagna, from which the dome of St. Peter's rises, is surveyed as far as the sea, r. rise Soracte and the Sabine Mts., then the Alban range; l. is the valley of the Sacco, bounded by the Volscian Mts. The picturesque, half-dilapidated *Fortezza* was erected by the Colonnas in 1322. The door is opened at the request of visitors (½—1 l.); the approach is uncomfortable, but the view from the interior is particularly fine.

The extensive ruins of the *Villa of Hadrian*, where the beautiful Antinous Braschi, now in the Rotonda of the Vatican (p. 248) was found, are near the church of *S. Maria della Villa*, ¾ M. from the town. In the forum of the ancient Præneste, in 1773 the calendar of Verrius Flaccus was found, now in the Palazzo Vidoni at Rome (159). The excavations at Palestrina have always yielded a rich harvest; the so-called cistæ (toilet-caskets), among them the celebrated Ficoronian (p. 119), have been exclusively found here. The great composer *Giov. Pierluigi da Palestrina*, who died at Rome in 1594 as director of the choir at St. Peter's, was born here in 1524. *Cicerchia de' Rossi* (in the Corso), formerly a singer in the papal choir, possesses a valuable collection of his celebrated compatriot's compositions, and is also well acquainted with the antiquities of Palestrina.

From Palestrina to Tivoli by *Zagarolo* and *Passerano* 4½ M. (comp. p. 287).

Olevano may be reached by carr. from Palestrina in 2½ hrs. The route is, however, also extremely interesting for pedestrians (4 hrs.); in the rear are the Alban Mts., to the r. the Volscian, to the l. and facing the traveller the Sabine. The circuit by Genazzano (see below) requires about 1 hr. more.

Palestrina is quitted by the Porta del Sole, and the road to the l. followed, which in ¾ hr. leads to *Cavi*, a village with 2000 inhab., in the property of the Colonna family. Above it, ¾ hr. walk, lies the small village of *Rocca di Cavi*, near which a brook is crossed by a viaduct of 7 arches, built in 1827.

The road from Cavi to Olevano leads in a straight direction. A little beyond Cavi the church of the *Madonna del Campo* is passed. 1½ M. farther a road diverges to the l. to **Genazzano**, a pleasant little town with 3000 inhab., possessing the rich and far-famed pilgrimage-chapel of the *Madonna del buon Consiglio*, which on festivals of the Virgin attracts devout multitudes in their picturesque costumes. The traveller may now return hence to the high road, or proceed through the valley direct to Olevano by an interesting, but rugged route.

The road to Olevano pursues a straight direction, until beyond the second bridge it divides, l. to Olevano, r. to *Puliano*. The former at first gradually ascends, and afterwards describes a long curve, causing Olevano to appear much nearer than it really is.

Olevano, a mediæval place with about 3000 inhab., the property of the Borghese, on the slope of a mountain and commanded by the ruins of an ancient castle, is strikingly picturesque. Insignificant remains of an ancient town-wall are to be seen, but the interior of the town, with its narrow and dirty streets, presents no attractions to the traveller. Immediately at the entrance to the town, the road to the r. should be taken, leading to the *Casa Baldi, much resorted to by artists, situated on the ridge of the mountain (unpretending, pension 4—5 l. per diem). The **view from this inn is singularly beautiful. To the r. are visible the barren summits of the Sabine Mts., with Civitella, S. Vito, Capranica and Rocca di Cavi, then the narrow plain, bounded by the Alban and Sabine Mts. In the distance Velletri is seen. Nearer is Valmontone with its château, situated on a mountain-summit; then Rocca Massima, Segni and Paliano. Towards the S. extends the valley of the Sacco, until lost to the eye. The town with its ruined castle forms the most charming foreground. The inn should if possible be reached an hour before sunset. It is well adapted for a prolonged stay. The environs are replete with beauties of nature.

From Olevano to Subiaco there are three different routes, all remarkable for their beauty. The carriage-road passing below *Civitella*, not yet completed, is the shortest and most convenient, but, like the two others, is at present available for riders and pedestrians only. Donkeys may be ordered of the landlord, 1½—2 l., attendant as much more. — The most beautiful route is by Civitella. Rocca S. Stefano and Rocca S. Francesco, 5 hrs. Continuing on the height from the Casa Baldi, the traveller reaches *Civitella* in 1¼ hr., a poor village situated on an isolated peak in a barren, mountainous district. On account of its secure situation it was inhabited even in ancient times, but its former name is unknown. The fragments of a fortification which commanded the narrow approach on the W. side, constructed of large masses of rock, are still visible. From the farther extremity of the village a beautiful view of the valleys and mountains towards Subiaco is enjoyed. Archæologists should not omit to follow the wall to the l. from this gate (although a rough walk), in order to inspect the *remains of the very ancient wall, constructed of unhewn blocks, by which this, the less precipitous side of the mountain, was guarded. The path then leads by *S. Stefano* and *Rocca S. Francesco* into the valley of the Anio, and to Subiaco, beautiful the whole way.

A third route, the longest, 5—6 hrs., and in some respects the most fatiguing, but also highly interesting, leads by *Rojate* and *Affile*. The longer half as far as Affile is by field and forest-paths, easily mistaken; a guide is therefore desirable. Rojate is a small village, Affile a place of more importance, boasting of a few relics of ancient walls and inscriptions. Hence to Subiaco the high road is followed. By the bridge over the Anio the road to the r. leads to the monasteries, that to the l. in ¼ hr. to the town.

Of the numerous beautiful Excursions which may be made among the Sabine Mts. two of the principal are here mentioned.

Monte Gennaro, one of the highest peaks (about 4500 ft.) of the Sabina, is a familiar object to the eye of the stranger who has visited Rome. The ascent from Tivoli occupies 5—6 hrs., and an entire day must be devoted to the excursion. Guides at Tivoli demand 5—6 l., those at S. Polo, which the traveller may reach unaided, 2—3 l.

Tivoli is quitted by the Porta S. Angelo, and the high road to Subiaco followed for 2 M. Here a bridle-path diverges to the l., leading along the mountain-slopes in 1½ hr. to the lofty (2400 ft.) village of *S. Polo*. (Those who do not object to rough accommodation should pass the night here.) The real ascent now commences (guide necessary), the last portion very fatiguing. The traveller should not omit to provide himself with refreshments for the excursion. The mountain is badly supplied with water, and the shepherds are compelled to drink rain-water collected in troughs and hollow trees. On the summit stands a rude pyramid of stone, which has served for trigonometrical surveys. The view is very extensive, comprising the coast from M. Circeio as far as the lake of Baccano, the broad plain with innumerable villages, from the Volscian and Alban Mts. as far as Soracte and the Ciminian Forest; then over the Apennines as far as the snowy peaks of the central range.

The descent may be made by the bridle-path, termed *La Scarpellata*, which traverses the S. slope of the mountain. The villages of *Monticelli* and *S. Angelo* are left on the r.

M. Gennaro may also be ascended from *Rocca Giovine* in 5—6 hrs. (guide 3—4 l.), and this excursion thus combined with the following, but the village affords very poor accommodation for the night.

Valley of Licenza. Travellers versed in classic lore will naturally be attracted to this spot, where the Sabine farm of Horace is reputed to have been situated, but its great natural beauty alone renders it an object of extreme interest. The excursion may either be undertaken from Tivoli, or combined with the journey to Subiaco, and may be almost entirely accomplished by carriage.

From Tivoli to Vicovaro 6½ M. (p. 288); thence to Rocca Giovine 3 M., the road is accessible to carriages; to Licenza 2 M. farther. *Rocca Giovine*, a small village standing on a precipitous rock, is charmingly situated; its name is supposed to be derived from *Arx Junonis*, and indeed a temple actually existed here once, possibly the Fanum Vacunæ of Horace. *Licenza*, another mountain-village, derives its appellation from the *Digentia*, now *Licenza*, which skirts the base of the hill ("me quoties reficit gelidus Digentia rivus", Hor. Ep. 1. 18, 104). Shortly before the village is attained (guide from Rocca Giovine ½ l.), the scanty remains of a villa are pointed out, which is said to have belonged to Horace. This, however, is a mere hypothesis; the most recent investigations tend to prove that the poet's Sabine farm was situated near Rocca Giovine, by the chapel of the *Madonna delle Case*, on an elevated plain at the base of *M. Corrignaleto*, which in this case would be the *Mons Lucretilis* of Horace, instead of M. Gennaro as formerly supposed. Near this chapel is a spring, termed *Fontana degli Oratini* by the natives, perhaps the *Fons Bandusiae* of the poet (Carm. III, 13).

On the route between Rocca Giovine and Subiaco a nearer path by *Cantalupo* (p. 288), the ancient *Mandela* ("rugosus frigore pagus", Ep. I. 18, 105) is generally taken.

The Volscian Mountains.

The mountain-range, separated on the E. from the principal chain of the Apennines by the valley of the Sacco, on the N. from the Alban Mts. by a narrow depression, extending S. as far as the Bay of Gaeta, and on the W. bounded by a dreary and in some places marshy plain adjoining the sea, and which attains an elevation of 5000 ft., was in ancient times the chief seat of the Volsci, but at an early period subjugated by the Romans and Latinized. Its towns, picturesquely rising on the mountain-slopes, still bear many traces of the republican epoch of Italy, which, in addition to then atural attractions, will highly interest the observant traveller. This mountainous district, however, is little frequented, partly on account of the poorness of the inns, but principally owing to its insecure state, the brigands expelled from the Neapolitan provinces having sought refuge here. An excursion to Cori may be accomplished in one day by means of the railway as far as Velletri, so also that to Segni. More extended journeys should not be undertaken without previous enquiry respecting the routes.

Rome should be quitted by the first train (in winter at 6. 30 a. m., fares 5 l. 65, 4 l. 50, 2 l. 75 c.), reaching Velletri about 8 a. m. — Railway-journey as far as Civitá Lavinia see p. 282.

From the station to the town of Velletri (Gallo, see p. 282). is an ascent of a few minutes. Hence to Cori 11 M., which may best be accomplished by carriage (one-horse there and back about 8 l.). The route, especially the first part, traversing a dreary plain, is uninteresting. To the l. of the road lies the (4½ M.) *Lago di Giulianello*, an extinct crater. A short distance farther is a wood, frequently infested by banditti, where the road is generally guarded. After 6½ M. the poor village of *Giulianello* is reached, whence the road l. ascends to *Rocca Massima*, whilst that to the r. leads to *Cori*. The slopes of the mountains here begin to present a more attractive appearance. About 3 M. from Giulianello, at a chapel of the *Madonna del Monte*, a road to the l. diverges to the upper part of the town. The road to the r., leading to the lower part, is preferable; it traverses olive plantations at the foot of the hill, and affords no view of the town until it is reached.

Cori *(Filippuccio* should be enquired for; the trattoria is near the Porta Romana, the sleeping-rooms farther up in the Piazza, accommodation rustic, but the people obliging). In order that no time may be lost, a guide to the principal points of interest had better be at once engaged (½—1 l.). Those who have arrived by the first train from Rome, and desire to return by the last from Velletri, have about 5 hrs. at their disposal. The ancient *Cora* was at an early period a member of the Latin League; it is mentioned B. C. 493 as one of the 30 confederate towns. During the empire it still prospered, but its name subsequently fell into oblivion. It now contains 4000 inhab.; tobacco is extensively cultivated in the neighbourhood. (Connoisseurs of the fragrant herb may occasionally purchase good, but strong cigars in the neighbourhood.)

Besides the modern walls, which to a great extent date from the 15th cent., considerable remains of ancient *walls of various periods are here preserved. Those of the earliest style consist of large blocks without mortar, the interstices being filled up with smaller stones; the best example of this is seen near the gate to Norma and S. Maria. The second and more perfect description is constructed of hewn polygonal blocks, the external sides of which alone are left rough. Finally walls of regularly hewn square stones, perhaps dating from the time of Sulla; e. g. those above S. Oliva and those separating the upper town (Arx) from the lower. The town appears to have been surrounded by differently situated walls at different periods.

A deep ravine outside the Porta Ninfesina is spanned by the *Ponte della Catena, a bridge constructed of blocks of tuffstone, in the style of the Cloaca Maxima at Rome. In order that the structure and its great solidity (an arch with double layers of masonry) may be appreciated, the survey must be made from the ravine below.

The traveller's attention, however, will be principally arrested by the colonnade of the so-called *Temple of Hercules (perhaps of Minerva), standing on the highest ground in the town. The cella of the temple is incorporated with the church of S. Pietro; the 8 columns of the Doric colonnade, with frieze of travertine bearing traces of stucco-decoration, are preserved. The inscription, recording the erection of the edifice by the duumviri, or chief magistrates of the place, dates from the time of Sulla. The *view hence over the town towards the sea, and of the plain with the isolated M. Circeio is remarkably fine.

S. Oliva is also erected on the foundations of an ancient temple, and possesses antique columns. In the street of S. Salvatore once stood a temple of Castor and Pollux, as the inscription, still preserved, records, but it is now incorporated with other buildings. The frieze and 2 columns of the Corinthian order, of admirable workmanship, are still to be seen. Other relics of antiquity, inscriptions, columns, reliefs, fragments of marble etc. are distributed throughout the whole town; also large masses of *opus reticulatum* of the imperial epoch.

From Cori a rugged bridle-path, endangered however of late years by bandits, traverses the mountains in 5—6 hrs. to Segni. Instead of returning to Velletri the traveller may prefer to proceed across the plain by *Giulianello* and *Montefortino* (12 M.) to stat. *Valmontone*, but this route is scarcely more secure. Segni is on the whole most conveniently accessible from the railway. The excursion to Cori may be prolonged to Norma, which is reached in 2 hrs. A shorter, but rough path (guide desirable, 1 l.) leads from Porta Ninfesina by the mountains, another by the plain. The former may be selected in going, the latter in returning. A walk of 1 3/4 hr. brings the traveller to the ruins of Norba, which became a Latin colony B. C. 492, and was conquered and destroyed by the troops of Sulla during the civil wars. The wall in the polygonal style, well preserved, was 1 1/2 M. in circumference; several gateways are still distinctly traceable. The interior contains various obscure relics. In 1/4 hr. the small mountain-village of *Norma* is reached hence. In the plain below it lie the ivy-clad remains of the mediæval town of *Ninfa*, surrounded by a marsh which has been the cause of its abandonment. A palace, monastery, church with faded frescoes, and streets are still easily distinguished. Cori may now be regained by the Cori and Sermoneta road.

Segni *(Locanda di Gaetanini)* may like Cori be visited in one day from Rome. (Two trains daily in 2 1/2 hrs., fares 8 l. 75, 7 l., 4 l. 25 c.). Beyond Velletri are the stations of *Valmontone*,

where the line enters the valley of the Sacco, and *Montefortino.*
From stat. Segni to the town is an ascent of 1½ hr. This is
the venerable *Signia,* said to have been colonized by the Romans
under Tarquinius Priscus, situated on a mountain-slope (the summit of which is 2290 ft. in height) in a secure position, commanding fine views of the valley with the towns of the Hernici.
The present town, with 3500 inhab., occupies the lower half of
the ancient.

Ascending through the streets, the traveller reaches the church
of *S. Pietro,* rising from the foundation of an ancient temple,
the walls of which are of rectangular blocks of tuff, below which
are two layers of polygonal masses of limestone. A fountain adjoining the church is also of the Roman epoch. The **Town-Walls,*
in the massive polygonal style, are for the most part well preserved.; From S. Pietro the remarkable *Porta Saracinesca* is
attained, apparently built before the discovery of the principle of
the arch, a substitute for which is formed by a gradual approach
of the lateral walls until they meet at an angle. From this point
the circuit of the wall may be followed for 1½ M.; the *Porta
Lucina,* similar to the above, is partially buried. Lower down
are remains of a second enclosing wall, inscriptions etc.

From stat. Segni, Anagni is about 4½ M. distant. Respecting
this and the other towns of the Hernici, comp. Part III. (S. Italy
and Sicily) of this Handbook.

Etruscan Towns.

That portion of the Roman Campagna which extends N. from the Tiber
to the Ciminian Forest and the mountains of Tolfa was the S. Etruria of
antiquity. Originally occupied by a tribe akin to the Latins, then subjugated by the Etruscans, it was finally, after protracted contests, with which
the first centuries of the annals of Rome abound, reconquered and Latinized. The fall of the mighty Veii, B. C. 396, principally contributed to
effect this memorable change. Excursions are frequently made to Cervetri
and Veii for the sake of visiting the remains of the Etruscan tombs; but,
apart from its archæological interest, this district deserves to be better
known on account of its imposing natural beauties. Malaria is unfortunately very prevalent here.

Veii.

Veii, near *Isola Farnese* may be visited from Rome, from which it is
11 M. distant, in one day. Carriage for the whole excursion 15—20 l. For
pedestrians the route is longer than agreeable; the first portion at least, perhaps as far as Tomba di Nerone (4½ M., fiacre 4 l.), or La Storta (8¼ M.),
should be performed by carriage. Those who are disposed may return from
Veii by a somewhat longer route, skirting the *Fosso di Valchetta,* the valley
of which descends to the Via Flaminia between the 6th and 7th milestones
(comp. p. 70). Provisions for the journey should be provided, as the tavern
at Isola is extremely poor.

The route is from Rome to the Ponte Molle; at the Osteria,
where the Via Flaminia (p. 272) diverges to the r., the *Via*

Cassia. gradually ascending to the l., must be followed. The district soon becomes desolate. About $4^1/_2$ M. from Rome, at the *Tomba di Nerone* (p. 42), an ancient route, somewhat shorter than the modern, diverges to Veii. As, however, an experienced eye alone can trace it across the Campagna, the high road is preferable. About $8^1/_4$ M. from Rome the post-station of *La Storta* (inn, see p. 42) is reached. One mile beyond it the road diverges to the r. to Isola Farnese; $1/_2$ M. farther, where the road divides, that to the r. is to be selected, l. is the route to *Formello*.

Isola Farnese, a poor village, numbering scarcely 100 inhab., and harassed by fever in summer, is the property of the Rospigliosi. It was a place of some consequence in the middle ages, having been founded on account of the natural security of its site. A guide is here engaged ($1-1^1/_2$ l., bargaining necessary) to conduct the traveller to the site of Veii. Imposing ruins must not be looked for here, but the landscape is interesting and picturesque. For the keys of the Grotta Campana (p. 299), although the property of the state, the farmer of the soil makes the exorbitant demand of 5 l., which moreover he cannot easily be persuaded to reduce. A minute inspection of the relics of the ancient city is interesting to the archæologist only. The following are the principal points, a visit to which occupies 2—3 hrs. The brook is first descended to the mill *(molino)*, where there is a picturesque waterfall, not far from which the brook is crossed by the antique *Ponte dell' Isola*. Farther on is the *Ponte Sodo*, hewn in the rock, beneath which the brook is conducted. Then the *Porta Spezieria* with remains of a columbarium, the recesses of which gave rise to the name. In the vicinity is the Grotta Campana. Hence by the banks of the *Cremera* to the *Piazza d'Armi*, the ancient citadel, commanding a fine view. Then back to Isola. Pedestrians, by descending the valley of the stream from the Piázza d'Armi, may reach the Via Flaminia in 2 hrs.

Veii, one of the most powerful Etruscan cities, after contests protracted for centuries [at first centred round *Fidenae (Castel Giubileo)*, the outwork of the Etruscans on the S. bank of the Tiber], and after manifold vicissitudes and a long siege, was at length captured by Camillus, B. C. 396. The circumference of the town, which may still be traced, is $5^1/_2$ M. After the conquest it fell to decay, and was subsequently re-peopled by Cæsar with a Roman colony, which however scarcely occupied one-third of the former area. Excavations here have led to the discovery of inscriptions, statues etc., and the columns which adorn the colonnades of the military casino in the Piazza Colonna (p. 117).

Veii stands on a table-land, around which on the N. and E. flows the ancient *Cremera*, now *Fosso di Formello*, on the W. towards Isola the *Fosso dell' Isola*. The ancient citadel, now *Piazza d'Armi*, occupies a position at the confluence of the two brooks, connected with the site of the town by a narrow isthmus only. The camp of the Fabii, whose entire family was destroyed by the Veientines, was situated on the heights on the r. bank of the *Valca*, as the *Cremera* is named in the lower part of its course, about $1^1/_2$ M. distant from the citadel. The *Grotta Campana, named after its discoverer, is the only tomb of Veii still preserved, and is left in the condition in which it was found in 1842. It is hewn in the tuffstone-rock and guarded by two lions at the entrance. The interior consists of two chambers; the walls are covered with grotesque paintings of great antiquity. Two skeletons were found here, but soon fell to pieces. Remains of the armour of a warrior, vessels of clay etc. are also seen.

Galera.

Galera, $14^1/_2$ M. from Rome, may be visited by the route to Bracciano (p. 300), or by carriage (15—20 l.), in a single day from Rome. A supply of provisions necessary. Vetturini also occasionally run (see below).

About $^1/_2$ M. beyond *La Storta* (p. 298) the *Via Clodia* diverges to the l. from the Via Cassia, which leads to *Baccano* (p. 42). The former, the old pavement of which is occasionally seen, is to be selected. The district is dreary. On the roadside is the entrance-shaft of the subterranean *Acqua Paola*, which descends from the lake of Bracciano and turns the mills on the Janiculus (p. 229). On the l., $4^1/_4$ M. from La Storta, appears the church of *S. Maria di Cesareo*; 1 M. farther the *Osteria Nuova*, where the carriage may be quitted. The land here is well watered, and occupied by several extensive farms. A path to the l. in the direction of these, then turning off to the r., leads in $^1/_2$ hr. to the ruins of *Galera*. The town arose in the middle ages near the *Carciae* of antiquity, at first ruled by powerful nobles, then 1226—1670 in possession of the Orsini, and now the property of the Collegium Hungaricum of the Jesuits. At the beginning of the present century the inhabitants were compelled by malaria to abandon the place. Even the solitary shepherd who now lives here quits it with his flock in summer. It stands on an abrupt tuffstone-rock, around which the *Arrone*, the outlet of the lake of Bracciano, flows. The walls are of the 14th and 15th centuries; two churches with their towers, the palace of the Orsini and many houses are recognisable, all densely overgrown with ivy and creepers. The surrounding wooded ravine enhances the romantic appearance of the spot.

Bracciano.

$23^1/_2$ M. from Rome. A vetturino conveys passengers thither every alternate day (occasional irregularity), from the Locanda del Sole in the

Piazza of the Pantheon, in 5—6 hrs., fare 4 l., returning on the following day. During May and June, the bathing-season at Vicarello (see below), the traffic is more animated.

Beyond the Osteria Nuova (see p. 299) the *Arrone* is soon reached. Then to the r. a road diverges to *Anguillara*, situated on the lake. The district continues dreary. About 3 M. before Bracciano is reached, the lake becomes visible, with *Trevignano* and *Rocca Romana*, the highest point (2200 ft.) of the surrounding range of hills. The lake *(Lacus Sabatinus* of antiquity) is 20 M. in circumference, and lies upwards of 500 ft. above the sea-level. Its form and the heights encircling it indicate that it was once a crater. It abounds in fish (eels celebrated), and the slopes are well cultivated, the upper parts being clothed with wood, but malaria is prevalent.

Near Bracciano the road divides, the upper l. leads to the Capuchin monastery, the other r. to the town.

Bracciano (*Locanda Piva, unpretending), a small modern town with 2000 inhab., possesses a picturesque castle of the 15th cent., and in the vicinity several iron-works. The town has no attraction except its situation. A visit to the *Castle, however, is extremely interesting. It was erected by the Orsini, is now the property of Prince Torlonia, and with its towers and fortifications serves to convey an accurate idea of a mediæval stronghold. It is said on this account to have arrested the attention of Sir Walter Scott far more powerfully than the more imposing ruins of antiquity. The interior, which is still inhabited, contains nothing worthy of note. The *view from the tower, extending over the beautiful lake to Trevignano and Anguillara, with Soracte and the Sabine Mts. in the background, is remarkably attractive.

A pleasant excursion may be made from Bracciano to *Trevignano*, 6½ M. distant. The road skirts the lake. After 1½ M. a path ascends to the l. to the old church of the martyrs SS. Marco, Marciano and Liberato, erected, as the inscription informs us, on the site of an ancient villa named *Pausilypon*, and affording a fine view. In the vicinity stood *Forum Clodii*, from which inscriptions and other relics are preserved. Pedestrians may regain the road to Vicarello by another forest-path. — *Vicarello* is 3¾ M. from Bracciano. The baths, ¾ M. from the road, with a hot sulphureous spring, now in possession of the Jesuits, are the *Aquæ Apollinares* of antiquity. A proof of the estimation in which they were held was afforded in 1852 by the discovery of great numbers of coins and votive offerings, most of which are now in the Museo Kircheriano (p. 119). Owing to the malaria, the bathing season is not prolonged beyond the early part of summer. — By the road are seen frequent remains of opus reticulatum, belonging to villas of the imperial epoch. *Trevignano*, occupying the site of the Etruscan town of *Sabate*, which early fell into oblivion, formerly the property of the Orsini, now of the Conti, is a poor village. Roman remains very scanty; in the principal church two pictures of the school of Perugino. The ruined castle above the village commands a fine view; its destruction was due to Cæsar Borgia.

A bridle-path leads hence in 1½ hr. to Sutri (p. 41), another in about 3 hrs. to *Anguillara*, the ancestral seat of the once powerful counts of that name. If the wind be favourable it is preferable to cross the lake from Trevignano by boat. From Anguillara to Bracciano an uninteresting route of 6½ M.; thus the tour of the lake may thus be accomplished in a single day. (One-horse carr. from Bracciano to Trevignano 3½ l.)

From Bracciano a road traverses a dreary district to Cervetri, 9 M. distant, so that the above excursion may be conveniently combined with the following.

Cære.

Cerretri, the ancient *Caere*, may be visited from Rome in a single day. The first train should be taken as far as Palo (p. 12) (three trains daily, fares 6 l. 65, 4 l. 25 c.); thence in 1¼ hr. to Cervetri, where a stay of 5 hrs. may be made, leaving time to regain Rome by the last train.

Caere, more anciently named *Agylla* (a Pelasgic city), is a place of very remote origin. Afterwards subject to the Etruscans, it carried on from its harbours *Pyrgos* (Palo) and *Alsion* (S. Severa) an extensive commerce. At the same time it was closely allied with Rome. In B. C. 351 it was received into the confederation of Roman states, and B. C. 390 gave refuge to the Vestal virgins on the subjugation of Rome by the Gauls. The Romans out of gratitude are said to have conferred upon the Cærites the franchise without the suffragium. In 1250 the town was abandoned by its inhabitants, who founded *Cere Nuovo* 3 M. distant, the present *Ceri*, with not more than 50 inhab. A number of them, it is uncertain when, afterwards returned to Cære Vetere, whence the name *Cervetri*. The present village, the property of the Ruspoli, with about 200 inhab., stands on the site of the ancient city, which was 4¼ M. in circumference. The interest of this locality was greatly increased by the discovery of numerous tombs in 1829; the excavations are still prosecuted. (Accommodation at the house of the vetturino *Pacifico Rosati;* keys of the tombs at *Passegieri's.*)

The tombs are either clustered together and hewn in the rock, or stand alone in conical mounds or tumuli. On the whole their state of preservation is far inferior to that of the tombs of Corneto: of painting hardly a trace remains. The more important may be visited in 3—4 hrs. Most of them lie on the hill opposite the village, and separated from it by a gorge. The traveller who desires to form an accurate idea of their arrangements should not confine his attention to the most interesting only.

1. *Grotta delle Sedie e Scudi*, so called from two seats and several shields hewn in the rock, contains an anteroom and five chambers. 2. *Grotta del Triclinio*, with almost entirely obliterated paintings representing a banquet. 3. *Grotta della bella Architettura*, with two chambers, supported by pillars. 4. *Grotta delle Urne*, with three marble sarcophagi. *5. *Grotta delle Iscrizioni* or *de' Tarquinii*, with two chambers, supported by pillars, contains numerous inscriptions with the name of *Tarchnas* (Lat. *Tar-*

quinius), thus corroborating the alleged Etruscan origin of the Roman kings. *6. *Grotta dei Bassorilievi*, excavated in 1850, contains two pillars, supporting the roof of the chamber, decorated with various bas-reliefs of scenes from every-day life, hewn in the tuffstone, and bearing traces of painting. — On the road to Palo lies: *7. *Grotta Regolini Galassi*, opened in 1836, a tomb of great antiquity. The roof is vaulted by means of the gradual approach of the lateral walls to each other, instead of by the arch-principle. The yield of this tomb, now in the Gregorian Museum, was very considerable, consisting of a bed, a four-wheeled chariot, shields, tripods, vessels of bronze, an iron altar, figures of clay, silver goblets, and golden ornaments used in decorating the deceased. — One mile from this is situated a tomb, opened in 1850, and still containing the vases, vessels and other objects then discovered. Besides these, there are numerous other tombs (e. g. *Grotta Torlonia*, the first chamber of which contains 54 recesses for the dead).

The Sea-coast of Latium.

Communication with the sea was of far higher importance to ancient than to modern Rome. Its former facility, indeed, mainly contributed to the proud rank held in the world by the city. The most imposing harbours and other structures were accordingly established at the estuary of the Tiber, the ruins of which are still visible. The coast stretching towards the S. was a favourite resort of the wealthy Romans, as the numerous villas testify. It is now entirely desolate, and is skirted by a broad belt of forest (macchia), where in the summer-months the malaria is more pestilential than in any other locality.

Very interesting excursions may be undertaken along the coast, especially in spring. They are most conveniently made by carriage, and should be so arranged that Rome may be regained in the evening.

Ostia.

14 M. from Rome. Two-horse carr. there and back 25 l., fee 2 l. The drive to *Castel Fusano* must be expressly stipulated for. A small steamboat of rather uninviting appearance starts in the morning for Fiumicino (see below), which it reaches in 2 hrs., returning in the evening in 3 hrs. A supply of provisions should be taken, as the osteria at Ostia is poor. Quarters for the night may be obtained, by applying to the Principe Chigi for permission, in his château of Castel Fusano, but not during the residence of the family (end of May and June).

The road quits the city by the Porta S. Paolo, passes the monastery of that name, and proceeds in the vicinity of the river. A short distance beyond the monastery a road leads to the l. to the three churches of *Tre Fontane* (p. 263) and to Ardea. $8^1/_4$ M. from Rome the *Rio di Decima* is reached, and $1^1/_2$ M. farther the *Ponte della Refolta*, an ancient viaduct of peperine. The road next traverses the hills of Decima, then a growth of underwood *(Macchia di Ostia)*, beyond which, 2 M. from Ostia, a fine view of the latter is obtained. A short distance from the village the *Stagno di Ostia*, which yielded salt as early as the epoch of the kings, is reached and crossed by an embankment.

Ostia, a poor village with scarcely 100 inhab., was founded by Gregory IV. in 830, several centuries after the destruction of the ancient town. Under Leo IV. (847—56) the Saracens here sustained a signal defeat, which Raphael has represented in the Stanze. Julius II. (1503—13), when Cardinal della Rovere, caused the fort to be erected by *Sangallo*. The importance which the town had hitherto enjoyed was lost, when, in 1612, Paul reopened the r. arm of the Tiber at Porto.

The beautiful church of *S. Aurea*, designed by Baccio Pintelli, was erected under Julius II. The adjacent *Episcopal Palace* contains numerous inscriptions and other relics, discovered during the excavations. These works, commenced in the last century, have been successfully prosecuted under the superintendence of M. Visconti since 1855. It is intended to erect a dwelling-house for the convenience of artists and savants who contemplate protracted researches. Two or three hours, however, suffice for a visit to the principal objects.

The Ostia of antiquity, founded by Ancus Martius, fourth King of Rome, extended along the left arm of the Tiber, $1/2$ M. from the present village, as far as *Torre di Boacciano*. It was a large commercial town, numbering 80,000 inhab., and continued to maintain its position even after the foundation of Portus. Among the numerous nationalities of which the population consisted, various foreign religions were professed; thus Christianity also was here introduced at an early period. The bishopric of Ostia, according to some accounts, is said to have been established by the apostles themselves, and is still regarded with great veneration by the Romish clergy. Monica, the mother of St. Augustine, died here.

At the entrance to the town (r.) is an osteria, which affords very poor fare. The custodian is generally to be found here, and may be recognised by his metal-badge (for the whole distance 2—3 l.). About 5 minutes' walk from the gate are the tombs, extending in a line beyond the Porta Romana of the ancient town. The greater number of the reliefs found here are now in the Lateran (p. 204). In 3 min. the gate of the old town is reached, and, after passing several streets and half-excavated edifices, the visitor arrives at a temple, with a well-preserved cella and raised basement, adjoining which is the store-room for the sacred vessels *(favissæ)*. Then, 2 min. farther, towards the river, is the building, which it is proposed to convert into a dwelling-house, containing the antiquities. The fragments of reliefs and inscriptions are interesting to the antiquarian only. In 10 min. more the *baths, discovered in 1867, are reached. They are of considerable size but unfortunately not sufficiently excavated to be here described: the situation of the furnace, a swimming-basin, hot-bath *(calidarium)* etc. may, however, be distinguished.

Proceeding towards the Tiber for 7 min., the visitor arrives at more extensive baths with a palæstra etc., probably erected by Antoninus Pius; adjacent is a small temple of Mithras, with an inscription on the mosaic-pavement. About $^3/_4$ M. hence (by the street skirting the E. side of the town) is *Laurentum*, where a number of graves and columbaria were discovered in 1867; the pictures found in them are now in the 16th room of the Lateran (p. 206).

A carriage-road leads from Ostia to (2 M.) *Castel Fusano* (to which the driver should be expressly desired to convey the traveller), situated in the midst of a beautiful forest of pines. It was erected by the Marchese Sacchetti in the 16th cent., and fortified against pirates; it is now the property of the Chigi family. A modern road, with ancient pavement of basalt, leads hence to the sea, 1 M. distant, the view of which however is excluded by a lofty sandbank. Similar formations, extending to the S. beyond the Pontine Marshes, bound the entire coast.

From Ostia the river may be crossed near Torre di Boacciano to the *Isola Sacra* (p. 305), which is then traversed till the r. arm of the Tiber is reached ($1^1/_2$ M.). Beyond the latter lies *Fiumicino*, whence the traveller proceeds to Porto.

From Castel Fusano to *Tor Paterno*, a farm in the vicinity of the ancient Laurentum, is a route of $6^1/_2$ M. Thence with guide to ($4^1/_2$ M.) *Pratica*, an insignificant village on the site of the *Lavinium* of antiquity. From Pratica to Albano $7^1/_4$ M., to Rome 14 M. *Ardea*, with remains of the ancient town, is $6^1/_2$ M. from Pratica.

Porto.

An excursion to this point is far less interesting than that to Ostia, and recommended to the archæologist more than to the ordinary traveller. Carriage to Fiumicino 20—25 l. The journey may also be performed by means of the small steamer already mentioned (p. 302), or by the Civita Vecchia railway. From *Ponte Galera* (p. 13), the second station, to Porto $5^1/_2$ M., to Fiumicino $7^1/_4$ M.

Owing to the extensive alluvial deposits of the Tiber (according to modern calculations its delta advances on an average $12^1/_2$ ft. annually), the harbour at Ostia was gradually filled with sand, and the lower quarters of the capital itself were frequently exposed to danger from inundations, on account of the diminished fall of the channel. The Emp. Claudius accordingly constructed a new harbour immediately on the coast, enclosed it by moles, and conducted into it a canal from the Tiber. In 103 Trajan considerably enlarged and improved this harbour, which was called after him *Portus Trajani*, and soon absorbed the entire traffic with Rome. At the same time he excavated a new canal (fossa

Trajani), which at present forms the principal arm of the Tiber. This harbour is now 2 M. distant from the sea.

Porto now consists of a *Cathedral*, dedicated to S. Rufina, an episcopal *Palace*, with inscriptions and antiquities, and a *Villa of Prince Torlonia*, who has caused excavations to be made here. The traveller first reaches the walls of the town, then, passing the farm-buildings, the harbour of Trajan, a large octagonal basin, surrounded by magazines, now a shallow lake only. In the meadows to the N. of this, the extent of the harbour of Claudius is still recognised. Towards the river are situated the episcopal palace, and the church of St. Rufina, of the 10th cent., now entirely modernized.

Fiumicino (Locanda), a modern place which derives some importance from the river-navigation, is 2 M. distant from Ostia. The castle, erected in 1773 close to the sea, is now nearly $1/_2$ M. distant from it. The tower commands a fine view.

The *Isola Sacra*, situated between the two arms of the river, was so termed at a very early period, either from having been the site of a heathen temple, or from having been granted by Constantine to the Church. Numerous herds of cattle are pastured here, against which travellers must be on their guard, especially in spring.

Porto d'Anzio,

$33^1/_2$ M. from Rome, is much frequented during the bathing-season (May and June), when direct tickets (5 l.) are issued by the post-office authorities. Duration of journey 5 hrs.; the excursion requires two days. Railway to *La Cecina*, the station for Albano. Thence to Porto d'Anzio $16^1/_2$ M. Every alternate day, in spring generally daily, a vetturino performs this part of the journey in 3 hrs. Another vetturino from Rome (Via Bocca di Leone 86) on Wednesdays and Saturdays at 5. 30 a. m., fare 6 l. Accommodation at the *Locanda di Ambrogio Pallastrini*, in private apartments, and also at the Palazzo Doria in the neighbouring village of Nettuno. A stay at Porto d'Anzio is extremely agreeable in the early summer, but fevers begin to prevail in July, often setting in with great suddenness.

Antium, the capital of the Volsci, and a prosperous seaport at a very early period, where, B. C. 490, Coriolanus sought refuge when banished from Rome, and perished after having spared the city at the entreaty of his mother, was compelled in 468 to succumb to the Romans. In 338, when all the Latins were subjugated, it received a Roman colony, and was thus permanently united with Rome. Extensive villas were subsequently established here. Cicero possessed an estate at Antium, the tranquillity and charms of which he cannot sufficiently extol (Att. IV, 8). Horace (Carm. I, 35) mentions the temple of Fortune at the "lovely Antium", where oracular responses were given, and which was consulted as late as the time of Theodosius the Great (about 390). Claudius and Nero were born at Antium, where the latter erected magnificent edifices. Domitian, Hadrian, Antoninus Pius and Lucius Verus resided at Antium in summer. The Goths and Saracens subsequently established themselves here. In the 14th cent. the place was at length entirely deserted, and in the 16th the popes endeavoured to restore the harbour. Since 1831 Porto d'Anzio and Nettuno have been the property of Prince Borghese, who here possesses a handsome villa, said to occupy the site of the ancient fortress. Extensive substructures, fragments of columns etc. have been discovered here. Under Julius II. the Apollo Belvedere, and probably the Diana of Versailles also, was extricated from the ruins near the so-called Arco Muto; subsequently the Borghese Gladiator (now in Paris). The town possesses beautiful villas of the Corsini (now Mencacci) and Doria families, likewise a bagno for convicts. Pius IX. generally spends part of the summer at Porto d'Anzio.

A picturesque road, passing villas and country-residences (or the beach may be followed, although somewhat fatiguing), leads to the small town of (1½ M.).

Nettuno, said to have been originally a settlement of the Saracens, situated on a fortified height with a single entrance only. The streets are narrow and precipitous; the inhabitants, principally fishermen, are generally engaged in their pursuits on the coast. The costume of the women is picturesque. Cicero once possessed a villa at *Astura*, ¼ M. distant. A tower, connected with the mainland by a bridge, is associated with the memory of the ill-fated prince *Conradin of Swabia*, who, after the loss of the Battle of Tagliacozzo sought refuge here with *Jacopo Frangipani*. The latter, however, delivered him up to Charles of Anjou, who caused him to be beheaded at Naples.

INDEX.

Abete, Monte dell' 22.
Acciajuolo 14.
Acquabuona 14.
Acqualagna 78.
Acquapendente 37.
Acqua Santa 269.
Acqua Traversa 43.
Aesis 82.
Aethalia 23.
Affile 293.
Agosta 288.
Agylla 301.
Aiguillette, Fort 6.
Alba Longa 278.
Albano 279.
—, Lago di 278.
Alban Mountains, the 273.
Albanum 280.
Albegna 16.
—, river 16.
Albinia 16.
Allia 271.
Almo, brook 264. 267.
Alsion 12. 301.
Amelia 66.
Ameria 66.
Amiata, Monte 32. 37.
Ampiglione 287.
Ancona 81.
Anemo 71.
S. Angelo 294.
— in Vado 78.
Anguillara 300.
Anio, river 270. 271. 284. 286.
Ansedonia 17.
Antemnae 271.
Anticoli 288.
Antium 305.
Aqua Alexandrina 291.
— *Ferentina* 277.
Aquae Albulae 284.
— *Apollinares* 300.
— *Tauri* 12.
Ardea 304.
Arezzo 45.
Argentario, Monte 16.
Ariccia 281.
Aricia 281.
Ariccianа, Valle 281.
Ariminum 73.
Arno, river 9. 50.
Arretium 45.

Arrone, river 17. 299.
Arsoli 288.
Artemisio, Monte 282.
Arx Junonis 294.
Asciano 31.
Asdrubale, Monte d' 78.
Asinalunga 32.
Assisi 58.
Astura 306.
Attidium 83.
Ausa, river 73.
Auximum 84.

Baccano 42.
Bachetona, La 22.
Bagnaia 40.
Bagnorea 35.
Ballaguier, Fort 6.
Balneum Regis 35.
Balze, Le 22. 57.
Bambolo 14.
Bassano 40.
Bastia 57.
Belcaro 31.
Belforte 85.
Benat, Cap. 7.
S. Benedetto 72.
Bertinoro 72.
Bettole 32.
Bevagna 61.
Bieda 40.
Bisentina 36.
Blera 40.
Bolsena 36.
—, Lago di 36.
Bomarzo 40.
Borghetto 50. 67.
Borgo S. Lorenzo 72.
— S. Sepolcro 57.
Bovillae 279.
Bracciano 299.
—, Lago di 300.
Bruna, river 16.
Buche de' Saracini, Le 21.
Bucine 45.
Bulicame 37.
Burano, river 78.
Busco 80.

Caecina 14.
Caduta delle Marmore, la 64.
Caffarella, brook 267.

Cagli 78.
Cales 78.
Calle 78.
Calmazzo 78.
Calseraigne, îles de 6.
Calvo, Monte 79.
Camaldoli 276.
Camaret, Cap 7.
Camerino 85.
Campagna di Roma 261.
Campello 62.
Campiglia 14.
Campo d'Annibale 277.
Camuscia 48.
Candigliano, river 78.
Cantalupo 288. 294.
Canterano 287.
Cantiano 79.
Capanne, Monte 23.
Capo d'Istria 81.
Capoliveri 23.
Capraja 22.
Caprarola 41.
Carciae 299.
Caere 301.
Carnaiola 33.
Carsulae 57.
Casale di Pantano 291.
— dei Pazzi 270.
Casape 287.
S. Casciano 67.
Cascina 9.
Case Bruciate 77.
Case Nuove 86.
Casino di Terra 19.
Cassidaine, Rochers de 6.
Cassis 6.
Castel Arcione 284.
— d'Asso 39.
— Bolognese 71.
— S. Elia 71.
Castelfidardo 84.
Castel Fiorentino 24.
— Fusano 304.
— Gandolfo 280.
— Giubileo 271. 298.
— di S. Leo 74.
— Nuovo 70.
— S. Pietro 71.
— Planio 83.
— Savelli 279.
— Todino 57.
Castello Madama 288.

INDEX.

Castiglione 290.
— del Lago 50.
— della Pescaia 16.
—, Palude di 16.
Castiglionfiorentino 48.
Castrimoenium 277.
Cattolica, La 74.
Cava, La 22.
Cava Beatina 65.
— Gregoriana 65.
— Paolina 65.
Cavi 338.
Cavo, Monte 277.
Cecina 14. 19.
—, La 279.
Centum Cellae 12.
Cerbara 288.
Cerboli 23.
—, Lagoni di Monte 22.
Ceri 301.
Certaldo 24.
Cervara, Grottoes of 270.
Cervetri 301.
Cesena 73.
Cesi 66.
Cessano, the 77.
Cetona, Monti di 32.
Chiana, river 31. 43. 48.
Chiaravalle 82.
Chiascio, river 57. 80. 83.
Chiavari 8.
Chienti, river 84.
Chiusi 32.
Chiusure 31.
Ciampino 279.
Ciminian Forest 40.
Ciotat, la 6.
Ciriaco, Monte 81.
Città di Castello 57.
— della Pieve 43.
Cittanova 81.
Cività Castellana 68.
— Lavinia 282.
Civitanuova 84.
Civita Vecchia 11.
Civitella 287. 293.
Clanis 48.
Claustra Etruriae 41.
Clitumnus, the 61. 62.
Clusium 32.
Colfiorito 85.
Collatia 270.
Colle Salvetti 14.
Collescipoli 66.
Colonia*Julia*Hispellum 60.
— *Julia Senensis* 25.
— *Junonia* 69.
— *Nepensis* 71.
Colonna 290.
Compartri 290.
Compiobbi 44.
Conca, river 74.

Conero, Monte 84.
Cora 295.
Cori 295.
Corneto 17.
Cornia, La 14.
Correse, Passo di 68.
Corrignaleto, Monte 294.
Corsica 7. 11.
Cortona 48.
Cosa 17.
S. Cosimato 288.
Cremera, the 42. 70. 298.
Crete 32.
Croisette, Cap de la 6.
Cures 68.

Daila 81.
Digentia 294.
S. Donnino 9.

Elba 23.
Ellera 51.
Elsa, river 24.
Empoli 9.
Empulum 287.
Era, river 9.
Esino, river 77. 82.
Etruscan Towns 297.

Fabriano 83.
S. Facondino 83.
Faenza 71.
Falconara 77. 82.
Falerii 68. 69.
Fano 76.
Fanum Fortunae 76.
— *Vacunae* 294.
— *Voltumnae* 37.
Faventia 71.
Felcino 80.
Ferentinum 37.
Ferento 37.
Ficulle 33.
Fidenae 271. 298.
Fiesole 44.
Figline 45.
Filettino 284.
Fiora, river 17.
Fiumicino 305.
Florence 9.
Foglia, river 74. 75.
Fojano 32.
Foligno 61.
Follonica 15.
Fons Bandusiae 294.
Fontana degli Oratini 294.
Forli 72.
Forlimpopoli 72.
Formello, Fosso di 298.
Formica, island 15.
Forum Cassii 39.
— *Clodii* 300.

Forum Cornelii 71.
— *Livii* 72.
— *Popilii* 72.
— *Sempronii* 78.
Fossato 80. 83.
Fossombrone 78.
Frascati 274.
Frassineto 48.
Fratocchie, le 279.
Fratta 57.
Fregenae 13.
Fulginium 61.
Furbara 12.
Furlo Pass 78.

Gabii 290.
Galera 299.
Galese 67.
Gelagno 85.
S. Gemine 57.
Genazzano 292.
Genga, La 83.
Gennaro, Monte 293.
Genoa 7.
Genzano 281.
Gerano 287.
Gericomio 287.
S. Giacomo 62.
Giannutri 11.
Giano 83.
Giano, brook 83.
Giglio 24.
S. Gimignano 24.
S. Giovanni 45.
— d'Asso 31.
Giulianello 295.
—, Lago di 295.
Gonfolina, the 9.
Gorgona 23.
Graviseae 18.
S. Gregorio 287.
Grosseto 16.
Grotta Ferrata 276.
Grotte, Le 40.
Gualdo Tadino 83.
Guasco, Monte 81.
Gubbio 79.

Horta 67.
Hyères, Iles d' 7.

Jesi 83.
If, château d' 6.
Igilium 24.
Iguvium 79.
Ilva 23.
Imola 71.
Imperiale, L' 74.
Imposta, L' 40.
Incisa 45.
Interamna 64.
Isaurus 74.

INDEX.

Isola, Fosso dell' 298.
Isola Farnese 298.
— Maggiore 50.
— Minore 50.
— Polvese 50.
— Sacra 305.
Labicum 290.
Lacus Albanus 278.
— Alsietinus 42.
— Ciminius 41.
— Nemorensis 282.
— Prelius 16.
— Sabatinus 300.
— Trasimenus 50.
— Vadimonis 40.
— Vulsiniensis 36.
Lamone, river 71.
Lanuvium 282.
Laterina 45.
Laurentum 304.
Lavinium 304.
Lecques, Baye de 6.
Leghorn 9.
Lévant, Ile du 7.
Licenza 294.
Livorno 9.
S. Lorenzo 37. 74.
Loreto 84.
Lucignano 32.
Luco, Monte 63.
Lucretilis, Mons 294.
Lunghezza 270.
Lugnano 290.

Maccarese 13.
Macerata 84.
Madonna del buon consiglio 292.
— del Campo 292.
— delle Case 294.
— di Mongiovino 44.
— del Monte 295.
— di Monte Nero 14.
— della Quercia 40.
— del Tufo 278.
Maggiore, Monte 81.
Magione 51.
Magliana 13.
Magliano 67.
Malgue, la, Fort 6.
Mandela 288. 294.
Marano, river 74.
Marciana 23.
Marecchia, river 73.
Maremme, the 15.
S. Maria degli Angeli 57.
— di Cesareo 299.
— delle Grazie 64.
S. Marinella 12.
S. Marino 74.
Marino 277.

Marotto 77.
Marradi 72.
Marseilles 2.
Marta, river 17. 18.
Martana 36.
Martignano, lake of 42.
S. Martino 19. 74.
Massa 15.
Massilia 2.
Matelica 83. 85.
Maures, Mont. des 7.
Meloria 22.
Mentana 270.
Metaurus 77.
Mevania 61.
Mignone, river 18.
S. Miniato dei Tedeschi 9. 24.
Miramar 81.
Mirandola 71.
Mola, la 281.
Mons Albanus 278.
— Ciminius 40.
— Lucretilis 294.
— Sacer 270.
Montalto 17.
Montarozzi 17.
Monte S. Bartolo 74.
— Catillo 286.
— Catini 22.
Montecchio 48. 75.
Monte Compatri 290.
— Cristo 24.
Montefalco 64.
Monteflascone 37.
Montefortino 296.
Montelupo 9.
Monte Massi 22.
— Oliveto maggiore 31.
Monte Pescali 16.
— Porzio 290.
— Pulciano 32.
— Riggioni 25.
— Romano 12.
Monterosi 41.
Monte Rotondo 68.
Montesanto 84.
Montevarchi 45.
Monticelli 284. 294.
Monti Pisani 9.
Mont' Olmo 85.
Montone, river 72.
Montorso 68.
Muccia, La 85.

Nar 66.
Narni 66.
Navacchio 9.
Nemi 282.
—, Lago di 282.
Nepete 71.
Nepi 71.

Nequinum 66.
Nera, river 57. 66.
Nero's Tomb 42.
Nervi 8.
Nettuno 306.
Ninfa 296.
Nocera 84.
Nomentum 270.
Norba 296.
Norchia 40.
Norma 296.
Notre Dame de la Garde 5.
Nuceria 84.

Olevano 292.
Ombrone, river 9. 16. 31.
Orbetello 16.
Orciano 14.
Orcle 40.
S. Oreste 70.
—, Monte di 69.
Orlando, Grotta d' 41.
Orsera 81.
Orte 67.
Orvieto 33.
Osa, river 16. 290.
Osimo 84.
Osservanza, La 31.
Osteria Bianca 24.
Ostia 302.
—, Stagno di 302.
Otricoli 67.

Paglia, river 33.
Palazzolo 83.
Palazzuola 278.
Pale 86.
—, Sasso di 86.
Palestrina 290.
Paliano 292.
Palidoro 12.
Palmaiola 23.
Palmaria 8.
Palo 12.
S. Paolo 288.
Papigno 64.
Parenzo 81.
Passerano 287. 292.
Passignano 51.
Passo di Correse 68.
Pausilypon 300.
Pellegrino 83.
Perugia 51.
S. Agnese 55.
S. Angelo 55.
Arco di Augusto 53.
S. Bernardino 55.
Cathedral 53.
Citadel 52.
S. Domenico 54.
S. Francesco dei Conventuali 55.

INDEX.

Perugia :
  Grotta de' Volunni 56.
  Libreria publica 56.
  Necropolis 56.
  Pal. Baldeschi 55.
  °— Comunale 52.
  — Conestabile 53.
  — Donini 56.
  — Penna 56.
  Piazza del Sopramuro 54.
  °S. Pietro de' Casinensi 55.
  Pinacoteca 53.
  S. Severo 54.
  University 53.
Perusia 51.
Pesa, river 9.
Pesaro 74.
Petrara, Monte 79.
Pianosa 23.
Piedilugo 66.
Pienza 32.
S. Pierino 9.
Pietralata 78.
Piombino 14.
Pirano 81.
Pisa 9.
Pisaurum 74.
Pisciatello, the 73.
Planasia 23.
Poggibonsi 24.
Poggio alla Croce 22.
  — Mirteto 68.
Polenta 72.
Polimartium 40.
S. Polo 294.
Pomarance 22.
Pomègues 6.
Ponente, Lago di 13.
Pons Milvius 43.
Pontassieve 44.
Ponte della Badia 17.
  — a Botte 79.
  — Centesimo 84.
Pontedera 9.
Ponte Felice 67.
  — Galera 13.
  — Ginori 19.
  — S. Giovanni 57.
  — Lucano 284.
  — Mammolo 284.
  — Molle 43.
  — di Nono 290.
  — Nuovo 56.
  — della Refolta 302.
  — del Terreno 69.
  — della Trave 85.
Ponticino 45.
Populonia 15.
Porquerolles 7.
Porta Furba 269.

Porta della Rosa 67.
Porteros 7.
Porto 304.
Porto d'Anzio 305.
  — Civitanuova 84.
  — Clementino 18.
  — Ercole 7.
  — Ferrajo 23.
  — Longone 23.
  — S. Stefano 16.
  — Venere 8.
Portus Trajani 12. 304.
Potassa 16.
Potenza, river 84.
Potenza-Picena 84.
Praeneste 291.
Pratica 304.
Prima Porta 70.
Pupluna 15.
Pussino, Val di 272.
Pyrgos 12. 301.

Quaderna 71.

Radicofani 37.
Rapallo 8.
Rapolano 32.
Ratonneau 6.
Ravenna 71. 72.
Recanati 84.
Recco 8.
Regillus, Lake 290.
Rignano 45. 69.
Rimini 73.
Rio 23.
Rio di Decima 302.
  — Fiume 12.
Ripoli, Monte 287.
Riviera di Levante 8.
Rocca Canterano 287.
  — S. Casciano 72.
  — di Cavi 292.
  — S. Francesco 293.
  — Giovine 294.
  — Massima 295.
  — di Papa 277.
  — Romana 300.
  — S. Stefano 287.
Rojate 293.
Rome 86.
  Accademia di Francia 112.
  — di S. Luca 181.
  Acqua Acetosa 271.
  — Felice 135. 269.
  — Paola 229.
  — Santa 269.
  — Vergine 115. 270.
  S. Adriano 174.
  S. Agata alla Suburra 140.
  S. Agnese 157.

Rome:
  °S. Agnese fuori le mura 136.
  °S. Agostino 151.
  S. Alessio 192.
  °Amphitheatrum Castrense 145.
  — Flavium 177.
  S. Anastasia 188.
  S. Andrea delle Fratte 114.
  — della Valle 159.
  SS. Angeli Custodi 114.
  S. Angelo, Castello 214.
  S. Antonio Abbate 141.
  S. Apollinare 152.
  °SS. Apostoli 121.
  Aqua Claudia 143. 269. 290.
  — Julia 143.
  — Marcia 269.
  — Trajana 229.
  — Virgo 115.
  Archæolog. Institut. 109.
  °Arch of Constantine 179.
  — of Dolabella 199.
  — of Drusus 197.
  — of Gallienus 143.
  — de' Pantani 182.
  °— of Septimius Severus 172.
  °— of Titus 176.
  °Arcus Argentarius 186.
  Armoury 256.
  Artists' Association 109. 114.
  Aventine, the 189.
  S. Balbina 195.
  Bank, the 161.
  Barcaccia, La 113.
  S. Bartolommeo 231.
  —, Isola di 231.
  °Basilica of Constantine 175.
  Basilica Julia 173.
  Basis of Nero 176.
  Belrespiro 230.
  S. Bernardo 135.
  S. Bibiana 144.
  Bibliotheca Angelica 152.
  — Casanatensis 156.
  °— Vaticana 254.
  Bibulus, Monument of 123.
  Bocca della Verità 186.
  S. Bonaventura 185.
  Borgo 215.
  Botanical Garden 224.
  °Braccio Nuovo 243.
  °Caecilia Metella, Tomb of 265.

Rome:
S. Cajo 135.
Caelius, the 198.
Campo Militare (di Macao) 138.
— Vaccino 171.
Capitol 169.
—, Collections of the 208.
°Cappella di Niccolò V. 242.
— Paolina 237.
°°— Sistina 235.
°Carcer Mamertinus 173.
Carceri Nuovi 164.
S. Carlo 132.
— a Catinari 164.
— al Corso 116.
Casa di Crescenzio 187.
— di Pilato 187.
— di Rienzi 187.
— Zuccari 113.
Caserma de' Gendarmi Pontefici 109.
— de' Vigili 148.
Catacombs 256.
S. Caterina de' Funari 165.
— di Siena 135.
S. Cecilia in Trastevere 233.
Cemetery, German 223.
—, Protestant 190.
S. Cesareo 196.
°Cestius, Pyramid of 190.
Chiesa Nuova 160.
Circus of Domitian 156.
— Flaminius 165.
°— of Maxentius 265.
— Maximus 188.
S. Clemente 200.
°Cloaca Maxima 186.
Collegio Nazareno 114.
— di Propaganda Fide 113.
— Romano 118.
Colonacce, Le 181.
Colonnade of Octavia 167.
— of the Twelve Gods 172.
°°Colosseum 177.
Columbaria 196. 197. 230.
Conservatori, Palace of the 209.
Corso, the 115.
Cortile di Belvedere 245.
— di S. Damaso 235.
°SS. Cosma e Damiani 174.
S. Costanza 137.

Rome:
S. Crisogono 232.
°S. Croce in Gerusalemme 144.
— di Monte Mario 273.
Dogana 117.
S. Domenico e Sisto 139.
Domine Quo Vadis 264.
English Church 109.
°Eurysaces, Monum. of 144.
S. Eusebio 143.
Farnese Gardens 183.
Fontana delle Tartarughe 165.
— di Termini 135.
°— di Trevi 114.
°— del Tritone 127.
Fontanone dell' Acqua Felice 135.
— di Ponte Sisto 164.
Forum of Augustus 182.
— Boarium 186.
— of Cæsar 182.
— of Nerva 181.
°°— Romanum 171.
°— of Trajan 182.
— Transitorium 181.
S. Francesca 127.
— Romana 175.
S. Francesco di Paola 146.
— a Ripa 233.
— delle Stimate 158.
S. Gallicano, Ospedale 232.
Gardens of Sallust 128.
Gesù 124.
Gesù e Maria 115.
Ghetto 166.
S. Giacomo 215.
— in Augusta (degli Incurabili) 115.
— alla Lungara 224.
— dei Spagnoli 157.
S. Giorgio in Velabro 186.
S. Giovanni Colabita 231.
— de' Fiorentini 224. 164.
°— in Fonte 204.
°— in Laterano 202.
°— e Paolo 198.
— a Porta Latina 196.
S. Girolamo degli Schiavoni 148.
S. Giuliano 143.
S. Giuseppe de' Falegnami 173.
S. Gregorio 198.
Grotto of Egeria 267.

Rome:
Grotte Vaticane 221.
House of Crescentius 187.
Janiculus, the 231.
°Janus Quadrifrons 186.
S. Ignazio 118.
S. Ildefonso 127.
Immacolata, Column of the 113.
S. Isidoro 127.
S. Ivo 153.
Lateran, the 202.
Longara 223.
S. Lorenzo in Damaso 161.
°— fuori le mura 142.
— in Lucina 116.
— in Miranda 174.
— in Paneperna 140.
SS. Luca e Martino 174.
S. Lucia 150.
S. Luigi de' Francesi 152.
Madonna Lucrezia 123.
S. Marcello 119.
S. Marco 123.
°Marcus Aurelius, Column of 117.
°—, Statue of 169.
Marforio, Via di 123.
°S. Maria degli Angeli 137.
°— dell' Anima 157.
°— in Araceli 168.
— Aventina 192.
— in Campitelli 166.
— della Concezione 127.
— in Cosmedin 186.
— in Domnica 199.
— Egiziaca 187.
— Liberatrice 173. 184.
— di Loreto 151. 183.
°°— Maggiore 140.
— sopra Minerva 155.
— de' Miracoli 109.
— di Monserrato 162.
— in Monte Santo 109.
— della Morte 164.
— della Navicella 199.
— Nuova 175. 266.
— dell' Orazione 164.
— dell' Orto 233.
°— della Pace 158.
— del Pianto 166.
°— del Popolo 110.
— del Priorato 192.
— del Rosario 273.
°°— Rotonda 153.
— Scala Cœli 263.
— del Sole 187.
— Traspontina 215.

Rome:
°S. Maria in Trastevere 232.
— in Via Lata 119.
— della Vittoria 136.
Marmorata, the 189.
S. Martino ai Monti 145.
Mausoleum of Augustus 147.
— of Hadrian 214.
Meta Sudans 179.
S. Michele, Ospizio di 233.
S. Michele in Sassia 216.
Mint 256.
Mons Sacer 270.
Monte Caprino 170.
— Cavallo 132.
— Citorio 117.
— Mario 272.
— di Pietà 163.
— Testaccio 190.
Mosaico, Studio del 256.
Museo Chiaramonti 244.
°— Gregoriano (Etrusc.) 250.
°— Kircheriano 118.
°°— Pio-Clementino 245.
Museum, Egyptian 252.
—, Capitoline 210.
°—, Christian 204.
—, Etruscan 250.
— Gregorianum Later. 204.
Neptune, Temple of 117.
SS. Nereo ed Achilleo 195.
S. Niccolò in Carcere 167.
S. Niccolò di Tolentino 127.
Nome di Maria 183.
°S. Onofrio 223.
Palatine Hill 183.
Palatium, the 185.
Pal. Albani 135.
— Altieri 124.
— Altemps 152.
— Antonelli 135.
°— Barberini 131.
— Bonaparte 121.
°— Borghese 148.
— Braschi 160.
— del Bufalo 114.
— Caffarelli 168.
— della Cancelleria 161.
— Cenci Bolognetti 166.
— Chigi 116.
°— Colonna 121.
— of the Conservatori 209.

Rome:
Pal. della Consulta 132.
°— Corsini 226.
— Costaguti 165.
— della Dataria 132.
°— Doria 119.
— Falconieri 164.
°— Farnese 162.
— Fiano 116.
— di Firenze 148.
— Galizin 150.
°— Giraud 215.
— Giustiniani 153.
— del Governo vecchio 160.
— Lancelotti 151.
— Maccarini 153.
— Madama 156.
— Massimi alle Colonne 159.
— Mattei 165.
— Nipoti 123.
— Odescalchi 121.
— Pacca 166.
— Pamfili 157.
— Patrizi 153.
— Piombino 117.
— Apost. al Quirinale 133.
— Righetti 164.
— Rinuccini 122.
— Rondinini 115.
°— Rospigliosi 134.
— Ruffo 121.
— Ruspoli 116.
— Sacchetti 164.
— Salviati 120. 224.
— Santacroce 163.
°— Sciarra Colonna 117.
— del Senatore 169.
— Simonetti 119.
°— Spada alla Regola 163.
— Strozzi 158.
— Teodoli 116.
— Terrajuoli 117.
— Torlonia 122.
— del SS. Uffizio 223.
— Valentini 121.
°— di Venezia 122.
— Verospi 116.
— Vidoni 158.
°Palazzetto Farnese 161.
S. Pantaleo 160.
°°Pantheon 153.
°°S. Paolo fuori le Mura 193.
— alle Tre Fontane 263.
Pasquino, Piazza di 160.
Pescheria 166.
°° St. Peter's 217.
Phocas, Column of 170.

Rome:
Piazza di SS. Apostoli 121.
— Araceli 168.
— Barberini 127.
°°— del Campidoglio 169.
— di Campo de' Fiori 161.
°— Colonna 117.
— di MonteCavallo 132.
— di Monte Citorio 117.
°— Navona 156.
°°— di S. Pietro 216.
°— del Popolo 109.
— della Rotonda 153.
— di Spagna 113.
— di Termini 135.
— S. Trinità 112.
— di Venezia 122.
S. Pietro in Carcere 174.
— in Montorio 227.
°°— in Vaticano 217.
°— in Vincoli 146.
Pincio, the 110.
Police-office 117.
Ponte S. Angelo 214.
— S. Bartolommeo 231.
— Molle 43.
— Nomentano 270.
— de' Quattro Capi 231.
— Rotto 187. 231.
— Salaro 271.
— Sisto 227.
Porta Angeli 272.
— Appia 147.
— Asinaria 202.
— Aurelia 229.
— Capena 195.
— S. Giovanni 202.
— Latina 196.
— S. Lorenzo 142.
°— Maggiore 144.
— Nomentana 136.
— S. Paolo 189.
— S. Pancrazio 229.
— Pia 136.
— del Popolo 109.
— Portese 234.
— Salara 128.
— S. Sebastiano 197.
— Settimiana 227.
— S. Spirito 223.
Post-office 153.
°S. Prassede 141.
Prati del Popolo Romano 190.
S. Prisca 192.
Propaganda 113.
S. Pudenziana 139.
°Pyramid of Cestius 190.
SS. Quattro Coronati 201.

INDEX   313

Rome:
Quirinal, the 133.
Railway Station 137.
°°Raphael's Loggie 237.
°°— Stanze 238.
°— Tapestry 249.
— Tomb 154.
Regia 173.
Ripa Grande 233.
Ripetta, Porto di 148.
Ripresa de' Barberi 123.
SS. Rocco e Martino 147.
Rostra 173.
°°Rotonda, La 154.
S. Saba 193.
S. Sabina 191.
S. Salvatore in Onda 164.
Scala Santa 202.
Schola Xantha 172.
°Scipios, Tomb of the 197.
S. Sebastiano 264.
Seminario Romano 152.
Servius, Wall of 138. 192.
Sette Sale 146.
S. Silvestro in Capite 116.
— a Monte Cavallo 134.
S. Sisto 196.
°°Sixtine Chapel 235.
Spanish Staircase 113.
S. Spirito, Ospedale di 215.
— in Sassia 215.
Stamperia Papale 114.
S. Stefano Rotondo 199.
S. Susanna 135.
Synagogue 166.
°Tabularium 170.
Tarpeian Rock 170.
Temple of Castor and Pollux 173.
— of Concordia 172.
°— of Deus Rediculus 267.
°— of Faustina 174.
— of Fortune 187.
— of Hercules Victor 187.
— of Juno Sospita 167.
— of Jupiter Capitolinus 170.
— of Jupiter Stator 184.
— of Jupiter Victor 185.
— of Mars Ultor 182.
— of Minerva Medica 144.

Rome:
Temple of Neptune 117.
°— of Saturn 171.
— of the Three Gods 187.
— of Venus and Roma 176.
°— of Vespasian 172.
— of Vesta 173. 187.
S. Teodoro 185.
S. Teresa 135.
Testaccio, Monte 190.
Theatre of Marcellus 167.
— of Pompey 164.
Thermæ of Agrippa 154.
°— of Caracalla 195.
— of Diocletian 137.
°— of Titus 180.
S. Tommaso in Formis 199.
Torraccio, the 266.
Torre de' Conti 135.
— delle Milizie 135.
— di Nerone 135.
°°Trajan's Column 182.
Trastevere 227.
Tre Fontane 263.
SS. Trinità de' Monti 112.
— de' Pellegrini 164.
Trofei di Mario 144. 169.
Università della Sapienza 153.
S. Urbano 267.
Vatican, the 234.
Velabrum 186.
Velia 175.
Via Appia 195. 264.
°Villa Albani 129.
— Aldobrandini 139.
— Bonaparte 136.
°— Borghese 124.
— Campana 202.
°— Doria Pamfili 229.
°— Farnesina 224.
°°— Ludovisi 127.
— Madama 273.
— Malta 127.
— Massimo 207.
— Mattei 199.
— Medici 112.
— Mellini 273.
— Mills 185. 188.
— di Papa Giulio 271.
— Patrizi 136.
— Spada 271.
— Torlonia 136.
— Wolkonsky 208.
SS. Vincenzo ed Anastasio 115. 263.
S. Vito 143.

Rome:
Zecca 256.
Roma vecchia 266.
S. Romano 9.
Ronciglione 41.
Ronco, the 72.
Rosaro 57.
Roselle 16.
Rosso, Monte 83.
Rotta, La 9.
Roviano 288.
Rovigno 81.
Rubicon, the 73.
Rusellae 16.

Sabate 300.
Sabina, the 68.
Sabine Mountains, the 283.
Saccomuro 288.
Salarco 32.
Saline 19.
S. Salvatore, Abbey 22.
Salvore 81.
Sambuci 288.
Santerno, river 71.
Sapis 72.
Saracinesco 288.
Sassoferrato 83.
Sassula 287.
Saturnia 17.
Savio, river 72.
Saxa Rubra 70.
Scannabechi, river 271.
Schieggia 79.
Segni 296.
Selagite, Mt. 22.
Sena Gallica 77.
— Julia 25.
Senio, river 71.
Sentinum 83.
Septempeda 85.
Serra S. Quirico 83.
Serravalle 85.
Sestri a Levante 8.
Sette Vene 41.
S. Severa 12.
S. Severino 85.
Sibilla, Mt. 84.
Siciliano 287.
Siena 25.
  Accademia degli Intronati 30.
  S. Agostino 28.
  Archives 30.
  °S. Bernardino 29.
  Carmine 29.
  Casa di S. Caterina 29.
  Casino de' Nobili 27.
  °°Cathedral 27.
  Citadel 31.
  S. Concezione 29.

Siena:
S. Domenico 28.
Fonte Branda 30.
— Fullonica 30.
— Gaja 27.
— Giusta 29.
Istituto delle belle Arti 29.
Library 31.
Lizza, la 31.
Loggia di S. Paolo 27.
S. Niccolò 29.
Palazzo Buonsignori 30.
— del Governo 30.
— del Magnifico 30.
— Piccolomini 30.
— Pollini 30.
— Pubblico 26.
— Saracini 30.
— Tolomei 30.
*Pellegrinajo 28.
*Piazza Vittorio Emanuele 26.
Spedale di S. Maria della Scala 27.
S. Spirito 29.
University 30.
Sieve, river 44.
Sigillo 80.
Signa 9.
Signia 297.
Sillaro, river 71.
S. Silvestro 70.
Sinalunga 32.
Sinigaglia 77.
Sinnus 71.
Somma, Monte 64.
Soracte, Mt. 69.
Sorana 17.
Spaccato, Monte 287.
Spello 60.
Spoleto 62.
Staggia 25.
S. Stefano 293.
Stimigliano 68.
Storta, la 42.
Stracciacappa, Lake of 42.
Subasio, Monte 60.
Subiaco 287.
Sublaqueum 288.
Sutri 41.
Sutrium 41.

Tadinum 84.
Talamone 16.
Talazzo 83.
Tarquinii 17.
Tartari, Lago de' 284.
Tavernelle 44.

Tavollo, river 74.
Tenna, river 85.
Terni 64.
Teverone, river 284.
Tiber, river 40. 43. etc.
Tifernum Tiberinum 57.
Tibur 283.
Titan, Ile du 7.
Tivoli 283.
Todi 56.
Tolentino 85.
Tolentinum Picenum 85.
Tolfa, La 12. 18.
Topina, Val 84.
Topino, the 61.
Tor Paterno 304.
— di Quinto 272.
— de' Schiavi 270. 290.
— di Selce 266.
— tre Teste 290.
Torre Bertaldo 18.
— di Boacciano 303.
— di Giove 23.
— Pignattara 269.
Torrenieri 31. 37.
Torretta, la 279.
Torrita 32.
Toscanella 40.
Toulon 6.
Trasimeno, Lago 50.
Trebia 62.
Tre Fontane 263.
Treja, the 69.
Trevi 62.
Trevignano 300.
Trieste 80.
Tuder 56.
Tuficum 83.
Turchina 17.
Turri, La 279.
Tuscania 40.
Tusculum 275.
Tutia 43.

Umago 81.
Umbertide 57.
Urbania 57.
Urbibentum 33.
Urbino 75.
Urbisaglia 85.
Urgone, the 73.

Valca, the 299.
Valchetta, the 42. 70.
Valcimara 85.
Vallombrosa 74.
Valmontone 296.
Varia 288.
Veji 297.
Velathri 19.

Velino, river 65.
Velitrae 282.
Velletri 282.
Vene, Le 62.
Venere, Monte 41.
Vetralla 39.
Vetulonia 15.
Via Appia nuova 264. 279.
Via Æmilia 71.
— *Appia* 264.
— *Aurelia* 12. 13.
— *Cassia* 37. 41.
— *Clodia* 299.
— *Collatina* 270.
— *Flaminia* 45. 77.
— *Labicana* 269. 290.
— *Latina* 268.
— *Nomentana* 136. 270.
— *Ostiensis* 263.
— *Praenestina* 269. 290.
— *Salara* 66. 271.
— *Sublacensis* 288.
— *Tiburtina* 142. 284.
— *Valeria* 288.
Vicarello 300.
Vico, Lago di 41.
Vicovaro 288.
Villa Aldobrandini 274.
— Ambrogiana 9.
— Braschi 287.
— of Cicero 275.
— Conti 275.
— d'Este 287.
— Falconieri 275.
— *ad Gallinas* 70.
— Graziani 65.
— of Hadrian 284.
— Inghirami 21.
— Lante 40.
— of Livia 70.
— Mondragone 275.
— Montalto 275.
— Piccolomini 274.
— Ruffinella 275.
— Taverna 275.
— Vittoria 75.
S. Vincenzo 14.
Vita, Capo della 23.
Viterbo 38.
—, Monte di 40.
S. Vito 67.
Volaterrae 19.
Volscian Mountains, the 294.
Volsinii 36.
Volterra 19.
Vulci 17.

Zagarolo 287. 292.

List of Streets in the Plan of Rome.

The plan is divided into three sections, the upper numbered I, the central II, the lower III. The three columns of figures in the subjoined list correspond to these sections; the numbers indicate the square of the section in which the place in question is to be found (thus: Accademia di S. Luca is in the 14th square of the 1st section). Where space has been too limited to admit of the names being inserted in the plan, they have been replaced by numbers, which in the following list are annexed to each name so omitted (thus: Banco di S. Spirito 15 is N⁰ 15 in the 10th square of the 2nd section). The key to these numbers in their order is also inserted in the plan itself, an arrangement which will often be found useful.

Abbreviations: V. = Via, Vic. = Vicolo, Vg. = Vigna, Pal. = Palazzo.

	I	II	III		I	II	III
Accademia Ecclesiastica 11	.	.	16	S. Andrea e Bernardino. 1	.	.	23
— di Francia	.	20		Anfiteatro Castrense	.	.	36
— di S. Luca	14			— Corea	.	14	
— di Napoli	.	.	11	— Flavio (o Coliseo)	.	.	24
Accoramboni, Pal. 2	.	7		S.S. Angeli Custodi. 8	.	19	
Acqua Felice, Acquedotto dell'	.	.	28	Angelo Custode, V. dell'	.	19	
				Angelica, Porta	.	.	8
— Giulia, Castello dell'	.	.	28	S. Angelo, Castello	.	.	10
— Paola	.	.	12	—, Ponte	.	.	10
Acquedotto Antoniniano	.	.	22	—, Vic.	.	.	7
— Neroniano dell' Acqua Claudia	.	.	33	— in Pescaria	.	.	17
				S. Aniano. 4	.	.	18
S. Adriano	.	.	20	Anicia, V.	.	.	15
S. Agata. 3	.	.	15	Anima, V. dell'	.	.	13
— in Suburra	.	.	22	S. Anna	.	.	10
S. Agnese	.	.	13	— 23.	.	.	17
S.S. Agonizzanti. 10	.	.	13	—, Monasterio	.	.	15
S. Agostino	.	13		— de' Calzettari	.	.	18
—, V.	.	13		— de' Palafrenieri. 1	.	7	
Albani, Pal.	.	22		SS. Anna e Gioacchino	.	22	
Alberini, Villa	.	26		S. Annunziata. 9	.	.	20
Alberoni, Pal. 10	.	19		Antonelli, Pal.	.	.	19
—, Vic.	.	30		Antonino, Tempio di	.	.	20
Aldobrandini, Villa	.	.	19	S. Antonio Abbate	.	.	25
Alessandrina, V.	.	.	20	— delle Fornaci, V.	.	.	1
S. Alessio	.	.	18	— di Padova. 10	.	.	13
Alibert, V.	18			S. Apollinare	.	.	13
—, Vic.	.	7		—, Piazza	.	.	13
Altemps, Pal. 6.	.	13		3. Apollonia	.	.	15
Altieri, Pal.	.	.	16	S.S. Apostoli	.	.	19
— — 29	.	.	17	—, Piazza	.	.	19
—, Villa	.	24	32	S.S. Apostoli, Vic.			16
Altoviti, Pal.	.	10		Appia, Via.	.	.	28
—, Villa	.	14		— —, nuova	.	.	36
S. Ambrogio della Minima	.	.	17	Aquiro, V. in	.	16	
S. Anastasia	.	.	21	Araceli, S. Maria in	.	.	20
S. Andrea	.	.	30	—, V. di	.	.	17
—	.	.	24	Arancio, V. dell'	.	17	
S. Andrea, con Collegio Scozzese. 1.	.	22		Arcaccio, Vic. dell'	.	.	15
				Arco di Ciambella. 8	.	.	16
—, Oratorio. 2	.	.	18	— di Costantino	.	.	24
—, delle Fratte	.	19		— di Dolabella	.	.	27
—, di Monte Cavallo	.	22		— di Druso	.	.	28
— della Valle	.	.	13	— di Gallieno	.	.	28
— in Vinci. 10	.	.	17	— di Giano	.	.	21

	I	II	III		I	II	III
Arco di M. Aurelio (sito). 7.			16	Bonaparte, Pal. 5			16
— degli Orefici. 1		21		—, Villa		26	
— di Settimio Severo		20		S. Bonaventura			24
— di Tito		23		Boncompagni, Pal. 5		17	
Ardeatina, Porta			28	— Simonetti, Pal. 15			16
Armata, V. dell'	13	10		Bonella, V.			20
Ascanio, V. di				S. Bonosa. 4			15
Asinaria, Porta			33	Borghese, Pal.		16	
Astalli, Villa		33		—, Piazza		16	
d'Aste, Villa	17	26		—, Villa		21	
S. Atanasio de' Greci. 6.				Borgo S. Agata			22
Aventino, Monte	19	18		— Angelico		8	
Avignonesi, V. degli				— S. Angelo		7	
Avila, Piazza d'	17	10		— nuovo		7	
Babuino, V. del				— Pio		7	
Baccina, V.		23		— S. Spirito		7	
S. Balbina			23	— vecchio		7	
Bambin Gesù		25		— Vittorio		7	
Banchi Nuovi, V. de'		10		Borgognona, V.		17	
— Vecchj, V. de'		10		Borromeo, Pal. 12			16
Banco di S. Spirito. 15		10		Boschetto, V. del			22
—, V. del		10		Bosco Parrasio dell' Accademia degli Arcadi			12
S. Barbara		14					
		24		Botteghe oscure, V. delle			17
Barberine, Monastero delle	22			Bovario, Campo		15	
Barberini, Pal.	7			Braccio, Str. del		4	
—		22		Branca, Piazza di			14
—, Piazza		19		Braschi, Pal. 17			13
—, Villa		26		S. Brigida. 3			13
Barchetta, Vic. della		14		Bucimazza, V.			18
S. Bartolommeo			18	Bufalo, Pal. del 6		19	
—. 19		16		Bufola, Vic. della			17
— de' Vaccinari		14		Buon Pastore			11
—, Isola		17		Caccagna, V.			13
—, Ponte		18		Cacciabove, V.		16	
Basilica di Costantino		20		Caffarelli, Pal. 9			17
— Giulia		20		S. Cajo. 5		22	
— Ulpia		19		Calabraga, Vic.			10
S. Basilio, V. di		23		Camerata, Pal. 18			10
Bastioni di Paolo III			17	Campana, Pal.			18
Battisterio di Costantino		30		—, V.			27
Baullari, V. de'		13		Campanaro, V. del			12
Belsiana, V.		17		Campanile, Str. del		7	
Benedetta, V.		11		Campidoglio			20
S. Benedetto		13		Campo Carleo			20
—. 7		16		Campo de' Fiori			13
S. Benedetto in Piscinula. 1		18		— Marzo, V. di		16	
Berardi, Pal. 10		16		— Militare		29	
S. Bernardo alle Terme	22			— Vaccino			20
Bernini, Pal. 15		19		Camposanto, Str. del		4	
S. Biagio		18		Cancelleria, Pal. della			13
— 4	16			—, Piazza della			13
— del Fosso. 21		13		Canestrari, V. de'			13
— della Pagnotta. 13		10		Canestraro, Vic. del			11
S. Bibiana		31		Capitolino, Monte			20
—, V. di		28		Capo di Ferro, Piazza			14
Bocca di Leone, V. di	17			Capo le Case, V.		19	
Bocca della verità, V. della		18		Cappellari, V. de'			13
Bologna, V.		11		Capponi, Pal. 17			10
Bolognetti, Pal. 3		16		Cappuccini, Convento de'		20	
Bonaccorsi-Sabini, Pal. 21	16			Capranica, Piazza			16

LIST OF STREETS. 317

	I	II	III		I	II	III
Carbonari, Vic. de'.		20		Cimeterio de' Protestanti			16
Cardelli, Pal. 14	13			Cini, Pal.		16	
—.	15			Cinque, V. del			11
— 14.		17		Cinque Lune, V.		13	
S. Carlino 2	22			Circo Adriano		11	
S. Carlo	17			— Massimo			21
— a Catenari		14		— Sallustiano		26	
— —, Piazza		14		S. Claudio. 23.		16	
Carpegna, Pal. 24	13			—, V.		16	
Carrette, Str. delle		4		S. Clemente		27	
—, V. delle		22		Clementina, V.		22	
Carrozza, V.	17			Cloaca Massima		18	
Cartari, V.		10		Codini, Vg.			23
Casa di Crescenzio (detta di Rienzi o di Pilato). 3		18		Colisco		24	
				Collegio Clementino	13		
Casa di Raffaelle	10			— de' Copti		4	
Casali, Pal. 9.	13			— Greco. 7		17	
Cascine, Vic. delle	15			— Inglese, Vg. del			21
Caserma de' Carabinieri	15			— Irlandese		20	
— de' Dragoni. 8		19		— Nazareno		19	
— de' Vigili. 5		16		— de Propaganda Fide. 16		19	
Castello, Porta		8		— Romano		16	
Catalone, Piazza		7		Colonna, Pal.		19	
Catena, Piazza della		17		—, Piazza		16	
—, Str. della		4		—, V.		16	
—, V. della		14		—, Villa		19	
S. Caterina de' Funari		17		Colonna di Foca		20	
— della Rota. 1		10		— Trajana		19	
— de' Sanesi. 2		19		Colonnelle, Vic. delle		17	
— di Siena. 7		19		Colonnesi, V. de'		19	
Cavaletti, Pal. 15		17		Colosseo, V. del		23	
Cavalieri di Malta, Pal. de' 9	17			Colosso di Nerone		23	
Cavalleggieri, Porta		4		Commendatore, Pal. del. 13	7		
S. Cecilia		15		Commercio, Casa del. 2		16	
— 20		10		Compagnia di Gesù, Casa della		16	
—, V. di		18					
Celio, Monte		30		Concezione		10	
S. Celso 4.	10			Condotti, V.	17		
Cenci, Pal.	17			Conservatore, P. del. 1		20	
—, Piazza	17			Conservatorio de' Fanciulli projetti. 14	7		
Cerchj, V. de'		21					
Certosa	26			Conservatorio della Divina Providenzia. 1	14		
S. Cesareo		26					
Cesarini, V.		16		Consolato, Vic. del		10	
—, Vic.		16		Consulta, Pal. della		19	
Cesi, Pal.	4			Consulta, V. della		19	
—, Villa	23			Conti, Pal. 12.		16	
— Piccolomini, Pal. 9	7			—, Villa		36	
Cestari, Vic. de'		16		Convento de' Padri della Missione. 14		16	
Cestio, Ponte		18					
—, Piramide di		16		Copelle, V. delle		13	
S. Chiara	22			Corallo, Vic. del			13
—.		16		Corea, Pal.		17	
—, Monastero		26		Cornacchie, Pozzo delle		13	
Chiavari, V.		14		Coronari, V. de'		13	
Chiesa Nuova		10		Corsini, Pal.			11
Chigi, Pal.	16			Corso, V. del		16	16
Ciampini, Pal.		25		Cortile di Belvedere. 1	4		
Ciancaleone, Vic.	22			— di S. Damaso (delle Logge). 2	4		
Cimarra, V.		22					
Cimatori, Vic. de'		10		— della Panateria. 5		19	

LIST OF STREETS.

	I	II	III		I	II	III
S. Cosimato, V. di			15	Fiamme, Vic. delle			23
S. Cosma. 6			13	Fiano, Pal. 8			16
S.S. Cosma e Damiano. 5			20	Filippine, Monast. delle		25	
Costaguti, Pal. 20			17	S. Filippo Neri. 8			10
Costantino, Basilica di			20	— 6			7
Cremona, V.			20	Firenze, Pal. di			13
Crescenzi, Vic.			13	—, Piazza			16
—, Villa			12	Fiumara, V. della			17
Croce, V. del		17		Fiume, V. del			14
S. Croce, V. di			33	Florida, V.			17
— de' Lucchesi. 13			19	Fonseca, Villa			27
— in Gerusalemme, Bas.			36	Fontanella, V.			18
Crocebianca, V. di			20	—			16
Crociata, V. della			15	Fontanone, V. del			14
Crociferi, V. de'		19		Fornaci, V. delle			11
Crocifisso, Cappella del		7		Foro di Augusto			20
—, Oratorio. 16			16	— di Nerva (avanzi). 7			20
—, Vic.			11	— Romano			20
Dame del Sacro Cuore, Conv.				— Trajano			19
delle			8	S. Francesca			17
Dataria, V. della		19		—		19	
Datti, Pal. 6			16	— Romana			23
Delfini, V.			17	S. Francesco, V. di			15
S. Dionisio		22		— di Paola			23
Dogana. 18		16		— a Ripa			15
S.S. Domenico e Sisto			19	—, V. di			15
— —, V.			19	— delle Stimate			16
Dominicani, Conv. de'			16	Frati, Vic. de'			7
Doria Pamfili, Pal.			16	Fratte, V. delle			15
S. Dorotea			11	Frattina, V.			16
—, V.			11	Frezza, V. della			17
Drago, Pal. del		13		Fruste, V. delle			12
— 12		19		Gabrielli, Pal.			10
S. Efremo		22		Gaetani, Giardino			29
S. Egidio			12	—, Pal.			25
S. Elena			17	Gaetano - Sermoneta, Pal. 26			17
S. Eligio. 4			10	Galitzin, Pal. 13			13
S. Elisabetta. 9			13	S. Galla			18
— 12			10	Galli, Orto			15
Esquilino, Monte			29	—, Pal.			13
Eurisace, Sepolcro di			35	Gallo, Pal. del. 5			19
S. Eusebio			28	Galluzze, le			32
—, V.			25	Gambaro, V. del		16	
S. Eustachio			13	Gatta, V. della			16
Fabbrica, Porta		4		Gelsomino, V. del			1
Fabricio, Ponte			17	Genovesi, V. de'			18
Falcone, Vic. del		23		Gentili, Villa			31
Falconieri, Pal.			11	Gesù, il			16
Falegnami, V. de'			17	—, V. del			16
Falzacappa, Villa		30		Gesù e Maria. 4			17
Farinoue, Vic. del		8		—, V.			17
Farnese, Pal.			14	Gesuiti, Noviziato de'			22
—, Piazza			14	Ghetto, il			17
Farnesiani, Orti			21	S. Giacomo, V.			17
Farnesina, Villa			11	—, Str.			11
Felice, V.		19		— in Aino. 6.			10
Fenili, V. de'			12	— in Augusto (de' Incura-			
—			21	bili). 2			17
—, Vic. de'			20	— Scossacavalli. 7			7
Ferajuoli, Pal. 20		16		— de' Spagnuoli. 23			13
Ferratella, V. della			30	Gianicolo, Monte			9

LIST OF STREETS

Street	I	II	III
Maccao, V. del		26	
Maccarani, Pal. 2		19	
—, Vg.			17
Maccelletto, V. del		15	
Macelli, V. de' due		19	
Macello, V.		18	
Madama, Piazza		13	
Maddalena, V.		16	
Madonna di Loreto. 3		19	
Maggiore, Porta		35	
Magnani, Pal.		16	
—, Vg.		32	
—, Villa		32	
Magnanapoli, V.		19	
Malabarba, Vic. di		34	
Malatesta, Pal. 13		17	
Malva, V. della		18	
Manfroni, Pal. 6		16	
— 10		13	
Mantellate, V. delle		10	
S. Marcello		16	
S. Marco		16	
—, V. di		19	
—, Piazza di		16	
Marescotti, Pal. 1	16		
— — 9		16	
Marforio, V. di		20	
Margana, Piazza		17	
S. Margherita. 1		15	
Margutta, V.		17	
—, Vic.		18	
Marj, Pal. (ora Gran - Guardia). 11	7		
S. Maria Addolorata		8	
— Agata. 6		20	
— degli Angeli	25		
— dell' Anima		13	
— in Aquiro 17		16	
— in Ara coeli		20	
— in Cacaberis. 3		14	
S. Maria in Campitelli		17	
— in Campo Marzo. 2	16		
— in Capella		18	
— del Carmine		19	
— della Concezione	23		
— della Consolazione		20	
— in Cosmedin		18	
— di Costantinopoli. 14		19	
— in Domnica			27
— Egiziaca		18	
— de' Fiori		15	
— —, V. di	17		
— delle Fornaci		4	
— delle Grazie	8		
— di Grottapinta. 5		13	
— Imperatrice		30	
— Liberatrice		20	
— Maddalena	16		
— —		19	
— Maggiore, Basilica		25	
— —, V. di		25	

Street	I	II	III
S. Maria sopra Minerva		16	
— —, Piazza di		16	
— de' Miracoli. 1		18	
— di Monserrato. 3		10	
— in Monterone. 12		13	
— in Monte Santo. 2		18	
— a' Monti. 3		23	
— —, V. di		23	
— a' Monti della Neve. 2		23	
— in Monticelli		14	
— della Morte		11	
— della Neve. 13		19	
— dell' Orto		15	
— della Pace. 3		13	
— del Pianto. 19		17	
— di Pietà (Oratorio di Caravita). 14		16	
— di Pietà con Camposanto (Cimeterio de' Tedeschi). 4	4		
— del Popolo		18	
— Porta Paradisi. 1		17	
— in Posterula		13	
— del Priorato di Malta			18
— in Publicolis. 21		17	
— della Purificazione		26	
— — 14		10	
— dell Purità. 3	7		
— di Quercia. 9		14	
— Regina Coeli		10	
— della Sanità		22	
— della Scala		11	
— —, V. di		11	
— de' sette dolori		12	
— del Sole		18	
— della Stella		1	
— del Suffragio 11		10	
— della Torre			15
— Traspontina. 5	7		
— in Trastevere		15	
— —, Piazza di		15	
S. Maria in Trivio		19	
— dell' Umiltà. 11		19	
— in Vallicella		10	
— delle Vergini. 1		19	
— in Via		16	
— —, V. di		16	
— in Via Lata		16	
— in Vinci. 6			17
— della Vittoria		23	
Marmorata		15	
—, Str. della			18
Marmorella, V.		20	
Marroniti, V. de'	19		
S. Marta	4		
— —		16	
—, Piazza	4		
S. Martino. 6		14	
— a' Monti		26	
— de' Svizzeri. 3	4		
Maschera d'oro, Piazza	13		
Mascherino, Vic. del	8		

LIST OF STREETS.

	I	II	III		I	II	III
Giardino, V. del		16		S. Ignazio, Piazza di		16	
— Papale, V. del		19		—, V.		16	
Ginnasi, Vic. de'		16		S. Ildefonso		19	
S. Giorgio in Velabro		21		Incarnazione, Cappella dell'. 3	22		
S. Giovanni		14		Incurabili, Vic. degli		17	
—, Porta		33		Inferno, Valle dell'		5	
—, V.		18		S. Isidoro		20	
—, V.		27		—, V.		20	
— Decollato. 5		18		Istituto Archeologico. 8		17	
— de' Fiorentini		10		S. Ivo. 12		13	
— in Fonte		30		— 26		13	
— de' Genovesi. 7		15		Labicana, V.		27	
— in Laterano, Bas.		30		Lancellotti, Pal. 1		13	
— e Collegio de' Maroniti. 9	19			— 16		13	
— in Oleo, Cappella			28	Lante, Pal.		13	
— della Pigna		16		—, Villa (Borghese)		8	
— ante Portam Latinam			28	Larga, V.		10	
— e Paolo		24		Laterano, S. Giovanni in		30	
—, V. di		24		Latina, Porta			23
— e Petronio. 8		14		—, V.			28
Giraud-Torlonia, Pal. 4		7		Lattanzi, Villa		28	
S. Girolamo. 1		13		Laurina, V.		17	
— de' Schiavoni	14			Lauro, Vic. del		20	
Giubbonari, V. de'		14		Lavaggi, Pal. 15		16	
Giudia, Piazza		17		Lavandare, Vic. delle		15	
Giulia, V.		10		Lavatore, V. del		19	
S. Giuliano		28		Leccosa, V.		13	
— 16		10		S. Leonardo		10	
— de' Fiaminghi. 7		13		Leoncino, V. del		16	
Giuoco di Pallone		22		—, Vic.		4	
S. Giuseppe		10		Leonina, V.		23	
—	19			Lepri, Pal.		17	
— de' Falegnami (Carcere Tulliano). 3		20		Longara, V. della		11	
				S. Lorenzino in Piscibus. 10	7		
Guistiniani, Pal.		13		S. Lorenzo, Monast.		22	
—, Vic.		13		—, Porta		31	
Governo Vecchio, Pal. del. 20		13		—, Vic.		34	
—, V. del		13		—, Vg.		22	
Granari, Vic.		13		— in Fonte		19	
Grazie, V. delle		20		— in Lucina		16	
Grazioli, Pal. 4		16		— —, Piazza di		16	
Graziosa, V.		25		S. Lorenzo in Miranda		20	
Greca, V.	17			— a' Monti		20	
Greci, V. de'	17			— in Paneperna, V. di		22	
Gregori, Pal.		20		S.S. Lorenzo e Damaso		13	
Gregoriana, V.		20		S.S. Luca e Martino. 4		20	
S. Gregorio		14		Lucchesi, V. de'		19	
—	17			S. Lucia. 10		10	
—, V. di	24			—		17	
— Magno			24	— del Gonfalone. 9		10	
— Taumaturgo. 10		20		— in Selci		26	
Grillo, V. del		19		—, V. di		26	
Grimaldi-Potenziani, Pal. 12		19		— della Tinta. 11		13	
S. Grisogono		15		Lucina, V. in		16	
—, V. di		15		Ludovisi, Villa		23	
Grotte, Vic. delle		14		S. Luigi de' Francesi		13	
Grottino, V. del	17			Lunetta, Vic. della		10	
Guardiola, V. della		16		Lungaretta V. della		15	
Guarnieri, Pal.		20		Lungarina, V. della		18	
Guglielmi, Pal. 25		17		Lupa, V. della		16	
S. Ignazio		16		Lupi, Villa			25

LIST OF STREETS. 321

	I	II	III		I	II	III
Mascherone, V. del	.	14		Morticelli, V. de'	.	15	
Massimi, Pal. 12	.	17		Muratte, V. delle	.	16	
— alle Colonne, Pal. 11	.	13		Muronova, V.	.	15	
Massimi-Sinibaldi, Pal. 13	.	13		Museo Capitolino. 12	.	20	
Massimi, Villa	26			— Lateranense	.	30	
—, ...	.	30		Muti-Paparuzzi, Pal. 9	.	19	
Massimo Negroni, Villa	25	25		Napoli, Orto di	17		
Mattei, Pal. 27	.	17		Nari, Pal. 14	.	13	
—, Villa	.	24		Navicella, Piazza della	.	27	
—	.	23		—, V. della	.	27	
S. Matteo, V. di	.	29		Navona, Piazza	.	13	
Mattonato, V. del	.	12		S.S. Nereo ed Achilleo	.	26	
S. Mauro. 13	.	16		Neroniano, Pal.	.	26	
Mausoleo di Adriano	10			Niccolini, Pal. 2	10		
— di Augusto	14			S. Nicola	.	16	
Mazzamurelli, Vic.	.	15		— in Carcere	.	17	
Mazzarina, V.	.	19		— in Arcione. 11	.	19	
Medici, Villa	.	18		— degli Incoronati. 7	.	10	
Melone, Vic. del	.	13		— de' Lorenesi. 8	.	13	
Merangelo, V. del	.	12		— de' Perfetti. 3	.	16	
Mercede, V. di	.	19		— di Tolentino	.	23	
de Merode, Villa	.	25		—, Vic. di	.	23	
Merulana, V.	.	29		Nicosia, Piazza	.	13	
Meta Sudante	.	24		Nome di Maria. 4	.	19	
Metronia, Porta	.	27		Nomentana, Porta	.	29	
S. Michele Arcangelo	.	4		S. Norberto	.	22	
S. Michele, V. di	.	15		Noviziato de' Gesuiti, Villa del	29		
S.S. Michele e Magno	7			Nuova, V.	.	19	
Mignanelli, Pal.	20			Nussiner, Vg.	.	21	
—, Piazza	20			Ova, Piazza dell'	.	15	
Mills (Spada), Villa	.	21		Odescalchi, Pal.	.	16	
Minerva Medica, Tempio di	.	32		S. Offizio, Pal. del	.	4	
Ministero delle Finanze	.	13		Olmo, V. dell'	.	25	
Minuzzi, Pal. 3	17			S. Omobuono. 7	.	17	
Miracoli, Vic. de'	15			S. Onofrio	.	7	
Missione, V. della	16			—, V.	.	7	
Molara, Piazza	18			Orfeo, Vic. di	.	7	
Mole, Vic. delle	.	27		Ornani, Pal. 22	.	13	
Monserrato, V. di	.	10		Oro, Monte d'	17		
Montanara, Piazza	.	17		Orologio, Piazza dell'.	.	10	
Monte Brianzo, V. di	13			Orsini, Pal.	.	10	
— Caprino, V. di	17			Orsini-Savelli, Pal.	.	17	
— Cavallo, Piazza di	.	19		Orso, V. dell'	.	13	
— Citorio, Pal. di (Ministero d'Interno e di Polizia). 21	16			S. Orsola. 1	10		
				— 8	17		
— Citorio, Piazza di	16			S.S. Orsola e Caterina. 11	.	17	
— della Farina, V. del	.	13		Ortaccio degli Ebrei	.	15	
— di Pietà	.	14		Orto botanico	.	12	
— —, Piazza di	.	14		Ospedale Ecclesiastico. 1	.	14	
Monte Tarpeo, V. di	20			— S. Gallicano	.	15	
Monterone, V.	.	13		— di S. Giovanni Calabita	.	17	
Monteverde, Vic. di	.	10		— di S. Giovanni Laterano	.	30	
Montoro, Pal.	10			— de' Incurabili	17		
—, V.	.	13		— S. Michele	.	15	
Monumento dell' Immacolata Concezione. 1	20			— Militare	.	7	
				— de' Pazzi	.	7	
Moretto, V. del	.	19		— di Tata Giovanni. 22	.	17	
Moro, V. del	.	15		Ospizio de' Poveri	26		
Moroni, Vic.	.	11		Osteria, Vic. dell'	31		
—, Vg.	.	25		Ottoboni, Villa	.	9	
Morte, V. della	.	14		Otto Cantoni, Vic. dei	17		

LIST OF STREETS.

Name	I	II	III	Name	I	II	III
Pace, Piazza della		13		Pigna, Giardino della 1	5		
Padella, Piazza		10		Pilotta, Piazza della		19	
Paganica, Piazza		17		—, V. della		19	
Palatino, Monte		21		Pinaco, V. del	13		
—, Ponte		18		Pinciana, Porta	21		
Palle, Vic. delle	7			—, V.	24		
— —.		10		Pincio, Monte	18		
Palma, Vic. della	19			Pinellari, V.	13		
Palombara, Pal. 11	16			Pio, Pal.		14	
—, Villa		29		Piombino, Pal. 22	16		
Pamfili, Giardino		18		Piombo, V. del		19	
—, Pal. 18		13		Piscinola, V.		18	
—, Villa		9		Polacchi, Vic. de'		17	
S. Pancrazio, Porta		9		Poli, Pal.	19		
Panico, V. di	10			—, Piazza	19		
S. Pantaleone		13		Polveriera, V. della		23	
— . . .		3		Ponte, Piazza di	10		
—, V. di		13		Ponte Nomentano, V. di	30		
Panteon		16		— Molle, V. di	15		
Paola, V.		25		— Sisto, Vic. di		14	
— . . .	10			Pontefici, V. de'	17		
S. Paolino		14		Popolo, Piazza del	18		
S. Paolo Eremita	22			—, Porta del	15		
S. Paolo, Porta		16		Porta, Pal. della	17		
—, Via di		16		Porta Angelica, V. di	8		
Paradisi, V.		22		— Castello, Str. di	8		
Paradiso, V. del		13		— Latina, V. di			26
Parione, V. in		13		— S. Lorenzo, V. di		28	
Pasquino, Piazza del		13		— Maggiore, V. di		32	
Passionisti, Giardino de'	24			— S. Pancrazio, V. di		12	
Pastini, V. de'		16		— Pia, V. di	26		
Patrizi, Pal.		13		— Pinciana, V. di	20		
—, Villa	30			— Portese			15
—, —			25	— Salara, V. di	27		
Pavone, V. del		10		— S. Sebastiano, V. di			26
Pedacchia, V. della		20		Portico di Ottavia. 18		17	
S. Pelegrino	5			Porto di Ripa Grande			18
Pellegrino, V. del		13		— di Ripetta	14		
Penitenzieri, Coll. de'	7			Portuense, Porto			14
Penna, Vic. della	15			Posta	13		
Perfetti, V. de'		16		Pozzetto, V. del	19		
Pergola, V.		17		Pozzi, V. de'	20		
Perucchi, Pal.		20		Pozzo, Vic. del	15		
Pescheria, V. della		17		S. Prassede	25		
Pettinari, V. de'		14		Prati del Popolo Romano		17	
Pia, Porta	30			Prenestina, Porta			31
—, Piazza	10			S. Prisca			21
Pianciani, Pal. 4	19			—, V. di			21
Pianto, V. del		17		S. Pudenziana	25		
Piè de Marmo, V. del		16		Purificazione, V. della	20		
Pieroni, Villa			19	Quaranta Santi	15		
Pietra, Piazza di	16			Quarantotto, Villa		28	
—, V. di	16			S.S. Quattro, V. de'		27	
S. Pietro in Vaticano, Bas.	4			S.S. Quattro Coronati		27	
—, Piazza di	7			Quattro Cantoni, V.		25	
S. Pietro in Montorio		12		—, Ponte		17	
— in Vincoli		23		Quattro Capi. 4		17	
— —, Piazza di		23		S.S. Quirico e Giuditta. 8		20	
— —, V. di		26		Quirinale, Pal. e Giardino del	19		
S.S. Pietro e Marcellino		30		—, V. del	19	22	
Pighini, Pal. 4		13		Raifi, V.			26

LIST OF STREETS. 323

Street	I	II	III	Street	I	II	III
Rasella, V.		19		Sciarra-Colonna, Pal.		16	
Ravenna, Pal.			25	Scimia, Vic. della			10
Regola, V. della			13	Scossa Cavalli, Piazza		7	
Renella, V. della			15	Scrofa, V. della		13	
Renzi, Piazza di			15	Scuole degli Ebrei. 2			17
Riarj, V. de'			11	S. Sebastianello, V.		17	
Rimesse, V. delle			15	S. Sebastiano de' Mercanti.			
Ripetta, V. di	14			24			17
Rita, Beata. 11			20	S. Sebastiano, Porta			23
S. Rocco		14		Sediola, V. della		13	
Romana, Piazza			15	Semenzaio comunale			26
de Romanis, Pal.		13		Seminario. 7		13	
S. Romualdo V.		19		—, V. del			16
Roncioni, Orto			21	Senatore, Pal. del. 2			20
Rondinini, Pal.		17		Sepolcro di Bibulo. 2			19
—, — 13		16		— de' Scipioni			25
—, Villa		28		Serlupi, Pal.			16
Rosa, V. della		16		— — 17			17
Rospigliosi, Pal.		19		Serpe, Vic. della			18
Rotonda, Piazza della		16		Serpenti, V. de'		22	
Rotto, Ponte		18		Serristori, Pal. 8		7	
Rua, V. di		17		Servio Tullio, recinto di			20
Ruaccia, Piazza			15	Sette Sale			26
S.S. Rufina e Seconda. 2			15	—, V. delle			26
Ruspoli, Pal.	16			Settimiana, Porta			11
Rusticucci, Piazza	7			Sforza, Piazza			10
S. Saba			20	Sforza-Cesarini, Pal.			10
—, V. di			20	S. Silvestro			19
S. Sabina			18	— in Capite		16	
Sacchetti, Pal.		10		— —, Piazza di		16	
—, V.			15	S. Silvia			24
Sacriponte, Pal. 5		13		S. Simone		13	
Salara, Porta		27		S. Simone e Giuditta. 5		10	
— —, V. della			18	Sistina, V.		20	
Salara vecchia, V.			20	S. Sisto			26
Salumi, V. de'			18	Sisto, Ponte		14	
Salvage, Villa		11		Soldato, V. del		13	
S. Salvatore		14		Sora, Pal.		13	
—		13		—, Piazza di		13	
—		18		Spada, Pal.		14	
—			16	— —, 19			10
— in Campo. 5		14		—, Villa			9
— della Corte. 6			15	Spagna, Pal. di		17	
— in Lauro		10		—, Piazza di		17	
— al Torrione. 5		4		—, Vic. di			11
Salviati, Pal.		7		Specchj, Piazza de'			14
—		19		S. Spirito, Oratorio di. 16		7	
Sampieri, Pal. (Cicciaporci). 3	10			—, Porta			7
Santacroce, Pal. 4		14		— in Sassia. 12.			7
Santinelli, Vg.			33	Spirito Santo de' Napoli-			
Saponari, Vic. de'		17		tani. 5			10
Sassi, Vg.			28	Sposata, Fossa della		12	
Saturno, Tempio di		20		Stamperia e Calcografia Ca-			
Savelli, V.		13		merale. 7		19	
Savorelli, Villa		9		Stamperia, V. della		19	
Scaccia, V.	1			S. Stanislao			17
Scala Santa		30		Stazione della Ferrovia		28	
Scalcaccia, Vic. della		18		S. Stefano		4	
Scalette, Vic. delle	15			—			18
—			11	— del Cacco			16
Schiavoni, V. de'		17		— in Piscinula. 21			10

324 LIST OF STREETS.

Street	I	II	III
S. Stefano Rotondo			27
—, V. di		27	
Stelletta, V. della		13	
Sterrato, Vic.		22	
Strozzi, Pal.			16
— 16			17
—, V.		25	
Struzzo, Vic. dello			10
Sublicio, Ponte			18
S. Sudario, Cappella del. 8		13	
—, V. del		13	
S. Susanna		23	
—, Vic.		23	
Tartaruga, Piazza			17
Teatro Apollo		10	
— Argentina		13	
— Capranica		16	
— di Marcello. 5			17
— Metastasio. 15		13	
— della Pace			13
— di Pompeo			13
— della Valle. 15			13
S. Tecla. 15		7	
Telline, Vic. delle		10	
Teodoli, Pal. 9		16	
S. Teodoro			20
S. Teresa			11
— 7			14
— 4		22	
Terme di Agrippa		16	
— di Caracalla			23
Terme di Costantino			19
— di Diocleziano		25	
— di S. Elena		35	
— di Tito		26	
Termini, Fontana di		22	
—, Piazza di		25	
Testa spaccata, V.			19
Testaccio, Monte			13
Tiburtina, Porta		28	
Tinta, V. della		13	
Tomacelli, V.		17	
S. Tommaso. 1			17
—			13
— Cantuari. 2			13
— in Formis			24
Tor Argentina, V. di			17
— Cantarelli		25	
— de' Conti		20	
—, V. di		23	
— Mellina			13
— Sanguinea. 4		13	
— de' Specchj, V. di			17
Tordinona, V. di		10	
Torlonia, Pal. 10		17	
— -Bolognetti, Pal. 1			19
—, Villa		20	
Torre delle Milizie. 6			19

Street	I	II	III
Torretta, Piazza			16
Trajana, Colonna			19
Tre Archi, V. de'		13	
Tre Cannelli. 3			17
Tre Cannette, V. delle			19
Tre Ladroni, Vic.			16
Trevi, Fontana di		19	
Triclinio Leoniano			33
S. Trifone. 2		13	
S. Trinità		16	
— 11		17	
— de' Monti		20	
— de' Pellegrini			14
Tritone, V. del		19	
Umiltà, V. dell'		19	
Università della Sapienza. 25			13
Urbana, V.			22
S. Urbano			20
Vaccarella, Vic.		13	
Valentini, Pal.			19
—, Villa			9
Valle, Piazza di			13
—, V. di			13
Vantaggio, V. del		14	
Vascellari, Vic. de'			18
Vaschette, Piazza delle		7	
Vaticano, Monte		1	
—, Pal.		4	
Vecchi, Villa de'		28	
Vecchiarelli, Vic.		10	
S. Venanzio			17
Venere e Roma, Tempio di			23
Venezia, Pal. di			16
—, Piazza di			16
Vergine Beata del Carmine. 5			15
Vergini, V. delle			19
Verospi, Pal. 10		16	
—, Villa		27	
Vetrina, V. della		13	
Vidoni, Pal.		13	
Vigne, V. delle			12
S.S. Vincenzo ed Anastasio		14	
— — 3		19	
Visitazione, Monastero della		21	
S. Vitale		22	
S. Vitale, V. di		22	22
Vite, V. della		16	
Vitelleschi, Pal. 1			16
S. Vito, V.			25
SS. Vito e Modesto			28
Vittoria, V.		17	
Volpe, V. del		13	
Wolkonsky, Villa			33
Zecca		4	
Zingari, Piazza			22
Zoccolette, Monast. delle. 2			14
Zuccheri, Palazzo		20	
Zucchette, V. delle			19

7. 1. S. Maria della Clemenza
2. S. Maria del Refugio
10. 1. S. Caterina della Rota
2. S. Caterina de' Sanesi
3. S. Maria di Monserrato
4. S. Eligio
5. S. Spirito Santo de' Napolitani
6. S. Giacomo in Ajno
7. S. Nicola degli Incoronati
8. S. Filippo Neri
9. S. Lucia del Gonfalone
10. S. Lucia
11. S. Maria del Suffragio
12. S. Elisabetta
13. S. Biagio della Pagnotta
14. S. Maria della Purificazione
15. Banco di S. Spirito
16. S. Giuliano
17. Pal. Capponi
18. Pal. Camerata
19. Pal. Spada
20. S. Cecilia
21. S. Stefano in Piscinula
13. 1. S. Girolamo
2. S. Tomaso Cantuariense
3. S. Brigida
4. Pal. Pighini
5. S. Maria di Grottapinta
6. S. Cosma
7. S. Giuliano de' Fiaminghi
8. Cappella del S. Sudario
9. S. Elisabetta
10. Pal. Manfroni
11. Pal. Massimi delle Colonne
12. S. Maria in Monterone
13. Pal. Massimi-Sinibaldi
14. Pal. Nari
15. Teatro della Valle
16. Pal. Lancellotti
17. Pal. Braschi
18. Pal. Panfili
19. S. S. Agonizzanti
20. Pal. del Governo Vecchio
21. S. Biagio del Fosso
22. Pal. Ornani
23. S. Giacomo de' Spagnuoli
24. Pal. Carpegna
25. Università della Sapienza
14. 1. Ospedale Ecclesiastico
2. Monasterio delle Zoccolette
3. S. Maria in Cacaberis
4. Pal. Santacroce
5. S. Salvatore in Campo
6. S. Martino
7. S. Teresa
8. S. S. Giovanni e Petronio
9. S. Maria di Quercia
15. 1. S. Margherita

2 S. S. Rufina e Seconda
3. S. Agata
4. S. Bonosa
5. Beata Vergine del Carmine
6. S. Salvatore della Corte
7. S. Giovanni de' Genovesi
16. 1. Pal. Vitelleschi
2. Casa del Commercio
3. Pal. Bolognetti
4. Pal. Grazioli
5. Pal. Buonaparte
6. Pal. Datti
7. S. Benedetto
8. Arco di Ciambella
9. Pal. Marescotti
10. Pal. Berardi
11. Accademia Ecclesiastica
12. Pal. Borromeo
13. S. Mauro
14. S. Maria di Pietà (Oratorio di Caravita)
15. Pal. Buoncampagni-Simonetti
16. Oratorio del Crocifisso
17. 1. S. Tommaso
2. Scuole degli Ebrei
3. Tre Cannelli
4. Quattro Capi
5. Teatro di Marcello
6. S. Maria in Vinci
7. S. Omobuono
8. Istituto Archeologico
9. Pal. Caffarelli
10. S. Andrea in Vinci
11. S. S. Orsola e Caterina
12. Pal. Massimi
13. Pal. Malatesta
14. Pal. Cardelli
15. Pal. Cavaletti
16. Pal. Strozzi
17. Pal. Serlupi
18. Portico di Ottapia
19. S. Maria del Pianto
20. Pal. Costaguti
21. S. Maria in Publicolis
22. Ospedale di Tita Giovanni
23. S. Anna
24. S. Sebastiano de' Mercanti
25. Pal. Guglielmi
26. Pal. Gaetano-Sermoneta
27. Pal. Mattei
28. S. Stanislao
29. Pal. Altieri
18. 1. S. Benedetto in Piscinula
2. Oratorio S. Andrea
3. Casa di Crescenzio detta di Rienzi o del
4. S. Aniano
5. S. Giovanni Decollato
19. 1 Pal. Torlonia Bolognetti
2. Sepolcro di Bibulo
3. Madonna di Loreto
4. Nome di Maria

www.ingramcontent.com/pod-product-compliance
Lightning Source LLC
Chambersburg PA
CBHW022113290426

44112CB00008B/662